Reading Literature and Writing Argument

THIRD EDITION

Missy James
Tallahassee Community College

Alan P. Merickel
Tallahassee Community College

PEARSON
Prentice
Hall

Upper Saddle River, New Jersey 07458

Library of Congress Cataloging-in-Publication Data

James, Missy.
 Reading literature and writing argument / Missy James, Alan P. Merickel. -- 3rd ed.
    p. cm.
 Includes index.
 ISBN-13: 978-0-13-224884-6
 ISBN-10: 0-13-224884-0
 1. English language--Rhetoric. 2. Persuasion (Rhetoric) 3. College readers. 4. Report writing.
 I. Merickel, Alan. II. Title.
 PE1408J36 2008
 808'.0427--dc22

                                                                    2006103225

Editorial Director: Leah Jewell
Acquisitions Editor: Vivian Garcia
Editorial Assistant: Christina Volpe
Production Liaison: Joanne Hakim
Marketing Manager: Vivian Garcia
Marketing Assistant: Christina Volpe
Manufacturing Buyer: Christina Amato
Permissions Specialist: Mary Dalton Hoffman
Cover Art Director: Jayne Conte
Cover Photo/Illustration: © 1986 Pat O'Hara/
 Pat O'Hara Photography, Inc. All Rights Reserved
 Worldwide.

Director, Image Resource Center: Melinda Patelli
Manager, Rights and Permissions: Zina Arabia
Manager, Visual Research: Beth Brenzel
Manager, Cover Visual Research & Permissions:
 Karen Sanatar
Image Permission Coordinator: Robert Farrell
Photo Researcher: Rachel Lucas
Full-Service Project Management: Jessica
 Balch/Pine Tree Composition
Composition: Laserwords Private Limited
Printer/Binder: The Courier Companies

Credits and acknowledgments for material borrowed from other sources and reproduced, with permission, in this textbook appear on pages 733–740.

Pearson Education LTD., London
Pearson Education Singapore, Pte. Ltd
Pearson Education, Canada, Ltd
Pearson Education-Japan
Pearson Education Australia PTY, Limited

Pearson Education North Asia Ltd
Pearson Educación de Mexico, S.A. de C.V.
Pearson Education Malaysia, Pte. Ltd
Pearson Education, Upper Saddle River,
 New Jersey

10 9 8 7 6 5 4 3 2 1

978-0-13-224884-6
0-13-224884-0

Contents

4   Individuality and Community   99

5 Nature and Place 259

6 **Family and Identity   401**

Preface

Any real study of great literature must take in human life at every possible level and search out every dark corner. And its natural territory is the whole human experience, no less. It does not astonish me that young people love to hear about these things, love to talk about them, and think about them.

—KATHERINE ANNE PORTER, "TO DR. WILLIAM ROSS"

Reading Literature and Writing Argument springs directly from our classroom experiences as teachers of two college composition courses: "Writing Argument and Persuasion" and "Writing about Literature." We want our students to experience the best of these two courses. In both courses, students are enriched, as readers and as writers, through their active engagement with ideas in written text. *Reading Literature and Writing Argument* is based on the premise that writing is valued when it makes readers think. This premise implies, of course, that a person must have ideas—something to say—in order to put pen to paper or fingers to keyboard. However, the notion that these ideas must have value can be daunting to the individual who is staring at the blank page or screen. Here is where literature—stories, poems, plays, essays—can play a vital role, one too often overlooked in students' overly busy, information-laden lives. Literature can unlock the gate to students' imaginations and open the window for creative envisioning. Likewise, the study of argument is vital to compelling students to think clearly and objectively.

Through their engagement with literature and application of the principles of argument, students practice the skills of analysis and evaluation and, in doing so, develop critical standards for judging ideas. For example, Henry David Thoreau's essay, "Civil Disobedience," presents an explicit argument; students learn when they examine his assertion that the individual's first responsibility is to maintain his or her own integrity. Similarly, students learn from examining the arguments made in a play by Aristophanes, in a poem by Gwendolyn Brooks, or in stories by Louise Erdrich, Randall Kenan, and Fae Myenne Ng.

Literature liberates thinking, and argument disciplines it. The combined forces are inspiring and empowering. With our students' experiences in the two composition courses as our guide, we have attempted to harness the courses' complementary strengths in *Reading Literature and Writing Argument*.

NEW TO THIS EDITION

The organizational structure of *Reading Literature and Writing Argument* has been well-received. In writing this edition, we added a chapter to address first-year college students' need for guidelines for writing academic argument. Additionally, reviewers universally have praised the diversity of reading selections in the first edition. We, therefore, dropped only a few works while adding twenty. In making our selections, we have continued to honor the value of classical literature (Jonathan Swift, Francis Bacon, and Ernest Hemingway), as well as to seek out fresh, contemporary voices (John Crawford, Lydia Davis, and Laura Hendrie). Also, to contextualize the literature, we have added research/writing topics; in creating these topics, we explicitly linked enduring themes to contemporary issues.

ORGANIZATION

Chapters One and Two introduce and explain the terms and tools of argument; Chapter Three presents the writing process for academic argument. Chapters Four through Seven present literature pieces centered on four enduring themes: "Individuality and Community," "Nature and Place," "Family and Identity," and "Power and Responsibility." Following each reading selection are questions that invite students to apply the argument terms and tools from Chapters One and Two. In this way, the literature pieces offer a practice field for the tools of critical thinking. Also, writing topics are provided to generate longer written responses and, thus, to prompt students' ideas for writing their own arguments.

Chapter One, Reading to Explore, Analyze, and Evaluate, opens with a brief discussion of academic argument and presents a core concept: reading literature is a prompt for rooting out and exploring the underlying values that inform our responses to the world around us. We introduce basic argument structure and several rhetorical concepts that relate argument to audience appeal and tone. In selecting terms and concepts to feature, we chose the tools our classroom experiences have shown to be particularly useful for our students, both as readers and as writers. The Chapter Activities reinforce the argument terms and concepts by giving students a chance to practice applying them to their reading of several literature pieces.

Chapter Two, Examining Thinking and Shaping an Argument, features the reasoning process—how we form opinions and arrive at conclusions. To begin, we challenge students to develop a habit of questioning the foundation of their opinions by evaluating their thinking processes. Again, taking a lead from our experiences in the composition classroom, we highlight the common fallacy of hasty generalization. Also brief overviews of inductive and deductive reasoning and common logical fallacies help students examine the reasoning process in argumentation and give them tools for evaluating their own thinking, ideas, and opinions, as well as those of others—from a speaker in a poem to a character in a play.

In Chapter Two, we move from the reasoning process to the process of writing argument, which we present as five basic tasks. We offer illustrations of writers, both professional and student, applying these tasks. The last section of the chapter presents a four-part written exploration and articulation, a process that draws on the concepts from Chapters One and Two and culminates in the students' writing their own arguments. The four-part activity directs students to explore their own thinking about a designated subject; to explore the subject in the context of several literature pieces; to explore the subject by doing some research; and, finally, to articulate an issue and claim, gather support, and compose their own arguments. The chapter presents four sample student essays, including two longer research projects: one illustrates the process of the four-part written exploration and articulation and one features the final product, the research-based argument paper. Last, Chapter Activities provide students with hands-on engagement with the concepts introduced in the chapter.

Chapter Three, Participating in an Academic Community, provides a detailed explanation of the writing process for research-based, academic argument. Student essays offer successful models, one organized around a claim of policy and one featuring Rogerian argument strategy. Moreover, we address the challenges students face when working with sources, including avoiding plagiarism, creating a draft, and using electronic sources. Finally, we present two extended writing projects, a model student essay, and two essay scoring rubrics.

For the anthology Chapters Four through Seven, we purposefully created theme headings that are broad and that directly affect students' lives. To echo Katherine Anne Porter's testimony, we believe that students appreciate the opportunity to explore their own thinking processes within these contexts. Also, the themes invite students to draw connections, not only among the readings within a single chapter, but also among readings throughout the four chapters. For example, some family issues that students may identify in Chapter Six readings can be related to responsibility issues in Chapter Seven readings. Students may draw on their reading experiences from several chapters as they explore an issue and move toward the writing of their own arguments. Chapter Activities are designed to stimulate students' thinking about their reading experiences and about potential issues for writing an argument.

To borrow from Robert Frost's statement on poetry, *Reading Literature and Writing Argument* is designed to bring both "delight" and "wisdom" to the first-year college student's composition experience. We believe that students will enjoy reading the literature pieces, practicing critical thinking skills, and exploring different perspectives on issues close to their own lives. And finally, students will discover they have a wealth of ideas, as well as the critical acumen to compose written arguments that will compel their readers to think. The blank page or computer screen will present a welcome invitation to speak out and to be heard, to make choices and to make a difference in one's own life and in the lives of others.

TEACHING NOTES AND RESOURCES

An accompanying *Teaching Notes and Resources* manual provides (1) notes on teaching Chapter One, including an outline for collaborative learning and writing a focus journal; (2) notes on Chapter Two, including suggestions for peer critiques; (3) notes on Chapter Three, including a student model Rogerian argument essay; (4) notes on Chapters four through seven, including a list of argument terms and related literature, as well as teaching notes for the literature selections. Finally, the manual offers a list connecting chapter themes to films.

ACKNOWLEDGMENTS

We are grateful to the following composition teachers whose comments and suggestions provided both encouragement and constructive guidance for the changes in this third edition:

Sue Crowson, Del Mar College; Dan Ferguson, Amarillo College; Karen Gardiner, University of Alabama; Arden Jensen, Lee University; Tori Mask, Blinn College; and Steve Street, SUNY-Buffalo.

To our persistent permissions editor, Mary Dalton-Hoffman, and to project manager, Jessica Balch, we offer a hearty thank you. At Prentice Hall, we thank literature acquisitions editor, Vivian Garcia, for her support and guidance. And most of all, we are ever grateful to Leah Jewell, Editorial Director. Were it not for her early-on interest, this book may not have gone past the conceptualization stage.

Missy James
Alan Merickel

ᴧᴧ CHAPTER 1 ᴧᴧ

Reading to Explore,
Analyze, and Evaluate

It is the mark of an educated mind to be able
to entertain a thought without accepting it.
                                          —*Aristotle*

The term *argument* evokes images of confrontation. As two people challenge one another over conflicting views, their voices rise, their moods darken, and their minds become fixed upon winning.

> "How can you say sexual harassment in the workplace is an overstated problem? Being a male, you've never experienced it. You don't know what you're talking about!"
>
> "Oh, so just because I'm a male, I can't understand this issue? What an unbelievably sexist thing to say!"

Of course, this confrontational form of argument can be heard throughout our society, from dorm rooms to courtrooms, from public hearings to legislative debates. The Fox News program *The O'Reilly Factor* is built around exactly such a form of argument as nationally known political analysts spend a half hour attacking one another during prime time. And the 1990s vintage talk shows—from Ricki Lake to Jerry Springer—thrived on divisiveness and confrontation. When people join a confrontational argument, they often close their minds. Their emotions displace their reason as their desire for victory overcomes any inclination to listen to their opposition's point of view.

In an academic setting, however, argument means more than confrontation. **Academic argument** implies a reasoned approach to issues. In an academic community, people also hold opposing viewpoints, but they debate in order to modify and strengthen their positions. Through the deliberative and respectful exchange of viewpoints, each side "wins" by attaining a deeper understanding of the issue. Two history professors, for example, may well view the World War II bombings of Hiroshima and Nagasaki quite differently. Two paleontology professors may debate the cause of the extinction of the dinosaurs. Two students may hold differing views regarding the use of capital punishment. However, in academic argument, despite the intensity of the debate, emotion should never replace reason.

Reason dictates that we not only make our own position clear, but also that we do our best to understand opposing positions. After all, the purpose of the college experience is learning, whether that learning comes through classroom discussion, through research, or through the general interaction of members in the academic community. Academic argument is an integral part of that learning process.

EXPLORE

> *"You go to a great school not so much for the knowledge as for arts and habits: for the habit of attention, for the art of expression, for the art of assuming at a moment's notice a new intellectual position, for the art of entering quickly into another person's thoughts, for the habit of submitting to censure and refutation, for the art of indicating assent or dissent in graduated terms, for the habit of regarding minute points of accuracy, for the art of working out what is possible in a given time, for taste, for discrimination, for mental courage and mental soberness."*

—WILLIAM JOHNSON CORY (1823–1892)[1]
ETON COLLEGE

Written over one hundred years ago, William Johnson Cory's description of the learning process endures. Each semester many contemporary social issues wash across a college campus, touching the academic disciplines both directly and indirectly: euthanasia, affirmative action, freedom of speech, genetic engineering, gender equity, global warming, immigration. Although in society at large, sharply focused debates emerge as people establish positions around these issues, in a college setting, students and faculty have the opportunity to step back from the moment and create some emotional distance. The college experience enables us to probe the values and belief systems which underlie issues and ideas. Looking inward and outward, we practice the *habit of attention* which enables us to make choices, deliberately and thoughtfully, and to participate in shaping a free society.

Imaginative literature allows us to explore *"the art of expression, . . . the art of assuming at a moment's notice a new intellectual position, . . . the art of entering into another person's thoughts."* Anchoring one of humanity's fundamental questions—how should I live my life?—in the concrete language of time and place, literature both personalizes and focuses this question for us. Reading literature we are transported from the particular details of our individual lives to the lives of other persons, their places, and their times. We emerge from the pages of the literary work with fresh perspectives. As the poet Wallace Stevens noted, "Imagination is one of the forces of nature." Through literature we may examine with a clear vision both the personal issues that sometimes cloud our daily lives and the social issues that often divide our communities. The literature provided in this textbook is grouped around four themes: Individuality and Community, Nature and Place, Family and Identity, and Power and Responsibility.

---

[1]William Johnson Cory was a British educator and lyric poet who taught at Eton College from 1845 to 1871. In 1882, he published *Guide to Modern History from 1815 to 1835.*

"Once upon a time . . ."

Listening to stories as young children, we were not only entertained but also informally instructed in values: honesty, competition, pride, loyalty, compassion, and empathy. As readers in a first-year college composition course, we continue to learn from stories about our beliefs and ideas, the **value assumptions,** which underlie our behavior and attitudes and inform our opinions and conclusions. Through our reading and our writing about literature, we can step back and explore these value assumptions; we can ferret out underlying beliefs and ideas and scrutinize their logic and reasonableness. To illustrate we briefly explore three stories, whose full texts are included in later chapters.

In reading Raymond Carver's "Cathedral" (Chapter Seven), we witness the narrator's personal growth through his reluctant interaction with his "wife's blind friend," Robert. As active readers, we can trace our evolving response to the narrator. For example, here are some excerpts from early in the story:

> My idea of blindness came from the movies. In the movies, the blind moved slowly and never laughed. Sometimes they were led by seeing-eye dogs.
>
> At first glance, his [Robert's] eyes looked like anyone else's eyes. But if you looked close, there was something different about them. Too much white in the iris, for one thing, and the pupils seemed to move around in the sockets without his knowing it or being able to stop it. Creepy.

While the narrator shows himself to be observant, his comments are likely to strike us as simpleminded, crass, and insensitive. By the end of the story, however, the narrator reveals a softer, more serious, and thoughtful side of his character. But careful readers will ask questions: Is the narrator's transformation authentic? Has this one night's encounter changed his outlook? By writing to record our reaction to the narrator at various points in the story, we can draw our individual conclusions about the character of the narrator. We also explore our personal reactions to each of the story's three characters—the narrator/husband, the wife, and the wife's friend Robert—which may reveal something about how we form judgments.

In writing an informal, reflective response to the story, we may recall our own experiences with individuals who were different from us—in physical or mental abilities, in ethnicity, in economic class, in religious faith—and around whom we felt uncomfortable. In the act of recalling and writing, we can become readers of our own "stories" and explore the underlying themes: *What assumptions, beliefs, or ideas accounted for our feelings about and actual reaction in that particular situation?* Also, using Carver's story as a model, we can "role-play"; we can imagine ourselves in a situation similar to the narrator's and write our own script. How would we respond to a visitor who is uncomfortably different from us? Again, from this outward perspective, viewing ourselves as a character in a story, we can explore and examine our range of feelings and reactions: What ideas or beliefs about how a person *should* act or look shape our reaction to and interaction with this "different" individual? Finally, as we move beyond ourselves, these underlying questions—how we view "the other," those who are not "like us"—may lead us to a deeper level of scrutiny of contemporary issues, for example, the scope of the American Disabilities Act, the purpose of affirmative action programs, or the reform of immigration policies.

Tim O'Brien's short story, "The Things They Carried" (Chapter Seven), introduces us, firsthand, to the Vietnam foot soldier, and Louise Erdrich's story, "The Red Convertible" (Chapter Four), to a recent Vietnam veteran. Reading O'Brien's story and empathizing with Lieutenant Jimmy Cross and his men, we may see today's middle-aged veterans as yesterday's young men with names and girlfriends and families back home, as individuals who are struggling to survive in a hostile environment: "afraid of dying . . . they were even more afraid to show it. . . . They used a hard vocabulary to contain the terrible softness. . . . *zapped while zipping.*" Likewise, reading Erdrich's story, we see Lyman Lamartine's brother, Henry, who has recently returned home after serving as a Marine in Vietnam. Here is how Lyman describes his brother, who spends much of his time watching TV: "He sat in front of it, watching it, and that was the only time he was completely still. But it was the kind of a stillness you see in a rabbit when it freezes and before it will bolt . . . his smile had changed, or maybe it was gone."

Living with these characters in the pages of O'Brien's and Erdrich's stories, we see the actual human faces behind the cliche "war is hell." As a result, we may look a bit differently upon the middle-aged man at the street corner with the weathered face, scraggly hair, and "Veteran, will work for food" sign. Perhaps, too, this deliberative reflection will lead us to investigate homeless issues or programs and benefits for veterans in our own communities.

ANALYZE: ARGUMENT STRUCTURE

If academic argument implies both understanding opposing positions as well as articulating our own positions, then we must begin with analysis. Thoughtfully and objectively analyzing the views of others, including their underlying assumptions, is a necessary first step in understanding our own beliefs. However, this task is not simple. First, we must understand some of the basic elements of argument.

The Greek philosopher Aristotle in his *Rhetoric* identifies several elements of argument which will be important for us. His three appeals, *logos, pathos,* and *ethos* (**rhetorical triangle**), mark three human characteristics: reason, emotion, and perception of character. Understanding these three elements will give us insights into the positions of others as well as our own. (These terms are further explained on pages 12–17.) In addition, Aristotle describes a three-part **syllogism,** consisting of a major premise, a minor premise, and a conclusion:

Major Premise:	College graduates are critical thinkers.
Minor Premise:	Michael and Meredith are college graduates.
Conclusion:	Michael and Meredith are critical thinkers.

Such a syllogism creates an outline, revealing the logical structure of an argument. Although not all arguments can be so neatly dissected and outlined, our attempts to reduce an argument to its bare elements can help us examine its underlying logic.

To allow more flexibility and openness in examining argument structure, a twentieth-century British philosopher, Stephen Toulmin, created new terminology to rework the elements of Aristotle's syllogism. According to the Toulmin model for argument, the warrant replaces the syllogism's major premise, the grounds or evidence replaces its minor premise, and the claim replaces its conclusion:

> Since dogs are bred for human companionship [the *warrant*], and schnauzers are dogs [the *grounds*], schnauzers would make companionable pets [the *claim*].

Because this textbook emphasizes reading, writing, and critical thinking rather than advanced logic and rhetoric, we focus on those elements of argument that will help us examine and articulate positions efficiently: claims, evidence, warrants, and rhetorical appeals.

Claims

The **claim** is the assertion made in an argument, the main point or thesis. We can also think of the claim as the conclusion the writer has drawn. Some claims are easily seen. For example, in the essay, "Truer to the Game," Randy Horick makes this statement: "The women play a superior brand of basketball." For readers, there can be no misunderstanding—in fact, every word in Horick's essay leads readers to accept his claim.

Truer to the Game

RANDY HORICK

Out in our driveway, where my 12-year-old daughter dreams of becoming the next Chamique Holdsclaw, we have been working together on a few of the finer points of competitive basketball. Like how to use your elbow semi-legally to establish position (an old Don Meyer bit of wisdom). Or how to inbound the ball to yourself by thunking it off the buttocks of an unsuspecting opponent. Or the deep personal satisfaction, to say nothing of the psychological advantage, gained from setting a teeth-rattling screen.

As part of this regimen, I have tried to use games on TV as teaching tools. I point out, for example, a good blockout on a rebound, a properly executed pick and roll, or the way to run a two-on-one fast break (or, more often, the way *not* to run a break).

Being a quick study, my daughter has observed one of the game's truths just from viewing two telecasts: the women's Final Four games on Friday and the corresponding men's contests on Saturday evening. "Dad," she observed, "the guys can't shoot."

This is either basketball's deep, dark secret or a cause for excitement, depending on your point of view. The truth is that the women take better shots than their male counterparts. As their respective NCAA tournaments made it ever clearer this March, when it comes to putting the pill in the hoop, girls' basketball rocks. Boys' basketball, well, doesn't.

But not only that: The women play a superior brand of basketball. These are not the tilted rantings of some addle-brained pot-stirrer, as accustomed as you may profess to be to seeing such things on these pages. You can find a whole pantheon of old NBA stars—including no less of a luminary than Bill Russell his own bad shot-blocking self—who proclaim

5

that women's basketball is much truer to the game they played than the men's version today.

Claims of superiority, of course, all depend upon your definitions. If you measure quality by physical measures—speed, play above the rim, dazzling one-on-one moves—it's still a man's world. (Don't imagine, however, that the women in the Final Four aren't superbly conditioned athletes.)

If you're looking for solid fundamentals and all-around team play, well, um, fellas, y'all got next. Ironically, the relative physical inferiority of today's women players provides the basis for a superior game.

The ability of men to complete acrobatic, soaring drives and dunks increasingly has led them to become infatuated with "taking it to the tin"— regardless of which defenders are in the way or which teammates may be open elsewhere. It's as if the guys have all graduated from some funky basketball camp that teaches that style points count for even more than real ones.

If you had $250 for every time during the men's NCAAs that a player passed up a jump shot, faked with the ball, then put his head down and headed toward the hole, they'd make you an honorary member of the bar association. The predictable results of such reckless driving, all too often, are offensive fouls, ugly collisions, and loads of bricks. For every dunk, we are forced to witness several thunks. For every electrifying play, there are several short-circuits. The literal rise of countless would-be Jordans has corresponded with a steady fall in field goal and free throw percentages in the men's game

10   Contrast that with the women's game, where the play is decidedly below the rim and dunks are rarer than incorruptible state legislators.

Because the girls aren't yet throwing it down, they're forced to concentrate on the aspects of the game that many of the boys seem to regard as beneath them. Like practicing free throws. Running patterned offenses. Looking for back-door cutters. Making routine shots. Executing the fundamentals.

For all of these reasons, if you want to teach someone to play the game, women's basketball today is far more instructive. In part, that's because their game runs at a slightly slower speed, allowing you more clearly to see plays develop. Much more, however, it has to do with better shot selection, better ball movement, and more faithful adherence to the concept of team play.

Off the court, of course, women's college basketball looks even better in comparison. At the Division I Level, men's hoops today less and less exemplifies the old ideals of amateur competition and more and more resembles a corporate leviathan.

In the way that drug cartels have corrupted the institutions in countries like Columbia and Mexico, those who control the money and labor supply have leeched into men's basketball. AAU coaches serve as talent brokers who wield inordinate influence. Shoe companies sponsor posh summer camps for top high school players and sign college coaches to cushy contracts, hoping to win future endorsements from those who become stars.

15   Meanwhile, the pressures to win are so enormous upon coaches, and the financial allure of an NBA career so powerful to players, that almost any action can be rationalized in the name of winning. Top high school players with marginal grades may be shipped off to basketball trade schools that pass themselves off as institutions of academic learning.

Collegiate coaches recruit the nation's elite players knowing all too well that they will be gone within a year or two, and that their only real interest in the college experience lies in gaining experience that will prepare them for the pros.

Things are so whomperdejawed that the NCAA, which blithely presided over the creation of this mess, is now declaring that the entire culture of men's basketball is diseased and needs a radical cure. (Good luck, guys.)

Against this backdrop, the women's game looks like a fount of purity. Star players don't bug out early for the professional league; they stay and earn their degrees.

Coaches don't have to hire bodyguards to protect their athletes from contact by predatory agents. The recruiting process does not begin in the eighth or ninth grades. There are no televised McDonald's all-American games or dunk contests that teach the best players that they belong to some sort of celebrity elite.

Those days may be coming. As the popularity of women's basketball continues to increase (Sunday's championship between Tennessee and Connecticut was the most watched women's game ever), so too will the pressures.   20

The retirement last week of Louisiana Tech coach Leon Barmore is a reminder of where the game is going. Tech and Old Dominion are perhaps the last of the "little" schools that remain powers in women's basketball today. It's easy to forget that, barely two decades ago, the game was dominated by colleges you never heard of: Delta State, Immaculata, Stephen F. Austin, Wayland Baptist.

Women's basketball belongs to the big schools now. With the WNBA successfully established, it is conceivable that collegians might turn pro early if salaries become attractive enough. Coaches might cut corners and grease palms to lure the best high schoolers to their programs. A whole industry might rise up and enshroud the game, as it has with men's basketball.

Until then, though, I'll keep offering up as role models the kind of unspoiled, we-first players who were evident in the women's tournament.

Meanwhile, we won't forget at our house that the men's pro league still offers enormous entertainment value. Just last Sunday, during the Knicks-Lakers game, my daughter came rushing in breathlessly. "Dad, dad, come check it out. Kobe Bryant and Chris Childs are having a fight!"

On the other hand, a claim can be implied or indirect rather than explicit or directly stated, particularly in imaginative literature. Do you recall reading *The Scarlet Letter* by Nathaniel Hawthorne? Like many high school students, you probably encountered this novel sometime during your four years, but can you state the claim Hawthorne makes? Something about deception perhaps? Maybe something about values? Readers are not likely to find a single sentence in Hawthorne's novel equivalent to Horick's assertion regarding women's basketball. However, in a classroom discussion, through the interplay of varying interpretations, readers can articulate a central claim or assertion for this novel.

Of course, some imaginative literature offers no claim whatsoever. Look, for example, at a short poem by Kenneth Rexroth:

Cold before Dawn

Cold before dawn,
Off in the misty night,
Under the gibbous moon,
The peacocks cry to each other,
As if in pain.

Do you see an implicit claim in this poem? If you do, you are probably reading too much into this five-line, imagist poem. As a further example, look at this Ezra Pound poem:

In a Station of the Metro

> The apparition of these faces in the crowd,
> Petals on a wet, black bough.

You will discover no claim here, no matter how proficiently you analyze this poem. But look at the following poem by the eighteenth-century British poet William Blake:

London

> I wander thro' each charter'd street,
> Near where the charter'd Thames does flow,
> And mark in every face I meet
> Marks of weakness, marks of woe.

5

> In every cry of every Man,
> In every Infant's cry of fear,
> In every voice, in every ban,
> The mind-forg'd manacles I hear.

> How the Chimney-sweeper's cry

10

> Every black'ning Church appalls;
> And the hapless Soldier's sigh
> Runs in blood down Palace walls.

> But most thro' midnight streets I hear
> How the youthful Harlot's curse

15

> Blasts the new born Infant's tear,
> And blights with plagues the Marriage hearse.

What do you see as the claim in this poem? Is the claim about the young children used as chimney sweeps and doomed to early deaths? Is it about venereal disease? Yes, the poem says something about both of these subjects; indeed, a number of subclaims usually can be identified in any example of writing. In this poem, however, Blake indirectly accuses the religious, military, and legal institutions of being responsible for the human suffering endured by so many people in the late 1700s. No single line makes such a claim, but when you reread the poem, you will see that the indictment is certainly the poem's central focus, the conclusion the writer wishes the reader to draw from this evidence.

Argument theorists identify several types of claims, including a claim of fact, a claim of policy, and a claim of value. If you state that the world loses ten acres of rainforest every minute, then you are making a **claim of fact,** which may be useful as evidence in an argument calling for new environmental laws to protect the rainforest. The call for new laws would be a **claim of policy** because it asks for a specific action to take place. If the argument makes a judgment labeling something good or bad, then you have a **claim of value:** Rainforests are an invaluable and irreplaceable natural resource.

Evidence

Evidence is the body of information used to support claims. This information may be based on subjective personal experience, on objective facts, on the authority of an expert. Toulmin calls this information the grounds for the claims. There are various types of evidence, but for our purposes, let's concentrate on three: personal experience, reports, and authority.

In an essay, a student claims euthanasia should be legalized and cites his experience of watching his grandmother suffer a prolonged and painful death as the result of cancer. The student's choice of descriptive details coupled with his sincere tone creates a strong, emotional response in his readers. His use of **personal experience** provides strong evidence for the validity of his argument, particularly among readers who have had similar experiences.

On the other hand, some readers may not have any experience with cancer and may never have experienced the death of a family member or loved one. For these people, despite the obvious emotional pull of the evidence, further proof will be required. In this case, the writer might want to provide some statistics of the numbers of patients on life support in this country, as well as the costs to families and health care providers. Taking this approach, the writer is using **reports,** objective facts gathered from outside sources, to support his argument.

The student writer might take one further step toward validating his argument for legalizing euthanasia by citing an **authority.** In this case, a quote from a health care professional would be a good choice. In fact, any field has authorities, people recognized as experts. Citing Dr. Spock as an authority on babies, Bill Gates when discussing the computer industry, or Michael Jordan in relation to professional basketball, a writer could be certain readers would recognize these people as authorities. They have credibility.

Applying the concept of evidence to imaginative literature complicates and enriches our reading experience. To begin with, we must address the **dramatic context** of the writing itself, including the actions, words, and thoughts of the characters within that work. Examining the characters' arguments, their positions, framed within the dramatic context, we look beyond ourselves and ultimately gain a better perception of our own positions.

For example, perhaps if you saw the film *Rain Man,* you recall watching Tom Cruise's character transform his attitude toward his mentally challenged, older brother (played by Dustin Hoffman) as the two travel together. That transformation is based on the evidence of personal experience within the context of the film. In fact, that particular film had a great impact on audiences, for many people left the theater examining their own perceptions of mentally challenged people. Similarly, readers of Harper Lee's novel, *To Kill a Mockingbird,* not only see the transformation of attitudes within the characters as they confront the issue of racial discrimination, but also they may come away from that reading experience examining their own attitudes about prejudice. Thus, analyzing the evidence in the dramatic context of a particular work leads you to understand the position of the character within the work and to explore your own beliefs and values.

Moving beyond the dramatic context, we also can examine the **social context** of a story, poem, or play as evidence of the writer's claim. However, an understanding of that evidence often requires us to gather additional information.

Look back at the poem "London," cited earlier. If William Blake wants the reader to believe the social institutions of eighteenth-century England were to blame for much of the suffering endured by its citizens, he must offer us some evidence. At that time, poor families often sold one of their children to the chimney sweeps who used them to slide down London's many tight chimneys. As they brushed the soot from those chimneys, the children's lungs filled with black dust, and they regularly died while still in their early teens. The fact that such an abuse of children was legal in London is clear evidence in support of Blake's claim. By acquainting yourself with this historical background, you enrich your understanding of Blake's implied argument.

Warrants

Warrants are the assumptions, general principles, or commonly accepted beliefs that underlie an argument. According to Toulmin's argument model, warrants link the evidence to the claim; they are the bonding element that justifies or warrants the audience's movement from evidence to claim. Although a warrant may be stated in an argument, it frequently is a hidden or an unstated assumption. Furthermore, warrants are often value based, that is, based on principles or beliefs that guide our behavior and inform our attitudes about people, events, and issues.

For example, in arguing for strict environmental regulation of rainforests (claim of policy), a writer may offer statistical data and scientific facts to show how rainforests are being destroyed (evidence). The warrant—rainforests are valuable resources—may be readily accepted by American readers and require no backing. However, for the Brazilian landowner, his property may seem more valuable as a clear-cut and plowed field than as a rainforest. Perhaps the writer should not assume all of her readers will accept her warrant. Depending on whom the writer envisions as her audience, she may need to back her warrant with evidence to show how rainforests are valuable. Of course, within our own boundaries, from the Pacific Northwest to the Everglades, similar disputes rage over how to use our wilderness areas. First, how do we define *wilderness?* And how is our view of wilderness impacted by the economic or cultural factors in our lives? Responses will vary among individuals. Yet these responses are crucial to any discussion of wilderness issues. Our personal definition informs the value we assign to wilderness areas; this value assignment (the warrant) then shapes our viewpoint about specific land use issues. Similarly, in the case of euthanasia or physician-assisted suicide, the sanctity and dignity of human life are values that influence our positions. In articulating a claim for physician-assisted suicide, the warrant would be based on our degree of allegiance to each of these values.

Because warrants are often value-based, they can be difficult for us to recognize. How often do we stop to examine the values that affect our judgment of a person or groups of people? When do we have the time for this deliberative introspection? Voice mail, cell phones, and e-mail are efficient means of communicating, for example, but they also make us even busier, as we rush to respond. In contrast, reading literature can relax us. It can take us out of the hectic rush of our daily lives and provide a window for us to look more deeply into ourselves and beyond ourselves—inside the lives and emotions of other persons. Literature, therefore, provides an ideal playing field for examining warrants.

For example, in Blake's poem, "London," we identified a claim (the social institutions of eighteenth-century England were to blame for much of the suffering of its citizens) and pointed out evidence (the practice of selling children to chimney sweeps). What warrant underlies the argument, binding the evidence to the claim? Interestingly, the warrant, a value assumption, is so readily accepted by contemporary readers that we don't think to question it: The use of child labor is an affront to the principles of compassionate people everywhere. In eighteenth-century England, however, children, especially children of poor families, were viewed as property; the selling and buying of children were not widely condemned. Fortunately, enlightened thinkers, such as Blake, stood apart and questioned social institutions that supported the exploitation and abuse of children.

But the child labor issue is still complicated for contemporary readers. What about those expensive athletic shoes or the designer silk shirt we may have recently purchased? Where were they manufactured? And by whom? Recently, the employment practices of several well-known U.S. manufacturers of name-brand shoes and clothing have come under critical scrutiny. Many U.S. manufacturers have opened factories in foreign countries where operating costs are far lower: Land is cheaper, and environmental and labor laws are often either nonexistent or far less stringent than in the United States. In some cases, boys and girls younger than sixteen work long hours in brutal working conditions for meager wages. Is this practice not abusive and exploitative, an affront to our principles of compassion? Even though we are not directly responsible for hiring the twelve-year-old girl who works in the factory where our silk shirts were manufactured, do we share some portion of responsibility? Reading Blake's poem as an argument and examining its warrant from this perspective, we bridge the centuries that seemed to divide us from eighteenth-century London.

EVALUATE: AUDIENCE APPEAL AND TONE

Over two thousand years ago, Aristotle's *Rhetoric* introduced the three appeals, *pathos, logos, ethos,* which focus on the specific effects of an argument—its language and tone—on its audience. Drawing on these three appeals, the writer of argument addresses the basic human characteristics of his or her audience: emotion and empathy (***pathos***), logic and reasoning (***logos***), and credibility and trust (***ethos***). Today any lawyer who expects to win over a jury understands the necessity for making these appeals. Martin Luther King Jr.'s essay, "Letter from Birmingham Jail," written in 1963 (Chapter Four), stands as a modern classic of argumentation, in part because of King's use of rhetorical appeals. Reading this essay, you will see how King builds trust with his audience (*ethos*): "I hope this letter finds you strong in the faith. I also hope that circumstances will soon make it possible for me to meet each of you, not as an integrationist or a civil rights leader, but as a fellow clergyman and a Christian brother"; reasons deliberately and analytically (*logos*): "How does one determine whether a law is just or unjust? A just law is a man-made code. . . . An unjust law is a code that is out of harmony with the moral law"; and evokes his audience's empathy and compassion (*pathos*): "when you suddenly find your tongue twisted and your speech stammering as you seek to explain to your six-year-old daughter why she can't go to the amusement park that has just been advertised on television, and see tears welling up in her eyes." Although addressed to a specific audience, eight "fellow" Alabama clergymen, more than thirty-five years ago, King's "Letter" speaks compellingly to a universal audience.

If we are not accustomed to examining essays as arguments, certainly we are familiar with the Western tradition of courtroom confrontation. Using Aristotle's rhetorical appeals to examine several poems, we can appreciate the poems as argumentation, as well as deepen our understanding of the appeals as ways that writers connect with their readers.

Pathos

"Federico's Ghost" by Martín Espada provides a striking illustration of *pathos* appeal. The poem tells the story of a boy's defiant gesture of protest against the abusive treatment of workers by those in positions of power:

Federico's Ghost

The story is
that whole families of fruitpickers
still crept between the furrows
of the field at dusk,
5   when for reasons of whiskey or whatever
the cropduster plane sprayed anyway,
floating a pesticide drizzle
over the pickers
who thrashed like dark birds
10   in a glistening white net,
except for Federico,
a skinny boy who stood apart
in his own green row,
and, knowing the pilot
15   would not understand in Spanish
that he was the son of a whore,
instead jerked his arm
and thrust an obscene finger.

The pilot understood
He circled the plane and sprayed again,   20
watching a fine gauze of poison
drift over the brown bodies
that cowered and scurried on the ground,
and aiming for Federico,
leaving the skin beneath his shirt   25
wet and blistered,
but still pumping his finger at the sky.

After Federico died,
rumors at the labor camp,
told of tomatoes picked and smashed at night,   30
growers muttering of vandal children
or communists in camp,
first threatening to call Immigration,
then promising every Sunday off
if only the smashing of tomatoes would stop.   35

Still tomatoes were picked and squashed
in the dark,
and the old women in camp
said it was Federico,
laboring after sundown   40
to cool the burns on his arms,
flinging tomatoes
at the cropduster
that hummed like a mosquito
lost in his ear,   45
and kept his soul awake.

Using sensory language and specific details, Espada pulls us inside—behind the words—to where we cannot avoid seeing the human faces of the tomato pickers, who are not unlike ourselves: "whole families," "a skinny boy," "old women." By acknowledging our common humanity, we must acknowledge the injustice and the oppression of the field laborers' lives. Poetic structure also heightens *pathos* appeal. Because we are accustomed to reading margin-to-margin prose, the poem's line breaks slow down our reading. We cannot rush, or skip over words, as we may do in reading an essay. Espada isolates images in short lines, which surprise and shock us as readers:

over the pickers
who thrashed like dark birds
in a glistening white net,
. . . .
leaving the skin beneath his shirt
wet and blistered,

With these images fixed in our imaginations, we are compelled to confront the reality of "man's inhumanity to man" and also to examine our own attitudes toward day laborers, migrant workers, and illegal aliens. Appealing to our emotions and moral values, Espada's poem makes a powerful statement about prejudice and power and about human dignity and heroism. "Federico's Ghost" may, indeed, keep our own "soul[s] awake."

Logos

Shakespeare's sonnets can provide excellent illustrations for the *logos* point of Aristotle's triangle. Compare the form of the English or Shakespearean sonnet itself, a logical, fixed structure (fourteen lines—three quatrains and a couplet) to Espada's free verse (open-form poetry), for example. The sonnet's structure reinforces the poem's argumentative emphasis. As noted earlier, Espada's free-form line breaks counter-logical structure and dramatize emotion. In the case of a Shakespearean sonnet, however, its ordered structure and regular rhythm underscore its pattern of reasoning and logic, as illustrated in "Sonnet 18":

Sonnet 18

Shall I compare thee to a summer's day?
Thou art more lovely and more temperate:
Rough winds do shake the darling buds of May,
And summer's lease hath all too short a date:
5 Sometime too hot the eye of heaven shines,
And often is his gold complexion dimmed;
And every fair from fair sometimes declines
By chance or nature's changing course untrimmed;
But thy eternal summer shall not fade,
10 Nor lose possession of that fair thou ow'st,
Nor shall death brag thou wander'st in his shade,
When in eternal lines to time thou grow'st:
   So long as men can breathe or eyes can see,
   So long lives this, and this gives life to thee.

In the sonnet, the poet's claim is explicitly stated in the final quatrain: For as long as men live, this poem shall live and so, too, shall his beloved. In the preceding twelve lines, the poet provides evidence for his claim. Beginning with "a summer's day," he lists comparisons, each of which he finds deficient: "Sometime too hot the eye of heaven shines, / And often is his gold complexion dimmed." As readers, we are invited to think and reason with the poet as he makes his case for his beloved's immortality.

Ethos

Questioning the speaker's reliability leads us to the last point of Aristotle's rhetorical triangle: *ethos* appeal—the attitude the speaker or writer conveys through specific word choices. In King's "Letter from Birmingham Jail" (chapter 4), King offers a verbal handshake to build trust with his audience: ". . . finds you strong in the faith. . . . as a fellow Christian and clergyman." However, as readers, we cannot always readily agree about a speaker's or writer's credibility. For example, read the following, "Sonnet 130" by Shakespeare:

Sonnet 130

My mistress' eyes are nothing like the sun;
Coral is far more red than her lips' red;
If snow be white, why then her breasts are dun;
If hairs be wires, black wires grow on her head.
I have seen roses damasked, red and white,   5
But no such roses see I in her cheeks;
And in some perfumes there is more delight
Than in the breath that from my mistress reeks.
I love to hear her speak, yet well I know
That music has a far more pleasing sound;   10
I grant I never saw a goddess go;
My mistress, when she walks, treads on the ground.
    And yet, by heaven, I think my love as rare
    As any she belied with false compare.

As in "Sonnet 18," the poet states his claim in the final quatrain: "And yet, by heaven, I think my love as rare / As any she belied with false compare." And again the poet laces the first twelve lines with comparisons as evidence for his claim.

However, studying the specific images, readers are led to scrutinize the poet's tone and to question the sincerity of his declaration of "love as rare." Would one whose love is "rare" describe his mistress' breasts as "dun," her hair as "black wires," her breath as "reek[ing]"? Does the poet intend to compliment her or to poke fun at her? And what does he mean by "rare"—rare as in precious, or rare as in unusual? Finally, how do we as individual readers respond to our perception of his character? Do we admire him for his down-to-earth honesty and witty outlook, or do we fault him for a mean-spirited, sexist attitude? Debates over the *ethos* of the poet/speaker can spark lively classroom discussions and prompt us to examine our own attitudes and assumptions about men and women and relationships.

For a different perspective on *ethos* appeal, read the following short fiction piece, "Girl," by Jamaica Kincaid:

Girl

JAMAICA KINCAID

Wash the white clothes on Monday and put them on the stone heap; wash the color clothes on Tuesday and put them on the clothesline to dry; don't walk barehead in the hot sun; cook pumpkin fritters in very hot sweet oil; soak your little clothes right after you take them off; when buying cotton to make yourself a nice blouse, be sure that it doesn't have gum on it, because that way it won't hold up well after a wash; soak salt fish overnight before you cook it; is it true that you sing benna in Sunday school?; always eat your food in such a way that it won't turn someone else's stomach; on Sundays try to walk like a lady and not like the slut you are so bent on becoming; don't sing benna in Sunday school; you must-n't speak to wharf-rat boys, not even to give directions; don't eat fruits on the street—flies will follow you; *but I don't sing benna on Sundays at all and never in Sunday school;* this is how to sew on a button; this is how to make a buttonhole for the button you have just sewed on; this is how to hem a dress when you see the hem coming down and so to prevent your-self from looking like the slut I know you are so bent on becoming; this is how you iron your father's khaki shirt so that it doesn't have a crease; this is how you iron your father's khaki pants so that they don't have a crease; this is how you grow okra—far from the house, because okra tree harbors red ants; when you are growing dasheen, make sure it gets plenty of water or else it makes your throat itch when you are eating it; this is how you sweep a corner; this is how you sweep a whole house; this is how you sweep a yard; this is how you smile to someone you don't like too much; this is how you smile to someone you don't like at all; this is how you smile to someone you like completely; this is how you set a table for tea; this is how you set a table for dinner; this is how you set a table for dinner with an im-portant guest; this is how you set a table for lunch; this is how you set a table for break-fast; this is how to behave in the presence of men who don't know you very well, and this way they won't recognize immediately the slut I have warned you against becoming; be sure to wash every day, even if it is with your own spit; don't squat down to play marbles—you are not a boy, you know; don't pick people's flowers—you might catch something; don't throw stones at blackbirds, because it might not be a blackbird at all; this is how to make a bread pudding; this is how to make doukona; this is how to make pepper pot; this is how to make a good medicine for a cold; this is how to make a good medicine to throw away a child before it even becomes a child; this is how to catch a fish; this is how to throw back a fish you don't like, and that way something bad won't fall on you; this is how to bully a man; this is how a man bullies you; this is how to love a man, and if this doesn't work there are other ways, and if they don't work don't feel too bad about giving up; this is how to spit up in the air if you feel like it, and this is how to move quickly so that it doesn't fall on you; this is how to make ends meet; always squeeze bread to make sure it's fresh; *but what if the baker won't let me feel the bread?;* you mean to say that after all you are really going to be the kind of woman who the baker won't let near the bread?

Kincaid's narrator would seem to be a mother lecturing her daughter, "girl." The mother's advice and admonitions are salt-of-the-earth, basic survival skills for a girl or woman: from how to cook, how to clean, and how to spit or smile to how to take care of a man or to administer her own birth control. Clearly the mother is intent on her daughter's listening; the daughter manages only two brief rebuttals: "*but I don't sing benna on Sundays . . . but what if the baker won't let me feel the bread?*" Furthermore, the mother's tone is authoritative and domineering; her lecture is spiked with imper-ative clauses: do this, do that, don't do that, never do this, and so on. Yet it also is a catalog of practical information: "this is how . . .; this is how . . ." The mother is pass-ing on to her daughter all of her own hard-earned knowledge. As readers, what is our attitude toward this mother? Is she a "good" mother? Do we respect her? Trust her? Why or why not? In response, we find ourselves scrutinizing the tone of the voice we hear as we read this short piece and examine the narrator's motives. Would we describe the tone as simple yet elegant, a message of "tough love," or crude and haranguing, a belittling message of misguided love? Like "Sonnet 130," Kincaid's short fiction piece can provoke energetic discussion and prompt us to explore our underlying assumptions about the role of a parent or an authority figure.

Rogerian Argument Strategy

Common sense dictates that successful argument depends on our success in engaging audiences—in particular, those audiences with opposing or conflicting viewpoints. Yet how often have we witnessed or participated in an argument, such as the following:

Michael: I think the use of animals for medical science research and laboratory testing should be banned. It's unethical, immoral, and inefficient to use animals for these experimentations.

Meredith: That's easy for you to say. But what if your own child or your mother or your brother had a life-threatening illness and needed a certain drug or maybe an organ transplant? Wouldn't you want the best medical science could do for your loved one? And wouldn't you want that treatment to have been laboratory-tested on animals?

Michael: No. Animals have as much right to life as we do. We're no better. In fact, when I look around the world today, I think we may be less deserving than animals.

Meredith: You're a fanatic. I love animals, too, but a human life is more valuable than an animal's.

. . . end of the argument. But what was accomplished? Each party has had his or her moment at the podium to justify his or her position. Each party walks away from the argument, unchanged, unmoved by the opposing viewpoint, indeed, perhaps even more entrenched in his or her position. How can we avoid these dead-end arguments? If we and our audience have strong viewpoints on a divisive issue, how can we build that essential bridge between our views and our audience's?

Earlier we noted that Stephen Toulmin adapted Aristotle's classical model of argument to suit the needs of modern and contemporary audiences. Similarly, in studying audience appeal and tone, the work of Carl R. Rogers, an American psychotherapist and communication theorist, complements Aristotle's rhetorical triangle. According to Rogers, we engage our audience by demonstrating empathy with their viewpoints; we present an objective summation of the opposing viewpoints. In this way, we acknowledge their validity and, therefore, open the doors for communication—a first and crucial step for argumentation. At the same time, we present ourselves as individuals of good will and character, thus building trust with our audience (*ethos* appeal).

Rogers's theory of argumentation and audience empathy, **Rogerian strategy**, appears frequently in argument textbooks. In fact, Rogerian strategy follows the common sense wisdom of the "golden rule": "Do unto others as you would have them do unto you." In other words, I will listen openly to your views; in exchange, you will agree to listen openly to mine. Furthermore, the conclusion or claim of Rogerian argument is a well-qualified, compromise position. For example, in the earlier dialogue, a Rogerian conclusion might read: "Recognizing that the use of animals for tests and laboratory experiments is inherently unfair to the animals, we must strictly regulate research laboratories to ensure that conditions are humane and to limit the use of animal testing." All in all, negotiation and compromise are the ruling principles of Rogerian argument strategy (see Chapter Three).

In theory, the Rogerian strategy seems wholly sensible, based, as it is, on a practical understanding of people and an awareness of human nature. But in our competitive society ("Winning's not everything—it's the only thing") and amidst a media culture that seems to thrive on an "in-your-face" hollering match, the Rogerian style takes a backseat. Indeed, in presenting Rogerian argument in the composition classroom, as teachers we find that students often protest its nonaggressive tone ("where's the fun?") and question its tactics ("manipulative, deceptive?"). We respond that Rogerian argument does not mean giving up one's beliefs, nor does it mean accepting whatever anyone says or writes; rather we ask our students to agree to listen to opposing viewpoints with the purpose of understanding them.

For example, let's consider one current and enduring environmental issue: the preservation of wilderness or "green spaces." Clearly these areas are shrinking, squeezed out by the needs of a growing population and technological culture. And in the case of some of the more popular national parks, Yellowstone, for example, the visitors themselves are literally the vehicles of much ecological degradation. Given these premises, the conclusion seems simple: Take action before it's too late, before there are no remaining wilderness areas to preserve. But action requires money—taxpayers' dollars. Meanwhile, other environments, not likely featured on a glossy Sierra Club calendar, are also threatened and endangered; these are our cities, our large urban areas where thousands of citizens live. We worry about the drug culture and violent crimes, yet send young children off to schools with overcrowded classrooms, overworked teachers, and too few textbooks. Again, given these premises, the conclusion seems simple: Take action now to improve urban schools and provide these children with a quality education. Again, action requires money—taxpayers' dollars.

The wilderness and urban environments would seem to be competing factions, and indeed, public discussion often fosters this division. Meanwhile, the media, hungry for drama, fan the flames of divisiveness by couching the different groups in extreme terms. Serious thinking evaporates. The fight is on: "us against them." In the headlong rush to win, each side must beat its drums more loudly and attempt to drown out others. Of course, serious thinking does not have to be overcome by contentious rhetoric. If we practice the habit of listening—of understanding and empathizing with other persons' perspectives—we are less likely to be waylaid by simplistic thinking.

Reading stories, poems, plays, and essays fosters empathetic understanding and provides practice in receptive listening. For example, we may never have lived in a large urban environment, but reading Lucille Clifton's poem, "For deLawd," gives us, at least for a moment, an insider's viewpoint:

For deLawd

people say they have a hard time
understanding how I
go on about my business
playing my Ray Charles
hollering at my kids—   5
seem like my Afro
cut off in some old image
would show I got a long memory
and I come from a line
of black and going on women   10
who got used to making it through murdered sons
and who kept on pushing
who fried chicken
ironed
swept off the back steps   15
who grief kept
for their still alive sons
for their sons coming
for their sons gone
just pushing   20
in the inner city
or
like we call it
home
we think a lot about uptown   25
and the silent nights
and the houses straight as
dead men
and the pastel lights
and we hang on to our no place   30
happy to be alive
and in the inner city
or
like we call it
home   35

This black woman and mother of sons, who lives in the "inner city," speaks to us directly and plainly about "home": we see people who are going about the daily doings of living; who love, who grieve, and who are proud, "happy to be alive." Thus, rather than an abstract slogan or label, the "inner city" becomes a real place for us.

Similarly, N. Scott Momaday's poem, "New World," invites us to go out in nature and witness the unfolding of a day:

New World

1.
First Man,
behold:
the earth
glitters
with leaves;
the sky
glistens
with rain.
Pollen
is borne
on winds
that low
and lean
upon
mountains.
Cedars
blacken the slopes—
and pines.

2.
At dawn
eagles
hie and
hover
above
the plain
where light
gathers
in pools.
Grasses
shimmer
and shine.
Shadows
withdraw
and lie
away
like smoke.

3.
At noon
turtles
enter
slowly
into
the warm
dark loam.
Bees hold
the swarm.
Meadows
recede
through planes
of heat
and pure
distance.

4.
At dusk
the gray
foxes
stiffen
in cold;
blackbirds
are fixed
in the
branches.
Rivers
follow
the moon,
the long
white track
of the
full moon.

The poem's short, one- or two-word lines demand our close attention as readers. We must practice patience and slow ourselves down to follow the text of the poem accurately. Then, like the "First Man," we can "behold" the treasures which the day reveals: "the earth / glitters . . . grasses shimmer."

The study of literature and the study of argument are complementary and mutually empowering; both contribute to critical thinking and creative envisioning. Even as we hold fast to opposing viewpoints, we share the common ground of our humanity. Literature can lead us to this common ground. By tapping into our imaginations, literature can help us see from a broader and a more in-depth perspective, our personal, day-to-day issues as well as enduring, public issues. In this way, we are better prepared to articulate a thoughtful position and to argue it with heartfelt emotion, clear logic, and valid reasoning. Through the interplay of arguments, we participate in shaping our lives and the affairs of our communities.

CHAPTER ACTIVITIES

1. In our culture we see arguments everywhere: from billboards to Web sites, from magazines to television. Record the subject of an argument you encounter. In doing so, complete this sentence: *The arguer wants us to believe that ___(claim)___ because ___(evidence)___*. Be prepared to share with your classmates.

2. In a group of three or more, select an issue that prompts local or national debate. Pick one side in the debate and write its *claim* in one sentence. List several examples of *evidence* this side uses to support its claim. What *warrants* (assumptions) do the followers of this side hold? List them. And finally, which rhetorical appeals (*logos, pathos, ethos*) does this side use? List them and include examples.

3. a. What assumption about suburban neighborhoods does the editorial cartoon below challenge?
   b. Bring to class an editorial cartoon which challenges a widely held assumption.

Mike Smith reprinted by permission of United Feature Syndicate, Inc.

4. After reading "Those Winter Sundays" by Robert Hayden, write out the poet's claim in one sentence. Now list the poem's evidence that supports that claim. Is the claim valid only within the dramatic context of the poem? Or is the claim valid

universally? Can you find evidence within your own personal experience that would support the claim? What warrant underlies the claim?

Those Winter Sundays

Sundays too my father got up early
and put his clothes on in the blueblack cold,
then with cracked hands that ached
from labor in the weekday weather made
5 banked fires blaze. No one ever thanked him.

I'd wake and hear the cold splintering, breaking.
When the rooms were warm, he'd call,
and slowly I would rise and dress,
fearing the chronic angers of that house,

10 Speaking indifferently to him,
who had driven out the cold
and polished my good shoes as well.
What did I know, what did I know
of love's austere and lonely offices?

5. Read Wilfred Owen's poem "*Dulce Et Decorum Est.*" How does the poet use Aristotle's three rhetorical appeals to convince us of his claim that the phrase, "*Dulce et decorum est / Pro patria mori,*"[2] lacks merit? Is there a logical presentation of evidence? Is there an emotional presentation of evidence? Does the speaker seem to have credibility?

Dulce Et Decorum Est

Bent double, like old beggars under sacks,
Knock-kneed, coughing like hags, we cursed through sludge,
Till on the haunting flares we turned our backs
And towards our distant rest began to trudge.
5 Men marched asleep. Many had lost their boots
But limped on, blood-shod. All went lame; all blind;
Drunk with fatigue; deaf even to the hoots
Of tired, outstripped Five-Nines that dropped behind.

Gas! GAS! Quick boys!—An ecstasy of fumbling,
10 Fitting the clumsy helmets just in time;
But someone still was yelling out and stumbling
And flound'ring like a man in fire or lime—
Dim, through the misty panes and thick green light,
As under a green sea, I saw him drowning.

---

[2]Quotation from Horace meaning, "It is sweet and dutiful to die for one's country."

In all my dreams, before my helpless sight,   15
He plunges at me, guttering, choking, drowning.

If in some smothering dreams you too could pace
Behind the wagon that we flung him in,
And watch the white eyes writhing in his face,
His hanging face, like a devil's sick of sin;   20
If you could hear, at every jolt, the blood
Come gargling from the froth-corrupted lungs,
Obscene as cancer, bitter as the cud

Of vile, incurable sores on innocent tongues,—
My friend, you would not tell with such high zest   25
To children ardent for some desperate glory,
The old Lie: *Dulce et decorum est*
Pro patria mori.

6. *Modeling a Master:* As editorial cartoons demonstrate, not all arguments rely on words. In the 12-panel poster, "A Short History of America" on page 24, cartoonist Robert Crumb uses only visual images to create the text for his argument.
   a. Write out a single, descriptive sentence for each of the twelve panels.
   b. Outline the argument's structure: Write out its *claim, evidence,* and *warrants/value assumptions.*
   c. To what extent do you agree or disagree with Crumb's argument?
   d. Create your own visual argument. Consider modeling Crumb's design concept, which traces a change over time—for example, *a short history of* family, . . . *of* marriage, . . . *of* college football, . . . *of* television, or . . . *of* the telephone. First, you will need to write out an outline for your argument: to state a claim, identify some evidence, and at least one warrant. Next, assemble a series of visual panels to depict your argument (cut out photos or illustrations, use computer graphics or clip art, or create your own drawings).

7. Examine the verbal and visual texts of Paul Madonna's "All Over Coffee" on page 25. How does Madonna suggest a counterargument to Crumb's "A Short History of America"?

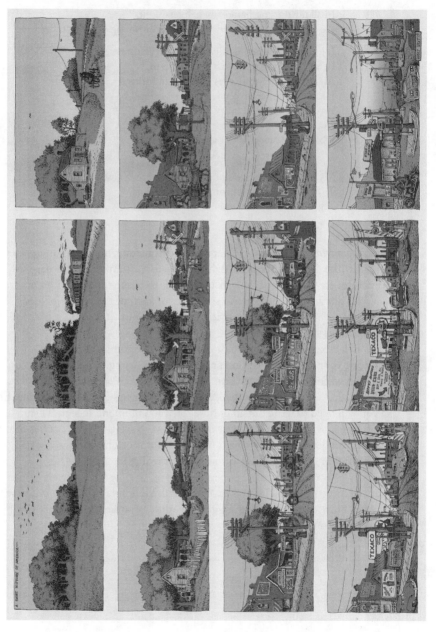

All Over Coffee

I was late, but as I stood to leave the sandwich shop, a song came on that I hadn't heard since childhood, and reminded me of my father.

So I sat back down, closed my eyes and listened.

My phone rang, and I turned it off.

On Sundays, Dad would take me on walks through the city.

He would hold my hand and we'd make up stories about why people built all the buildings.

Then randomly, he'd stop us on a corner, even if the walk sign was lit. He'd bend in close to me, smile and flutter his eyebrows.

"Let's wait until the next one," he'd say, "make old fate rearrange her plans."

© 2005 Paul Madonna

CHAPTER 2

Examining Thinking and Shaping an Argument

"Everyone agrees in theory we can't judge a new point of view unless we enter into it and try it out, but the practice itself is rare."
—*Peter Elbow*

Mark Twain, well known for his skepticism about the human race, was particularly scathing in his comments about man's ability to think independently. "We are creatures of outside influences; as a rule we do not think, we only imitate," Twain writes in his essay, "Corn-Pone Opinions."[1] Indeed, everyone has an opinion: "You have your opinion; I have mine." How often have we heard this comment? We arrive at these opinions through our reasoning. This reasoning process secures our status as a higher order of animal than, say, a mole, which reacts to stimuli (although when ranking reasoning abilities, Twain probably would have placed the mole above humans). Throughout our waking moments, we are forming opinions, many of these quickly and subconsciously, seemingly without thinking or at least without examining our reasoning process.

The enormous influence of mass media in our culture undermines any impulse toward independent thought. In an increasingly complex world, any one person cannot hope to have more than a rudimentary understanding of such issues as welfare reform in the United States, inflation and interest rates, global warming, or ethnic conflicts in the Balkan region. In their efforts to fill our information gap, news magazines serve us up predigested facts leading to undeniably *correct* conclusions, and televised news programs often seem to make little distinction between fact and opinion. Movies also present us with distinct perspectives of current affairs. Whether another's opinion or our own, we must constantly question the foundation of that opinion: What assumptions do we make about the world? What inferences do we unwittingly want to accept? And to what extent is our thinking based on flawed logic?

[1]Mark Twain, *The Family Mark Twain* (New York and London: Harper & Brothers Publishers, 1935), p. 1402.

Copyright © 1998 by Don Wright. Used by permission of Don Wright/The Palm Beach Post.

EXAMINING THINKING

If we pay attention to the media, we are likely to believe crime is a major problem in the United States. Our newspapers and television programs are filled with graphic reports of criminal activities, from fraudulent corporate schemes to random mass shootings. Popular films regularly depict criminal situations culminating in extreme violence. Let's put ourselves in the place of a person living alone in a suburban neighborhood. Through the influence of the media, such a person might fear for his life. And such fears may well restrict this person's daily activities—he may no longer feel safe taking the bus to his doctor's appointments; he may avoid the local mall where he encounters, in his view, many oddly dressed adolescents; and he may feel too insecure to take an evening walk in his neighborhood. On the other hand, living where he does, the probability of this man's becoming a victim of crime is minimal. Nevertheless, acting on his **assumption**—crime is epidemic—he has narrowed his life. From his perspective of the world, shaped by the media's daily news reports, his argument is clear: Because I do not want to become a victim of crime, I must stay at home where I feel somewhat secure.

This individual's thinking is based on flawed reasoning. Although it is true that crime can occur anywhere, he has used inadequate evidence to generalize about the crime risk in his own suburban community. His error in reasoning, moving from inadequate evidence to a broad generalization, illustrates a common logical fallacy: **hasty generalization.** We also know this fallacy as the clichéd expression, *jumping to conclusions.*

When we move from particular evidence to make a broad assertion, we are thinking inductively. Although hasty generalization is a fallacy, **inductive reasoning** also sparks creative thinking which can lead us to personal insights or profound discoveries. Based on a careful examination of *what is,* we envision *what could be.* For example, when a college instructor notices her students are experiencing difficulty understanding the assigned readings and notes that her students' scores on the verbal portion of the SAT have fallen, she could reasonably conclude that students at her particular institution are reflecting a national trend toward weaker reading skills. This conclusion would provide the motivation for the professor to seek a creative solution to the problem. A conclusion reached through inductive reasoning is also called an **inference,** which the linguist S. I. Hayakawa defined as "a statement about the unknown based on the known."[2] Although we cannot know for certain that an inference is 100 percent true, based on what we do know, we can feel convinced it is probably true.

Not uncommonly, however, people make their inductive leaps too soon; they jump to a conclusion when their evidence is inadequate. For example, a toddler may burn his fingers on a stove, and after that incident he may say, "Hot! Hot!" whenever entering a kitchen and seeing a stove. The toddler's parents, although amused by his simplistic conclusion (of course, not all stoves are hot at all times), are also glad that he views the stove as a dangerous beast. However, in some cases, a person's hasty generalization can have tragic consequences. For example, you may have read Shakespeare's *Romeo and Juliet* in high school or have seen a movie adaptation. In the end, although Juliet is merely pretending to have taken her own life, Romeo immediately jumps to the conclusion she is dead and takes his own life. In Act 5, Romeo meets his servant on the streets of Mantua:

Romeo:	News from Verona! How now Balthasar?	
	Dost thou not bring me letters from the friar?	
	How doth my lady? Is my father well?	
	How fares my Juliet? That I ask again,	
	For nothing can be ill if she be well.	5
Balthasar:	Then she is well, and nothing can be ill.	
	Her body sleeps in Capel's monument,	
	And her immortal part with angels lives,	
	I saw her laid low in her kindred's vault	
	And presently took post to tell it you.	10
	O, pardon me for bringing thee ill news,	
	Since you did leave it for my office, sir.	
Romeo:	Is it e'en so? Then I defy you, stars!	
	Thou knowest my lodging. Get me ink and paper	
	And hire post horses. I will hence tonight.	15
Balthasar:	I do beseech you, sir, have patience.	
	Your looks are pale and wild and do import	
	Some misadventure.	

---

[2]S. I. Hayakawa, *Language in Thought and Action* (New York: Harcourt, Brace, Jovanovich, 1978), p. 35.

[Although the servant has delivered terrible news to Romeo, he can also see that Romeo is in no state of mind to think the situation through clearly. The key word in Balthasar's speech is "patience," something Romeo does not possess at the moment. Nor has he gained any patience when, later arriving at the tomb, he kills Paris and lays him in the tomb near Juliet. And as he turns his attention to Juliet herself, Romeo still is not thinking clearly.]

Romeo:	. . . O my love, my wife!	
	Death, that hath sucked the honey of thy breath,	
	Hath had no power yet upon thy beauty.	
	Thou art not conquered. Beauty's ensign yet	
5	Is crimson in thy lips and in thy cheeks.	
	And death's pale flag is not advanced there.	
	. . . Ah, dear Juliet,	
	Why art thou yet so fair? Shall I believe	
	That unsubstantial Death is amorous,	
10	And that the lean abhorrèd monster keeps	
	Thee here in dark to be his paramour?	
	For fear of that I will stay with thee	
	And never from this pallet of dim night	
	Depart again	

* * *

15   [*Drinks*] O true apothecary!
Thy drugs are quick. Thus with a kiss I die.

[Of course, as we know, Juliet is not dead but merely drugged. Romeo's confusion is understandable; after all, his servant has told him Juliet is dead, and he himself has seen her lying in a tomb. However, Romeo also has seen quite clearly that she does not look dead ("crimson in thy lips and in thy cheeks"). Even so, his emotional state overpowers his reason, and he ignores this important piece of evidence. Romeo jumps to a fatal conclusion: He drinks the poison he has brought with him and dies beside his, yet living, beloved Juliet.]

Arthur Miller's twentieth-century play, *The Crucible*, based on the Salem witch trials of 1692, also illustrates how emotion, in this case, fear, can derail reasoning and clear thinking. In the play, as in historical Salem, Massachusetts, the townspeople jump to the conclusion that the women are witches, although their evidence, the testimony of young girls, is inadequate. At the close of Act 1, the girls, Abigail and Betty, begin their accusations:

Hale: Take courage, you must give us all their names. How can you bear to see this child suffering? Look at her, Tituba. *He is indicating Betty on the bed.* Look at her God-given innocence; her soul so tender; we must protect her Tituba; the Devil is out and preying on her like a beast upon the flesh of the pure lamb. God will bless you for your help.

Abigail rises, staring as though inspired, and cries out.

Abigail: I want to open myself! *They turn to her, startled. She is enraptured, as though in a pearly light.* I want the light of God, I want the sweet love of Jesus! I danced for the Devil; I saw him; I wrote in his book; I go back to Jesus; I kiss His hand. I saw Sarah Good with the Devil! I saw Goody Osburn with the Devil! I saw Bridget Bishop with the Devil!

As she is speaking, Betty is rising from the bed, a fever in her eyes, and picks up the chant.

Betty, *staring too:* I saw George Jacobs with the Devil! I saw Goody Howe with the Devil!
Parris: She speaks! *He rushes to embrace Betty.* She speaks!
Hale: Glory to God! It is broken, they are free!
Betty, *calling out hysterically and with great relief:* I saw Martha Bellows with the Devil!
Abigail: I saw Goody Sibber with the Devil! *It is rising to a great glee.*
Putnam: The marshal, I'll call the marshal!

Parris is shouting a prayer of thanksgiving.

Betty: I saw Alice Barrow with the Devil!

The curtain begins to fall.

Hale, *as Putnam goes out:* Let the marshal bring irons!

[The dialogue and stage directions depict the strong emotions that surround this situation. The men, who very much *want* to believe the girls' accusations, readily make the inductive leap to condemn the accused women. And once made, they secure exactly what they want: the accused women's guilty verdict. In contrast, at the start of Act 2, Miller shows us two people for whom the evidence is inadequate.]

Elizabeth: . . .There be fourteen people in jail now. *Proctor simply looks at her, unable to grasp it.* And they'll be tried, and the courts have power to hang them too.
Proctor, *scoffing, but without conviction:* Ah, they'd never hang—
Elizabeth: The Deputy Governor promises hangin' if they'll not confess, John. The town's gone wild, I think. She speaks of Abigail, and I thought she were a saint, to hear her. Abigail brings the other girls into the court, and where she walks the crowd will part like the sea for Israel. And folks are brought before them, and if they scream and howl and fall to the floor—the person's clapped in the jail for bewitchin' them.
Proctor, *wide-eyed:* Oh, it is a black mischief.
Elizabeth: I think you must go to Salem, John. *He turns to her.* I think so. You must tell them it is a fraud.

[John Proctor does, indeed, go to Salem, but to no avail. The town has "gone wild," allowing emotion to overcome all reason. Based on inadequate evidence, the people of Salem have made a hasty generalization. As a result, fourteen people are hanged.]

Perhaps we are inclined to tell ourselves that these events in Salem took place over three hundred years ago and, therefore, do not apply to our contemporary world. However, we need only to look back to the mid-twentieth century to see a series of events dominated by emotion rather than reason—the McCarthy hearings in which the House UnAmerican Activities Commission investigated persons accused of being communists. In fact, this occurrence inspired Miller to write *The Crucible.* Appealing to fear—the post–World War II threat of communism, the "Red Scare"—this group in Congress thwarted or ruined the careers of many journalists and actors in this country. Again, as in colonial Salem, reason was overcome by emotion. Indeed, the term "witch hunt" has as much viability today as it did in the late 1600s. We must remain vigilant to avoid becoming victims of our own flawed reasoning, slaves to purely emotional appeals. Examining literature, like *Romeo and Juliet* and *The Crucible,* helps us to practice this vigilance.

Hasty generalization, when it fosters **stereotyping,** can have considerable negative impact on individuals and far-reaching implications on our policies and institutions. When we form quick judgments about other persons, based on their outward appearance—their dress, their hairstyle, their accent, or their gender, race, or age—we may be making a hasty generalization. As we suggested in Chapter One, for example, the narrator in the short story "Cathedral" (Chapter Seven) has formed simplistic generalizations about "blindness" from images in movies. Standing apart as readers, we clearly see the narrator's own blindness, his narrow-mindedness and prejudicial thinking. In contrast, we may not so readily detect our own narrow thinking when it is reinforced by popular culture and media images.

Of course, we should take individual responsibility for our opinions about others and about issues and events. Taking this responsibility, however, demands hard thinking—the continuous questioning of the underlying evidence that affects our generalizations and inferences. But hard thinking sounds like hard work. Perhaps, "ignorance is bliss"? Of course not. Most of us would not knowingly choose to be prejudicial thinkers. In reading literature, our imaginations allow us to practice using our mental energy: We journey with characters to Vietnam, we hear about the inner city, or we see the boy in the tomato field thrust his finger toward the sky in protest. In writing about literature, we develop the habit of inquiry and scrutiny. We explore the roots of our thinking, examine the underlying logic of our assumptions, evaluate the validity of our generalizations, and articulate our conclusions. And once committed to living the examined life—to scrutinizing assumptions, to questioning evidence, and to analyzing arguments—we cannot turn away from the task of taking responsibility for our choices and opinions.

DEDUCTION AND INDUCTION: AN OVERVIEW

Logicians use the terms **inductive** (specific to general) and **deductive** (general to specific) to describe our reasoning process. Inductive reasoning is an open-ended process in that the conclusion reached is *always* based on probability. Deductive reasoning, on the other hand, aims to *prove* its conclusion by confining or limiting its scope. To practice the habit of self-inquiry and evaluation, inductive and deductive thinking are useful tools of analysis. For example, let's consider Percy Bysshe Shelley's poem, "Ozymandias":

Ozymandias

I met a traveler from an antique land
Who said: Two vast and trunkless legs of stone
Stand in the desert . . . Near them, on the sand,
Half sunk, a shattered visage lies, whose frown,
And wrinkled lip, and sneer of cold command,   5
Tell that its sculptor well those passions read
Which yet survive, stamped on these lifeless things,
The hand that mocked them, and the heart that fed:
And on the pedestal these words appear:
"My name is Ozymandias, king of kings: 10
Look on my works, ye Mighty and despair!"
Nothing beside remains. Round the decay
Of that colossal wreck, boundless and bare
The lone and level sands stretch far away.

Using the model of Aristotle's syllogism (Toulmin terms in parentheses), we can outline Ozymandias's reasoning:

Major premise (warrant):	The monuments of great and powerful leaders will last forever.
Minor premise (support):	I am a great and powerful leader who has built monuments.
Conclusion (claim):	Therefore, my monuments will last forever.

Ozymandias bases his argument on an underlying, unstated assumption that seems true to him—the monuments of kings are eternal. However, on what evidence is his assumption based? Propelled by self-pride and arrogance, the "king of kings" has made an inductive leap to arrive at his major premise. From this premise, he reasons deductively that his "works" will last forever. In the last lines of the poem, however, the poet proclaims the error of Ozymandias's reasoning:

Nothing beside remains. Round the decay
Of that colossal wreck, boundless and bare
The lone and level sands stretch far away.

Inductive reasoning, often occurring beneath the surface, that is, subconsciously, is risky, prone to error, as in the case of Ozymandias. However, as noted earlier, inductive reasoning also can lead to profound discoveries. For example, the research scientist first must risk an inductive leap in her search for a cure for a disease. After observing patterns of reactions of certain viruses to a particular agent in laboratory experiments, she may predict (hypothesize) that this virus would react similarly to this agent within a human subject. She then would use deductive reasoning to test her hypothesis: She would set up specific laboratory conditions to prove or disprove her theory. We see, therefore, how inductive and deductive reasoning are intertwined in argumentation. The two processes are not contradictory; rather, they are complementary, as inextricably linked as wings are to a bird: one does not "fly" without the other.

LOGICAL FALLACIES

Common Fallacies

Ad hominem   the fallacy of personal attack. Instead of arguing with someone's position, one attacks the person. Ex.: Mrs. X has had a extramarital affair and does not deserve our vote.

Begging the question   to use an argument that assumes exactly what the argument attempts to prove. Ex.: Capital punishment deters crimes because it prevents criminals from committing crimes.

Either-or reasoning   sometimes called the *black and white* or *false dilemma fallacy;* in argument, such reasoning is characterized by oversimplification that presents an issue only in two ways, either X or Y. Ex: Either you vote for this school bond, or we may as well shut down our public schools.

Equivocation   in argument, the intentional use of a word which has more than one interpretation and thus misleads the reader or listener. Ex.: I am simply adjusting some figures; I am not cheating on my tax return.

False analogy   a false comparison, sometimes expressed as "comparing apples to oranges." Ex.: People might say that like Rome, America is destined for destruction; however, modern America is quite unlike ancient Rome.

Hasty generalization   a fallacy of induction in which someone jumps to a broad conclusion based on too little evidence. Stereotyping is an example of hasty generalization. Ex.: English professors are nonathletic bookworms.

***Post hoc* fallacy**   incorrectly attributing a cause and effect relationship; often called the false cause fallacy. Ex.: If you follow a vegetarian diet, you will stunt your growth.

Red herring   the fallacy of leading the reader astray by bringing up a different issue as bait to capture the reader's interest, thus distracting him or her from the real issue. Ex: You must give me a "B" in this class; I need the grade to keep my scholarship.

Slippery slope   suggests a single event or situation will trigger a series of seemingly catastrophic effects; a false appeal to fear. Ex.: If the drinking age is lowered to 18, we will end up with a nation of alcoholics.

> **Two wrongs make a right**   justifying wrongdoing by pointing to another's wrongdoing. Ex.: So maybe I did fudge a bit when I reported my income to the IRS, but so do many of the nation's richest people.

The unexamined bone is not worth chewing.[3]

SHAPING AN ARGUMENT

When we sit down to write our own arguments, we face several tasks:

1. We must be certain we have clearly identified the *issue*.
2. We must gather and analyze the information logically.
3. We must create a *claim* which uses well-defined terminology and is limited in scope.
4. We must provide adequate support by selecting specific, accurate, and relevant *evidence*.
5. We must organize our evidence in a way that effectively presents our argument to the audience.

---

[3]This cartoon alludes to Socrates's famous aphorism, "The unexamined life is not worth living."

To see how these five elements come together in writing an argument, let's look at two excerpts from Martin Luther King Jr.'s "Letter from Birmingham Jail" (Chapter Four).

In the following example of **deductive** organization, King makes a general statement as a major premise (*warrant*), then states his *claim*, and, finally in the succeeding five paragraphs, supports his claim with *evidence:*

> In any nonviolent campaign there are four basic steps: collection of the facts to determine whether injustices exist; negotiation; self-purification; and direct action [*major premise*]. We have gone through all of these steps in Birmingham [*claim*]. . . . Birmingham is probably the most thoroughly segregated city in the United States. . . . [*evidence* for collection of facts].
>
> Then, last September, came the opportunity to talk to leaders of Birmingham's economic community. . . . [*evidence* for negotiation] Mindful of the difficulties involved, we decided to undertake a process of self-purification. We began a series of workshops on non-violence. . . . [*evidence* for self-purification]
>
> Then it occurred to us that Birmingham's mayoral election was coming up in March, and we speedily decided to postpone direct action until after election day. . . . Having aided in this community need, we felt our direct-action program could be delayed no longer. [*evidence* for direct action]

King later uses a pattern of **inductive** organization to refute his audience's position that his direct-action program was "untimely" and that he should have waited for the new civic administration to remedy segregation. First, King piles on specific examples and personal testimonies as his *evidence,* and then he presents his *claim:*

> We have waited for more than 340 years for our constitutional and Godgiven rights. The nations of Asia and Africa are moving with jetlike speed toward gaining political independence, but we still creep at horse-and-buggy pace toward gaining a cup of coffee at a lunch counter. Perhaps it is easy for those who have never felt the stinging darts of segregation to say, "Wait." But when you have seen vicious mobs lynch your mothers and fathers at will and drown your sisters and brothers at whim; when you have seen hate-filled policemen curse, kick and even kill your black brothers and sisters; when you see the vast majority of your twenty million Negro brothers smothering in an airtight cage of poverty in the midst of an affluent society; when you suddenly find your tongue twisted and your speech stammering as you seek to explain to your six-year-old child why she can't go to the amusement park that has just been advertised on television, and see tears welling up in her eyes when she is told that Funtown is closed to colored children, and see ominous clouds of inferiority beginning to form in her little mental sky, and see her beginning to distort her personality by developing an unconscious bitterness toward white people; when you have to concoct an answer for a five-year-old son who is asking: "Daddy, why do white people treat colored people so mean?"; when you take a cross-country drive and find it necessary to sleep night after night in your automobile because no motel will accept you; when you are humiliated day in and day out by nagging signs reading "white" and "colored"; when your first name becomes "nigger," your middle name becomes "boy" (however old you are) and your last name becomes "John," and your wife and mother are never given the respected title "Mrs."; when you are harried by day and haunted by night by the fact that you are a Negro, living constantly at tiptoe stance, never quite knowing what to do next, and are plagued with inner fears and outer resentments;

when you are forever fighting a degenerating sense of "nobodiness" [*evidence*]—then you will understand why we find it difficult to wait. There comes a time when the cup of endurance runs over, and men are no longer willing to be plunged into the abyss of despair [*claim*].

Despite his strong emotional involvement, King obviously has analyzed the situation logically. Within his letter, he has composed claims that are narrowly focused and thus provable. His examples in support of these claims are concrete rather than general. And, finally, King has used both deductive and inductive patterns of organization to structure his argument effectively for his audience.

While not everyone will be able to write as skillfully as Martin Luther King Jr., creating clear, effective position statements is certainly within the grasp of any college student. In his Birmingham jail cell, King had many long hours to compose his letter, and the result shows this hard work. Although time is a scarce commodity for most college students, several sessions of concentrated effort should produce a presentable argument. For example, let's examine a topic which is relevant and familiar to college students, *working while attending college:*

1. What do you know about working and attending college (your job, friends' jobs, classmates' jobs and academic experiences, student expenses, etc.)?
2. Do you hold any principles (warrants) that direct your thinking on this subject? Or have specific experiences led you to draw conclusions about working and attending college?
3. Can you make a claim of value (good/bad) or a claim of policy (should do/should not do) regarding this subject? Or does your experience lead you to make a claim of fact (true/false)? Is your claim focused and therefore supportable?
4. Do you have sufficient concrete examples, gleaned from your experience and observations, to prove your claim?
5. How can you most effectively organize your argument? Should you follow a deductive pattern, first, stating the claim and then supporting it with examples; or should you follow an inductive pattern, first, offering examples and then concluding with the claim? Or does the length of your argument allow you to use both organizational patterns effectively?

In reading the following student essay, notice how Shawn Mullin has addressed the five writing tasks listed above:

Yes, the Future Looks Bright, but the Moment Is Hell

My share of the rent, all $220 of it, is due next Friday. Today my business management professor asked the class to buy another textbook and read chapter one before we meet again; that's $46.50 I'll need by Wednesday. The utility bill is probably already in the mail, and my girlfriend is expecting me to take her out to dinner Saturday to celebrate our "six-month anniversary." I have $36.87 in my checking account and a big problem.

According to my calculations, I need to come up with about $300 by the end of the week. Perhaps I could make one of those desperation calls to Mom and Dad although I can already hear their answer: "Shawn, we are paying your tuition and sending some spending money. We expect you to contribute as well. After all, both your brothers will be attending college in the coming years. You wouldn't want us to spend their money on you, would you!" At this point, I wouldn't object, but I know I'll never make that call. No, I already have a job; what I need are more hours— more hours in the day so I can find the time to work, study, attend class, sleep, and, when all else is done, even have a social life.

Since my boss typically pays me in cash on Fridays, all I need to do is work more hours. But at $6.50 an hour, I'll need to add quite a few hours by Friday afternoon. When school began last fall, I promised myself I would not work more than 25 hours a week, and my position at the print shop has worked out well when compared to my friends' working conditions. Their bosses also promised to hold down their hours and be considerate of exams and research papers; however, those promises were hardly made before the managers began demanding more and more time at work. My friends' protests about chemistry exams or English papers were completely ignored. They regularly work 35 to 40 hours a week; their grades reflect the lack of study time. And now I am about to join them.

Dr. Robert Jones, my history professor, recently told me that due to working while attending school, most students now take five years to complete a four-year degree. And further corroborating that news is my academic counselor, Dr. Elizabeth French, who told me that she found that the grades of students working more than 20 hours per week fell with each increase of five hours. She also explained that she found a significant decrease in participation in campus life as working hours increased because these students have no extra time for student government, clubs, or other campus organizations. That information is not good news for me since I have no choice in this situation. It's work more hours or live on the streets.

Working more than twenty hours a week has negative effects on college students. That much is clear. Nevertheless, this time I'll ask for the extra hours and accept the consequences. However, I intend to find a cheaper place to live, so I will not be in this position again next term. And who knows? Maybe my girlfriend will be just

as happy celebrating our one-year anniversary over coffee at Star-
bucks.

For this short, first-person point of view argument, the writer chose to follow an
inductive pattern of organization. The first four paragraphs present the *evidence*—
personal experience and testimony—which leads to an explicit *claim* (position statement) in the conclusion paragraph: *Working more than twenty hours a week has negative
effects on college students.* Using the same set of considerations that guided this writer,
students can create an argumentative essay in response to assigned readings in literature. Look, for example, at Daphne Beckham's essay below, prompted by two poems,
Walt Whitman's "I Saw in Louisiana a Live-Oak Growing" (page 56) and T. S. Eliot's
"The Love Song of J. Alfred Prufrock" (Chapter Four):

Perspective on Men

When I was a little girl, I thought my father was a rock, hard and
unmoving. I come from a family of strong men. These male relatives were bread-winners, stoic, and without a doubt the leaders of
their respective prides. Later, I realized these rocks had cracks
which defined their characters and souls. These men cried, they
made mistakes, and they could feel.

My earlier attitudes towards men can be summed up in the poem
by Walt Whitman entitled, "I Saw in Louisiana a Live-Oak Growing."
In the poem, the speaker compares himself to a live-oak tree:

> I saw in Louisiana a live-oak growing,
> All alone stood it and the moss hung down from the branches,
> Without any companion it grew there uttering joyous leaves
>   of dark green,
> And its look, rude, unbending, lusty, made me think of myself.

Like the tree, the speaker believes himself to be deeply rooted. He
has a vision of himself as a dominating figure who is in control of
his environment.

As I got older, I began to realize that men are not the stereotypi-
cal figures I once believed. In T. S. Eliot's poem, "The Love Song of J.
Alfred Prufrock," a different kind of man is introduced. This man
feels insecure, fragmented, and confused. Prufrock states, "I am not
Prince Hamlet, nor was meant to be." Unlike Whitman's speaker who
thinks of himself as a master of his environment, Prufrock is unsure
of his ability to command respect, admiration, or to choose the direction of his own life. He calls himself, "an attendant lord," who is not
worthy of leadership privileges, and, "Almost, at times, the fool."
When I was young, the men around me seemed strong, secure, and

certain, like Whitman's live-oak tree. Later, however, I noticed a trace of Prufrock's insecurities.

In Whitman's poem, the speaker is confident of his physical and sexual appeal. The poem makes allusions to this confidence through the use of such phrases as, "lusty," and, "manly love." In contrast, Prufrock suffers doubts about his physical attractiveness:

> And indeed there will be time,
> To wonder, "Do I dare?" and, "Do I dare?"
> Time to turn back and descend the stair,
> With a bald spot in the middle of my hair—
> [They will say: "How his hair is growing thin!"]

When I was young, the last thing I would expect to see was my father, fretting in front of the mirror, worrying about a few extra pounds, or some new wrinkle around his eyes. But now I know better—he dyes his hair!

Prufrock, moreover, is deeply concerned about growing old; he places an inordinate value on youth. In contrast, Whitman's speaker celebrates the older man. He envisions his aging self like the unyielding oak tree and identifies with the noble characteristics of the tree, growing strong and more appealing with age. Prufrock's self-comparisons are cynical and demeaning. In one instance, he makes an analogy between himself and an insect, a mere bug put on display: "And when I am formulated, sprawling on a pin, / When I am pinned and wriggling on the wall." In another line, Prufrock compares himself to an insignificant crustacean laboring in obscurity on the bottom of the sea: "I should have been a pair of ragged claws, / Scuttling across the floors of silent seas." Clearly, Prufrock holds a low opinion of himself.

Reflecting on these two poems, I am reminded of an incident with my father when I was around eleven years old. I sat on the rough, splintered, wood of the community dock of the small Gulf coast village of Cedar Key, Florida. I was waiting for my father. He paid the bills and fed the family by working on the water. It was sticky and summer, and I was swatting mosquitoes while I watched a stray mutt rummage through an overturned garbage can. "Can we take him home?" I pleaded, when my father showed up. "He looks so hungry and kinda pitiful."

"What do we need with a mutt like that?" he snapped. "The damn thing looks like more trouble than it's worth. Leave it be."

I knew better than to argue, but later that evening, the dog showed up at our house, and my father was feeding him table scraps. "Must have followed us home," he grumbled as the dog gobbled up the food, "But tomorrow he's gotta go." The dog stayed, and, despite the constant complaining from my father, they were friends for many years.

Many years later, I learned that the dog did not follow us home; my father went back to get him. I guess a man can be Prufrock and a live-oak at the same time.

In writing this essay, Daphne chose to follow a deductive pattern of organization. The *claim* is presented in the introduction paragraph—*These men cried, they made mistakes, and they could feel*—and is followed by the *evidence*, examples from her personal experience and selected quotations from each of the poems.

As Daphne's essay illustrates, when we examine a theme dramatized in literature, we have the opportunity to gain insight into our own thinking. We move forward, attempting to clarify our own position on an aspect of the theme and, finally, to present our position to an audience. Moving beyond the personal perspective argument to construct an academic argument, we then face the challenging task of identifying an issue within that theme, researching that issue, and articulating a defensible position for an audience.

The following response activities provide a process for moving from self-reflection and exploration (examining thinking) to the articulation of a defensible position (shaping an argument).

Four-Part Written Exploration and Articulation

I. **Exploration.** Examine your own thinking on a subject. As an example, let's use *materialism*.

You can try one of the following prewriting techniques:

a. Write the word *materialism* at the top of a page, and write nonstop about it for five to ten minutes just to see what ideas emerge.

b. Write the word *materialism* and list all the ideas, concepts, and terms that are associated with the word. List but do not edit; allow your creative mind to work.

c. Similar to listing, you can cluster. Write *materialism* in the center of a page, circle the word, and cluster around it any ideas and concepts that come to mind. Once you have become familiar with your own thinking on the subject, examine your reasoning process. To do so, respond to the following questions:

1. What assumptions or broad generalizations about materialism are revealed in your prewriting?

2. Can you identify specific, personal experiences that may have led you to make an inductive leap in reaching those generalizations?

II. **Exploration.** Read four or five pieces of literature focusing on your chosen subject [*materialism*, in our example] and examine each one separately by looking at the argument made within its dramatic context.
   a. What is a significant *claim* in the piece?
   b. What *evidence* is offered in support of that claim?
   c. What rhetorical appeals (*ethos, logos, pathos*) does the writer use in order to move the reader toward acceptance of the claim?
   d. Upon reflection, how might you defend, refute, and or qualify each writer's claim?

III. **Exploration.** Research your subject [we will continue to use *materialism*] in its social context.
   a. Look for additional examples of literature, art, and film that address this subject of materialism.
   b. Find any statistics related to materialism. Perhaps you can locate the number of pounds of raw resources consumed by an American as compared with the pounds consumed by a Brazilian. Or perhaps you can discover the amount of money spent annually on clothes and music by American teenagers.
   c. Gather commentaries from sources with different perspectives on materialism. For example, if you look in the magazine *The Utne Reader*, where you will find a social critic's perspective, also look in *Forbes* magazine, where you will find a business perspective.
   d. Interview an authority on the subject and/or create your own survey instrument and implement it locally.
   e. Compile your research under specific, descriptive headings.

IV. **Articulation.** Create your own argument on the subject you have explored.
   a. Narrow the general subject to a particular issue.
   b. Identify a specific issue question and formulate a tentative claim for the issue.
   c. Gather support for your claim.
   d. Write your argument.

Student Sample

Continuing with our example of *materialism*, here is Lisa Coletti's response to the four-part assignment:

I. **Exploration.** Examine your own thinking on the subject you have selected. [Lisa chose option a: Write the word *materialism* at the top of a page, and write nonstop about it for five or ten minutes just to see what ideas emerge.]

Materialism

It's about buying things. About things being important to you.
About things being more important to you than people. The 1980s,
the "me" generation, consuming. Consumers. Americans and their

wealth, so much wealth they forget what is important and so buy things. . . . They try to buy love instead of earning it. Shopping malls. Rows of people going up and down on the escalators, people clustered around the fountains tossing pennies in. People looking at their watches. Crying children, angry wives. People, gluttons of consumer-ism. Capitalism? The evil one that Marx was trying to arm the worker against. PROFIT, the guiding principle. Cal, Adam's son in *East of Eden,* a pile of thousand-dollar bills (or hundred-dollar bills?) setting fire to them one by one. Think of the way children crowd around a piñata that has just been broken. GREED. The difference between wanting and needing things. When we invest meaning in things instead of people . . . "You can't take it with you."

II. **Exploration.** Read four or five pieces of literature focusing on your chosen subject and examine each one separately by looking at the argument within its dramatic context.
   a. What is a significant *claim* in the piece?
   b. What is the *evidence* offered in support of the claim?
   c. What rhetorical appeals (*ethos, logos, pathos*) does the writer use in order to move the reader toward acceptance of the claim?
   d. How might you defend, refute, and/or qualify each writer's claim?
   [Lisa read a dramatic monologue, "Rodeo" by Jane Martin, and poems by William Wordsworth, Marge Piercy, and Gary Snyder. (The four works occur later in the chapter, beginning on page 56) Here are her responses to each of these readings.]

"Rodeo" by Jane Martin

Claim: This piece seems to claim that there is a certain integrity to traditional things which is lost when they are commercialized.

Evidence: The evidence which is presented is the fact that the elements of commercialism which have been brought into the rodeo have lowered its quality and authenticity.

Rhetorical Appeals: In the first part of the monologue, the first three paragraphs, Big Eight focuses on the rodeo she was raised with. From her description of how she started riding to stories of rodeo tradition and the original procedure, she communicates a feeling of belonging, which she expresses with the word "us." By showing her firsthand commitment and connection to the rodeo, the narrator creates *ethos.* Because of her involvement, I respect her viewpoints, even though her language is a bit rough.

In the second part of the monologue, Big Eight moves on to describe "them," the big-time hot shots who have taken over rodeo. To convey her feelings about these newcomers, Big Eight begins by rattling off a list of famous names with contempt: "Them. Coca-Cola, Pepsi Cola, Marlboro damn cigarettes. You know the ones I mean. Them." With her tone and repetition of the word "them," Martin establishes Big Eight's negative feelings toward the forces of commercialism, therefore, appealing to *pathos.* Further developing these feelings in Big Eight's character, Martin continues to splice the word "damn" into otherwise recognizable famous names: "Marlboro damn cigarettes," "Ice damn Capades," and "Minnie damn Mouse." This selective use of an expressive word, especially in the case of "Ice Capades" and "Minnie Mouse"—generally not seen as malevolent influences—leaves no doubt as to the speaker's distaste for the popular commercial influence in rodeo. Big Eight's disapproval of commercial values, her disdain for "them," also appeals to *pathos.*

Defend: From my experience, money interests often corrupt. College football is one example. Also, it's not unusual to see a nice stand of trees bulldozed to build a shopping center directly across from another one.

"The World Is Too Much with Us" by William Wordsworth

Claim: Wordsworth is claiming that modern life has lost its magic because we are preoccupied with material things.

Evidence: The evidence put forth for this claim is the fact that despite the knowledge that modern people have, they are not as happy as ancient peoples who had to rely much more on imagination and mythology for explanation.

Rhetorical Appeals: The main appeal is *logos.* Wordsworth uses logic in drawing a contrast between his nineteenth-century world, the world which is "too much with us" (line 1), and the ancient pagan world in which connections between humans and nature were considered fundamental to an understanding of life. Also, the poem's Elizabethan sonnet form appeals to *logos.* The poet presents his evidence in a coherent and logical structure. After stating his main premise in the first line, he follows with his evidence, rhythmically ordered, line by line. The language of this poem is vivid, but it doesn't really grab my emotions, although it may have worked on an emotional level for nineteenth-century readers. I can appreciate Wordsworth's metaphors, such as in line 5, "The sea that bares her bosom to the moon," but it doesn't really strike an emotional chord for me.

Qualify: Wordsworth leaves me thinking about his claim. The sentiment of yearning for a simpler time and a purer form of joy which the poet communicates is common still today, nearly two hundred years later. This suggests that materialism and short-sightedness are not just characteristic of humans in the twentieth century. Contrary to what we might think, materialism is not unique to modern society; however, just because a person drives a BMW doesn't necessarily mean that he or she is insensitive. For example, I enjoy possessing material things, but I also enjoy nature, taking a walk in the park at sunset.

"To Be of Use" by Marge Piercy

Claim: This poem claims that well-done, necessary work has a substance to it which is lacking in more frivolous pursuits.

Evidence: The evidence which is offered to support this claim is that men and women of action are more likable than those who sit still and live in fear.

Rhetorical Appeals: Overall, this poem appeals to my emotions (*pathos*) because of its language—choice of images and sounds of words and phrases. In the first stanza, Piercy talks about the people who go at their work with confidence and assertiveness. She uses words like "sure" (line 4), "sleek" (line 6), and "bouncing" (line 7) to convey these qualities. Also, for me, the image of the seals and bouncing ball (lines 6 to 7) is happy. She makes work sound like fun! In the second stanza, Piercy pays tribute to people who persist in slow, laborious work. Using words like "harness" (line 8), "massive" (line 9), "strain," and "muck" (line 10), Piercy relates the lack of glamour in such work, and yet dignifies it at the same time. In the third stanza, the speaker admires the rhythm of those who work communally and for a common purpose. In the last line of this stanza, Piercy applies this idea of "common rhythm" to the poem itself: "when the food must come in or the fire be put out," (line 17).

Additionally, with the last two lines, "The pitcher cries for water to carry / and a person for work that is real" (line 25), Piercy sets up an analogy which states that water is to a pitcher as real work is to a human; the former fulfills the latter. This analogy appeals to reasoning (*logos*). Finally, Piercy does not try to say that only one way of working or one type of work is useful. This open-mindedness, looking at her subject from several perspectives, creates *ethos*.

Defend: I never thought about work in quite this way. Piercy takes the drudgery out of the word. Also, I like how she celebrates the common worker, the laborer—that would include students who wait tables to pay their tuition.

"After Work" by Gary Snyder

Claim: Happiness comes from simple things.

Evidence: The couple in the poem do not have many material goods, and yet they are happy.

Rhetorical Appeals: Like Piercy, Snyder appeals to my emotions (*pathos*) through his choice of words and images. To communicate feelings of "home" which his audience can identify with, Snyder uses words that appeal to the senses. The phrases, "peeling garlic" (line 7), "hot iron stove" (line 8), and "stew simmering" (line 13), all evoke sensory responses. Also, in the second stanza, in the repetitive phrasing of "the axe, the rake / the wood" (line 9), Snyder uses heavy words to describe heavy objects. All the things mentioned in the poem are simple, and many words are monosyllabic. Yet Snyder communicates to me a very deep feeling of happiness and pleasure. This is definitely a feel-good poem, one to read when I need to change my mood!

Also, I find myself really liking Snyder's speaker. This is a guy with down-home (nonmaterialistic) values that I respect (*ethos*).

Defend: Snyder's speaker supports what I said earlier in qualifying Wordworth's claim. In our material world, people can still appreciate the simpler things in life.

Summary: These four pieces of literature all relate to materialism. In their own way, they each make a claim which is based on the same underlying value assumptions: Material things are impermanent; happiness can be found in simple things, like a pot of stew, a hard day's work, a daydream, and a good old-fashioned rodeo. Also, commercial values should not rule our lives and undercut our respect for traditions and for other beings.

III. **Exploration.** Research *materialism* in its **social context.**
   a. Look for additional examples of literature, art, and film that address this subject of *materialism.*
   b. Find any statistics or other factual data related to *materialism.*
   c. Gather commentaries from sources with different perspectives on *materialism.* For example, if you look in the magazine, *The Utne Reader,* where you will find a liberal perspective, also look in *The National Review,* where you will find a conservative perspective.
   d. Interview an authority on the subject and/or create your own survey instrument and implement it locally.

Research on *materialism:*

• Statistics: *Time* magazine online article; book by Robbins on cultural capitalism
• Background information: book by Storey on cultural consumption
• Commentaries: *Working Paper Series* articles; book by Twitchell on American materialism; *Time* magazine online article

IV. **Articulation.** Create your own argument on the subject you have explored.
   a. Narrow the general subject to a particular issue.
   b. Identify a specific issue question and formulate a tentative claim for the issue.
   c. Gather support for your claim.
   d. Write your argument.
[For this section of the assignment, Lisa narrowed her subject from the broad topic of *materialism* to focus on consumerism and fast food. She created a claim, found support for that claim, and wrote her essay.]

Super-Size It!

Modern Americans are, by definition, consumers. Whether it be satellite dishes or diamonds, SUVs, or gold jewelry, Americans spend a great deal of resources on the acquisition of goods. People's reasons for consumption of specific goods vary widely, but undoubtedly, our culture's emphasis on material possessions has in some way affected each of us. Just a glance at our waistlines offers jiggling proof of our misplaced values.

The British poet, William Wordsworth, saw our consumer society coming two hundred years ago when he wrote the famous lines, "The world is too much with us; late and soon, / Getting and spending, we lay waste our powers. . ." He continues, "We have given our hearts away. . ." (Wordsworth 433). And perhaps we have given our hearts away, traded our appreciation for nature and the simple pleasures in life for a stereo with wrap-around sound and a big-screen television. In a consumer society like ours, that's called marketing. That we prefer a Little Debbie to a carrot or sixteen ounces of rare steak to a serving of beans and rice may have more to do with marketing than any conscious decision on our part to ruin our health.

The Western, and more specifically, American focus on consumption has been held responsible for the nation's tendency toward obesity. The seriousness of this ailment is specific to the United States in that fully 20 percent of Americans are obese (30 percent or more over one's ideal weight), up from about 12.5 percent in 1991 (Reaves). That is a shocking statistic—20 percent of us are not merely fat, we are obese. In light of the position of the United States as a leading consumer society and the fact of rising American obesity rates, it seems Americans' problem with weight control is directly related to the country's economic prosperity and tendency toward materialism.

Materialism is not a purely American invention, however. Some historians begin the study of consumer society in relatively recent times, but others place its birth much earlier. For example, in John Storey's *Cultural Consumption and Everyday Life,* Julia Bermingham is said to have argued that the beginnings of consumer society can be traced to "the sixteenth, and certainly no later than the eighteenth century" (1). Once scarce and, hence, expensive commodities, fat and sugar slowly became more available to the general population, and what was once coveted—for example a couple of pieces of hard candy at holiday time—now is so common we hardly take notice. Feeling a little hungry? Just buy a candy bar from a nearby machine. For that matter, buy two. Or perhaps opt for the super-sized bar offering a full half pound of instant satisfaction.

The consumer society came to the United States on a large scale with the development of the assembly line by Henry Ford in the manufacture of his Model T's (Robbins 13). With the money he saved in the manufacturing process of these cars, Ford raised wages and lowered the cost of the automobile. This rise in wages led to more money being made available to workers to spend on consumer goods (13). But in addition to rising wages, a more widespread change in the economy which greatly increased spending power was instigated by the introduction of credit. Credit allowed consumers to buy with only the promise to pay. This new spending power, in effect, "created" money and led to, among other things, a housing boom throughout the 1940s, 50s, and 60s (20). The post–World War II housing boom is critical in an examination of the components of contemporary American consumer culture, for this increase in homes led to an increase in demand for such products as appliances, furnishings, and automobiles (20). While the products which entered the market directly after World War II, for instance, were much less technologically advanced than the devices which line store shelves today, there is little doubt that these symbols of convenience and middle-class prosperity were the precursors of today's Cuisinarts, bagel slicers, and pasta makers.

Along with this flood of new consumer products came the increase in social emulation, which is seen as a "key factor in the dramatic birth of consumerism" (Storey 4). The modern consumer society began to take root, and as the economy grew, so did Americans' desire for material possessions. In the rush for spending power, Americans grew busier and busier, adjusting their working patterns to accommodate their desires. Americans' busy lifestyles are blamed for the tendency of Americans to be overweight, literally driving Americans to fast-food restaurants.

Beef and sugar, primary ingredients in most fast-food meals, are both inefficient to produce and detrimental to our diet. For example, the production of 28 metric tons of animal protein from beef requires 150 million tons of vegetable and cereal protein, not particularly efficient use of the land (Robbins 220). At the same time, beef, which is high in fat and cholesterol, has been linked to cardiovascular disease, colon cancer, breast cancer, and osteoporosis. Yet, in spite of these drawbacks, beef remains the most popular meat in America, having replaced pork as the top choice in the 1960s (220). Every year, 6.7 billion hamburgers are sold in the United States in fast-food restaurants alone (220). A popular sandwich choice, McDonald's Big Mac, has a "whopping" 530 total calories (Twitchell 211).

But what is the effect of the Big Mac on the growth of American obesity? Perhaps the answer lies not in the Big Mac itself but rather in the technology which makes the Big Mac both necessary and possible. Technology has allowed Americans to produce more while expending less energy. As is stated in "The Long-Run Growth in Obesity as a Function of Technological Change" by Tomas J. Philipson and Richard A. Posner,

> Technological change caused the price of calories to fall because food prices have declined while at the same time the

amount of physical exertion required when supplying labor
has also fallen. In an agricultural or industrial society, work is
strenuous; in effect, the worker is paid to exercise. . . . In a
postindustrial and redistributive society, such as that of the
United States today, most work entails little exercise. . . . As a
result, people must pay for undertaking. . . physical activity. . .
leisure weight control must be substituted for job weight
control. (4)

In effect, an attempt to control this weight problem, brought on by
too much consumption, is made by (what else?) more consumption.
Americans spent $8.4 billion on diet products and services in 1991,
with total sales, including things like artificial sweeteners and
health club memberships, reaching $33 billion. This figure is, inci-
dentally, roughly equal to the gross national product of Pakistan,
Egypt, or Hungary (Averett and Korenman 6). As with everything
else having to do with consumption, whether it is a Jenny Craig
Weight Reduction Program or a Weight Watchers Frozen Dinner,
Americans lead the world on weight-loss expenditures.

So why, if Americans are weight-conscious enough to spend so
much on diet aids, do they continue to become obese and at increasingly higher rates? One argument that has been put forth is that
the $33 billion has not been spent to lose weight, but rather to feel
better about not losing weight. As *Time* writer Joel Stein says in an
article by Jessica Reaves, ". . . spending $33 billion on weird fad
diets is actually quite easy when you look at the options. . . . It's a
lot easier to fumble around with complicated diets and then blame
the diet for a failure than it is to take responsibility for gaining
weight" (qtd. in Reaves). Meanwhile, the diet industry's growth
helps keep the economy plump.

Given that obesity is a complicated problem which cannot be
completely attributed to any one cause, one can conclude that while
American prosperity and materialism are not solely responsible for
the rise in obesity, these factors contribute to the problem. But perhaps our desire for comfort and convenience is also to blame. After
all, when the fast-food patron pulls up to the drive-through window
and says, "Super-size it!", he knows what he is buying—a large
serving of fat and sugar packaged for immediate consumption as
he sits behind the wheel of his new SUV talking on his cell phone. . .
"Let me put you on hold just a minute. I gotta mop a little mayo off
my tie."

American society is not going to change soon. It will continue to fuel its economy with elevated consumer spending. And, of course, there is an undeniable pleasure in owning nice things. However, individually we can choose how we spend our time and resources. We can make rational decisions. We can protect our health and need not have heart attacks at age 48. . . nor awaken some day to realize we have "given our hearts away."

Works Cited

Averett, Susan and Sandern Korenman. "The Economic Reality of *The Beauty Myth." Working Paper Series # 4521.* The National Bureau of Economic Research, Inc. Cambridge, MA: Nov. 1993.

Philipson, Tomas J., and Richard A. Posner. "The Long-Run Growth in Obesity as a Function of Technical Change." *Working Paper Series #7423.* Nov. 1999.

Reaves, Jessica. "The Unbearable Heaviness of Being American." *Time.com.* 7 Oct. 1999. 22 March 2000. <http://www.time.com/time/daily/0,2960,33259,00.html>.

Robbins, Richard H. *Global Problems and the Culture of Capitalism.* Needham Heights, Massachusetts: Allyn and Bacon, 1999.

Stein, Joel. "I Wouldn't Eat That If I Were You." *Time.com.* 31 May 1999. 22 March 2000. <http://www.time.com/time/magazine/article/0,3266,25700,00.html>.

Storey, John. *Cultural Consumption and Everyday Life.* New York: Oxford University Press, 1999.

Twitchell, James B. *Lead Us Into Temptation: The Triumph of American Materialism.* New York: Columbia University Press, 1999.

Wordsworth, William. "The World Is Too Much With Us." *Literature: Reading and Writing the Human Experience.* 7th ed. Richard Abcarian and Marvin Klotz, eds. New York: St. Martin's Press, 1998. 433.

Any part of the assignment sequence is valuable; however, it is the end product, an articulated expression of your own particular position, that promises the most rewards. Here is another example of that final product, in this case, student Meredith Newmon Blanco's essay dealing with alcoholism and the family. (For some discussion of Meredith's writing process, see Chapter Three.)

Who Are the Real Victims of Alcoholism?

The knocking at the door was so loud that I thought my heart was going to explode. We had been asleep for hours. Neither one of us was prepared to be awakened so abruptly. Once the sleepy fog began to lift from my head, I realized that it was my father-in-law who was making so much noise outside of my door. Like so many other times, he was drunk and yelling in a high-pitched babble about needing to borrow ten dollars. Ten dollars, I thought to myself. It's two o'clock in the morning; he's got to be out of his mind! My husband jumped to his feet and, as always, dismissed his father with money in hand and tried to salvage some of his own dignity. As he came back to the room, he had an unusual look on his face. Enrique said to me, "My mother was driving him, this time." He turned the light off and went to sleep. I realized at that moment, there was a substance abuse problem that involved everyone and would eventually explain some of my husband's peculiar habits and behaviors. Molly Peacock's poem, "Say You Love Me," brilliantly illustrates the emotional and sometimes physical damage done to children of alcoholics.

Children of alcoholic parents suffer from a variety of problems directly linked to their parents' alcohol abuse. The abuse is widespread and not particular. It doesn't seek out the poor and disadvantaged; it seeks out any soul who will give it a home, no matter what or who is lost in the process. Researchers Charles D. Weddle and Phillip Wishon state, "There are estimates of some twenty-eight million children of alcoholics in this country" (8). Children of alcoholics are challenged by their own development as well as their experiences of living in a dysfunctional home environment. Moreover, children of alcoholics are a unique group of people, in that, if they can survive, their survival skills are unparalleled.

Children in homes with alcoholics grow up with inconsistency and disciplinary fluctuations that may cause them to take on certain types of identity roles as a defense mechanism. These roles are the "hero," who is often the elder child and who takes on responsibility and shoulders adult responsibilities. The "scapegoat" is another role. This child typically shoulders all the blame for the family problems and disturbances. The middle child is typically the ignored child, or the "lost-one." The last child, the youngest, is often shielded from the family problems and nasty secrets (Weddle and Wishon 9). All of these children have a variety of characteristics,

each unique to its own circumstances. Regardless of how differently these children may be labeled, they each long for their parent's approval, whether or not the parent is sober. This longing is
illustrated in "Say You Love Me": "Do you love me? Say You Do. / I
love you Dad, I whispered leveled by defeat" (Peacock 1036). This
child displays the same type of behavior that children of alcoholics
do. The pattern of succumbing to the dependent parent's needs is a
typical behavior in children who grow up in these environments.

Alcoholic parents may not realize the devastation they impose
on those they love. Peacock writes, "He'll get mean, my sister
hissed, just tell him. / I brought my knee up to kick him, but I was
too scared" (1035). Children of alcoholics live in an environment
laced with fear and darkness ("Alcoholism and Alcohol"). As a consequence, these children have more psychological, health, and social problems. These problems range from migraines to frequent
illnesses, poor schoolwork, and, the most devastating one, suicide
attempts ("Answers to Frequently"). These children cannot cope
with their problems alone, nor should they have to.

If one is going to help a child of an alcoholic, one must know
what alcoholism is. Alcoholism is defined as,

> primary chronic disease with genetic, psychosocial and envi-
> ronmental factors influencing its development and manifesta-
> tions. The disease is often progressive and fatal. It is
> characterized by continuous or periodic: impaired control over
> drinking, preoccupation with the drug alcohol, use of alcohol
> despite adverse consequences, and distortions in thinking most
> notably denial. ("Definition")

This is a very clinical and detailed definition of the disease and its
effects; however, aside from the effects on the consumer of alcohol,
it fails to mention the other victims affected by this disease. The
victims in an alcoholic family are primarily the other family members. The victims in "Say You Love Me" are clearly the two young
girls: "He gazed through hysteria as a wet baby thing repeating 'do
you love me?' 'Say you do,' in baby chokes, only loud because he
was man. / There wouldn't be any rescue from my mother" (Peacock 1036). The children in this poem, like so many other children
of alcoholics, are the true victims of this illness.

Alcoholism is extremely prevalent in the United States. It is a
vicious cycle that, left untreated, will replicate itself: "Sons of alcoholic father are 4 or 5 times more likely to become alcoholics than

sons of non-alcoholics. Daughters of alcoholic parents are also more likely to marry alcoholic men and have children with high risk for addictive behavior" ("Answers"). This cycle of dysfunctional behavior will not be broken if the abuse is not treated and intervention is not accomplished. The world can seem like a horrible, dangerous place for children whose parents drink, as Peacock's poem depicts, "There was no world out there, so there we remained, completely alone" (1036). Children in these dysfunctional environments often have a grim and dark outlook on life and themselves. These views will carry over into their adult lives and adult relationships. The views and feelings of these children are supported by a multitude of statistics on alcoholism.

The statistics on alcoholism are staggering: "76 million people have been exposed to alcoholism in the family. . . . Alcohol attributes to 100,000 deaths annually making it the third leading cause of preventable mortality in the US" ("Alcoholism"). Children of alcoholics experience higher levels of conflict within the family. Their development is delayed, and they are four times more likely than other children to develop alcoholism. There is a higher risk that a child of an alcoholic will marry into families where alcoholism is prevalent ("Children"). Also, their communication skills and problem-solving skills are often delayed and ineffective. These children have a lower self-esteem than children who grow up in homes where alcohol is not abused. As the research conclusively demonstrates, children of alcoholics face a multitude of challenges, both in the family they are born into and in the family they create.

As we know, art imitates life, and Molly Peacock's poem, "Say You Love Me," paints a starkly realistic and dark portrait of a chronic social problem. The poem dramatizes the extremely volatile relationship between an alcoholic father and his two young daughters. In the family home, if an alcoholic adult's illness is left untreated, the chances of its resurfacing or being passed on to the next generation are extremely high. Children of alcoholics face a variety of complex challenges in their homes, and once they "leave the nest," they will confront a whole new set of challenges. If these children are not taught conflict resolution tools and effective communication skills, they will be sorely disadvantaged throughout their childhoods and adult lives. These children need to be provided with community resources to teach them skills to help them cope and manage their lives. Adults in our community must realize the severity of this problem and work towards this common goal. The children in our society are the real victims of alcoholism, and we, the adults, are the responsible party.

Works Cited

"Alcoholism and Alcohol-Related Problems: A Sobering Look." *Infinet Internet Service. National Council on Alcohol and Drug Dependency.* 13 Nov. 1999. <http://www.ncadd.org>.

"Answers to Frequently Asked Questions about Being a Child of an Alcoholic." *Infinet Internet Service. National Council of Alcohol and Drug Dependency.* 11 Nov. 1999. <http://www.alcoholism help.com>.

"Children of Alcoholics: Important Facts." *Infinet Internet Service.* August, 1998. *National Association of Children of Alcoholics.* 13 Nov. 1999. <http://www.healthorg/nacoa/impfacts.htm>.

"Definition of Alcoholism." *Infinet Internet Service.* 25 Feb. 1990. *National Council on Alcoholism and Drug Dependency.* 11 Nov. 1999. <http://www.ncadd.org>.

Peacock, Molly. "Say You Love Me." *Literature: Reading and Writing the Human Experience.* 7th ed. Richard Abcarian and Marvin Klotz, eds. New York: St. Martin's Press, 1998. 1035–1036.

Weddle, Charles D. and Phillip Wishon. "Children of Alcoholics." *Children Today* Jan–Feb. 1986: 8–12.

Walt Whitman (1819–1892)

I Saw in Louisiana a Live-Oak Growing

I saw in Louisiana a live-oak growing,
All alone stood it and the moss hung down from the branches,
Without any companion it grew there uttering joyous leaves of dark green,
And its look, rude, unbending, lusty, made me think of myself,
5   But I wonder'd how it could utter joyous leaves standing alone there
        without its friend near, for I knew I could not,
And I broke off a twig with a certain number of leaves upon it, and
        twined around it a little moss,
And brought it away, and I have placed it in sight in my room,
It is not needed to remind me as of my own dear friends,
(For I believe lately I think of little else than of them,)
10   Yet it remains to me a curious token, it makes me think of manly love;
For all that, and though the live-oak glistens there in Louisiana solitary
        in a wide flat space,
Uttering joyous leaves all its life without a friend a lover near,
I know very well I could not.

Jane Martin

Rodeo

A young woman in her late twenties sits working on a piece of tack. Beside her is a Lone Star beer in the can. As the lights come up we hear the last verse of a Tanya Tucker song or some other female country-western vocalist. She is wearing old worn jeans and boots plus a long-sleeved workshirt with the sleeves rolled up. She works until the song is over and then speaks.

Big Eight: Shoot—Rodeo's just goin' to hell in a handbasket. Rodeo used to be somethin'. I loved it. I did. Once Daddy an' a bunch of 'em was foolin' around with some old bronc over to our place and this ol' red nose named Cinch got bucked off and my Daddy hooted and said he had him a nine-year-old girl, namely me, wouldn't have no damn trouble cowboyin' that horse. Well, he put me on up there, stuck that ridin' rein in my hand, gimme a kiss, and said, "Now there's only on thing t' remember Honey Love, if ya fall off you jest don't come home." Well I stayed up. You gotta stay on a bronc eight seconds. Otherwise the ride don't count. So from that day on my daddy called me Big Eight. Heck! That's all the name I got anymore . . . Big Eight.

Used to be fer cowboys, the rodeo did. Do it in some open field, folks would pull their cars and pick-ups round it, sit on the hoods, some ranch hand'd bulldog him some rank steer and everybody'd waver their hats and call him by name. Ride us some buckin' stock, rope a few calves, git throwed off a bull, and then we'd jest git us to a bar and tell each other lies about how good we were.

Used to be a family thing. Wooly Billy Tilson and Tammy Lee had them five kids on the circuit. Three boys, two girls and Wooly and Tammy. Wasn't no two-beer rodeo in Oklahoma didn't have a Tilson entered. Used to call the oldest girl Tits. Tits Tilson. Never seen a girl that top-heavy could ride so well. Said she only fell off when the gravity got her. Cowboys used to say if she landed face down you could plant two young trees in the holes she'd leave. Ha! Tits Tilson.

Used to be people came to a rodeo had a horse of their own back home. Farm   5 people, ranch people—lord, they *knew* what they were lookin' at. Knew a good ride from a bad ride, knew hard from easy. You broke some bones er spent the day eatin' dirt, at least ya got appreciated.

Now they bought the rodeo. Them. Coca-Cola, Pepsi Cola, Marlboro damn cigarettes. You know the ones I mean. Them. Hire some New York faggot t' sit on some ol' stuffed horse in front of a sagebrush photo n' smoke that junk. Hell, to-bacco wasn't made to smoke, honey, it was made to chew. Lord wanted ya filled up with smoke he would've set ya on fire. Damn it gets me!

There's some guy in a banker's suit runs the rodeo now. Got him a pinky ring and a digital watch, honey. Told us we oughta have a watchamacallit, choriographus or somethin', some ol' ballbuster used to be with the Ice damn Capades. Wants us to ride around dressed up like Mickey Mouse, Pluto, crap like that. Told me I had to haul my butt through the barrel race done up like Minnie damn Mouse in a tu-tu. Huh uh, honey! Them people is so screwed-up they probably eat what they run over in the road.

Listen, they got the clowns wearin' Astronaut suits! I ain't lyin'. You know what a rodeo clown does! You go down, fall off whatever—the clown runs in front of the bull so's ya don't git stomped. Pin-stripes, he got 'em in space suits tellin' jokes on a microphone. First horse see 'em, done up like the Star Wars went crazy. Best buckin' horse on the circuit, name of Piss 'N' Vinegar, took one look at them clowns, had him a heart attack and died. Cowboy was ridin' him got hisself squashed. Twelve hundred pounds of coronary arrest jes fell right through 'em. Blam! Vio con dios. Crowd thought that was funnier than the astronauts. I swear it won't be long before they're strappin' ice-skates on the ponies. Big crowds now. Ain't hardly no ranch people, no farm people, nobody I know. Buncha disco ba-bies and dee-vorce lawyers—designer jeans and day-glo Stetsons. Hell, the whole bunch of 'em wears French perfume. Oh it smells like money now! Got it on the cable T and V—hey, you know what, when ya rodeo yer just bound to kick yerself up some dust—well now, seems like that fogs up the ol' TV camera, so they told us a while back that from now on we was gonna ride on some new stuff called Astro-dirt. Dust free. Artificial damn dirt, honey. Lord have mercy.

Banker Suit called me in the other day said "Lurlene . . ." "Hold it," I said, "Who's this Lurlene? Round here they call me Big Eight." "Well, Big Eight," he said, "My name's Wallace." "Well that's a real surprise t' me," I said, "Cause aroun' here everybody jes calls you Dumb-ass." My, he laughed real big, slapped his big ol' desk, an' then he said I wasn't suitable for the rodeo no more. Said they was lookin' fer another type, somethin' a little more in the showgirl line, like the Dallas Cowgirls maybe. Said the ridin' and ropin' wasn't the thing no more. Talked on about floats, costumes, dancin' choreog-aphy. If I was a man I woulda pissed on his shoe. Said he'd give me a lifetime pass though. Said I could come to his rodeo any time I wanted.

10   Rodeo used to be people ridin' horses for the pleasure of people who rode horses—made you feel good about what you could do. Rodeo wasn't worth no money to nobody. Money didn't have nothing to do with it! Used to be seven Tilsons riding in the rodeo. Wouldn't none of 'em dress up like that Donald damn Duck so they quit. That there's the law of gravity!

There's a bunch of assholes in this country sneak around until they see ya havin' fun and then they buy the fun and start in sellin' it. See, they figure if ya love it, they can sell it. Well you look out, honey! They want to make them a dollar out of what you love. Dress *you* up like Minnie Mouse. Sell your rodeo. Turn *yer* pleasure into Ice damn Capades. You hear what I'm sayin'? You're jus' merchandise to them, sweetie. You're jus' merchandise to them.

Blackout.

William Wordsworth (1770–1850)
The World Is Too Much With Us

The world is too much with us; late and soon,
Getting and spending, we lay waste our powers;
Little we see in nature that is ours;
We have given our hearts away, a sordid boon.
5   This sea that bares her bosom to the moon,
The winds that will be howling at all hours,
And are up-gathered now like sleeping flowers,
For this, for everything, we are out of tune;
It moves us not.—Great God! I'd rather be
10   A pagan suckled in a creed outworn;
So might I, standing on this pleasant lea,

Have glimpses that would make me less forlorn;
Have sight of Proteus rising from the sea;
Or hear old Triton blow his wreathèd horn.

Marge Piercy (b. 1936)
To Be of Use

The people I love the best
jump into work head first
without dallying in the shallows
and swim off with sure strokes almost out of sight.
They seem to become natives of that element,   5
the black sleek heads of seals
bouncing like half-submerged balls.

I love people who harness themselves, an ox to a heavy cart,
who pull like water buffalo, with massive patience,
who strain in the mud and the muck to move things forward,   10
who do what has to be done, again and again.

I want to be with people who submerge
in the task, who go into the fields to harvest
and work in a row and pass the bags along,
who are not parlor generals and field deserters   15
but move in a common rhythm
when the food must come in or the fire be put out.

The work of the world is common as mud.
Botched, it smears the hands, crumbles to dust.
But the thing worth doing well done   20
has a shape that satisfies, clean and evident.
Greek amphoras for wine or oil,
Hopi vases that held corn, are put in museums
but you know they were made to be used.

The pitcher cries for water to carry   25
And a person for work that is real.

Gary Snyder (b. 1930)

After Work

The shack and a few trees
float in the blowing fog

I pull out your blouse,
warm my cold hands
5   on your breasts.
you laugh and shudder
peeling garlic by the
              hot iron stove.
bring in the axe, the rake,
10   the wood

we'll lean on the wall
against each other
stew simmering on the fire
as it grows dark
15   drinking wine.

Molly Peacock (b. 1947)

Say You Love Me

What happened earlier I'm not sure of.
Of course he was drunk, but often he was.
His face looked like a ham on a hook above

me—I was pinned to the chair because
5 he'd hunkered over me with arms like jaws
pried open by the chair arms. "Do you love

me?" he began to sob. "Say you love me!"
I held out. I was probably fifteen.
What had happened? Had my mother—had she

said or done something? Or had he just been
10 drinking too long after work? "He'll get *mean,*"
my sister hissed, "just *tell* him." I brought my knee

up to kick him, but was too scared. Nothing
could have got the words out of me then. Rage
shut me up, yet "DO YOU?" was beginning   15

to peel, as of live layers of skin, age
from age from age from him until he gazed
through hysteria as a wet baby thing

repeating, "Do you love me? Say you do,"
in baby chokes, only loud, for they came   20
from a man. There wouldn't be a rescue

from my mother, still at work. The same
choking sobs said, "Love me, love me," and my game
was breaking down because I couldn't do

anything, not escape into my own   25
refusal, *I won't, I won't,* not fantasize
a kind, rich father, not fill the narrowed zone,

empty except for confusion until the size
of my fear ballooned as I saw his eyes,
blurred, taurean—my sister screamed—unknown,   30

unknown to me, a voice rose and leveled
off "I love you," I said. "*Say 'I love you,
Dad!'*" "I love you, Dad," I whispered, leveled

by defeat into a cardboard image, untrue,
unbending. I was surprised I could move   35
as I did to get up, but he stayed, burled

onto the chair—my monstrous fear—she screamed,
my sister, "Dad, the phone! Go answer it!"
The phone wasn't ringing, yet he seemed

to move toward it, and I ran. He had a fit—   40
"*It's not ringing!*"—but I was at the edge of it
as he collapsed into the chair and blamed

both of us at a distance. No, the phone
was not ringing. There was no world out there,
so there we remained, completely alone.   45

CHAPTER ACTIVITIES

1. In a group of three or more, select several categories of people with whom you are familiar, such as college athletes, rappers, motorcyclists, or sorority women. Make a list of five or so commonly held characteristics associated with each group. Under each list, write out the underlying evidence that has fostered these perceptions.

2. Read through the cartoon below.
   a. What stereotypes does the cartoonist illustrate?
   b. What *inference* is suggested by the juxtaposition of the two bumper stickers?

DOUG MARLETTE/Newsday

3. a. What conclusions did you make about college before you came to campus? What evidence led you to make these conclusions? Which proved to be inaccurate? Which accurate?
   b. What conclusions do you think people might make about you? Why? What are these conclusions based on?

4. Can you recall a specific situation in which you jumped to a conclusion? Spend several minutes writing about it. Try to step back and analyze the situation. What caused you to "jump" too quickly? Would you characterize it as an "innocent mistake," or did you have a strong emotional interest in coming to that conclusion?

5. Using a newspaper's letters to the editor, find examples of both **inductive** and **deductive** thinking. Is the writer reasoning from specific evidence to reach a broader conclusion (induction)? Or does the writer's conclusion follow from the specific application of a general principle (deduction)?

6. Look back at the explanation of **logical fallacies** on pages 34–35. Decide which fallacy this cartoon best illustrates and explain why. Pick another fallacy and create a simple cartoon illustration. Be prepared to share your cartoon with a small group. Can your group members identify the fallacy you have illustrated?

"We weren't cheating. We were consulting."

7. Read Jane Martin's "Rodeo," beginning on page 56. Notice that the narrator, Big Eight, makes broad conclusions about corporate culture.
   a. State Big Eight's conclusions.
   b. Identify Big Eight's **evidence** for her conclusions.
   c. Cast yourself in Banker Suit's position and create counterarguments to Big Eight's conclusions.
   d. Identify the **value assumptions** that underlie both Big Eight's and Banker Suit's conclusions.
   e. Recalling the **Rogerian Argument strategy** from page 17 of Chapter One, offer a middle-ground position which Big Eight and Banker Suit might both find acceptable.

8. Read "The World Is Too Much with Us" by William Wordsworth, beginning on page 58. The poet states his **claim** in the title and in the first line.
   a. Identify the **warrants** or **value assumptions** underlying Wordsworth's idea.
   b. To what degree do these **value assumptions** apply to today's world?

⋙ CHAPTER 3 ⋙

Participating in an Academic Community

The educated person is, above all, one who is "open to new
knowledge and able to advance it."
—William J. Bouwsma[1]

The college classroom provides a unique opportunity for you to encounter new knowledge. In this academic community, you sit with a group of strangers from diverse backgrounds and discuss ideas and issues. As a participant in this community, you have the responsibility to bring your best thinking to this conversation: to read background information about the issue and to listen to the perspectives other students may offer, including those which clash with your beliefs. In the spirit of academic discourse, have the courage to entertain all possibilities—to contribute your own perspective and to listen openly to other persons' viewpoints.

In an academic community, you also have the opportunity to advance knowledge and shape your own and other persons' thinking about ideas and issues. You, therefore, have the responsibility to move beyond discussing issues to expressing your informed opinion in an **academic argument**. The writing process for academic argument is neither simple nor fast; it requires a steadfast commitment to hard work—to reading, thinking, writing; to rereading, rethinking, rewriting.

In developing an academic argument, we suggest following these fundamental steps:

1. Explore multiple perspectives on a subject through reading, writing, and conversation in order to expand, deepen, and complicate your thinking.
2. Analyze and evaluate those perspectives in order to construct your own argument, centered on a clear claim that you can support with credibility and specificity.

---

[1]Qtd. in Carol L. Smith and Karen I. Spear, *The Purposes and Practices of Scholarship: A Primer*, rev. ed. (Durango, CO: Fort Lewis College, 1998), p. 1.

3. Design an organizational plan/mapping out an argument strategy based on your specific goals with your audience.
4. Draft and seek feedback in order to "field-test" your argument with alive audience; as a result, you will value your writing as "real" writing for "real" readers and, thus, recharge your commitment to working further on it, asking new questions and creating new knowledge.
5. Rethink and revise, edit and proofread in order to present an argument that will compel your readers (an academic community) to respect your position and to rethink their own: *Good writing makes readers think.*

CLARIFYING A SUBJECT, PURPOSE, AND AUDIENCE

In Chapter One, we introduced a specific rhetorical triangle from Aristotle's *Rhetoric*, which denotes three types of appeals to audience—*ethos, logos, pathos*. Another rhetorical triangle, commonly associated with the writing process, denotes the relationship among the writer's subject, purpose, and audience. For example, in the sample essay in Chapter Two (page 37), "Yes, the Future Looks Bright, but the Moment Is Hell," student writer Shawn Mullin addresses the *subject* of college students' working. His *audience* is his peers, college students, and his *purpose* is to convince his fellow students that if they do choose to get a job, they should not work more than 20 hours a week. However, in the longer, research-based argument (page 52), "Who Are the Real Victims of Alcoholism?", student writer Meredith Newmon Blanco envisions a broader and more general *audience*—not only her college peers but also adults, younger and older, in the community. Her *subject* is victims of alcoholism, and her *purpose* is to inform her readers about often overlooked victims and to *move* them to feel concern for these victims. For both Shawn and Meredith, finding their *subject* (*what do I want to write about?*), designating their *audience* (*whom do I want to target?*), and clarifying their *purpose* (*what effect do I want to have on readers?*) were critical, early stage steps in their writing process.

For many writers, finding a subject presents the biggest challenge. Here is where journal/freewriting, reading, and talking with others/class discussions can provide the requisite spark. For example, in a National Public Radio interview, poet Stephen Dunn said that if he waited for his "muse" or inspiration before beginning to write, he would not get any poems written. Dunn said he must sit down and begin to write, and in the process of writing, he finds a subject for his poem. Like the poet Dunn, student writers Shawn and Meredith began their search for a subject by writing *freely* and *for themselves*. In considering his essay assignment criteria (a short, first-person argument based on personal experience), Shawn began freewriting about an immediate personal predicament—how to celebrate his six-month anniversary with his girlfriend—which led him to his subject, working and the college student. Similarly, Meredith, in writing a journal response to Molly Peacock's poem, "Say You Love Me," found her subject for a longer, research-based, argument essay on alcoholism. With a palpable connection to their subjects, Shawn and Meredith were motivated to move forward from the private to the public realm of communication—to the process of producing writing about a specific *subject*, with a specific *purpose*, and for a specific *audience*.

ORGANIZING A RESEARCH-BASED ARGUMENT ESSAY

The Heart of an Argument Is Its *Claim:* Claims of Fact, Value, and Policy

The *subject* of an argument is, by definition, an *issue,* a debatable topic. One way for a writer to ascertain that his or her subject is debatable is to frame the topic as an *issue question.* Prompted by her response to Peacock's poem, Meredith narrowed her research focus from the general topic of alcoholism to children of alcoholic parents. Meredith articulated her issue as the question, "Who Are the Real Victims of Alcoholism?", which she later decided to use as her essay title, thus setting a tone of inquiry and also suggesting an argumentative stance toward her subject.

The *purpose* of an argument is wedded to the writer's *claim.* In articulating the claim, the writer asserts his or her response to the issue question or subject of the argument. Because the claim of an argument is the thesis or main point of the essay, its clarity and scope are crucial in producing a successful argument. Chapter One discusses three central types of claims: *claim of fact, claim of value, claim of policy.* Determining which type of claim best suits one's purpose provides a key organizing tool for creating an effective argument.

For example, let's consider the subject of global warming. Alarmed by record heat and droughts, one may be motivated to find out what action could be taken to slow down or reverse this recent warming trend. By framing the issue question—how can we alleviate the detrimental effects of global warming?—one has set the stage for writing a *claim of policy* argument. Preliminary research, however, would reveal that the scientific community itself is debating the "fact or myth" of global warming. In constructing his argument, the writer could not *assume* the "fact" of global warming without also ignoring compelling counterarguments. Thus, if he persists with a claim of policy argument on global warming, he first would need to address the issue question— what is global warming?—and then proceed to propose his specific action for reducing the harm caused by global warming. All in all, quite a task! Returning to the initial question of choosing a type of claim, the writer may well decide to limit himself to a *claim of fact* argument: *Key factors contributing to the harmful effects of global warming are directly related to humans, including. . . .* Similarly, in writing her argument on victims of alcoholism, Meredith settled on a *claim of fact* argument. Later, by concluding her argument with a "call to action," Meredith seeks to motivate her audience to act on this information; however, the thrust of her argument has been to establish a factual basis for her claim that children are the real victims of alcoholism.

Some issues readily lend themselves to a *claim of policy* argument. For example, the link between tobacco smoke and lung cancer has long been documented; recent debate has centered on *what to do* about the public health problems caused by tobacco smoke (hence, a *claim of policy* issue). Similarly, let's consider the policy debate over mandatory uniforms in public schools. Most reasonable persons fully endorse the value of orderly conduct and respect for others in the public school classroom; however, many reasonable persons dispute the policy of mandating school uniforms as a means of creating a constructive climate in the classroom.

Intrinsic to many claim of policy arguments is a subclaim of value. A *claim of policy* argument, for example, might advocate the legalization of physician-assisted suicide for terminally ill persons. In supporting this policy proposal, the writer would need to address the ethical dilemma of the quality of life/dignity of dying, thus establishing a *claim of value.* She would attempt to convince her readers that the individual's right to choose when and how one dies is preferable to the experience of unremitting pain and suffering. On the other hand, to argue against physician-assisted suicide, a writer might *evaluate* the procedure, hoping to convince readers that it would be a detrimental policy for society to sanction. In this case, the writer would assert a *claim of value* as his main argument: *Physician-assisted suicide endorses an immoral principle by using the practice of medicine to terminate rather than to sustain human life.* When a writer's central purpose is to critique or evaluate his subject, he formulates a *claim of value* for his argument.

The Body of an Argument Is Its *Support:* Appeals to *Ethos, Logos,* and *Pathos*

Just as a heart requires a body, so does a claim require support. The writer of an argument not only must state a claim but also demonstrate to her audience why her claim is worthy of thoughtful consideration. To support the claim, the writer must draw on sources—*primary* (firsthand experience, observations, interviews, and personal accounts) and *secondary* (reported facts and information). Because one of the writer's principal concerns is to build respect and trust *(ethos)* with her target audience, the writer evaluates and selects evidence (support) with her audience's needs in mind. She must envision her audience as "real" persons with their own emotions and biases, beliefs and values, and intellectual and social backgrounds. As with all levels of communication, the key to success is to establish a bond of respect: to demonstrate respect *for* and to earn respect *from* one's audience.

In selecting evidence to build support and establish credibility, a writer draws on material that will appeal to an audience's emotions and beliefs, *pathos,* and to an audience's logic and reasoning, *logos.* Or course, there often is an overlap among materials that appeal to the audience's emotions and reasoning. But for the purpose of *organizing* support for his argument, a writer decides which of his evidence primarily appeals to *logos* and which primarily appeals to *pathos* and, thus, groups or "chunks" his supporting materials accordingly. For example, in her argument essay on victims of alcoholism, Meredith's main body of evidence—statistical data and factual information from researchers—appeals to *logos.* However, to appeal to *pathos,* she breaks up the factual evidence with quotes from Peacock's poem to evoke her audience's emotions. Moreover, Meredith frames her essay with appeals to *pathos:* by leading in with a personal anecdote and by concluding with the articulation of a common ground belief (a stated *warrant*) in the value of children.

Counterarguments: Concessions and Refutations

Depending on the *rhetorical context*—the current climate of controversy surrounding an issue—some arguments are more sharply divisive than others. The climate of controversy surrounding Meredith's argument, for example, might be described as seasonably comfortable. Her purpose was not to argue for or against her subject (of course, no one "supports" victims of alcoholism, be they children or adults) but to heighten her audience's awareness and concern about certain victims of alcoholism. On the other hand, the issue of physician-assisted suicide draws clear dissension among reasonable and compassionate individuals; likewise, the enduring issue surrounding the value of civil disobedience for protesting an injustice can evoke clashing opinions. Thus, in developing an organizational strategy for his support, the writer should assess the current climate of controversy. The writer also should be willing to evaluate and reconsider his own opinions as he confronts new information about an issue. All in all, throughout the research process, the writer should be formulating his claim based on a thorough and critical investigation of information involving multiple and diverse perspectives on the issue.

To compose her argument, the writer determines which opposing views or *counterarguments* are significant in arguing her claim. Based on her investigation and evaluation of the evidence, the writer may choose to make some *concessions,* that is, to acknowledge the merit of aspects of opposing viewpoints. For example, in the case of global warming, the writer might acknowledge that factual records of climate factors are relatively recent and, therefore, offer some credence to the challenge that global warming is not directly linked to modern industrial and technological factors but, instead, is a naturally recurring climatic phenomenon. By acknowledging this possibility, the writer would offer a *limited concession;* however, the writer could follow her concession with a *refutation* to provide compelling factual evidence that weighs in more heavily on the side of industrial and technological factors as primary causes of global warming.

In addressing opposing viewpoints, the writer strengthens her position with a broader audience—those who are undecided or skeptical about global warming, as well as those who are predisposed to see technological advancement as a threat to the purity of the environment. Through the dialectical process of counterargument, concession, and refutation, the writer demonstrates fair-mindedness and reasonableness (appeal to *ethos*) and reinforces the bond of respect and trust between writer and audience.

Argument Outline

The following outline can be useful for students who want specific organizational guidelines, or it can serve as a starting point for those students who want to devise their own organizational plans:

Introduction

- Lead-in "hook" sentences
- Concise overview of issue/rhetorical context
- Explicit claim of fact, value, or policy

Opposition

- Concise summary of keys points of opposing viewpoint
- Concession/acknowledgement of legitimacy of aspects of this viewpoint
- Refutation/counterargument to address weak aspects of opposition

Supporting Argument

- Specific proof of claim
- Evidence grouped under three or so key points
- Strongest point presented last

Conclusion

- Restatement of claim
- Resolution, compromise, or call to action

Strategy Questions for Organizing Your Argument Essay

1. How will you *introduce* your issue? What will be your *lead-in "hook"* (an example, anecdote, scenario, startling statistic, provocative questions or statements, vivid description)? Is there an interesting fact or quotation you have come across which might make a catchy beginning for your introduction?

2. How much *background* (*rhetorical context*) will your readers need to understand this issue?

3. Where will you present the strongest statement of your *claim:* early on/at the end of your introduction (the conventional location) or delayed/in your conclusion?

4. What are your three (or so) main supporting arguments (*subclaims*)? How should they be ordered? These subclaims should probably serve as body paragraph topic sentences.

5. What *authoritative evidence* do you have to support the subclaims you identified above? Have you found authorities whom you can quote? Are there statistics or facts you need to present? Do you have the option to use personal experience?

   a. What evidence do you have that will appeal to your readers' *logos*?

   b. What evidence do you have that will appeal to your readers' *pathos?* Will any of the creative literature you have read provide direct support for your claim? Will including it add an emotional impact to your argument, and, if so, where do you want that impact to appear in your essay?

   c. Where in the argument will the appeals work the best to build your *ethos* with your readers?

6. Where will you address *opposing* viewpoints—in the first, middle, or last section of your body? What are the main points of the opposing arguments? Should these points serve as *paragraph topic sentences?*

7. Acknowledging that readers' objections will have some validity, *how* will you address those objections? Will you make some *concessions?* How will you *refute* opposing arguments?

8. What questions of *style* and *tone* do you need to keep in mind as you write to ensure that you keep readers open to and interested in your argument? How do you want your *voice* to sound?
9. How will you *conclude* your essay? Will you use a value-based appeal (assert a *warrant*) in an attempt to strike common ground? Will you issue a specific "call to action"—suggest steps "we" can take. . .?

[*Hint:* As you design your organizational plan, keep in mind this overall guideline: Lay out coherent "chunks" of evidence in a logical order to lead your readers to believe that your claim is the *thinking* person's response to the issue question.]

Annotated Student Essay

In the following essay, student Josh Griep presents a research-based argument, centered on a *claim of policy* (stated in the last sentence of paragraph two):

Josh Griep
Professor James
ENC 1102–028
31 March 2003

Wild Captives: The Exotic Animal Trade

An estimated five thousand tigers live freely in the wild today; the number of tigers living in captivity is approximately the same (Brook). The latter figure, however, is only the tip of the animal   *Lead-in* trading iceberg. Each year, approximately thirty thousand animals are taken from the wild to be sold to private owners (Elton). It has been estimated that fifty to ninety percent of these animals die before ever reaching the United States to be sold.

    Clearly, the traders of these animals care only about profits; the animals' welfare is the least of their concerns. Jorge Risemberg, who heads up the Ecological Police's Animal Division   *Rhetorical* in Peru, says, "On the global level, after drug trafficking and the   *Context* contraband arms trade, the contraband trade of animals is the most profitable" (Elton). The animals that are strong enough to survive are sold for as little as fifty dollars in the United States. These animals were not put on this earth to be conversation pieces or to simply look exotic in someone's backyard in Ohio. These wild animals belong in their natural habitats where they can roam their native habitat freely. The United States   *Claim of* Government must step in and outlaw the shipping of exotic   *Policy* animals into this country.

Twelve states currently have bans against large exotic animals, and seven have partial bans. There is no federal law, however, that restricts anyone from selling or owning non-endangered, exotic animals ("HSUS"). U.S. Representative George Miller has been the prime supporter of HR 5226, a bill which would halt private ownership of many exotic animals: "Wild animals, especially such large and uniquely powerful animals as lions and tigers, should be kept in captivity by professional

Opposing Viewpoint

zoological facilities" (Woolf, "Lions"). Opponents of the bill argue that some people have the resources to care for these animals as well as or even better than zoos. This may be true, but this justification also begs the central question: the humane treatment

Refutation

of the wild animals. If zoos are unable to provide sufficient habitat, they should not be allowed to house the animals. Furthermore, how would the animals' living conditions be evaluated and qualified as suitable or not? Who would continue to monitor these facilities to make sure living conditions remain sufficient? Partial bans, while suggesting a compromise solution, would only serve the selfish needs of the human owners, not the basic needs of the captive animals. Therefore, a complete federal ban must be established to protect these wild creatures and to preserve the natural balance of species of the native lands from which they have been stolen.

Not only is a total ban necessary to maintain the well being of the animals and their native habitats, but it also is a prime

Supporting Evidence

factor in the safety of humans. The director of governmental affairs for the Humane Society states, "Each wild animal kept as a pet in a community is a time bomb waiting to go off. They're genetically programmed to kill" (Brook). Most people are not qualified to own wild animals. The United States Department of Agriculture "believes that only qualified, trained professionals should keep these animals, even if they are only to be pets" (Woolf, "Movie Stars"). However, owners of exotic animals

Opposing Viewpoint

disagree: "Ninety-nine percent of the people with exotic animals look after them properly. Of course, you only hear about that one percent that don't," claims Mark Killman, owner of the Killman

Concession

Zoo which keeps exotic pets (Nikolovsky). One percent seems extremely low, so perhaps Mr. Killman has a point. However, that minute percentile includes the following: a Toronto man who was killed by one of his twenty Burmese pythons (Nikolovsky); the wild boar and three lions, found roaming around small towns, that had to be executed (Brook); the leopard found in a freezing garage; and the two thousand exotic animals found in an animal breeder's home—all must be factored in to Mr. Killman's so-called "one percent" (Elton). Apparently, Mr. Killman and other opponents of the ban need a math lesson. Ten thousand exotics or less survive being imported each year, and two thousand are found in a single home. That adds up to one-fifth or twenty percent of the animals imported that, Mr. Killman claims, are "properly taken care of."

Refutation

The problem extends far beyond the animals' having to be put down when they are beyond rehabilitation. These animals are killing machines, and unpredictably they will return to their basic predatory instincts. For example, a three-year-old boy in Texas was killed by a "pet" tiger; another three-year-old had part of his arm ripped off; and a woman was bitten on the head by a 750-pound Siberian-Bengal tiger mix ("HSUS"). Cases such as these convincingly demonstrate that these wild creatures are not only dangerous to their owners, but to other people as well.

Supporting Evidence

Paris Griep, who has been a wildlife biologist for thirty years, believes that no one should be allowed to own these animals: "Well-regulated and monitored zoos are the only facilities with highly trained personnel who can truly care for these animals properly. They cannot be stuck in an 8' by 8' cage and expect to live any kind of a life." Not only does this importation of wild animals harm the individual animals, but it also endangers the ecosystem from which they are captured. "Whenever those animals are taken out of the wild, it depletes the natural diversity from the place where they are taken from," Griep points out. These animals already have a difficult time trying to maintain their species populations without humans further interfering through the exotic trade.

Authoritative Testimony

Wild animals are called wild for a reason; they should be allowed to live freely in their native habitats. Furthermore,wild animals are by their natures unpredictable and cannot safely interact with people. A complete federal ban on the selling and housing of exotic animals is the only rational and humane policy. Such a ban would not remove these animals from the public eye; in fact, that is quite the contrary. If a complete ban is established by law, the populations of these animals can be returned to the flourishing populations they once were. These animals can still be loved and viewed in the safety of well-regulated zoos and licensed wildlife preserves. If owners of exotic pets truly care for their animals, as they insist, they will realize that keeping the animals in a cage or in an environment that they are not accustomed to is unreasonable, unsafe, and inhumane.

Restatement of Claim

Written almost a century ago, the poem, "The Panther" by Rainer Maria Rilke, offers powerful support for a complete ban on the wild animal trade:

His vision, from the constantly passing bars,
has grown so weary that it cannot hold
anything else. It seems to him there are
a thousand bars; and behind the bars, no world.

Let's not take away these animals' vision. We must make sure that they can roam freely in a world without bars.

Works Cited

Brook, Tom Vanden. "Exotic pets growing more accessible in USA." December, 2002. *USA TODAY Online article*. 26 Mar. 2003 <http://USATODAY.com/news>.

Elton, Catherine. "Peru's Eco-Police Make Barely a Dent in Trade of Exotic Pets." *Christian Science Monitor* 5 May 1998. *Academic Search Premier*. EBSCO. 21 Mar. 2003 <http://web22.epnet.com>.

Griep, Paris. Personal Interview. 20 Mar. 2003.

"HSUS Applauds Rep. George Miller for Introducing Legislation." July, 2002. *The Humane Society of the United States article*. 24 Mar. 2003 <http://hsus.org>.

Nikolovsky, Boris. "Critics growl over keeping of exotic pets: Zoo animals live in basements and backyards." August, 1994. *Zoocheck Canada Inc. Online article*. 26 Mar. 2003 <http://www.zoocheck.com/programs>.

Rilke, Rainer Maria. "The Panther." In *Reading Literature and Writing Argument*. Missy James and Alan Merickel. Upper Saddle River, NJ: Prentice Hall, 2002. 296.

Woolf, Norma Bennett. "Lions and tigers and bears, oh no!" July, 2002. *National Animal Interest Alliance Online article*. 19 Mar. 2003 <http://naiaonline.org.html>.

Woolf, Norma Bennett. "Movie stars want federal restrictions on private ownership of exotic animals." Feb. 2000. *National Animal Interest Alliance Online article*. 19 Mar. 2003 <http://naiaonline.org.html>.

THE ROGERIAN ARGUMENT

Introduced in Chapter One, the Rogerian approach to argument places the value of consensus building above "winning" an argument. Carl R. Rogers suggested that more is to be gained through compromise than through confrontation. Thus, the Rogerian argument seeks out an area where both sides' positions overlap—common ground upon which to base a compromise. Of course, compromise means individuals, regardless of their firm beliefs in their positions, must be willing to relinquish a piece of their positions; however, in the end, no one goes away defeated and angry.

Rogerian Argument Organizational Plan

Here is a basic structure for organizing a Rogerian argument essay. Of course, you may choose to adapt these guidelines to suit your particular material and your individual writing styles. Two principles, however, should hold for all Rogerian arguments: (1) maintaining a mask of neutrality/*persona* of fair-mindedness and (2) advocating a compromise/middle-ground position.

Introduction

- Lead-in sentences ("hook" strategies: a scenario or an example, a related current event in the news, a startling statistic, a provocative question or statement)
- Synopsis of the discussion surrounding the issue/rhetorical context
- Issue stated as an issue question to set a neutral tone of inquiry and investigation

Body

- Two or three paragraphs to examine key supporting points that support one prominent position on the issue
- Two or three paragraphs to examine supporting points that support alternative positions
  (The writer's use of transitional "signal sentences"—*On the other hand, critics argue . . .*; or *Despite these compelling arguments for . . ., many persons strongly oppose*—helps prepare readers for the writer's switch from examining one position to an opposing viewpoint.)

Conclusion

- Paragraph that presents a balanced and concise summation of the most compelling points representing different sides of the argument
- Paragraph(s) that present(s) and advocate(s) the writer's middle-ground position, drawing on elements from the diverse positions examined earlier

---

Sample Student Essay

In writing his essay on marriage and divorce, Matt Morrison demonstrates the Rogerian approach to argument: he maintains a *persona* of fair-mindedness throughout the essay, and, in its conclusion, he seeks to bring all sides together with a common ground value appeal and then advocates a compromise.

Matt Morrison

Professor James

ENC 1102

3 April 2006

"Separating" the Arguments

In a time when divorce seems to be just as common as marriage, rarely is talk focused on the children who must suffer through the separation. Normally, the consoling surrounds the adults. These young bystanders are usually brought to the negotiating tables as mere property: similar to an automobile or house—who gets to keep the children. Is it worth keeping a broken marriage alive to save children from being harmed, emotionally and socially, not only in the short- but also the long-term? Or does a broken marriage do just as much, if not more, harm by setting a bad example for the children in their future relationships?

Even as the marriage rate is dropping, according to the U.S. Census Bureau, almost fifty percent of marriages in the United States end in divorce (Masci, "Future"). In a related statistic, roughly forty-five percent of American children will experience their parents' filing for divorce before they reach eighteen (Masci, "Children"). This is an alarming number, considering many argue that a child should be raised in a nurturing household with both maternal and paternal figures present. Of course, reasons vary as to why some marriages fail, from a spouse's more determined focus on a career to an irresistible extramarital affair. "The Storm" by Kate Chopin tells of a marriage seemingly suffering from everyday routine. Although the wife Calixta has become used to this changeless pace of marriage, she is awakened from its routineness by the presence of a former lover: "His voice and her own startled her as if from a trance" (Chopin 341). Awakened from this trance, Calixta remembers how passion and desire feel; even so, she knows she is committed to her husband Bobinôt and her son Bibi. So when Bobinôt and Bibi return from the store, Calixta chooses to act as though nothing had occurred and to resume the routine of her marriage and household.

Without both parental figures, a child, such as the young Bibi, might not understand that marriage is a sacred institution and that couples work together through day to day affairs, both the routines and the crises, and that a marriage can weather a storm. Without both the mother and father present in the household, the child misses out on a valuable lesson, how to treat one's partner. Also, lack of proper role models could become a serious issue down the road when the child becomes an adult and enters into his or her own relationships. This viewpoint supports the claim of those who believe that a marriage, even flawed, provides a child with the best example of how two adults in love should behave toward each other.

Still, many persons oppose this strong belief in the enduring value of marriage for the sake of the children. Just because two people are joined in marriage does not always mean they will love each other "till death do us part" and treat one another respectfully. John Updike's story, "Separation," illustrates a marriage that has fallen apart; both the husband Richard and the wife Joan seem settled on the notion of separating. Updike uses the unfinished tennis court in the family's backyard as an analogy for the couple's love, once powerful and strong but now an unfinished project that no longer excites them: "The next spring, waking each day at dawn to a sliding sensation as if the bed were being tipped, Richard found the barren tennis court, its net and tapes still rolled in the barn, an environment congruous with his mood of purposeful desolation" (Updike 387). Although marriage could have been the right choice for a couple at one time, that does not mean it will always provide the best environment for raising children.

Those persons who hold this viewpoint make a valid point that a marriage tearing at the seams, but held together for the sake of a child, often would be more harmful to the child than the actual divorce. The negative atmosphere that an unhappy marriage can foster is definitely not the home of choice for a child who is learning who he or she is. Also, if the husband and wife are constantly bickering, it might create a distorted sense of what marriage should be and, in this way, negatively impact the child's own relationships later in life. Since example is a powerful teacher, one must question the reasoning for maintaining a broken marriage for the child's sake.

Instead of focusing on the problems that arise from a separation, some argue the real problem is the ease of obtaining a divorce as a result of "no-fault" divorce laws. Most critics of divorce tend to be politically conservatives; however, some well-known liberals, such as former First Lady Hillary Clinton, have spoken out against divorce. In her book, *It Takes a Village,* she claims divorce is too easy and laws as well as couples' attitudes are to blame (Clark). Also, contemporary social norms have made divorce socially acceptable. Half a century ago, divorce was almost unheard of; marriage was meant to last until death, not until the going got tough. In Updike's "Separation," Richard is so focused on being free of his marital bond so that he can pursue a relationship with another woman, that he hasn't paused to consider the consequences. This realization only hits him after he and Joan have told their three teenage children about their separation plans and his son asks him *why:* "Richard had forgotten why" (Updike 394). In contrast, without an "easy way out," as in the 1950s and earlier, most marriages lasted "till death do us part," perhaps, preventing many people from making rash decisions.

Of course, not all marriages were successful and provided role model conditions for youths, but social disapproval of divorce ruled out the option of calling it quits quickly when a few problems arose. The vice president of the Family Research Council, William Maddox Jr., backs this viewpoint by stating that "the thing that distinguishes 50-year-old marriages isn't that they're scot-free of problems, but they've confronted those difficulties and persevered when others gave up" (Clark). Moreover, when a couple who are having marriage problems have few alternatives to sticking with it and working it out, the solution to the problem and the teamwork to overcome it almost always makes the marriage stronger than it was before. Perhaps, no-fault divorce laws should be reviewed.

Even as we debate viewpoints on issues surrounding marriage and divorce, we share a strong concern for the children involved. As the future leaders of the world, it is important that these young impressionable children can grow and thrive in the best environment available to them. One of the leading women authors of Austria in the late 1800's, Marie Ebner von Eschenbach, asserted that "whenever two good people argue over principles, they are both right" (Chastain). This is assuredly the case when the welfare of children is discussed.

We can take several steps to ensure that children are given the best opportunity for a bright future, not just in their relationships

but in financial and other social aspects as well. First, a social reform should be considered to raise the seriousness of marriage to
more than just economic benefits for a couple. The word marriage
should have the connotation of love and respect. To promote these
values, couples who have demonstrated time-tested marriages
should share their knowledge with younger couples who are having trouble. Rarely is there a new problem to marriage, so society
should use the valuable resource of elders to help solve marital issues. Such counsel, combined with slightly stricter laws on divorce, would encourage couples to work out their problems
within their marriage rather than abandon ship when the waves
get rough. This course of action also addresses the question of
whether or not a couple should split for the sake of the child: divorce is the last option, only exercised after all available alternatives have been exhausted. By putting in place constructive
steps to support mending rather than terminating marriages and
by modifying laws to make divorce a last option rather than a so-
called quick fix, we would ensure the best possible future for our
children. Then, perhaps, fewer children would need to ask a parent, *"Why?"*

Works Cited

Chastain, James. "Marie von Ebner-Eschenbach." *Encyclopedia of
    1848 Revolutions.* 13 October 2004. Ohio University. 3 April
    2006. <http://www.ohiou.edu/~chastain/dh/ebner.htm>.

Chopin, Kate. "The Storm." *Reading Literature and Writing Argu-
    ment.* 2nd Ed. Missy James and Alan P. Merickel. Pearson
    Prentice Hall, 2006. 341–344.

Clark, Charles S. "Marriage and Divorce." *The CQ Researcher* 6.18
    (1996). 3 April 2006 <http://library.cqpress.com/cqresearcher/
    cqresrre1996051000>.

Masci, David. "Children and Divorce." *The CQ Researcher* 11.2
    (2001). 31 March 2006
    <http://library.cqpress.com/cqresearcher/cqresrre2001011900>.

Masci, David. "Future of Marriage." *The CQ Researcher* 14.17
    (2004). 3 April 2006 <http://library.cqpress.com/cqresearcher/
    cqresrre2004050700>.

Updike, John. "Separating." *Reading Literature and Writing Argu-
    ment.* 2nd Ed. Missy James and Alan P. Merickel. Upper Saddle
    River, NJ: Pearson Prentice Hall, 2006. 386–394.

WORKING WITH SOURCES

You certainly can write a college-level essay that expresses your opinions and insights on an issue by using personal experience to support your claims. This personal perspective argument, such as Shawn Mullin's essay on page 37 in Chapter Two, is characterized by a subjective approach to argument. However, in an academic community, professors often expect you to move beyond the use of personal experience as evidence. In these cases, you will need to make use of evidence from *authoritative sources*. When using information from books and periodicals, databases and Web sites, or personal interviews with experts, you face several tasks.

First, you must make accurate and fair use of the material in your essay. This task involves taking good notes and then deciding whether to *quote* directly or *paraphrase* that information as you integrate it into your essay. Secondly, you must follow a *documentation system* to give credit to the original sources of your information and to allow your reader to see the sources of this information.

Avoiding Plagiarism with Note-Taking

Most first-year college students hear several lectures on the sins of plagiarism. *Plagiarism* means making use of someone else's ideas or facts without giving him or her credit. In other words, plagiarism is equivalent to theft, and thieves, when caught, are punished. While a few students knowingly take others' ideas and pass them off as their own, many more students unknowingly commit plagiarism because they do not understand how to make fair use of ideas and facts from outside sources. In particular, because information is so readily available through the Internet, some students do not realize that they still must document its sources. Although seemingly free-for-the-taking, information from Web sites must be cited throughout the essay, and full details of its source listed on the Works Cited page.

To avoid charges of plagiarism, begin by taking *accurate notes*. As you examine materials from your preliminary bibliography, you will need to record the facts and ideas you think you might find useful for your essay. Whether you take your notes on 3 × 5 index cards, on a legal pad, or in a Word document, one concept is particularly important—*make a clear distinction between your words and the words of the author; always put quotes around any words or phrases that are the author's*. Unless you put quotation marks around the author's words, later, when you are writing your essay, you will be unable to distinguish your words from the author's.

[*Hint:* Many writing handbooks advocate the use of note cards; you might want to read through a handbook's discussion of note cards.]

Some information from sources may not require documentation; this information is called *common knowledge*. For instance, you may read that the U.S. military suffered many casualties during the worst battles of World War II; however, because that information is common knowledge, you are not required to document its source, even though you also make that statement in your essay. On the other hand, if you read that 3,200 Americans were wounded or killed at the Battle of the Bulge—information that is not common knowledge—you would have to document the source of that statistic in your essay.

[*Hint:* Deciding what is or is not common knowledge can be confusing. When in doubt, cite the source, and, if time allows, check with your campus writing center specialists or professor.]

PARAPHRASING

As you take notes, you may encounter long passages which you want to record. In those cases, students traditionally *paraphrase* the material; that is, they read the passage and then, *using their own words,* express the ideas briefly but accurately. Paraphrasing means completely rephrasing a quotation so that only the core or central idea of the original is retained. It is not enough just to change a few words, here and there; indeed, such a practice is considered plagiarism. Also, although paraphrased material is not enclosed in quotation marks, you still must document its source with an in-text parenthetical citation.

[*Hint:* Paraphrasing a passage can be quite difficult, especially for inexperienced writers, because the task involves making judgments and interpretations. Unintentional plagiarism can be the result. If your college has a writing center, it would provide a good place for you to practice this skill.]

DIRECT QUOTATIONS

A *direct quotation* is an exact, word-for-word, restatement of a writer's or a speaker's words. A direct quotation must be documented in two ways: it must be enclosed in quotation marks, and it must be noted with an in-text parenthetical citation that refers to its source on the Works Cited page. Longer direct quotations—more than four typed lines—are introduced with your own sentence and then indented ten spaces from the left margin and double-spaced, omitting the quotation marks unless they are included in the original text. Here is an example:

If one is going to help a child of an alcoholic, one must know what alcoholism is. Alcoholism is defined as,

> primary chronic disease with genetic, psychosocial and environmental factors influencing its development and manifestations. The disease is often progressive and fatal. It is characterized by continuous or periodic: impaired control over drinking, preoccupation with the drug alcohol, use of alcohol despite adverse consequences, and distortions in thinking most notably denial. ("Definition")

Documentation Systems

All academic disciplines require a systematic approach to research and documentation. Whether your essay is in anthropology or chemistry, economics or English, geology or art history, you will need to learn to use outside sources accurately and correctly. Academic disciplines make use of several documentation systems. For example, the social sciences often use a system devised by the American Psychological Association (APA), while the humanities typically use one created by the Modern Language Association (MLA). Other academic documentation systems include Turabian and *The Chicago Manual of Style*. However, since essays written for this English course will fall under the category *humanities,* the following explanation will center on the MLA documentation system. For information on using the other documentation systems, we suggest you consult your campus writing center, library, or the following Web sites: *www.apastyle.org/tools.html* and *www.chicagomanualofstyle.org.*

The Preliminary Bibliography

As you begin to search for authoritative sources, you will want to maintain a list of the sources you examine; this list is called a *preliminary bibliography.* In creating this list, get into the habit of recording as much bibliographic information as is available—author, title, publisher, date of publication, Web address, page or paragraph numbers, and so forth. You will need this information when you compose the Works Cited page for your essay. Nothing is more frustrating than finishing an essay, only to discover you must try to locate the source of a quotation you found three weeks earlier when you began the project. In fact, when you have the opportunity, photocopy or print the page containing the information you think you might use in your essay. Check to make sure the photocopy or printout includes the bibliographic information you need, and if not, record those details on the copy.

CREATING A DRAFT

You have thought about your issue, discussed it with friends and classmates, and read about it in various periodicals, books, and electronic sources. You have a collection of notes, photocopies of sources, and a preliminary bibliography, and you have created a rough outline for your argument. Now comes the time to sit down and create a draft. In writing a research-based argument, this stage of the process can be quite challenging. Many students over rely on their sources and lose ownership of their writing.

[*Hint:* To avoid this common pitfall, we suggest you put your sources aside—*out of sight!*—and write a first, fast-draft by using only your outline and the knowledge you have gained through your reading and study of the issue. Now return to your sources/notes and identify relative information to flesh out your draft and provide the authoritative basis for your argument.]

As you incorporate quotations into your writing, you will want them to flow smoothly into the context of what you have to say rather than dropping them in awkwardly. Introduce a paraphrase or quotation with a *signal phrase,* which includes the author's name as well as a verb (usually in *present tense*). Here are commonly used source signal verbs:

acknowledges	allows	charges
advises	answers	claims
advocates	asserts	concedes
affirms	avows	concludes
agrees	believes	confirms

contends	interprets	remarks
criticizes	lists	reports
declares	objects	responds
denies	observes	states
disagrees	offers	suggests
discusses	opposes	thinks
emphasizes	recommends	writes
expresses	refutes	

In-Text Parenthetical Citations

Once you begin to write and make use of your research, you will encounter several challenges. First, you will need to integrate your facts, quotations, and paraphrased material into your essay. To achieve coherence and clarity, always introduce each piece of outside evidence, making clear to the reader the purpose of placing this quotation or paraphrase in this particular spot in your essay. Some students' first research-based essays neglect this important element, and, as a consequence, their essays read as if they merely dropped their quotations randomly onto the pages. Second, you will need to document your statements with in-text parenthetical citations showing the sources of your information.

In MLA style, the in-text parenthetical citations usually include the author's last name or, if an author's name is not given with the source, the title and the page number, all enclosed in parentheses. Remember this key principle: *You must use in-text parenthetical citations for direct quotations, for paraphrases or summaries of another person's words, and for facts, figures, or concepts that originated in someone else's work.* For example, if you are citing a fact you found in an article by Sharon Johnson, called "Cosmetic Surgery" and published on page 114 of the magazine *Science* on October 14, 1992, the parenthetical citation would look like this: (Johnson 114). It would be placed *before* the punctuation at the end of the sentence containing that fact. In cases where your source does not include an author, use key words of the title to identify the source ("Postmodern Culture" 398). If there is no actual page number, as is often the case with electronic sources (printout page numbers are not original source page numbers), include only the author's last name (Johnson) or key words of the title in your parenthetical note: ("Postmodern Culture"). The *MLA Handbook for Writers of Research Papers*, 6th ed. (2003) is an excellent source for bibliographic information. Also, you can look at the organization's Web site (*http://www.mla.org*) for updates and further explanations.

[*Hint:* As you type in your in-text, parenthetical citations, keep this guideline in mind: The author's last name or the key words from the title in your in-text parenthetical citation should match the first word of the source citation on your Works Cited page (excluding articles—*A, An, The*).]

Using Electronic Sources

Today, many students will find they can do their research for an essay without ever entering a library. However, students often do not realize that by doing only an Internet search through Google, Yahoo, or any of the other popular search engines available on the Web, they will not pick up the majority of scholarly sites and journals that academic writing usually requires. Of course, a Google search often will bring up pages and pages of links on a subject, but the challenge is to sift through and discern what is credible and authoritative and what is not. And, indeed, a discerning user can make these distinctions: for example, no, to Joe Schmo's blog on legalizing pot, but, yes, to the Centers for Disease Control Web site with health information on medicalizing marijuana. However, given the pages and pages of "hits," this grab-bag approach to research can be both time-consuming and inefficient for time-constrained students.

A *smart-student-search-strategy* is for you to begin your research process with your campus library, an academic library, which means information is presifted to include only sources that contribute credible information to the academic community. Also, an academic library houses thousands of peer-reviewed, scholarly journals, including articles written by professionals in a specific discipline for students and professionals of that discipline. Thus, to find articles from *The Journal of the American Medical Association* (*JAMA*), from *Women's Studies*, or from *Film Journal International*, you must use an academic library database, such as Academic Search Premier.

Although documenting electronic sources can be confusing, keep in mind the same basic principle of identifying the source within the essay: Identify the source within the context of the writing and with an in-text parenthetical citation followed by a full bibliographic entry for the source on the Works Cited page. The in-text parenthetical citation identifies the source either by the author's last name, if the source has an author, or by the first key words in the title: (Bishop) or ("Newsroom Integrity"). However, unlike hard copy sources that require page numbers in their citations, electronic sources only include the page number if the source is formatted in "page display format" or PDF: (Johnson 5) or ("Fighting with Microbes" 11). If the electronic source includes paragraph numbers in the original site, you do include the paragraph number corresponding to the specific spot where you took your quote, fact, or paraphrase: (Vickers, par. 14) or ("Finding Your Future," par. 23).

Although the primary purpose of documentation is to give credit to the originators of any material that is not your own, documentation also serves another important purpose: to allow your readers to locate the information you used and evaluate it for themselves. In effect, you are sharing the information you have found, a consideration that becomes increasingly important as you become an active participant in an academic community.

In order to fulfill these two purposes, your readers must be able to find the complete bibliographic information for each of your sources. To this end, within your essay, you provide the key name or title in your parenthetical citation, *immediately after* your use of the information. Now the reader can turn to the last page of your essay and locate the full bibliographic entry for each of these sources; therefore, you must create a Works Cited page.

The Works Cited Page

The final page of your essay is the Works Cited page, a list of the sources you directly cited in your essay. These citations are arranged alphabetically by the author's last name or by the first word in the title (excluding *A, An,* or *The*). The specific details to be included in each entry vary, according to the nature of the source—book, article, Web site, interview; hard copy or electronic. Following are some sample source citations typically found in first-year college essays:

Book by one author

Greenlaw, Linda. *The Hungry Ocean.* New York: Hyperion, 1999.

Story, poem, or essay from a collection in a book

Kenan, Randall. "The Foundations of the Earth." *Reading Literature and Writing Argument,* Second Edition. Missy James and Alan Merickel. Upper Saddle River, NJ: Prentice Hall, 2005. 89–101.

Article from a hard-copy periodical

Hallowell, Christopher. "A Mighty Challenge." *Audubon.* May/June 2006. 36–41.

Personal interview

Pekins, John. Personal interview. 10 May 2006.

Film

Bridget Jones's Diary. Dir. Sharon Maguire. Perf. Renee Zellweger, Colin Firth, Hugh Grant, Jim Broadbent, and Gemma Jones. 2001. DVD. Miramax, 2004.

Article in an online journal

McQueen, Tena F. and Robert A. Fleck Jr. "Changing Patterns of Internet Usage and Challenges at Colleges and Universities." *First Monday* 9.12 (2004) <http://www.firstmonday.dk/issues/issue9_12/mcqueen/>.

[Note: *First Monday* is an online, peer-reviewed journal.]

Article with no author from an electronic database

"Being Stalked by Intelligent Design." *American Scientist* 93 (November/December 2005): n.pag. <u>OmniFile Full Text Mega</u>. Wilson. 18 Jan. 2006 <http://linccweb.org>.

[Note: Since this entry is in html format, there are no page numbers.]

Article with authors from an electronic database

Beard, Lawrence A., Cynthia Harper, and Gena Riley. "Online Versus On-Campus Instruction: Student Attitudes & Perceptions." *TechTrends: Linking Research & Practice to Improve Learning* 48

(November/December 2004): 29–31. Academic Search Premier.
EBSCO. 19 Jan. 2006 <http://linccweb.org>

[Note: Since this article is in PDF format, this reference does include page
numbers.]

A literary work from an electronic database

Yeats, W. B. "To a Wealthy Man." *Responsibilities and Other Poems.*
New York: The McMillan Company, 1916; Bartleby.com, 1999. 20
March 2006 <http://www.bartleby.com/147>.

Online article

Ozols, Jennifer Barrett. "At Risk." *Newsweek.* 15 March 2005. 10 February
2006 <http://www.msnbc.msn.com/id/7184214/site/newsweek>.

Web sites

The Zora Neale Hurston Plays at the Library of Congress. 7 Jan. 2004.
Lib. Of Congress, Washington. 18 Jan. 2006
<http://memory.loc.gov/ammem/znhhtml/znhhome.html>.

Documenting the American South. 19 Dec. 2005. Library, U North
Carolina at Chapel Hill. 19 Jan. 2006 <http://docsouth.unc.edu>.

Sample Student Works Cited Page

Works Cited

"Alcoholism and Alcohol-Related Problems: A Sobering Look."
*Infinet Internet Service. National Council on Alcohol and Drug
Dependency.* 13 Nov. 1999. <http://www.ncadd.org>.
"Answers to Frequently Asked Questions about Being a Child of an
Alcoholic." *Infinet Internet Service. National Council of Alcohol
and Drug Dependency.* 11 Nov. 1999. <http://www.alcoholism
help.com>.
"Chemical Dependency: Myths and Facts about Alcoholism." *Infinet
Internet Service. Baptist Hospital East.* 13 Nov. 1999.
<http://www.baptisteast.com>.
"Children of Alcoholics: Important Facts." *Infinet Internet Service.*
August, 1998. *National Association of Children of Alcoholics.*
13 Nov. 1999. <http://www.healthorg/nacoa/impfacts.htm>.
"Definition of Alcoholism." *Infinet Internet Service.* 25 Feb 1990.
National Council on Alcoholism and Drug Dependency. 11 Nov.
1999. <http://www.ncadd.org>.

"FYI: Drinking in America." *Infinet Internet Service. National Council of Alcohol and Drug Dependency.* 12 Nov. 1999. <http://www.ncadd.org/fyidina.html>.

Peacock, Molly. "Say You Love Me." *Literature: Reading and Writing the Human Experience.* 7th ed. Richard Abcarian and Marvin Klotz, eds. New York: St. Martin's Press, 1998. 1056–1057.

Weddle, Charles D. and Phillip Wishon. "Children of Alcoholics." *Children Today* Jan–Feb. 1986: 8–12.

TWO SAMPLE WRITING PROJECTS

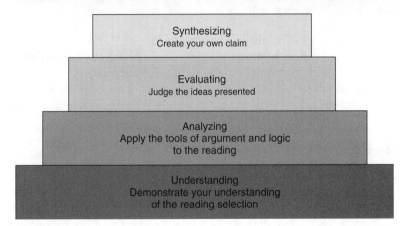

Justice and Ethical Responsibility

Issue Question: What governs ethical behavior? How do we decide on an ethical course of action?

"Yet my love of country comes over me like a strong wind and bears me irresistibly with all those chains to the battlefield."

—*Major Sullivan Ballou, "Last Letter to His Wife"*

"I here pledge my word, a word that has never been broken, that if your great father will set aside a part of my own country, where I and my little band can live, we will remain at peace with your people forever."

—*Cochise, [I am alone]*

"It's a start, a work of art To revolutionize, make a change, nothin' strange"

—*Public Enemy, "Fight the Power"*

"I joined the Wild and killed him with knowledgeable unknowing."

—*Gwendolyn Brooks, "The Boy Died in My Alley"*

"It is curious; but till that moment I had never realized what it means to destroy a healthy, conscious man."

—*George Orwell, "A Hanging"*

jus·tice   *n.*   (Dictionary.com)

1. The quality of being just; fairness.
2. a. The principle of moral rightness; equity.
   b. Conformity to moral rightness in action or attitude; righteousness.

eth·ic   *n.*   (Dictionary.com)

1. a. A set of principles of right conduct.
   b. A theory or a system of moral values: "An ethic of service is at war with a craving for gain" (Gregg Easterbrook).
2. ethics *(used with a sing. verb)* The study of the general nature of morals and of the specific moral choices to be made by a person; moral philosophy.

Understanding ⇒ Analyzing ⇒ Evaluating

I. **Exploration.**
   - Examine your own thinking by freewriting on the topic, justice and ethical responsibility.
   Here are some prompts to spark thinking and get your pen moving or fingers pecking: Spin-off of one or more of the above quotations. . . . Should one "fight for the power," and, if so, how? Can you think of firsthand examples where an individual has exercised his or her "power" in a fight for a just cause (i.e., "the good fight")? What were the circumstances? How did the "fight" play out? Who were the winners. . . the losers? On the other hand, can you think of individuals who abused their power either by specific action or by *not* acting? Finally, a "tongue-in-cheek" bumper sticker reads: *"Whoever has the most when he dies, wins."* What are the connotations of "most" and "wins"? What principles and ethics do the saying implicitly endorse?
   - Once you have become familiar with your own thinking, examine your reasoning process: What assumptions or broad generalizations about justice and ethical responsibility are revealed in your prewriting?

II. **Exploration.** Read the following poems, stories, and essays/speeches:
   - "In Response to Executive Order 9066" by Dwight Okita (Chapter Four)

- "Letter from Birmingham Jail by Martin Luther King Jr. (Chapter Four)
- "The Black Walnut Tree" by Mary Oliver (Chapter Six)
- "Major Sullivan Ballou's Last Letter to His Wife" by Sullivan Ballou (Chapter Six)
- "Terminal" by Nadine Gordimer (Chapter Seven)
- "The Boy Died in My Alley" by Gwendolyn Brooks (Chapter Seven)
- "Ethics" by Linda Pastan (Chapter Seven)
- "Fight the Power" by Public Enemy (Chapter Seven)
- [I am alone] by Cochise (Chapter Seven)
- "Inaugural Address" by John F. Kennedy (Chapter Seven)
- "A Hanging" by George Orwell (Chapter Seven)

Examine three of the above readings by writing responses to these questions; write in *complete sentences* and *write out responses for each of the three selected pieces* (four separate responses for each piece of literature):

a. What is an implied **claim** on the subject of justice and ethical responsibility? [UNDERSTANDING]

b. What **evidence** is offered in support of that claim? [ANALYZING]

c. What **rhetorical appeals** *ethos, logos, pathos*) move the reader toward acceptance of the claim? [ANALYZING]

d. Upon reflection, how might you **defend, refute,** and/or **qualify** each claim? [EVALUATING]

⇒ Creating

I. Articulation: Writing the Essay

- Based on your "exploration," create your own claim on the subject of justice and ethical responsibility. [SYNTHESIZING/CREATING]
- To support and exemplify your claim, discuss and analyze specific examples from:
  - three (or more) literature pieces (any selections from *Reading Literature and Writing Argument*)
  - your own experience, direct observation, firsthand knowledge

Essay Requirements

- MLA format for presentation; 12-pt. Times New Roman font
- Minimum word count: 1,100 words
- Paper trail

Reading/Exploration Schedule

- Okita, King, Brooks
- Oliver, Pastan, Gordimer
- Orwell, Cochise, Kennedy, Public Enemy

Workshop Schedule for Writing Your Argument

- Designing Your Argument/Mapping Paragraphs/Drafting

- Drafting/Revising
- Peer Argument Analysis
- Final copy with "paper trail"

Suggested Topics with Related Readings

- *How should an individual respond to an injustice that is embedded in the larger culture that surrounds him or her?*
  "In Response to Executive Order 9066" by Dwight O'Kita
  "Letter from Birmingham Jail" by Martin Luther King. Jr.
  "Fight the Power" by Public Enemy
  [*I am alone*] by Cochise
- *When and how should an individual act in the face of the destruction of life?*
  "The Things They Carried" by Tim O'Brien
  "The Boy Died in My Alley" by Gwendolyn Brooks
  "Ethics" by Linda Pastan
  "A Hanging" by George Orwell
- *How does an individual determine his or her ethical responsibility in a personal or an intimate dilemma?*
  "The Black Walnut Tree" by Mary Oliver
  "Last Letter to His Wife" by Sullivan Ballou
  "Terminal" by Nadine Gordimer

Sample Student Essay: Justice and Ethical Responsibility

Jeff Smith
Ms. Missy James
ENC 1102
12 December 2005

The Power of Inaction

What is the going rate for someone to give up the most fundamental of values? Apparently it is equivalent to the cost of a Big Mac ($4.50); this was the finding of psychologist Stanley Milgram and his team at Yale University in 1961. In the study, they proved that 26 out of 40 paid subjects could be made to apply lethal levels of voltage to a restrained person, provided the subject was urged to do so by an authoritative figure (Weiten 673). The study was conducted in response to the Nuremberg trials in which high-ranking Nazi officials, such as Adolf Eichmann, pleaded, "I was just following orders." If people can be coaxed into betraying their fundamental ethical values such as intentionally harming people, how far of a stretch would it be to get them to kill another human being? Looking back through the history of human civilization, it would appear our fundamental ethical and moral beliefs only work part time. The dictionary defines ethics as moral principles or practices. But what this definition does not say is that more often than not, our moral boundaries are defined not by religion or even family, but by the government, the media, and society. A strong sense of ethical responsibility is an important attribute for one to have, but history shows it can also take on a much darker role as a tool of the upper class and power elite to control the lower classes.

Ethical responsibility has been used to legitimatize multiple atrocities throughout the history of mankind. In fact, if one were to ask Germans during the rounding up of ethnic Jews in 1933, if it was the right thing to do, the overwhelming response would have been yes; after all, in their eyes, Jews were responsible for Germany's defeat in World War One. Centuries earlier, was it not also deemed ethically responsible for soldiers to go off and fight in the Crusades against the Muslim infidels? In retrospect, it almost seems laugh-able that reasonable people expected that God wanted millions to die for something as insignificant as land. But let's not be hypocritical. One doesn't have to look too far back into modern American history to realize our new moral and ethical code isn't much better. It isn't too far of a stretch to imagine President Truman defending himself for crimes against humanity after the atomic bombings of Hiroshima and Nagasaki, that is, if the war had gone differently. But in the end, the difference between morality and immorality, much like the history books, is written by the victor of such conflicts.

The ethical values of a society can best be represented by the laws it upholds, laws that prohibit crimes such as murder, stealing, and adultery. These are a direct reflection of the moral boundaries we as a society seek to defend. This is also where one can find the greatest hypocrisy as these laws and values come into conflict with the greater needs of society. The poem, "In Response to Executive Order 9066" by Dwight Okita, is a telling portrayal of one such law in which the rights of Japanese-Americans were disavowed due to the threat of Japanese saboteurs and spies on American soil during

World War Two. The poem also shows how these laws change our individual values. Denise, the friend of the speaker, accuses her of "giving secrets away to the enemy" and "trying to start a war" (Okita 137). If laws can have such an effect on two teenage friends, what levels of animosity and hate could be fomented among strangers of the same society? One might begin to wonder if the very foundation of our laws, the Declaration of Independence, was written in disappearing ink.

Laws, however ethical they may sound, can be one of the most effective tools for controlling the lower classes. Laws that prohibit stealing (even if a necessity for survival, such as food) seem unjust in a society with so much disparity of wealth between the rich and the poor. Unfortunately, in the end we can only blame human nature for the creation of a class social system; after all, in the beginning, it took at least two people to start our insatiable thirst for wealth, one to build a fence around some land and the other to be stupid enough to abide by it. Unfortunately, for us today, laws prohibiting stealing are so imbedded in and crucial to our society that we could never go back and recreate ourselves as equals. What is even more unfortunate is that wealth has ways of creating more wealth because with it comes power, and with power one has the ability to influence and manipulate laws to secure and maintain this wealth. As a result, the rich get richer and the poor get poorer. Therefore, a seemingly ethical law against stealing keeps equality far out of reach of the rest of society.

Do two wrongs make a right? In the case of capital punishment, it is an immoral response to an immoral action. State-sponsored murder (capital punishment) had its place, and that was fifty years ago, when the rest of Western World ceased to utilize this archaic form of justice. In the short essay, "A Hanging," George Orwell vividly describes the execution process, giving a human face and character to an individual facing the noose: "He and we were a party of men walking together, seeing, hearing, feeling, understanding the same world; and in two minutes, with a sudden snap, one of use would be gone—one mind less, one world less" (Orwell 629). It is the realization of the permanence of this act that eludes most Americans that have been brought up with a media of violence, for example, cartoons of road runner blowing up the unsuspecting coyote, only to return to get blown up again in the next scene. Most importantly, capital punishment is ineffective as a tool of punishment, given that murder tends to be a crime of passion in which the threat of execution is probably the farthest from the conscience of the perpetrator. Capital punishment is an immoral act and the most prolific example of hypocrisy in our modern justice system.

Historically, there can be no greater example of upper class control than through the church; for centuries the upper-classes and clergy have used the authority of God to push their values on the lower-classes. In the short story, "The Foundations of the Earth" by Randall Kenan, the main character Maggie comes to this realization when she finds that the message of the church has been one of arrogance toward and hatred of alternative lifestyles. This condemnation comes in conflict with her newfound knowledge that her recently deceased grandson had been " 'living with another man all these years. . . . Like man and wife' " (Kenan 93). Throughout the history of man, we have conformed our ways to the wishes of what someone else says are God's, rarely stopping to think through the situation for ourselves. Therefore, through the church, values can be placed on society, and values have ways of becoming laws—laws such as those against same-sex marriage or abortion. As such, moral decisions, that should be decided in private among the people to whom they matter the most, are turned into public issues. As a result, countless hours and dollars are wasted in the courts and on talk shows, debating issues that are not ours to judge for others.

"The tree of liberty must be refreshed from time to time with the blood of patriots and tyrants"—The famous words of Thomas Jefferson still ring true today, as we are reminded that our fundamental rights, were not always so. In the end people need to learn to become independent thinkers who question the laws and the authority behind them. The government, media, and religions all play a role in influencing our beliefs and actions; it is through this dynamic that both ethical—and unethical—laws and practices come into being. During the desegregation movement of the 1960's, Martin Luther King, Jr. defined the concepts embedded in just and unjust laws in his "Letter from Birmingham Jail." The civil rights activist defines unjust laws as, "laws that are not rooted in eternal law and natural law"; he goes on to claim that "any law that uplifts human personality is just. Any law that degrades human personality is unjust" (King 155). Therefore, in the interest of human personality and equality, we should take it upon ourselves, as our moral responsibility, to defy any law we deem to be unjust: "The only thing necessary for the triumph of evil is for good men to do nothing."—British statesman Edmund Burke

Works Cited

Kenan, Randall. "Foundations of the Earth." Rpt. in *Reading Literature and Writing Argument.* 2nd Ed. Missy James and Alan P. Merickel. Upper Saddle River, New Jersey: Pearson Prentice Hall, 2005. 89–101.

King, Jr., Martin Luther. "Letter from Birmingham Jail." Rpt. in. *Reading Literature and Writing Argument.* 2nd Ed. Missy James and Alan P. Merickel. Upper Saddle River, New Jersey: Pearson Prentice Hall, 2005. 151–162.

Okita, Dwight. "In Response to Executive Order 9066." Rpt. in *Reading Literature and Writing Argument.* 2nd Ed. Missy James and Alan P. Merickel. Upper Saddle River, New Jersey: Pearson Prentice Hall, 2005. 137.

Orwell, George. "A Hanging." Rpt. in *Reading Literature and Writing Argument.* 2nd Ed. Missy James and Alan P. Merickel. Upper Saddle River, New Jersey: Pearson Prentice Hall, 2005. 627–630.

Wayne, Weiten. *Psychology, Themes and Variations.* Las Vegas: Thompson Wadsworth, 2004.

Knowledge and Individual Power

I. **Exploration.** Examine your own thinking on the subject of *knowledge and individual power.*

Try one of the following prewriting techniques:

a. Write the words *knowledge and individual power* at the top of a page, and write nonstop about it for five to ten minutes just to see what ideas emerge.

b. List all the ideas, concepts, and terms that are associated with the words *knowledge and individual power.* List, but do not edit; allow your creative mind to work.

c. Write *knowledge and individual power* in the center of a page, circle the words, and cluster around the circle any ideas and concepts that come to mind.

Once you have become familiar with your own thinking on the subject, examine your reasoning process. To do so, read back over your prewriting and respond to the following questions:

1. What **assumptions** or broad generalizations about knowledge and individual power are revealed in your prewriting?
2. Can you identify specific, personal experiences that may have led you to make an **inductive leap** in reaching those generalizations?

II. **Exploration.** Read the following stories, poems, and essays:

Kenan, "The Foundations of the Earth" (Chapter Four)

Dickinson, "Much madness is divinest sense" (Chapter Four)

Villanueva, "Crazy Courage" (Chapter Four)

Alexie, "Superman and Me" (Chapter Four)

Bambara, "The Lesson" (Chapter Seven)

Carver, "Cathedral" (Chapter Seven)

Hawthorne, "The Birth-Mark" (Chapter Seven)

Hughes, "Theme for English 'B'" (Chapter Seven)

Examine three of the above selections by writing responses to these questions:

a. What is an implied **claim** on the subject of knowledge and individual power? [UNDERSTANDING]
b. What **evidence** is offered in support of that claim? [ANALYZING]
c. What **rhetorical appeals** (*ethos, logos, pathos*) move the reader toward acceptance of the claim? [ANALYZING]
d. Upon reflection, how might you defend, refute, and/or qualify each claim? [EVALUATING]

III. **Articulation**
   • Based on Explorations I and II, create your own claim for the subject of knowledge and individual power. [SYNTHESIZING]
   • To support and exemplify your claim, select and discuss specific examples from three (or more) literature pieces you have examined, as well as from your own experience and observations.

Project Requirements
   • MLA format for presentation and documentation; 12-pt. Times New Roman font
   • Minimum word count: Explorations I and II, 400 words; Articulation III, 1,000 words
   • Paper trail

Workshop Schedule

- Exploration I & II activities
- Articulation/designing & drafting your argument
- Revising, editing, submitting final copy with "paper trail"

ESSAY SCORING RUBRIC—FOR PEER REVIEWS AND SELF-EVALUATIONS

6=Superior	3=Minimally Adequate
5=Strong	2=Inadequate
4=Competent	1=Incompetent

1. **Engagement with texts/perspectives; critical thinking and insights**

   The essay demonstrates successful *engagement* with readings/various perspectives related to the topic. It includes well-reasoned *analyses* and shows the student responding to various perspectives in thoughtful and distinctive ways.

   Superior   **Strong**   **Competent**

   Minimally Adequate   **Inadequate**   **Incompetent**

2. **Clarity of claim/perspective**

   The essay demonstrates the student's ability to *synthesize* the various perspectives and to *create* and advocate a specific and compelling *claim* in response to the assignment's topic.

   Superior   **Strong**   **Competent**

   Minimally Adequate   **Inadequate**   **Incompetent**

3. **Development**

   Key points of the claim are exemplified with *specific and substantive information,* including details from texts and, as appropriate, details from personal experiences and observations.

   Superior   **Strong**   **Competent**

   Minimally Adequate   **Inadequate**   **Incompetent**

4. Organization

- Each part of the essay flows logically from the preceding point.
- *Paragraphs* support the writer's goal to provide clear understanding and engaged reading throughout the essay.
- *Transitions* create coherence between and within paragraphs.

Superior   **Strong**   **Competent**

Minimally Adequate   **Inadequate**   **Incompetent**

5. Presentation and Style

- Presentation of the essay, including its format and *MLA documentation,* point of view, and tone, is appropriate to the writing context.
- The essay demonstrates fresh and precise *diction* and a sophisticated *sentence style.*

Superior   **Strong**   **Competent**

Minimally Adequate   **Inadequate**   **Incompetent**

6. Mechanics

Errors in *spelling, grammar, or mechanics* are minimal and minor. The reader is never distracted by them. (Frequent and serious errors will lower an essay's overall grade to below a C.)

Superior   **Strong**   **Competent**

Minimally Adequate   **Inadequate**   **Incompetent**

ESSAY SCORING RUBRIC FOR ROGERIAN ARGUMENT— FOR PEER REVIEWS AND SELF-EVALUATIONS

- **Introduction: [Understanding]**

Introduces the issue to the reader. Offers adequate background enabling the reader to understand the origin and importance of the issue. Focuses the issue as a succinct and clear statement or question.

Superior   Strong   Competent

Minimally Adequate   **Inadequate**   **Incompetent**

- **Presentation of Opposing Perspectives: [Analyzing]**

  Presents opposing sides of the issue in a balanced and neutral manner. Uses an objective tone and avoids biased language. Shows the student exploring opposing perspectives in thoughtful and distinctive ways, *including details from texts and, as appropriate, references to personal experiences and observations.* Points out the evidence and appeals commonly found in these argumentative positions.

  Superior   Strong   Competent

  Minimally Adequate   Inadequate   Incompetent

- **Finding the Middle Ground: [Evaluating and Synthesizing/Creating]**

  Presents a concise synopsis of the main points of both sides of the argument. Offers a compromise to the two conflicting positions. Articulates and advocates a specific and an engaging *middle-ground position/ claim of policy.*

  Superior   Strong   Competent

  Minimally Adequate   Inadequate   Incompetent

- **Organization: [Applying]**

  - Uses *paragraphs* to demonstrate the student's ability to develop topics and connect ideas in a unified and logical fashion.
  - Includes *transitions* to create coherence between and within paragraphs.

  Superior   Strong   Competent

  Minimally Adequate   Inadequate   Incompetent

- **Presentation and Style: [Applying]**

  - *Presentation* of the essay, including its format and *MLA documentation,* point of view, and tone, is appropriate to the writing context.
  - The essay demonstrates fresh and precise *diction* and sophisticated *sentence style.*

  Superior   Strong   Competent

  Minimally Adequate   Inadequate   Incompetent

- **Grammar and mechanics**

  Errors in spelling, grammar, or mechanics are minimal and minor. The reader is never distracted by writing errors.

  [Note: Frequent or serious errors will lower an essay's overall grade to below a C.]

  Superior   Strong   Competent

  Minimally Adequate   Inadequate   Incompete

⋙ CHAPTER 4 ⋙

Individuality
and Community

The goals of an individual sometimes conflict with the goals of the society in which he or she lives. People naturally want to live in an orderly environment and, as a result, generally choose to obey the rules of their society. For example, a person cannot choose to grow cabbages in a public park just because the park makes a convenient spot for a garden: usurping public land for private enterprise is against the law. Similarly, although the temperature soars to 100 degrees on an August afternoon, a person cannot elect to walk the streets naked: Public nudity is usually prohibited by local law. And, of course, even beyond the authority of the law, society may enforce codes of behavior simply through the power of its approval or its disapproval. Yet what teenager has not enjoyed the thrill of nonconformity accompanying socially unacceptable behavior, whether it comes in the form of purple hair, a pierced navel, or simply lighting a cigarette? Nevertheless, in most areas of life, adults generally are forced to conform to community standards of conduct, and while some people may find such conformity comforting, others find it irritating, even demeaning.

History is filled with examples of conflicts created when individuals have felt their own paths blocked by the constraints of the societies in which they lived. Galileo was certain the earth revolved around the sun and ultimately paid a high price for his iconoclastic belief. Other than seeing his innovative art ridiculed by contemporary critics, Vincent van Gogh received almost no recognition during his lifetime; however, today we view him as one of the most talented Impressionists, and his paintings are valued in the millions of dollars. James Joyce's *Ulysses* was banned in the United States when it was first published in Paris in 1922, yet by the end of the century, it was acclaimed as one of the world's most important novels. Whether, in the end, such conflicts affect the flow of history or merely create friction for people as they go about their daily lives, they create powerful emotions which inform our literature.

Many of us have read *Huckleberry Finn* by Mark Twain. Huck, certainly the prototype rebellious American child, at first simply finds ways to get around both his father's and his aunt's demands, but later defies the values and laws of the larger society as he befriends the freed slave Jim in their trip down the Mississippi River. We tend to approve of Huck's rebelliousness and applaud the trouble it causes for those around him. Similarly, readers often find the language and behavior of the main character, Holden Caulfield, in J. D. Salinger's *Catcher in the Rye* acceptable, even insightful, as he displays the characteristic teenage behavior that questions rather than accepts the standards of adults. In these two instances, as well as innumerable other examples in literature, the emotions surrounding conflicts between individuals and their communities create powerfully moving experiences for readers.

In order to evaluate our own behavior, we can analyze the motives and reasoning behind the actions of individuals who accept the constraints of society and bend to its wishes, as well as those individuals who choose to resist. Clearly, history and literature provide many examples. Plato's *Crito,* included in this chapter, is an account of the ancient Greek philosopher Socrates's suicide. A renowned teacher and respected thinker, Socrates finds himself accused by the Athenian government of corrupting the youth of the city. For this crime, Socrates is sentenced to death. His friends urge him to flee, for another city-state is sure to offer him refuge; however, Socrates believes so strongly in the need for order and in his duty to uphold civil law that he yields to his sentence and drinks poisonous hemlock. In accepting his death, was Socrates holding on to the generalization that civic duty is more important than personal happiness? Is he to be honored for this ultimate personal sacrifice? Or is he to be judged a fool for not taking the advice of his friends and students?

Thomas Jefferson argued that all citizens must respect the law or face the threat of anarchy, yet he also helped author the Declaration of Independence, which itself justifies instances of civil disobedience. Later in American history, Henry David Thoreau and Martin Luther King Jr. willingly risked anarchy in the hopes of evoking social change. Included in this chapter are essays by Thoreau and King, both of whom, in contrast to Socrates, chose to resist the demands of their governments. During the Vietnam War, thousands of young men were drafted to serve in the military to fight a war which many Americans considered to be immoral. Upon receiving their draft notices, some young men chose to resist their orders and, in protest, fled to Canada; others, however, accepted their military orders as their patriotic and civic duty.

In each selection in this chapter, we encounter the question of the individual's place in his or her society. In some cases, such as "The Bride Comes to Yellow Sky," the situation evokes humor; however, in others, such as "The Red Convertible," the conflict is one of life and death. Both our personal experiences and our reading of works by such writers as Claude McKay, Richard Rodriguez, and John Hope Franklin demonstrate that finding our place as individuals in a complex society such as ours is always a struggle. And in a democratic society such as ours, we are granted the privilege and obliged with the responsibility to articulate and to defend our positions, our choices, to others. Thus, in creating an argument based on morals and values, we must define and clarify, explain and elaborate those principles which have guided our decisions.

When we argue that this particular action is the right action because it is the morally right thing to do, we create arguments that are not quite like the standard argument. For example, we might well argue that having multiple sex partners is dangerous to one's health. To support our claim, we could easily find reliable statistics showing a higher incidence of sexually transmitted diseases among people who do have multiple sex partners when compared with people who do not have multiple sex partners. That would be strong evidence for our claim, and those statistics alone might be adequate to convince readers to avoid sexual promiscuity. We would be making an appeal to fear, and that fear would be well founded. On the other hand, if we argue that people should avoid sexual promiscuity because having sex before marriage is immoral, then we have created an argument whose support would be quite different.

When we make a claim of policy based on a moral judgment, we cannot so easily find statistics or objective facts to use as evidence. Rather we will have to look for support in the form of authoritative opinions and testimonies and personal experience. Perhaps promiscuity is unhealthy, but that is not our point; this time we want to prove to our readers that promiscuity violates a moral code. And to make our case, we will have to cite moral authorities our audience will recognize and respect. Most religions have recognizable leaders who have commented on the immorality of multiple sexual partners, but what if we are unsure about our readers' adherence to an organized religion? Where do we turn for evidence then? Certainly a person does not have to be religious to have strong moral convictions. In families, grandparents are often enforcers of moral code: "Don't do that. You know your grandfather would not approve." Most cultures respect the wisdom gained through years of living, so we might look for an older person with some positive name recognition. We might also turn to philosophers whose writings address ethical principles and matters of right and wrong. Or perhaps we might cite respected public figures who have a generally credible quality to their actions and words; former President Jimmy Carter and Nelson Mandela, for example, both seem to have achieved that kind of credibility with a wide range of people today. As a result, many readers would take seriously their comments on promiscuity even though their expertise and experience have nothing directly to do with the subject.

Personal experience also sometimes supports a moral claim. Reading Martin Luther King, Jr.'s "Letter from Birmingham Jail," we will notice that King cites religious authorities, St. Augustine and St. Thomas Aquinas, as well as modern philosopher Martin Buber. But he also offers his readers evidence in the form of personal experience as he recounts incidents of segregation that affected his children. In our argument about promiscuity, we could offer readers our own experience watching promiscuous friends suffer due to their choice of having multiple sexual partners. As with most personal experience, the emotional impact of such anecdotes is often strong, making this type of evidence effective in persuading an audience.

Sexual promiscuity is a personal choice that certainly affects an individual, yet there are also many moral choices whose ripples of influence more overtly extend far out into society. For example, in the 1980s, some citizens of the United States chose to harbor illegal aliens from Central American countries because deportation by the Immigration Service might mean torture or death at the hands of conflicting groups vying for power. These people knowingly violated U.S. law, making that choice on moral grounds. Earlier in our history, abolitionists hid runaway slaves traveling the underground railroad; they, too, made the choice to violate U.S. law since it conflicted with their own sense of what was right. Although we may respect those who made that decision in the 1800s and those who did so in the 1980s and admire them for the risks they took in making that moral decision, we must also recognize that no country can afford to have its citizens deciding which laws they will obey and which they will ignore.

Any time a person chooses to break the law, that decision has an impact on the rest of society. How many people illegally use marijuana to relieve the effects of chemotherapy or the pain of glaucoma? And at what point will their numbers be so large that the nation will begin to reexamine its drug laws? Perhaps the impact of our moral decisions is minor, or perhaps, as in former President Clinton's case, the impact can be felt by the entire nation.

How does an individual know right from wrong? In a given situation, why is one action preferable to another? Is an action based on personal conviction? Does an individual choose a path based on a community's social code? Or is there some innate instinct within all humans guiding individuals toward right action? Literature often portrays an individual's struggle to justify a choice that conflicts with his or her community's standards. For example, in Randall Kenan's "The Foundations of the Earth," Maggie faces this conflict. As Maggie demonstrates, acknowledging this struggle provides opportunities for individuals to "realign" their thinking.

PREWRITING AND DISCUSSION

1. What do we mean when we use the word *community?* Is a community merely a group of people joined by the fact that they live in the same small geographic area? Or are there other ways in which a group can be held together to form a community?

2. Consider both the positive as well as the negative effects of belonging to a community. What pressures are exerted on individuals by communities? Think about a community you or a friend has experienced. How does this community describe itself, and is the description consistent with the way outsiders would describe it?

3. Write for a few minutes about what it means to be an individual in our contemporary society. What qualities signal one's individuality? List some people you consider to be strong, independent individuals. In small groups of four or five, discuss your ideas of individuality.

FICTION

∧∧

Kate Chopin (1851–1904)
Désirée's Baby

As the day was pleasant, Madame Valmondé drove over to L'Abri to see Désirée and the baby.

It made her laugh to think of Désirée with a baby. Why, it seemed but yesterday that Désirée was little more than a baby herself; when Monsieur in riding through the gateway of Valmondé had found her lying asleep in the shadow of the big stone pillar.

The little one awoke in his arms and began to cry for "Dada." That was as much as she could do or say. Some people thought she might have strayed there of her own accord, for she was of the toddling age. The prevailing belief was that she had been purposely left by a party of Texans, whose canvas-covered wagon, late in the day, had crossed the ferry that Coton Maïs kept, just below the plantation. In time Madame Valmondé abandoned every speculation but the one that Désirée had been sent to her by a beneficent Providence to be the child of her affection, seeing that she was without child of the flesh. For the girl grew to be beautiful and gentle, affectionate and sincere,—the idol of Valmondé.

It was no wonder, when she stood one day against the stone pillar in whose shadow she had lain asleep, eighteen years before, that Armand Aubigny riding by and seeing her there, had fallen in love with her. That was the way all the Aubignys fell in love, as if struck by a pistol shot. The wonder was that he had not loved her before; for he had known her since his father brought him home from Paris, a boy of eight, after his mother died there. The passion that awoke in him that day, when he saw her at the gate, swept along like an avalanche, or like a prairie fire, or like anything that drives headlong over all obstacles.

Monsieur Valmondé grew practical and wanted things well considered: that is, the girl's obscure origin. Armand looked into her eyes and did not care. He was reminded that she was nameless. What did it matter about a name when he could give her one of the oldest and proudest in Louisiana? He ordered the *corbeille* from Paris, and contained himself with what patience he could until it arrived; then they were married. 5

Madame Valmondé had not seen Désirée and the baby for four weeks. When she reached L'Abri she shuddered at the first sight of it, as she always did. It was a sad looking place, which for many years had not known the gentle presence of a mistress, old Monsieur Aubigny having married and buried his wife in France, and she having loved her own land too well ever to leave it. The roof came down steep and black like a cowl, reaching out beyond the wide galleries that encircled the yellow stuccoed house. Big, solemn oaks grew close to it, and their thick-leaved, far-reaching branches shadowed it like a pall. Young Aubigny's rule was a strict one, too, and under it his negroes had forgotten how to be gay, as they had been during the old master's easy-going and indulgent lifetime.

The young mother was recovering slowly, and lay full length, in her soft white muslins and laces, upon a couch. The baby was beside her, upon her arm, where he had fallen asleep, at her breast. The yellow nurse woman sat beside a window fanning herself.

Madame Valmondé bent her portly figure over Désirée and kissed her, holding her an instant tenderly in her arms. Then she turned to the child.

10   "This is not the baby!" she exclaimed, in startled tones. French was the language spoken at Valmondé in those days.

"I knew you would be astonished," laughed Désirée, "at the way he has grown. The little *cochon de lait!* Look at his legs, mamma, and his hands and fingernails—real fingernails. Zandrine had to cut them this morning. Isn't it true, Zandrine?"

The woman bowed her turbaned head majestically, "Mais si, Madame."

"And the way he cries," went on Désirée, "is deafening. Armand heard him the other day as far away as La Blanche's cabin."

Madame Valmondé had never removed her eyes from the child. She lifted it and walked with it over to the window that was lightest. She scanned the baby narrowly, then looked as searchingly at Zandrine, whose face was turned to gaze across the fields.

"Yes, the child has grown, has changed," said Madame Valmondé, slowly, as she replaced it beside its mother. "What does Armand say?"

15   Désirée's face became suffused with a glow that was happiness itself.

"Oh, Armand is the proudest father in the parish, I believe, chiefly because it is a boy, to bear his name; though he says not,—that he would have loved a girl as well. But I know it isn't true. I know he says that to please me. And mamma," she added, drawing Madame Valmondé's head down to her, and speaking in a whisper, "he hasn't punished one of them—not one of them—since baby is born. Even Négrillon who pretended to have burnt his leg that he might rest from work—he only laughed, and said Négrillon was a great scamp. Oh, mamma, I'm so happy; it frightens me."

What Désirée said was true. Marriage, and later the birth of his son had softened Armand Aubigny's imperious and exacting nature greatly. This was what made the gentle Désirée so happy, for she loved him desperately. When he frowned she trembled, but loved him. When he smiled, she asked no greater blessing of God. But Armand's dark, handsome face had not often been disfigured by frowns since the day he fell in love with her.

When the baby was about three months old, Désirée awoke one day to the conviction that there was something in the air menacing her peace. It was at first too subtle to grasp. It had only been a disquieting suggestion; an air of mystery among the blacks; unexpected visits from far-off neighbors who could hardly account for their coming. Then a strange, an awful change in her husband's manner, which she dared not ask him to explain. When he spoke to her, it was with averted eyes, from which the old love-light seemed to have gone out. He absented himself from home; and when there, avoided her presence and that of her child, without excuse. And the very spirit of Satan seemed suddenly to take hold of him in his dealings with the slaves. Désirée was miserable enough to die.

She sat in her room, one hot afternoon, in her *peignoir,* listlessly drawing through her fingers the strands of her long, silky brown hair that hung about her shoulders. The baby, half-naked, lay asleep upon her own great mahogany bed, that was like a sumptuous throne, with its satin-lined half-canopy. One of La Blanche's little quadroon boys—half naked too—stood fanning the child slowly with a fan of peacock feathers. Désirée's eyes had been fixed absently and sadly upon the baby, while she was striving to penetrate the threatening mist that she felt closing about her. She looked from her child to the boy who stood beside him, and back again; over and over. "Ah!" It was a cry that she could not help; which she was not conscious of having uttered. The blood turned like ice in her veins, and a clammy moisture gathered upon her face.

She tried to speak to the little quadroon boy; but no sound would come, at first.   20
When he heard his name uttered, he looked up, and his mistress was pointing to the door. He laid aside the great, soft fan, and obediently stole away, over the polished floor, on his bare tiptoes.

She stayed motionless, with gaze riveted upon her child, and her face the picture of fright.

Presently her husband entered the room, and without noticing her, went to a table and began to search among some papers which covered it.

"Armand," she called to him, in a voice which must have stabbed him, if he was human. But he did not notice. "Armand," she said again. Then she rose and tottered towards him. "Armand," she panted once more, clutching his arm, "look at our child. What does it mean? tell me."

He coldly but gently loosened her fingers from about his arm and thrust the hand away from him. "Tell me what it means!" she cried despairingly.

"It means," he answered lightly, "that the child is not white; it means that you are   25
not white."

A quick conception of all that this accusation meant for her nerved her with unwonted courage to deny it. "It is a lie; it is not true, I am white! Look at my hair, it is brown; and my eyes are gray, Armand, you know they are gray. And my skin is fair," seizing his wrist. "Look at my hand; whiter than yours, Armand," she laughed hysterically.

"As white as La Blanche's," he returned cruelly; and went away leaving her alone with their child.

When she could hold a pen in her hand, she sent a despairing letter to Madame Valmondé.

"My mother, they tell me I am not white. Armand has told me I am not white. For God's sake tell them it is not true. You must know it is not true. I shall die. I must die. I cannot be so unhappy, and live."

The answer that came was as brief: 30
"My own Désirée: Come home to Valmondé; back to your mother who loves you. Come with your child."

When the letter reached Désirée she went with it to her husband's study, and laid it open upon the desk before which he sat. She was like a stone image: silent, white, motionless after she placed it there.

In silence he ran his cold eyes over the written words. He said nothing.

"Shall I go, Armand?" she asked in tones sharp with agonized suspense.

35   "Yes, go."

"Do you want me to go?"

"Yes, I want you to go."

He thought Almighty God had dealt cruelly and unjustly with him; and felt, somehow, that he was paying Him back in kind when he stabbed thus into his wife's soul. Moreover he no longer loved her, because of the unconscious injury she had brought upon his home and his name.

She turned away like one stunned by a blow, and walked slowly towards the door, hoping he would call her back.

40   "Good-by, Armand," she moaned.

He did not answer her. That was his last blow at fate.

Désirée went in search of her child. Zandrine was pacing the sombre gallery with it. She took the little one from the nurse's arms with no word of explanation, and descending the steps, walked away, under the live-oak branches.

It was an October afternoon; the sun was just sinking. Out in the still fields the negroes were picking cotton.

Désirée had not changed the thin white garment nor the slippers which she wore. Her hair was uncovered and the sun's rays brought a golden gleam from its brown meshes. She did not take the broad, beaten road which led to the far-off plantation of Valmondé. She walked across a deserted field, where the stubble bruised her tender feet, so delicately shod, and tore her thin gown to shreds.

45   She disappeared among the reeds and willows that grew thick along the banks of the deep, sluggish bayou; and she did not come back again.

Some weeks later there was a curious scene enacted at L'Abri. In the centre of the smoothly swept back yard was a great bonfire. Armand Aubigny sat in the wide hallway that commanded a view of the spectacle; and it was he who dealt out to a half dozen negroes the material which kept this fire ablaze.

A graceful cradle of willow, with all its dainty furbishings, was laid upon the pyre, which had already been fed with the richness of a priceless *layette*. Then there were silk gowns, and velvet and satin ones added to these; laces, too, and embroideries; bonnets and gloves; for the *corbeille* had been of rare quality.

The last thing to go was a tiny bundle of letters; innocent little scribblings that Désirée had sent to him during the days of their espousal. There was the remnant of one back in the drawer from which he took them. But it was not Désirée's; it was part of an old letter from his mother to his father. He read it. She was thanking God for the blessing of her husband's love:—

"But, above all," she wrote, "night and day, I thank the good God for having so arranged our lives that our dear Armand will never know that his mother, who adores him, belongs to the race that is cursed with the brand of slavery."

CRITICAL THINKING QUESTIONS

1. What is Armand's argument for disowning Désirée and their baby? What assumption about race underlies Armand's argument?

2. Community standards are sometimes applied by those in control for the purpose of maintaining their control. This situation can be positive; for example, most societies find ways to curb the impulses of their adolescent males. On the other hand, Chopin describes a situation in which those in control unfairly manipulate others in the name of community standards. Can you think of situations in which such control occurs today?

Stephen Crane (1871–1900)

The Bride Comes to Yellow Sky

The great Pullman was whirling onward with such dignity of motion that a glance from the window seemed simply to prove that the plains of Texas were pouring eastward. Vast flats of green grass, dull-hued spaces of mesquit and cactus, little groups of frame houses, woods of light and tender trees, all were sweeping into the east, sweeping over the horizon, a precipice.

A newly married pair had boarded this coach at San Antonio. The man's face was reddened from many days in the wind and sun, and a direct result of his new black clothes was that his brick-colored hands were constantly performing in a most conscious fashion. From time to time he looked down respectfully at his attire. He sat with a hand on each knee, like a man waiting in a barber's shop. The glances he devoted to other passengers were furtive and shy.

The bride was not pretty, nor was she very young. She wore a dress of blue cashmere, with small reservations of velvet here and there, and with steel buttons abounding. She continually twisted her head to regard her puff sleeves, very stiff, straight, and high. They embarrassed her. It was quite apparent that she had cooked, and that she expected to cook, dutifully. The blushes caused by the careless scrutiny of some passengers as she had entered the car were strange to see upon this plain, under-class countenance, which was drawn in placid, almost emotionless lines.

They were evidently very happy. "Ever been in a parlor-car before?" he asked, smiling with delight.

"No," she answered; "I never was. It's fine, ain't it?"   5

"Great! And then after a while we'll go forward to the diner, and get a big layout. Finest meal in the world. Charge a dollar."

"Oh, do they?" cried the bride. "Charge a dollar? Why, that's too much—for us—ain't it, Jack?"

"Not this trip, anyhow," he answered bravely. "We're going to go the whole thing."

Later he explained to her about the trains. "You see, it's a thousand miles from one end of Texas to the other; and this train runs right across it, and never stops but four times." He had the pride of an owner. He pointed out to her the dazzling fittings of the coach; and in truth her eyes opened wider as she contemplated the sea-green figured velvet, the shining brass, silver, and glass, the wood that gleamed as darkly brilliant as the surface of a pool of oil. At one end a bronze figure sturdily held a support for a separated chamber, and at convenient places on the ceiling were frescos in olive and silver.

10   To the minds of the pair, their surroundings reflected the glory of their marriage that morning in San Antonio; this was the environment of their new estate; and the man's face in particular beamed with an elation that made him appear ridiculous to the negro porter. This individual at times surveyed them from afar with an amused and superior grin. On other occasions he bullied them with skill in ways that did not make it exactly plain to them that they were being bullied. He subtly used all the manners of the most unconquerable kind of snobbery. He oppressed them; but of this oppression they had small knowledge, and they speedily forgot that infrequently a number of travellers covered them with stares of derisive enjoyment. Historically there was supposed to be something infinitely humorous in their situation.

"We are due in Yellow Sky at 3:42," he said, looking tenderly into her eyes.

"Oh, are we?" she said, as if she had not been aware of it. To evince surprise at her husband's statement was part of her wifely amiability. She took from a pocket a little silver watch; and as she held it before her, and stared at it with a frown of attention, the new husband's face shone.

"I bought it in San Anton' from a friend of mine," he told her gleefully.

"It's seventeen minutes past twelve," she said, looking up at him with a kind of shy and clumsy coquetry. A passenger, noting this play, grew excessively sardonic, and winked at himself in one of the numerous mirrors.

15   At last they went to the dining-car. Two rows of negro waiters, in glowing white suits, surveyed their entrance with the interest, and also the equanimity, of men who had been forewarned. The pair fell to the lot of a waiter who happened to feel pleasure in steering them through their meal. He viewed them with the manner of a fatherly pilot, his countenance radiant with benevolence. The patronage, entwined with the ordinary deference, was not plain to them. And yet, as they returned to their coach, they showed in their faces a sense of escape.

To the left, miles down a long purple slope, was a little ribbon of mist where moved the keening Rio Grande. The train was approaching it at an angle, and the apex was Yellow Sky. Presently it was apparent that, as the distance from Yellow Sky grew shorter, the husband became commensurately restless. His brick-red hands were more insistent in their prominence. Occasionally he was even rather absent-minded and far-away when the bride leaned forward and addressed him.

As a matter of truth, Jack Potter was beginning to find the shadow of a deed weigh upon him like a leaden slab. He, the town marshal of Yellow Sky, a man known, liked, and feared in his corner, a prominent person, had gone to San Antonio to meet a girl he believed he loved, and there, after the usual prayers, had actually induced her to marry him, without consulting Yellow Sky for any part of the transaction. He was now bringing his bride before an innocent and unsuspecting community.

Of course people in Yellow Sky married as it pleased them, in accordance with a general custom; but such was Potter's thought of his duty to his friends, or of their idea of his duty, or of an unspoken form which does not control men in these matters, that he felt he was heinous. He had committed an extraordinary crime. Face to face with this girl in San Antonio, and spurred by his sharp impulse, he had gone headlong over all the social hedges. At San Antonio he was like a man hidden in the dark. A knife to sever any friendly duty, any form, was easy to his hand in that remote city. But the hour of Yellow Sky—the hour of daylight—was approaching.

He knew full well that his marriage was an important thing to his town. It could only be exceeded by the burning of the new hotel. His friends could not forgive him. Frequently he had reflected on the advisability of telling them by telegraph, but a new cowardice had been upon him. He feared to do it. And now the train was hurrying him toward a scene of amazement, glee, and reproach. He glanced out of the window at the line of haze swinging slowly in toward the train.

Yellow Sky had a kind of brass band, which played painfully, to the delight of the 20 populace. He laughed without heart as he thought of it. If the citizens could dream of his prospective arrival with his bride, they would parade the band at the station and escort them, amid cheers and laughing congratulations, to his adobe home.

He resolved that he would use all the devices of speed and plains-craft in making the journey from the station to his house. Once within that safe citadel, he could issue some sort of vocal bulletin, and then not go among the citizens until they had time to wear off a little of their enthusiasm.

The bride looked anxiously at him. "What's worrying you, Jack?"

He laughed again. "I'm not worrying, girl; I'm only thinking of Yellow Sky."

She flushed in comprehension.

A sense of mutual guilt invaded their minds and developed a finer tenderness. 25 They looked at each other with eyes softly aglow. But Potter often laughed the same nervous laugh; the flush upon the bride's face seemed quite permanent.

The traitor to the feelings of Yellow Sky narrowly watched the speeding landscape. "We're nearly there," he said.

Presently the porter came and announced the proximity of Potter's home. He held a brush in his hand, and, with all his airy superiority gone, he brushed Potter's new clothes as the latter slowly turned this way and that way. Potter fumbled out a coin and gave it to the porter, as he had seen others do. It was a heavy and muscle-bound business, as that of a man shoeing his first horse.

The porter took their bag, and as the train began to slow they moved forward to the hooded platform of the car. Presently the two engines and their long string of coaches rushed into the station of Yellow Sky.

"They have to take water here," said Potter, from a constricted throat and in mournful cadence, as one announcing death. Before the train stopped his eye had swept the length of the platform, and he was glad and astonished to see there was none upon it but the station-agent, who, with a slightly hurried and anxious air, was walking toward the watertanks. When the train had halted, the porter alighted first, and placed in position a little temporary step.

30   "Come on, girl," said Potter, hoarsely. As he helped her down they each laughed on a false note. He took the bag from the negro, and bade his wife cling to his arm. As they slunk rapidly away, his hang-dog glance perceived that they were unloading the two trunks, and also that the station-agent, far ahead near the baggage-car, had turned and was running toward him, making gestures. He laughed, and groaned as he laughed, when he noted the first effect of his marital bliss upon Yellow Sky. He gripped his wife's arm firmly to his side, and they fled. Behind them the porter stood, chuckling fatuously.

2

The California express on the Southern Railway was due at Yellow Sky in twenty-one minutes. There were six men at the bar of the Weary Gentleman saloon. One was a drummer who talked a great deal and rapidly; three were Texans who did not care to talk at that time; and two were Mexican sheep-herders, who did not talk as a general practice in the Weary Gentleman saloon. The barkeeper's dog lay on the board walk that crossed in front of the door. His head was on his paws, and he glanced drowsily here and there with the constant vigilance of a dog that is kicked on occasion. Across the sandy street were some vivid green grassplots, so wonderful in appearance, amid the sands that burned near them in a blazing sun, that they caused a doubt in the mind. They exactly resembled the grass mats used to represent lawns on the stage. At the cooler end of the railway station, a man without a coat sat in a tilted chair and smoked his pipe. The fresh-cut of the Rio Grande circled near the town, and there could be seen beyond it a great plum-colored plain of mesquit.

Save for the busy drummer and his companions in the saloon, Yellow Sky was dozing. The new-comer leaned gracefully upon the bar, and recited many tales with the confidence of a bard who has come upon a new field.

"—and at the moment that the old man fell downstairs with the bureau in his arms, the old woman was coming up with two scuttles of coal, and of course—"

The drummer's tale was interrupted by a young man who suddenly appeared in the open door. He cried: "Scratchy Wilson's drunk, and has turned loose with both hands." The two Mexicans at once set down their glasses and faded out of the rear entrance of the saloon.

35   The drummer, innocent and jocular, answered: "All right, old man. S'pose he has? Come in and have a drink, anyhow."

But the information had made such an obvious cleft in every skull in the room that the drummer was obliged to see its importance. All had become instantly solemn. "Say," said he, mystified, "what is this?" His three companions made the introductory gesture of eloquent speech; but the young man at the door forestalled them.

"It means, my friend," he answered, as he came into the saloon, "that for the next two hours this town won't be a health resort."

The barkeeper went to the door, and locked and barred it; reaching out of the window, he pulled in heavy wooden shutters, and barred them. Immediately a solemn, chapel-like gloom was upon the place. The drummer was looking from one to another.

"But say," he cried, "what is this, anyhow? You don't mean there is going to be a gun-fight?"

"Don't know whether there'll be a fight or not," answered one man, grimly; "but there'll be some shootin'—some good shootin'." 40

The young man who had warned them waved his hand. "Oh, there'll be a fight fast enough, if any one wants it. Anybody can get a fight out there in the street. There's a fight just waiting."

The drummer seemed to be swayed between the interest of a foreigner and a perception of personal danger.

"What did you say his name was?" he asked.

"Scratchy Wilson," they answered in chorus.

"And will he kill anybody? What are you going to do? Does this happen often? Does he rampage around like this once a week or so? Can he break in that door?" 45

"No; he can't break down that door," replied the barkeeper. "He's tried it three times. But when he comes you'd better lay down on the floor, stranger. He's dead sure to shoot at it, and a bullet may come through."

Thereafter the drummer kept a strict eye upon the door. The time had not yet been called for him to hug the floor, but, as a minor precaution, he sidled near to the wall. "Will he kill anybody?" he said again.

The men laughed low and scornfully at the question.

"He's out to shoot, and he's out for trouble. Don't see any good in experimentin' with him." 50

"But what do you do in a case like this? What do you do?"

A man responded: "Why, he and Jack Potter—"

"But," in chorus the other men interrupted, "Jack Potter's in San Anton'."

"Well, who is he? What's he got to do with it?"

"Oh, he's the town marshal. He goes out and fights Scratchy when he gets on one of these tears."

"Wow!" said the drummer, mopping his brow. "Nice job he's got." 55

The voices had toned away to mere whisperings. The drummer wished to ask further questions, which were born of an increasing anxiety and bewilderment; but when he attempted them, the men merely looked at him in irritation and motioned him to remain silent. A tense waiting hush was upon them. In the deep shadows of the room their eyes shone as they listened for sounds from the street. One man made three gestures at the barkeeper; and the latter, moving like a ghost, handed him a glass and a bottle. The man poured a full glass of whisky, and set down the bottle noiselessly. He gulped the whisky in a swallow, and turned again toward the door in immovable silence. The drummer saw that the barkeeper, without a sound, had taken a Winchester from beneath the bar. Later he saw this individual beckoning to him, so he tiptoed across the room.

"You better come with me back of the bar."

"No, thanks," said the drummer, perspiring; "I'd rather be where I can make a break for the back door."

Whereupon the man of bottles made a kindly but peremptory gesture. The drummer obeyed it, and, finding himself seated on a box with his head below the level of the bar, balm was laid upon his soul at sight of various zinc and copper fittings that bore a resemblance to armor-plate. The barkeeper took a seat comfortably upon an adjacent box.

60   "You see," he whispered, "this here Scratchy Wilson is a wonder with a gun—a perfect wonder; and when he goes on the war-trail, we hunt our holes—naturally. He's about the last one of the old gang that used to hang out along the river here. He's a terror when he's drunk. When he's sober he's all right—kind of simple—wouldn't hurt a fly—nicest fellow in town. But when he's drunk—whoo!"

There were periods of stillness. "I wish Jack Potter was back from San Anton'," said the barkeeper. "He shot Wilson up once—in the leg—and he would sail in and pull out the kinks in this thing."

Presently they heard from a distance the sound of a shot, followed by three wild yowls. It instantly removed a bond from the men in the darkened saloon. There was a shuffling of feet. They looked at each other. "Here he comes," they said.

3

A man in a maroon-colored flannel shirt, which had been purchased for purposes of decoration, and made principally by some Jewish women on the East Side of New York, rounded a corner and walked into the middle of the main street of Yellow Sky. In either hand the man held a long, heavy, blue-black revolver. Often he yelled, and these cries rang through a semblance of a deserted village, shrilly flying over the roofs in a volume that seemed to have no relation to the ordinary vocal strength of a man. It was as if the surrounding stillness formed the arch of a tomb over him. These cries of ferocious challenge rang against walls of silence. And his boots had red tops with gilded imprints, of the kind beloved in winter by little sledding boys on the hillsides of New England.

The man's face flamed in a rage begot of whisky. His eyes, rolling, and yet keen for ambush, hunted the still doorways and windows. He walked with the creeping movement of the midnight cat. As it occurred to him, he roared menacing information. The long revolvers in his hands were as easy as straws; they were moved with an electric swiftness. The little fingers of each hand played sometimes in a musician's way. Plain from the low collar of the shirt, the cords of his neck straightened and sank, straightened and sank, as passion moved him. The only sounds were his terrible invitations. The calm adobes preserved their demeanor at the passing of this small thing in the middle of the street.

65   There was no offer of fight—no offer of fight. The man called to the sky. There were no attractions. He bellowed and fumed and swayed his revolvers here and everywhere.

The dog of the barkeeper of the Weary Gentleman saloon had not appreciated the advance of events. He lay yet dozing in front of his master's door. At sight of the dog, the man paused and raised his revolver humorously. At sight of the man, the dog sprang up and walked diagonally away, with a sullen head, and growling. The man yelled, and the dog broke into a gallop. As it was about to enter an alley, there was a loud noise, a whistling, and something spat the ground directly before it. The dog screamed, and, wheeling in terror, galloped headlong in a new direction. Again there was a noise, a whistling, and sand was kicked viciously before it. Fear-stricken, the dog turned and flurried like an animal in a pen. The man stood laughing, his weapons at his hips.

Ultimately the man was attracted by the closed door of the Weary Gentleman saloon. He went to it and, hammering with a revolver, demanded drink.

The door remaining imperturbable, he picked a bit of paper from the walk, and nailed it to the framework with a knife. He then turned his back contemptuously upon this popular resort and, walking to the opposite side of the street and spinning there on his heel quickly and lithely, fired at the bit of paper. He missed it by a half-inch. He swore at himself, and went away. Later he comfortably fusilladed the windows of his most intimate friend. The man was playing with this town; it was a toy for him.

But still there was no offer to fight. The name of Jack Potter, his ancient antagonist, entered his mind, and he concluded that it would be a glad thing if he should go to Potter's house, and by bombardment induce him to come out and fight. He moved in the direction of his desire, chanting Apache scalp-music.

When he arrived at it, Potter's house presented the same still front as had the   70 other adobes. Taking up a strategic position, the man howled a challenge. But this house regarded him as might a great stone god. It gave no sigh. After a decent wait, the man howled further challenges, mingling with them wonderful epithets.

Presently there came the spectacle of a man churning himself into deepest rage over the immobility of a house. He fumed at it as the winter wind attacks a prairie cabin in the North. To the distance there should have gone the sound of a tumult like the fighting of two hundred Mexicans. As necessity bade him, he paused for breath or to reload his revolvers.

4

Potter and his bride walked sheepishly and with speed. Sometimes they laughed together shamefacedly and low.

"Next corner, dear," he said finally.

They put forth the efforts of a pair walking bowed against a strong wind. Potter was about to raise a finger to point the first appearance of the new home when, as they circled the corner, they came face to face with a man in a maroon-colored shirt, who was feverishly pushing cartridges into a large revolver. Upon the instant the man dropped his revolver to the ground and, like lightning, whipped another from its holster. The second weapon was aimed at the bridegroom's chest.

There was a silence. Potter's mouth seemed to be merely a grave for his tongue.   75 He exhibited an instinct to at once loosen his arm from the woman's grip, and he dropped the bag to the sand. As for the bride, her face had gone as yellow as old cloth. She was a slave to hideous rites, gazing at the apparitional snake.

The two men faced each other at a distance of three paces. He of the revolver smiled with a new and quiet ferocity.

"Tried to sneak up on me," he said. "Tried to sneak up on me!" His eyes grew more baleful. As Potter made a slight movement, the man thrust his revolver venomously forward. "No; don't you do it, Jack Potter. Don't you move a finger toward a gun just yet. Don't you move an eyelash. The time has come for me to settle with you, and I'm goin' to do it my own way, and loaf along with no interferin'. So if you don't want a gun bent on you, just mind what I tell you."

Potter looked at his enemy. "I ain't got a gun on me, Scratchy," he said. "Honest, I ain't." He was stiffening and steadying, but yet somewhere at the back of his mind a vision of the Pullman floated: the sea-green figured velvet, the shining brass, silver, and glass, the wood that gleamed as darkly brilliant as the surface of a pool of oil— all the glory of the marriage, the environment of the new estate. "You know I fight when it comes to fighting, Scratchy Wilson; but I ain't got a gun on me. You'll have to do all the shootin' yourself."

His enemy's face went livid. He stepped forward, and lashed his weapon to and fro before Potter's chest. "Don't you tell me you ain't got no gun on you, you whelp. Don't tell me no lie like that. There ain't a man in Texas ever seen you without no gun. Don't take me for no kid." His eyes blazed with light, and his throat worked like a pump.

80   "I ain't takin' you for no kid," answered Potter. His heels had not moved an inch backward. "I'm takin' you for a damn fool. I tell you I ain't got a gun, and I ain't. If you're goin' to shoot me up, you better begin now; you'll never get a chance like this again."

So much enforced reasoning had told on Wilson's rage; he was calmer. "If you ain't got a gun, why ain't you got a gun?" he sneered. "Been to Sunday-school?"

"I ain't got a gun because I've just come from San Anton' with my wife. I'm married," said Potter. "And if I'd thought there was going to be any galoots like you prowling around when I brought my wife home, I'd had a gun, and don't you forget it."

"Married!" said Scratchy, not at all comprehending.

"Yes, married. I'm married," said Potter, distinctly.

85   "Married?" said Scratchy. Seemingly for the first time, he saw the drooping, drowning woman at the other man's side. "No!" he said. He was like a creature allowed a glimpse of another world. He moved a pace backward, and his arm, with the revolver, dropped to his side. "Is this the lady?" he asked.

"Yes; this is the lady," answered Potter.

There was another period of silence.

"Well," said Wilson at last, slowly, "I s'pose it's all off now."

"It's all off if you say so, Scratchy. You know I didn't make the trouble." Potter lifted his valise.

90   "Well, I 'low it's off, Jack" said Wilson. He was looking at the ground. "Married!" He was not a student of chivalry; it was merely that in the presence of this foreign condition he was a simple child of the earlier plains. He picked up his starboard revolver, and, placing both weapons in their holsters, he want away. His feet made funnel-shaped tracks in the heavy sand.

CRITICAL THINKING QUESTIONS

1. Scratchy's behavior is based on several *assumptions,* and in the end he is disappointed to learn that they no longer hold true. What assumptions does he hold?

2. If we generalize from this story, we might say that Crane is arguing that women are a force that serves to diminish men's natural tendency to fight and brawl. Do you think this is a fair statement to make about the Old West? Does it hold true today?

WRITING TOPIC

People naturally shape their behavior and attitudes to the social conditions they encounter. When those conditions change, people are thrown off balance. Have you witnessed social changes that have forced you to confront your behavior and attitudes?

Louise Erdrich (b. 1954)

The Red Convertible

Lyman Lamartine

I was the first one to drive a convertible on my reservation. And of course it was red, a red Olds. I owned that car along with my brother Henry Junior. We owned it together until his boots filled with water on a windy night and he bought out my share. Now Henry owns the whole car, and his youngest brother Lyman (that's myself), Lyman walks everywhere he goes.

How did I earn enough money to buy my share in the first place? My own talent was I could always make money. I had a touch for it, unusual in a Chippewa. From the first I was different that way, and everyone recognized it. I was the only kid they let in the American Legion Hall to shine shoes, for example, and one Christmas I sold spiritual bouquets for the mission door to door. The nuns let me keep a percentage. Once I started, it seemed the more money I made the easier the money came. Everyone encouraged it. When I was fifteen I got a job washing dishes at the Joliet Cafe, and that was where my first big break happened.

It wasn't long before I was promoted to busing tables, and then the short-order cook quit and I was hired to take her place. No sooner than you know it I was managing the Joliet. The rest is history. I went on managing. I soon became part owner, and of course there was no stopping me then. It wasn't long before the whole thing was mine.

After I'd owned the Joliet for one year, it blew over in the worst tornado ever seen around here. The whole operation was smashed to bits. A total loss. The fryalator was up in a tree, the grill torn in half like it was paper. I was only sixteen. I had it all in my mother's name, and I lost it quick, but before I lost it I had every one of my relatives, and their relatives, to dinner, and I also bought that red Olds I mentioned, along with Henry.

5   The first time we saw it! I'll tell you when we first saw it. We had gotten a ride to Winnipeg, and both of us had money. Don't ask me why, because we never mentioned a car or anything, we just had all our money. Mine was cash, a big bankroll from the Joliet's insurance. Henry had two checks—a week's extra pay for being laid off, and his regular check from the Jewel Bearing Plant.

We were walking down Portage anyway, seeing the sights, when we saw it. There it was, parked, large as life. Really as *if* it was alive. I thought of the word *repose*, because the car wasn't simply stopped, parked, or whatever. That car reposed, calm and gleaming, a FOR SALE sign in its left front window. Then, before we had thought it over at all, the car belonged to us and our pockets were empty. We had just enough money for gas back home.

We went places in that car, me and Henry. We took off driving all one whole summer. We started off toward the Little Knife River and Mandaree in Fort Berthold and then we found ourselves down in Wakpala somehow, and then suddenly we were over in Montana on the Rocky Boy, and yet the summer was not even half over. Some people hang on to details when they travel, but we didn't let them bother us and just lived our everyday lives here to there.

I do remember this place with willows. I remember I laid under those trees and it was comfortable. So comfortable. The branches bent down all around me like a tent or a stable. And quiet, it was quiet, even though there was a powwow close enough so I could see it going on. The air was not too still, not too windy either. When the dust rises up and hangs in the air around dancers like that, I feel good. Henry was asleep with his arms thrown wide. Later on, he woke up and we started driving again. We were somewhere in Montana, or maybe on the Blood Reserve—it could have been anywhere. Anyway it was where we met the girl.

All her hair was in buns around her ears, that's the first thing I noticed about her. She was posed alongside the road with her arm out, so we stopped. That girl was short, so short her lumber shirt looked comical on her, like a nightgown. She had jeans on and fancy moccasins and she carried a little suitcase.

10   "Hop on in," says Henry. So she climbs in between us.

"We'll take you home," I says. "Where do you live?"

"Chicken," she says.

"Where the hell's that?" I ask her.

"Alaska."

15   "Okay," says Henry, and we drive.

We got up there and never wanted to leave. The sun doesn't truly set there in summer, and the night is more a soft dusk. You might doze off, sometimes, but before you know it you're up again, like an animal in nature. You never feel like you have to sleep hard or put away the world. And things would grow up there. One day just dirt or moss, the next day flowers and long grass. The girl's name was Susy. Her family really took to us. They fed us and put us up. We had our own tent to live in by their house, and the kids would be in and out of there all day and night. They couldn't get over me and Henry being brothers, we looked so different. We told them we knew we had the same mother, anyway.

One night Susy came in to visit us. We sat around in the tent talking of this and that. The season was changing. It was getting darker by that time, and the cold was even getting just a little mean. I told her it was time for us to go. She stood up on a chair.

"You never seen my hair," Susy said.

That was true. She was standing on a chair, but still, when she unclipped her buns the hair reached all the way to the ground. Our eyes opened. You couldn't tell how much hair she had when it was rolled up so neatly. Then my brother Henry did something funny. He went up to the chair and said, "Jump on my shoulders." So she did that, and her hair reached down past his waist, and he started twirling, this way and that, so her hair was flung out from side to side.

"I always wondered what it was like to have long pretty hair," Henry says. Well, 20 we laughed. It was a funny sight, the way he did it. The next morning we got up and took leave of those people.

On to greener pastures, as they say. It was down through Spokane and across Idaho then Montana and very soon we were racing the weather right along under the Canadian border through Columbus, Des Lacs, and then were in Bottineau County and soon home. We'd made most of the trip, that summer, without putting up the car hood at all. We got home just in time.

I don't wonder that the army was so glad to get my brother that they turned him into a Marine. He was built like a brick outhouse anyway. We liked to tease him that they really wanted him for his Indian nose. He had a nose big and sharp as a hatchet, like the nose on Red Tomahawk, the Indian who killed Sitting Bull, whose profile is on signs all along the North Dakota highways. Henry went off to training camp, came home once during Christmas, then the next thing you know we got an overseas letter from him. It was 1970, and he said he was stationed up in the northern hill country. Whereabouts I did not know. He wasn't such a hot letter writer, and only got off two before the enemy caught him. I could never keep it straight, which direction those good Vietnam soldiers were from.

I wrote him back several times, even though I didn't know if those letters would get through. I kept him informed all about the car. Most of the time I had it up on blocks in the yard or half taken apart, because that long trip did a hard job on it under the hood.

I always had good luck with numbers, and never worried about the draft myself. I never even had to think about what my number was. But Henry was never lucky in the same way as me. It was at least three years before Henry came home. By then I guess the whole war was solved in the government's mind, but for him it would keep on going. In those years I'd put his car into almost perfect shape. I always thought of it as his car while he was gone, even though when he left he said, "Now it's yours," and threw me his key.

25   "Thanks for the extra key," I'd said. "I'll put it in your drawer just in case I need it." He laughed.

When he came home, though, Henry was very different, and I'll say this: the change was no good. You could hardly expect him to change for the better, I know. But he was quiet, so quiet, and never comfortable sitting still anywhere but always up and moving around. I thought back to times we'd sat still for whole afternoons, never moving a muscle, just shifting our weight along the ground, talking to whoever sat with us, watching things. He'd always had a joke, then, too, and now you couldn't get him to laugh, or when he did it was more the sound of a man choking, a sound that stopped up the throats of other people around him. They got to leaving him alone most of the time, and I didn't blame them. It was a fact: Henry was jumpy and mean.

I'd bought a color TV set for my mom and the rest of us while Henry was away. Money still came very easy. I was sorry I'd ever bought it though, because of Henry. I was also sorry I'd bought color, because with black-and-white the pictures seem older and farther away. But what are you going to do? He sat in front of it, watching it, and that was the only time he was completely still. But it was the kind of stillness that you see in a rabbit when it freezes and before it will bolt. He was not easy. He sat in his chair gripping the armrests with all his might, as if the chair itself was moving at a high speed and if he let go at all he would rocket forward and maybe crash right through the set.

Once I was in the room watching TV with Henry and I heard his teeth click at something. I looked over, and he'd bitten through his lip. Blood was going down his chin. I tell you right then I wanted to smash that tube to pieces. I went over to it but Henry must have known what I was up to. He rushed from his chair and shoved me out of the way, against the wall. I told myself he didn't know what he was doing.

My mom came in, turned the set off real quiet, and told us she had made something for supper. So we went and sat down. There was still blood going down Henry's chin, but he didn't notice it and no one said anything, even though every time he took a bite of his bread his blood fell onto it until he was eating his own blood mixed in with the food.

30   While Henry was not around we talked about what was going to happen to him. There were no Indian doctors on the reservation, and my mom couldn't come around to trusting the old man, Moses Pillager, because he courted her long ago and was jealous of her husbands. He might take revenge through her son. We were afraid that if we brought Henry to a regular hospital they would keep him.

"They don't fix them in those places," Mom said; "they just give them drugs."

"We wouldn't get him there in the first place," I agreed, "so let's just forget about it."

Then I thought about the car.

Henry had not even looked at the car since he'd gotten home, though like I said, it was in tip-top condition and ready to drive. I thought the car might bring the old Henry back somehow. So I bided my time and waited for my chance to interest him in the vehicle.

One night Henry was off somewhere. I took myself a hammer. I went out to that   35
car and I did a number on its underside. Whacked it up. Bent the tail pipe double.
Ripped the muffler loose. By the time I was done with the car it looked worse than
any typical Indian car that has been driven all its life on reservation roads, which they
always say are like government promises—full of holes. It just about hurt me, I'll tell
you that! I threw dirt in the carburetor and I ripped all the electric tape off the seats. I
make it look just as beat up as I could. Then I sat back and waited for Henry to find it.

Still, it took him over a month. That was all right, because it was just getting
warm enough, not melting, but warm enough to work outside.

"Lyman," he says, walking in one day, "that red car looks like shit."

"Well, it's old," I says. "You got to expect that."

"No way!" says Henry. "That car's a classic! But you went and ran the piss right
out of it, Lyman, and you know it don't deserve that. I kept that car in A-one shape.
You don't remember. You're too young. But when I left, that car was running like a
watch. Now I don't even know if I can get it to start again, let alone get it anywhere
near its old condition."

"Well you try," I said, like I was getting mad, "but I say it's a piece of junk."   40

Then I walked out before he could realize I knew he'd strung together more than
six words at once.

After that I thought he'd freeze himself to death working on that car. He was
out there all day, and at night he rigged up a little lamp, ran a cord out the window,
and had himself some light to see by while he worked. He was better than he had
been before, but that's still not saying much. It was easier for him to do the things the
rest of us did. He ate more slowly and didn't jump up and down during the meal to
get this or that or look out the window. I put my hand in the back of the TV set, I
admit, and fiddled around with it good, so that it was almost impossible now to get
a clear picture. He didn't look at it very often anyway. He was always out with that car
or going off to get parts for it. By the time it was really melting outside, he had it
fixed.

I had been feeling down in the dumps about Henry around this time. We had always been together before. Henry and Lyman. But he was such a loner now that I didn't
know how to take it. So I jumped at the chance one day when Henry seemed friendly.
It's not that he smiled or anything. He just said, "Let's take that old shitbox for a
spin." Just the way he said it made me think he could be coming around.

We went out to the car. It was spring. The sun was shining very bright. My only
sister, Bonita, who was just eleven years old, came out and made us stand together for
a picture. Henry leaned his elbow on the red car's windshield, and he took his other
arm and put it over my shoulder, very carefully, as though it was heavy for him to lift
and he didn't want to bring the weight down all at once.

"Smile," Bonita said, and he did.   45

That picture. I never look at it anymore. A few months ago, I don't know why, I
got his picture out and tacked it on the wall. I felt good about Henry at the time,
close to him. I felt good having his picture on the wall, until one night when I was looking at television. I was a little drunk and stoned. I looked up at the wall and Henry

was staring at me. I don't know what it was, but his smile had changed, or maybe it was gone. All I know is I couldn't stay in the same room with that picture. I was shaking. I got up, closed the door, and went into the kitchen. A little later my friend Ray came over and we both went back into that room. We put the picture in a brown bag, folded the bag over and over tightly, then put it way back in a closet.

I still see that picture now, as if it tugs at me, whenever I pass that closet door. The picture is very clear in my mind. It was so sunny that day Henry had to squint against the glare. Or maybe the camera Bonita held flashed like a mirror, blinding him, before she snapped the picture. My face is right out in the sun, big and round. But he might have drawn back, because the shadows on his face are deep as holes. There are two shadows curved like little hooks around the ends of his smile, as if to frame it and try to keep it there—that one, first smile that looked like it might have hurt his face. He has his field jacket on and the worn-in clothes he'd come back in and kept wearing ever since. After Bonita took the picture, she went into the house and we got into the car. There was a full cooler in the trunk. We started off, east, toward Pembina and the Red River because Henry said he wanted to see the high water.

The trip over there was beautiful. When everything starts changing, drying up, clearing off, you feel like your whole life is starting. Henry felt it, too. The top was down and the car hummed like a top. He'd really put it back in shape, even the tape on the seats was very carefully put down and glued back in layers. It's not that he smiled again or even joked, but his face looked to me as if it was clear, more peaceful. It looked as though he wasn't thinking of anything in particular except the bare fields and windbreaks and houses we were passing.

The river was high and full of winter trash when we got there. The sun was still out, but it was colder by the river. There were still little clumps of dirty snow here and there on the banks. The water hadn't gone over the banks yet, but it would, you could tell. It was just at its limit, hard swollen, glossy like an old gray scar. We made ourselves a fire, and we sat down and watched the current go. As I watched it I felt something squeezing inside me and tightening and trying to let go all at the same time. I knew I was not just feeling it myself; I knew I was feeling what Henry was going through at that moment. Except that I couldn't stand it, the closing and opening. I jumped to my feet. I took Henry by the shoulders and I started shaking him. "Wake up," I says, "wake up, wake up, wake up!" I didn't know what had come over me. I sat down beside him again.

50   His face was totally white and hard. Then it broke, like stones break all of a sudden when water boils up inside them.

"I know it," he says. "I know it. I can't help it. It's no use."

We start talking. He said he knew what I'd done with the car. It was obvious it had been whacked out of shape and not just neglected. He said he wanted to give the car to me for good now, it was no use. He said he'd fixed it just to give it back and I should take it.

"No way," I says. "I don't want it."

"That's okay," he says, "you take it."

55   "I don't want it, though," I says back to him, and then to emphasize, just to emphasize, you understand, I touch his shoulder. He slaps my hand off.

"Take that car," he says.

"No," I say. "Make me," I say, and then he grabs my jacket and rips the arm loose. That jacket is a class act, suede with tags and zippers. I push Henry backwards, off the log. He jumps up and bowls me over. We go down in a clinch and come up swinging hard, for all we're worth, with our fists. He socks my jaw so hard I feel like it swings loose. Then I'm at his rib cage and land a good one under his chin so his head snaps back. He's dazzled. He looks at me and I look at him and then his eyes are full of tears and blood and at first I think he's crying. But no, he's laughing. "Ha, ha!" he says. "Ha! Ha! Take good care of it."

"Okay," I says. "Okay, no problem. Ha! Ha!"

I can't help it, and I start laughing, too. My face feels fat and strange, and after a while I get a beer from the cooler in the trunk, and when I hand it to Henry he takes his shirt and wipes my germs off. "Hoof-and-mouth disease," he says. For some reason this cracks me up, and so we're really laughing for a while, and then we drink all the rest of the beers one by one and throw them in the river and see how far, how fast, the current takes them before they fill up and sink.

"You want to go on back?" I ask after a while. "Maybe we could snag a couple nice Kashpaw girls." 60

He says nothing. But I can tell his mood is turning again.

"They're all crazy, the girls up here, every damn one of them."

"You're crazy too," I say, to jolly him up. "Crazy Lamartine boys!"

He looks as though he will take this wrong at first. His face twists, then clears, and he jumps up on his feet. "That's right!" he says. "Crazier 'n hell. Crazy Indians!"

I think it's the old Henry again. He throws off his jacket and starts springing his 65 legs up from the knees like a fancy dancer. He's down doing something between a grass dance and a bunny hop, no kind of dance I ever saw before, but neither has anyone else on all this green growing earth. He's wild. He wants to pitch whoopee! He's up and at me and all over. All this time I'm laughing so hard, so hard my belly is getting tied up in a knot.

"Got to cool me off!" he shouts all of a sudden. Then he runs over to the river and jumps in.

There's boards and other things in the current. It's so high. No sound comes from the river after the splash he makes, so I run right over. I look around. It's getting dark. I see he's halfway across the water already, and I know he didn't swim there but the current took him. It's far. I hear his voice, though, very clearly across it.

"My boots are filling," he says.

He says this in a normal voice, like he just noticed and he doesn't know what to think of it. Then he's gone. A branch comes by. Another branch. And I go in.

By the time I get out of the river, off the snag I pulled myself onto, the sun is down. 70 I walk back to the car, turn on the high beams, and drive it up the bank. I put it in first gear and then I take my foot off the clutch. I get out, close the door, and watch it plough softly into the water. The headlights reach in as they go down, searching, still lighted even after the water swirls over the back end. I wait. The wires short out. It is all finally dark. And then there is only the water, the sound of it going and running and going and running and running.

CRITICAL THINKING QUESTIONS

1. The word *pariah* means outcast or outsider. When Vietnam vets returned to American society, some said they felt like pariahs. In what way does the brother demonstrate this attitude in Erdrich's story?

2. Read Louise Erdrich's biographical information (see "Appendix B"). In what ways do you think her heritage influences her story?

3. At the Red River, Henry and Lyman fight over their car, then laugh and joke— "pitch whoopee." When Lyman says, "Crazy Lamartine boys!", Henry responds, "Crazier 'n hell. Crazy Indians!" Is Henry crazy? Does his final act suggest that he is in control or out of control? Use evidence from the story to discuss how you arrived at your *claim of value* in judging Henry.

RESEARCH/WRITING TOPIC—Veterans' Benefits

Do you know any war veterans (World War II, the Korean, Vietnam, Persian Gulf wars, the war in Iraq)? If so, interview him or her to learn about his or her war and postwar experiences. Also, contact your local veterans' affairs office to find out information about the benefits for veterans who have sustained disabilities. Are disabled or wounded veterans receiving adequate treatment and fair compensation?

Laura Hendrie (b. 1954)

Corsage

The porch is the best place to be. It used to be that under the honey locust was best, where even when the afternoons were white-hot, the air smelled blue and green. But since Baby Annie's come, I haven't been back there.

From here, though, from this porch swing, I can know everything. I can know what's going on right now in the kitchen and the parlor and the upstairs and the hallway that ties all the rooms of this house together, and I can know what's going on out in the street, too. Where Harley Barrows will stop his car when the crickets start, where he'll toot his horn and whistle hello to me if I'm still here. Tonight he'll smell like linen and limes instead of gasoline. He'll have that Camaro tuned up like a cat, and best of all, Mama Jewell says he'll bring a gardenia with him. I've never smelled a gardenia, but Baby Annie says it's her favorite flower and Mama Jewell says it leaves a trail of beauty behind it, so I guess that must be so.

Baby Annie's in the bathroom with the door locked. She's been in there all afternoon. I have to use the bathroom again, but I don't mind waiting. Not for Baby Annie.

Mama Jewell is in the kitchen. She loves to cook, but today, mixed up with the smells of her and her cooking oil and zinnias and all the other smells of this house and this thick afternoon heat, I smell Spraystarch. She's told Hallie and me she's too busy to breathe. That's why I'm on the porch—because of Mama Jewell and the gardenia. Baby Annie's dress is taffeta, and it rustles when Mama Jewell turns it.

"You know it'll break everyone's heart if you move out of Stygo after you're married." 5
She's shouting on account of the bathroom door being shut. "I realize things are awfully backward around here for you, Baby Annie, but I've been thinking if Harland wanted to, he could move his trailer into the backyard. I wouldn't mind. Better yet, we could fix up the back bedroom where Mr. Peske and I used to sleep," she says. "Harland seems to like that room, don't you think?" Mama Jewell stops to listen. "Darling? You could open the door. It's not like we're strangers. Besides, I don't like the idea of closed doors in my home. They make me feel lonesome and mean. You hear me?" Then she sighs and starts again, rowing back and forth and back and forth over the taffeta. "Oh, Baby Annie!" she cries. "With you in this peach-colored dress, that poor boy won't be able to take his eyes off—"

"Don't call me Baby Annie."

"What, Baby Annie?" she says. But I know she's listening for something besides Baby Annie's answer, and I know what it is, too. "Hallorie?" Mama Jewell sets the can of starch on the counter and crosses the kitchen. The linoleum floor has grown soft in the summer's heat and her sneakers squeak. She crosses the wood floor in the hall to the front parlor, where the rug is thick enough to grab in bare toes, and I feel more than hear her cross to where I know Hallie's hiding behind the couch.

"What are you up to?" she says. "What have you got there? Oh—Hallorie!" Back to the hallway, back to the kitchen, to the broom closet. "You think I enjoy this? You think I like cleaning up after you six times a day?" The vacuum tubes ding against the closet walls as she pulls them out. Then she gives a yip and tubes go clanging and banging everywhere.

"For God's sake!" she cries. "Why do you have to sneak up on people like that, Hallorie? You want to give me heart failure, or what? What? Why are you always at me? And what's that in your mouth?"

I shake my head. Days like this Hallie can be so bad. 10

"How many times have we talked about calories?" says Mama Jewell. "How many times have I told you? Come on. Spit it out. Here, Hallorie. Right here in my hand." Steps and a clank in the wastebasket. "Now go," she says. "Go out to the porch with your stepsister or something. She's probably lonesome out there. Don't you think?"

Mama Jewell picks up the tubes and rolls the vacuum cleaner out into the kitchen, across the wood in the hall, the rug in the parlor. I don't like vacuum cleaners. They take over everything with their sound and then they take it away. The wheels squeak like baby mice caught by the tail. I'm glad Hallie's coming outside. She doesn't like vacuum cleaners either.

What she does like is sneaking up on people. She doesn't care whether you're blind or not. But she never wins. This time the smell of chocolate tells me, and the way Tip starts whacking his tail on the porch in welcome. But mostly it's a knowing I all at once get. You don't need eyes for that. "Hallie," I say and catch hold of her fat-soft hand holding something.

It's a cattail from the river, an old one, crusted hard on the outside, only she's broken it open to let the silk out. The stem is smooth and cold and it smells like the river. She holds the silk under my nose and slides her face against the back of my neck. And even now, with the vacuum blasting in the parlor, Hallie's hum sinks down inside me. It feels like my stomach growling. "Hallie," I say. She knows I don't like vacuum cleaners.

* * *

15   Hallie's never talked. When they first brought her here, she didn't even hum. She was so skinny back then, her skin felt like pink ribbon wrapped around bone, and all she could do was sit behind the stove and poop on herself. Mama Jewell was about to give up on her and make Sheriff Whatly and the social workers take her back. Later, when Hallie got better, Mama Jewell said she'd known all along that Christian love and patience would do the trick. But that's a lie. The truth is, Hallie got better because of Tip. One day he went to her so sure she would scratch under his harness for him that she did. That was the first day she made noise. Only a little noise, a hum down inside of her, and only when Tip came to her. But then it got stronger and she started crawling, and then tiptoeing and walking, and then running, too. And nowadays her hum never stops and neither does she, not until late at night after everybody else is asleep. Now, even if Mama Jewell orders her to stand still and be quiet, Hallie can't. She hums through her food and through her afternoon naps, and even when she holds her mouth shut with both hands, trying to please Mama Jewell, still there is that hum. Like a bumblebee living down in her throat, the big fat slow kind that floats around Mama Jewell's parlor in the thick heat of an afternoon. It's a lot more touch than sound.

* * *

When Mama Jewell's done, she winds up the cord and wheels the vacuum back to the kitchen. She crams the tubes and brushes in the closet and then she takes out the air freshener and goes back to fill up the parlor with smells. Hallie lets go and sinks down under the swing. Tip groans when she scratches him the way he likes best.

Baby Annie says Tip is the ugliest dog she ever saw and Mama Jewell tries to keep him out of the house, so I guess that must be so. But Tip can't help it if he's losing his hair. He thumps his tail on the porch when Hallie slides his water dish closer.

It's a Tootsie Roll she's got, I can smell it melting in this dead, still heat. She opens one for me and two for herself, but I give mine back. I don't need it. I'm on Baby Annie's Seven Day Beauty Plan. "Maybe I'll eat it later," I say. But I won't. Hallie lays her head on my foot, puts her arm around my ankle and pushes Tootsie Rolls in her mouth. When Tip's done with his, she unwraps two more for him and two for herself. With her mouth so full she has to breathe through her nose. And still through it she hums.

Her socks are stuffed with Tootsie Rolls—that's why she wears socks—and I know her hat and shirt and pockets are, too. Nowadays they always are. Mama Jewell says it's sickening. When Hallie first came, Mama Jewell tried to think up ways to make her eat, but now all she does is try to think up ways to make Hallie stop. She says if Hallie watched her diet, she'd have a face nearly as beautiful as Baby Annie's. But Hallie likes candy too much. She's backward. Mama Jewell says it's hopeless.

And it is hopeless. Hallie has a hole of hunger in her that nothing will ever fill 20 up. It makes her itchy and quick and sometimes it makes her smell sour. It makes her hurt and sometimes it makes her steal. When it gets bad, it changes her hum—till it's not just one big bumblebee living down in her throat anymore, but a whole swarm of little bees squeezed up behind her teeth and trying to sting through the cracks. When it gets bad she pulls her lips back and runs around the house bumping into things and falling down. Then if she wants, I'll give her all the candy she can eat. Like today, when I feel it building in her. Because I know how it is, how the things you've lost are the only things they remember to talk about, day after day after day.

* * *

I hope Baby Annie's finished in the bathroom. I hope she's standing up and flushing and pulling down her slip and just leaning a little to unlock the door. I hope she calls Mama Jewell soon and says "If Christina wants to, she can use the bathroom." I don't mind waiting. I don't. But it is hot out here, and this time I have to go. I really do.

* * *

A lot has changed since Baby Annie. Now there's the new rug in the parlor and the sachet in the coat closet and the lock on the bathroom door. Nowadays, Mama Jewell wears powder and lipstick and sometimes, when she thinks no one will notice, Baby Annie's perfume. Now every Tuesday, Hallie and I have to go with Pearl Stiles while Mama Jewell takes Baby Annie for voice lessons. It used to be that Mama Jewell hardly ever left the house unless it was to take Hallie and me to see specialists in Mason City, but now Pearl says she wonders some Tuesdays if Mama Jewell's coming back. Pearl Stiles is okay, except she won't let Tip in her house. It makes Tip fret, but Pearl says her cats don't like dogs. She can't let us outside to be with him, either, because she could never forgive herself if something happened. Which is what Mama Jewell used to say all the time about Hallie and me. At first, I was glad she quit saying it. But it's one thing to want to be alone and know you never will be, and a whole other thing when you all at once are.

So it's no fun hiding under the honey locust from Mama Jewell anymore. Hallie doesn't understand. She's always at me to sneak away. But somebody has to be Baby Annie's look-out, and it won't be Hallie because all Hallie cares about is Tip and candy and me.

* * *

Back when Baby Annie first showed up with all her beauty books and swimsuits and diets, I hated her. I sat out on the porch just like this, and I hated Baby Annie all day long. Worse than I hate vacuum cleaners or heat waves or strangers who pat Tip without my permission. Worse than darkness or social workers or Mama Jewell's air fresheners. Mama Jewell told Hallie and me that Baby Annie was a gift from Jesus to prove beauty comes to those who suffer; but all I knew was that, with her here, it was like I wasn't.

At night it was worse. At night the smell of her coating my eyeballs and teeth and 25 the insides of my nose woke me up. I'd hear Mama Jewell dreaming in one bed and Baby Annie in another and Hallie behind the stove downstairs or under the couch or somewhere else I don't know and all the other beds folded up and put away because now we are the last ones, and I'd get lost because out of all of it, I couldn't hear me. Things came unstuck those nights. Sometimes the closets opened up and the beds unfolded and came out into the dark. Other times it was my head that opened up and unfolded, floating around above my bed, bump bump bump against the ceiling. But either way, the dark inside me mixed with the dark all around the beds until everywhere and every one of us was dark. Like a mouth that will never stop swallowing, like a hole in the world that everything, living and unliving, beautiful and unbeautiful, sleeping and unsleeping, falls into. Dark and dark and dark. And even if Tip came to me then, creeping up on my bed in apology and inching his way up to my face until the sad wet cold of his nose touched my chin and breathed warmth there—even then, I wasn't always sure I was there, too.

Hallie knew how I felt, but she couldn't hate Baby Annie, any more than she could hate Tip or me or anyone else. Tip knew too, in a different dog-way, but the same too, because late at night he'd go off through the house by himself. Listening to the dark, uneasy, I know, sniffing at cracks under closet doors, around cabinets and laundry piles. Like he'd lost something, only he couldn't remember what it was or where he'd lost it. But it was me he went looking for on those nights when he nosed around under Baby Annie's milk breath and beauty guides and lists for Mama Jewell, me he went to find.

At first, I thought Sheriff Whatly's social workers had ordered Mama Jewell to please Baby Annie—just like they had ordered Mama Jewell to put Hallie on a diet and close her in the bedroom when she hummed, just like they had ordered Mama Jewell to be firm with me about independence. I figured Mama Jewell would get sick of Baby Annie and send her away, which is what happened to a few others I could name. But when nothing happened, when Mama Jewell acted as if it was a miracle every time Baby Annie came down to breakfast, I caught on. Mama Jewell wasn't getting orders from anybody. Mama Jewell was just being smart.

Because Baby Annie is beautiful. Not just nice or sweet or brave—things they tell Tip and Hallie and me.

Baby Annie is *beautiful*.

30   And when you are beautiful, the rest doesn't matter. It leaks out of itself. When you are beautiful you don't need anything, but everybody needs you, and if you go away, you leave a hole behind.

Which is why we're so lucky to have Baby Annie. We never want her to leave. Mama Jewell says Harley worships the ground Baby Annie walks on, and now so do I, along with everybody else. I'm not stupid.

I try explaining it to Hallie, but she won't listen. She's a good kid, but she's hopeless. Mama Jewell says so and I know so. Hallie eats too much and messes the house and won't take baths or comb her hair. She doesn't want to learn. She has eyes to see what Baby Annie is, but she acts like Baby Annie is nobody different. Sometimes she makes me furious. Because one of these days Mama Jewell will say enough's enough, and Hallie will end up going back to wherever she came from, and she'll wonder why, and I won't be there to tell her. Because I'll be here, probably on this very same porch, and I'm the only one who cares.

I wish it was ten minutes more than right now, and I wish I didn't have to go anymore, because then I'd have gone already and Baby Annie would be unlocking the door and Harley Barrows would already be on his way with the gardenia. I wish I never had to use the bathroom when Baby Annie is in there, but I always do. Sometimes sitting on your foot takes the need away. Mama Jewell says when she has to wait, she takes deep breaths.

But I wish I hadn't taken the Kool-Aid Hallie stole for me. I really do. Kool-Aid makes it worse.

Breathe. The problem was I forgot the diet. I was thirsty.   35

Breathe. Drinking it also made Hallie calmer, which is a good thing because with Mama Jewell so busy with Harley's visit to Baby Annie, Hallie is worse than ever.

There. Breathe. Today. Of all days.

*   *   *

I never told anybody, but I used to hear voices inside. After Baby Annie came, it was like somebody closed the window; I'd think I could hear something far away, but when I'd listen, I couldn't make it out anymore. Once I stopped hiding under the honey locust, I couldn't hear anything at all except my stomach growling. Some days I wonder if that's why Hallie hums, to forget the quiet. But when you hum, sooner or later you have to quit, and then the quiet is even worse.

I don't think about this much anymore, not if I can help it. It doesn't matter anymore, not to anybody. Not now that Baby Annie lives here.

*   *   *

Mama Jewell's about to come out on the porch. I can feel her mind turn to it as she takes   40
the first batch out of the oven. The smell is fudge and it floats out the windows and doors, oily and thick. When it's strong enough, Hallie's hum shoves her off the porch and around the corner. She'll be on her hands and knees under the kitchen window, going back and forth and back in the dead petunias there. The smell of fresh fudge scares her. It's like when somebody's playing ball in the playground across the street and Tip starts whining from the porch, wanting and wanting. But Hallie can't be good, she can't hold back, not like Tip and me. The bees in her mouth start stinging if she tries. She'll have to get in the kitchen and swipe as much as she can. I know this and I know she's already sorry because Mama Jewell and Baby Annie will be so mad. But that's all she knows how to do, and she knows how thankful Tip will be. That's why she'll have to do it.

Mama Jewell's sneakers coming down the hall sound like Tip's feet with no claws. The screen door cries open. "Whatever are you doing sitting out in that sweater, Christina? It's hot enough out here to choke a horse."

I don't say boo. Mama Jewell thinks I'm backward like Hallie. She thinks I don't know what hot is or what day it is or that Baby Annie is beautiful. She thinks, like everybody else, that I sit here empty until she comes along to explain things.

"All right," she says, slapping her apron. "Be that way. Drown to death in your own perspiration." Then her voice brightens, sliding upwards. Someone must be across the street in the playground or maybe over at Sheriff Whatly's, watching. "Here you are, Christina," she says, putting a plate in my lap. "Lean over now when you eat. Use your napkin. And please don't let me catch you trying to give any to Hallorie. She's already been into the candy dish." When Mama Jewell pauses, I feel her eyes looking around the yard. "Now, I thought I told that child to stay put—"

"I don't want any," I say.

45 She turns to me. "But you love my fudge." She clucks her tongue and speaks louder. "Why, from the look of it, people must think I'm some kind of monster that never feeds her children. Are you trying to starve yourself to death?"

"Baby Annie didn't eat."

"Baby Annie's on a diet. Harland likes a slim figure and we have to be—"

"Careful of complexions," I say.

Mama Jewell leans over the back of the swing so no one will hear. "What's the matter now," she says, straightening my sweater.

"Nothing."

50 Mama Jewell's hands stop and then disappear. "Don't sit with your leg under you like that in public. Only dogs sit that way."

The plate in my lap goes away. "Suit yourself, Miss Particular," she says loud and bright. "In any case, I made these for Harland—but honest to Betsy," she says, opening the screen door. "Sometimes you look like the Grim Reaper the way you mope. Haven't you learned to smile yet?"

"I have to pee," I say.

She stops, holding the door. "But you just went."

"That was then."

55 "Young lady," she says. "That was no more than fifteen minutes ago."

"It feels longer."

"Then take deep breaths," she says. "You can't keep bothering Baby Annie. She's trying to fix herself up for her young man."

As if I didn't know who her young man was or why he's coming or what he's bringing. "I did," I say.

60 But her mind has already gone back inside to see if the next batch of fudge bars is done. "You did what?" she says.

"I already took deep breaths."

"Then take some more. You've got to realize that today is—"

But I can't hear the rest. With my foot not under me anymore, I have to go worse than ever. "I can go out in the garden if you want—"

"My God!" I feel her mind come rushing back to where we are. "You'll do no such thing!" she says. She leans into my face. "I am sorry," she whispers, "but if you think this is some kind of animal farm we're running, I don't mind telling you—why, my God, what would happen if Pearl was to look out her window or Harland drove by—or Oren Whatly! To see you up to such a thing! It would be dreadful, it would be . . . *appalling,* I'd lose—"

65 I can smell Baby Annie's lipstick. "Mama Jewell?"

"Don't you Mama Jewell." Her voice is sharp enough to stop us both. Then she sighs, rich and smooth as fudge. "Oh, all *right,*" she says. "Baby Annie's told me to keep you out of her hair and I've done my best—but you just remember, she's nervous and you're not helping." She bangs the screen behind her and starts down the hall. "And leave that mangy thing of yours outside," she calls. "I've just cleaned and I don't plan to do it again."

I take a deep breath and then another before I can stand up. Tip's harness squeaks. "Tip. Stay." I take one more deep breath, all the way down to the bottom of me until I'm not even sure I have to go anymore. Then I turn and follow the wall into the house.

When Tip isn't with me, I get "watch out for the throw rug in the hall," or "use the handrail," or "don't forget the door's shut." I tell Mama Jewell not to, because it gets me mixed up and then I go and do wrong exactly the thing she expects me to do wrong. Because then sounds don't make sense and smells don't count, and all that's left is dark and her voice and maybe the cane going tap tap. Like you're buried alive and listening to somebody trying to get through from the other side of somewhere else you don't know. That's when I make mistakes. I forget if I'm standing or sitting or walking or talking or alive or dead. Then it's darker than ever.

But today she's forgotten. Today she's worried about Harley's fudge bars. She scurries down the hall that runs through this house like a train tunnel and pushes through the swinging door to the kitchen. I go to the bathroom door and wait there for her to remember. The smell of fudge is sweet, sticky smoke. Even though she's tried to trap it in the kitchen, it's leaked out into the hall. It's like a fever in the walls, like our home is on fire. Behind me on the porch, Tip is beginning to fret.

*   *   *

Mama Jewell says dogs can't be sad, but Tip, he's filled fat with sadness. He can feel 70
sad when his tail wags just like I can feel all dark and glassed-in when they tell me to smile. Why else would he go check his food dish every hour, when he knows full well it stays empty till dinner? And why else does he lie out in the middle of the street when the air is too hot to breathe? I feel him out there sometimes, his head turned away from our home, watching the playground hour after hour, panting, panting.

And why else but for sadness does he get up in the middle of the night? His harness squeaks when he sits up, and then his panting stops and he gets off my bed and goes to the head of the stairs. Sometimes he just stands there listening, but more often than not, he goes wandering. When he's finished, he'll come back. But I'll feel him watching me before he lays down his head and goes to sleep. Like he has a thought that needs finishing first. Or like he is wondering if I could ever understand or explain such a sadness to him.

"I'm sorry, but how can you think that?" cried Mama Jewell when I told her. "Why do you always have to be so morbid? Tip's got everything you need to be happy. There isn't anything else, can't you see that?"

She talked then like she meant it. But sometimes after everything is cooked and cleaned and sprayed and swept, she soaks her corns in a bowl of Epsom salts and weeps. And late at night when Baby Annie's off with Harley, we hear her talk in her sleep. "For me?" she cries and turns over. "Why it's lovely! But you shouldn't have gone to so much trouble! You really shouldn't have!" Her voice rises and falls in our dark house on those nights like a sparrow trapped up in the attic with Baby Annie's suitcases and the extra mattresses, trying to find a way out.

*   *   *

Mama Jewell says it's natural I smell things she can't, but she doesn't know all of it. To her it will only be a gardenia. To her, the only things that smell are burnt food and air fresheners and rum on Pearl Stiles' breath. She doesn't know I can smell the river in a fish or the color of the air under the honey locust or the day Baby Annie will have blood in her panties. She doesn't want to know. She wants to believe I'm blank until she fills me up, until she makes fudge for me or wears perfume.

If she could smell, she wouldn't smoke clove cigarettes when Harley comes and she wouldn't make fudge bars when it's hot out, and she'd run around the house this minute and open the windows to stir out the dark. But the only time she can smell is when Tip poops behind the couch, and then all she does about it is slap Tip, throw out the poop, and cover the sweet smell of poop over with more air freshener.

75   Sometimes, when Baby Annie is in the bathroom putting on smells and Mama Jewell is in the kitchen fussing with smells and it is hot and flat out like today, all the smells pile up on one another in here until you can't tell day from night or hard from soft or walls from blankets or blankets from air. All the smells of all the years and years that have been lived through in this house, that have seeped into the walls to return in the heat of an afternoon, when they swell up and bust. Like today.

Mama Jewell. Hurry up.

"I'm coming, I'm coming," she sighs. The oven door cries shut and she starts across the kitchen, but halfway over she stops. I know what's coming next. I can hear it as if it's already come and gone.

"All right. Where is the sheet of fudge bars I just took out of the oven?" Her sneakers squeal as she turns. "I'm not kidding," she warns. "Hallorie?"

She blasts through the swinging door like a train, passing by in a roar of fire and fudge smell. "Hallorie?" She goes in the parlor, looks behind the couch. "Hallorie!"

But the parlor is too quiet, too humless. She comes back, passes me again and opens the door to the cellar. "Hallorie!"

80   I start moaning. "Mama Jewell."

"Just a minute," she snaps, and I feel her trying to listen.

"If Baby Annie doesn't let me in right now," I say, "I have to go on the floor."

"Oh good lord, do I have to do everything around here? Can't you simply knock on the door yourself? There's nothing wrong with your hands, you know." But all the same, she's coming. She waits and taps with one finger. "Baby Annie?" she calls. "Our friend's got to piddle again. She'll just slip in and out. I promise."

"Which one is it?" says Baby Annie.

85   "Christina," says Mama Jewell. Her voice is soft and pink. "Do you mind horribly? These children, you know—"

"In a minute."

Mama Jewell takes my arm and pulls me to the door. "There," she whispers. "Satisfied?" She walks back to the kitchen humming "Moon River." Sometimes I think Mama Jewell is as afraid of Baby Annie as Harley is.

After the kitchen door stops swinging, I slip down the hallway. The cellar door is still open and sure enough, I can hear her. Back behind the furnace, even though she's scared of spiders, shoving everything she can into her mouth and breaking the

rest into her socks and hat for us. I ease the cellar door shut, follow the wall back to
the bathroom, and lean against the door. Music—Baby Annie's new transistor radio—
and a clink of something in the sink.

"Baby Annie?" 90

"What."

"I really do this time. I have to go."

"That's what you said last time."

I lean against the door and listen to the music. I lean with all of me. "Baby Annie?"
I lick the wood, rub the inside of my lips against its paint softness, almost as sweet-
tasting as fudge.

"I didn't steal the fudge bars," I say. "They're for Harley, I know." 95

"What?" At least I think that's what she says.

"Baby Annie?" I say.

"Jesus."

"Will you let me smell the gardenia," I say. "I mean if he doesn't—"

The door opens so suddenly I'm lost in a flood of her wet dark pink smell. "What 100
do you *want?*"

But I forget. Because she is the smell of everything and everything that is her
has made me forget. I can barely breathe.

"Well?" she asks. But she's not angry, not really. She closes the door halfway so
she can face the full-length mirror Mama Jewell put up for her. I can smell the heat
of her curling iron through her perfume. It's burning her hair, but the bathroom is too
full of smells for her to notice.

"I'm hungry," I say. "But Hallie stole all our fudge bars. I heard her in the cellar,
behind the furnace. With spiders."

"Well, goody for her," says Baby Annie. "Cripes, Har's on the team diet anyhow.
I told Mama already." Her voice fades into the smell of her as she opens the curling
iron, hair zithering free of the metal bar. And then on top of it all—incredible—Baby
Annie lights a cigarette in there, the match sound and smell and then smoke drifting
out in the hall in the powdery steam of everything else.

"Me too," I say. 105

"You too what?" she says. Her voice has lost all of its edge now. We could be
friends this way, she and I talking like this, like it was nothing at all to do. I let go of
the wall and stand straighter, stand alone in the middle of the hallway.

"I'm on a diet, too," I say.

But she chokes on her cigarette and then the door swings open in a rush of air. I
feel her staring with a force that could push me down. But me, I will stay where I am,
I won't budge.

"You? On a *diet?*" she says. "Give me a break, kid. You don't weigh more than a
mouse." She picks up the ashtray and takes a puff, watching me. Then she closes the
door so she can look at the mirror again. "You're not like me. Everything I eat makes
me big." I hear the curling iron click open and shut on more hair. "If Mama would quit
trying to shove it down me all the time. All she wants is to watch me blow up into a

barrel of lard, just like her. Well, fat chance, Mama." She pulls the curling iron free. "I'm not ever going to lose control like that."

110   "Baby Annie?"

    "I don't want to sound mean or anything," she says, leaning around the door, "but I'm awful busy. Why don't you get lost or something? Your dog's whining for you anyhow. Hear him?" The door starts to close, and then by magic, opens. "And kid, like, I know you don't mean it, but don't call me Baby Annie anymore. The name's Annie. Just plain Annie. Okay?"

    "Okay—" A woosh of air and a bang of the door that pushes me off balance again, and it's over. When Mama Jewell breezes through the swinging door again saying "you're not still bothering our Baby Annie, are you?" she finds me holding onto the baseboard.

    "Well, for heaven's sake!" she cries, bending over me. "I might have knocked you to Kingdom Come, you behind the door like that. Come away from there, child."

    When she tries to pull me up, I grab hold of her hands. They are wet and smell— they always do—like she just washed them in cantaloupes.

115   "How much am I?"

    "What do you mean," she says, " 'how much are you?' "

    "How much do I weigh?"

    "Weigh?" she says. "Whatever do you want to know that for?"

    "How much?"

120   "Much? Much what?" She leans back and I feel her watching. "In heaven's name—" she says. "What is the matter with you?" She puts her hand on my forehead. I can smell her teeth, she's so close. "You're shaking."

    "Too much," I say. "Am I too much weight?" But the words don't make sense, I can't keep my teeth from biting them apart, and my head, even though it's not night yet, even though I'm not in my bed alone, rising like a balloon to the ceiling, bump bump bump.

    "Why no, child. You don't have to worry." Her voice is careful. "You're skin and bones. Why do you think I spend all my time trying to get you to eat something?"

    "Skin and bones?"

    "What *is* the matter? Why Tip weighs more than you . . . now, Christina, don't do that. Look here." She gets down on her knees with a grunt. "Look at the size of your arm—here, baby—compared to mine. Can you feel the difference? You couldn't be more than 80 pounds soaking wet. You're thin as a thread, Christina. One or two pounds less and you'd be nothing at all."

125   "Nothing?"

    But Tip is waiting at the end of the hall. Whining for me to let him in, whining for me to come out, whining for me to remember, whining and whining and whining. And I see it then, how my life will be as straight and unchanging as this hallway itself, with me waiting at one end and Tip waiting at the other and nothing in between and all the doors shut and everybody behind them busy. Because I'm not like Baby Annie, not in a million years.

    So I let Mama Jewell fuss. I let her lead me back to where Tip is whining. She pulls up my sock and unbuttons my sweater and brings me a plate of sandwiches she's made for Harley. She pats my head and sits down with a sigh of relief, and together we rock the swing.

Tip is glad I'm back. He puts his head in my lap and groans. Because Mama Jewell is still worried, she pats his head. "There now," she says. "Isn't that cute?" Me, I sit still. Sooner or later she'll remember the last batch of fudge bars I can smell burning right now, and then she'll run off to save them and leave me in peace.

"Pity Moses!" she cries. "Harland's fudge bars!" The swing lurches back on a slap of chains and she is gone, her sneakers like bugs' feet skittering up the hall.

Tip starts to lie down, but I pull him up by his harness. Inside, Mama Jewell is 130 whying over her burnt fudge.

"Hallie," I whisper. I take a cookie and split it with him. "*Hallie,* Tip." Eager to please, Tip swallows his half in a gulp and pulls me up. To the sidewalk and around the corner, either through the cellar window or across the street to the honey locust. Because Hallie's been right all along. Hallie, who understood from the first, who doesn't care what is beautiful and what is not, Hallie who cares most of all. "Hallie, Tip. Hallie." I urge Tip until he's whining with desire, until I feel his tail beat against my leg as he tugs me down the steps, the love and sadness leaking out of him, hungry, gentled, and bleak.

CRITICAL THINKING QUESTIONS

1. Hendrie's narrator Christina observes, "And when you are beautiful, the rest doesn't matter. It leaks out of itself. When you are beautiful you don't need anything, but everybody needs you, and if you go away, you leave a hole behind" (par. 30). What does the narrator mean by "the rest"? What does she mean by the *metaphor* (*see* Glossary), "a hole [left] behind"?

2. Without her sense of sight, the narrator Christina depends on her other physical senses, especially, smell, sound, and touch, to navigate her world. Besides helping her to physically move about Mama Jewell's household, how do her senses help her to "see" what is really happening in the household? Point to specific examples as you describe how Christina attempts to make sense of the world around her.

3. Christina's guide dog Tip, of course, has a clearly functional role. But he also seems to have a thematic role as a character: How is he a *foil* (*see* Glossary) to some of the human characters in the story?

WRITING TOPICS

1. Create your own claim about the value of beauty and then list of evidence drawn from personal experience and observation. Now do some research to discover other perspectives on beauty. How does society tend to value beauty? Does this new information prompt you to revise your claim?

2. As Americans, we champion independence and self-reliance; we applaud individuals who "pull themselves up by their own bootstraps." However, "Corsage" portrays individuals who clearly are incapable of attaining either independence or self-reliance. What obligation does an individual or a community have to help such individuals?

Edward P. Jones (b. 1950)

The Store

I'd been out of work three four months when I saw her ad in the *Daily News;* a few lines of nothing special, almost as if she really didn't want a response. On a different day in my life I suppose I would have passed right over it. I had managed to squirrel away a little bit of money from the first slave I had, and after that change ran out, I just bummed from friends for smokes, beer, the valuables. I lived with my mother, so rent and food weren't a problem, though my brother, when he came around with that family of his, liked to get in my shit and tell me I should be looking for another job. Usually, my mother was okay, but I could tell when my brother and his flat-butt wife had been around when I wasn't there, because for days after that my mother would talk that same shit about me getting a job, like I'd never slaved a day before in my life.

That first slave I had had just disappeared out from under me, despite my father always saying that the white people who gave me that job were the best white people he'd known in his life. My father never had a good word to say about anybody white, and I believed him when he said I could go far in that place. I started working there—the Atlas Printing Co. ("75 YEARS IN THE SAME LOCATION")—right after I graduated from Dunbar, working in the mailroom and sometimes helping out the printers when the mail work was slow. My father had been a janitor there until he got his third heart attack, the one that would put him in the ground when I was in my sophomore year at Dunbar.

At twenty I was still in the mailroom: assistant chief mail clerk or something like that, still watching the white boys come in, work beside me, then move on. My mother always said that every bullfrog praises his own poem, but I know for a natural fact that I was an excellent worker. Never late, never talked back, always volunteering; the product of good colored parents. Still . . . In the end, one bitching cold day in January, the owner and his silly-ass wife, who seemed to be the brains of the outfit, came to me and said they could no longer afford to keep me on. Times were bad, said the old man, who was so bald you could read his thoughts. They made it sound like I was the highest-paid worker in the joint, when actually I was making so little the white guys used to joke about it.

I said nothing, just got my coat and took my last check and went home. Somewhere along K Street, I remembered I'd left some of my personal stuff back there—some rubbers I'd bought just that morning at Peoples, a picture of the girl I was going with at the time, a picture of my father, my brother, and me at four years old on one of our first fishing trips. I had the urge to go back—the girl was already beginning not to mean anything to me anymore, so I didn't care about her picture, but the fishing trip picture was special. But I didn't turn back because, first of all, my balls were beginning to freeze.

My father always said that when the world pisses on you, it then spits on you to   5
finish the job. At New York Avenue and 5th I crossed on the red light. A white cop twirling his billy club saw me and came to spit on me to finish up what Atlas had done: He asked me if I didn't know it was against D.C. and federal law to cross on the red light. I was only a few blocks from home and maybe heat and thawing out my nuts were the only things on my mind, because I tried to be funny and told him the joke my father had always told—that I thought the green light was for white folks and the red light was for colored people. His face reddened big-time.

When my brother and I were in our early teens, my mother said this to us with the most seriousness she had ever said anything: "Never even if you become kings of the whole world, I don't want yall messin with a white cop." The worst that my mother feared didn't happen to her baby boy that day. The cop only made me cross back on the green light and go all the way back to 7th Street, then come back to 5th Street and cross again on the green light. Then go back to 7th to do it all over again. Then I had to do it twice more. I was frozen through and through when I got back to 5th the second time and as I waited for the light to change after the fourth time and he stood just behind me I became very afraid, afraid that doing all that would not be enough for him, that he would want me to do more and then even more after that and that in the end I would be shot or simply freeze to death across the street from the No. 2 police precinct. Had he told me to deny my mother and father, I think I would have done that too.

I got across the street and went on my way, waiting for him to call me back. I prayed, "Just get me back to one fifteen New York Avenue safely and I'll never come to their world again. . . . Just get me back to one fifteen New York Avenue safely. . . ." For days after that I just hung out at home. My mother believed that a day had the best foundation if you had breakfast, so after she fixed our breakfast, and went off to work, I went back to bed and slept to about noon.

When I got some heart back, I started venturing out again, but I kept to my own neighborhood, my own world. Either my aceboon, Lonney McCrae, would come get me or I would go looking for him and we'd spend the rest of the afternoon together until our friends got off work. Then all of us would go off and fuck with the world most of the night.

Lonney was going to Howard, taking a course here and there, doing just enough to satisfy his father. I'd seen his old man maybe once or twice in all the time I knew Lonney, and I'd been knowing him since kindergarten. His father had been one of the few bigshot Negro army officers in the Korea war, and Lonney was always saying that after the war his father would be home for good. He was still saying it that January when Kennedy was inaugurated.

Lonney liked to fuck bareback and that was how he got Brenda Roper preg-   10
nant. I think he liked her, maybe not as much as she liked him, but just enough so it

wasn't a total sacrifice to marry her. I was to be his best man. One night, all of us—me and Lonney and his mother and Brenda and her parents—were sitting around his living room, talking about the wedding and everything. Someone knocked on the door and Lonney opened it. It was his old man, standing there tall and straight as a lamppost in his uniform. You know something's wrong when a man doesn't even have a key to his own house.

The soldier didn't say Hello or Good to see you, son. He just stood in the doorway and said—and I know he could see everybody else in the room—"You don't have anything better to do with your time than marrying this girl?" Lonney's mother stood up, in that eager, happy way women do when they want to greet their husbands home from a foreign land. Brenda's father stood up too, but he had this goofy look on his face like he wanted to greet his soon-to-be in-law. "I asked you something," Lonney's father said. Lonney said nothing, and his father walked by him, nodded at Mrs. McCrae, and went on upstairs with his suitcase. The next morning he was gone again.

Lonney married Brenda that March, a few weeks before I saw the ad in the *Daily News*. I think that he wanted to make things work with Brenda, if only to push the whole thing in his father's face, but the foundation, as my mother would have said, was built on shifting sand. In about a year or so he had separated from her, though he continued to be a good father to the child, a chubby little girl they named after his mother. And some two years after he married, he had joined the army and before long he himself was in a foreign land, though it was a different one from where his father was.

The day before I saw the ad I spent the evening at Lonney and Brenda's place. They fought, maybe not for the first time as newly-weds, but for the first time in front of me. I felt as if I were watching my own folks arguing, as if the world I knew and depended on was now coming apart. I slept till one the next day, then went down to Mojo's near North Capitol and Florida Avenue and hung out there for most of the day. Late in the day, someone left a *Daily News* at a table and over my second beer, with nothing better to do, I read the want ads. Her ad said:

> STORE HELPER. *Good pay. Good hours.*
> *Good Opportunity for Advancement.*

Then she had the store's location—5th and O streets Northwest. The next morning I forced myself to stay awake after my mother had left then went off about eight o'clock to see what the place was about. I didn't want any part of a white boss and I stood outside the store, trying to see just who ran the place. Through the big windows I could see a colored woman of fifty or so in an apron, and she seemed to be working alone. Kids who attended Bundy Elementary School down the street went in and out of the store buying little treats. I walked around the block until about nine, then went in. A little bell over the door tinkled and the first thing I smelled was coal oil from the small pump just inside the door. The woman was now sitting on a tall stool behind the counter, reading the *Post*, which she had spread out over the glass counter.

15   She must have known I was there, but even after I was halfway to her, she just wet a finger and turned the page. I was inches from the counter, when she looked up. "Somethin you want?" she said. Oh shit, I thought, she's one of those bitches. I could feel my balls trying to retreat back up into my body.

"I come about the job in the paper," I said.

"Well, you pass the first test: At least you know how to read. What else you know how to do? You ever work in a store before? A grocery store like this?"

I gave her my work history, such as it was, and all the while she looked like she wanted to be someplace else. She kept reading and turning those pages. She seemed skeptical that the printing company had let me go without just cause.

"What you been doin since you lost that job?" she said.

"Lookin. I just never found anything I liked."   20

That was not the right answer, I could see that right away, but by then I didn't care. I was ready to start mouthing off like somebody was paying me to do it.

"The job pays thirty a week," she said finally. "The work is from eight in the mornin till eight in the evenin. Every day but Sunday and maybe a holiday here and there. Depends. You got questions?" But she didn't wait for me to ask, she just went on blubbering. "I'll be interviewin everybody else and then make my decision. Affix your name and phone number and if you're crowned queen of the ball, I'll let you know, sweetie." She tossed a pencil across the counter and pointed to the top of a newspaper page where she wanted me to put my telephone number. I wrote down my name and number, and just before I opened the door to leave, I heard her turn the next page.

The next day was Tuesday, and I spent most of that morning and the next few mornings cleaning up what passed for the backyard of Al's and Penny's Groceries. I had been surprised when she called me Monday night, too surprised to even tell her to go to hell. Then, after she hung up, I figured I just wouldn't show up, but on Tuesday morning, way long before dawn, I woke up and couldn't get back to sleep. And so for a change I was up when my mother rose and I fixed our breakfast. She did days work for some white people in Chevy Chase, and that morning I noticed how fast she ate, "wolfing down" her food, she would have called it.

For the first time in a long while, I stood at the window and watched her skinny legs take her down New York Avenue to hop the first of two D.C. Transits that would take her to Chevy Chase. Maybe it was watching her that sent me off that morning to the store. Or maybe it was that I came back to the table and saw that she hadn't finished all of her coffee. My mother would have sold me back into slavery for a good cup of coffee, and no one made it to her satisfaction the way she did.

"Good," the store owner said to me after she parked her lavender Cadillac and   25
was opening the store's door. "You passed the second test: You know how to show up on time." It was about 7:30 and I'd been waiting about fifteen minutes.

She took me straight to the backyard, through the store itself, through a smaller room that served mostly as a storage area, to the back door, which took a hell of an effort for us to open. In the yard, two squirrels with something in their hands stood on their hind legs, watching us. No one had probably been in the yard for a coon's age and the squirrels stood there for the longest time, perhaps surprised to see human beings. When they realized we were for real, they scurried up the apple tree in a corner of the yard. The store owner brought out a rake, shovel, wheelbarrow, everything I needed to do to the yard what no one had done for years. I hadn't worn any good clothes and I was glad of that. Right off I took my tools and went to the far end of the yard to begin.

"By the way," she said, standing in the back door, "my name's Penelope Jenkins. Most people call me Penny. But the help call me Mrs. Jenkins, and you, buddy boy, you the help."

Beyond the high fence surrounding the yard there were the sounds of school-children getting into their day. Well into the second hour of work, after I knew I was getting dirty and smelly as hell, after the children were all in school, I started throwing stones at the damn squirrels, who, jumping back and forth from tree to fence, seemed to be taunting me. Just like on the cold evening of the green light, I began to feel that I would be doing that shit forever.

The first thick layer of crap in the yard was slimy dead leaves from the autumn before, maybe even years before, and the more I disturbed the leaves the more insects and slugs crawled out from the home they had created and made a run for it under the fence and to other parts of the yard. The more spiteful and stupid bugs crawled up my pants legs. Beneath the layer of leaves there was a good amount of soda bottles, candy wrappers, the kind of shit kids might have thrown over the fence. But I didn't get to that second layer until Thursday morning, because the yard was quite large, big enough for little kids to play a decent game of kickball. Sometimes, when I heard voices on the other side of the fence, I would pull myself up to the top and look over.

30   My father always told the story of working one week for an undertaker in Columbia, South Carolina, one of his first jobs. He didn't like the undertaker and he knew the undertaker didn't like him. But, and maybe he got this from his old man, my father figured that he would give the undertaker the best goddamn week of work a fourteen-year-old was capable of. And that's what he did—for seven days he worked as if that business was his own. Then he collected his pay and never went back. The undertaker came by late one evening and at first, thinking my father wasn't showing up because he was just lazy, the undertaker acted big and bad. Then, after my father told him he wouldn't be coming back, the undertaker promised a raise, even praised my father's work, but my father had already been two days at a sawmill.

I didn't think Mrs. Jenkins was the kind of woman who would beg me to come back, but I did like imagining her sitting on her high stool, reading her damn paper and thinking of what a good worker she had lost. That was the image I took home each evening that week, so sore and depressed I could not think of fucking the world or anybody else. My mother would fix me dinner and I would sit hunched down in my chair close to the food because I had little strength left to make the long distance from the plate to my mouth if I sat up straight. Then, before I could fall asleep in the chair, my mother would run water for me to take a bath, the same thing I had seen her do for my father so often when I was a child that I didn't notice it anymore.

In the late mornings that week, after she thought I had done enough in the yard, Mrs. Jenkins would have me sweep the area around the front of the store or provide some order to the merchandise in the storage room. On Tuesday she wanted the boxes of stuff arranged just so, but then, as if she had some revelation during the night, she wanted everything rearranged on Wednesday. Then on Thursday I had to do things different again, and then different still again on Friday. And because she claimed she planned to repaint, she also had me up on a ladder, scraping away the peeling orange paint of the store's exterior. The paint chips would fly off into my eyes and hair, and it took me until Thursday to get smart about wearing a stocking cap and the goggles my father had once used.

Saturday morning I woke up happy. Again, I was there waiting for her to open up and again I did all the shit work while she chatted and made nice-nice with all the customers. I had already planned my weekend, had, in my mind, spent every dollar I was to be paid. But I was also prepared to get cheated. Cheating folks was like some kind of religion with people like Mrs. Jenkins—they figured that if they didn't practice it they'd go to hell. Actually, I was kind of hoping she would cheat me, just so I could come back late that night and break all the fucking windows or something.

At the end of the day, after she had locked the front door to any more customers and pulled down the door's shade with the little CLOSED sign on it, she opened the cash register and counted out my money. It came to about twenty-five dollars after she took out for taxes and everything. She explained where every dollar I wasn't getting was going, then she gave me a slip with that same information on it.

"You did a good job," she said. "You surprised me, and no one in the world sur- 35 prises me anymore."

The words weren't much and I had heard better in my time, but as I stood there deliberately counting every dollar a second and third time, I found I enjoyed hearing them, and it came to me why some girls will give their pussys to guys who give them lines full of baby this and baby that and I'll do this and I'll be that forever and ever until the end of time. . . .

I just said yeah and good night and thanks, because my mother had always taught me and my brother that the currency of manners didn't cost anything. Mrs. Jenkins had untied her apron, but she still had it on and it hung loosely from her neck. She followed me to the door and unlocked it. "I'll see you bright and early Monday mornin," she said, like that was the only certainty left in my whole damn life. I said yeah and went out. I didn't look back.

Despite my aches, I went dancing with Mabel Smith, a girl I had gone to Dunbar with. We stepped out with Lonney and Brenda. I didn't get any trim that night, and it didn't bother me, because there was something satisfying in just dancing. I danced just about every dance, and when Mabel said she was tired, couldn't take it anymore, I took Brenda out on the dance floor, and when I had worn her out, I danced away what was left of the night with girls at other tables.

I got home about six that Sunday morning. In the dark apartment, I could see that slice of light along the bottom of my mother's closed door.

I didn't go back to the store on Monday. In fact, I slept late and spent the rest of the 40 day running the streets. Tuesday, I couldn't get back to sleep after my old lady left, and about ten I wandered over to the store, then wandered in. She didn't act mad and she sure didn't act like she was glad to see me. She just put me to work like the week before had been a rehearsal for the real thing. And she enjoyed every bad thing that happened to me. Tuesday I restocked the cereal section of shelves behind the counter with the cash register. As I bent down to dust the bottom shelves, a box of oatmeal fell on my head from three or four shelves up. Hit me so hard I'm sure some of my descendants will be born dumb because of it. Mrs. Jenkins went into a laugh that went on and on for minutes, and throughout the rest of the day she'd come up behind me and shout "Oatmeal!" and go into that laugh again.

"In the grocery business," she said after I replaced the box, "the first law of supply in them shelves is to supply em so that nothin falls over."

And late that Friday afternoon, as I was checking the coal oil pump to see how much was in it, a customer rushed in and the door pushed me against the pump, soiling a good shirt with oily dirt and dust. None of Mrs. Jenkins's aprons fit me and she had said she was ordering one for me. "Sorry, sport," the customer said.

"The first law of customer relations," Mrs. Jenkins said after the guy was gone, "is to provide your customers with proper egress to and from your product." Such bullshit would have been enough in itself, but then, for the rest of that day, she'd look at me and ask, "What am I thinkin?" And before I could say anything, she would say, "Wrong! Wrong! I'm thinkin oil." Then the laugh again.

That was how it was for months and months. But each Monday morning, like a whipped dog that stayed because he didn't know any other master but the one that whipped him, I was at the store's front door, waiting for her to open up. And a thousand times during the week I promised myself I would give her a week of work that only my father could surpass and then, come Saturday night, get my pay and tell her to kiss my ass. But always there was something during the week to bring me back on Monday—she allowed me, for example, to wait on customers (but didn't allow me to open the cash register and make change); and I got two new aprons with my name stitched in script over the left pocket; and I got a raise of one dollar more a week after I had been there six months; and eventually she allowed me to decide how much of what things we had to reorder. Often, at home in the evening, I would go over the day and rate it according to how many times Mrs. Jenkins had laughed at me, and it became a challenge to get through the next day and do things as perfectly as possible. By the time I got my raise I felt comfortable enough to push that laugh back in her face whenever she slipped up on something. I'd say, "The first law of bein a grocery store boss is to be perfect."

45   Then, too, I found that there was something irresistible to girls about a man in an apron with his name stitched on it. I had to suffer with a lot of giggly little girls from Bundy, who would hang around the store just to look at me, but there were also enough high school and older girls to make working there worth my while. Before my first year was out, I was borrowing from next week's pay to finance the good life of the current week.

The first time I waited on Kentucky Connors was just after Lonney separated from Brenda and went back to a room in his father's house. Mrs. Jenkins didn't tolerate the type of friendliness with customers that led to what she called "exploiratation," so when I wanted a date with someone who came into the store, I'd arrange to set up things after I got off. The night Kentucky came in that first time, I purposely failed to put her pack of gum in the bag and ran after her.

"Why, of all the men on this earth," she said after I caught up with her and boldly told her to clear her calendar for that Saturday night, "would I think of going out with someone like you?" You can tell when girls are just being coy and want you to lay it on just a little thicker before they say yes. But there are others who have no facade, who are not seeking to be wooed, who give out smiles like each time they do it takes them a mile farther from heaven. And after they speak you're a year older and a foot shorter. That was Kentucky.

She actually stood there for several long seconds as if waiting for me to give her some kind of fucking resume. Then she said, "I thought so," and walked away. A thousand and one comebacks came much later, when I was trying to go to sleep.

You do manage to go on with your life. Over the next weeks and months, I had to put up with her coming in a few times a week, but for her there seemed to be no memory of me asking her out and she acted as though I was no more or less than the fellow who took her money and bagged her groceries. But her you're welcome in response to my thanking her for her purchases contained no sense of triumph, of superiority, as I would have expected. I learned in bits and pieces over time that she lived in an apartment on Neal Place a few doors from 5th Street, was a year out of Dunbar, was a secretary with the government people, that her family lived in a house on N Street that her mother's parents had bought. . . .

About a fifth of Mrs. Jenkins's customers bought things on credit and each purchase   50 was carefully noted. On a chain beside the cash register she kept an elongated accounting book for nonmeat credit purchases. The meat case, with its small array of dressed chickens and parts, wrapped hamburger and stew beef, rolls of lunch meats, pork chops, etc., was catty-corner to the counter with the register. The meats had their own credit book, and perhaps no one—except maybe Mrs. Gertrude Baxter—had a longer bill than the Turner family. I rarely ever saw the father of the two Turner children and I came to know that he worked as a night watchman. The mother seemed to live and die for her stories on television, and I rarely saw her either. The boy and girl were in and out all the time.

"My mama said gimme a small box of soap powder," one of them would say. "Gimme" meant the mother wanted it on credit. "My mama said give her a pound of baloney and a loaf a Wonda Bread." "My mama said give her two cans a spaghetti. The kind with the meatballs, not the other kind. She said you gave me the wrong kind the last time." If you got a please with any of that, it was usually from the little girl, who was about seven or so. Mrs. Jenkins had a nice way with every customer as long as they didn't fuck with her, but the Turner girl seemed to have a special place in her heart. Which is why, despite what Mrs. Baxter went about telling the whole world, I know that Penny Jenkins would have done anything to avoid killing the Turner girl.

The ten-year-old Turner boy, however, was an apprentice thug. He never missed a chance to try me, and he was particularly fond of shaking the door just to hear that tinkling bell. He never messed with Mrs. Jenkins, of course, but he seemed to think

God had put me on the earth just for his amusement. He also liked to stand at the cooler with the sodas and move his hand about, knocking the bottles over and getting water on the floor. Whenever I told him to get a soda and get out of the box, he would whine, "But I want a *reeaal* cold one. . . ." He would persist at the box and I usually had to come and pull his arm out, and he'd back away to the door.

He'd poke his tongue out at me and, no matter how many old church ladies were in the store, would say in his loudest voice: "You don't tell me what to do, mothafucka!" Then he'd run out.

Just before he dashed out, his sister, Patricia, who often came with him, would say, "Ohh, Tommy. I'm gonna tell mama you been cursin." Then she would look up at me with this exasperated look as if to say, "What can you do?"

55 "Where me and you gonna retire to?" was the standard question Mrs. Jenkins would ask the girl after she had bagged the girl's stuff.

"To Jamaica," Patricia would say, giggling that standard little-girl giggle.

"Now don't you grow up and run off somewhere else," Mrs. Jenkins said. "There's some fine, fine men in Jamaica, and we gon get us some."

"Oh, no," Patricia said as if Mrs. Jenkins had implied that the girl was capable of doing something horrible.

"And how we gon get to Jamaica?"

60 "On a slow boat by way a China."

None of that meant very much to me then, of course. It was just so much bullshit heard over the hours of a long day.

By the summer of 1962 I was making forty dollars a week and that November I had enough to buy a used Ford from a longtime friend of my parents. "Always know where the seller lives in case the thing turns out to be a piece of junk," my father once said. The first long trip I took in the car was to Fort Holabird in Baltimore, where Lonney was inducted into the man's army. I came back to Washington and dropped his mother off at her house and then went back to work, though Penny had said I could take the day off. Perhaps it was the effort of trying to get through the day, of trying not to think about Lonney, that made me feel reckless enough to ask Kentucky out again.

Penny had waited on her, and I followed Kentucky out of the store. I waited until we were across O Street and asked with words that would have done my mother proud if I could take her to Howard Theater to see Dinah Washington that Saturday night.

"I'd like that," she said without much hesitation. And because she was the kind of woman she was, I knew it was the simple truth, no more, no less. She set down her bag of stuff and pulled a pen and a slip of paper from her pocketbook. She began to write. "This is my telephone number. If you're going to be late," she said, "I'd like the courtesy of knowing. And if you are late and haven't called, don't come. I love Dinah Washington, but I don't love her that much."

65 I found her family a cold and peculiar lot, except for her little sisters, who were as passionate about the Washington Senators as I was. A few times a month we had

dinner at their place on N Street. Her father was a school principal and talked as if every morning when he got up, he memorized an awfully big word from the dictionary and forced himself to use that word in his conversations throughout the day, whether the word actually fit what he was saying or not. Kentucky's mother was the first Negro supervisor at some office in the Department of Commerce. She was a bit better to take than her husband, but she was a terrible cook and I seemed to be the only person at her dinner table who realized this.

The first time we slept together was that January. I had waited a long time, something quite unusual for me. I had started to think I would be an old man with a dick good for nothing but peeing before she would let me get beyond heavy petting. So when she turned to me as we were sitting at the counter at Mile Long one Sunday night, I didn't think anything was up.

She turned to look at me. "Listen," she said and waited until I had chewed up and swallowed the bite of steak sandwich I had in my mouth. "Listen: Thou shall have no other woman before me. I can take a lot but not that." Which didn't mean anything to me until we got back to her apartment. We had just gotten in and shut the door. She took my belt in both her hands and pulled me to her until our thighs and stomachs met. Until then I'd made all the moves, and so what she did took my breath away. She kissed me and said again, "Thou shall have no other woman before me." Then she asked if I wanted to stay the night.

A very mischievous wind came through Washington that night and the rattling windows kept waking us, and each time we woke we would resettle into each other's arms, to drift away with sleep and return with another rattling. I can be twenty-two forever as long as I can remember that evening and that night.

When you work in a grocery store the world comes to buy: tons of penny candy and small boxes of soap powder because the next size up—only pennies more—is too expensive and rubbing alcohol and baby formula and huge sweet potatoes for pies for church socials and spray guns and My Knight and Dixie Peach hair grease and Stanback ("snap back with Stanback") headache powder and all colors of Griffin shoe polish and nylon stockings and twenty-five cents worth of hogshead cheese cut real thin to make more sandwiches and hairnets for practically bald old women trudging off to work at seventy-five and lard and Argo starch not for laundry but to satisfy a pregnant woman's craving and mousetraps and notebook paper for a boy late with his what-I-did-on-my-summer-vacation paper and Kotex and clothespins and Bat 'N' Balls and coal oil for lamps in apartments where landlords decline to provide electricity and Sneaky Pete dream books and corn flakes with the surprise in the box and light bulbs for a new place and chocolate milk and shoe-strings and Wonder Bread to help "build strong bodies 12 ways" and RC Cola and Valentine's Day specials to be given with all your heart and soul and penny cookies and enough chicken wings to feed a family of ten and bottles of bluing. . . .

By the time I came on the scene, Penelope Jenkins had been selling all that and 70 more for about fifteen years. She and her husband ("the late Mr. Al Jenkins") had bought the place from a Jewish family not long after World War II. Al had died ten years before I showed up, and Penny had had a succession of helpers, including a son who went off and died in Korea, never to come back to Al's and Penny's Groceries.

Because of my life at the store, my sense of neighborhood began to expand; then, too, it's easier to love a neighborhood when you love the girl in it. My allegiances had always been to the world around New York Avenue and 1st Street, around Dunbar, because that was Home. In fact, I hadn't much cared for the world around 5th and O; when I was still in junior high I'd gotten my ass whipped by a boy who lived around 5th and O. Lonney and I and people from our world had always associated the whole 5th and O area with punk fighters, and the boy I fought turned out to be one of the biggest punks around. From the get-go, this guy went for my privates with a hard kick and it took everything out of me; you never recover from shit like that, so even though I lost, I didn't lose fair.

The second time I realized my allegiances were expanding, that I was making room in my soul for more than one neighborhood, was when I was asked to be godfather to two babies within one month; Penny got to be the godmother and I stood beside her as the godfather. The first time, though, was the afternoon Penny gave me the combination to the safe she kept in the little room off the main room. She had me practice the combination that afternoon until I knew it by heart. After a few turns I got tired of that and ended up looking through some of what was in the safe. There was a stack of pictures Al Jenkins had taken in those early years, mostly pictures of people in the 5th and O Street neighborhood. Many of the people in the pictures still lived around there; having served them in the store for so long, I recognized them despite what time had done to them. I sat on the floor and read what Al had written on the backs of the black-and-white pictures. One picture showed Joy Lambert, the mother of Patricia and Tommy Turner. Surrounded by several girlfriends, Joy was standing on what must have been a sunny day in front of the store in her high-school graduation cap and gown. Al had written on the back of the picture, "June 1949. The world awaits." This picture, above all the others, captivated me. You could tell that they were innocents, with good hearts. And the more I looked at those smiling girls, especially Joy, the more I wanted only good things for them, the way I wanted only good things for my nieces and nephews. Perhaps it was tiredness, but I began to feel that I was looking at a picture of the dead, people who had died years and years before, and now there was nothing I could do.

"Now you know why I keep all those in the safe." Penny had come up behind me and was looking down on me and the pictures spread out before me. "Out of harm's way," she said, "way in back, behind the money."

Kentucky and I fell into an easy, pleasant relationship, which is not to say that I didn't tip out on her now and again. But it was never anything to upset what we had, and, as far as I know, she never found out about any of it. More and more I got to staying at her place, sleeping at my mother's only a few times a month. "I hope you know what you doin," my mother would say sometimes. Who knew? Who cared?

75   In fact, my mother said those very words that August Thursday night when I went to get clean clothes from her place. That Friday was hot, but bearably humid, and the next day would be the same. The weather would stay the same for a week or so more. After that, I remember nothing except that it stayed August until it became September. The air-conditioning unit installed over the front door, which Penny had bought second-hand, had broken down again that Wednesday, and we had managed to get

the repairman, a white man with three fingers missing on one hand, to come out on Thursday and do his regular patch-up job. In the summer, we had two, sometimes three, deliveries a week of sodas and stuff like Popsicles and Creamsicles that the kids couldn't seem to do without. For years and years after that, my only dreams of the store were of a summer day and of children coming to buy those sodas and ice cream. We always ran out of the product in my dreams and the delivery men were either late or never showed up and a line of nothing but children would form at the door, wanting to buy the stuff that we didn't have, and the line would go on down 5th Street, past N, past M, past New York Avenue, past F, past Pennsylvania Avenue, all the way down into Southwest, until it went on out Washington and into another land. In the dreams I would usually be yelling at Penny that I wanted her to do something about that line of children, that we weren't in business to have a line like that, that I wanted it gone pretty damn soon. Eventually, in the dreams, she would do something to placate me—sometimes, she would disappear into the back and return with a tub of stuff that I recognized immediately as the home-made ice cream my mother said her parents always made when she was a little girl.

About a half hour or so before closing that Friday, Kentucky came by. She had bought a new stereo and all week I had been borrowing records from friends because we planned a little party, just the two of us, to break in the stereo. Penny left the locking up to me and got ready to go.

"Who's the man tonight?" Kentucky asked Penny. I think she must have had more boyfriends than Carter had liver pills. I had just finished covering the meat for the night, something Penny and I called putting the chickens to bed.

"Ask me no questions . . . ," Penny said and winked. She whispered in Kentucky's ear, and the two laughed. Then Kentucky, looking dead at me, whispered to Penny, and they laughed even louder. Finally, Penny was ready to leave.

If the sign said we closed at nine, that was precisely the time Penny wanted the store closed and I wasn't allowed to close any sooner. I could close later for a late-arriving customer, but not any sooner. And as it happened, someone did come in at the last minute and I had to pull out some pork chops. Penny said good night and left. I locked the door after the pork chop customer. I may or may not have heard the sound of a car slamming on brakes, but I certainly heard little Carl Baggot banging at the door.

"You little squirt," I said to him. "If you break that window, I'm gonna make   80 your daddy pay for it." I'd pulled down the door shade to an inch or so of where the glass ended, and I could see the kid's eyes beaming through that inch of space. "Can't you read, you little punk. We closed. *We closed!*" and I walked away. Kentucky was standing near the door and the more the kid shouted, the closer she got to the door.

"He's hysterical, honey," she said, unlocking the door. She walked out, and I followed.

Penny's lavender Cadillac was stopped in the middle of 5th Street, one or two doors past O Street. From everywhere people were running to whatever had happened. Penny was standing in front of the car. I pushed my way through the crowd, and as I got closer I saw that her fists were up, shaking, and she was crying.

"She hit my sista," Tommy Turner was saying, pounding away at Penny's thigh. "This bitch hit my sista! This bitch hit my sista!" Some stranger picked the boy up. "All right, son," the man said, "thas anough of that."

Patricia Turner lay in the street, a small pool of blood forming around her head. She had apparently been chasing a rolling Hula Hoop, and she and the hoop, now twisted, had fallen in such a way that one of her arms was embracing the toy. Most of what light there was came from the street lamps, but there were also the Cadillac's headlights, shining out on the crowd on the other side of the girl. "You should watch where you goin with that big ole car," Mrs. Baxter said to Penny. "Oh, you know it was a accident," a man said. "I don't know no such thing," Mrs. Baxter said.

85   The girl's eyes were open and she was looking at me, at the people around her, at everything in the world, I suppose. The man still had hold of Tommy, but the boy was wiggling violently and still cursing Penny. Penny, crying, bent down to Patricia and I think I heard her tell the child that it would be all right. I could tell that it wouldn't be. The girl's other arm was stretched out and she had a few rubber bands around the wrist. There was something about the rubber bands on that little wrist and they, more than the blood perhaps, told me, in the end, that none of it would be all right.

    Soon Joy, the girl's mother, was there. "You murderin fuckin monster!" she kept yelling at Penny, and someone held her until she said that she wanted to go to her baby. "Look what that murderin monster did to my baby!"

    The police arrived, but they did not know what else to do except handcuff Penny and threaten to arrest the man who held Tommy if he didn't control the boy. Then the ambulance arrived and in little or no time they took the girl and her mother away, the flashing light on the roof shining on all the houses as it moved down 5th Street. A neighbor woman took Tommy from the stranger and took the boy inside. Wordlessly, the crowd parted to let them by, as it had parted to let the ambulance through. The police put Penny in the back of the scout car and I followed, with Kentucky holding tight to my arm. Through the rolled down window, she said to me, "Bail me out, if they'll let me go." But most of what she said was just a bunch of mumbles, because she hadn't managed to stop crying. I reached in the window and touched her cheek.

I opened the store as usual the next day, Saturday. The child died during the night. No one, except people from out of the neighborhood, spoke when they came in the store; they merely pointed or got the items themselves and set them on the counter. I sold no meat that day. And all that day, I kept second-guessing myself about even the simplest of things and kept waiting for Penny to come and tell me what to do. Just before I closed, one girl, Snowball Patterson, told me that Mrs. Baxter was going about saying that Penny had deliberately killed Patricia.

    Penny called me at Kentucky's on Sunday morning to tell me not to open the store for two weeks. "We have to consider Pat's family," she said. I had seen her late that Friday night at No. 2 police precinct, but she had said little. I would not see her again for a month. I had parked the Cadillac just in front of the store, and sometime over the next two weeks, the car disappeared, and I never found out what happened to it, whether Penny came to get it late one night or whether it was stolen. "Pay it no mind," Penny told me later.

90   She called me again Monday night and told me she would mail me a check for two thousand dollars, which I was to cash and take the money to Patricia's family for her funeral. The police were satisfied that it had been an accident, but on the phone Penny always talked like old lady Baxter, as if she had done it on purpose. "Her

mother," Penny said, "wouldn't let me come by to apologize. Doesn't want me to call anymore." All that month, and for some months after, that was the heart of the phone conversation, that the mother wouldn't allow her to come to see her and the family.

Joy came in one day about three months after Pat died. Tommy came with her, and all the time they were in the store, the boy held his mother's hand.

"You tell her to stop callin me," Joy said to me. "You tell her I don't want her in my life. You tell her to leave me alone, or I'll put the law on her. And you"—she pointed at me—"my man say for you not to bring me no more food." Which is what Penny had been instructing me to do. The boy never said a word the whole time, just stood there close to his mother, with his thumb in his mouth and blinking very, very slowly as if he were about to fall asleep on his feet.

About once a week for the next few years, Penny would call me at Kentucky's and arrange a place and time to meet me. We always met late at night, on some fairly deserted street, like secret lovers. And we usually met in some neighborhood in far, far Northeast or across the river in Anacostia, parts of the world I wasn't familiar with. I would drive up, park, and go to her car not far away. She wanted to know less about how I was operating the store than what was going on with the people in the neighborhood. She had moved from her apartment in Southwest, and because I had no way of getting in touch with her, I always came with beaucoup questions about this and that to be done in the store. She dispensed with all the questions as quickly as possible, and not always to my satisfaction. Then she wanted to know about this one and that one, about so-and-so and whoever. Because it was late at night, I was always tired and not always very talkative. But when I began to see how important our meetings were, I found myself learning to set aside some reserve during the day for that night's meeting, and over time, the business of the store became less important in our talks than the business of the people in the neighborhood.

And over time as well, nearly all the legal crap was changed so that my name, just below hers, was on everything—invoices, the store's bank account, even the stuff on the door's window about who to call in case of emergency. After she had been gone a year or so, I timidly asked about a raise because I hadn't had one in quite a while. "Why ask me?" she said. We were someplace just off Benning Road and I didn't know where I would get the strength to drive all the way back to Kentucky's. "Why in the world are you askin me?"

I went about my days at first with tentativeness, as if Penny would show up at any moment in her dirty apron and make painful jokes about what I had done wrong. When she was there, I had, for example, always turned the bruised fruit and vegetables bad side up so people could see from jump what was what, but Penny always kept the bruised in with all the healthy pieces and sold the good and the not-so-good at the same price. Now that she was not there, I created a separate bin for the bruised and sold it at a reduced price, something she had always refused to do. But the dividing line of that separate bin was made of cardboard, something far from permanent. Every week or so the cardboard would wear out and I had to replace it.

Because there were many nights when I simply was too exhausted to walk the 95 two blocks or so to Kentucky's, I made a pallet for myself in the back room, which would have been an abomination to Penny. "Work is work, and home is home," she always said, "and never should those trains meet."

When Mrs. Baxter came in to buy on credit, which was about twice a day, she would always ask, "How the murderer doin?" I tried to ignore it at first, but began trying to get back at her by reminding her of what her bill was. Generally, she owed about a hundred dollars; and rarely paid more than five dollars on the bill from month to month. Since Penny had told me to wipe the slate clean for Patricia's mother, Old Lady Baxter became the biggest deadbeat. Baxter always claimed that her retirement check was coming the next day. After I started pressing her about the bill, she stopped bad-mouthing Penny, but I found out that that was only in the store, where I could hear.

When I told her that I wouldn't give her any more credit until she paid up, she started crying. My mother once told me that in place of muscles God gave women the ability to cry on a moment's notice.

"I'll tell," Mrs. Baxter boo-hooed. "I'm gonna tell."

"Oh, yeah," I said, loud enough for everyone in the store to hear. "Who you gonna tell? Who you gonna go to?"

100   "Penny," she said. "I'll tell Penny. She oughta know how you runnin her sto into the ground. I'ma tell her you tryin to starve me to death."

Within a few weeks her account was settled down to the last penny, but I still told her never to step foot in the store again. Surprisingly, the old lady took it like a man. It was a full month before I got the courage to tell Penny what I had done. I could see that she did not approve, but she only had this look that my mother had the day my brother came home with the first piece of clothing my parents allowed him to buy on his own. A look of resignation—Thank God I don't have to live with it.

At first, with Penny's blessing, I hired my more trustworthy friends or cousins or a few people in the neighborhood, but either they could only work part time or they didn't do the job well enough to suit me. Kentucky even helped out some, but after she got into an executive training program at what she called her "real job," she didn't want to work in the store anymore.

Then, in the spring of 1965, I lucked onto a Muslim who lived on 6th Street. She was on public assistance and had three children, which made me skeptical about her working out, but I gave her a one-week tryout, then extended it another week. Then extended two weeks more, then I took her on full time, permanent, and gave her two aprons with her named stitched over the left pockets. I was always afraid that I'd find the place overrun with her kids every day, but in all the time I knew her, despite the fact that she lived only a block away, I met her kids only a few times and came to know them only by the pictures she showed me. Her name was Gloria 5X, but before she lost her slave name, the world—and she seemed to know three fourths of it—had called her Puddin. And that was what I learned to call her.

After I got where I could leave things in Puddin's hands, I was able to take off now and again and spend more time than I had been with Kentucky. We did two weeks in Atlantic City in the summer of 1965, back when the only rep the city had was what the ocean gave it, and that seemed to revive what we had had. That fall I set about redoing the store—repainting, rearranging shelves, and, at long last, getting a new meat case. The renovations left me, again, spending more and more nights on the pallet in the back. There were fewer people buying coal oil and I wanted to tear out the pump, but Penny vetoed that. "Wait," she said. "Wait till the day after the very last person comes to buy some, then you tear it out."

I passed the halfway mark in the new work before the end of winter and wanted   105 to celebrate with a good meal and a movie. I was to meet Kentucky at her office one evening in February, but I was late getting there for a reason I don't remember, for a reason that, when it is all said and done, will not matter anyway. When I did get there, she iced me out and said she was no longer interested in going out, which pissed me off. I kept telling her we could have a good evening, but she insisted we go home.

"You know," she said as I continued trying to coax her to go, "you spend too much time at that damn store. You act like you own it or something." I was making $110 a week, had a full-time employee and one part-time worker, and I didn't particularly want to hear that shit.

"It's my job," I said. "You don't hear me complainin and everything when you come home and sit all evening with your head in those books."

"It's not every single day, not like you do. Maybe once every three weeks. You come first, and you know it."

When we got home, she began to thaw.

"Why are we letting all this come between you and me?" she said. "Between us?"   110 She repeated that "us" three or four times and put her arms around me.

Because she was thawing, I felt I was winning. And I think I got to feeling playful, because the first thing that came to mind after all those *us*es was that joke about Tonto and the Lone Ranger looking up to see a band of Indians bearing down on them: "What they gonna do to us, Tonto?" "Whatcha mean 'us,' Kemo Sabe?"

I don't think I said that line out loud. Maybe I did. Or maybe she just read my mind. In any case, she withdrew from me, then went to the window, her arms hugging her body. "I thought so," she said after a bit. "Clean your things out of here," she said, in the same quiet way she used to tell me to remember to set the clock's alarm. "Clean everything out as soon as possible."

Despite what she had said, I left her place feeling pretty cocky and went to Mojo's. After four beers, I called Kentucky to say we should wipe the slate clean. She calmly told me not to call her again. "You fuckin bitch!" I said. "Who the fuck do you think you are!" After a while I went to my mother's place. For the most part, I had sobered up by the time I got there. I found my mother at the kitchen table, listening to gospel on the radio. I don't recall what conversation we had. I do remember noticing that she had lost, somewhere in time, three or four of her teeth, and it pained me that I did not even know when it had happened.

It took me three days to clean out my life from Kentucky's place. She stayed at work until I had finished each day. And on each of those days, I left a note telling her I wanted to stay.

I suppose any man could take rejection by any woman as long as he knew that   115 the morning after he was cast out, the woman would be bundled up with her best memories of him and taken away to a castle in the most foreign of lands to live there forever, guarded by a million eunuchs and by old women who had spent their lives equating sex with death. No, no, the woman would have to say to the old women for the rest of her life, I remember different.

If you approached Al's and Penny's Groceries coming down O Street from 6th you could see the bright new orange color I myself put on, a color announcing to the world an establishment of substance, a place I tried to make as friendly as a customer's own home. Joy and Tommy and Tommy's father moved away when the paint was still fresh and bright. And it was still bright when Mrs. Baxter went on to her reward, and though she had not been in the store since the day I told her not to come back, Penny had me send flowers to the funeral home in both our names. The paint was still radiant when the babies I was godfather to learned to walk in the store on their own and beg for candy from me.

One evening—the season it was is gone from my mind now—I let Puddin go home early. Alone in the store, I sat on my high stool behind the counter, reading the *Afro*, a rare treat. At one point I stood to stretch and looked out the O Street window to see Penny, with shorter hair and in her apron, looking in at me. I smiled and waved furiously and she smiled and waved back. I started from behind the counter and happened to look out the 5th Street window and saw my father coming toward me. When I saw that he too had on an apron, I realized that my mind, exhausted from a long day, was only playing tricks.

I do not know what would have happened had Penny not decided to sell. Perhaps I would be there still, and still going home each evening with the hope that I would not see, again, Kentucky arm-in-arm with someone else. Penny and I had continued to meet in her car about once a week. The night she told me she was selling the place, we met on Q Street, between 5th and 6th. And the very last meeting was on O Street, in front of Bundy's playground. From meetings far, far from the neighborhood, we had now come to one that was just down the street from the store. I came out of the store about midnight, locked it, stepped back to take one final look at the place as I usually did, and walked only a few yards. In a few minutes, Penny drove up.

"You been a good friend to me," she said as soon as I got in the car. She handed me two envelopes—one with a month's pay for Puddin and the other with four thousand dollars for me. "Severin pay," she said. "Don't spend it on all the whores, for a man does not live on top of whores alone."

120   She hugged me, kissed me hard on the cheek. After a while, I got out and watched her make a U turn and go back down the way she had come. I had a feeling that that would be the last time I would ever see her and I stood there with my heart breaking, watching her until I lost her in the night.

The next week I took the G2 bus all the way down P Street, crossing 16th Street into the land of white people. I didn't drive because my father had always told me that white people did not like to see Negroes driving cars, even a dying one like my Ford. In the fall, I was sitting in classes at Georgetown with glad-handing white boys who looked as if they had been weaned only the week before. I was twenty-seven years old, the age my mother was when she married. Sometimes, blocks before my stop on my way home from Georgetown in the evening, I would get off the G2 at 5th Street. I would walk up to O and sit on the low stone wall of the apartment building across the street from what had been Al's and Penny's Groceries. The place became a television repair shop after it stopped being a store, then it became a church of Holy Rollers. But whatever it was over the years, I could, without trying very hard, see myself sitting in the window eating my lunch the way I did before I knew Kentucky, before Pat was killed. In those early days at the store, I almost always had a lunch of one half smoke heavy with mustard and a large bottle of Upper 10 and a package of Sno-Ball cupcakes. I sat on the stone wall and watched myself as I ate my lunch and checked out the fine girls parading past the store, parading as if for me and me alone.

CRITICAL THINKING QUESTIONS

1. Early in the story, the narrator takes three paragraphs to describe his reaction to an encounter with a white policeman. In a short story, there is no room for superfluous material and every word has to count; why do you suppose the author decided to keep these three paragraphs in his story? What do they contribute to our understanding of the narrator and his situation?

2. Although the narrator of "The Store" eventually finds recognition and meaning in work, his first job in a mailroom offered him neither of these rewards. What characteristics of his second job make it a positive experience? Can you generalize and suggest characteristics any job must have in order to make the work worthwhile? How did the second job, even though it ended abruptly, lead him to taking classes at Georgetown University?

WRITING TOPIC

Read the following quotation from Barry Lopez's fictional work, *Resistance:*

> We reject the assertion, promoted today by success-mongering bull terriers in business, in government, in religion, that humans are goal-seeking animals. We believe they are creatures in search of proportion in life, a pattern of grace. It is balance and beauty we believe people want, not triumph.[1]

At the beginning of the story, the narrator does not seem to be a "goal-seeking animal," but by the end, he has enrolled in Georgetown University. He appears to have triumphed over circumstances, internal and external, that often stifle a person's desire to succeed. How do you think the narrator would respond to Lopez's perspective? (For another perspective, read "The Lesson" in Chapter Seven.)

---

[1]Barry Lopez, *Resistance* (New York: Alfred A. Knopf, 2004), p. 11.

Randall Kenan (b. 1963)

The Foundations of the Earth

I

Of course they didn't pay it any mind at first: just a tractor—one of the most natural things in the world to see in a field—kicking dust up into the afternoon sky and slowly toddling off the road into a soybean field. And fields surrounded Mrs. Maggie Mac-Gowan Williams's house, giving the impression that her lawn stretched on and on until it dropped off into the woods far by the way. Sometimes she was certain she could actually see the earth's curve—not merely the bend of the small hill on which her house sat but the great slope of the sphere, the way scientists explained it in books, a monstrous globe floating in a cold nothingness. She would sometimes sit by herself on the patio late of an evening, in the same chair she was sitting in now, sip from her Coca-Cola, and think about how big the earth must be to seem flat to the eye.

She wished she were alone now. It was Sunday.

"Now I wonder what that man is doing with a tractor out there today?"

They sat on Maggie's patio, reclined in that after-Sunday-dinner way—Maggie; the Right Reverend Hezekiah Barden, round and pompous as ever; Henrietta Fuchee, the prim and priggish music teacher and president of the First Baptist Church Auxiliary Council; Emma Lewis, Maggie's sometimes housekeeper; and Gabriel, Mrs. Maggie Williams's young, white, special guest—all looking out lazily into the early summer, watching the sun begin its slow downward arc, feeling the baked ham and the candied sweet potatoes and the fried chicken with the collard greens and green beans and beets settle in their bellies, talking shallow and pleasant talk, and sipping their Coca-Colas and bitter lemonade.

5   "Don't they realize it's Sunday?" Reverend Barden leaned back in his chair and tugged at his suspenders thoughtfully, eyeing the tractor as it turned into another row. He reached for a sweating glass of lemonade, his red bow tie afire in the penultimate beams of the day.

"I . . . I don't understand. What's wrong?" Maggie could see her other guests watching Gabriel intently, trying to discern why on earth he was present at Maggie MacGowan Williams's table.

"What you mean, what's wrong?" The Reverend Barden leaned forward and narrowed his eyes at the young man. "What's wrong is: it's Sunday."

"So? I don't . . ." Gabriel himself now looked embarrassed, glancing to Maggie, who wanted to save him but could not.

" 'So?' 'So?' " Leaning toward Gabriel and narrowing his eyes, Barden asked: "You're not from a churchgoing family, are you?"

10   "Well, no. Today was my first time in . . . Oh, probably ten years."

"Uh-huh." Barden corrected his posture, as if to say he pitied Gabriel's being an infidel but had the patience to instruct him. "Now you see, the Lord has declared Sunday as His day. It's holy. 'Six days shalt thou labor and do all thy work: but the seventh day is the sabbath of the Lord thy God: in it thou shalt not do any work, thou, nor thy son, nor thy daughter, thy manservant, nor thy maidservant, nor thy cattle, nor thy stranger that is within thy gates: for in six days the Lord made heaven and earth, the sea, and all that in them is, and rested the seventh day: wherefore, the Lord blessed the sabbath day, and hallowed it.' Exodus. Chapter twenty, verses nine and ten."

"Amen." Henrietta closed her eyes and rocked.

"Hez." Maggie inclined her head a bit to entreat the good Reverend to desist. He gave her an understanding smile, which made her cringe slightly, fearing her gesture might have been mistaken for a sign of intimacy.

"But, Miss Henrietta—" Emma Lewis tapped the tabletop, like a judge in court, changing the subject. "Like I was saying, I believe that Rick on. *The Winds of Hope* is going to marry that gal before she gets too big with child, don't you?" Though Emma kept house for Maggie Williams, to Maggie she seemed more like a sister who came three days a week, more to visit than to clean.

"Now go on away from here, Emma." Henrietta did not look up from her empty   15
cake plate, her glasses hanging on top of her sagging breasts from a silver chain. "Talking about that worldly foolishness on TV. You know I don't pay that mess any attention." She did not want the Reverend to know that she secretly watched afternoon soap operas, just like Emma and all the other women in the congregation. Usually she gossiped to beat the band about this rich heifer and that handsome hunk whenever she found a fellow TV-gazer. Buck-toothed hypocrite, Maggie thought. She knew the truth: Henrietta, herself a widow now on ten years, was sweet on the widower minister, who in turn, alas, had his eye on Maggie.

"Now, Miss Henrietta, we was talking about it t'other day. Don't you think he's apt to marry her soon?" Emma's tone was insistent.

"I *don't know*, Emma." Visibly agitated, Henrietta donned her glasses and looked into the fields. "I wonder who that is anyhow?"

Annoyed by Henrietta's rebuff, Emma stood and began to collect the few remaining dishes. Her purple-and-yellow floral print dress hugged her ample hips. "It's that ole Morton Henry that Miss Maggie leases that piece of land to." She walked toward the door, into the house. "He ain't no God-fearing man."

"Well, that's plain to see." The Reverend glanced over to Maggie. She shrugged.

They are ignoring Gabriel, Maggie thought. She had invited them to dinner after   20
church services thinking it would be pleasant for Gabriel to meet other people in Tims Creek. But generally they chose not to see him, and when they did it was with illconcealed scorn or petty curiosity or annoyance. At first the conversation seemed civil enough. But the ice was never truly broken, questions still buzzed around the talk like horseflies, Maggie could tell. "Where you from?" Henrietta had asked. "What's your line of work?" Barden had asked. While Gabriel sat there with a look on his face somewhere between peace and pain. But Maggie refused to believe she had made a mistake. At this stage of her life she depended on no one for anything, and she was certainly not dependent on the approval of these self-important fools.

She had been steeled by anxiety when she picked Gabriel up at the airport that Friday night. But as she caught sight of him stepping from the jet and greeted him, asking about the weather in Boston; and after she had ushered him to her car and watched him slide in, seeming quite at home; though it still felt awkward, she thought: I'm doing the right thing.

II

"Well, thank you for inviting me, Mrs. Williams. But I don't understand . . . Is something wrong?"

"*Wrong?* No, nothing's wrong, Gabriel. I just thought it'd be good to see you. Sit and talk to you. We didn't have much time at the funeral."

"Gee . . . I—"

25   "You don't want to make an old woman sad, now do you?"

"Well, Mrs. Williams, if you put it like that, how can I refuse?"

"Weekend after next then?"

There was a pause in which she heard muted voices in the wire.

"Okay."

30   After she hung up the phone and sat down in her favorite chair in the den, she heaved a momentous sigh. Well, she had done it. At last. The weight of uncertainty would be lifted. She could confront him face to face. She wanted to know about her grandboy, and Gabriel was the only one who could tell her what she wanted to know. It was that simple. Surely, he realized what this invitation meant. She leaned back looking out the big picture window onto the tops of the brilliantly blooming crepe myrtle trees in the yard, listening to the grandfather clock mark the time.

III

Her grandson's funeral had been six months ago, but it seemed much longer. Perhaps the fact that Edward had been gone away from home so long without seeing her, combined with the weeks and days and hours and minutes she had spent trying not to think about him and all the craziness that had surrounded his death, somehow lengthened the time.

At first she chose to ignore it, the strange and bitter sadness that seemed to have overtaken her every waking moment. She went about her daily life as she had done for thirty-odd years, overseeing her stores, her land, her money; buying groceries, paying bills, shopping, shopping; going to church and talking to her few good living friends and the few silly fools she was obliged to suffer. But all day, dusk to dawn, and especially at night, she had what the field-workers called "a monkey on your back," when the sun beats down so hot it makes you delirious; but her monkey chilled and angered her, born not of the sun but of a profound loneliness, an oppressive emptiness, a stabbing guilt. Sometimes she even wished she were a drinking woman.

The depression had come with the death of Edward, though its roots reached farther back, to the time he seemed to have vanished. There had been so many years of asking other members of the family: Have you heard from him? Have you seen him? So many years of only a Christmas card or birthday card a few days early, or a cryptic, taciturn phone call on Sunday mornings, and then no calls at all. At some point she realized she had no idea where he was or how to get in touch with him. Mysteriously, he would drop a line to his half-sister, Clarissa, or drop a card without a return address. He was gone. Inevitably, she had to ask: Had she done something evil to the boy to drive him away? Had she tried too hard to make sure he became nothing like his father and grandfather? I was as good a mother as a woman can claim to be, she thought: from the cradle on he had all the material things he needed, and he certainly didn't want for attention, for care; and I trained him proper, he was a well-mannered and upright young fellow when he left here for college. Oh, I was proud of that boy, winning a scholarship to Boston University. Tall, handsome like his granddad. He'd make somebody a good . . .

So she continued picking out culprits: school, the cold North, strange people, strange ideas. But now in her crystalline hindsight she could lay no blame on anyone but Edward. And the more she remembered battles with the mumps and the measles and long division and taunts from his schoolmates, the more she became aware of her true anger. He owes me respect, damn it. The least he can do is keep in touch. Is that so much to ask?

But before she could make up her mind to find him and confront him with her   35 fury, before she could cuss him out good and call him an ungrateful, no-account bastard just like his father, a truck would have the heartless audacity to skid into her grandchild's car one rainy night in Springfield and end his life at twenty-seven, taking that opportunity away from her forever. When they told her of his death she cursed her weakness. Begging God for another chance. But instead He gave her something she had never imagined.

Clarissa was the one to finally tell her. "Grandma," she had said, "Edward's been living with another man all these years."

"So?"

"No, Grandma. Like man and wife."

Maggie had never before been so paralyzed by news. One question answered, only to be replaced by a multitude. Gabriel had come with the body, like an interpreter for the dead. They had been living together in Boston, where Edward worked in a bookstore. He came, head bowed, rheumy-eyed, exhausted. He gave her no explanation; nor had she asked him for any, for he displayed the truth in his vacant and humble glare and had nothing to offer but the penurious tribute of his trembling hands. Which was more than she wanted.

In her world she had been expected to be tearless, patient, comforting to other   40 members of the family; folk were meant to sit back and say, "Lord, ain't she taking it well. I don't think I could be so calm if my grandboy had've died so young." Magisterially she had done her duty; she had taken it all in stride. But her world began to hopelessly unravel that summer night at the wake in the Raymond Brown Funeral Home, among the many somber-bright flower arrangements, the fluorescent lights, and the gleaming bronze casket, when Gabriel tried to tell her how sorry he was . . . How dare he? This pathetic, stumbling, poor trashy white boy, to throw his sinful lust for her grandbaby in her face, as if to bury a grandchild weren't bad enough. Now this abomination had to be flaunted.—Sorry, indeed! The nerve! Who the hell did he think he was to parade their shame about?

Her anger was burning so intensely that she knew if she didn't get out she would tear his heart from his chest, his eyes from their sockets, his testicles from their sac. With great haste she took her leave, brushing off the funeral director and her brother's wives and husband's brothers—they all probably thinking her overcome with grief rather than anger—and had Clarissa drive her home. When she got to the house she filled a tub with water as hot as she could stand it and a handful of bath oil beads, and slipped in, praying her hatred would mingle with the mist and evaporate, leaving her at least sane.

Next, sleep. Healing sleep, soothing sleep, sleep to make the world go away, sleep like death. Her mama had told her that sleep was the best medicine God ever made. When things get too rough—go to bed. Her family had been known as the family that retreated to bed. Ruined crop? No money? Get some shut-eye. Maybe it'll be better in the morning. Can't be worse. Maggie didn't give a damn where Gabriel was to sleep that night; someone else would deal with it. She didn't care about all the people who would come to the house after the wake to the Sitting Up, talking, eating, drinking, watching over the still body till sunrise; they could take care of themselves. The people came; but Maggie slept. From deeps under deeps of slumber she sensed her granddaughter stick her head in the door and whisper, asking Maggie if she wanted something to eat. Maggie didn't stir. She slept. And in her sleep she dreamed.

She dreamed she was Job sitting on his dung heap, dressed in sackcloth and ashes, her body covered with boils, scratching with a stick, sending away Eliphaz and Bildad and Zophar and Elihu, who came to counsel her, and above her the sky boiled and churned and the air roared, and she matched it, railing against God, against her life—*Why? Why? Why did you kill him, you heartless old fiend? Why make me live to see him die? What earthly purpose could you have in such a wicked deed? You are God, but you are not good. Speak to me, damn it. Why? Why? Why?* Hurricanes whipped and thunder ripped through a sky streaked by lightning, and she was lifted up, spinning, spinning, and Edward floated before her in the rushing air and quickly turned around into the comforting arms of Gabriel, winged, who clutched her grandboy to his bosom and soared away, out of the storm. Maggie screamed and the winds grew stronger, and a voice, gentle and sweet, not thunderous as she expected, spoke to her from the whirlwind: *Who is this that darkeneth counsel by words without knowledge? Gird up now thy loins like a man; for I will demand of thee, and answer thou me. Where wast thou when I laid the foundations of the earth? Declare if thou hast understanding . . .* The voice spoke of the myriad creations of the universe, the stupendous glory of the Earth and its inhabitants. But Maggie was not deterred in the face of the maelstrom, saying: *Answer me, damn you: Why?*, and the winds began to taper off and finally halted, and Maggie was alone, standing on water. A fish, what appeared to be a mackerel, stuck its head through the surface and said: *Kind woman, be not aggrieved and put your anger away. Your arrogance has clouded your good mind. Who asked you to love? Who asked you to hate?* The fish dipped down with a plip and gradually Maggie too began to slip down into the water, down, down, down, sinking, below depths of reason and love, down into the dark unknown of her own mind, down, down, down.

Maggie MacGowan Williams woke the next morning to the harsh chatter of a bluejay chasing a mockingbird just outside her window, a racket that caused her to open her eyes quickly to blinding sunlight. Squinting, she looked about the room, seeing the chest of drawers that had once belonged to her mother and her mother's mother before that, the chairs, the photographs on the wall, the television, the rug thickly soft, the closet door slightly ajar, the bureau, the mirror atop the bureau, and herself in the mirror, all of it bright in the crisp morning light. She saw herself looking, if not refreshed, calmed and within her the rage had gone, replaced by a numb humility and a plethora of questions. Questions. Questions. Questions.

Inwardly she had felt beatific that day of the funeral, ashamed at her anger of the   45
day before. She greeted folk gently, softly, with a smile, her tones honey-flavored but solemn, and she reassumed the mantle of one-who-comforts-more-than-needing-comfort.

The immediate family had gathered at Maggie's house—Edward's father, Tom, Jr.; Tom, Jr.'s wife, Lucille; the grandbaby, Paul (Edward's brother); Clarissa. Raymond Brown's long black limousine took them from the front door of Maggie's house to the church, where the yard was crammed with people in their greys and navy blues, dark browns, and deep, deep burgundies. In her new humility she mused: When, oh when will we learn that death is not so somber, not something to mourn so much as celebrate? We should wear fire reds, sun oranges, hello greens, ocean-deep blues, and dazzling, welcome-home whites. She herself wore a bright dress of saffron and a blue scarf. She thought Edward would have liked it.

The family lined up and Gabriel approached her. As he stood before her—raven-haired, pink-skinned, abject, eyes bloodshot—she experienced a bevy of conflicting emotions: disgust, grief, anger, tenderness, fear, weariness, pity. Nevertheless she *had* to be civil, *had* to make a leap of faith and of understanding. Somehow she felt it had been asked of her. And though there were still so many questions, so much to sort out, for now she would mime patience, pretend to be accepting, feign peace. Time would unravel the rest.

She reached out, taking both his hands into her own, and said, the way she would to an old friend: "How have you been?"

IV

"But now, Miss Maggie . . ."

She sometimes imagined the good Reverend Barden as a toad-frog or an impo-   50
tent bull. His rantings and ravings bored her, and his clumsy advances repelled her; and when he tried to impress her with his holiness and his goodness, well . . .

". . . that man should know better than to be plowing on a Sunday. Sunday! Why, the Lord said . . ."

"Reverend, I know what the Lord said. And I'm sure Morton Henry knows what the Lord said. But I am not the Lord, Reverend, and if Morton Henry wants to plow the west field on Sunday afternoon, well, it's his soul, not mine."

"But, Maggie. Miss Maggie. It's—"

"Well,"—Henrietta Fuchee sat perched to interject her five cents into the debate—"but, Maggie. It's your land! Now, Reverend, doesn't it say somewhere in Exodus that a man, or a woman in this case, a woman is responsible for the deeds or misdeeds of someone in his or her employ, especially on her property?"

55 "But he's not an emplo—"

"Well,"—Barden scratched his head—"I think I know what you're talking about, Henrietta. It may be in Deuteronomy . . . or Leviticus . . . part of the Mosaic Law, which . . ."

Maggie cast a quick glance at Gabriel. He seemed to be interested in and entertained by this contest of moral superiority. There was certainly something about his face . . . but she could not stare. He looked so *normal* . . .

"Well, I don't think you should stand for it, Maggie."

"Henrietta? What do you . . . ? Look, if you want him to stop, *you* go tell him what the Lord said. I—"

60 The Right Reverend Hezekiah Barden stood, hiking his pants up to his belly. "Well, *I* will. A man's soul is a valuable thing. And I can't risk your own soul being tainted by the actions of one of your sharecroppers."

"My soul? Sharecropper—he's not a sharecropper. He leases that land. I—wait! . . . Hezekiah! . . . This doesn't . . ."

But Barden had stepped off the patio onto the lawn and was headed toward the field, marching forth like old Nathan on his way to confront King David.

"Wait, Reverend." Henrietta hopped up, slinging her black pocketbook over her left shoulder. "Well, Maggie?" She peered at Maggie defiantly, as if to ask: *Where do you stand?*

"Now, Henrietta, I—"

65 Henrietta pivoted, her moral righteousness jagged and sharp as a shard of glass. "Somebody has to stand up for right!" She tromped off after Barden.

Giggling, Emma picked up the empty glasses. "I don't think ole Morton Henry gone be too happy to be preached at this afternoon."

Maggie looked from Emma to Gabriel in bewilderment, at once annoyed and amused. All three began to laugh out loud. As Emma got to the door she turned to Maggie. "Hon, you better go see that they don't get into no fist-fight, don't you think? You know that Reverend don't know when to be quiet." She looked to Gabriel and nodded knowingly. "You better go with her, son," and was gone into the house; her molasses-thick laughter sweetening the air.

Reluctantly Maggie stood, looking at the two figures—Henrietta had caught up with Barden—a tiny cloud of dust rising from their feet. "Come on, Gabe. Looks like we have to go referee."

Gabriel walked beside her, a broad smile on his face. Maggie thought of her grandson being attracted to this tall white man. She tried to see them together and couldn't. At that moment she understood that she was being called on to realign her thinking about men and women, and men and men, and even women and women. Together . . . the way Adam and Eve were meant to be together.

V

Initially she found it difficult to ask the questions she wanted to ask. Almost impossible.   70

They got along well on Saturday. She took him out to dinner; they went shopping. All the while she tried with all her might to convince herself that she felt comfortable with this white man, with this homosexual, with this man who had slept with her grandboy. Yet he managed to impress her with his easygoing manner and openness and humor.

"Mrs. W." He had given her a *nickname*, of all things. No one had given her a nickname since . . . "Mrs. W., you sure you don't want to try on some swimsuits?"

She laughed at his kind-hearted jokes, seeing, oddly enough, something about him very like Edward; but then that thought would make her sad and confused.

Finally that night over coffee at the kitchen table she began to ask what they had both gingerly avoided.

"Why didn't he just tell me?"   75

"He was afraid, Mrs. W. It's just that simple."

"Of what?"

"That you might disown him. That you might stop . . . well, you know, loving him, I guess."

"Does your family know?"

"Yes."   80

"How do they take it?"

"My mom's fine. She's great. Really. She and Edward got along swell. My dad. Well, he'll be okay for a while, but every now and again we'll have these talks, you know, about cures and stuff and sometimes it just gets heated. I guess it'll just take a little more time with him."

"But don't you *want* to be normal?"

"Mrs. W., I *am*. Normal."

"I see."   85

They went to bed at one-thirty that morning. As Maggie buttoned up her nightgown, Gabriel's answers whizzed about her brain; but they brought along more damnable questions and Maggie went to bed feeling betrayal and disbelief and revulsion and anger.

In church that next morning with Gabriel, she began to doubt the wisdom of having asked him to come. As he sat beside her in the pew, as the Reverend Barden sermonized on Jezebel and Ahab, as the congregation unsuccessfully tried to disguise their curiosity—("What is that white boy doing here with Maggie Williams? Who is he? Where he come from?")—she wanted Gabriel to go ahead and tell her what to think: *We're perverts* or *You're wrong-headed, your church has poisoned your mind against your own grandson; if he had come out to you, you would have rejected him. Wouldn't you?* Would she have?

Barden's sermon droned on and on that morning; the choir sang; after the service people politely and gently shook Gabriel and Maggie's hands and then stood off to the side, whispering, clearly perplexed.

On the drive back home, as if out of the blue, she asked him: "Is it hard?"

90 "Ma'am?"

"Being who you are? What you are?"

He looked over at her, and she could not meet his gaze with the same intensity that had gone into her question. "Being gay?"

"Yes."

"Well, I have no choice."

95 "So I understand. But is it hard?"

"Edward and I used to get into arguments about that, Mrs. W." His tone altered a bit. He spoke more softly, gently, the way a widow speaks of her dead husband. Or, indeed, the way a widower speaks of his dead husband. "He used to say it was harder being black in this country than gay. Gays can always pass for straight; but blacks can't always pass for white. And most can never pass."

"And what do you think now?"

"Mrs. W., I think *life* is hard, you know?"

"Yes. I know."

VI

100 Death had first introduced itself to Maggie when she was a child. Her grandfather and grandmother both died before she was five; her father died when she was nine; her mother when she was twenty-five; over the years all her brothers except one. Her husband ten years ago. Her first memories of death: watching the women wash a cold body: the look of brown skin darkening, hardening: the corpse laid out on a cooling board, wrapped in a winding-cloth, before interment: fear of ghosts, bodyless souls: troubled sleep. So much had changed in seventy years; now there were embalming, funeral homes, morticians, insurance policies, bronze caskets, a bureaucratic wall between deceased and bereaved. Among the many things she regretted about Edward's death was not being able to touch his body. It made his death less real. But so much about the world seemed unreal to her these dark, dismal, and gloomy days. Now the flat earth was said to be round and bumblebees were not supposed to fly.

What was supposed to be and what truly was. Maggie learned these things from magazines and television and books; she loved to read. From her first week in that small schoolhouse with Miss Clara Oxendine, she had wanted to be a teacher. School: the scratchy chalkboard, the dusty-smelling textbooks, labyrinthine grammar and spelling and arithmetic, geography, reading out loud, giving confidence to the boy who would never learn to read well, correcting addition and subtraction problems, the taste and the scent of the schoolroom, the heat of the potbellied stove in January. She liked that small world; for her it was large. Yet how could she pay for enough education to become a teacher? Her mother would smile, encouragingly, when young Maggie would ask her, not looking up from her sewing, and merely say: "We'll find a way."

However, when she was fourteen she met a man named Thomas Williams, he sixteen going on thirty-nine. Infatuation replaced her dreams and murmured to her in languages she had never heard before, whispered to her another tale: *You will be a merchant's wife.*

Thomas Williams would come a-courting on Sunday evenings for two years, come driving his father's red Ford truck, stepping out with his biscuit-shined shoes, his one good Sunday suit, his hat cocked at an impertinent angle, and a smile that would make cold butter drip. But his true power lay in his tongue. He would spin yarns and tell tales that would make the oldest storyteller slap his knee and declare: "Hot damn! Can't that boy lie!" He could talk a possum out of a tree. He spoke to Maggie about his dream of opening his own store, a dry-goods store, and then maybe two or three or four. An audacious dream for a seventeen-year-old black boy, son of a farmer in 1936—and he promised, oh, how he promised, to keep Maggie by his side through it all.

Thinking back, on the other side of time and dreams, where fantasies and wishing had been realized, where she sat rich and alone, Maggie wondered what Thomas Williams could possibly have seen in that plain brown girl. Himself the son of a farmer with his own land, ten sons and two daughters, all married and doing well. There she was, poorer than a skinned rabbit, and not that pretty. Was he looking for a woman who would not flinch at hard work?

Somehow, borrowing from his father, from his brothers, working two, three jobs 105 at the shipyards, in the fields, with Maggie taking in sewing and laundry, cleaning houses, saving, saving, saving, they opened their store; and were married. Days, weeks, years of days, weeks of days, weeks of inventory and cleaning and waiting on people and watching over the dry-goods store, which became a hardware store in the sixties while the one store became two. They were prosperous; they were respected; they owned property. At seventy she now wanted for nothing. Long gone was the dream of a schoolhouse and little children who skinned their knees and the teaching of the ABCs. Some days she imagined she had two lives and she preferred the original dream to the flesh-and-blood reality.

Now, at least, she no longer had to fight bitterly with her pompous, self-satisfied, driven, blaspheming husband, who worked seven days a week, sixteen hours a day, money-grubbing and mean though—outwardly—flamboyantly generous; a man who lost interest in her bed after her first and only son, Thomas Jr., arrived broken in heart, spirit, and brain upon delivery; a son whose only true achievement in life was to illegitimately produce Edward by some equally brainless waif of a girl, now long vanished; a son who practically thrust the few-week-old infant into Maggie's arms, then flew off to a life of waste, sloth, petty crime, and finally a menial job in one of her stores and an ignoble marriage to a woman who could not conceal her greedy wish for Maggie to die.

Her life now was life that no longer had bite or spit or fire. She no longer worked. She no longer had to worry about Thomas's philandering and what pretty young thing he was messing with now. She no longer had the little boy whom Providence seemed to have sent her to maintain her sanity, to moor her to the Earth, and to give her vast energies focus.

In a world not real, is there truly guilt in willing reality to cohere through the life of another? Is that such a great sin? Maggie had turned to the boy—young, brown, handsome—to hold on to the world itself. She now saw that clearly. How did it happen? The mental slipping and sliding that allowed her to meld and mess and confuse her life with his, his rights with her wants, his life with her wish? He would not be like his father or his grandfather; he would rise up, go to school, be strong, be honest, upright. He would be; she would be . . . a feat of legerdemain; a sorcery of vicariousness in which his victory was her victory. He was her champion. Her hope.

Now he was gone. And now she had to come to terms with this news of his being "gay," as the world called what she had been taught was an unholy abomination. Slowly it all came together in her mind's eye: Edward.

110   He should have known better. I should have known better. I must learn better.

VII

They stood there at the end of the row, all of them waiting for the tractor to arrive and for the Reverend Hezekiah Barden to save the soul of Morton Henry.

Morton saw them standing there from his mount atop the green John Deere as it bounced across the broken soil. Maggie could make out the expression on his face: confusion. Three blacks and a white man out in the fields to see him. Did his house burn down? His wife die? The President declare war on Russia?

A big, red-haired, red-faced man, his face had so many freckles he appeared splotched. He had a big chew of tobacco in his left jaw and he spat out the brown juice as he came up the edge of the row and put the clutch in neutral.

"How you all today? Miss Maggie?"

115   "Hey, Morton."

Barden started right up, thumbs in his suspenders, and reared back on his heels. "Now I spect you're a God-fearing man?"

"Beg pardon?"

"I even spect you go to church from time to time?"

"Church? Miss Maggie, I—"

120   The Reverend held up his hand. "And I warrant you that your preacher—where *do* you go to church, son?"

"I go to—wait a minute. What's going on here? Miss Maggie—"

Henrietta piped up. "It's Sunday! You ain't supposed to be working and plowing fields on a Sunday!"

Morton Henry looked over to Maggie, who stood there in the bright sun, then to Gabriel, as if to beg him to speak, make some sense of this curious event. He scratched his head. "You mean to tell me you all come out here to tell me I ain't suppose to plow this here field?"

"Not on Sunday you ain't. It's the Lord's Day."

"The Lord's Day?" Morton Henry was visibly amused. He tongued at the wad of 125
tobacco in his jaw. "The Lord's Day." He chuckled out loud.

"Now it ain't no laughing matter, young man." The Reverend's voice took on a dark
tone.

Morton seemed to be trying to figure out who Gabriel was. He spat. "Well, I tell
you, Reverend. If the Lord wants to come plow these fields I'd be happy to let him."

"You . . ." Henrietta stomped her foot, causing dust to rise. "You can't talk about
the Lord like that. You're using His name in vain."

"I'll talk about Him any way I please to." Morton Henry's face became redder by
the minute. "I got two jobs, five head of children, and a sick wife, and the Lord don't
seem too worried about that. I spect I ain't gone worry to much about plowing this here
field on His day none neither."

"Young man, you can't—"   130

Morton Henry looked to Maggie. "Now, Miss Maggie, this is your land, and if
you don't want me to plow it, I'll give you back your lease and you can pay me my
money and find somebody else to tend this here field!"

Everybody looked at Maggie. How does this look, she couldn't help thinking, a
black woman defending a white man against a black minister? Why the *hell* am I here
having to do this? she fumed. Childish, hypocritical idiots and fools. Time is just slipping, slipping away and all they have to do is fuss and bother about other folk's business while their own houses are burning down. God save their souls. She wanted to
yell this, to cuss them out and stomp away and leave them to their ignorance. But in
the end, what good would it do?

She took a deep breath. "Morton Henry. You do what you got to do. Just like the
rest of us."

Morton Henry bowed his head to Maggie, "Ma'am," turned to the others with a
gloating grin, "Scuse me," put his gear in first, and turned down the next row.

"Well—"   135

Barden began to speak but Maggie just turned, not listening, not wanting to hear,
thinking: When, Lord, oh when will we learn? Will we ever? *Respect,* she thought. Oh
how complicated.

They followed Maggie, heading back to the house, Gabriel beside her, tall and
silent, the afternoon sunrays romping in his black hair. How curious the world had become that she would be asking a white man to exonerate her in the eyes of her own
grandson; how strange that at seventy, when she had all the laws and rules down pat,
she would have to begin again to learn. But all this stuff and bother would have to come
later, for now she felt so, so tired, what with the weekend's activities weighing on her
three-score-and-ten-year-old bones and joints; and she wished it were sunset, and
she alone on her patio, contemplating the roundness and flatness of the earth, and
slipping softly and safely into sleep.

CRITICAL THINKING QUESTIONS

1. If Reverend Barden and Henrietta can be said to represent the values of their community, Tims Creek, then Edward, Gabriel, and Morton Henry represent an implicit challenge to those values.
   a. List the values that the Reverend and Henrietta represent.
   b. List the values that Edward, Gabriel, and Morton represent.
   c. Identify specific passages which show Maggie as one who is caught between these two forces.

2. On page 158, Maggie says she must "realign her thinking." Describe the stages of Maggie's realigned thinking as she navigates her way between the two forces you described in question 1.

3. Consider the following examples of *figurative language* (see Glossary) in Kenan's story:

   • the flatness of the Earth
   • the angel Gabriel
   • the dream and sleep

   How do these images reveal aspects of Maggie's conflict?

WRITING TOPICS

1. Readers might identify two quite different implied claims in the story: Some might believe Maggie is presented as a positive force for change in her provincial society, a person who becomes more tolerant and will likely influence others; on the other hand, some readers might believe Maggie is presented as a negative force in her community, a person who has lost her bearing and threatens the stability of her community. Choose one of these ways of reading the story and defend your choice.

2. In the last paragraph of the story, Maggie says she must "begin to learn." Describe a time when you had to learn a new way of thinking.

3. "The Foundations of the Earth" presents an implied claim about homosexuality and about religion. Write an essay in which you *briefly* articulate that argument; then develop your own argument to defend, challenge, or qualify Kenan's implied claim. Use textual evidence, as well as evidence from your own direct observations and experience to support your claim.

Maile Meloy (b. 1972)

Ranch Girl

If you're white, and you're not rich or poor but somewhere in the middle, it's hard to have worse luck than to be born a girl on a ranch. It doesn't matter if your dad's the foreman or the rancher—you're still a ranch girl, and you've been dealt a bad hand.

She's the foreman's daughter. She grew up on Ted Haskell's Running-H cattle ranch, in the foreman's house, on the dirt road between Haskell's place and the barn. There are two bedrooms with walls made of particleboard, one bathroom (no tub), muddy boots and jackets in the living room, and a kitchen that's never used. The front door is painted with Haskell's brand—an H slanted to the right—and for a long time she didn't know that an H normally stands up straight. No one from school ever visits the ranch, so she's kept her room the way she decorated it at ten: a pink comforter on the bed, horse posters on the walls, plastic horse models on the shelves. There's a cow dog with a ruined hip, a barn cat who sleeps in the rafters, and, until he dies, a runt calf named Minute, who cries at night outside the front door.

She helps her dad when the other hands are busy, wading after him into an irrigation ditch, or rounding up a stray cow-calf pair. Her mother used to help, too—she sits a horse better than any of the hands—but then she took an office job in town, and bought herself a house to be close to work. That was the story, anyway; her mom hasn't shown up at the ranch since junior high. Her dad works late now, comes home tired and opens a beer. She brings him cheese and crackers, and watches him fall asleep in his chair.

Down the road, at the ranch house, Ted Haskell grills steaks from his cows every night. He's been divorced for years, but he's never learned how to cook anything except grilled steak. Whenever she's there to visit Haskell's daughter Carla, who's in her class at school, Haskell tries to get her to stay for dinner. He says that she's too thin and that a good beefsteak will make her strong. But she doesn't like leaving her dad alone, and Haskell's joking embarrasses her, so she walks home hungry.

When she's sixteen and starts going out at night, Haskell's ranch house is the   5
best place to get ready. Carla has her own bathroom, with a big mirror, where they curl their hair into ringlets and put on blue eyeshadow. She and Carla wear matching Wranglers, and when it gets cold she wears knitted gloves with rainbow-striped fingers that the boys love to look at when they get drunk out on the Hill.

The Hill is the park where everyone stands and talks after they get bored driving their cars in circles on the drag. The cowboys are always on the Hill, and there's a fight every night; on a good night, there are five or six. On a good night, someone gets slid across the asphalt on his back, T-shirt riding up over his bare skin. It doesn't matter what the fights are about—no one ever knows—all that matters is that Andy Tyler always wins. He's the one who slides the other guy into the road. Afterward, he gets casual, walks over with his cowboy-boot gait, takes a button from the school blood drive off his shirt (and he always seems to have a button), and reads it aloud: "'I Gave Blood

Today', " he says. "Looks like you did, too," and then he pins the button to the other guy's shirt. He puts his jean jacket back on and hides a beer inside it, his hand tucked in like Napoleon's, and smiles that invincible smile of his.

"Hey," he says. "Do that rainbow thing again."

She waves her gloved hands in fast arcs, fingers together so the stripes line up.

Andy laughs, and grabs her hands, and says, "Come home and fuck me."

10   But she doesn't. She walks away. And Andy leaves the Hill without saying good-bye, and rolls his truck in a ditch for the hundredth time, but a buddy of his dad's always tows him, and no one ever calls the cops.

Virginity is as important to rodeo boys as it is to Catholics, and she doesn't go home and fuck Andy Tyler because, when she finally gets him, she wants to keep him. But she likes his asking. Some nights, he doesn't ask. Some nights, Lacey Estrada climbs into Andy's truck, dark hair bouncing in soft curls on her shoulders, and moves close to Andy on the front seat as they drive away. Lacey's dad is a doctor, and she lives in a big white house where she can sneak Andy into her bedroom without waking anyone up. But cowboys are romantics; when they settle down they want the girl they haven't fucked.

When Haskell marries an ex-hippie, everyone on the ranch expects trouble. Suzy was a beauty once; now she's on her third husband and doesn't take any shit. Suzy reads tarot cards, and when she lays them out to answer the question of Andy Tyler, the cards say to hold out for him.

On the spring cattle drive, she shows Suzy how to ride behind the mob and stay out of the dust. Suzy talks about her life before Haskell: she has a Ph.D. in anthropology, a police record for narcotics possession, a sorority pin, and a ski-bum son in Jackson Hole. She spent her twenties throwing dinner parties for her first husband's business clients—that, she says, was her biggest mistake—and then the husband ran off with one of her sorority sisters. She married a Buddhist next. "Be interesting in your twenties," Suzy says. "Otherwise you'll want to do it in your thirties or forties, when it wreaks all kinds of havoc, and you've got a husband and kids."

She listens to Suzy talk and says nothing. What's wrong with a husband and kids? A sweet guy, a couple of brown-armed kids running around outside—it wouldn't be so bad.

15   There's a fall cattle drive, too, but no one ever wants to come on it. It's cold in November, and the cows have scattered in the National Forest. They're half wild from being out there for months, especially the calves, who are stupid as only calves can be. The cowboys have disappeared, gone back to college or off on binges or to other jobs. So she goes out with her dad and Haskell, the three of them sweating in their heavy coats as they chase down the calves, fighting the herd back to winter pasture before it starts to snow. But it always snows before they finish, and her dad yells at her when her horse slips on the wet asphalt and scrapes itself up.

In grade school, it's O.K. to do well. But by high school, being smart gives people ideas. Science teachers start bugging her in the halls. They tell her Eastern schools have Montana quotas, places for ranch girls who are good at math. She could get scholarships, they say. But she knows, as soon as they suggest it, that if she went to one of those schools she'd still be a ranch girl—not the Texas kind who are débutantes and just happen to have a ranch in the family, and not the horse-farm kind who ride English. Horse people are different, because horses are elegant and clean. Cows are mucusy, muddy, shitty, slobbery things, and it takes another kind of person to live with them. Even her long, curled hair won't help at a fancy college, because prep-school girls don't curl their hair. The rodeo boys like it, but there aren't any rodeo boys out East. So she comes up with a plan: she has to start flunking. She has two and a half years of straight A's, and she has to flunk quietly, not to draw attention. Western Montana College, where Andy Tyler wants to go, will take anyone who applies. She can live cheap in Dillon, and if things don't work out with Andy she already knows half the football team.

When rodeo season begins, the boys start skipping school. She'd skip, too, but the goal is to load up on D's, not to get kicked out or sent into counselling. She paints her nails in class and follows the rodeo circuit on week-ends. Andy rides saddle bronc, but his real event is bull riding. The bull riders have to be a little crazy, and Andy Tyler is a little crazy. He's crazy in other ways, too: two years of asking her to come home and fuck him have made him urgent about it. She dances with him at the all-night grad-uation party, and he catches her around the waist and says he doesn't know a more beautiful girl. At dawn, he leaves for spring rodeo finals in Reno, driving down with his best friend, Rick Marcille, and she goes with Carla to Country Kitchen in a happy fog. She orders a chocolate shake and thinks about dancing with Andy. Then she falls asleep on Carla's bedroom floor, watching cartoons, too tired to make it down the road to bed.

Andy Tyler calls once from Reno, at 2 A.M. She answers the phone before it wakes her dad. Andy's taken second place in the bull riding and won a silver belt buckle and three thousand dollars. He says he'll take her to dinner at the Grub Stake when he gets home. Rick Marcille shouts "Ro-*day*-o!" in the background.

There's a call the next night, too. But it's from Rick Marcille's dad. Rick and Andy rolled the truck somewhere in Idaho, and the doctors don't think Rick will make it, though Andy might. Mr. Marcille sounds angry that Andy's the one who's going to live, but he offers to drive her down there. She doesn't wake her dad; she just goes.

The doctors are wrong. It's Andy who doesn't make it. When she gets to Idaho, he's already dead. Rick Marcille is paralyzed from the neck down. The cops say the boys weren't drinking, that a wheel came loose and the truck rolled, but she guesses the cops are just being nice. It's her turn to be angry, at Mr. Marcille, because his son will live and Andy is dead. But when they leave the hospital, Mr. Marcille falls down on his knees, squeezing her hand until it hurts.

At Andy's funeral, his uncle's band plays, and his family sets white doves free. One won't go, and it hops around the grass at her feet. The morning is already hot and blue, and there will be a whole summer of days like this to get through.

Andy's obituary says he was engaged to Lacey Estrada, which only Lacey or her doctor father could have put in. If she had the guts, she'd buy every paper in town and burn them outside the big white house where Lacey took him home and fucked him. Then Lacey shows up on the Hill with an engagement ring and gives her a sad smile as if they've shared something. If she were one of the girls who gets in fights on the Hill, she'd fight Lacey. But she doesn't; she looks away. They'll all be too old for the Hill once school starts, anyway.

At Western, in the fall, in a required composition class, her professor accuses her of plagiarism because her first paper is readable. She drops his class. Carla gets an A on her biology midterm at the university in Bozeman. She's going to be a big-animal vet. Her dad tells everyone, beaming.

But the next summer, Carla quits college to marry a boy named Dale Banning. The Bannings own most of central Montana, and Dale got famous at the family's fall livestock sale. He'd been putting black bulls on Herefords when everyone wanted purebreds. They said he was crazy, but at the sale Dale's crossbred black-baldies brought twice what the purebreds did. Dale stood around grinning, embarrassed, like a guy who'd beaten his friends at poker.

25   Carla tells her about the engagement in Haskell's kitchen, and says she'll still be working with animals, without slogging through all those classes. "Dale's never been to vet school," Carla says. "But he can feel an embryo the size of a pea inside a cow's uterus."

She's heard Dale use that line on girls before, but never knew it to work so well. Carla's voice has a dreamy edge.

"If I don't marry him now," Carla says, "he'll find someone else."

In his head, Haskell has already added the Banning acreage to his own, and the numbers make him giddy. He forgets about having a vet for a daughter, and talks about the wedding all the time. If Carla backed out, he'd marry Dale himself. For the party, they clear the big barn and kill a cow. Carla wears a high-collared white gown that hides the scar on her neck—half a Running-H—from the time she got in the way at branding, holding a struggling calf. Dale wears a string tie and a black ten-gallon hat, and everyone dances to Andy's uncle's band.

Her mother drives out to the ranch for the wedding; it's the first time she's seen her parents together in years. Her dad keeps ordering whiskeys and her mother gets drunk and giggly. But they sober up enough not to go home together.

30   That winter, her dad quits his job, saying he's tired of Haskell's crap. He leaves the foreman's house and moves in with his new girlfriend, who then announces he can't stay there without a job. He hasn't done anything but ranch work for twenty-five years, so he starts day riding for Haskell again, then working full-time hourly, until he might as well be the foreman.

When she finishes Western, she moves into her mother's house in town. Stacks of paperwork for the local horse-racing board cover every chair and table, and an old leather racing saddle straddles an arm of the couch. Her mother still thinks of herself as a horsewoman, and buys unbroken thoroughbreds she doesn't have time or money to train. She doesn't have a truck or a trailer, or land for pasture, so she boards the horses and they end up as big, useless pets she never sees.

Summer evenings, she and her mother sit on the front step and eat ice cream with chocolate-peanut-butter chunks for dinner. She thinks about moving out, but then her mother might move in with her—and that would be worse.

She isn't a virgin anymore, thanks to a boy she found who wouldn't cause her trouble. He drops by from time to time, to see if things might start up again. They don't. He's nothing like Andy. He isn't the one in her head.

She drives out to see Carla's baby when Carla leaves Dale and moves back home to the Running H. It feels strange to be at the ranch now, with the foreman's house empty and Carla's little boy in the yard, and everything else the same.

"You're so lucky to have a degree and no kid," Carla says. "You can still leave." 35

And Carla is right: She could leave. Apply to grad school in Santa Cruz and live by the beach. Take the research job in Chicago that her chemistry professor keeps calling about. Go to Zihuatenejo with Haskell's friends, who need a nanny. They have tons of room, because in Mexico you don't have to pay property tax if you're still adding on to the house.

But none of these things seem real; what's real is the payments on her car and her mom's crazy horses, the feel of the ranch road she can drive blindfolded, and her dad needing her in November to bring in the cows.

Suzy lays out the tarot cards on the kitchen table. The cards say, Go on, go away. But, she thinks, out there in the world you get old. You don't get old here. Here you can always be a ranch girl. Suzy knows. When Haskell comes in wearing muddy boots, saying, "Hi, baby, Hi, hon," his wife stacks up the tarot cards and kisses him hello. She pours him fresh coffee and puts away the cards that say go.

CRITICAL THINKING QUESTIONS

1. What stereotypes are associated with a "ranch girl"? How do Carla and the narrator reinforce, challenge, or qualify these stereotypes?

2. Read back over the last few paragraphs where the narrator decides to stay where she is, living with her mom and close by the ranch.
   a. What value assumptions about life "out there in the world" and about ranch life does the narrator hold?
   b. Evaluate the narrator's decision to stay rather than to "Go on, go away," as the tarot cards say. Do you think her decision is reasonable and valid? Why or why not?

WRITING TOPIC

What does the author imply about the role of one's childhood environment in shaping individual character and one's life path choices? To what degree do you agree with this claim? Does a person's childhood environment always/often/sometimes/rarely determine his or her character and life path? What evidence can you provide to support your claim?

Ernesto Quiñonez (b. 1966)

from *Bodega Dreams*

Back in Julia de Burgos Junior High, back in the days of my growing up and all that Piri Thomas kinda crap that I will spare you from, there was the English teacher, Mr. Blessington. He kept telling us boys we were all going to end up in jail and that all the girls were going to end up hooking. He would say these things right out loud and the administration wouldn't do anything. I hated Blessington and he knew it. He looked at Blanca with the eyes of a repressed rapist. He thought he was smooth but what he came out looking was creepy. He'd come to school in a suit and tell us that a man with a suit is a man that is valuable and that a man without a suit has no worth. He always did Robert Frost poems with us, which were all right, but after a while we started to hate Robert Frost. Blessington thought he was doing us a service, and that was his error. He was one of those upper-middle-class people who think highly of themselves because they could be making money or something, but no, they have taken the high road and have chosen to "help" poor kids from the ghetto.

On the other hand the science teacher, Jose Tapia, was always lecturing us on how fortunate we were because we were young and Latin. His speeches were at times so fiery and full of passion that every year the principal would try to make Tapia the gym teacher, in hopes of cutting down Tapia's influence over us. But as a science teacher Tapia was state certified and was appointed to our school so there was no way for the principal to get rid of him.

And he didn't want to be called Mr. Tapia, simply Tapia.

One day when Sapo and me were in the eighth grade, Tapia told us, "You speak two languages, you are worth two people." Sapo retorted, "What about the pope? He speaks like a hundred languages, but he ain't worth jack." The class was rolled.

5   "Sapo, do you think the pope would be the pope if he didn't know his hundred languages?" Tapia asked after the laughter died down.

"Nah, if he didn't speak a hundred languages he'd still be pope, because he's white. All popes are white. I ain't never seen no black pope. I ain't seen a Spanish pope, either."

"Hey, Tapia," I said, "I never even seen a black nun." Of course we were just stalling. The truth was we hadn't done our homework and wanted to kill time.

"Or a Chinese nun. All I've ever seen are white nuns," Edwin jumped in, so I figured he hadn't done his homework either. "You can't have a black pope if there are no black nuns." I hated Edwin. When he borrowed a pencil he never gave it back and when school was almost over, he always borrowed loose-leaf paper because he didn't see the point of buying a new notebook.

10   "Yeah, a black nun!" Sapo shouted in agreement.

"Julio, can you shut him up?" Blanca whispered to me. I always sat next to Blanca. I would leave my science book at home on purpose so I could use the excuse of sharing hers. Tapia understood this and, even though we had assigned seats, would always let me move.

"No," I whispered back at Blanca. "Sapo has a point."

"The point is Sapo hasn't done his homework."

"I haven't done mine, either," I said.

"Then this book"—she pulled the science text we were sharing toward her side of the desk—"does you no good."

"Look, forget about the pope," Tapia continued. "I don't care about the pope. The 15 pope is not one of my students. The pope has a good job and there are black nuns and Chinese nuns, too, but that doesn't matter. All that matters is you. I care about you. And I played the same games when I was your age. If you haven't done your homework just tell me." Hands shot up.

Tapia sighed loudly. "Edwin, you didn't do your homework?"

"Yeah, I did."

"Well?"

"Well, I did it, I just didn't bring it." The class laughed and Tapia looked at his roll book. 20

"All right, Edwin, you live on 102nd and Third. That's three blocks from here. You better get your homework at lunchtime or you'd better have it done by then." Edwin nodded his head.

"Sapo, your homework?"

"I didn't do it."

"Why didn't you do it?"

"Because Mr. Blessington told me I was going to end up in jail, so why waste my time doing homework?" We all laughed.

"Sapo, don't you want to prove Blessington wrong?" 25

"Nah, I'd rather not do my homework."

Tapia got upset. He threw down the roll book and began to yell at us. "I don't care what Blessington's been telling you! If you are here it is because you want to be, right? Otherwise don't even come to school, just stay on the street. You can make more money selling pot on the stairwells than coming to my classroom, but if you come— and I want you to come, I like having you here—all I ask is that you make an effort! That's all I ask. Don't give me this nonsense about what Mr. Blessington is telling you. You guys are smart enough to know that it's up to you to become what you want to be. So why even listen to him? I've heard what he says. It's all nonsense." Tapia pointed at one of the girls. "Rita Moreno, she was once like you, is Rita Moreno hooking?" Tapia then pointed at one of the guys. "Reggie Jackson, he was once as young as you, he's half Puerto Rican, is Reggie in jail? They worked hard. That's what you have to do. Just do your work and don't pay attention to Blessington."

So we all quieted down and did our work, even Sapo, although he copied off me. Sapo always copied me but it was no big deal. The next period was English and we hated it because it was Blessington. I was in no mood for Robert Frost, that white-assed crusty old man from some cow state. But I couldn't say that to Blessington. Instead, as politely as I could, I asked, "Mr. Blessington, why do we always do Robert Frost, why can't we do someone else?"

"Because Robert Frost," he said, slowly shaking his head in disbelief as if I was asking something real stupid, "is a major American poet."

30 "Well, I heard that Julia de Burgos was a poet; why don't we do some of her poems?" I said, and the class jumped in with me.

"That's right," Lucy, Blanca's Pentecostal friend whom we used to call Chewbacca, chimed in, "why did they name the school after her? She must have been important."

"Yeah, they didn't name the school Robert Frost Junior High, why we always reading him?" someone else asked. Truth was, I was happy we were killing time. I wanted those forty-five minutes in his class to fly. I wanted to keep this discussion going for as long as possible.

"If any of you have noticed since September," Blessington pointed out, "this is English class, not Spanish. Julia-day-Burgos"—he pronounced her name with a thick accent—"wrote only in Spanish."

"But maybe she wrote in English too. I write in Spanish and in English sometimes," Blanca said to him. Every time Blanca spoke Blessington would leer. It was one of those cartoon monster smiles, where the monster rubs his hands as he thinks of something dastardly.

35 "Listen, you people"—he always called us you people—"Julia-day-Burgos is so obscure it would be hard to find a single poem of hers. In any language." I turned to Blanca and, whispering, asked what *obscure* meant. Sapo was quietly drawing all this time. He drew terribly, but it never stopped him. He mostly did it because he was bored. But I knew he was listening and could jump in any minute.

"But if she is so unknown," I said confidently, emphasizing the word Blanca had provided to let Blessington know that I knew what *obscure* meant, "then I agree with Lucy, why did they name an entire school after her? Why not after someone famous?"

"Finally, a good question," Blessington said, adjusting his tie and buttoning up his blazer. "I'll tell you why: because the people in this district are simpletons, that's why. District Four has no idea what it's doing. The name they chose for this school was probably the worst name they could choose. Why, we teachers didn't even know who she was when they renamed this place."

"Mr. Tapia did," Sapo piped up, leaving his drawing for a minute. We all knew what Blessington was saying was that none of the white teachers knew who she was, and they were the only teachers that mattered.

"Oh, him," Blessington said in a tired voice. "Him again. Well, I heard he's a good science teacher," he said with a smirk, "but we're in English now. You people need to get on with today's work." And it was all right with me because we had chopped off at least fifteen minutes of the period. Blessington then went to the board and wrote, "Analogies Between Frost's Poems and New York City." I turned around and asked Blanca what *analogies* meant. She told me. I laughed.

40 "What similarities?" I called out. Blessington was upset now.

"End of discussion," he said. "Get out your homework." Blessington walked over to Sapo's desk.

"Enrique, where's your homework?" Blessington asked.

"I'm going to jail, so why bother, right?" Sapo kept drawing. "Yo'r the smart guy here, right, can't you figure that out yo'self?" The class went "Oooooh," which Blessington took as a challenge.

"You'll be lucky to even make jail," he said to Sapo.

"Why you snapping at me? I said you were right."   45

"I know I'm right. I'm doing all you people a favor. I say these things to you so you can maybe prove me wrong. Now, it's sad to say, but I've yet to see one of my Puerto Rican students, just one, prove me wrong. And I know it's not going to be Sapo here." Blessington then leaned over and took Sapo's drawing from him and crumpled it in his hands. Sapo got so mad, he shot straight up from his seat and thrust himself at Blessington so they were face to face.

"Thass right, I won't prove you wrong b'cause I'm going to jail for jamming your wife." The class was silent because that wasn't a snap any longer but an insult. They stared each other down for a second or two before Sapo turned around and headed for the door. "Where do you think you're going?" Blessington yelled, and went after Sapo, grabbing him by the shoulder.

"Don't touch me, man!" Sapo yelled, but Blessington didn't listen. I got up from my seat and went over to Sapo.

"Yo, take a chill pill," I said to Sapo. Blessington yelled at me, "I can handle this. Sit back down!" He didn't let go of Sapo. Sapo started to pull himself away and that's when Blessington made the mistake of putting Sapo in a headlock.

"Yo, you choking him!" I yelled, but Blessington kept at it, all the while cursing   50
at Sapo. Blanca and her friend Lucy started to run out of the room to get the teacher next door. Blessington released Sapo and went after Blanca. And that's when Sapo jumped him from behind. Sapo crawled on Blessington as if Blessington were going to give him a piggyback ride. Before Blessington could shake Sapo free, Sapo dug his teeth into the base of the teacher's neck. Blessington screamed; the blood spurted out, running down his back and staining his white shirt collar crimson. Sapo scrambled off Blessington's back as Blessington fell to his knees, pressing the wound with his hands. Then Sapo came around and grabbed Blessington's face in his hands and pulled it toward his own. Sapo spat out a chunk of Blessington's flesh, bouncing it off Blessington's left cheekbone. Covered in blood and saliva, Blessington's eyes were frozen in disbelief. He wasn't screaming. He was in shock. It was only when he saw a piece of his own flesh on the floor that he registered what had happened, and passed out.

Standing in front of the classroom Sapo smiled as only Sapo could; he slowly turned to the class, showing us his shining red teeth. He then calmly walked out of the room. Everyone was stunned. Blanca was the first one to shake herself and ran out of the room. "Help us, help us, Blessington's dying!" she kept yelling down the hall. A minute later the school nurse arrived. When she saw all that blood on the floor she took off her smock and put pressure on Blessington's neck. Meanwhile I went looking for Sapo. He had stopped by the bathroom to rinse his mouth and when he saw me he laughed.

"The nigga had that shit coming." He spat water.

"Sapo, bro, what you gonna do?"

"I could give two fucks," he said. "I never felt better. It's as if I let some fucken courier pigeon go free." At that minute Tapia walked into the bathroom, his face red with fury. It was the same anger he would show us when we let him down by not behaving, by not doing work or getting in trouble.

55   "Did he really have you in a headlock?" Tapia asked Sapo.

"Yeah, I saw it all, Ta—"

"Shut up! I'm asking Sapo!" I quieted down and backed away. Sapo nodded and Tapia paced the bathroom. He sighed loudly. He stopped in front of Sapo and placed both arms on top of Sapo's shoulders.

"Look at me," Tapia said. "Don't say that he had you in a headlock—"

I jumped in. "But he did, Tapia—"

60   "Shut up, Chino! *Coño*, just shut up!" This time I did for good. Tapia breathed hard. His eyes were watery. "Sapo, look at me. If you say he had you in a headlock, when he recovers he will deny it. And it won't matter which of your friends backs you up, they will believe Blessington. Now, you listen to me and you listen good because I don't want you to go to Juvie. The police are on their way. When they ask you why you bit Blessington, you tell them you heard voices. You got that?" Sapo nodded. "You tell them the voices said to bite Blessington. You don't say Blessington said all this bullshit to you or that he had you in a headlock, you just say you heard voices. You got that?" Sapo understood and a slow smirk began to form on his big lips as he nodded. When he had completely registered what Tapia had told him, that smirk became a fullblown smile.

That whole year Sapo saw a shrink and thus avoided juvenile detention. He must have lied, and I bet for a while he loved the opportunity to have an audience for those stories he was so good at making up. It was like getting away with biting Blessington's neck all over again. But then he got tired of it, started blowing off sessions, and ultimately he dropped out of school and moved out on his own. That year something happened to Sapo. He had always been Sapo but that year, after biting Blessington, he started turning into someone who wasn't afraid to die. It was the beginning of the adult Sapo. His was the sneaker you wouldn't want to step on because "sorry" wouldn't cut it. He became that person you wouldn't want to cut off in traffic because he'd pull a knife and slice you. He became that person you wanted on your side so you could unleash him on your enemies. Like the rest of us, Sapo was still a kid, but he was already turning into something else. He had reached that point in existence where he wasn't afraid to hurt anyone who threatened his only source of meaning, his love for himself.

CRITICAL THINKING QUESTIONS

1. Identify the two opposing arguments Mr. Blessington and Mr. Tapia present regarding their students' potential.

2. Do negative arguments carry a stronger emotional impact than positive ones? Support your conclusion with evidence from the story, as well as examples from history.

RESEARCH/WRITING TOPIC—Youth Violence in High Schools

Since the tragedy of the Columbine High School shootings in Colorado in 1999, discussion among school officials, parents, and students has centered on understanding what causes a young person to engage in such violence and how to prevent it. Often the individual seems to be one who feels like an outsider, one who does not feel integrated into the high school community. Do some research on this topic, as well as recall and analyze your own experiences and observations as a high school student. Based on your research and analysis, what factors do you think push some students to the fringe? Advocate specific approaches and strategies high schools might take to reduce the anger within such individuals.

POETRY

⋀⋀

Sherman Alexie (b. 1966)

The Reservation Cab Driver

waits outside the Breakaway Bar
in the '65 Malibu with no windshield.

It's a beer a mile. No exceptions.

He picks up Lester FallsApart
who lives in the West End
5   twelve miles away, good for a half-rack.

When congress raised the minimum wage
the reservation cab driver upped his rates
made it a beer and a cigarette each mile.

10   HUD evicted him
so he wrapped himself in old blankets
and slept in the front seat of his cab.

When the BIA rescinded his benefits
he added a can of commodities for every mile.

15   Seymour climbed in the cab
said, this is a hell of a pony.
Ain't no pony, the reservation cab driver
said, it's a car.

During the powwow, he works 24 hours a day
20   gets paid in quilts, beads, fry bread, firewood.

3 a.m., he picks up Crazy Horse hitchhiking.
Where are you going, asks the reservation cab driver.
Same place you are, Crazy Horse answers
somewhere way up the goddamn road.

CRITICAL THINKING QUESTIONS

1. As you read the poem, you naturally compare this odd situation to the reality most of us accept. Certainly no cab driver in New York City or Los Angeles would work for beer and cigarettes. What does the author wish us to see by creating this contrast?

2. Does the situation described in the poem challenge any assumptions you hold concerning Native Americans?

RESEARCH/WRITING TOPIC—Native American Reservations

A Justice Department report showed that during 1998, there were 110 victims of violent crime for every 1,000 Native Americans, compared with 43 victims per 1,000 blacks, 38 per 1,000 whites, and 22 per 1,000 Asians. Read about the situation on Native American reservations, and write an essay which argues that X is the cause of the disparity indicated by these figures.

Michael Cleary (b. 1945)

Burning Dreams on the Sun

LONG BEACH, Calif. (AP)—A truck driver with 45 weather balloons rigged to a lawn chair took a 45 minute ride ... up to 16,000 feet before he got cold, shot some balloons with a BB gun and crashed into a power line.

Were there too many turnaround loads,
distance measured by all-night diners,
hours yawning through too much coffee,
kidneys throbbing again at 3 a.m.?
Were there too many nights on your hands   5
that hung like chains from the wheel,
monotonous, humdrum motion
droning away the sound of your dream?
And did the darkness ever whisper,
it might not work, it might not,   10
nearly grounding you in mortal shame,
too foolish ever to dream again?
Icarus, too, must have felt like you,
restless with impudent wonder.
No labyrinth could hold him;   15

he flew on wings of feathers and wax
until he burned his dreams on the sun.
But no matter. For a time,
you dared to leave the darkful land,
20   rising high in wacky flight
like an uncouth god, purified by light.

CRITICAL THINKING QUESTIONS

1. What stereotypes are associated with truck drivers?

2. How does Cleary's poem refute those stereotypes?

3. What is the poet's implied *claim of value* about Icarus's and the truck driver's flights? Are you convinced?

Countee Cullen (1903–1946)

Incident

Once riding in old Baltimore,
   Heart-filled, head-filled with glee,
I saw a Baltimorean
   Keep looking straight at me.

5   Now I was eight and very small,
   And he was no whit bigger,
And so I smiled, but he poked out
   His tongue and called me, "Nigger."

I saw the whole of Baltimore
10   From May until December:
Of all the things that happened there
   That's all that I remember.

WRITING TOPICS

1. Sometimes an incident carries with it such emotional force that it blocks any positive experiences that might have been enjoyed. Intellectually, you might argue that it is best to ignore the negative and focus on the positive, but emotions are so powerful they usually prevail. Can you recall and describe an incident when the power of your emotions overwhelmed all the rational arguments you knew to be correct?

2. "Sticks and stones may break my bones, but words will never hurt me." This playground jingle suggests that name calling is harmless, at least, physically. But is it? What happens when we label certain individuals, for example, "enviros," "right wing Bible-thumpers," "illegal aliens"? To what degree, if any, are such labels harmful?

Emily Dickinson (1830–1886)

Much madness is divinest sense

> Much Madness is divinest Sense—
> To a discerning Eye—
> Much Sense—the starkest Madness—
> 'Tis the Majority
> In this, as All, prevail—   5
> Assent—and you are sane—
> Demur—you're straightway dangerous—
> And handled with a Chain—

CRITICAL THINKING QUESTIONS

1. What *value assumptions* about "Madness" does Dickinson's poem refute? To what extent do you agree or disagree with the poet? Cite evidence from your own observation and experience to support your viewpoint. For example, if you have seen the movie, *A Beautiful Mind,* how does it affect your thinking?

2. Majority rule is a democratic principle that we value. As the antithesis of monarchical dictatorship, it is meant to guarantee a government that is "for the people, by the people." Dickinson's poem, however, implies that "Majority" is anything but liberating (lines 7–8). Do you agree or disagree with the poet's perspective on the majority?

WRITING TOPIC

Read "Crazy Courage" by Alma Luz Villanueva (page 198). Does Michael's "crazy courage" support Dickinson's viewpoint on madness? Build on your response to question 1 above and create your own argument about individuality. Cite evidence from the poems, as well as your own experience and observation.

T. S. Eliot (1888–1965)

The Love Song of J. Alfred Prufrock

S o'io credesse che mia risposta fosse
A persona che mai tornasse al mondo,
Questa fiamma staria senza piu scosse.
Ma perciocche giammai di questo fondo
5   *Non torno vivo alcun, s 'i'odo il vero,*
Senza tema d'infamia ti rispondo.[2]

Let us go then, you and I,
When the evening is spread out against the sky
Like a patient etherised upon a table;
10   Let us go, through certain half-deserted streets,
The muttering retreats
Of restless nights in one-night cheap hotels
And sawdust restaurants with oyster-shells:
Streets that follow like a tedious argument
15   Of insidious intent
To lead you to an overwhelming question . . .
Oh, do not ask, "What is it?"
Let us go and make our visit.

In the room the women come and go
20   Talking of Michelangelo.

The yellow fog that rubs its back upon the window-panes,
The yellow smoke that rubs its muzzle on the window-panes
Licked its tongue into the corners of the evening,
Lingered upon the pools that stand in drains,
25   Let fall upon its back the soot that falls from chimneys,
Slipped by the terrace, made a sudden leap,
And seeing that it was a soft October night,
Curled once about the house, and fell asleep.

And indeed there will be time
30   For the yellow smoke that slides along the street,
Rubbing its back upon the window-panes;
There will be time, there will be time
To prepare a face to meet the faces that you meet;

---

[2]"If I believed that my reply were made / to one who could ever climb to the world again/this flame would shake me no more. But since no shade/ever returned—if what I am told is true— / from this blind world into the living light, / without fear of dishonor I answer you."—John Ciardi, trans., *Dante Alighieri, The Inferno* (New American Library, 1954), p. 229.

There will be time to murder and create,
And time for all the works and days of hands　　35
That lift and drop a question on your plate;
Time for you and time for me,
And time yet for a hundred indecisions,
And for a hundred visions and revisions,
Before the taking of a toast and tea.　　40

　In the room the women come and go
Talking of Michelangelo.

　And indeed there will be time
To wonder, "Do I dare?" and, "Do I dare?"
Time to turn back and descend the stair,　　45
With a bald spot in the middle of my hair—
[They will say: "How his hair is growing thin!"]
My morning coat, my collar mounting firmly to the chin,
My necktie rich and modest, but asserted by a simple pin—
[They will say: "But how his arms and legs are thin!"]　　50
Do I dare
Disturb the universe?
In a minute there is time
For decisions and revisions which a minute will reverse.

　For I have known them all already, known them all:—　　55
Have known the evenings, mornings, afternoons,
I have measured out my life with coffee spoons;
I know the voices dying with a dying fall
Beneath the music from a farther room.
　So how should I presume?　　60

　And I have known the eyes already, known them all—
The eyes that fix you in a formulated phrase,
And when I am formulated, sprawling on a pin,
When I am pinned and wriggling on the wall,
Then how should I begin　　65
To spit out all the butt-ends of my days and ways?
　And how should I presume?

　And I have known the arms already, known them all—
Arms that are braceleted and white and bare
[But in the lamplight, downed with light brown hair!]　　70
Is it perfume from a dress
That makes me so digress?
Arms that lie along a table, or wrap about a shawl.
　And should I then presume?　　75
　And how should I begin?

　　　　　*　*　*

Shall I say, I have gone at dusk through narrow streets
And watched the smoke that rises from the pipes
Of lonely men in shirt-sleeves, leaning out of windows? . . .

I should have been a pair of ragged claws
80   Scuttling across the floors of silent seas.

*   *   *

And the afternoon, the evening, sleeps so peacefully!
Smoothed by long fingers,
Asleep . . . tired . . . or it malingers,
Stretched on the floor, here beside you and me.
85   Should I, after tea and cakes and ices,
Have the strength to force the moment to its crisis?
But though I have wept and fasted, wept and prayed,
Though I have seen my head [grown slightly bald] brought in upon a platter,
I am no prophet—and here's no great matter;
90   I have seen the moment of my greatness flicker,
And I have seen the eternal Footman hold my coat, and snicker,
And in short, I was afraid.

And would it have been worth it, after all,
After the cups, the marmalade, the tea,
95   Among the porcelain, among some talk of you and me,
Would it have been worth while,
To have bitten off the matter with a smile,
To have squeezed the universe into a ball
To roll it toward some overwhelming question,
100   To say: "I am Lazarus, come from the dead,
Come back to tell you all, I shall tell you all"—
If one, settling a pillow by her head,

Should say: "That is not what I meant at all.
That is not it, at all."

105   And would it have been worth it, after all,

Would it have been worth while,
After the sunsets and the dooryards and the sprinkled streets,
After the novels, after the teacups, after the skirts that trail along the floor—
And this, and so much more?—
110   It is impossible to say just what I mean!
But as if a magic lantern threw the nerves in patterns on a screen:
Would it have been worth while
If one, settling a pillow or throwing off a shawl,
And turning toward the window, should say:

115   "That is not it at all,
That is not what I meant, at all."

*   *   *

No! I am not Prince Hamlet, nor was meant to be;
Am an attendant lord, one that will do
To swell a progress, start a scene or two,   120
Advise the prince; no doubt, an easy tool,
Deferential, glad to be of use,
Politic, cautious, and meticulous;
Full of high sentence but a bit obtuse;
At times, indeed, almost ridiculous—   125
Almost, at times, the Fool.

  I grow old . . . I grow old . . .
I shall wear the bottoms of my trousers rolled.

  Shall I part my hair behind? Do I dare to eat a peach?
I shall wear white flannel trousers, and walk upon the beach.   130
I have heard the mermaids singing, each to each.

  I do not think that they will sing to me.

  I have seen them riding seaward on the waves
Combing the white hair of the waves blown back
When the wind blows the water white and black.   135

  We have lingered in the chambers of the sea
By sea-girls wreathed with seaweed red and brown
Till human voices wake us, and we drown.

CRITICAL THINKING QUESTIONS

1. In presenting the reader with J. Alfred Prufrock, Eliot is also presenting an argument about an individual's sense of self in modern society. Articulate a claim for this argument.

2. What specific evidence is offered in the poem to support the claim you wrote in question 1?

WRITING TOPIC

Does the claim you articulated apply exclusively to Prufrock, or would you extend it to apply generally to persons today? Write your own argument that either limits or extends the poem's claim; use evidence from the poem and your own experience to support your claim.

Jack Gilbert (b. 1925)

Trying to Sleep

The girl shepherd on the farm beyond has been
taken from school now she is twelve, and her life is over.
I got my genius brother a summer job in the mills
and he stayed all his life. I lived with a woman four
5   years who went crazy later, escaped from the hospital,
hitchhiked across America terrified and in the snow
without a coat, and was raped by most men who gave her
a ride. I crank my heart even so and it turns over.
Ranges high in the sun over continents and eruptions
10   of mortality, through winds and immensities of rain
falling for miles. Until all the world is overcome
by what goes up and up in us, singing and dancing
and throwing down flowers as we continue north taking
the maimed with us, keeping the sad parts carefully.

CRITICAL THINKING QUESTIONS

1. Gilbert lists examples of events that should be very discouraging, if not depressing, to anyone. However, he tell us, "I crank my heart even so and it turns over." What idea is he expressing through this metaphorical language? The short story writer Laura Hendrie writes, "There was no moon yet and the stars were thick, the land stretching out under them as flat and black as a pool of tar." We see her metaphor easily because the image of a pool of tar is quite readily apparent to us. But what does Gilbert mean by "crank and "turn over"?

2. Explain what these last words of the poem mean to you: "taking the maimed with us, keeping the sad parts carefully."

3. In a single sentence, state a claim the poet seems to be making about the human spirit.

Judy Grahn (b. 1940)

Ella, in a square apron, along Highway 80

She's a copperheaded waitress,
tired and sharp-worded, she hides
her bad brown tooth behind a wicked
smile, and flicks her ass
out of habit, to fend off the pass   5
that passes for affection.
She keeps her mind the way men
keep a knife—keen to strip the game
down to her size. She has a thin spine,
swallows her eggs cold, and tells lies.   10
She slaps a wet rag at the truck drivers
if they should complain. She understands
the necessity for pain, turns away
the smaller tips, out of pride, and
keeps a flask under the counter. Once,   15
she shot a lover who misused her child.
Before she got out of jail, the courts had pounced
and given the child away. Like some isolated lake,
her flat blue eyes take care of their own stark
bottoms. Her hands are nervous, curled, ready to scrape.   20
The common woman is as common
as a rattlesnake.

CRITICAL THINKING QUESTIONS

1. Compare and contrast your response to the snake imagery in the poem's opening and closing lines.

2. What is the speaker's *claim of value* about Ella as "the common woman"?

3. On which rhetorical appeal is this poem's argument based? Is this an effective persuasive strategy?

WRITING TOPIC

How does Grahn's waitress attempt to maintain her individuality within her environment? Are her efforts successful? What pressures does your environment exert on your sense of individuality?

Etheridge Knight (1933–1991)

Hard Rock Returns to Prison
from the Hospital for the Criminal Insane

Hard Rock was "known not to take no shit
From nobody," and he had the scars to prove it:
Split purple lips, lumped ears, welts above
His yellow eyes, and one long scar that cut
5   Across his temple and plowed through a thick
Canopy of kinky hair.

The WORD was that Hard Rock wasn't a mean nigger
Anymore, that the doctors had bored a hole in his head,
Cut out part of his brain, and shot electricity
10 Through the rest. When they brought Hard Rock back,
Handcuffed and chained, he was turned loose,
Like a freshly gelded stallion, to try his new status.
And we all waited and watched, like indians at a corral,
To see if the WORD was true.

15 As we waited we wrapped ourselves in the cloak
Of his exploits: "Man, the last time, it took eight
Screws to put him in the Hole." "Yeah, remember when he
Smacked the captain with his dinner tray?" "He set
The record for time in the Hole—67 straight days!"
20 "Ol Hard Rock! man, that's one crazy nigger."
And then the jewel of a myth that Hard Rock had once bit
A screw on the thumb and poisoned him with syphilitic spit.

The testing came, to see if Hard Rock was really tame.
A hillbilly called him a black son of a bitch
25 And didn't lose his teeth, a screw who knew Hard Rock
From before shook him down and barked in his face.
And Hard Rock did *nothing*. Just grinned and looked silly,
His eyes empty like knot holes in a fence.
And even after we discovered that it took Hard Rock
30 Exactly 3 minutes to tell you his first name,
We told ourselves that he had just wised up,
Was being cool; but we could not fool ourselves for long,

And we turned away, our eyes on the ground. Crushed.
He had been our Destroyer, the doer of things
35 We dreamed of doing but could not bring ourselves to do,
The fears of years, like a biting whip,
Had cut grooves too deeply across our backs.

CRITICAL THINKING QUESTIONS

1. How does the poem's speaker use *pathos* appeal?

2. Describe the speaker and assess his *ethos* appeal.

3. How does this poem affect your attitude toward or feelings about prisoners?

RESEARCH WRITING TOPIC—High-Security Prisions

The hospital procedure which Hard Rock was forced to undergo is no longer allowed; however, solitary time is a form of punishment still used in some prisons for misbehavior. Do some research on high-security prisons and the treatment of individuals for infractions of prison rules, particularly, the use of solitary confinement as punishment. Based on your research, write a claim of policy argument on the use of solitary confinement (or other punishments) as a correction method for individual prisoners.

Don Marquis (1878–1937)

the lesson of the moth

i was talking to a moth
the other evening
he was trying to break into
an electric light bulb
and fry himself on the wires   5

why do you fellows
pull this stunt i asked him
because it is the conventional
thing for moths or why
if that had been an uncovered   10
candle instead of an electric
light bulb you would
now be a small unsightly cinder
have you no sense

15
plenty of it he answered
but at times we get tired
of using it
we get bored with the routine
and crave beauty
20
and excitement
fire is beautiful
and we know that if we get
too close it will kill us
but what does that matter
25
it is better to be happy
for a moment

and be burned up with beauty
than to live a long time
and be bored all the while
30
so we wad all our life up
into one little roll
and then we shoot the roll
that is what life is for

it is better to be a part of beauty
35
for one instant and then cease to
exist than to exist forever
and never be a part of beauty
our attitude toward life
is come easy go easy
40
we are like human beings
used to be before they became
too civilized to enjoy themselves

and before i could argue him
out of his philosophy
45
he went and immolated himself
on a patent cigar lighter
i do not agree with him
myself i would rather have
half the happiness and twice
50
the longevity

but at the same time i wish
there was something i wanted
as badly as he wanted to fry himself

CRITICAL THINKING QUESTION

The narrator moth says, "we are like humans beings used to be before they became too civilized to enjoy themselves." However, besides the example of his own life and death, he offers no other concrete examples to show how his claim applies to everyday life. Provide several examples to support the moth's claim.

WRITING TOPIC

Select another insect or animal and, as Marquis has done with the moth, use its voice to articulate its attitude toward life.

Claude McKay (1890–1948)

Outcast

For the dim regions whence my fathers came
My spirit, bondaged by the body, longs.
Words felt, but never heard, my lips would frame;
My soul would sing forgotten jungle songs.
I would go back to darkness and to peace,   5
But the great western world holds me in fee,
And I may never hope for full release
While to its alien gods I bend my knee.
Something in me is lost, forever lost,
Some vital thing has gone out of my heart,   10
And I must walk the way of life a ghost
Among the sons of earth, a thing apart.
For I was born, far from my native clime,
Under the white man's menace, out of time.

CRITICAL THINKING QUESTIONS

1. Use the rhetorical triangle to analyze and evaluate this poem as an argument.
   a. How does the speaker create *ethos* appeal?
   b. How does the speaker use *logos* appeal?
   c. How does the speaker use *pathos* appeal?

2. In your view, is one appeal more persuasive?

Dwight Okita (b. 1958)

In Response to Executive Order 9066

All Americans of Japanese Descent Must Report to Relocation Centers

Dear Sirs:
Of course I'll come. I've packed my galoshes
and three packets of tomato seeds. Janet calls them
"love apples." My father says where we're going
5   they won't grow.
I am a fourteen-year-old girl with bad spelling
and a messy room. If it helps any, I will tell you
I have always felt funny using chopsticks
and my favorite food is hot dogs.
10   My best friend is a white girl named Denise—
we look at boys together. She sat in front of me
all through grade school because of our names:
O'Connor, Ozawa. I know the back of Denise's head very well.
I tell her she's going bald. She tells me I copy on tests.
15   We're best friends.
I saw Denise today in Geography class.
She was sitting on the other side of the room.
"You're trying to start a war," she said, "giving secrets away
to the Enemy, Why can't you keep your big mouth shut?"
20   I didn't know what to say.
I gave her a packet of tomato seeds
and asked her to plant them for me, told her
when the first tomato ripens
to miss me

CRITICAL THINKING QUESTIONS

1. Why does the author choose a fourteen-year-old girl to write this letter? What does this persona or voice offer the reader?

2. Would the letter be less or more convincing if it were written by the girl's father?

3. What evidence might the father select to prove that this order is unfair to innocent people?

**RESEARCH/WRITING TOPIC—Reparations: Japanese
Internment Camps**

During World War II, on February 19, 1942, President Franklin D. Roosevelt is-
sued "Executive Order 9066," which authorized the removal of over 100,000
Americans of Japanese descent from their homes to internment camps. The Civil
Liberties Act of 1989 provided a settlement to these people for their mistreatment.
Research this topic and then write an argument defending or refuting such pay-
ments (reparations).

Mary Oliver (b. 1935)

Wild Geese

You do not have to be good.
You do not have to walk on your knees
for a hundred miles through the desert, repenting.
You only have to let the soft animal of your body love what it loves.
Tell me about despair, yours, and I will tell you mine.   5
Meanwhile the world goes on.
Meanwhile the sun and the clear pebbles of the rain
are moving across the landscapes,
over the prairies and the deep trees,
the mountains and the rivers.   10
Meanwhile the wild geese, high in the clean blue air,
are heading home again.
Whoever you are, no matter how lonely,
the world offers itself to your imagination,
calls to you like the wild geese, harsh and exciting—   15
over and over announcing your place
in the family of things.

CRITICAL THINKING QUESTIONS

1. What *assumptions* about being "good" does Oliver challenge in the poem's first five
   lines?

2. How does the phrase, "family of things," create a distinct perspective on the idea
   of community? What *implied claim* does the poet make about an individual's place
   within his or her community?

3. On which rhetorical appeal—*pathos, logos, ethos*—does the poet rely? Cite examples and discuss their effects on you as the reader.

4. How might the calls of the wild geese be both "harsh and exciting" (line 15)?

WRITING TOPIC

Read Wallace Stevens's "Disillusionment at Ten O'Clock" (page **197**). Compare and contrast the ideas about the value of imagination in Stevens's and Oliver's poems. What role does imagination play in your daily life? Create your own claim about the value of imagination and support your argument with evidence from the two poems and your own experiences and observations. For a different perspective on imagination, you can read and cite evidence from Michael Cleary's "Burning Dreams on the Sun" (page **177**).

Edwin Arlington Robinson (1869–1935)

Richard Cory

Whenever Richard Cory went down town,
We people on the pavement looked at him:
He was a gentleman from sole to crown,
Clean favored, and imperially slim.

5   And he was always quietly arrayed,
And he was always human when he talked;
But still he fluttered pulses when he said;
"Good-morning," and he glittered when he walked.
And he was rich—yes, richer than a king—

10 And admirably schooled in every grace:
In fine, we thought that he was everything
To make us wish that we were in his place.
So on we worked, and waited for the light,
And went without the meat, and cursed the bread;

15 And Richard Cory, one calm summer night,
Went home, and put a bullet through his head.

CRITICAL THINKING QUESTIONS

1. What assumptions do the townspeople make about Richard Cory? On what evidence are those assumptions based?

2. The poem urges the reader to accept another generalization—money does not make people happy. Does your experience cause you to support or reject that generalization?

Muriel Rukeyser (b. 1913–1980)

The Lost Romans

Where are they, not those young men, not those young women
Who walked among the bullet-headed Romans with their roads,
their symmetry, their iron rule—
We know the dust and bones they are gone to, those young Romans
Who stood against the bitter imperial, their young green life with its
poems—
Where are the poems made music against the purple   5
Setting their own purple up for a living sign,
Bright fire of some forgotten future against empire,
Their poems in the beautiful Roman tongue
Sex-songs, love-poems, freedom-songs?
Not only the young, but the old and in chains,   10
The slaves in their singing, the fierce northern gentle blond rhythms,
The Judean cantillations, lullabies of Carthage,
Gaul with her cries, all the young Roman rebels,
Where are their songs? Who will unlock them,
Who will find them for us, in some undiscovered painted cave   15
For we need you, sisters, far brothers, poems of our lost Rome.

CRITICAL THINKING QUESTIONS

1. Reading this poem as an argument that is a "call to action," whom is the poet addressing and what action is she advocating?

2. On which rhetorical appeal does the poet's argument rely? Provide some examples and evaluate their persuasiveness.

WRITING TOPIC

Does Rukeyser's argument speak directly to you as an individual? Why or why not?

Cathy Song (b. 1955)

Lost Sister

1

In China,
even the peasants
named their first daughters
Jade—
5   the stone that in the far fields
could moisten the dry season,
could make men move mountains
for the healing green of the inner hills
glistening like slices of winter melon.
10   And the daughters were grateful:
They never left home.
To move freely was a luxury
stolen from them at birth.
Instead, they gathered patience;
15   learning to walk in shoes
the size of teacups,
without breaking—
the arc of their movements
as dormant as the rooted willow,
20   as redundant as the farmyard hens.
But they traveled far
in surviving,
learning to stretch the family rice,
to quiet the demons,
25   the noisy stomachs.

2

There is a sister
across the ocean,
who relinquished her name,
diluting jade green
30   with the blue of the Pacific.
Rising with a tide of locusts,
she swarmed with others
to inundate another shore.
In America,
35   there are many roads
and women can stride along with men.

But in another wilderness,
the possibilities,
the loneliness,
can strangulate like jungle vines. 40
The meager provisions and sentiments
of once belonging—
fermented roots, Mah-Jong tiles and firecrackers—set but
a flimsy household
in a forest of nightless cities. 45
A giant snake rattles above,
spewing black clouds into your kitchen.
Dough-faced landlords
slip in and out of your keyholes,
making claims you don't understand, 50
tapping into your communication systems
of laundry lines and restaurant chains.
You find you need China:
your one fragile identification,
a jade link 55
handcuffed to your wrist.
You remember your mother
who walked for centuries,
footless—
and like her, 60
you have left no footprints,
but only because
there is an ocean in between,
the unremitting space of your rebellion.

CRITICAL THINKING QUESTIONS

1. What *value assumptions* about the individual and freedom does this poem challenge?

2. The poet implies that the sister should have stayed in China. Do you agree? Why or why not?

Gary Soto (b. 1952)

Mexicans Begin Jogging

At the factory I worked
In the fleck of rubber, under the press
Of an oven yellow with flame,
Until the border patrol opened
5   Their vans and my boss waved for us to run.
"Over the fence, Soto," he shouted,
And I shouted that I was American.
"No time for lies," he said, and pressed
A dollar in my palm, hurrying me
10   Through the back door.
Since I was on his time, I ran
And became the wag to a short tail of Mexicans—
Ran past the amazed crowds that lined
The streets and blurred like photographs, in rain.
I ran from that industrial road to the soft
15   Houses where people paled at the turn of an autumn sky.
What could I do but yell *vivas*
To baseball, milkshakes, and those sociologists
Who would clock me
20   As I jog into the next century
On the power of a great, silly grin.

CRITICAL THINKING QUESTIONS

1. Word choice or *diction* can be a strong element in a successful argument because words carry with them a range of subtle meanings beyond their literal meaning. Look up the terms *denotation* and *connotation* in the book's Glossary and then in a paragraph explain the connotative meaning of the word *jogging* as Soto uses it in his poem. How do jogging, baseball, and milk shakes correlate to the world the Mexican workers experience? When, in fact, he is running away from the immigration authorities, why would Soto say, I "jog into the next century"? Why would Mexican immigrants want to begin jogging?

2. In the poem Soto says he is an American; however, his coworkers are illegal immigrants and face deportation. These workers and their employers break the law, and yet our economy seems to depend on just such illegal immigrants to maintain productivity. After reading about immigration as it impacts the U.S. economy, create your own *claim of policy* regarding this issue, and list at least three pieces of evidence you might use in its support.

WRITING TOPIC

Reread the discussion of moral argument in the introduction to this chapter. Do you believe the United States has a moral obligation to assist people living in Third World countries? Write an essay supporting your position.

Wallace Stevens (1879–1955)

Disillusionment at Ten O'Clock

The houses are haunted
By white night-gowns.
None are green,
Or purple with green rings,
Or green with yellow rings,   5
Or yellow with blue rings.
None of them are strange,
With socks of lace
And beaded ceintures.
People are not going   10
To dream of baboons and periwinkles.
Only, here and there, an old sailor,
Drunk and asleep in his boots,
Catches tigers
In red weather.   15

CRITICAL THINKING QUESTIONS

1. Stevens seems to regret the fact that residents of these houses are lacking in imagination; hence, the key word in the title of the poem, "Disillusionment." Bring to mind a quiet, middle-class, residential street in this country. Do you believe the people living on this street have traded their imaginations for the comfort of conformity?

2. The poet's underlying *assumption* here is that not having an imagination is a bad thing; he assumes you agree. Do you? Is it somehow better to be "an old sailor, Drunk and asleep in his boots" than to be someone living without an imagination?

WRITING TOPIC

Read "Wild Geese" by Mary Oliver (page 191) and "Burning Dreams on the Sun" by Michael Cleary (page 177). Also, read a definition of the term *imagination*. For this task, go beyond the dictionary and consult a psychology textbook or similar academic work. Write an essay in which you argue that a person can or cannot lead a fully productive life without imagination.

Alma Luz Villanueva (b. 1944)

Crazy Courage

To Michael B.
Why do I think of Michael . . .
He came to my fiction class
as a man (dressed in men's
clothes); then he came
5   to my poetry class
as a woman (dressed in women's
clothes; but he was still
a man under the clothes).
Was I moved in the face of
10   such courage (man/woman
woman/man) . . .
Was I moved by the gentleness
of his masculinity; the strength
of his femininity . . .
15   His presence at the class poetry
reading, dressed in a miniskirt,
high boots, bright purple tights,
a scooped-neck blouse, carrying
a single, living, red rose, in a
20   vase, to the podium (the visitors,
not from the class, shocked—
the young, seen-it-all MTV crowd—
into silence as he's introduced,
"Michael . . . ") And what it was, I think,
25   was his perfect dignity, the offering
of his living, red rose to the perceptive,
to the blind, to the amused, to the impressed,

to those who would kill him, and
to those who would love him.
And of course I remember the surprise   30
of his foamy breasts as we hugged
goodbye, his face blossomed
open, set apart, the pain of it,
the joy of it (the crazy courage
to be whole, as a rose is   35
whole, as a child is
whole before they're
punished for including
everything in their
innocence.)   40

CRITICAL THINKING QUESTIONS

1. In judging Michael, what is the speaker's *claim of value* about courage? On what evidence is this claim based? Are you convinced?

2. What values underlie our attitudes about nonconformist or unconventional behavior? How do these value assumptions inform our judgments about those individuals who exhibit nonconformist behavior?

WRITING TOPIC

In the United States, we often say we value expressions of individuality, yet people who run counter to prevailing cultural norms sometimes face some degree of discrimination. Using at least two specific examples, argue that this discrimination is either justified or unjustified.

NONFICTION

∿∿

Sherman Alexie (b. 1966)
Superman and Me

I learned to read with a Superman comic book. Simple enough, I suppose. I cannot recall which particular Superman comic book I read, nor can I remember which villain he fought in that issue. I cannot remember the plot, nor the means by which I obtained the comic book. What I can remember is this: I was 3 years old, a Spokane Indian boy living with his family on the Spokane Indian Reservation in eastern Washington state. We were poor by most standards, but one of my parents usually managed to find some minimum-wage job or another, which made us middle-class by reservation standards. I had a brother and three sisters. We lived on a combination of irregular paychecks, hope, fear, and government surplus food.

My father, who is one of the few Indians who went to Catholic school on purpose, was an avid reader of westerns, spy thrillers, murder mysteries, gangster epics, basketball player biographies, and anything else he could find. He bought his books by the pound at Dutch's Pawn Shop, Goodwill, Salvation Army, and Value Village. When he had extra money, he bought new novels at supermarkets, convenience stores, and hospital gift shops. Our house was filled with books. They were stacked in crazy piles in the bathroom, bedrooms, and living room. In a fit of unemployment-inspired creative energy, my father built a set of book-shelves and soon filled them with a random assortment of books about the Kennedy assassination, Watergate, the Vietnam War, and the entire 23-book series of the Apache westerns. My father loved books, and since I loved my father with an aching devotion, I decided to love books as well.

I can remember picking up my father's books before I could read. The words themselves were mostly foreign, but I still remember the exact moment when I first understood, with a sudden clarity, the purpose of a paragraph. I didn't have the vocabulary to say "paragraph," but I realized that a paragraph was a fence that held words. The words inside a paragraph worked together for a common purpose. They had some specific reason for being inside the same fence. This knowledge delighted me. I began to think of everything in terms of paragraphs. Our reservation was a small paragraph within the United States. My family's house was a paragraph, distinct from the other paragraphs of the LeBrets to the north, the Fords to our South, and the Tribal School to the west. Inside our house, each family member existed as a separate paragraph but still had genetics and common experiences to link us. Now, using this logic, I can see my changed family as an essay of seven paragraphs: mother, father, older brother, the deceased sister, my younger twin sisters, and our adopted little brother.

At the same time I was seeing the world in paragraphs, I also picked up that Superman comic book. Each panel, complete with picture, dialogue, and narrative was a three-dimensional paragraph. In one panel, Superman breaks through a door. His suit is red, blue, and yellow. The brown door shatters into many pieces. I look at the narrative above the picture. I cannot read the words, but I assume it tells me that "Superman is breaking down the door." Aloud, I pretend to read the words and say, "Superman is breaking down the door." Words, dialogue, also float out of Superman's mouth. Because he is breaking down the door, I assume he says, "I am breaking down the door." Once again, I pretend to read the words and say aloud, "I am breaking down the door." In this way, I learned to read.

This might be an interesting story all by itself. A little Indian boy teaches himself to read at an early age and advances quickly. He reads "Grapes of Wrath" in kindergarten when other children are struggling through "Dick and Jane." If he'd been anything but an Indian boy living on the reservation, he might have been called a prodigy. But he is an Indian boy living on the reservation and is simply an oddity. He grows into a man who often speaks of his childhood in the third person, as if it will somehow dull the pain and make him sound more modest about his talents. 5

A smart Indian is a dangerous person, widely feared and ridiculed by Indians and non-Indians alike. I fought with my classmates on a daily basis. They wanted me to stay quiet when the non-Indian teacher asked for answers, for volunteers, for help. We were Indian children who were expected to be stupid. Most lived up to those expectations inside the classroom but subverted them on the outside. They struggled with basic reading in school but could remember how to sing a few dozen powwow songs. They were monosyllabic in front of their non-Indian teachers but could tell complicated stories and jokes at the dinner table. They submissively ducked their heads when confronted by a non-Indian adult but would slug it out with the Indian bully who was 10 years older. As Indian children, we were expected to fail in the non-Indian world. Those who failed were ceremonially accepted by other Indians and appropriately pitied by non-Indians.

I refused to fail. I was smart. I was arrogant. I was lucky. I read books late into the night, until I could barely keep my eyes open. I read books at recess, then during lunch, and in the few minutes left after I had finished my classroom assignments. I read books in the car when my family traveled to powwows or basketball games. In shopping malls, I ran to the bookstores and read bits and pieces of as many books as I could. I read the books my father brought home from the pawnshops and secondhand. I read the books I borrowed from the library. I read the backs of cereal boxes. I read the newspaper. I read the bulletins posted on the walls of the school, the clinic, the tribal offices, the post office. I read junk mail. I read auto-repair manuals. I read magazines. I read anything that had words and paragraphs. I read with equal parts joy and desperation. I loved those books, but I also knew that love had only one purpose. I was trying to save my life.

Despite all the books I read, I am still surprised I became a writer. I was going to be a pediatrician. These days, I write novels, short stories, and poems. I visit schools and teach creative writing to Indian kids. In all my years in the reservation school system, I was never taught how to write poetry, short stories, or novels. I was certainly never taught that Indians wrote poetry, short stories, and novels. Writing was something beyond Indians. I cannot recall a single time that a guest teacher visited the reservation. There must have been visiting teachers. Who were they? Where are they now? Do they exist? I visit the schools as often as possible. The Indian kids crowd the classroom. Many are writing their own poems, short stories, and novels. They have read my books. They have read many other books. They look at me with bright eyes and arrogant wonder. They are trying to save their lives. Then there are the sullen and already defeated Indian kids who sit in the back rows and ignore me with theatrical precision. The pages of their notebooks are empty. They carry neither pencil nor pen. They stare out the window. They refuse and resist. "Books," I say to them. "Books," I say. I throw my weight against their locked doors. The door holds. I am smart. I am arrogant. I am lucky. I am trying to save our lives.

CRITICAL THINKING QUESTIONS

1. Before he could read, Alexie says he "understood with a sudden clarity, the purpose of a paragraph. . . . a fence that held words" (par. 3). Pick a paragraph from Alexie's essay and analyze it as an example of his fence *metaphor* (see Glossary). You may choose to articulate your analysis with visual, as well as textual, images.

2. Alexie states, "A smart Indian is a dangerous person, widely feared by Indians and non-Indians alike" (par. 5). Does his claim about being smart generally apply to other specific groups? Which ones and why? Are there specific groups where it is okay to be smart? Or are these generalizations no longer valid? Even so, why are some kids, as Alexie says, "sullen and already defeated" (par. 8)? For another example, you can read the selection "from *Bodega Dreams*" by Ernesto Quiñonez (page **170**). Recall your own earlier educational experiences and list specific details to support your perspective.

WRITING TOPIC

Read Scott Russell Sanders's "The Men We Carry in Our Minds" (page 510) and Richard Wright's excerpt from *Black Boy* (page 702). Sanders and Wright provide perspectives on specific individuals who, like Alexie, feel a passion for words, for knowledge as a way to "save my life" (par. 3). What are the similarities and differences between each author's experiences and viewpoints? What does education mean to you? Write an essay in which you examine the value of reading. Draw on your own experiences and observations, as well as ideas in Sanders's, Wright's, and Alexie's essays.

John Hope Franklin (b. 1915)

The Train from Hate

My pilgrimage from racial apprehension—read just plain confusion—to racial tolerance was early and brief. I was 7 years old, and we lived in the all-black town of Rentiesville, Oklahoma. My father had moved to Tulsa where he hoped to have a law
practice that would make it possible for him to support his family. Meanwhile, my
mother, sister, and I would occasionally make the journey to Checotah, six miles away,
to shop for supplies.

One day, we went down, as usual, by railroad. My mother flagged the train and
we boarded. It so happened that when the train stopped, the only place we could enter
was the coach reserved for white people. We did not take notice of this, and as the train
picked up speed, the conductor entered and told us that we would have to move to the
"colored" coach. My mother explained that we were not responsible for where the
coach stopped and we had no other alternative to climbing aboard and finding seats
as soon as possible. She told him that she could not risk the possible injury of her and
her children by going to the "colored" coach while the train was moving. The conductor
seemed to agree and said that he would signal to the engineer to stop the train. When
the train came to a halt, the conductor did not guide us to the coach for African Americans. Instead, he commanded us to leave the train. We had no alternative to stepping
off the train into the woods and beginning the trek back to Rentiesville.

As we trudged along, I began to cry. Taking notice of my sadness, my mother
sought to comfort me by saying that it was not all that far to Rentiesville. I assured
her that I did not mind the walk, but that man, the conductor, was so mean. Why
would he not permit us to ride the train to Checotah?

My mother then gave me my first lesson in race relations. She told me that the
laws required racial separation, but that they did not, could not, make us inferior in
any way. She assured me that the conductor was not superior because he was white,
and I was not inferior because I was black. I must always remember that simple fact,
she said. Then she made a statement that is as vivid and clear to me today as the day
she uttered it. Under no circumstances, she said, should I be upset or distressed because someone sought to demean me. It took too much energy to hate or even to fight
intolerance with one's emotions. She smiled and added that in going home we did not
have far to walk.

It would be too much to claim that my mother's calm talk removed a burden   5
from my shoulders. But it is not too much to say that her observations provided a
sound basis for my attitudes and conduct from that day to this. At that early age, I had
made an important journey. In the future, I remembered that I should not waste my
time or energy lamenting the inability of some members of society to take me as I was.
Instead, I would use my energies to make me a better person and to distance myself
from the perpetrators and purveyors of hate and misunderstanding. I shall always be
happy that my mother taught me that the journey to understanding and tolerance
was more important than the journey to Checotah.

CRITICAL THINKING QUESTIONS

1. Through his personal experience, Franklin argues for a *claim of policy.* Can you articulate that claim?

2. What *assumptions* underlie the thinking of those who put the Mother, Sister, and Son off that train?

Martin Luther King, Jr. (1929–1968)

Letter from Birmingham Jail

April 16, 1963

My Dear Fellow Clergymen:

While confined here in the Birmingham city jail, I came across your recent statement calling my present activities "unwise and untimely." Seldom do I pause to answer criticism of my work and ideas. If I sought to answer all the criticisms that cross my desk, my secretaries would have little time for anything other than such correspondence in the course of the day, and I would have no time for constructive work. But since I feel that you are men of genuine good will and that your criticisms are sincerely set forth, I want to try to answer your statement in what I hope will be patient and reasonable terms.

I think I should indicate why I am here in Birmingham, since you have been influenced by the view which argues against "outsiders coming in." I have the honor of serving as president of the Southern Christian Leadership Conference, an organization operating in every southern state, with headquarters in Atlanta, Georgia. We have some eighty-five affiliated organizations across the South, and one of them is the Alabama Christian Movement for Human Rights. Frequently we share staff, educational and financial resources with our affiliates. Several months ago the affiliate here in Birmingham asked us to be on call to engage in a nonviolent direct-action program if such were deemed necessary. We readily consented, and when the hour came we lived up to our promise. So I, along with several members of my staff, am here because I was invited here. I am here because I have organizational ties here.

But more basically, I am in Birmingham because injustice is here. Just as the prophets of the eighth century B.C. left their villages and carried their "thus saith the Lord" far beyond the boundaries of their home towns, and just as the Apostle Paul left his village of Tarsus and carried the gospel of Jesus Christ to the far corners of the Greco-Roman world, so am I compelled to carry the gospel of freedom beyond my own home town. Like Paul, I must constantly respond to the Macedonian call for aid.

Moreover, I am cognizant of the interrelatedness of all communities and states. I cannot sit idly by in Atlanta and not be concerned about what happens in Birmingham.

Injustice anywhere is a threat to justice everywhere. We are caught in an inescapable network of mutuality, tied in a single garment of destiny. Whatever affects one directly, affects all indirectly. Never again can we afford to live with the narrow, provincial "outside agitator" idea. Anyone who lives inside the United States can never be considered an outsider anywhere within its bounds.

You deplore the demonstrations taking place in Birmingham. But your statement, I am sorry to say, fails to express a similar concern for the conditions that brought about the demonstrations. I am sure that none of you would want to rest content with the superficial kind of social analysis that deals merely with effects and does not grapple with underlying causes. It is unfortunate that demonstrations are taking place in Birmingham, but it is even more unfortunate that the city's white power structure left the Negro community with no alternative.

In any nonviolent campaign there are four basic steps: collection of the facts to   5
determine whether injustices exist; negotiation; self-purification; and direct action. We have gone through all these steps in Birmingham. There can be no gainsaying the fact that racial injustice engulfs this community. Birmingham is probably the most thoroughly segregated city in the United States. Its ugly record of brutality is widely known. Negroes have experienced grossly unjust treatment in the courts. There have been more unsolved bombings of Negro homes and churches in Birmingham than in any other city in the nation. These are the hard, brutal facts of the case. On the basis of these conditions, Negro leaders sought to negotiate with the city fathers. But the latter consistently refused to engage in good-faith negotiation.

Then, last September, came the opportunity to talk with leaders of Birmingham's economic community. In the course of the negotiations, certain promises were made by the merchants—for example, to remove the stores' humiliating racial signs. On the basis of these promises, the Reverend Fred Shuttlesworth and the leaders of the Alabama Christian Movement for Human Rights agreed to a moratorium on all demonstrations. As the weeks and months went by, we realized that we were the victims of a broken promise. A few signs, briefly removed, returned; the others remained.

As in so many past experiences, our hopes had been blasted, and the shadow of deep disappointment settled upon us. We had no alternative except to prepare for direct action, whereby we would present our very bodies as a means of laying our case before the conscience of the local and the national community. Mindful of the difficulties involved, we decided to undertake a process of self-purification. We began a series of workshops on nonviolence, and we repeatedly asked ourselves: "Are you able to accept blows without retaliating?" "Are you able to endure the ordeal of jail?" We decided to schedule our direct-action program for the Easter season, realizing that except for Christmas, this is the main shopping period of the year. Knowing that a strong economic-withdrawal program would be the by-product of direct action, we felt that this would be the best time to bring pressure to bear on the merchants for the needed change.

Then it occurred to us that Birmingham's mayoral election was coming up in March, and we speedily decided to postpone action until after election day. When we discovered that the Commissioner of Public Safety, Eugene "Bull" Connor, had piled up enough votes to be in the run-off, we decided again to postpone action until the day after the run-off so that the demonstrations could not be used to cloud the issues. Like many others, we waited to see Mr. Connor defeated, and to this end we endured postponement after postponement. Having aided in this community need, we felt that our direct action program could be delayed no longer.

You may well ask: "Why direct action? Why sit-ins, marches and so forth? Isn't negotiation a better path?" You are quite right in calling for negotiation. Indeed, this is the very purpose of direct action. Nonviolent direct action seeks to create such a crisis and foster such a tension that a community which has constantly refused to negotiate is forced to confront the issue. It seeks so to dramatize the issue that it can no longer be ignored. My citing the creation of tension as part of the work of the nonviolent-resister may sound rather shocking. But I must confess that I am not afraid of the word "tension." I have earnestly opposed violent tension, but there is a type of constructive, nonviolent tension which is necessary for growth. Just as Socrates felt that it was necessary to create a tension in the mind so that individuals could rise from the bondage of myths and half-truths to the unfettered realm of creative analysis and objective appraisal, so must we see the need for nonviolent gadflies to create the kind of tension in society that will help men rise from the dark depths of prejudice and racism to the majestic heights of understanding and brotherhood.

10   The purpose of our direct-action program is to create a situation so crisis-packed that it will inevitably open the door to negotiation. I therefore concur with you in your call for negotiation. Too long has our beloved Southland been bogged down in a tragic effort to live in monologue rather than dialogue.

One of the basic points in your statements is that the action that I and my associates have taken in Birmingham is untimely. Some have asked: "Why didn't you give the new city administration time to act?" The only answer that I can give to this query is that the new Birmingham administration must be prodded about as much as the outgoing one, before it will act. We are sadly mistaken if we feel that the election of Albert Boutwell as mayor will bring the millennium to Birmingham. While Mr. Boutwell is a much more gentle person than Mr. Connor, they are both segregationists, dedicated to maintenance of the status quo. I have hope that Mr. Boutwell will be reasonable enough to see the futility of massive resistance to desegregation. But he will not see this without pressure from devotees of civil rights. My friends, I must say to you that we have not made a single gain in civil rights without determined legal and nonviolent pressure. Lamentably, it is an historical fact that privileged groups seldom give up their privileges voluntarily. Individuals may see the moral light and voluntarily give up their unjust posture; but, as Reinhold Niebuhr has reminded us, groups tend to be more immoral than individuals.

We know through painful experience that freedom is never voluntarily given by the oppressor; it must be demanded by the oppressed. Frankly, I have yet to engage in a direct-action campaign that was "well timed" in the view of those who have not suffered unduly from the disease of segregation. For years now I have heard the word "Wait!" It rings in the ear of every Negro with piercing familiarity. This "Wait" has almost always meant "Never." We must come to see, with one of our distinguished jurists, that "justice too long delayed is justice denied."

We have waited for more than 340 years for our constitutional and God-given rights. The nations of Asia and Africa are moving with jetlike speed toward gaining political independence, but we still creep at horse-and-buggy pace toward gaining a cup of coffee at a lunch counter. Perhaps it is easy for those who have never felt the stinging darts of segregation to say, "Wait." But when you have seen vicious mobs lynch your mothers and fathers at will and drown your sisters and brothers at whim; when you have seen hate-filled policemen curse, kick and even kill your black brothers and sisters; when you see the vast majority of your twenty million Negro brothers smothering in an airtight cage of poverty in the midst of an affluent society; when you suddenly find your tongue twisted and your speech stammering as you seek to explain to your six-year-old daughter why she can't go to the public amusement park that has just been advertised on television, and see tears welling up in her eyes when she is told that Funtown is closed to colored children, and see ominous clouds of inferiority beginning to form in her little mental sky, and see her beginning to distort her personality by developing an unconscious bitterness toward white people; when you have to concoct an answer for a five-year-old son who is asking: "Daddy, why do white people treat colored people so mean?"; when you take a cross-country drive and find it necessary to sleep night after night in the uncomfortable corners of your automobile because no motel will accept you; when you are humiliated day in and day out by nagging signs reading "white" and "colored"; when your first name becomes "nigger," your middle name becomes "boy" (however old you are) and your last name becomes "John," and your wife and mother are never given the respected title "Mrs."; when you are harried by day and haunted by night by the fact that you are a Negro, living constantly at tiptoe stance, never quite knowing what to expect next, and are plagued with inner fears and outer resentments; when you are forever fighting a degenerating sense of "nobodiness"—then you will understand why we find it difficult to wait. There comes a time when the cup of endurance runs over, and men are no longer willing to be plunged into the abyss of despair. I hope, sirs, you can understand our legitimate and unavoidable impatience.

You express a great deal of anxiety over our willingness to break laws. This is certainly a legitimate concern. Since we so diligently urge people to obey the Supreme Court's decision of 1954 outlawing segregation in the public schools, at first glance it may seem rather paradoxical for us consciously to break laws. One may well ask: "How can you advocate breaking some laws and obeying others?" The answer lies in the fact that there are two types of laws: just and unjust. I would be the first to advocate obeying just laws. One has not only a legal but a moral responsibility to obey just laws. Conversely, one has a moral responsibility to disobey unjust laws. I would agree with St. Augustine that "an unjust law is no law at all."

Now, what is the difference between the two? How does one determine whether 15 a law is just or unjust? A just law is a man-made code that squares with the moral law or the law of God. An unjust law is a code that is out of harmony with the moral law. To put it in the terms of St. Thomas Aquinas: An unjust law is a human law that is not rooted in eternal law and natural law. Any law that uplifts human personality is just. Any law that degrades human personality is unjust. All segregation statutes are unjust because segregation distorts the soul and damages the personality. It gives the segregator a false sense of superiority and the segregated a false sense of inferiority. Segregation, to use the terminology of the Jewish philosopher Martin Buber, substitutes an "I-it" relationship for an "I-thou" relationship and ends up relegating persons to the status of things. Hence segregation is not only politically, economically and sociologically unsound, it is morally wrong and sinful. Paul Tillich has said that sin is separation. Is not segregation an existential expression of man's tragic separation, his awful estrangement, his terrible sinfulness? Thus it is that I can urge men to obey the 1954 decision of the Supreme Court, for it is morally right; and I can urge them to disobey segregation ordinances, for they are morally wrong.

Let us consider a more concrete example of just and unjust laws. An unjust law is a code that a numerical or power majority group compels a minority group to obey but does not make binding on itself. This is *difference* made legal. By the same token, a just law is a code that a majority compels a minority to follow and that it is willing to follow itself. This is *sameness* made legal.

Let me give another explanation. A law is unjust if it is inflicted on a minority that, as a result of being denied the right to vote, had no part in enacting or devising the law. Who can say that the legislature of Alabama which set up that state's segregation laws was democratically elected? Throughout Alabama all sorts of devious methods are used to prevent Negroes from becoming registered voters, and there are some counties in which, even though Negroes constitute a majority of the population, not a single Negro is registered. Can any law enacted under such circumstances be considered democratically structured?

Sometimes a law is just on its face and unjust in its application. For instance, I have been arrested on a charge of parading without a permit. Now, there is nothing wrong in having an ordinance which requires a permit for a parade. But such an ordinance becomes unjust when it is used to maintain segregation and to deny citizens the First-Amendment privilege of peaceful assembly and protest.

I hope you are able to see the distinction I am trying to point out. In no sense do I advocate evading or defying the law, as would the rabid segregationist. That would lead to anarchy. One who breaks an unjust law must do so openly, lovingly, and with a willingness to accept the penalty. I submit that an individual who breaks a law that conscience tells him is unjust, and who willingly accepts the penalty of imprisonment in order to arouse the conscience of the community over its injustice, is in reality expressing the highest respect for law.

20   Of course, there is nothing new about this kind of civil disobedience. It was evidenced sublimely in the refusal of Shadrach, Meshach and Abednego to obey the laws of Nebuchadnezzar, on the ground that a higher moral law was at stake. It was practiced superbly by the early Christians, who were willing to face hungry lions and the excruciating pain of chopping blocks rather than submit to certain unjust laws of the Roman Empire. To a degree, academic freedom is a reality today because Socrates practiced civil disobedience. In our own nation, the Boston Tea party represented a massive act of civil disobedience.

We should never forget that everything Adolf Hitler did in Germany was "legal" and everything the Hungarian freedom fighters did in Hungary was "illegal." It was "illegal" to aid and comfort a Jew in Hitler's Germany. Even so, I am sure that, had I lived in Germany at the time, I would have aided and comforted my Jewish brothers. If today I lived in a Communist country where certain principles dear to the Christian faith are suppressed, I would openly advocate disobeying that country's antireligious laws.

I must make two honest confessions to you, my Christian and Jewish brothers. First, I must confess that over the past few years I have been gravely disappointed with the white moderate. I have almost reached the regrettable conclusion that the Negro's great stumbling block in his stride toward freedom is not the White Citizen's Counciler or the Ku Klux Klanner, but the white moderate, who is more devoted to "order" than to justice; who prefers a negative peace which is the absence of tension to a positive peace which is the presence of justice; who constantly says: "I agree with you in the goal you seek, but I cannot agree with your methods of direct action"; who paternalistically believes he can set the timetable for another man's freedom; who lives by a mythical concept of time and who constantly advises the Negro to wait for a "more convenient season." Shallow understanding from people of good will is more frustrating than absolute misunderstanding from people of ill will. Lukewarm acceptance is much more bewildering than outright rejection.

I had hoped that the white moderate would understand that law and order exist for the purpose of establishing justice and that when they fail in this purpose they become the dangerously structured dams that block the flow of social progress. I had hoped that the white moderate would understand that the present tension in the South is a necessary phase of the transition from an obnoxious negative peace, in which the Negro passively accepted his unjust plight, to a substantive and positive peace, in which all men will respect the dignity and worth of human personality. Actually, we who engage in nonviolent direct action are not the creators of tension. We merely bring to the surface the hidden tension that is already alive. We bring it out in the open, where it can be seen and dealt with. Like a boil that can never be cured so long as it is covered up but must be opened with all its ugliness to the natural medicines of air and light, injustice must be exposed, with all the tension its exposure creates, to the light of human conscience and the air of national opinion before it can be cured.

In your statement you assert that our actions, even though peaceful, must be condemned because they precipitate violence. But is this a logical assertion? Isn't this like condemning a robbed man because his possession of money precipitated the evil act of robbery? Isn't this like condemning Socrates because his unswerving commitment to truth and his philosophical inquiries precipitated the act by the misguided populace in which they made him drink hemlock? Isn't this like condemning Jesus because his unique God-consciousness and never-ceasing devotion to God's will precipitated the evil act of crucifixion? We must come to see that, as the federal courts have consistently affirmed, it is wrong to urge an individual to cease his efforts to gain his basic constitutional rights because the quest may precipitate violence. Society must protect the robbed and punish the robber.

I had also hoped that the white moderate would reject the myth concerning time 25 in relation to the struggle for freedom. I have just received a letter from a white brother in Texas. He writes: "All Christians know that the colored people will receive equal rights eventually, but it is possible that you are in too great a religious hurry. It has taken Christianity almost two thousand years to accomplish what it has. The teachings of Christ take time to come to earth." Such an attitude stems from a tragic misconception of time, from the strangely irrational notion that there is something in the very flow of time that will inevitably cure all ills. Actually, time itself is neutral; it can be used either destructively or constructively. More and more I feel that the people of ill will have used time much more effectively than have the people of good will. We will have to repent in this generation not merely for the hateful words and actions of the bad people but for the appalling silence of the good people. Human progress never rolls in on wheels of inevitability; it comes through the tireless efforts of men willing to be co-workers with God, and without this hard work, time itself becomes an ally of the forces of social stagnation. We must use time creatively, in the knowledge that time is always ripe to do right. Now is the time to make real the promise of democracy and transform our pending national elegy into a creative psalm of brotherhood. Now is the time to lift our national policy from the quicksand of racial injustice to the solid rock of human dignity.

You speak of our activity in Birmingham as extreme. At first I was rather disappointed that fellow clergymen would see my nonviolent efforts as those of an extremist. I began thinking about the fact that I stand in the middle of two opposing forces in the Negro community. One is a force of complacency, made up in part of Negroes who, as a result of long years of oppression, are so drained of self-respect and a sense of "somebodiness" that they have adjusted to segregation; and in part of a few middle-class Negroes who, because of a degree of academic and economic security and because in some ways they profit by segregation, have become insensitive to the problems of the masses. The other force is one of bitterness and hatred, and it comes perilously close to advocating violence. It is expressed in the various black nationalist groups that are springing up across the nation, the largest and best-known being Elijah Muhammad's Muslim movement. Nourished by the Negro's frustration over the continued existence of racial discrimination, this movement is made up of people who have lost faith in America, who have absolutely repudiated Christianity, and who have concluded that the white man is an incorrigible "devil."

I have tried to stand between these two forces, saying that we need emulate neither the "do-nothingism" of the complacent nor the hatred and despair of the black nationalist. For there is the more excellent way of love and nonviolent protest. I am grateful to God that, through the influence of the Negro church, the way of nonviolence became an integral part of our struggle.

If this philosophy had not emerged, by now many streets of the South would, I am convinced, be flowing with blood. And I am further convinced that if our white brothers dismiss as "rabble-rousers" and "outside agitators" those of us who employ nonviolent direct action, and if they refuse to support our nonviolent efforts, millions of Negroes will, out of frustration and despair, seek solace and security in blacknationalist ideologies—a development that would inevitably lead to a frightening racial nightmare.

Oppressed people cannot remain oppressed forever. The yearning for freedom eventually manifests itself, and that is what has happened to the American Negro. Something within has reminded him of his birthright of freedom, and something without has reminded him that it can be gained. Consciously or unconsciously, he has been caught up by the *Zeitgeist,* and with his black brothers of Africa and his brown and yellow brothers of Asia, South America and the Caribbean, the United States Negro is moving with a sense of great urgency toward the promised land of racial justice. If one recognizes this vital urge that has engulfed the Negro community, one should readily understand why public demonstrations are taking place. The Negro has many pent-up resentments and latent frustrations, and he must release them. So let him march; let him make prayer pilgrimages to the city hall; let him go on freedom rides—and try to understand why he must do so. If his repressed emotions are not released in nonviolent ways, they will seek expression through violence; this is not a threat but a fact of history. So I have not said to my people: "Get rid of your discontent." Rather, I have tried to say that this normal and healthy discontent can be channeled into the creative outlet of nonviolent direct action. And now this approach is being termed extremist.

But though I was initially disappointed at being categorized as an extremist, as I   30
continued to think about the matter I gradually gained a measure of satisfaction from the label. Was not Jesus an extremist for love: "Love your enemies, bless them that curse you, do good to them that hate you, and pray for them which despitefully use you, and persecute you." Was not Amos an extremist for justice: "Let justice roll down like waters and righteousness like an ever-flowing stream." Was not Paul an extremist for the Christian gospel: "I bear in my body the marks of the Lord Jesus." Was not Martin Luther an extremist: "Here I stand; I cannot do otherwise, so help me God." And John Bunyan: "I will stay in jail to the end of my days before I make a butchery of my conscience." And Abraham Lincoln: "This nation cannot survive half slave and half free." And Thomas Jefferson: "We hold these truths to be self-evident, that all men are created equal . . ." So the question is not whether we will be extremists, but what kind of extremists we will be. Will we be extremists for hate or for love? Will we be extremists for the preservation of injustice or for the extension of justice? In that dramatic scene on Calvary's hill three men were crucified. We must never forget that all three were crucified for the same crime—the crime of extremism. Two were extremists for immorality, and thus fell below their environment. The other, Jesus Christ, was an extremist for love, truth and goodness, and thereby rose above his environment. Perhaps the South, the nation and the world are in dire need of creative extremists.

I had hoped that the white moderate would see this need. Perhaps I was too optimistic; perhaps I expected too much. I suppose I should have realized that few members of the oppressor race can understand the deep groans and passionate yearnings of the oppressed race, and still fewer have the vision to see that injustice must be rooted out by strong, persistent and determined action. I am thankful, however, that some of our white brothers in the South have grasped the meaning of this social revolution and committed themselves to it. They are still all too few in quantity, but they are big in quality. Some—such as Ralph McGill, Lillian Smith, Harry Golden, James McBride Dabbs, Ann Braden and Sarah Patton Boyle—have written about our struggle in eloquent and prophetic terms. Others have marched with us down nameless streets of the South. They have languished in filthy, roach-infested jails, suffering the abuse and brutality of policemen who view them as "dirty nigger-lovers." Unlike so many of their moderate brothers and sisters, they have recognized the urgency of the moment and sensed the need for powerful "action" antidotes to combat the disease of segregation.

Let me take note of my other major disappointment. I have been so greatly disappointed with the white church and its leadership. Of course, there are some notable exceptions. I am not unmindful of the fact that each of you has taken some significant stands on this issue. I commend you, Reverend Stallings, for your Christian stand on this past Sunday, in welcoming Negroes to your worship service on a non-segregated basis. I commend the Catholic leaders of this state for integrating Spring Hill College several years ago.

But despite these notable exceptions, I must honestly reiterate that I have been disappointed with the church. I do not say this as one of those negative critics who can always find something wrong with the church. I say this as a minister of the gospel, who loves the church; who was nurtured in its bosom; who has been sustained by its spiritual blessings and who will remain true to it as long as the cord of life shall lengthen.

When I was suddenly catapulted into the leadership of the bus protest in Montgomery, Alabama, a few years ago, I felt we would be supported by the white church. I felt that the white ministers, priests and rabbis of the South would be among our strongest allies. Instead, some have been outright opponents, refusing to understand the freedom movement and misrepresenting its leaders; all too many others have been more cautious than courageous and have remained silent behind the anesthetizing security of stained-glass windows.

35   In spite of my shattered dreams, I came to Birmingham with the hope that the white religious leadership of this community would see the justice of our cause and, with deep moral concern, would serve as the channel through which our just grievances could reach the power structure. I had hoped that each of you would understand. But again I have been disappointed.

I have heard numerous southern religious leaders admonish their worshipers to comply with a desegregation decision because it is the law, but I have longed to hear white ministers declare: "Follow this decree because integration is morally right and because the Negro is your brother." In the midst of blatant injustices inflicted upon the Negro, I have watched white churchmen stand on the sideline and mouth pious irrelevancies and sanctimonious trivialities. In the midst of a mighty struggle to rid our nation of racial and economic injustice, I have heard many ministers say: "Those are social issues, with which the gospel has no real concern." And I have watched many churches commit themselves to a completely otherworldly religion which makes a strange, un-biblical distinction between body and soul, between the sacred and the secular.

I have traveled the length and breadth of Alabama, Mississippi and all the other southern states. On sweltering summer days and crisp autumn mornings I have looked at the South's beautiful churches with their lofty spires pointing heavenward. I have beheld the impressive outlines of her massive religious-education buildings. Over and over I have found myself asking: "What kind of people worship here? Who is their God? Where were their voices when the lips of Governor Barnett dripped with words of interposition and nullification? Where were they when Governor Wallace gave a clarion call for defiance and hatred? Where were their voices of support when bruised and weary Negro men and women decided to rise from the dark dungeons of complacency to the bright hills of creative protest?"

Yes, these questions are still in my mind. In deep disappointment I have wept over the laxity of the church. But be assured that my tears have been tears of love. There can be no deep disappointment where there is not deep love. Yes, I love the church. How could I do otherwise? I am in the rather unique position of being the son, the grandson and the great-grandson of preachers. Yes, I see the church as the body of Christ. But, oh! How we have blemished and scarred that body through social neglect and through fear of being nonconformists.

There was a time when the church was very powerful—in the time when the early Christians rejoiced at being deemed worthy to suffer for what they believed. In those days the church was not merely a thermometer that recorded the ideas and principles of popular opinion; it was a thermostat that transformed the mores of society. Whenever the early Christians entered a town, the people in power became disturbed and immediately sought to convict the Christians for being "disturbers of the peace" and "outside agitators." But the Christians pressed on, in the conviction that they were "a colony of heaven," called to obey God rather than man. Small in number, they were big in commitment. They were too God-intoxicated to be "astronomically intimidated." By their effort and example they brought an end to such ancient evils as infanticide and gladiatorial contests.

Things are different now. So often the contemporary church is a weak, ineffectual voice with an uncertain sound. So often it is an arch-defender of the status quo. Far from being disturbed by the presence of the church, the power structure of the average community is consoled by the church's silent—and often even vocal—sanction of things as they are. 40

But the judgment of God is upon the church as never before. If today's church does not recapture the sacrificial spirit of the early church, it will lose its authenticity, forfeit the loyalty of millions, and be dismissed as an irrelevant social club with no meaning for the twentieth century. Every day I meet young people whose disappointment with the church has turned into outright disgust.

Perhaps I have once again been too optimistic. Is organized religion too inextricably bound to the status quo to save our nation and the world? Perhaps I must turn my faith to the inner spiritual church, the church within the church, as the true *ekklesia* and the hope of the world. But again I am thankful to God that some noble souls from the ranks of organized religion have broken loose from the paralyzing chains of conformity and joined us as active partners in the struggle for freedom. They have left their secure congregations and walked the streets of Albany, Georgia, with us. They have gone down the highways of the South on tortuous rides for freedom. Yes, they have gone to jail with us. Some have been dismissed from their churches, have lost the support of their bishops and fellow ministers. But they have acted in the faith that right defeated is stronger than evil triumphant. Their witness has been the spiritual salt that has preserved the true meaning of the gospel in these troubled times. They have carved a tunnel of hope through the dark mountain of disappointment.

I hope the church as a whole will meet the challenge of this decisive hour. But even if the church does not come to the aid of justice, I have no despair about the future. I have no fear about the outcome of our struggle in Birmingham, even if our motives are at present misunderstood. We will reach the goal of freedom in Birmingham and all over the nation, because the goal of America is freedom. Abused and scorned though we may be, our destiny is tied up with America's destiny. Before the pilgrims landed at Plymouth, we were here. Before the pen of Jefferson etched the majestic words of the Declaration of Independence across the pages of history, we were here. For more than two centuries our forebears labored in this country without wages; they made cotton king; they built the homes of their masters while suffering gross injustice and shameful humiliation—and yet out of a bottomless vitality they continued to thrive and develop. If the inexpressible cruelties of slavery could not stop us, the opposition we now face will surely fail. We will win our freedom because the sacred heritage of our nation and the eternal will of God are embodied in our echoing demands.

Before closing I feel impelled to mention one other point in your statement that has troubled me profoundly. You warmly commended the Birmingham police force for keeping "order" and "preventing violence." I doubt that you would have so warmly commended the police force if you had seen its dogs sinking their teeth into unarmed, nonviolent Negroes. I doubt that you would so quickly commend the policemen if you were to observe their ugly and inhumane treatment of Negroes here in the city jail; if you were to watch them push and curse old Negro women and young Negro girls; if you were to see them slap and kick old Negro men and young boys; if you were to observe them, as they did on two occasions, refuse to give us food because we wanted to sing our grace together. I cannot join you in your praise of the Birmingham Police Department.

45   It is true that the police have exercised a degree of discipline in handling the demonstrators. In this sense they have conducted themselves rather "nonviolently" in public. But for what purpose? To preserve the evil system of segregation. Over the past few years I have consistently preached that nonviolence demands that the means we use must be as pure as the ends we seek. I have tried to make clear that it is wrong to use immoral means to attain moral ends. But now I must affirm that it is just as wrong, or perhaps even more so, to use moral means to preserve immoral ends. Perhaps Mr. Connor and his policemen have been rather nonviolent in public, as was Chief Pritchett in Albany, Georgia, but they have used the moral means of nonviolence to maintain the immoral end of racial injustice. As T. S. Eliot has said: "The last temptation is the greatest treason: To do the right deed for the wrong reason."

I wish you had commended the Negro sit-inners and demonstrators of Birmingham for their sublime courage, their willingness to suffer and their amazing discipline in the midst of great provocation. One day the South will recognize its real heroes. They will be the James Merediths, with the noble sense of purpose that enables them to face jeering and hostile mobs, and with the agonizing loneliness that characterizes the life of the pioneer. They will be old, oppressed, battered Negro women, symbolized in a seventy-two-year-old woman in Montgomery, Alabama, who rose up with a sense of dignity and with her people decided not to ride segregated buses, and who responded with ungrammatical profundity to one who inquired about her weariness: "My feets is tired, but my soul is at rest." They will be the young high school and college students, the young ministers of the gospel and a host of their elders, courageously and nonviolently sitting in at lunch counters and willingly going to jail for conscience sake. One day the South will know that when these disinherited children of God sat down at lunch counters, they were in reality standing up for what is best in the American dream and for the most sacred values in our Judaeo-Christian heritage, thereby bringing our nation back to those great wells of democracy which were dug deep by the founding fathers in their formulation of the Constitution and the Declaration of Independence.

Never before have I written so long a letter. I'm afraid it is much too long to take your precious time. I can assure you that it would have been much shorter if I had been writing from a comfortable desk, but what else can one do when he is alone in a narrow jail cell, other than write long letters, think long thoughts and pray long prayers?

If I have said anything in this letter that overstates the truth and indicates an unreasonable impatience, I beg you to forgive me. If I have said anything that understates the truth and indicates my having a patience that allows me to settle for anything less than brotherhood, I beg God to forgive me.

I hope this letter finds you strong in the faith. I also hope that circumstances will soon make it possible for me to meet each of you, not as an integrationist or a civil-rights leader but as a fellow clergyman and a Christian brother. Let us all hope that the dark clouds of racial prejudice will soon pass away and the deep fog of misunderstanding will be lifted from our fear-drenched communities, and in some not too distant tomorrow the radiant stars of love and brotherhood will shine over our great nation with all their scintillating beauty.

Yours for the cause of Peace and Brotherhood,
Martin Luther King, Jr.

CRITICAL THINKING QUESTIONS

1. How does Martin Luther King, Jr. create an *appeal to our emotions?* Cite examples of what you consider the most effective instances of that appeal.

2. What types of *evidence* does King use in his argument? Cite examples.

3. Are there places in the letter where the argument seems to be more oral than written, places where you can *hear* the words?

WRITING TOPIC

1. If you were to become an activist, what cause would you support today? Write to a friend inviting that person to join you in your support, citing evidence in the form of reports, personal experience, and authority.

2. **Modeling a Master:**   Using King's "Letter from Birmingham Jail" as your model, compose a letter to a target audience that examines a situation that you deem to be unfair and advocates specific action to right the wrong. First, you will need to spend some time studying the master. After reading the "Letter," use the following outline to analyze King's rhetorical strategies; mark passages and make marginal notes to denote each component listed:

I. King's Introduction
   - Presents the issue
   - Explains how this situation came about
   - Establishes common ground with his audience
   - Adopts a tone that is both personal and academic
   - Provides logical analysis of the situation at hand (appeal to *logos*) and invokes value appeals (*pathos*)

II. King's Concession
   - Anticipates and articulates the opposition's case
   - Shows his understanding of the opposition's views
   - Addresses the opposition's case; introduces his refutation with a key word, "Wait!"
   - Appeals to *pathos* through the use of personal experience; creates audience empathy, even as he asserts his case against the opposition

III. King's Rebuttal—Evidence and Appeals
   - Uses definition and analysis/appeal to *logos*
   - Uses appeals to authority/*logos*
   - Uses examples/*logos* and *pathos*
   - Uses a veiled threat, based on a stated warrant/*pathos*
   - Uses comparison/*logos* and *pathos*
   - Uses common ground value appeals (stated warrants)/*pathos*

IV. King's Closing
   - Regains audience empathy
   - Strikes common ground by expressing shared needs and values
   - States a clear "call to action"
   - Creates a final sentence that capitalizes on use of first-person plural and resonates with "scintillating" imagery

Now it's your turn. Make your case with a specific audience who you envision to be unsympathetic to your position. Use King's rhetorical tactics and win them over.

Following are some suggested situations:

- The draft has been reinstated, and you are required to sign up. You write a letter to the Selective Service Board (located in your hometown or country) to convince them to give you an exemption.
- You are applying to law school. Recorded on your college transcript is a plagiarism violation. Although you were, indeed, guilty as charged, you write a letter to convince the law school admissions board to give serious consideration to your application.
- Home from college for spring break, you learn that the Oklawahah City Council has approved construction of a Happy-Mart Superstore in a wooded area with a nearby pond. You write a letter to the council to convince its members to rescind their action.
- You and your partner, who are the same sex, wish to adopt a child through an adoption agency. You write the agency to convince its board members to allow you to do so.
- Create a situation/scenario, which places you in the role of writing a letter to a specific audience to defend your act of *civil disobedience.*

Plato (427–347 B.C.)

from *Crito*

Socrates: . . . Ought a man to do what he admits to be right, or ought he to betray the right?

Crito: He ought to do what he thinks right.

Socrates: But if this is true, what is the application? In leaving the prison against the will of the Athenians, do I wrong any? Or rather do I not wrong those whom I ought least to wrong? Do I not desert the principles which are acknowledged by us to be just—what do you say?

Crito: I cannot tell, Socrates; for I do not know.

Socrates: Then consider the matter in this way:—Imagine that I am about to play truant (you may call the proceeding by any name which you like), and the laws of the government come and interrogate me: "Tell us, Socrates," they say: "what are you about? Are you not going by an act of yours to overturn us—the laws, and the whole state, as far as in you lies? Do you imagine that a state can subsist and not be overthrown, in which the decisions of law have no power, but are set aside and trampled upon by individuals?" What will be our answer, Crito, to these and the like words? Any one, and especially a rhetorician, will have a good deal to say on behalf of the law which requires a sentence to be carried out. He will argue that this law

5

should not be set aside; and shall we reply, "Yes, but the state has injured us and given an unjust sentence." Suppose I say that?

Crito: Very good, Socrates.

Socrates: "And was that our agreement with you?" the law would answer; "or were you to abide by the sentence of the state?" And if I were to express my astonishment at their words, the law would probably add: "Answer, Socrates, instead of opening your eyes—you are in the habit of asking and answering questions. Tell us,—What complaint have you to make against us which justifies you in attempting to destroy us and the state? In the first place did we not bring you into existence? Your father married your mother by our aid and begat you. Say whether you have any objection to urge against those of us who regulate marriage?" None, I should reply. "Or against those of us who after birth regulate the nurture and education of children, in which you also were trained? Were not the laws, which have the charge of education, right in commanding your father to train you in music and gymnastics?" Right, I should reply. "Well then, since you were brought into the world and nurtured and educated by us, can you deny in the first place that you are our child and slave, as your fathers were before you? And if this is true you are not on equal terms with us; nor can you think that you have a right to do to us what we are doing to you. Would you have any right to strike or revile or do any other evil to your father or your master, if you had one, because you have been struck or reviled by him, or received some other evil at his hands?—you would not say this? And because we think right to destroy you, do you think that you have any right to destroy us in return, and your country as far as in you lies? Will you, O professor of true virtue, pretend that you are justified in this? Has a philosopher like you failed to discover that our country is more to be valued and higher and holier far than mother or father or any ancestor, and more to be regarded in the eyes of the gods and of men of understanding? Also to be soothed, and gently and reverently entreated when angry, even more than a father, and either to be persuaded, or if not persuaded, to be obeyed? And when we are punished by her, whether with imprisonment or stripes, the punishment is to be endured in silence, and if she leads us to wounds or death in battle, thither we follow as is right; neither may any one yield or retreat or leave his rank, but whether in battle or in a court of law, or in any other place, he must do what his city and his country order him; or he must change their view of what is just: and if he may do no violence to his father or mother, much less may he do violence to his country." What answer shall we make to this, Crito? Do the laws speak truly, or do they not?

Crito: I think that they do.

Socrates: Then the laws will say, "Consider, Socrates, if we are speaking truly that in your present attempt you are going to do us an injury. For, having brought you into the world, and nurtured and educated you, and given you and every other citizen a share in every good which we had to give, we further proclaim to any Athenian by the liberty which we allow him, that if he does not like us when he has become of age and has seen the ways of the city, and made our acquaintance, he may go where he pleases and take his goods with him. None of our laws will forbid him or interfere with him. Any one who does not like us and the city, and who wants to emigrate to a colony or to any other city, may go where he likes, retaining his property. But he who has experience of the manner in which we order justice and administer the state, and still remains, has entered into an implied contract that he will do as we command him. And he who disobeys us is, as we maintain, thrice wrong; first, because in disobeying us he is disobeying his parents; secondly, because we are the authors of his education; thirdly, because he has made an agreement with us that he will duly obey our commands; and he neither obeys them nor convinces us that our commands are unjust; and we do not rudely impose them, but give him the alternative of obeying or convincing us;—that is what we offer, and he does neither.

"These are the sort of accusations to which, as we were saying, you, Socrates, 10 will be exposed if you accomplish your intentions; you, above all other Athenians." Suppose now I ask, why I rather than anybody else? They will justly retort upon me that I above all other men have acknowledged the agreement. "There is clear proof," they will say, "Socrates, that we and the city were not displeasing to you. Of all Athenians you have been the most constant resident in the city, which, as you never leave, you may be supposed to love. For you never went out of the city either to see the games, except once when you went to the Isthmus, or to any other place unless when you were on military service; nor did you travel as other men do. Nor had you any curiosity to know other states or their laws: your affections did not go beyond us and our state; we were your special favorites, and you acquiesced in our government of you; and here in this city you begat your children, which is a proof of your satisfaction. Moreover, you might in the course of the trial, if you had liked, have fixed the penalty at banishment; the state which refuses to let you go now would have let you go then. But you pretended that you preferred death to exile, and that you were not unwilling to die. And now you have forgotten these fine sentiments, and pay no respect to us the laws, of whom you are the destroyer; and are doing what only a miserable slave would do, running away and turning your back upon the compacts and agreements which you made as a citizen. And first of all answer this very question: Are we right in saying that you agreed to be governed according to us in deed, and not in word only? Is that true or not?" How shall we answer, Crito? Must we not assent?

Crito: We cannot help it, Socrates.

Socrates: Then will they not say: "You, Socrates, are breaking the covenants and agreements which you made with us at your leisure, not in any haste or under any compulsion or deception, but after you have had seventy years to think of them, during which time you were at liberty to leave the city, if we were not to your mind, or if our covenants appeared to you to be unfair. You had your choice, and might have gone either to Lacedaemon or Crete, both which states are often praised by you for their good government, or to some other Hellenic or foreign state. Whereas you, above all our Athenians, seemed to be so fond of the state, or, in other words, of us her laws (and who would care about a state which has no laws?), that you never stirred out of her; the halt, the blind, the maimed were not more stationary in her than you were. And now you run away and forsake your agreements. Not so, Socrates, if you will take our advice; do not make yourself ridiculous by escaping out of the city.

"For just consider, if you transgress and err in this sort of way, what good will you do either to yourself or to your friends? That your friends will be driven into exile and deprived of citizenship, or will lose their property, is tolerably certain; and you yourself, if you fly to one of the neighboring cities, as, for example, Thebes or Megara, both of which are well governed, will come to them as an enemy, Socrates, and their government will be against you, and all patriotic citizens will cast an evil eye upon you as a subverter of the laws, and you will confirm in the minds of the judges the justice of their own condemnation of you. For he who is a corrupter of the laws is more than likely to be a corrupter of the young and foolish portion of mankind. Will you then flee from well-ordered citizens and virtuous men? and is existence worth having on these terms? Or will you go to them without shame, and talk to them, Socrates? And what will you say to them? What you say here about virtue and justice and institutions and laws being the best things among men? Would that be decent of you? Surely not. But if you go away from wellgoverned states to Crito's friends in Thessaly, where there is a great disorder and licence, they will be charmed to hear the tale of your escape from prison, set off with ludicrous particulars of the manner in which you were wrapped in a goatskin or some other disguise, and metamorphosed as the manner is of runaways; but will there be no one to remind you that in your old age you were ashamed to violate the most sacred laws from a miserable desire of a little more life? Perhaps not, if you keep them in a good temper; but if they are out of temper you will hear many degrading things; you will live, but how?—as the flatterer of all men, and the servant of all men; and doing what?—eating and drinking in Thessaly, having gone abroad in order that you may get a dinner. And where will be your fine sentiments about justice and virtue? Say that you wish to live for the sake of your children—you want to bring them up and educate them—will you take them into Thessaly and deprive them of Athenian citizenship? Is this the benefit which you will confer upon them? Or are you under the impression that they will be better cared for and educated here if you are still alive, although absent from them; for your friends will take care of them? Do you fancy that if you are an inhabitant of Thessaly they will take care of them, and if you are an inhabitant of the other world that they will not take care of them? Nay: but if they who call themselves friends are good for anything, they will—to be sure they will.

"Listen, then, Socrates, to us who have brought you up. Think not of life and children first, and of justice afterwards, but of justice first, that you may be justified before the princes of the world below. For neither will you nor any that belong to you be happier or holier or juster in this life, or happier in another, if you do as Crito bids. Now you depart in innocence, a sufferer and not a doer of evil; a victim, not of the laws of men. But if you go forth, returning evil for evil, and injury for injury, breaking the covenants and agreements which you have made with us, and wronging those whom you ought least of all to wrong, that is to say, yourself, your friends, your country, and us, we shall be angry with you while you live, and our brethren, the laws in the world below, will receive you as an enemy; for they will know that you have done your best to destroy us. Listen, then, to us and not to Crito."

This, dear Crito, is the voice which I seem to hear murmuring in my ears, 15 like the sound of the flute in the ears of the mystic; that voice, I say, is humming in my ears, and prevents me from hearing any other. And I know that anything more which you may say will be vain. Yet speak, if you have anything to say.

Crito: I have nothing to say, Socrates.

Socrates: Leave me then, Crito, to fulfill the will of God, and to follow whither he leads.

CRITICAL THINKING QUESTIONS

1. Socrates rejects the argument that he should escape even though escape would be quite easily accomplished. On what principles does he base this rejection? Do you admire his willingness to adhere to his principles?

2. Socrates feels he must model appropriate behavior as a citizen despite the dire consequences. Are there any situations you can imagine where your own individual needs must be placed behind the needs of the society as a whole even when such situations demand individual sacrifice?

WRITING TOPIC

What would Dr. Martin Luther King, Jr. say in response to Socrates? Write a dialogue you imagine the two men might have as they discuss Socrates's decision.

Richard Rodriguez (b. 1944)

The Chinese in All of Us

A Mexican American Explores Multiculturalism

The other day, the phone rang; it was a woman who identified herself as the "talent coordinator" for the "Oprah Winfrey Show." She said Oprah was planning a show on self-hating ethnics. "You know," she confided, "Norwegians who don't want to be Norwegian, Greeks who hate Greek food." Anyway, she said breezily, wouldn't I like to make an appearance?

About 10 years ago I wrote a thin book called *Hunger of Memory*. It was a book about my education, which is to say, a book about my Americanization. I wrote of losses and triumphs. And, in passing, I wrote about two issues particularly, affirmative action and bilingual education.

I was a nay-sayer. I became, because of my book, a notorious figure among the Ethnic Left in America. Consider me the brown Uncle Tom. I am a traitor, a sell-out. The Spanish word is *pocho*. A *pocho* is someone who forgets his true home. (A shame.) A Richard Rodriguez.

Last year, I was being interviewed by Bill Moyers. "Do you consider yourself American or Hispanic?" he asked.

5   "I think of myself as Chinese," I answered.

A smart-aleck answer, but one that is true enough. I live in San Francisco, a city that has become, in my lifetime, predominantly Asian, predominantly Chinese. I am becoming like them. Do not ask me how, it is too early to tell. But it is inevitable, living side by side, that we should become like each other. So think of me as Chinese.

Oh, my critics say: Look at you Mr. Rod-ree-guess. You have lost your culture.

They mean, I think, that I am not my father, which is true enough. I did not grow up in the state of Jalisco, in the western part of Mexico. I grew up here, in this country, amongst you. I am like you.

My critics mean, when they speak of culture, something solid, something intact. You have lost your culture, they say, as though I lost it at the Greyhound bus station. You have lost your culture, as though culture is a coat I took off one warm afternoon and then forgot.

10   I AM MY CULTURE. Culture is not something opposite us, it is rather something we breathe and sweat and live. My culture? Lucille Ball is my culture. (I love Lucy, after all.) And Michael Jackson. And Benjamin Franklin is my culture. And Elvis Presley and Walter Cronkite. Walt Disney is my culture. The New York Yankees.

My culture is you. You created me; if you don't like it, if I make you uncomfortable now by being too much like you, too bad.

When I was a little boy in Sacramento, California, the son of Mexican immigrant parents, Spanish-speaking mainly, even then, in those years, America came at me. America was everywhere around me. America was in the pace of the traffic lights, the assertion of neon, the slouch of the crowd, the impatience of the fast food counter. America was everywhere.

I recognized America best, in those years, standing outside the culture. I recognized its power, and from the first I knew that it threatened to swallow me up. America did not feel like something to choose or not choose. America felt inevitable.

Truman Capote said somewhere that he never met a true bisexual. He meant, I think, that finally people are one thing or the other.

15   Well, I must tell you that I have never met a truly bicultural person. Oh, I have met people who speak two languages, and all that. But finally, their allegiance belongs more to one side of the border than the other.

And yet, I believe in multiculturalism—my kind of multiculturalism.

I think the adventure of living in a multi-racial, multi-ethnic America leaves one vulnerable to a variety of cultures, a variety of influences. Consider me, for example, Chinese. I am also Irish.

About 10 years ago, I was going to school in England. One weekend, Aer Lingus, the Irish national airline, was offering a reduced fare to Dublin. I thought, "What a lark—it'd be fun to go off to Ireland for the weekend." Strange thing, once I got off the plane, I suddenly felt myself at home. I knew these people. I recognized their faces and their irony and their wit and their sadness.

I'll tell you why. I was educated by Irish Catholic nuns. They were my first, my most important foreign culture, intruding on my Mexican soul, reshaping my soul with their voices.

Sometime after Dublin, I realized something more about myself: All of my best   20 friends from childhood to now, the people I have been closest to, have been Irish-Americans, Irish Catholics.

How is this possible? How is it possible for a Mexican kid from Sacramento, California, to discover himself to be Irish?

In the orthodox American scheme of things, it is nonsense. America is a Protestant country. A low-church Protestant country. America was founded by Puritans who resisted the notion of the group. The most important founding idea of America was the notion of individualism—your freedom from the group, my freedom from you. A most glamorous idea.

Consider this paradox: The belief we share in common as Americans is the belief that we are separate from one another.

There is already with this paradox implied an important tension, one basic to American experience. Our culture, by which I mean our daily experience, is at war with our ideology, by which I mean our Protestant belief in separateness.

Diversity is our strength, we say. There is not an American president who would   25 say anything else: We are a country made stronger by our individuality, by our differences. Which is, in a way, true. But only partly true.

The other truth, I call it my catholic truth about puritan America, is that America exists. America exists as a culture, a sound, an accent, a walk.

Thousands of hotel clerks in thousands of hotels around the world will tell you that America exists. There is a recognizable type. Here they come, the Americans. Bermuda shorts. High-pitched voices. Too easy familiarity. Big tip, insecure tip. A slap on the back.

And when we ourselves are far from home, when we are in the Hilton lobby in Cairo or in Paris, we, too, recognize one another immediately. Across the crowded hotel lobby Americans find one another immediately, either with relief or with slight, acknowledging embarrassment.

It is only when we are home working alongside one another and living next to one another that we wonder whether America exists. We wonder about our individuality. And we talk about our traditional Protestant virtues. We talk about respecting our diversity.

Nativist politicians are saying these days that maybe we should think twice about   30 allowing non-European immigrants into this country. Can America, after all, sustain such diversity?

Liberal American educators end up echoing the point, in a way. They look at faces like mine and they see only what they call "diversity." They wonder, now, if the purpose of education shouldn't be diversity. We should teach our children about their separate cultures—forget the notion of a common culture.

The other day in Las Vegas I was speaking to a group of high school principals. One man, afterward, came up and told me that his school has changed in recent years. In little more than a decade the student body has changed its color, changed its complexion; the school is no longer black and white, but now suddenly Asian and Hispanic.

This principal smiled and said his school has dropped Black History Month in favor of what he calls, "Newcomers Month."

I think this is absurd. I think this is nonsense.

35   There isn't an American whose history is not black history. All of us, by virtue of being Americans, share in the history of black America—the oppression, the endurance, the triumph.

Do not speak to me of your diversity. My cultural forefathers are black slaves and black emancipators. I am an American.

America exists. Nothing more will I tell you, can I tell you.

Let me tell you some stories.

A friend of mine—let's call him Michael—tells me he's confused by America. Mike goes to junior high school in San Francisco. His teacher is always telling him to stand up, look up. "Speak up, Michael, we can't hear you! Look at me, Michael!"

40   Then Michael goes home. His Chinese father is always complaining at home. His Chinese father says that Michael is picking up American ways. "And since when have you started to look your father in the eye?"

America exists, dear Michael.

At the family picnic, the boy listens to his relatives argue and laugh. The spices are as familiar as the jokes. There are arguments about old civil wars and faceless politicians. The family is talking Greek or Chinese or Spanish. The boy grows restless; the boy gets up and wanders away from the family picnic to watch some other boys playing baseball in the distance.

America exists.

My Mexican father looks out at America from the window of his morning newspaper. After all these years in this country, he still doubts that America exists. Look at this place, he says. So many faces. So many colors. So many grandmothers and religions and memories here. This is not a real country. Not a real country like China or Germany or Mexico.

45   It falls to the son to say, America exists, Papa.

There is an unresolved tension between the "I" and the "we." We trust most the "I," though grudgingly we admit the necessity of the "we." The most important communal institution we have is the classroom. We build classrooms, recognize their necessity. But we don't like them.

In the most famous American novel, our greatest book about ourselves, Mark Twain's *Adventures of Huckleberry Finn*, the school marm plays the comic villain. She is always trying to tie down Huck. She tries to make him speak regular. She is always trying to civilize.

We recognize the value of having Huck Finn learn to speak regular, even if we don't like it. And we don't like it. Something in us as Americans forces us to fear the coming of fall, the chill in the woods, the starched shirt, the first day of school.

Let me tell you about my first day of school. I came to the classroom clutching a handful of English. A bilingual child?

The important distinction I want to make here is not between Spanish and English, but between private and public language.

50

I was the son of working class, immigrant parents. I stress working class. Too often in recent years, we have considered ethnicity and race at the expense of economic standing. Thus, we speak of "minorities" in America and we mean only certain races or so-called "non-white" groups. We use the term minority in a numerical sense. Am I a minority? Well, yes, if we mean that Hispanics generally are "under represented" in American public life. But the term minority is richer as a cultural term. There are certain people in this country who do not imagine themselves to belong to majority society. White. Black. Brown. Most of them are poor. Many of them are uneducated. All of them share a diffidence, a fear, an anxiety about public institutions.

When I walked into the classroom, I was such a minority. I remember the nun wrote my name on the black board: RICHARD RODRIGUEZ. She pronounced it. Then she said, repeat it after me.

It was not that I could not say it. Rather, I would not say it. Why should I? Who was this nun?

She said: Repeat your name after me loud enough so all the boys and girls can understand.

The nun was telling me not just to speak English, but to use language publicly. To speak in a voice loud enough to be heard by strangers. (She was calling me to the first and most crucial lesson of grammar school.)

55

I was a minority child. It wasn't a question of English versus Spanish. It was a question of public language. I didn't want to speak to you—*los gringos*, boys and girls.

I would not. I could not. I refused to speak up, to look up.

Half a year passed. The nuns worried over me. Speak up, Richard. Stand up, Richard. A year passed. A second year began.

Then one Saturday three nuns appeared at our door. They walked into our house and sat on our sagging blue sofa.

Would it be possible, Mrs. Rodriguez, for you and your husband to use English around the house?

60

Of course, my mother complied. (What would she not do for her children's public success?)

At first, it seemed a kind of game. We practiced English after dinner. But it was still your language.

Until one other Saturday. I remember my mother and father were speaking Spanish to one another in the kitchen. I did not realize they were speaking Spanish until, the moment they saw me, they switched to English.

I felt pushed away. I remember going over to the sink and turning on the water; standing there dumbly, feeling the water on my hand. I wanted to cry. The water was tepid, then warm, then scalding. I wanted to scream. But I didn't. I turned off the faucet and walked out of the room.

65   And now you have forgotten how I used to go after school to your house. I used to watch you. I watched television with you, there on the floor. I used to watch the way you laughed. I used to listen to the way you used words. I wanted to swallow you up, to become you. Five-thirty and your mom said, Well, Rickey, we're going to eat in half an hour. Do you want to stay? And I did. I became you.

Something happens to you in the classroom if you are a very good student. You change.

A friend of mine, who went to Bryn Mawr College in the 1950s—when she was the only black student in her class—remembers coming home to North Carolina. She remembers getting off the Greyhound bus. She remembers walking up the sidewalk on the hot early summer day.

When she got home and walked up the five steps of the front porch, her mother was waiting for her behind the screen door.

"I don't want you talkin' white in here," her mother said.

70   There is a sad story in America about "making it." It is the story of summer vacations. Of no longer being able to speak to one's parents. Of having your Chinese father mock your American ways. ("And since when have you started to look your father in the eye?") It is the story of the girl who learns a different kind of English at school and then is embarrassed to use it at the dinner table.

Bilinguists speak of the necessity of using what they call "family language" in the classroom. If I know anything about education, it is that such a bilingual scheme is bound to fail. Classroom language can never be family language. It is a matter not of different words, but of different contexts.

We don't like to hear such things. We don't like the school marm to change us. We want to believe that August will go on forever and that we can avoid wearing shoes. Huck Finn is America's archetypal bilingual student. He speaks one way—his way, his free way—the school marm wants him to speak another.

As Americans, we must root for Huck.

Americans have lately been searching for a new multi-cultural metaphor for America. We don't like the melting pot. Hispanic Americans particularly have been looking for a new metaphor. Our political coming of age in the late 1960s was accompanied by a stern resistance to the melting pot model of America.

75   America is a stew. (All of us, presumably chunks of beef in a common broth.)

Or America is a mosaic. A Mexican-American bishop recently said that to me. He pointed at a mosaic of the Virgin of Guadalupe. "That is how I think of America," he said. "We are each of us different colors, but united we produce a wonderful, a beautiful effect."

The trouble, I thought to myself, the trouble is that the tiny pieces of glass are static. In our real lives, we are not static.

America is fluid. The best metaphors of America for me are metaphors suggesting fluidity. Our lives melting into one another.

For myself, I like the metaphor of the melting pot. I like it for two reasons.

First, its suggestion of pain—and there is pain. The school teacher can put a sombrero   80
on my head and tell me to feel proud of my heritage, but I know I am becoming a different person than my father. There is pain in the melting pot. Fall in and you are burned.

But there is to the metaphor also a suggestion of alchemy or magic. Fall into the melting pot and you become a new person, changed, like magic, to gold.

Why do we even talk about multiculturalism?

For several reasons, most of them positive. First and foremost is the influence of the great black civil rights movement of the 1950s and 1960s. We are more apt today to recognize the colors of America than perhaps we were several decades ago. On the TV ad, on the football field, in the bank, in a room like this—we have grown used to different shades of America. But that is only to say that we are more apt to be struck by our differences now that we are side by side than in earlier times when segregation legalized separation.

Less positively, the black civil rights movement was undermined by a romantic separatism. Americans were romanced by the moral authority of the outsider, and the benefits of claiming outsider status. White women. Hispanics. Asians. Suddenly, in the 1970s there was a rush to proclaim one's separate status. The benefit was clear: America confronted real social problems. But the decadence also was clear: middle class Americans ended up competing with one another to proclaim themselves society's victims.

The second factor that gives rise to this multicultural preoccupation has recently   85
been the epic migration of non-Europeans into this country.

A friend of mine teaches at a school in Los Angeles where, she says, there are children from 54 language groups. "What possibility is there," she asks, "to teach such a diverse student body anything in common?"

These children do have something in common, however. They may be strangers to Los Angeles, but they are becoming Americans in Los Angeles. That is the beginning.

While I believe in the notion of a common culture, I believe also in the notion of a dynamic culture. Even while America changes the immigrants, the immigrants are changing us. They have always changed us. Assimilation is reciprocal.

Consider American English, for example. It is not British English. The British forced it down our throats, but the language we speak is changed. We speak American here. There are the sighs of German grandmothers and the laughter of Africans in the speech we use. There are in our speech thousands of words imported and brought unregistered through Ellis Island. Swedish words. Yiddish. Italian.

Listen to my voice and you will hear your Lithuanian grandmother. Listen to my   90
American voice and you will hear the echoes of my Chinese neighbors.

Yes, Mr. Bill Moyers, we are all destined to become Chinese.

CRITICAL THINKING QUESTIONS

1. Richard Rodriguez has angered many advocates of bilingual education, as well as those arguing for ethnic pride. Can you see why his *assertions* would stir hostility among these groups?

2. How does Rodriguez make use of personal experience, not only as evidence in support of his assertion, but also in establishing an appeal to *ethos?*

WRITING TOPIC

In what specific ways do you think our society is influenced by ethnic diversity? You might look for examples in food, music, fashion, and language. Write an essay in which you offer at least four pieces of evidence to support your claim.

Fred Setterberg (b. 1951)

The Usual Story

I ambled through the Quarter, down Dumaine Street, up Bourbon, along Chartres, heading no place in particular. The narrow streets thronged with drunks and musicians. In Jackson Square, I rested on the cement steps to finish a bottle of beer I had carried out of a dark, noisy joint near Patout's. The moon arched above the statue of General Jackson saddled upon his horse, his hat doffed in one hand to hail the light. A boy with a trumpet stood at the foot of the invader's statue. He bleated and blahed his way through Miles Davis's "All Blues."

I slipped back into the alleyways and zigzagged for another half-hour until I found myself standing in front of Preservation Hall.

I have never been a fan of traditional jazz. Worse, I have always imagined that the traditional jazz featured inside Preservation Hall would be a shuck, like Disneyland Dixieland—an artifice, unfelt, an impersonation for the tourists. The line in front of Preservation Hall was very long, but a good tenor sax player was wandering up and down the street, playing for free, and so I took my place at the end of the line, as much to rest and listen to the sax man as gain entry. When we were finally ushered into the building, I saw that a lack of artifice was Preservation Hall's greatest asset. The hall looked about twice the size of my hotel room, dimly lit like the gloomy altar of some small country church where a few candles sputtered bravely. Six musicians sat upon wooden chairs atop a small stage raised about eighteen inches from the floor. A half-dozen wooden bench pews filed back from the stage; everybody else—maybe seventy-five people—crowded together in the darkness, shoulder to shoulder.

I didn't recognize the band's first tune, but when the trumpet player took the lead, he shaved the melody close, in the style of King Oliver. After the clarinet solo, he stood up once again and sang out to the audience. His woman had left him, giving him the blues; it was the usual story.

5   Traditional jazz has never seemed risky enough to me. But as the band inside Preservation Hall continued to bang out one number after another, the piano, bass,

drums, banjo, clarinet, and trumpet swelling into a sea of collective fakery with sufficient spirit and peculiarity to challenge all the conventional harmonies, I caught for an inspired instant how truly daring the music must have felt at its inception. Even now the friction of creation showed sparks—the painful *hilarity* of squeezing something unheard before from a motley collection of instruments only recently transported to these shores. The band rambled on, and I realized there was nothing at all quaint about this music; it had always been full of risk, unstable, and liable to combust.

"Everyone is familiar with the Negro's modification of the whites' musical instruments," wrote Zora Neale Hurston in a 1911 essay, "Characteristics of Negro Expression," "so that his interpretation has been adopted by the white man himself and then reinterpreted. In so many words, Paul Whiteman is giving an imitation of a Negro orchestra making use of white-invented musical instruments in a Negro way. Thus has arisen a new art in the civilized world, and thus has our so-called civilization come. The exchange and re-exchange of ideas between groups."

The bass player at Preservation Hall seemed determined to prove this point. He launched into a flutter of notes that were both too rapid and dissonant for New Orleans vintage jazz, playing more like Charles Mingus than Pops Foster. He scurried up the instrument's neck from the bridge to the scroll, shattering the tune. The other players grunted encouragement. Together they were demonstrating how music—culture—argues, blends, dissolves, mutates, advances. The odd bird who hears something different plucks his strings too quickly or queerly or flat out plunks the *wrong* note, but he does it over and over until it sounds right. He finds his own groove and fashions new music from the old.

And that's exactly what American music—American culture—has managed to do. As Hurston understood, as the bass player was now showing, our nation's truest anthem contains the funeral dirge of the New Orleans street band combined with the whore-house piano and the last slave's work song and the bickering melodies of two hundred disparate points of origin, from Marseilles to Dakar, from Manaus to Guangzhou, now stretched out over the American plains like the hide of some mythical beast: the confluence of influences that nobody will ever be able to pick apart note-for-note. It has long been a sophisticated complaint to jeer that America has "no culture," but there couldn't be a sillier idea. We have more culture than one people will ever be able to digest. And that helps explain why the melting pot sometimes bubbles up—and when we least expect it, explodes.

CRITICAL THINKING QUESTIONS

1. List musical groups and songs which you enjoy.

2. What cultures and influences are reflected in the music you listed in question one?

3. Read paragraph 88 in Richard Rodriguez's essay, "The Chinese in All of Us." In what ways does Setterberg's essay support Rodriguez's *warrant* expressed in that paragraph?

Jonathan Swift (1667–1745)

A Modest Proposal

For Preventing the Children of Poor People in Ireland from Being a Burden to Their Parents or Country, and for Making Them Beneficial to the Public

It is a melancholy object to those who walk through this great town or travel in the country, when they see the streets, the roads, and cabin doors crowded with beggars of the female sex, followed by three, four, or six children, all in rags and importuning every passenger for an alms. These mothers, instead of being able to work for their honest livelihood, are forced to employ all their time in strolling to beg sustenance for their helpless infants, who, as they grow up, either turn thieves for want of work, or leave their dear native country to fight for the Pretender in Spain, or sell themselves to the Barbadoes.

I think it is agreed by all parties that this prodigious number of children in the arms, or on the backs, or at the heels of their mothers, and frequently of their fathers, is in the present deplorable state of the kingdom a very great additional grievance; and therefore whoever could find out a fair, cheap, and easy method of making these children sound and useful members of the commonwealth would deserve so well of the public as to have his statue set up for a preserver of the nation.

But my intention is very far from being confined to provide only for the children of professed beggars; it is of a much greater extent, and shall take in the whole number of infants at a certain age who are born of parents in effect as little able to support them as those who demand our charity in the streets.

As to my own part, having turned my thoughts for many years upon this important subject, and maturely weighed the several schemes of other projectors, I have always found them grossly mistaken in their computation. It is true a child just dropped from its dam may be supported by her milk for a solar year with little other nourishment, at most not above the value of two shillings, which the mother may certainly get, or the value in scraps, by her lawful occupation of begging; and it is exactly at one year old that I propose to provide for them in such a manner as instead of being a charge upon their parents or the parish, or wanting food and raiment for the rest of their lives, they shall, on the contrary, contribute to the feeding and partly to the clothing of many thousands.

5   There is likewise another great advantage in my scheme, that it will prevent those voluntary abortions, and that horrid practice of women murdering their bastard children, alas! too frequent among us, sacrificing the poor innocent babes, I doubt, more to avoid the expense than the shame, which would move tears and pity in the most savage and inhuman breast.

The number of souls in this kingdom being usually reckoned one million and a hair, of these I calculate there may be about two hundred thousand couples whose wives are breeders; from which number I subtract thirty thousand couples who are able to maintain their own children, although I apprehend there cannot be so many, under the present distress of the kingdom; but this being granted, there will remain an hundred and seventy thousand breeders. I again subtract fifty thousand for those women who miscarry, or whose children die by accident or disease within the year. There only remain an hundred and twenty thousand children of poor parents annually born. The question therefore is, how this number shall be reared and provided for, which, as I have already said, under the present situation of affairs is utterly impossible by all the methods hitherto proposed. For we can neither employ them in handicraft or agriculture; we neither build houses (I mean in the country) nor cultivate land: they can very seldom pick up a livelihood by stealing till they arrive at six years old, except where they are of towardly parts; although I confess they learn the rudiments much earlier, during which time they can, however, be properly looked upon only as probationers, as I have been informed by a principal gentleman in the county of Cavan, who protested to me that he never knew above one or two instances under the age of six, even in a part of the kingdom so renowned for the quickest proficiency in that art.

I am assured by our merchants that a boy or girl before twelve years old is no salable commodity; and even when they come to this age they will not yield above three pounds or three pounds and half-a-crown at most on the Exchange; which cannot turn to account either to the parents or the kingdom, the charge of nutriment and rags having been at least four times that value.

I shall now therefore humbly propose my own thoughts, which I hope will not be liable to the least objection.

I have been assured by a very knowing American of my acquaintance in London that a young healthy child well nursed is at a year old a most delicious, nourishing, and wholesome food, whether stewed, roasted, baked, or boiled; and I make no doubt that it will equally serve in a fricassee or a ragout.

I do therefore humbly offer it to public consideration that of the hundred and 10 twenty thousand children already computed, twenty thousand may be reserved for breed, whereof only one-fourth part to be males, which is more than we allow to sheep, black cattle or swine; and my reason is that these children are seldom the fruits of marriage, a circumstance not much regarded by our savages; therefore one male will be sufficient to serve four females. That the remaining hundred thousand may at a year old be offered in sale to the persons of quality and fortune through the kingdom, always advising the mother to let them suck plentifully in the last month, so as to render them plump and fat for a good table. A child will make two dishes at an entertainment for friends; and when the family dines alone, the fore or hind quarter will make a reasonable dish, and seasoned with a little pepper or salt will be very good boiled on the fourth day, especially in winter.

I have reckoned upon a medium that a child just born will weigh twelve pounds, and in a solar year if tolerably nursed increaseth to twenty-eight pounds.

I grant this food will be somewhat dear, and therefore very proper for landlords, who, as they have already devoured most of the parents, seem to have the best title to the children.

Infants' flesh will be in season throughout the year, but more plentiful in March, and a little before and after; for we are told by a grave author, an eminent French physician, that fish being a prolific diet, there are more children born in Roman Catholic countries about nine months after Lent than at any other season; therefore reckoning a year after Lent, the markets will be more glutted than usual, because the number of popish infants is at least three to one in this kingdom; and therefore it will have one other collateral advantage, by lessening the number of Papists among us.

I have already computed the charge of nursing a beggar's child (in which list I reckon all cottagers, laborers, and four-fifths of the farmers) to be about two shillings per annum, rags included; and I believe no gentleman would repine to give ten shillings for the carcass of a good fat child, which, as I have said, will make four dishes of excellent nutritive meat, when he hath only some particular friend or his own family to dine with him. Thus the squire will learn to be a good landlord, and grow popular among his tenants; the mother will have eight shillings net profit, and be fit for work till she produces another child.

15   Those who are more thrifty (as I must confess the times require) may flay the carcass; the skin of which artificially dressed will make admirable gloves for ladies, and summer boots for fine gentlemen.

As to our city of Dublin, shambles may be appointed for this purpose in the most convenient parts of it, and butchers we may be assured will not be wanting; although I rather recommend buying the children alive, and dressing them hot from the knife, as we do roasting pigs.

A very worthy person, a true lover of his country, and whose virtues I highly esteem, was lately pleased, in discoursing on this matter, to offer a refinement upon my scheme. He said that many gentlemen of this kingdom, having of late destroyed their deer, he conceived that the want of venison might be well supplied by the bodies of young lads and maidens, not exceeding fourteen years of age nor under twelve, so great a number of both sexes in every country being now ready to starve for want of work and service: and these to be disposed of by their parents, if alive, or otherwise by their nearest relations. But with due deference to so excellent a friend and so deserving a patriot, I cannot be altogether in his sentiments. For as to the males, my American acquaintance assured me from frequent experience that their flesh was generally tough and lean, like that of our schoolboys, by continual exercise, and their taste disagreeable; and to fatten them would not answer the charge. Then as to the females, it would, I think, with humble submission, be a loss to the public, because they soon would become breeders themselves: and besides, it is not improbable that some scrupulous people might be apt to censure such a practice (although indeed very unjustly) as a little bordering upon cruelty; which, I confess, hath always been with me the strongest objection against any project, how well soever intended.

But in order to justify my friend, he confessed that this expedient was put into his head by the famous Psalmanazar, a native of the island Formosa, who came from thence to London above twenty years ago, and in conversation told my friend that in his country when any young person happened to be put to death, the executioner sold the carcass to persons of quality as a prime dainty, and that in his time the body of a plump girl of fifteen, who was crucified for an attempt to poison the emperor, was sold to his Imperial Majesty's prime minister of state, and other great mandarins of the court, in joints from the gibbet, at four hundred crowns. Neither indeed can I deny that if the same use were made of several plump young girls in this town, who, without one single groat to their fortunes, cannot stir abroad without a chair, and appear at the playhouse and assemblies in foreign fineries, which they never will pay for, the kingdom would not be the worse.

Some persons of a desponding spirit are in great concern about that vast number of poor people, who are aged, diseased, or maimed, and I have been desired to employ my thoughts what course may be taken to ease the nation of so grievous an encumbrance. But I am not in the least pain upon that matter, because it is very well known that they are every day dying and rotting, by cold and famine, and filth and vermin, as fast as can be reasonably expected. And as to the younger laborers, they are now in almost as hopeful a condition. They cannot get work, and consequently pine away for want of nourishment, to a degree that if at any time they are accidentally hired to common labor, they have not strength to perform it; and thus the country and themselves are happily delivered from the evils to come.

I have too long digressed, and therefore shall return to my subject. I think the advantages by the proposal which I have made are obvious and many, as well as of the highest importance. 20

For first, as I have already observed, it would greatly lessen the number of Papists, with whom we are yearly overrun, being the principal breeders of the nation as well as our most dangerous enemies; and who stay at home on purpose with a design to deliver the kingdom to the Pretender, hoping to take their advantage by the absence of so many good Protestants, who have chosen rather to leave their country than stay at home and pay tithes against their conscience to an Episcopal curate.

Secondly, the poorer tenants will have something valuable of their own, which by law may be made liable to distress, and help to pay their landlord's rent; their corn and cattle being already seized, and money a thing unknown.

Thirdly, whereas the maintenance of an hundred thousand children, from two years old and upwards, cannot be computed at less than ten shillings apiece per annum, the nation's stock will be thereby increased fifty thousand pounds per annum, besides the profit of a new dish introduced to the tables of all gentlemen of fortune in the kingdom who have any refinement in taste. And the money will circulate among ourselves, the goods being entirely of our own growth and manufacture.

Fourthly, the constant breeders, besides the gain of eight shillings sterling per annum by the sale of their children, will be rid of the charge of maintaining them after the first year.

Fifthly, this food would likewise bring great custom to taverns, where the vintners 25 will certainly be so prudent as to procure the best receipts for dressing it to perfection, and consequently have their houses frequented by all the fine gentlemen, who justly value themselves upon their knowledge in good eating; and a skillful cook, who understands how to oblige his guests, will contrive to make it as expensive as they please.

Sixthly, this would be a great inducement to marriage, which all wise nations have either encouraged by rewards or enforced by laws and penalties. It would increase the care and tenderness of mothers toward their children, when they were sure of a settlement for life to the poor babes, provided in some sort by the public, to their annual profit instead of expense. We should see an honest emulation among the married women, which of them could bring the fattest child to the market. Men would become as fond of their wives during the time of their pregnancy as they are now of their mares in foal, their cows in calf, or sows when they are ready to farrow; nor offer to beat or kick them (as is too frequent a practice) for fear of miscarriage.

Many other advantages might be enumerated. For instance, the addition of some thousand carcasses in our exportation of barreled beef, the propagation of swine's flesh, and improvement in the art of making good bacon, so much wanted among us by the great destruction of pigs, too frequent at our tables, and are no way comparable in taste or magnificence to a well-grown, fat yearling child, which roasted whole will make a considerable figure at a lord mayor's feast, or any other public entertainment. But this and many others I omit, being studious of brevity.

Supposing that one thousand families in this city would be constant customers for infants' flesh, besides others who might have it at merry meetings, particularly weddings and christenings, I compute that Dublin would take off annually about twenty thousand carcasses, and the rest of the kingdom (where probably they will be sold somewhat cheaper) the remaining eighty thousand.

I can think of no one objection that will possibly be raised against this proposal, unless it should be urged that the number of people will be thereby much lessened in the kingdom. This I freely own, and it was indeed one principal design in offering it to the world. I desire the reader will observe that I calculate my remedy for this one individual kingdom of Ireland, and for no other that ever was, is, or, I think, ever can be upon earth. Therefore let no man talk to me of other expedients: of taxing our absentees at five shillings a pound; of using neither clothes nor household furniture except what is of our own growth and manufacture; of utterly rejecting the materials and instruments that promote foreign luxury; of curing the expensiveness of pride, vanity, idleness, and gaming in our women; of introducing a vein of parsimony, prudence, and temperance; of learning to love our country, in the want of which we differ even from Laplanders and the inhabitants of Topinamboo; of quitting our animosities and factions, nor act any longer like the Jews, who were murdering one another at the very moment their city was taken; of being a little cautious not to sell our country and consciences for nothing; of teaching landlords to have at least one degree of mercy toward their tenants; lastly, of putting a spirit of honesty, industry, and skill into our shopkeepers, who, if a resolution could now be taken to buy only our native goods, would immediately unite to cheat and exact upon us in the price, the measure, and the goodness, nor could ever yet be brought to make one fair proposal of just dealing, though often and earnestly invited to it.

30   Therefore I repeat, let no man talk to me of these and the like expedients, till he has at least some glimpse of hope that there will be ever some hearty and sincere attempt to put them in practice.

But as to myself, having been wearied out for many years with offering vain, idle, visionary thoughts, and at length utterly despairing of success, I fortunately fell upon this proposal, which, as it is wholly new, so it has something solid and real, of no expense and little trouble, full in our own power, and whereby we can incur no danger in disobliging England. For this kind of commodity will not bear exportation, the flesh being of too tender a consistence to admit a long continuance in salt, although perhaps I could name a country which would be glad to eat up our whole nation without it.

After all, I am not so violently bent upon my own opinion as to reject any offer proposed by wise men, which shall be found equally innocent, cheap, easy, and effectual. But before something of that kind shall be advanced in contradiction to my scheme, and offering a better, I desire the author or authors will be pleased maturely to consider two points. First, as things now stand, how they will be able to find food and raiment for an hundred thousand useless mouths and backs. And secondly, there being a round million of creatures in human figure throughout this kingdom, whose whole subsistence put into a common stock would leave them in debt two millions of pounds sterling, adding those who are beggars by profession to the bulk of farmers, cottagers, and laborers, with their wives and children, who are beggars in effect; I desire those politicians who dislike my overture, and may perhaps be so bold as to attempt an answer, that they will first ask the parents of these mortals whether they would not at this day think it a great happiness to have been sold for food at a year old in the manner I prescribe, and thereby have avoided such a perpetual scene of misfortunes as they have since gone through by the oppression of landlords, the impossibility of paying rent without money or trade, the want of common sustenance, with neither house nor clothes to cover them from the inclemencies of the weather, and the most inevitable prospect of entailing the like or greater miseries upon their breed for ever.

I profess, in the sincerity of my heart, that I have not the least personal interest in endeavoring to promote this necessary work, having no other motive than the public good of my country, by advancing our trade, providing for infants, relieving the poor, and giving some pleasure to the rich. I have no children by which I can propose to get a single penny; the youngest being nine years old, and my wife past child-bearing.

CRITICAL THINKING QUESTIONS

1. List the incentives Swift suggests will result from his proposal that people begin to eat the babies born to poor Irish mothers.

2. What adjectives would you use to describe the tone of Swift's writing? What adjectives might be applied to writing that does not employ Swift's tone but takes an opposite approach?

WRITING TOPIC

While Swift's proposal was not serious, it did point out very serious problems that needed to be addressed. Select a contemporary issue, such as immigration, and offer an equally outrageous solution which helps point out the importance of the situation.

Studs Terkel (b. 1912)

Frank Chin

A Chinese-American Playwright and Novelist

"When I was a little kid, during World War II, I was raised by white folks: a retired vaude-ville acrobat and a retired silent-screen bit player. We lived in a tarpaper shanty, outside Sacramento.

"A war veteran, with one eye missing and a few drinks, said to them, 'What are you doin' with that Jap kid?' I said, 'I'm no Jap kid. I'm an American of Chinese descent.' I didn't know what it was, but he didn't either. The rest of my life, I've been trying to find out ex-actly what it is." [Laughs.]

He later moved in with his grandmother and aunts in Oakland. "All we spoke in the family was Cantonese."

I hung out with blacks. I learned if I could make them laugh, I wouldn't get beat up and I could walk away and maintain my dignity. They actually came to respect me because I could talk my way out of fights in a way that would make them feel good. They would walk me to school.

5   Some people looked at this as a rejection of things Chinese. On the other hand, the blacks would say, and the whites, too, why was I talking about all this Chinese stuff? "We think of you as a member of the family." That always bothered me.

The Tower of Babel story always bothered me, too.

Oakland is the Tower of Babel. All these languages. And nobody even speaks English like everybody else. I've come to believe that monotheism encourages racism, whoever practices it. There is only one God and everyone else is an infidel, a pagan, or a goy. The Chinese look on all behavior as tactics and strategy. It's like war. You have to know the terrain. You don't destroy the terrain, you deal with it. We get along, not because we share a belief in God or Original Sin or a social contract, but because we make little deals and alliances with each other.

I like whites and blacks. I take them as individuals. I admire white culture: Shake-speare, the great ideas of Western Civilization. I also like black culture. In the sixties, it became a force in Asian-America. It always had a large presence in Oakland. I grew up with rhythm-and-blues, jazz, our original American art forms.

The fifties was still our age of innocence: the Eisenhower era. Everything was looking up: Perry Como. Since I grew up a loner, without any idea of parents, I thought Mommy and Daddy were just nicknames, like Shorty and Skinny. The idea that par-ents had a proprietary right over children was alien to me. A lot of the ideas of Chi-nese inferiority came late to me, from the outside. The one thing that saved me from being raised in the stereotype was my isolation during World War II, being raised by these white folks.

10   The sixties and the civil-rights movement came along, and the blacks were as-serting themselves and getting our attention with phrases like "Power to the People."

These wonderful black-leather jackets and the shades and the black berets were new even to the blacks themselves. It was like a parade, everyone in uniform.

As for the yellows, the civil-rights movement made us aware that we had no presence, no image in American culture as men, as people. We were perceived as being bright but with less physical prowess than the blacks and whites. We were more favored than the blacks, but we lacked their manhood. So a bunch of us began to appropriate "blackness." We'd wear the clothes, we'd affect the walk and we began talking black. We'd call our selves "Bro" and began talking Southern: "Hey, man."

We started talking about the sisters in the street and the brothers in the joint. I'd been in the joint and I didn't see any yellows there. I didn't see so many of our sisters walking the streets. That wasn't our thing. If it had been, we might have had a better sex life. [*Laughs.*]

[*He imitates the Black Panther rap.*] "Brothers and sisters, we've gotta organize, get together, and fight the *pig*. Brothers and sisters, Power to the People. Right on!" I said, "*What is this?* This isn't Chinese. It's a yellow minstrel show."

At this time, the government was throwing a lot of money at the gangs. The War on Poverty was on. Chinatown gangs, whose main business was being criminals, suddenly had social significance. They were perfectly happy to collect chump change.

I was teaching a class in Asian-American studies. My students were Chinese-Americans and Japanese-Americans. They were from the suburbs, outside Chinatown. My purpose was to break down stereotypes. So I decided to do an agit-prop thing, having them *play* the stereotypes.

We were rehearsing, doing a rock-and-roll version of

Ching-chong Chinaman,
sitting on a rail,
along come a choo-choo train,
cut off his tail.

Guitars, everything. The Lum gang walks in, walks up to the singer [*Simulates a deep, menacing voice.*]: "Stop singing that song. We don't like it." Lum comes up to me, he's holding his fist down, staring a hole through my chest. A student, a quiet little girl, who'd become a militant, is behind me saying, "Don't take no shit from nobody." I'm saying, "Shhh, shhh!" Porky, who's standing behind Lum, is yelling, "Kill 'im! Kill 'im!"

Lum is growling, "Stop singing that song. It makes fun of Chinese people." I say, in my gentlest voice, "Have you ever heard of satire? We *know* it's a racist song. That's why we're singing it. We're making fun of the people who make fun of Chinese. Do you understand?" I could see I wasn't cutting it. Porky is hollering, "Kill 'im! Kill 'im!" Finally, in frustration, because I wasn't responding to a fight, they walk out.

The gang council decides that we're too controversial. They call me to a meeting. The leader of the Chinatown Red Guard taps me on the shoulder and says, "I want to talk to you." I turn around and just like in the movies, his fist is coming toward me. He knocks me down, my glasses go flying, he punches me in the stomach. Just like in the movies, he hits me in the back of the neck. While I'm on my hands and knees, he stomps on me and starts kicking me. I'm saying [*in a whining voice*], "This is the wrong movie, guys."

He says, "Identify with China!" I say, "Wait a minute. We're in America. This is where we are, where we live and where we're going to die. There's not going to be any revolution. That's crazy." He can't hit me anymore. He's already done that and it's not working. I've interrupted his speech. This had never happened to him before. He curls his lip and says, "You cultural nationalist!" I go, "*What?* What's a cultural nationalist? Don't you know how to swear? Call me motherfucker, call me asshole, call me anything you want, but what's a cultural nationalist?" He doesn't know what to say to that, so they leave.

20   George Woo, a big guy, who's now teaching Asian-American Studies at San Francisco State, was pretty tight with the gangs then. He runs after the Red Guard and tells them if they ever beat me up again, he'll take it personally, that I'm his friend. All of a sudden, the leader of the gang council comes up to me and says, "I want to shake your hand. No one ever talked back to Alex that way before." We're all buddy-buddy now, because George said he'll take it personally.

The word flashes through Chinatown. Twenty-five minutes later, another gang of kids shows up. Must be fifteen, sixteen years old. One of them has a Tommy gun. "*Where are they?* We heard someone beat up a friend of George's." [*Laughs.*] I said, "No, no, that's not my style. Let's do it with words."

The civil-rights movement of the sixties affected the Chinese-American community in a number of ways. In ways that aren't very flattering to us. When I went to interview some Asian-American actors who played Charlie Chan's Number One, Two, Three, and Four sons, they were blaming the blacks for the yellows not getting more parts. "Here we've been good people, keeping our noses clean—" Suddenly they realized what I was up to and they saw *me* as a threat. I was making ChineseAmericans controversial by speaking out against racism.

It's an old story. The good Chinese were the Christian Chinese. The good Chinese were the ones who shucked all Chinese ways. They revere Pearl Buck and the missionaries that worked Chinatown. That's what bothered me, our history in Chinatown, San Francisco.

In Chinatown's twelve blocks, there are forty-two Christian churches. On the walls of Chinatown, there's a plaque honoring Ross Hunter, who produced *The Flower Drum Song;* a plaque honoring the song "Grant Avenue"; a plaque marking the birthplace of the first white child in San Francisco; a monument to the first white school. *Nothing* for the Chinese. There is one exception: a monument to Sun Yat Sen. He was a Christian.

25   Most in the community saw the civil-rights movement as a threat. They objected to school integration because they didn't want their children to be influenced by blacks. The fact is the mimicking of blacks that I experienced were of a few. White journalists have emphasized that aspect. As though the Chinese don't think of themselves as Chinese-Americans. As though we're an enclave, like Americans working for Aramco in Saudi Arabia.

Chinatown may be a stronghold of Chinese culture, but we're Chinese-Americans. We saw the movement as a threat because we might be identified as a minority. We were thinking of ourselves as being assimilated. We had worked so hard at being acculturated that we didn't know anything about China anymore.

During the Depression, my uncle was raised in a Chinese Baptist Home for Boys. To raise money, they put on a show. It was the first Chinese-American blackface minstrel show in the history of the world. I came across the autobiography of the founder. I showed my uncle a picture in the book; the boys in blackface. He burst into tears. He was one of the Chung-mai minstrels. He got sad and I got angry. It was humiliating.

At the same time, we thought we were above the blacks. My family owned some property in the black district of Oakland. I once went with my mother to collect the rent. I said, "These places are terrible." She says, "Yeah, but they drive Cadillacs. It's what you call nigger-rich." That struck me so hard. I had never heard my folks put down blacks, denigrate people that way. Yet we were slumlords, taking advantage, exploiting them. It was a moment of moral confusion. I was eight at the time.

We feel because we're more civilized, quote unquote, because we're more middle-class, that we deserve more acceptance than the blacks. We don't riot, we don't make waves, we didn't protest, we're more American. We don't see that we've described ourselves as a race of Helen Kellers, mute, blind and deaf. We're the perfect minority.

We embrace Charlie Chan as an image of racist love. Most of us still think the   30 good Chinaman is the Christian, Charlie Chan. There's a Chinese-American sociologist who said, "The Chinese, much to their credit, have never been overly bitter about racial prejudice. They have gone into jobs that reduced visibility and are moving out of population vortices of New York and San Francisco's Chinatown to outlying areas. Such a movement should be encouraged, because dispersion discourages visibility." The stereotype is embraced as a strategy for white acceptance.

The prejudice against blacks still continues, but we're smart enough to know it isn't quite civilized. We're also smart enough to use it to get our share. It happened to me. It was in the sixties. The railroads were taken to court for failing to integrate. They fell under ICC [Interstate Commerce Commission] rules. So they put up a call: they were hiring brakemen. I was encouraged to apply. I was a clerk for a railroad company. It was the lowest of the low. I was fairly assured I'd be hired, implying I'd be more acceptable than a black. By default, I became the first Chinese-American brakeman on the Southern Pacific. I was the lesser of the two evils.

We believed what whites believed about blacks. We adopted all the white prejudice. The blacks adopted the same prejudices about us. David Hilliard of the Black Panthers got up in Portsmouth Square—luckily most Chinese there didn't understand English—and said, "You Chinese are the Uncle Toms of the colored peoples." It was apt. At the same time, the solution was not for us to become black.

The new immigrants, the Indochinese, are a revelation. They still speak all the dialects of Indochina: Lao, Viet, or Cambodian. They pick up English as a matter of necessity, as a language of commerce. It's strategic. It's a white-man's world and you have to get along. Yet, all these languages are being spoken. They're using English as a dialect of Chinese and not following the rules. In Chinese-America, it is the new immigrants threatening our relationship with the whites, not the blacks. They are the unredeemed Chinese Chinese. It's an interesting, exciting time.

CRITICAL THINKING QUESTIONS

1. The narrator creates a frank discussion of his experience as a Chinese-American. What is his attitude toward assimilation by minorities in this country?

2. At the close of his piece, the narrator calls the new Chinese immigrants "unredeemed Chinese Chinese." What does he mean by that phrase?

Henry David Thoreau (1817–1862)

Civil Disobedience

I heartily accept the motto,—"That government is best which governs least"; and I should like to see it acted up to more rapidly and systematically. Carried out, it finally amounts to this, which also I believe,—"That government is best which governs not at all;" and when men are prepared for it, that will be the kind of government which they will have. Government is at best but an expedient; but most governments are usually, and all governments are sometimes, inexpedient. The objections which have been brought against a standing army, and they are many and weighty, and deserve to prevail, may also at last be brought against a standing government. The standing army is only an arm of the standing government. The government itself, which is only the mode which the people have chosen to execute their will, is equally liable to be abused and perverted before the people can act through it. Witness the present Mexican war, the work of comparatively a few individuals using the standing government as their tool; for, in the outset, the people would not have consented to this measure.

This American government—what is it but a tradition, though a recent one, endeavoring to transmit itself unimpaired to posterity, but each instant losing some of its integrity? It has not the vitality and force of a single living man; for a single man can bend it to his will. It is a sort of wooden gun to the people themselves. But it is not the less necessary for this; for the people must have some complicated machinery or other, and hear its din, to satisfy that idea of government which they have. Governments show thus how successfully men can be imposed on, even impose on themselves, for their own advantage. It is excellent, we must all allow. Yet this government never of itself furthered any enterprise, but by the alacrity with which it got out of its way. *It* does not keep the country free. *It* does not settle the West. *It* does not educate. The character inherent in the American people has done all that has been accomplished; and it would have done somewhat more, if the government had not sometimes got in its way. For government is an expedient by which men would fain succeed in letting one another alone; and, as has been said, when it is most expedient, the governed are most let alone by it. Trade and commerce, if they were not made of India-rubber, would never manage to bounce over the obstacles which legislators are continually putting in their way; and, if one were to judge these men wholly by the effects of their actions and not partly by their intentions, they would deserve to be classed and punished with those mischievous persons who put obstructions on the railroads.

But, to speak practically and as a citizen, unlike those who call themselves no-government men, I ask for, not at once no government, but *at once* a better government. Let every man make known what kind of government would command his respect, and that will be one step toward obtaining it.

After all, the practical reason why, when the power is once in the hands of people, a majority are permitted, and for a long period continue, to rule is not because they are most likely to be in the right, nor because this seems fairest to the minority, but because they are physically the strongest. But a government in which the majority rule in all cases cannot be based on justice, even as far as men understand it. Can there not be a government in which majorities do not virtually decide right and wrong, but conscience?—in which majorities decide only those questions to which the rule of expediency is applicable? Must the citizen ever for a moment, or in the least degree, resign his conscience to the legislator? Why has every man a conscience, then? I think that we should be men first, and subjects afterward. It is not desirable to cultivate a respect for the law, so much as for the right. The only obligation which I have a right to assume is to do at any time what I think right. It is truly enough said, that a corporation has no conscience; but a corporation of conscientious men is a corporation *with* a conscience. Law never made men a whit more just; and, by means of their respect for it, even the well-disposed are daily made the agents of injustice. A common and natural result of an undue respect for law is, that you may see a file of soldiers, colonel, captain, corporal, privates, powder-monkeys, and all, marching in admirable order over hill and dale to the wars, against their will, ay, against their common sense and consciences, which makes it very steep marching indeed, and produces a palpitation of the heart. They have no doubt that it is a damnable business in which they are concerned; they are all peaceably inclined. Now, what are they? Men at all? or small movable forts and magazines, at the service of some unscrupulous man in power? Visit the Navy-Yard, and behold a marine, such a man as an American government can make, or such as it can make a man with its black arts,—a mere shadow and reminiscence of humanity, a man laid out alive and standing, and already, as one may say, buried under arms with funeral accompaniments, though it may be,—

Not a drum was heard, not a funeral note,
As his corse to the rampart we hurried;
Not a soldier discharged his farewell shot
O'er the grave where our hero we buried.

The mass of men serve the state thus, not as men mainly, but as machines, with their bodies. They are the standing army, and the militia, jailers, constables, posse comitatus, etc. In most cases there is no free exercise whatever of the judgment or of the moral sense; but they put themselves on a level with wood and earth and stones; and wooden men can perhaps be manufactured that will serve the purpose as well. Such command no more respect than men of straw or a lump of dirt. They have the same sort of worth only as horses and dogs. Yet such as these even are commonly esteemed good citizens. Others—as most legislators, politicians, lawyers, ministers, and office-holders—serve the state chiefly with their heads; and, as they rarely make any moral distinctions, they are as likely to serve the Devil, without *intending* it, as God. A very few, as heroes, patriots, martyrs, reformers in the great sense, and *men*, serve the state with their consciences also, and so necessarily resist it for the most part; and they are commonly treated as enemies by it. A wise man will only be useful as a man, and will not submit to be "clay," and "stop a hole to keep the wind away," but leave that office to his dust at least:—

> I am too high-born to be propertied,
> To be a secondary at control,
> Or useful serving-man and instrument
> To any sovereign state throughout the world.

He who gives himself entirely to his fellow-men appears to them useless and self-ish; but he who gives himself partially to them is pronounced a benefactor and phil-anthropist.

How does it become a man to behave toward this American government to-day? I answer, that he cannot without disgrace be associated with it. I cannot for an instant recognize that political organization as *my* government which is the *slave's* government also.

All men recognize the right of revolution; that is, the right to refuse allegiance to, and to resist, the government, when its tyranny or its inefficiency are great and unen-durable. But almost all say that such is not the case now. But such was the case, they think, in the Revolution of '75. If one were to tell me that this was a bad government because it taxed certain foreign commodities brought to its ports, it is most probable that I should not make an ado about it, for I can do without them. All machines have their friction; and possibly this does enough good to counterbalance the evil. At any rate, it is a great evil to make a stir about it. But when the friction comes to have its machine, and oppression and robbery are organized, I say, let us not have such a machine any longer. In other words, when a sixth of the population of a nation which has undertaken to be the refuge of liberty are slaves, and a whole country is unjustly overrun and con-quered by a foreign army, and subjected to military law, I think that it is not too soon for honest men to rebel and revolutionize. What makes this duty the more urgent is the fact that the country so overrun is not our own, but ours is the invading army.

Paley, a common authority with many on moral questions, in his chapter on the "Duty of Submission to Civil Government," resolves all civil obligation into expedi-ency; and he proceeds to say, "that so long as the interest of the whole society requires it, that is, so long as the established government cannot be resisted or changed with-out public inconveniency, it is the will of God that the established government be obeyed, and no longer. . . . This principle being admitted, the justice of every partic-ular case of resistance is reduced to a computation of the quantity of the danger and grievance on the one side, and of the probability and expense of redressing it on the other." Of this, he says, every man shall judge for himself. But Paley appears never to have contemplated those cases to which the rule of expediency does not apply, in

which a people, as well as an individual, must do justice, cost what it may. If I have unjustly wrested a plank from a drowning man, I must restore it to him though I drown
myself. This, according to Paley, would be inconvenient. But he that would save his
life, in such a case, shall lose it. This people must cease to hold slaves, and to make war
on Mexico, though it cost them their existence as a people.

In their practice, nations agree with Paley; but does any one think that Massa-   10
chusetts does exactly what is right at the present crisis?

> A drab of state, a cloth-o'-silver slut,
> To have her train borne up, and her soul trail in the dirt.

Practically speaking, the opponents to a reform in Massachusetts are not a hundred
thousand politicians at the South, but a hundred thousand merchants and farmers
here, who are more interested in commerce and agriculture than they are in humanity, and are not prepared to do justice to the slave and to Mexico, *cost what it may*. I
quarrel not with far-off foes, but with those who, near at home, coöperate with, and
do the bidding of, those far away, and without whom the latter would be harmless. We
are accustomed to say, that the mass of men are unprepared; but improvement is slow,
because the few are not materially wiser or better than the many. It is not so important that many should be as good as you, as that there be some absolute goodness
somewhere; for that will leaven the whole lump. There are thousands who are *in opinion* opposed to slavery and to the war, who yet in effect do nothing to put an end to
them; who, esteeming themselves children of Washington and Franklin, sit down with
their hands in their pockets, and say that they know not what to do, and do nothing;
who even postpone the question of freedom to the question of free-trade, and quietly
read the prices-current along with the latest advices from Mexico, after dinner, and,
it may be, fall asleep over them both. What is the price-current of an honest man and
patriot to-day? They hesitate, and they regret, and sometimes they petition; but they
do nothing in earnest and with effect. They will wait, well disposed, for others to remedy the evil, that they may no longer have it to regret. At most, they give only a cheap
vote, and a feeble countenance and Godspeed, to the right, as it goes by them. There
are nine hundred and ninety-nine patrons of virtue to one virtuous man. But it is easier to deal with the real possessor of a thing than with the temporary guardian of it.

All voting is a sort of gaming, like checkers or backgammon, with a slight moral
tinge to it, a playing with right and wrong, with moral questions; and betting naturally
accompanies it. The character of the voters is not staked. I cast my vote, perchance, as
I think right; but I am not vitally concerned that that right should prevail. I am willing to leave it to the majority. Its obligation, therefore, never exceeds that of expediency.
Even voting *for the right* is *doing* nothing for it. It is only expressing to men feebly your
desire that it should prevail. A wise man will not leave the right to the mercy of chance,
nor wish it to prevail through the power of the majority. There is but little virtue in the
action of masses of men. When the majority shall at length vote for the abolition of slavery, it will be because they are indifferent to slavery, or because there is but little slavery left to be abolished by their vote. *They* will then be the only slaves. Only *his* vote
can hasten the abolition of slavery who asserts his own freedom by his vote.

I hear of a convention to be held at Baltimore, or elsewhere, for the selection of a candidate for the Presidency, made up chiefly of editors, and men who are politicians by profession; but I think, what is it to any independent, intelligent, and respectable man what decision they may come to? Shall we not have the advantage of his wisdom and honesty, nevertheless? Can we not count upon some independent votes? Are there not many individuals in the country who do not attend conventions? But no: I find that the respectable man, so called, has immediately drifted from his position, and despairs of his country, when his country has more reason to despair of him. He forthwith adopts one of the candidates thus selected as the only *available* one, thus proving that he is himself *available* for any purposes of the demagogue. His vote is of no more worth than that of any unprincipled foreigner or hireling native, who may have been bought. O for a man who is a *man*, and, as my neighbor says, has a bone in his back which you cannot pass your hand through! Our statistics are at fault: the population has been returned too large. How many *men* are there to a square thousand miles in his country? Hardly one. Does not America offer any inducement for men to settle here? The American has dwindled into an Odd Fellow,—one who may be known by the development of his organ of gregariousness, and a manifest lack of intellect and cheerful self-reliance; whose first and chief concern, on coming into the world, is to see that the Almshouses are in good repair; and, before yet he has lawfully donned the virile garb, to collect a fund for the support of the widows and orphans that may be; who, in short, ventures to live only by the aid of the Mutual Insurance company, which has promised to bury him decently.

It is not a man's duty, as a matter of course, to devote himself to the eradication of any, even the most enormous wrong; he may still properly have other concerns to engage him; but it is his duty, at least, to wash his hands of it, and, if he gives it no thought longer, not to give it practically his support. If I devote myself to other pursuits and contemplations, I must first see, at least, that I do not pursue them sitting upon another man's shoulders. I must get off him first, that he may pursue his contemplations too. See what gross inconsistency is tolerated. I have heard some of my townsmen say, "I should like to have them order me out to help put down an insurrection of the slaves, or to march to Mexico;—see if I would go"; and yet these very men have each, directly by their allegiance, and so indirectly, at least, by their money, furnished a substitute. The soldier is applauded who refuses to serve in an unjust war by those who do not refuse to sustain the unjust government which makes the war; is applauded by those whose own act and authority he disregards and sets at naught; as if the state were penitent to that degree that it hired one to scourge it while it sinned, but not to that degree that it left off sinning for a moment. Thus, under the name of Order and Civil Government, we are all made at last to pay homage to and support our own meanness. After the first blush of sin comes its indifference; and from immoral it becomes, as it were, *un*moral, and not quite unnecessary to that life which we have made.

The broadest and most prevalent error requires the most disinterested virtue to sustain it. The slight reproach to which the virtue of patriotism is commonly liable, the noble are most likely to incur. Those who, while they disapprove of the character and measures of a government, yield to it their allegiance and support are undoubtedly its most conscientious supporters, and so frequently the most serious obstacles to reform. Some are petitioning the state to dissolve the Union, to disregard the requisitions of the President. Why do they not dissolve it themselves,—the union between themselves and the state,—and refuse to pay their quota into its treasury? Do not they stand in the same relation to the state that the state does to the Union? And have not the same reasons prevented the state from resisting the Union which have prevented them from resisting the state?

How can a man be satisfied to entertain an opinion merely, and enjoy *it?* Is there 15 any enjoyment in it, if his opinion is that he is aggrieved? If you are cheated out of a single dollar by your neighbor, you do not rest satisfied with knowing that you are cheated, or with saying that you are cheated, or even with petitioning him to pay you your due; but you take effectual steps at once to obtain the full amount, and see that you are never cheated again. Action from principle, the perception and the performance of right, changes things and relations; it is essentially revolutionary, and does not consist wholly with anything which was. It not only divides states and churches, it divides families; ay, it divides the *individual,* separating the diabolical in him from the divine.

Unjust laws exist: shall we be content to obey them, or shall we endeavor to amend them, and obey them until we have succeeded, or shall we transgress them at once? Men generally, under such a government as this, think that they ought to wait until they have persuaded the majority to alter them. They think that, if they should resist, the remedy would be worse than the evil. But it is the fault of the government itself that the remedy *is* worse than the evil. *It* makes it worse. Why is it not more apt to anticipate and provide for reform? Why does it not cherish its wise minority? Why does it cry and resist before it is hurt? Why does it not encourage its citizens to be on the alert to point out its faults, and *do* better than it would have them? Why does it always crucify Christ, and excommunicate Copernicus and Luther, and pronounce Washington and Franklin rebels?

One would think, that a deliberate and practical denial of its authority was the only offense never contemplated by government; else, why has it not assigned its definite, its suitable and proportionate penalty? If a man who has no property refuses but once to earn nine shillings for the state, he is put in prison for a period unlimited by any law that I know, and determined only by the discretion of those who placed him there; but if he should steal ninety times nine shillings from the state, he is soon permitted to go at large again.

If the injustice is part of the necessary friction of the machine of government, let it go, let it go; perchance it will wear smooth,—certainly the machine will wear out. If the injustice has a spring, or a pulley, or a rope, or a crank, exclusively for itself, then perhaps you may consider whether the remedy will not be worse than the evil; but if it is of such a nature that it requires you to be the agent of injustice to another, then, I say, break the law. Let your life be a counter friction to stop the machine. What I have to do is to see, at any rate, that I do not lend myself to the wrong which I condemn.

As for adopting the ways which the state has provided for remedying the evil, I know not of such ways. They take too much time, and a man's life will be gone. I have other affairs to attend to. I came into this world, not chiefly to make this a good place to live in, but to live in it, be it good or bad. A man has not everything to do, but something; and because he cannot do *everything*, it is not necessary that he should do *something* wrong. It is not my business to be petitioning the Governor or the Legislature any more than it is theirs to petition me; and if they should not hear my petition, what should I do then? But in this case the state has provided no way; its very Constitution is the evil. This may seem to be harsh and stubborn and unconciliatory; but it is to treat with the utmost kindness and consideration the only spirit that can appreciate or deserves it. So is all change for the better, like birth and death, which convulse the body.

20   I do not hesitate to say, that those who call themselves Abolitionists should at once effectually withdraw their support, both in person and property, from the government of Massachusetts, and not wait till they constitute a majority of one, before they suffer the right to prevail through them. I think that it is enough if they have God on their side, without waiting for that other one. Moreover, any man more right than his neighbors constitutes a majority of one already.

I meet this American government, or its representative, the state government, directly, and face to face, once a year—no more—in the person of its tax-gatherer; this is the only mode in which a man situated as I am necessarily meets it; and it then says distinctly, Recognize me; and the simplest, the most effectual, and, in the present posture of affairs, the indispensablest mode of treating with it on this head, of expressing your little satisfaction with and love for it, is to deny it then. My civil neighbor, the tax-gatherer, is the very man I have to deal with,—for it is, after all, with men and not with parchment that I quarrel,—and he has voluntarily chosen to be an agent of the government. How shall he ever know well what he is and does as an officer of the government, or as a man, until he is obliged to consider whether he shall treat me, his neighbor, for whom he has respect, as a neighbor and well-disposed man, or as a maniac and disturber of the peace, and see if he can get over this obstruction to his neighborliness without a ruder and more impetuous thought or speech corresponding with his action. I know this well, that if one thousand, if one hundred, if ten men whom I could name,—if ten *honest* men only,—ay, if *one* HONEST man, in this State of Massachusetts, *ceasing to hold slaves,* were actually to withdraw from this co-partnership, and be locked up in the county jail therefor, it would be the abolition of slavery in America. For it matters not how small the beginning may seem to be; what is once well done is done forever. But we love better to talk about it: that we say is our mission. Reform keeps many scores of newspapers in its service, but not one man. If my esteemed neighbor, the State's ambassador, who will devote his days to the settlement of the question of human rights in the Council Chamber, instead of being threatened with the prisons of Carolina, were to sit down the prisoner of Massachusetts, that State which is so anxious to foist the sin of slavery upon her sister,—though at present she can discover only an act of inhospitality to be the ground of a quarrel with her,—the Legislature would not wholly waive the subject the following winter.

Under a government which imprisons any unjustly, the true place for a just man is also a prison. The proper place to-day, the only place which Massachusetts has provided for her freer and less desponding spirits, is in her prisons, to be put out and locked out of the State by her own act, as they have already put themselves out by their principles. It is there that the fugitive slave, and the Mexican prisoner on parole, and the Indian come to plead the wrongs of his race should find them; on that separate, but more free and honorable ground, where the State places those who are not *with* her, but *against* her,—the only house in a slave State in which a free man can abide with honor. If any think that their influence would be lost there, and their voices no longer afflict the ear of the State, that they would not be as an enemy within its walls, they do not know by how much truth is stronger than error, nor how much more eloquently and effectively he can combat injustice who has experienced a little in his own person. Cast your whole vote, not a strip of paper merely, but your whole influence. A minority is powerless while it conforms to the majority; it is not even a minority then; but it is irresistible when it clogs by its whole weight. If the alternative is to keep all just men in prison, or give up war and slavery, the State will not hesitate which to choose. If a thousand men were not to pay their tax-bills this year, that would not be a violent and bloody measure, as it would be to pay them, and enable the State to commit violence and shed innocent blood. This is, in fact, the definition of a peaceable revolution, if any such is possible. If the tax-gatherer, or any other public officer, asks me, as one has done, "But what shall I do?" my answer is, "If you really wish to do anything, resign your office." When the subject has refused allegiance, and the officer has resigned his office, then the revolution is accomplished. But even suppose blood should flow. Is there not a sort of blood shed when the conscience is wounded? Through this wound a man's real manhood and immortality flow out, and he bleeds to an everlasting death. I see this blood flowing now.

I have contemplated the imprisonment of the offender, rather than the seizure of his goods,—though both will serve the same purpose,—because they who assert the purest right, and consequently are most dangerous to a corrupt State, commonly have not spent much time in accumulating property. To such the State renders comparatively small service, and a slight tax is wont to appear exorbitant, particularly if they are obliged to earn it by special labor with their hands. If there were one who lived wholly without the use of money, the State itself would hesitate to demand it of him. But the rich man—not to make any invidious comparison—is always sold to the institution which makes him rich. Absolutely speaking, the more money, the less virtue; for money comes between a man and his objects, and obtains them for him; and it was certainly no great virtue to obtain it. It puts to rest many questions which he would otherwise be taxed to answer; while the only new question which it puts is the hard but superfluous one, how to spend it. Thus his moral ground is taken from under his feet. The opportunities of living are diminished in proportion as what are called the "means" are increased. The best thing a man can do for his culture when he is rich is to endeavor to carry out those schemes which he entertained when he was poor. Christ answered to Herodians according to their condition. "Show me the tribute-money," said he;—and one took a penny out of his pocket;—if you use money which has the image of Caesar on it, and which he has made current and valuable, that is, *if you are men of the State,* and gladly enjoy the advantages of Caesar's government, then pay him back some of his own when he demands it. "Render therefore to Caesar that which is Caesar's, and to God those things which are God's,"—leaving them no wiser than before as to which was which; for they did not wish to know.

When I converse with the freest of my neighbors, I perceive that, whatever they may say about the magnitude and seriousness of the question, and their regard for the public tranquillity, the long and the short of the matter is, that they cannot spare the protection of the existing government, and they dread the consequences to their property and families of disobedience to it. For my own part, I should not like to think that I ever rely on the protection of the State. But, if I deny the authority of the State when it presents its tax-bill, it will soon take and waste all my property, and so harass me and my children without end. This is hard. This makes it impossible for a man to live honestly, and at the same time comfortably, in outward respects. It will not be worth the while to accumulate property; that would be sure to go again. You must hire or squat somewhere, and raise but a small crop, and eat that soon. You must live within yourself, and depend upon yourself always tucked up and ready for a start, and not have many affairs. A man may grow rich in Turkey even, if he will be in all respects a good subject of the Turkish government. Confucius said: "If a state is governed by the principles of reason, poverty and misery are subjects of shame; if a state is not governed by the principles of reason, riches and honors are the subjects of shame." No: until I want the protection of Massachusetts to be extended to me in some distant Southern port, where my liberty is endangered, or until I am bent solely on building up an estate at home by peaceful enterprise, I can afford to refuse allegiance to Massachusetts, and her right to my property and life. It costs me less in every sense to incur the penalty of disobedience to the State than it would to obey. I should feel as if I were worth less in that case.

25   Some years ago, the State met me in behalf of the Church, and commanded me to pay a certain sum toward the support of a clergyman whose preaching my father attended, but never I myself. "Pay," it said, "or be locked up in the jail." I declined to pay. But, unfortunately, another man saw fit to pay it. I did not see why the schoolmaster should be taxed to support the priest, and not the priest the schoolmaster; for I was not the State's schoolmaster, but I supported myself by voluntary subscription. I did not see why the lyceum should not present its tax-bill, and have the State to back its demand, as well as the Church. However, at the request of the selectmen, I condescended to make some such statement as this in writing:—"Know all men by these presents, that I, Henry Thoreau, do not wish to be regarded as a member of any incorporated society which I have not joined." This I gave to the town clerk; and he has it. The State, having thus learned that I did not wish to be regarded as a member of that church, has never made a like demand on me since; though it said that it must adhere to its original presumption that time. If I had known how to name them, I should then have signed off in detail from all the societies which I never signed on to; but I did not know where to find a complete list.

I have paid no poll-tax for six years. I was put into jail once on this account, for one night; and, as I stood considering the walls of solid stone, two or three feet thick, the door of wood and iron, a foot thick, and the iron grating which strained the light, I could not help being struck with the foolishness of that institution which treated me as if I were mere flesh and blood and bones, to be locked up. I wondered that it should have concluded at length that this was the best use it could put me to, and had never thought to avail itself of my services in some way. I saw that, if there was a wall of stone between me and my townsmen, there was still a more difficult one to climb or break through before they could get to be as free as I was. I did not for a moment feel confined, and the walls seemed a great waste of stone and mortar. I felt as if I alone of all my townsmen had paid my tax. They plainly did not know how to treat me, but behaved like persons who are underbred. In every threat and in every compliment there was a blunder; for they thought that my chief desire was to stand the other side of that stone wall. I could not but smile to see how industriously they locked the door on my meditations, which followed them out again without let or hindrance, and *they* were really all that was dangerous. As they could not reach me, they had resolved to punish my body; just as boys, if they cannot come at some person against whom they have a spite, will abuse his dog. I saw that the State was half-witted, that it was timid as a lone woman with her silver spoons, and that it did not know its friends from its foes, and I lost all my remaining respect for it, and pitied it.

Thus the State never intentionally confronts a man's sense, intellectual or moral, but only his body, his senses. It is not armed with superior wit or honesty, but with superior physical strength. I was not born to be forced. I will breathe after my own fashion. Let us see who is the strongest. What force has a multitude? They only can force me who obey a higher law than I. They force me to become like themselves. I do not hear of *men* being *forced* to live this way or that by masses of men. What sort of life were that to live? When I meet a government which says to me, "Your money or your life," why should I be in haste to give it my money? It may be in a great strait, and not know what to do: I cannot help that. It must help itself; do as I do. It is not worth the while to snivel about it. I am not responsible for the successful working of the machinery of society. I am not the son of the engineer. I perceive that, when an acorn and a chestnut fall side by side, the one does not remain inert to make way for the other, but both obey their own laws, and spring and grow and flourish as best they can, till one, perchance, overshadows and destroys the other. If a plant cannot live according to its nature, it dies; and so a man.

The night in prison was novel and interesting enough. The prisoners in their shirt-sleeves were enjoying a chat and the evening air in the doorway, when I entered. But the jailer said, "Come, boys, it is time to lock up;" and so they dispersed, and I heard the sound of their steps returning into the hollow apartments. My room-mate was introduced to me by the jailer as "a first-rate fellow and a clever man." When the door was locked, he showed me where to hang my hat, and how he managed matters there. The rooms were whitewashed once a month; and this one, at least, was the whitest, most simply furnished, and probably the neatest apartment in the town. He naturally wanted to know where I came from, and what brought me there; and, when I had told him, I asked him in my turn how he came there, presuming him to be an honest man, of course; and, as the world goes, I believe he was. "Why," said he, "they accuse me of burning a barn; but I never did it." As near as I could discover, he had probably gone to bed in a barn when drunk, and smoked his pipe there; and so a barn was burnt. He had the reputation of being a clever man, had been there some three months waiting for his trial to come on, and would have to wait as much longer; but he was quite domesticated and contented, since he got his board for nothing, and thought that he was well treated.

He occupied one window, and I the other; and I saw that if one stayed there long, his principal business would be to look out the window. I had soon read all the tracts that were left there, and examined where former prisoners had broken out, and where a grate had been sawed off, and heard the history of the various occupants of that room; for I found that even here there was a history and a gossip which never circulated beyond the walls of the jail. Probably this is the only house in the town where verses are composed, which are afterward printed in a circular form, but not published. I was shown quite a long list of verses which were composed by some young men who had been detected in an attempt to escape, who avenged themselves by singing them.

30   I pumped my fellow-prisoner as dry as I could, for fear I should never see him again; but at length he showed me which was my bed, and left me to blow out the lamp.

It was like traveling into a far country, such as I had never expected to behold, to lie there for one night. It seemed to me that I never had heard the town-clock strike before, nor the evening sounds of the village; for we slept with the windows open, which were inside the grating. It was to see my native village in the light of the Middle Ages, and our Concord was turned into a Rhine stream, and visions of knights and castles passed before me. They were the voices of old burghers that I heard in the streets. I was an involuntary spectator and auditor of whatever was done and said in the kitchen of the adjacent village-inn,—a wholly new and rare experience to me. It was a closer view of my native town. I was fairly inside of it. I never had seen its institutions before. This is one of its peculiar institutions; for it is a shire town. I began to comprehend what its inhabitants were about.

In the morning, our breakfasts were put through the hole in the door, in small oblong-square tin pans, made to fit, and holding a pint of chocolate, with brown bread, and an iron spoon. When they called for the vessels again, I was green enough to return what bread I had left; but my comrade seized it, and said that I should lay that up for lunch or dinner. Soon after he was let out to work at haying in a neighboring field, whither he went every day, and would not be back till noon; so he bade me good-day, saying that he doubted if he should see me again.

When I came out of prison,—for some one interfered, and paid that tax,—I did not perceive that great changes had taken place on the common, such as he observed who went in a youth and emerged a tottering and gray-headed man; and yet a change had to my eyes come over the scene,—the town, and State, and country,—greater than any that mere time could effect. I saw yet more distinctly the State in which I lived. I saw to what extent the people among whom I lived could be trusted as good neighbors and friends; that their friendship was for summer weather only; that they did not greatly propose to do right; that they were a distinct race from me by their prejudices and superstitions, as the Chinamen and Malays are; that in their sacrifices to humanity they ran no risks, not even to their property; that after all they were not so noble but they treated the thief as he had treated them, and hoped, by a certain outward observance and a few prayers, and by walking in a particular straight though useless path from time to time, to save their souls. This may be to judge my neighbors harshly; for I believe that many of them are not aware that they have such an institution as the jail in their village.

It was formerly the custom in our village, when a poor debtor came out of jail, for his acquaintances to salute him, looking through their fingers, which were crossed to represent the grating of a jail window, "How do ye do?" My neighbors did not thus salute me, but first looked at me, and then at one another, as if I had returned from a long journey. I was put into jail as I was going to the shoemaker's to get a shoe which was mended. When I was let out the next morning, I proceeded to finish my errand, and, having put on my mended shoe, joined a huckleberry party, who were impatient to put themselves under my conduct; and in half an hour,—for the horse was soon tackled,—was in the midst of a huckleberry field, on one of our highest hills, two miles off, and then the State was nowhere to be seen.

This is the whole history of "My Prisons."   35

I have never declined paying the highway tax, because I am as desirous of being a good neighbor as I am of being a bad subject; and as for supporting schools, I am doing my part to educate my fellow-countrymen now. It is for no particular item in the tax-bill that I refuse to pay it. I simply wish to refuse allegiance to the State, to withdraw and stand aloof from it effectually. I do not care to trace the course of my dollar, if I could, till it buys a man or a musket to shoot one with,—the dollar is innocent,—but I am concerned to trace the effects of my allegiance. In fact, I quietly declare war with the State, after my fashion, though I will still make what use and get what advantage of her I can, as is usual in such cases.

If others pay the tax which is demanded of me, from a sympathy with the State, they do but what they have already done in their own case, or rather they abet injustice to a greater extent than the State requires. If they pay the tax from a mistaken interest in the individual taxed, to save his property, or prevent his going to jail, it is because they have not considered wisely how far they let their private feelings interfere with the public good.

This, then, is my position at present. But one cannot be too much on his guard in such a case, lest his action be biased by obstinacy or an undue regard for the opinions of men. Let him see that he does only what belongs to himself and to the hour.

I think sometimes, Why, this people mean well, they are only ignorant; they would do better if they knew how: why give your neighbors this pain to treat you as they are not inclined to? But I think again, This is no reason why I should do as they do, or permit others to suffer much greater pain of a different kind. Again, I sometimes say to myself, When many millions of men, without heat, without ill will, without personal feeling of any kind, demand of you a few shillings only, without the possibility, such is their constitution, of retracting or altering their present demand, and without the possibility, on your side, of appeal to any other millions, why expose yourself to this overwhelming brute force? You do not resist cold and hunger, the winds and the waves, thus obstinately; you quietly submit to a thousand similar necessities. You do not put your head into the fire. But just in proportion as I regard this as not wholly a brute force, but partly a human force, and consider that I have relations to those millions as to so many millions of men, and not of mere brute or inanimate things, I see that appeal is possible, first and instantaneously, from them to the Maker of them, and, secondly, from them to themselves. But if I put my head deliberately into the fire, there is no appeal to fire or to the Maker of fire, and I have only myself to blame. If I could convince myself that I have any right to be satisfied with men as they are, and to treat them accordingly, and not according, in some respects, to my requisitions and expectations of what they and I ought to be, then, like a good Mussulman and fatalist, I should endeavor to be satisfied with things as they are, and say it is the will of God. And, above all, there is this difference between resisting this and a purely brute or natural force, that I can resist this with some effect; but I cannot expect, like Orpheus, to change the nature of the rocks and trees and beasts.

40   I do not wish to quarrel with any man or nation. I do not wish to split hairs, to make fine distinctions, or set myself up as better than my neighbors. I seek rather, I may say, even an excuse for conforming to the laws of the land. I am but too ready to conform to them. Indeed, I have reason to suspect myself on this head; and each year, as the tax-gatherer comes round, I find myself disposed to review the acts and position of the general and State governments, and the spirit of the people, to discover a pretext for conformity.

> We must affect our country as our parents,
> And if at any time we alienate
> Our love or industry from doing it honor,
> We must respect effects and teach the soul
> Matter of conscience and religion,
> And not desire of rule or benefit.

I believe that the State will soon be able to take all my work of this sort out of my hands, and then I shall be no better a patriot than my fellow-countrymen. Seen from a lower point of view, the Constitution, with all its faults, is very good; the law and the courts are very respectable; even this State and this American government are, in many respects, very admirable, and rare things, to be thankful for, such as a great many have described them; but seen from a point of view a little higher, they are what I have described them; seen from a higher still, and the highest, who shall say what they are, or that they are worth looking at or thinking of at all?

However, the government does not concern me much, and I shall bestow the fewest possible thoughts on it. It is not many moments that I live under a government, even in this world. If a man is thought-free, fancy-free, imagination-free, that which *is not* never for a long time appearing *to be* to him, unwise rulers or reformers cannot fatally interrupt him.

I know that most men think differently from myself; but those whose lives are by profession devoted to the study of these or kindred subjects content me as little as any. Statesmen and legislators, standing so completely within the institution, never distinctly and nakedly behold it. They speak of moving society, but have no resting-place without it. They may be men of a certain experience and discrimination, and have no doubt invented ingenious and even useful systems, for which we sincerely thank them; but all their wit and usefulness lie within certain not very wide limits. They are wont to forget that the world is not governed by policy and expediency. Webster never goes behind government, and so cannot speak with authority about it. His words are wisdom to those legislators who contemplate no essential reform in the existing government; but for thinkers, and those who legislate for all time, he never once glances at the subject. I know of those whose serene and wise speculations on this theme would soon reveal the limits of his mind's range and hospitality. Yet, compared with the cheap professions of most reformers, and the still cheaper wisdom and eloquence of politicians in general, his are almost the only sensible and valuable words, and we thank Heaven for him. Comparatively, he is always strong, original, and above all, practical. Still, his quality is not wisdom, but prudence. The lawyer's truth is not Truth, but consistency or a consistent expediency. Truth is always in harmony with herself, and is not concerned chiefly to reveal the justice that may consist with wrong doing. He well deserves to be called, as he has been called, the Defender of the Constitution. There are really no blows to be given by him but defensive ones. He is not a leader, but a follower. His leaders are the men of '87. "I have never made an effort," he says, "and never propose to make an effort; I have never countenanced an effort, and never mean to countenance an effort, to disturb the arrangement as originally made, by which the various States came into the Union." Still thinking of the sanction which the Constitution gives to slavery, he says, "Because it was a part of the original compact,—let it stand." Notwithstanding his special acuteness and ability, he is unable to take a fact out of its merely political relations, and behold it as it lies absolutely to be disposed of by the intellect,—what, for instance, it behooves a man to do here in America to-day with regard to slavery,—but ventures, or is driven, to make some such desperate answer as the following, while professing to speak absolutely, and as a private man,— from which what new and singular code of social duties might be inferred? "The manner," says he, "in which the governments of those States where slavery exists are to regulate it is for their own consideration, under their responsibility to their constituents, to the general laws of propriety, humanity, and justice, and to God. Associations formed elsewhere, springing from a feeling of humanity, or any other cause, have nothing whatever to do with it. They have never received any encouragement from me, and they never will."

They who know of no purer sources of truth, who have traced up its stream no higher, stand, and wisely stand, by the Bible and the Constitution, and drink at it there with reverence and humility; but they who behold where it comes trickling into this lake or that pool, gird up their loins once more, and continue their pilgrimage toward its fountain-head.

No man with a genius for legislation has appeared in America. They are rare in the history of the world. There are orators, politicians, and eloquent men, by the thousand; but the speaker has not yet opened his mouth to speak who is capable of settling the much-vexed questions of the day. We love eloquence for its own sake, and not for any truth which it may utter, or any heroism it may inspire. Our legislators have not yet learned the comparative value of free-trade and of freedom, of union, and of rectitude, to a nation. They have no genius or talent for comparatively humble questions of taxation and finance, commerce and manufactures and agriculture. If we were left solely to the wordy wit of legislators in Congress for our guidance, uncorrected by the seasonable experience and the effectual complaints of the people, America would not long retain her rank among the nations. For eighteen hundred years, though perchance I have no right to say it, the New Testament has been written; yet where is the legislator who has wisdom and practical talent enough to avail himself of the light which it sheds on the science of legislation?

45   The authority of government, even such as I am willing to submit to,—for I will cheerfully obey those who know and can do better than I, and in many things even those who neither know nor can do so well,—is still an impure one; to be strictly just, it must have the sanction and consent of the governed. It can have no pure right over my person and property but what I concede to it. The progress from an absolute to a limited monarchy, from a limited monarchy to a democracy, is a progress toward a true respect for the individual. Even the Chinese philosopher was wise enough to regard the individual as the basis of the empire. Is a democracy, such as we know it, the last improvement possible in government? Is it not possible to take a step further towards recognizing and organizing the rights of man? There will never be a really free and enlightened State until the State comes to recognize the individual as a higher and independent power, from which all its own power and authority are derived, and treats him accordingly. I please myself with imagining a State at last which can afford to be just to all men, and to treat the individual with respect as a neighbor; which even would not think it inconsistent with its own repose if a few were to live aloof from it, not meddling with it, nor embraced by it, who fulfilled all the duties of neighbors and fellow-men. A State which bore this kind of fruit, and suffered it to drop off as fast as it ripened, would prepare the way for a still more perfect and glorious State, which also I have imagined, but not yet anywhere seen.

CRITICAL THINKING QUESTIONS

1. Thoreau states, "The mass of men serve the state thus, not as men mainly, but as machines. . . . In most cases there is not free exercise whatever of the judgment or of the moral sense." Do you think he is being too harsh on his fellow citizens?

2. "If I devote myself to other pursuits and contemplations, I must first see, at least, that I do not pursue them sitting upon another man's shoulders." If you agree with Thoreau's *assertion,* to what extent would you modify your behavior to follow this concept?

RESEARCH/WRITING TOPIC—The Rule of Law and the Nuremberg Trials

Some legal experts argue that the law is totally sacred, that a society cannot tolerate disobedience to the law because that is an open-door invitation to anarchy. The Nazi officials involved in the Holocaust used this reasoning as a defense during the Nuremberg Trials following World War II; they claimed they were following the laws in Germany. Read about these trials and the judgments passed. Defend, refute, and/or qualify the Nazi defense. You can extend your study of this topic by researching the Geneva Conventions, four treaties that establish standards related to humanitarian concerns in the realm of international law. Also, both King's "Letter from Birmingham Jail" and Plato's dialogue from *Crito* speak to the topic of the sanctity of law.

CHAPTER ACTIVITIES
AND TOPICS FOR WRITING ARGUMENTS

1. Write about your concept of the American Dream? As you write, think about specific individuals whom you know who have achieved the dream—or those who have not. What has contributed to their successes or failures? Form a group with several classmates and read each others' writings to compare and contrast your perspectives. Now as a group, read the poems, "Burning Dreams on the Sun" (page 177) and "Richard Cory" (page 192). How do these poems extend your group's ideas? Be prepared to share your insights with the class as a whole.

2. Puritans came to these shores seeking freedom, yet ironically created one of the more restrictive societies in our country's history. Our ambivalence toward questions of freedom and conformity, therefore, go back to our very beginnings. Look at the short story, "The Foundations of the Earth," and the poem, "Crazy Courage," which might help you gain some perspective on this subject. Where do you observe or personally encounter that ambivalence today? Based on your observations, create a *claim of fact*, and list at least three examples as *evidence* to support your claim.

3. Snowboarders have provoked a great deal of criticism from the skiing community over the past ten years. They do not behave like downhill skiers on the slopes, nor do they choose to wear the glitzy clothing downhill skiers typically choose. They are often rebels and enjoy that role. Now, however, the sport has been recognized and accepted into the Winter Olympics, an action some say means snowboarding is becoming mainstream. In fact, societies often do absorb their rebels, co-opting their philosophies and symbols. In this chapter, read the short stories, "The Bride Comes to Yellow Sky" and "Ranch Girl," to help you see this problem in a wider context. Are nonconformists presently being absorbed into mainstream society? How do their positions change as a result? What compromises are demanded? What *evidence* do you see confirming such compromises? Write an essay arguing that this process is or is not beneficial to society as a whole.

4. In Washington, Congress regularly considers an amendment to the Constitution, making the unconventional use of the flag for social protests or artistic expression illegal. To gain some insight into the concept of just and unjust laws, read the essay, "Letter from Birmimgham Jail," and the poem, "In Response to Executive Order 9066." Also, read about laws governing the use of the American flag. Write a *claim of policy*, and argue that these laws are just or unjust.

5. What is a hero? How do others define this concept? How do you define it? Think about some of the characters in the selections you have read in this chapter. Do they fit a definition of hero? Think about real people you have encountered in your life. Do any of them fit the definition? How does a hero relate to his or her society? Broaden your understanding of a hero by reading the short selection, "from *Bodega Dreams*," the poem, "Hard Rock Returns to Prison from the Hospital for the Criminal Insane," and the essay, "The Train from Hate." Do some library research in order to extend your understanding of the concept of the hero. Now create your own definition. Support your argument with evidence from your library reserch, personal experience, and specific examples from your reading in this chapter.

COLLABORATION ACTIVITY:
CREATING A ROGERIAN ARGUMENT

For this activity, you will work in small teams to research, write, and present a Rogerian argument on a contemporary issue that has emerged from your exploration of readings in this chapter. The Writing Topics following many of the selections can help you identify an issue. For a discussion of the Rogerian Argument and a suggested organizational approach to the assignment, please see Chapter Three.

Following are guidelines for this collaboration activity:

- Identify an *issue.*
- Divide the research/writing responsibilities as follows:
  - Student one: introduction section
  - Student two: body section, affirmative position
  - Student three: body section, opposing position
  - Student four: conclusion, summation, and middle-ground position

Following are characteristics of effective collaboration. The team member should:

- *Contribute* by collecting information related to the issue.
- *Take responsibility* by completing his or her assigned work on time.
- *Engage* with team members by listening to and considering other viewpoints.

Sample Issue: Immigration Policy
Lines from the poem inscribed on the Statue of Liberty say, "'Give me your tired, your poor / Your huddled masses yearning to breathe free.'" Traditionally, the United States has offered immigrants the opportunity to join the community and to add their contributions to the culture. Many Americans continue to value that tradition; however, since the continued terrorist threats to internal security, others now wish to limit immigration. For example, in 2006, President Bush advocated the use of National Guard troops to secure the Mexican border. Concurrently, the U.S. Congress debated the construction of a fence along the border, while others advocated amnesty for illegal immigrants. Should the United States adopt policies to further restrict immigration?

Literature suggestions: "Mexicans Begin Jogging" and "The Chinese in All of Us" in Chapter Four; "Safe" in Chapter Six; "He Becomes Deeply and Famously Drunk" in Chaper Seven.

MAKING CONNECTIONS

Chapter Four: Individuality and Community

The individual as cultural outsider
Chopin, "Désireé's Baby"; Erdrich, "The Red Convertible"; Okita, "In Response to Executive Order 9066"; Rodriguez, "The Chinese in All of Us"

The individual on society's fringe
Jones, "The Store"; Alexie, "The Reservation Cab Driver"; Soto, "Mexicans Begin Jogging"; Grahn, "Ella, in a square apron, along Highway 80"; Terkel, "Frank Chin"

The individual as rebel
Quinonez, from *Bodega Dreams;* Knight, "Hard Rock Returns to Prison from the Hospital for the Criminally Insane"; Rukeyser, "The Lost Romans"; Thoreau, "Civil Disobedience"

The individual confronting oppression
McKay, "Outcast"; Song, "Lost Sister"; Alexie, "Superman and Me," Franklin, "The Train from Hate"; King, "Letter from Birmingham Jail"

Cross-Chapter Connections

The individual's obligation to his or her community
Keenan, "The Foundations of the Earth" and Plato, from *Crito* (Chapter Four); Cooper, "The Slaughter of the Pigeons" and Carson, "The Obligation to Endure" (Chapter Five); Ballou, "Major Sullivan Ballou's Last Letter to His Wife" (Chapter Six); Public Enemy, "Fight the Power" (Chapter Seven)

ᴧᴧ CHAPTER 5 ᴧᴧ

Nature and Place

This land is your land, / this land is my land—Woodie Guthrie's 1950s' folk ballad celebrates the American people's proud possession of the continent. In the last half of the twentieth century, the responsibility that that possession imposes on us became starkly apparent in the form of clearcut mountainsides, smog-ridden cities, and fouled waterways. Entering the twenty-first century, we accept our role as custodians of the earth, water, and sky; in some ways, the "state" of the environment is healthier than it was fifty years ago. We recognize, too, the complexities of our stewardship as we wrestle with finding a balance between the economic and aesthetic values of our natural resources. Moreover, research shows that preserving species of plants and animals is intrinsically related to the preservation of our own viability as a species. Preservationist advocates also argue that humankind's connection to nature, our sense of community with other living things on this earth—whether in an urban or a rural setting—nurtures our humanity and, likewise, the well-being of the human community. Adding to this ethical argument, they underscore our moral imperative to preserve this legacy of the land for our children. To understand the urgency of these arguments, we need look only to our past.

Only two hundred years ago, the continent of North America was a largely uncharted wilderness area. In 1803, President Thomas Jefferson enlisted the services of Meriwether Lewis to follow the Missouri River and its tributaries westward to the Pacific Ocean in order to chart a transcontinental water route. And in May 1804, Lewis, William Clark, and a small party of men set off on their historical journey. Following is an excerpt from *The Journals of Lewis and Clark,* dated Friday, June 3, 1805:

> Capt. C. & myself stroled out to the top of the hights in the fork of the rivers from whence we had an extensive and most inchanting view; the country in every derection around us was one vast plain in which innumerable herds of Buffalow were seen attended by their shepperds the wolves; the solatary antelope were distributed over

it's face; some herds of Elk were also seen; . . . to the South we saw a range of lofty mountains . . . these were partially covered with snow.[1]

Although the explorers failed to discover a continuous transcontinental water route, they did document the bounty and beauty of the American West and, thus, inspired a century of westward expansion. European and American settlers pushed westward throughout the 1800s, forcing Native Americans from their lands; acres of virgin forests were cleared, and wild animals slaughtered and displaced. By the end of the nineteenth century, the transformation of the continent was well underway.

In addition to a transcontinental railroad, factories, and metropolises, the nineteenth century spawned some of America's best-known nature writers, notably, Henry David Thoreau and Ralph Waldo Emerson. Whether or not we have read Thoreau in a book, many of us can recite some Thoreau lines, popularized on posters and notecards: "Simplicity, simplicity, simplicity!"; "Time is but the stream I go a-fishing in"; "in Wildness is the preservation of the World." In his celebrated book, *Walden, or Life in the Woods* (1854), Thoreau writes, "I went to the woods because I wished to live deliberately, . . . to live deep and suck out the marrow of life." Inspiring Thoreau was his contemporary Emerson. Emerson's first published book, *Nature* (1836), launched the transcendentalist movement in nineteenth-century America, a philosophy that spiritualized nature, equating it with the soul of the individual:

> Standing on the bare ground,—my head bathed by the blithe air, and uplifted into infinite space,—all mean egotism vanishes. I become a transparent eye-ball. I am nothing. I see all. The currents of the Universal Being circulate through me; I am part or particle of God. . . . In the wilderness, I find something more dear and connate than in streets or villages. In the tranquil landscape, and especially in the distant line of the horizon, man beholds somewhat as beautiful as his own nature. (*Nature*, Chapter 1)

Singing his praises of nature, poet Walt Whitman contributed to Emerson's and Thoreau's legacy—the elevation of nature to a mystical experience, a spiritual communion between the self and nature:

> I believe a leaf of grass is no less than the journey-work of the stars,
> And the pismire is equally perfect, and a grain of sand, and the egg of the wren,
> And the tree-toad is a chief-d'oeuvre for the highest,
> And the running blackberry would adorn the parlors of heaven,
> And the narrowest hinge in my hand puts to scorn all machinery,
> And the cow crunching with depress'd head surpasses any statue,
> And a mouse is miracle enough to stagger sextillions of infidels.

(Song of Myself, 31)

Observing the world of nature, Whitman celebrates its simple yet celestial beauty.

The spiritual concept of nature is neither uniquely American nor uniquely nineteenth century. Its roots reach back to pre-Christian times and span the globe. However, Thoreau and his contemporaries were instrumental in resurrecting and renewing the spiritual concept of nature for nineteenth- and twentieth-century readers and authors. Indeed, Annie Dillard's 1974 Pulitzer Prize–winning book, *Pilgrim at Tinker Creek*, is

---

[1] *The Journals of Lewis and Clark,* ed. Bernard DeVoto (Boston: Houghton Mifflin, Co.), p. 125.

a direct literary descendant of Thoreau's *Walden*. Dillard's first-person narrative is rendered with minute, descriptive details and laced with meditative musings:

> Trees stir memories; live waters heal them. The creek is the mediator, benevolent, impartial, subsuming my shabbiest evils and dissolving them, transforming them into live moles, and shiners, and sycamore leaves. It is a place even my faithfulness hasn't offended; it still flashes for me, now and tomorrow, that intricate, innocent face. It waters an undeserving world, saturating cells with lodes of light. I stand by the creek over rock under trees. ("The Present")

In the 1970s, Dillard's book found a highly receptive audience. As the protest causes of the 1960s (the Vietnam War and civil rights) cooled, the call to "save the environment" helped fill the vacuum for a new decade of protesters.

Environmental causes became central themes in popular culture—in art, literature, music, and movies. Most of us know Dr. Seuss's modern children's classics, *The Cat in the Hat* and *Green Eggs and Ham*. In 1971, he published *The Lorax*, the story of the destruction of an ecosystem—the chopping down of the Truffula Trees to build a factory to produce Thneeds: "and BIGGERING and BIGGERING and BIGGERING, turning MORE Truffula Trees into Thneeds which everyone, EVERYONE, EVERYONE needs!" Singer Randy Newman took up the cause of urban pollution in his 1972 song, "Burn on":

> There's a red moon rising
> On the Cuyahoga River
> Rolling into Cleveland to the lake
>
> *   *   *
>
> And the Lord can make you overflow
> But the Lord can't make you burn
> Burn on, big river, burn on

And raising the banner of endangered species for moviegoers in *Star Trek IV: The Voyage Home*, Captain Kirk and the crew of the Enterprise travel back in time to 1988 to save the humpback whale from extinction. Today, in this new millennium, interest in the environment is mainstream, central to the lives of individuals of all economic and ethnic backgrounds and a potent issue at the local community level as well as national and global levels. We share a common concern about our planet's environmental quality.

This chapter presents readings that invite you to explore different ways of seeing, feeling, and thinking about the themes of nature and place. For Emerson and Thoreau, for example, nature provides a place for a spiritual cleansing, the path to a higher state of being. However, for the narrator in Jack London's "To Build a Fire" and for Phoenix Jackson in Eudora Welty's "A Worn Path," nature presents physical challenges, throwing out obstacles that may even prove to be deadly. Several selections focus on human relationships to animals. Specifically, the slaying of wildlife is featured in James Fenimore Cooper's "The Slaughter of the Pigeons" and Sarah Orne Jewett's short story, "A White Heron." Ursula K. Le Guin's "May's Lion" depicts a mystical communion between an old woman and a dying mountain lion.

However, the poem, "The Panther" by Rainer Maria Rilke, dramatizes the disquieting disharmony between animals and humans, when an animal is caged as an exotic creature, on view for humans. In William Stafford's poem, "Traveling through the Dark," the speaker confronts a dilemma that illustrates the inherent conflict between the human and wilderness communities: "I stood in the glare of the warm exhaust turning red; / around our group, I could hear the wilderness sing." In contrast, poet James Wright's "A Blessing" displays a harmonious and tranquil moment of contact between humans and animals.

Furthermore, the literature in this chapter presents varying perspectives on one's sense of place, the values an individual associates with his or her physical setting. N. Scott Momaday, for example, weaves together the vibrant threads of his Kiowa heritage—its myths, legends, histories—to create a sense of place as palpable as the mountain that titles his book, *The Way to Rainy Mountain*. For poet Theodore Roethke, in "Meditation at Oyster River," a rocky ledge above a river quite literally provides a seat for reflection, and for essayist Verlyn Klinkenborg, a flock of Katahdin sheep creates a moment of "luminosity." On the other hand, as we suggested in Chapter One, for the speaker of Lucille Clifton's poem, "For deLawd," an urban setting, "the inner city," is "home" where she is "happy to be alive." And in Virginia Woolf's short story, "Kew Gardens," the details about the flowers and insects of a formal botanic garden in suburban London overshadow the human element, the garden's visitors.

Finally, as readers, we bring the authority of our particular experiences and ideas to our readings of the story, poem, play, or essay text. Before reading the selections that follow, let's explore our personal perspectives on nature and on place.

PREWRITING AND DISCUSSION

1. a. What is *nature?* Spend several minutes thinking about your views on nature. Write about your own personal experiences with nature and about images of nature you can recall from movies, songs, photographs, paintings, or books. In reading back over your writing, does anything surprise you? Write a sentence or two that sums up the most important impression or ideas that emerge in your writing.

   b. Spend several minutes writing about *place*, a particular physical setting or landscape, that has meaning or value for you as an individual. What makes this place special? How do you relate to it? Is it a part of your self-identity—of who you are? How so?

2. In groups of three or four, discuss your writings. Look for common ground, for shared values and attitudes, and note different viewpoints or ideas. Drawing from each group member's writings, list key impressions and ideas for both *nature* and *place*, and be prepared to report your findings to the rest of the class.

FICTION

∧∧

Rick Bass (b. 1959)

Antlers

Halloween brings us all closer, in the valley. The Halloween party at the saloon is when we all, for the first time since last winter, realize why we are all up here—all three dozen of us—living in this cold, blue valley. Sometimes there are a few tourists through the valley in the high green grasses of summer, and the valley is opened up a little. People slip in and out of it; it's almost a regular place. But in October the snows come, and it closes down. It becomes our valley again, and the tourists and less hardy-of-heart people leave.

Everyone who's up here is here because of the silence. It is eternity up here. Some are on the run, and others are looking for something ; some are incapable of living in a city, among people, while others simply love the wildness of new untouched country. But our lives are all close enough, our feelings, that when winter comes in October there's a feeling like a sigh, a sigh after the great full meal of summer, and at the Halloween party everyone shows up, and we don't bother with costumes because we all know one another so well, if not through direct contact then through word of mouth—what Dick said Becky said about Don, and so forth—knowing more in this manner, sometimes. And instead of costumes, all we do is strap horns on our heads—moose antlers, or deer antlers, or even the high throwback of elk antlers—and we have a big potluck supper and get drunk as hell, even those of us who do not drink, that one night a year, and we dance all night long, putting nickels in the jukebox (Elvis, the Doors, Marty Robbins) and clomping around in the bar as if it were a dance floor, tables and stools set outside in the falling snow to make room, and the men and women bang their antlers against each other in mock battle. Then around two or three in the morning we all drive home, or ski home, or snowshoe home, or ride back on horses—however we got to the party is how we'll return.

It usually snows big on Halloween—a foot, a foot and a half. Sometimes whoever drove down to the saloon will give the skiers a ride home by fastening a long rope to the back bumper, and we skiers will hold on to that rope, still wearing our antlers, too drunk or tired to take them off, and we'll ride home that way, being pulled up the hill by the truck, gliding silently over the road's hard ice across the new snow, our heads tucked against the wind, against the falling snow . . .

Like children being let off at a bus stop, we'll let go of the rope when the truck passes our dark cabins. It would be nice to leave a lantern burning in the window, for coming home, but you don't ever go to sleep or leave with a lantern lit like that—it can burn your cabin down in the night and leave you in the middle of winter with nothing.

We come home to dark houses, all of us. The antlers feel natural after having been up there for so long. Sometimes we bump them against the door going in and knock them off. We wear them only once a year: only once a year do we become the hunted.

5   We believe in this small place, this valley. Many of us have come here from other places and have been running all our lives from other things, and I think that everyone who is up here has decided not to run anymore.

There is a woman up here, Suzie, who has moved through the valley with a regularity, a rhythm, that is all her own and has nothing to do with our—the men's— pleadings or desires. Over the years, Suzie has been with all the men in this valley. All, that is, except Randy. She won't have anything to do with Randy. He still wishes very much for his chance, but because he is a bowhunter—he uses a strong compound bow and wicked, heart-gleaming aluminum arrows with a whole spindle of razor blades at one end for the killing point—she will have nothing to do with him.

Sometimes I wanted to defend Randy, even though I strongly disagreed with bowhunting. Bowhunting, it seemed to me, was wrong—but Randy was just Randy, no better or worse than any of the rest of us who had dated Suzie. Bowhunting was just something he did, something he couldn't help; I didn't see why she had to take it so personally.

Wolves eviscerate their prey; it's a hard life. Dead's dead, isn't it? And isn't pain the same everywhere?

I would say that Suzie's boyfriends lasted, on the average, three months. Nobody ever left her. Even the most sworn bachelors among us enjoyed her company—she worked at the bar every evening—and it was always Suzie who left the men, who left us, though I thought it was odd and wonderful that she never left the valley.

Suzie has sandy-red hair, high cold cheeks, and fury-blue eyes; she is short, no
10   taller than anyone's shoulders. But because most of us had known her for so long—and this is what the other men had told me after she'd left them—it was fun, and even stirring, but it wasn't really that *great*. There wasn't a lot of heat in it for most of them— not the dizzying, lost feeling kind you get sometimes when you meet someone for the first time, or even glimpse them in passing, never to meet. . . . That kind of heat was missing, said most of the men, and it was just comfortable, they said—*comfortable.*

When it was my turn to date Suzie, I'm proud to say that we stayed together for five months—longer than she's ever stayed with anyone—long enough for people to talk, and to kid her about it.

Our dates were simple enough; we'd go for long drives to the tops of snowy mountains and watch the valley. We'd drive into town, too, seventy miles away down a one-lane, rutted, cliff-hanging road, just for dinner and a movie. I could see how there was not heat and wild romance in it for some of the other men, but for me it was warm, and *right,* while it lasted.

When she left, I did not think I would ever eat again, drink again. It felt like my heart had been torn from my chest, like my lungs were on fire; every breath burned. I couldn't understand why she had to leave; I didn't know why she had to do that to me. I'd known it was coming, someday, but still it hurt. But I got over it; I lived. She's lovely. She's a nice girl. For a long time, I wished she would date Randy.

Besides being a bowhunter, Randy was a carpenter. He did odd jobs for people in the valley, usually fixing up old cabins rather than ever building any new ones. He kept his own schedule, and stopped working entirely in the fall so that he could hunt to his heart's content. He would roam the valley for days, exploring all of the wildest places, going all over the valley. He had hunted everywhere, had seen everything in the valley. We all hunted in the fall—grouse, deer, elk, though we left the moose and bear alone because they were rarer and we liked seeing them—but none of us were clever or stealthy enough to bowhunt. You had to get so close to the animal, with a bow.

Suzie didn't like any form of hunting. "That's what cattle are for," she'd say. "Cat- 15 tle are like city people. Cattle expect, even deserve, what they've got coming. But wild animals are different. Wild animals enjoy life. They live in the woods on purpose. It's cruel to go in after them and kill them. It's cruel."

We'd all hoo-rah her and order more beers, and she wouldn't get angry, then— she'd understand that it was just what everyone did up here, the men and the women alike, that we loved the animals, loved seeing them, but that for one or two months out of the year we loved to hunt them. She couldn't understand it, but she knew that was how it was.

Randy was so good at what he did that we were jealous, and we admired him for it, tipped our hats to his talent. He could crawl right up to within thirty yards of wild animals when they were feeding, or he could sit so still that they would walk right past him. And he was good with his bow—he was deadly. The animal he shot would run a short way with the arrow stuck through it. An arrow wouldn't kill the way a bullet did, and the animal always ran at least a little way before dying—bleeding to death, or dying from trauma—and no one liked for that to happen, but the blood trail was easy to fol- low, especially in the snow. There was nothing that could be done about it; that was just the way bowhunting was. The men looked at it as being much fairer than hunting with a rifle, because you had to get so close to the animal to get a good shot—thirty-five, forty yards was the farthest away you could be—but Suzie didn't see it that way.

She would serve Randy his drinks and would chat with him, would be polite, but her face was a mask, her smiles were stiff.

What Randy did to try to gain Suzie's favor was to build her things. Davey, the bartender—the man she was dating that summer—didn't really mind. It wasn't as if there were any threat of Randy stealing her away, and besides, he liked the objects Randy built her; and, too, I think it might have seemed to add just the smallest bit of that white heat to Davey and Suzie's relationship—though I can't say that for sure.

Randy built her a porch swing out of bright larch wood and stained it with 20 tung oil. It was as pretty as a new truck; he brought it up to her at the bar one night, having spent a week sanding it and getting it just right. We all gathered around, admiring it, running our hands over its smoothness. Suzie smiled a little—a polite smile, which was, in a way, worse than if she had looked angry—and said nothing, not even "thank you," and she and Davey took it home in the back of Davey's truck. This was in June.

Randy built her other things, too—small things, things she could fit on her dresser: a little mahogany box for her earrings, of which she had several pairs, and a walking stick with a deer's antler for the grip. She said she did not want the walking stick, but would take the earring box.

Some nights I would lie awake in my cabin and think about how Suzie was with Davey, and then I would feel sorry for Davey, because she would be leaving him eventually. I'd lie there on my side and look out my bedroom window at the northern lights flashing above the snowy mountains, and their strange light would be reflected on the river that ran past my cabin, so that the light seemed to be coming from beneath the water as well. On nights like those I'd feel like my heart was never going to heal—in fact, I was certain that it never would. I didn't love Suzie anymore—didn't think I did, anyway—but I wanted to love someone, and to be loved. Life, on those nights, seemed shorter than anything in the world, and so important, so precious, that it terrified me.

Perhaps Suzie was right about the bowhunting, and about all hunters.

In the evenings, back when we'd been together, Suzie and I would sit out on the back porch after she got in from work—still plenty of daylight left, the sun not setting until very late—and we'd watch large herds of deer, their antlers covered with summer velvet, wade out into the cool shadows of the river to bathe, like ladies. The sun would finally set, and those deer bodies would take on the dark shapes of the shadows, still out in the shallows of the rapids, splashing and bathing. Later, well into the night, Suzie and I would sit in the same chair, wrapped up in a single blanket, and nap. Shooting stars would shriek and howl over the mountains as if taunting us.

25   This past July, Randy, who lives along a field up on the side of the mountains at the north end of the valley up against the brief foothills, began practicing: standing out in the field at various marked distances—ten, twenty, thirty, forty yards—and shooting arrow after arrow into the bull's-eye target that was stapled to bales of hay. It was unusual to drive past in July and not see him out there in the field, practicing—even in the middle of the day, shirtless, perspiring, his cheeks flushed. He lived by himself, and there was probably nothing else to do. The bowhunting season began in late August, months before the regular gun season.

Too many people up here, I think, just get comfortable and lazy and lose their real passions—for whatever it is they used to get excited about. I've been up here only a few years, so maybe I have no right to say that, but it's what I feel.

It made Suzie furious to see Randy out practicing like that. She circulated a petition in the valley, requesting that bowhunting be banned.

But we—the other men, the other hunters—would have been doing the same thing, hunting the giant elk with bows for the thrill of it, luring them in with calls and rattles, right in to us, hidden in the bushes, the bulls wanting to fight, squealing madly and rushing in, tearing at trees and brush with their great dark antlers. If we could have gotten them in that close before killing them, we would have, and it would be a thing we would remember longer than any other thing. . . .

We just weren't good enough. We couldn't sign Suzie's petition. Not even Davey could sign it.

"It's wrong," she'd say.   30

"It's personal choice," Davey would say. "If you use the meat, and apologize to the spirit right before you do it and right after—if you give thanks—it's okay. It's a man's choice, honey," he'd say—and if there was one thing Suzie hated, it was that man-woman stuff.

"He's trying to prove something," she said.

"He's just doing something he cares about, dear," Davey said.

"He's trying to prove his manhood—to me, to all of us," she said. "He's danger-ous."

"No," said Davey, "that's not it. He likes it and hates it both. It fascinates him is   35
all."

"It's sick," Suzie said. "He's dangerous."

I could see that Suzie would not be with Davey much longer. She moved from man to man almost with the seasons. There was a wildness, a flightiness, about her—some sort of combination of strength and terror—that made her desirable. To me, anyway, though I can only guess for the others.

I'd been out bowhunting with Randy once to see how it was done. I saw him shoot an elk, a huge bull, and I saw the arrow go in behind the bull's shoulder where the heart and lungs were hidden—and I saw, too, the way the bull looked around in wild-eyed surprise, and then went galloping off through the timber, seemingly uninjured, running hard. For a long time Randy and I sat there, listen-ing to the clack-clack of the aluminum arrow banging against trees as the elk ran away with it.

"We sit and wait," Randy said. "We just wait." He was confident and did not seem at all shaky, though I was. It was a record bull, a beautiful bull. We sat there and waited. I did not believe we would ever see that bull again. I studied Randy's cool face, tiger-striped and frightening with the camouflage painted on it, and he seemed so cold, so icy.

After a couple of hours we got up and began to follow the blood trail. There wasn't   40
much of it at all, at first—just a drop or two, drops in the dry leaves, already turning brown and cracking, drops that I would never have seen—but after about a quarter of a mile, farther down the hill, we began to see more of it, until it looked as if entire buck-ets of blood had been lost. We found two places where the bull had lain down beneath a tree to die, but had then gotten up and moved on again. We found him by the creek, a half mile away, down in the shadows, but with his huge antlers rising into a patch of sun and gleaming. He looked like a monster from another world; even after his death, he looked noble. The creek made a beautiful trickling sound. It was very quiet. But as we got closer, as large as he was, the bull looked like someone's pet. He looked friendly. The green-and-black arrow sticking out of him looked as if it had hurt his feelings more than anything; it did not look as if such a small arrow could kill such a large and strong animal.

We sat down beside the elk and admired him, studied him. Randy, who because of the scent did not smoke during the hunting season—not until he had his elk—pulled out a pack of cigarettes, shook one out, and lit it.

"I'm not sure why I do it," he admitted, reading my mind. "I feel kind of bad about it each time I see one like this, but I keep doing it." He shrugged. I listened to the sound of the creek. "I know it's cruel, but I can't help it. I have to do it," he said.

"What do you think it must feel like?" Suzie had asked me at the bar. "What do you think it must feel like to run around with an arrow in your heart, knowing you're going to die for it?" She was furious and righteous, red-faced, and I told her I didn't know. I paid for my drink and left, confused because she was right. The animal had to be feeling pain—serious, continuous pain. It was just the way it was.

In July, Suzie left Davey, as I'd predicted. It was gentle and kind—amicable—and we all had a party down at the saloon to celebrate. We roasted a whole deer that Holger Jennings had hit with his truck the night before while coming back from town with supplies, and we stayed out in front of the saloon and ate steaming fresh meat on paper plates with barbecue sauce and crisp apples from Idaho, and watched the lazy little river that followed the road that ran through town. We didn't dance or play loud music or anything—it was too mellow. There were children and dogs. This was back when Don Terlinde was still alive, and he played his accordion: a sad, sweet sound. We drank beer and told stories.

45   All this time, I'd been uncertain about whether it was right or wrong to hunt if you used the meat and said those prayers. And I'm still not entirely convinced, one way or the other. But I do have a better picture of what it's like now to be the elk or deer. And I understand Suzie a little better, too: I no longer think of her as cruel for hurting Randy's proud heart, for singling out, among all the other men in the valley, only Randy to shun, to avoid.

     She wasn't cruel. She was just frightened. Fright—sometimes plain fright, even more than terror—is every bit as bad as pain, and maybe worse.

     What I am getting at is that Suzie went home with me that night after the party; she had made her rounds through the men of the valley, had sampled them all (except for Randy and a few of the more ancient ones), and now she was choosing to come back to me.

     "I've got to go somewhere," she said. "I hate being alone. I can't stand to be alone." She slipped her hand in mine as we were walking home. Randy was still sitting on the picnic table with Davey when we left, eating slices of venison. The sun still hadn't quite set. Ducks flew down the river.

     "I guess that's as close to 'I love you' as I'll get," I said.

50   "I'm serious," she said, twisting my hand. "You don't understand. It's *horrible.* I can't *stand* it. It's not like other people's loneliness. It's worse."

     "Why?" I asked.

     "No reason," Suzie said. "I'm just scared, is all. Jumpy. Spooky. Some people are that way. I can't help it."

     "It's okay," I said.

We walked down the road like that, holding hands, walking slowly in the dusk. It was about three miles down the gravel road to my cabin. Suzie knew the way. We heard owls as we walked along the river and saw lots of deer. Once, for no reason, I turned and looked back, but I saw nothing, saw no one.

If Randy can have such white-hot passion for a thing—bowhunting—he can, I un-   55
derstand full well, have just as much heat in his hate. It spooks me the way he does-n't bring Suzie presents anymore in the old, hopeful way. The flat looks he gives me could mean anything: they rattle me.

It's like I can't *see* him.

Sometimes I'm afraid to go into the woods.

But I do anyway. I go hunting in the fall and cut wood in the fall and winter, fish in the spring, and go for walks in the summer, walks and drives up to the tops of the high snowy mountains—and there are times when I feel someone or something is just behind me, following at a distance, and I'll turn around, frightened and angry both, and I won't see anything, but still, later on into the walk, I'll feel it again.

But I feel other things, too: I feel my happiness with Suzie. I feel the sun on my face and on my shoulders. I like the way we sit on the porch again, the way we used to, with drinks in hand, and watch the end of day, watch the deer come slipping down into the river.

I'm frightened, but it feels delicious.   60

This year at the Halloween party, it dumped on us; it began snowing the day before and continued on through the night and all through Halloween day and then Hal-loween night, snowing harder than ever. The roof over the saloon groaned that night under the load of new snow, but we had the party anyway and kept dancing, all of us leaping around and waltzing, drinking, proposing toasts, and arm-wrestling, then leap-ing up again and dancing some more, with all the antlers from all the animals in the valley strapped to our heads—everyone. It looked pagan. We all whooped and danced. Davey and Suzie danced in each other's arms, swirled and pirouetted; she was so light and so free, and I watched them and grinned. Randy sat on the porch and drank beers and watched, too, and smiled. It was a polite smile.

All of the rest of us drank and stomped around. We shook our heads at each other and pretended we were deer, pretended we were elk.

We ran out of beer around three in the morning, and we all started gathering up our skis, rounding up rides, people with trucks who could take us home. The rumble of trucks being warmed up began, and the beams of headlights crisscrossed the road in all directions, showing us just how hard it really was snowing. The flakes were as large as the biggest goose feathers. Because Randy and I lived up the same road, Davey drove us home, and Suzie took hold of the tow rope and skied with us.

Davey drove slowly because it was hard to see the road in such a storm.

Suzie had had a lot to drink—we all had—and she held on to the rope with both   65
hands, her deer antlers slightly askew, and she began to ask Randy some questions about his hunting—not razzing him, as I thought she would, but simply questioning him—things she'd been wondering for a long time, I supposed, but had been too angry

to ask. We watched the brake lights in front of us, watched the snow spiraling into our faces and concentrated on holding on to the rope. As usual, we all seemed to have forgotten the antlers that were on our heads.

"What's it like?" Suzie kept wanting to know. "I mean, what's it *really* like?"

We were sliding through the night, holding on to the rope, being pulled through the night. The snow was striking our faces, caking our eyebrows, and it was so cold that it was hard to speak.

"You're a real asshole, you know?" Suzie said, when Randy wouldn't answer. "You're too cold-blooded for me," she said. "You scare me, mister."

Randy just stared straight ahead, his face hard and flat and blank, and he held on to the rope.

70   I'd had way too much to drink. We all had. We slid over some rough spots in the road.

"Suzie, honey," I started to say—I have no idea what I was going to say after that—something to defend Randy, I think—but then I stopped, because Randy turned and looked at me, for just a second, with fury, terrible fury, which I could *feel* as well as see, even in my drunkenness. But then the mask, the polite mask, came back down over him, and we continued down the road in silence, the antlers on our heads bobbing and weaving, a fine target for anyone who might not have understood that we weren't wild animals.

CRITICAL THINKING QUESTIONS

1. Explain what the narrator means when he says, "We believe in this small place, this valley."

2. Why does Suzie object to Randy's bowhunting? How does the narrator view bowhunting? What are some of the other men's viewpoints?

3. Randy declines to defend or explain his choice to bowhunt. Based on what you know about Randy, why do you think he bowhunts?

4. Why is Suzie frightened? What does the narrator mean when he says, "I'm frightened, but it feels delicious"?

WRITING TOPICS

1. Identify the different viewpoints that are presented about the ethics of hunting. Which viewpoint do you support and why?

2. Examine the significance of the title. In your study, consider what the narrator says early on about the annual Halloween party costume: "The antlers feel natural after having been up there for so long. . . . We wear them only once a year: only once a year do we become the hunted." Also, read carefully the closing scene when Suzie questions Randy about his bowhunting; note, in particular, the images in the last sentence.

James Fenimore Cooper (1789–1851)

The Slaughter of the Pigeons

from *The Pioneers*

"Men, boys, and girls.
Desert th' unpeopled village; and wild crowds
Spread o'er the plain, by the sweet frenzy driven."

—SOMERVILLE

From this time to the close of April, the weather continued to be a succession of great and rapid changes. One day, the soft airs of spring would seem to be stealing along the valley, and, in unison with an invigorating sun, attempting, covertly, to rouse the dormant powers of the vegetable world; while on the next, the surly blasts from the north would sweep across the lake, and erase every impression left by their gentle adversaries. The snow, however, finally disappeared, and the green wheat fields were seen in every direction, spotted with the dark and charred stumps that had, the preceding season, supported some of the proudest trees of the forest. Ploughs were in motion, wherever those useful implements could be used, and the smokes of the sugarcamps were no longer seen issuing from the summits of the woods of maple. The lake had lost all the characteristic beauty of a field of ice, but still a dark and gloomy covering concealed its waters, for the absence of currents left them yet hid under a porous crust, which, saturated with the fluid, barely retained enough of its strength to preserve the contiguity of its parts. Large flocks of wild geese were seen passing over the country, which would hover, for a time, around the hidden sheet of water, apparently searching for an opening, where they might obtain a resting-place; and then, on finding themselves excluded by the chill covering, would soar away to the north, filling the air with their discordant screams, as if venting their complaints at the tardy operations of nature.

For a week, the dark covering of the Otsego was left to the undisturbed possession of two eagles, who alighted on the centre of its field, and sat proudly eyeing the extent of their undisputed territory. During the presence of these monarchs of the air, the flocks of migrating birds avoided crossing the plain of ice, by turning into the hills, and apparently seeking the protection of the forests, while the white and bald heads of the tenants of the lake were turned upward, with a look of majestic contempt, as if penetrating to the very heavens, with the acuteness of their vision. But the time had come, when even these kings of birds were to be dispossessed. An opening had been gradually increasing, at the lower extremity of the lake, and around the dark spot where the current of the river had prevented the formation of ice, during even the coldest weather; and the fresh southerly winds, that now breathed freely up the valley, obtained an impression on the waters. Mimic waves begun to curl over the margin of the frozen field, which exhibited an outline of crystallizations, that slowly receded towards the north. At each step the power of the winds and the waves increased, until, after a struggle of a few hours, the turbulent little billows succeeded in setting the whole field in an undulating motion, when it was driven beyond the reach of the eye, with a rapidity, that was as magical as the change produced in the scene by this expulsion of the lingering remnant of winter. Just as the last sheet of agitated ice was disappearing in the distance, the eagles rose over the border of crystals, and soared with a wide sweep far above the clouds, while the waves tossed their little caps of snow into the air, as if rioting in their release from a thraldom of five months duration.

The following morning Elizabeth was awakened by the exhilarating sounds of the martins, who were quarrelling and chattering around the little boxes which were suspended above her windows, and the cries of Richard, who was calling, in tones as animating as the signs of the season itself—

"Awake! awake! my lady fair! the gulls are hovering over the lake already, and the heavens are alive with the pigeons. You may look an hour before you can find a hole, through which, to get a peep at the sun. Awake! awake! lazy ones! Benjamin is overhauling the ammunition, and we only wait for our breakfasts, and away for the mountains and pigeon-shooting."

5   There was no resisting this animated appeal, and in a few minutes Miss Temple and her friend descended to the parlour. The doors of the hall were thrown open, and the mild, balmy air of a clear spring morning was ventilating the apartment, where the vigilance of the ex-steward had been so long maintaining an artificial heat, with such unremitted diligence. All of the gentlemen, we do not include Monsieur Le Quoi, were impatiently waiting their morning's repast, each being equipt in the garb of a sportsman. Mr. Jones made many visits to the southern door, and would cry—

"See, cousin Bess! see, 'duke! the pigeon-roosts of the south have broken up! They are growing more thick every instant. Here is a flock that the eye cannot see the end of. Three is food enough in it to keep the army of Xerxes for a month, and feathers enough to make beds for the whole county. Xerxes, Mr. Edwards, was a Grecian king, who—no, he was a Turk, or a Persian, who wanted to conquer Greece, just the same as these rascals will overrun our wheat-fields, when they come back in the fall.—Away! away! Bess; I long to pepper them from the mountain."

In this wish both Marmaduke and young Edwards seemed equally to participate, for really the sight was most exhilarating to a sportsman; and the ladies soon dismissed the party, after a hasty breakfast.

If the heavens were alive with pigeons, the whole village seemed equally in motion, with men, women, and children. Every species of fire-arms, from the French ducking-gun, with its barrel of near six feet in length, to the common horseman's pistol, was to be seen in the hands of the men and boys; while bows and arrows, some made of the simple stick of a walnut sapling, and others in a rude imitation of the ancient cross-bows, were carried by many of the latter.

The houses, and the signs of life apparent in the village, drove the alarmed birds from the direct line of their flight, towards the mountains, along the sides and near the bases of which they were glancing in dense masses, that were equally wonderful by the rapidity of their motion, as by their incredible numbers.

We have already said, that across the inclined plane which fell from the steep as-   10
cent of the mountain to the banks of the Susquehanna, ran the highway, on either side of which a clearing of many acres had been made, at a very early day. Over those clearings, and up the eastern mountain, and along the dangerous path that was cut into its side, the different individuals posted themselves, as suited their inclinations; and in a few moments the attack commenced.

Amongst the sportsmen was to be seen the tall, gaunt form of Leather-stocking, who was walking over the field, with his rifle hanging on his arm, his dogs following close at his heels, now scenting the dead or wounded birds, that were beginning to tumble from the flocks, and then crouching under the legs of their master, as if they participated in his feelings, at this wasteful and unsportsmanlike execution.

The reports of the fire-arms became rapid, whole volleys rising from the plain, as flocks of more than ordinary numbers darted over the opening, covering the field with darkness, like an interposing cloud; and then the light smoke of a single piece would issue from among the leafless bushes on the mountain, as death was hurled on the retreat of the affrighted birds, who would rise from a volley, for many feet into the air, in a vain effort to escape the attacks of man. Arrows, and missiles of every kind, were seen in the midst of the flocks; and so numerous were the birds, and so low did they take their flight, that even long poles, in the hands of those on the sides of the mountain, were used to strike them to the earth.

During all this time, Mr. Jones, who disdained the humble and ordinary means of destruction used by his companions, was busily occupied, aided by Benjamin, in making arrangements for an assault of a more than ordinarily fatal character. Among the relics of the old military excursions, that occasionally are discovered throughout the different districts of the western part of New York, there had been found in Templeton, at its settlement, a small swivel, which would carry a ball of a pound weight. It was thought to have been deserted by a war-party of the whites, in one of their inroads into the Indian settlements, when, perhaps, their convenience or their necessities induced them to leave such an encumbrance to the rapidity of their march, behind them in the woods. This miniature cannon had been released from the rust, and mounted on little wheels, in a state for actual service. For several years, it was the sole organ for extraordinary rejoicings that was used in those mountains. On the mornings of the Fourth of July, it would be heard, with its echoes ringing among the hills, and telling forth its sounds, for thirteen times, with all the dignity of a two-and-thirty pounder; and even Captain Hollister, who was the highest authority in that part of the country on all such occasions, affirmed that, considering its dimensions, it was no despicable gun for a salute. It was somewhat the worse for the service it had performed, it is true, there being but a trifling difference in size between the touch-hole and the muzzle. Still, the grand conceptions of Richard had suggested the importance of such an instrument, in hurling death at his nimble enemies. The swivel was dragged by a horse into a part of the open space, that the sheriff thought most eligible for planting a battery of the kind, and Mr. Pump proceeded to load it. Several handfuls of duck-shot were placed on top of the powder, and the Major-domo soon announced that his piece was ready for service.

The sight of such an implement collected all the idle spectators to the spot, who, being mostly boys, filled the air with their cries of exultation and delight. The gun was pointed on high, and Richard, holding a coal of fire in a pair of tongs, patiently took his seat on a stump, awaiting the appearance of a flock that was worthy of his notice.

15   So prodigious was the number of the birds, that the scattering fire of the guns, with the hurling of missiles, and the cries of the boys, had no other effect than to break off small flocks from the immense masses that continued to dart along the valley, as if the whole creation of the feathered tribe were pouring through that one pass. None pretended to collect the game, which lay scattered over the fields in such profusion, as to cover the very ground with the fluttering victims.

Leather-stocking was a silent, but uneasy spectator of all these proceedings, but was able to keep his sentiments to himself until he saw the introduction of the swivel into the sports.

"This comes of settling a country" he said—"here have I known the pigeons to fly for forty long years, and, till you made your clearings, there was nobody to scare or to hurt them. I loved to see them come into the woods, for they were company to a body; hurting nothing; being, as it was, as harmless as a garter-snake. But now it gives me sore thoughts when I hear the frighty things whizzing through the air, for I know it's only a motion to bring out all the brats in the village at them. Well! the Lord won't see the waste of his creaters for nothing, and right will be done to the pigeons, as well as others, by-and-by.—There's Mr. Oliver, as bad as the rest of them, firing into the flocks as if he was shooting down nothing but the Mingo warriors."

Among the sportsmen was Billy Kirby, who, armed with an old musket, was loading, and, without even looking into the air, was firing, and shouting as his victims fell even on his own person. He heard the speech of Natty, and took upon himself to reply—

"What's that, old Leather-stocking!" he cried; "grumbling at the loss of a few pigeons! If you had to sow your wheat twice, and three times, as I have done, you wouldn't be so massyfully feeling'd to'ards the divils.—Hurrah, boys! scatter the feathers. This is better than shooting at a turkey's head and neck, old fellow."

20   "It's better for you, maybe, Billy Kirby," returned the indignant old hunter, "and all them as don't know how to put a ball down a rifle-barrel, or how to bring it up ag'in with a true aim; but it's wicked to be shooting into flocks in this wastey manner; and none do it, who know how to knock over a single bird. If a body has a craving for pigeon's flesh, why! it's made the same as all other creaters, for man's eating, but not to kill twenty and eat one. When I want such a thing, I go into the woods till I find one to my liking, and then I shoot him off the branches without touching a feather of another, though there might be a hundred on the same tree. But you couldn't do such a thing, Billy Kirby—you couldn't do it if you tried."

"What's that you say, you old, dried cornstalk! you sapless stub!" cried the wood-chopper. "You've grown mighty boasting, sin you killed the turkey; but if you're for a single shot, here goes at that bird which comes on by himself."

The fire from the distant part of the field had driven a single pigeon below the flock to which it had belonged, and, frightened with the constant reports of the muskets, it was approaching the spot where the disputants stood, darting first from one side, and then to the other, cutting the air with the swiftness of lightning, and making a noise with its wings, not unlike the rushing of a bullet. Unfortunately for the wood-chopper, notwithstanding his vaunt, he did not see his bird until it was too late for him to fire as it approached, and he pulled his trigger at the unlucky moment when it was darting immediately over his head. The bird continued its course with incredible velocity.

Natty had dropped his piece from his arm, when the challenge was made, and, waiting a moment, until the terrified victim had got in a line with his eyes, and had dropped near the bank of the lake, he raised his rifle with uncommon rapidity, and fired. It might have been chance, or it might have been skill, that produced the result; it was probably a union of both; but the pigeon whirled over in the air, and fell into the lake, with a broken wing. At the sound of his rifle, both his dogs started from his feet, and in a few minutes the "slut" brought out the bird, still alive.

The wonderful exploit of Leather-stocking was noised through the field with great rapidity, and the sportsmen gathered in to learn the truth of the report.

"What," said young Edwards, "have you really killed a pigeon on the wing, Natty, with a single ball?"   25

"Haven't I killed loons before now, lad, that dive at the flash?" returned the hunter. "It's much better to kill only such as you want, without wasting your powder and lead, than to be firing into God's creaters in such a wicked manner. But I come out for a bird, and you know the reason why I like small game, Mr. Oliver, and now I have got one I will go home, for I don't like to see these wasty ways that you are all practysing, as if the least thing was not made for use, and not to destroy."

"Thou sayest well, Leather-stocking," cried Marmaduke, "and I begin to think it time to put an end to this work of destruction."

"Put an ind, Judge, to your clearings. An't the woods his work as well as the pigeons? Use, but don't waste. Wasn't the woods made for the beasts and birds to harbour in? and when man wanted their flesh, their skins, or their feathers, there's the place to seek them. But I'll go to the hut with my own game, for I wouldn't touch one of the harmless things that kiver the ground here, looking up with their eyes at me, as if they only wanted tongues to say their thoughts."

With this sentiment in his mouth, Leather-stocking threw his rifle over his arm, and, followed by his dogs, stepped across the clearing with great caution, taking care not to tread on one, of the hundreds of the wounded birds that lay in his path. He soon entered the bushes on the margin of the lake, and was hid from view.

Whatever might be the impression the morality of Natty made on the Judge, it was utterly lost on Richard. He availed himself of the gathering of the sportsmen, to   30 lay a plan for one "fell swoop" of destruction. The musket-men were drawn up in battle array, in a line extending on each side of his artillery, with orders to await the signal of firing from himself.

"Stand by, my lads," said Benjamin, who acted as an aid-de-camp on this momentous occasion, "stand by, my hearties, and when Squire Dickens heaves out the signal for to begin the firing, d'ye see, you may open upon them in a broadside. Take care and fire low, boys, and you'll be sure to hull the flock."

"Fire low!" shouted Kirby—"hear the old fool! If we fire low, we may hit the stumps, but not ruffle a pigeon."

"How should you know, you lubber?" cried Benjamin, with a very unbecoming heat, for an officer on the eve of battle—"how should you know, you grampus? Havn't I sailed aboard of the Boadishy for five years? and wasn't it a standing order to fire low, and to hull your enemy? Keep silence at your guns, boys, and mind the order that is passed."

The loud laughs of the musketmen were silenced by the authoritative voice of Richard, who called to them for attention and obedience to his signals.

35   Some millions of pigeons were supposed to have already passed, that morning, over the valley of Templeton; but nothing like the flock that was now approaching had been seen before. It extended from mountain to mountain in one solid blue mass, and the eye looked in vain over the southern hills to find its termination. The front of this living column was distinctly marked by a line, but very slightly indented, so regular and even was the flight. Even Marmaduke forgot the morality of Leather-stocking as it approached, and, in common with the rest, brought his musket to his shoulder.

"Fire!" cried the Sheriff, clapping his coal to the priming of the cannon. As half of Benjamin's charge escaped through the touch-hole, the whole volley of the musketry preceded the report of the swivel. On receiving this united discharge of small-arms, the front of the flock darted upward, while, at the same instant, myriads of those in their rear rushed with amazing rapidity into their places, so that when the column of white smoke gushed from the mouth of the little cannon, an accumulated mass of objects was gliding over its point of direction. The roar of the gun echoed along the mountains, and died away to the north, like distant thunder, while the whole flock of alarmed birds seemed, for a moment, thrown into one disorderly and agitated mass. The air was filled with their irregular flights, layer rising over layer, far above the tops of the highest pines, none daring to advance beyond the dangerous pass; when, suddenly, some of the leaders of the feathered tribe shot across the valley, taking their flight directly over the village, and the hundreds of thousands in their rear followed their example, deserting the eastern side of the plain to their persecutors and the fallen.

"Victory!" shouted Richard, "victory! we have driven the enemy from the field."

"Not so, Dickon," said Marmaduke; "the field is covered with them; and, like the Leather-stocking, I see nothing but eyes, in every direction, as the innocent sufferers turn their heads in terror, to examine my movements. Full one half of those that have fallen are yet alive: and I think it is time to end the sport; if sport it be."

"Sport!" cried the Sheriff; "it is princely sport. There are some thousands of the blue-coated boys on the ground, so that every old woman in the village may have a pot-pie for the asking."

"Well, we have happily frightened the birds from this pass," said Marmaduke, 40 "and our carnage must of necessity end, for the present.—Boys, I will give thee sixpence a hundred for the pigeons' heads only; so go to work, and bring them into the village, when I will pay thee."

This expedient produced the desired effect, for every urchin on the ground went industriously to work to wring the necks of the wounded birds. Judge Temple retired towards his dwelling with that kind of feeling, that many a man has experienced before him, who discovers, after the excitement of the moment has passed, that he has purchased pleasure at the price of misery to others. Horses were loaded with the dead; and, after this first burst of sporting, the shooting of pigeons became a business, for the remainder of the season, more in proportion to the wants of the people. Richard, however, boasted for many a year, of his shot with the "cricket;" and Benjamin gravely asserted, that he thought that they killed nearly as many pigeons on that day, as there were Frenchmen destroyed on the memorable occasion of Rodney's victory.

CRITICAL THINKING QUESTIONS

1. What is the author's claim about the ethics of hunting?

2. Point out specific wording and details that the author uses to *stack the evidence* (see Glossary) for his claim.

3. Which *rhetorical appeal* is most prevalent?

WRITING TOPIC

What is Leather-stocking's viewpoint on the ethics of hunting? Compare Leather-stocking's viewpoint to Davey's in Bass's "Antlers." Both characters use similar ethical standards to justify hunting; however, Leather-stocking lived in early nineteenth-century America while Davey lives in contemporary America. Does Davey's viewpoint on the ethics of hunting represent a reasonable middle-ground position (Rogerian argument)?

Pam Houston (b. 1962)

A Blizzard under Blue Sky

The doctor said I was clinically depressed. It was February, the month in which depression runs rampant in the inversion-cloaked Salt Lake Valley and the city dwellers escape to Park City, where the snow is fresh and the sun is shining and everybody is happy, except me. In truth, my life was on the verge of more spectacular and satisfying discoveries than I had ever imagined, but of course I couldn't see that far ahead. What I saw was work that wasn't getting done, bills that weren't getting paid, and a man I'd given my heart to weekending in the desert with his ex.

The doctor said, "I can give you drugs."

I said, "No way."

She said, "The machine that drives you is broken. You need something to help you get it fixed."

5 I said, "Winter camping."

She said, "Whatever floats your boat."

One of the things I love the most about the natural world is the way it gives you what's good for you even if you don't know it at the time. I had never been winter camping before, at least not in the high country, and the weekend I chose to try and fix my machine was the same weekend the air mass they called the Alaska Clipper showed up. It was thirty-two degrees below zero in town on the night I spent in my snow cave. I don't know how cold it was out on Beaver Creek. I had listened to the weather forecast, and to the advice of my housemate, Alex, who was an experienced winter camper.

"I don't know what you think you're going to prove by freezing to death," Alex said, "but if you've got to go, take my bivvy sack; it's warmer than anything you have."

"Thanks," I said.

10 "If you mix Kool-Aid with your water it won't freeze up," he said, "and don't forget lighting paste for your stove."

"Okay," I said.

"I hope it turns out to be worth it," he said, "because you are going to freeze your butt."

When everything in your life is uncertain, there's nothing quite like the clarity and precision of fresh snow and blue sky. That was the first thought I had on Saturday morning as I stepped away from the warmth of my truck and let my skis slap the snow in front of me. There was no wind and no clouds that morning, just still air and cold sunshine. The hair in my nostrils froze almost immediately. When I took a deep breath, my lungs only filled up halfway.

I opened the tailgate to excited whines and whimpers. I never go skiing without Jackson and Hailey: my two best friends, my yin and yang of dogs. Some of you might know Jackson. He's the oversized sheepdog-and-something-else with the great big nose and the bark that will shatter glass. He gets out and about more than I do.

People I've never seen before come by my house daily and call him by name. He's all grace, and he's tireless; he won't go skiing with me unless I let him lead. Hailey is not so graceful, and her body seems in constant indecision when she runs. When we ski she stays behind me, and on the downhills she tries to sneak rides on my skis.

The dogs ran circles in the chest-high snow while I inventoried my backpack   15 one more time to make sure I had everything I needed. My sleeping bag, my Thermarest, my stove, Alex's bivvy sack, matches, lighting paste, flashlight, knife. I brought three pairs of long underwear—tops and bottoms—so I could change once before I went to bed, and once again in the morning, so I wouldn't get chilled by my own sweat. I brought paper and pen, and Kool-Aid to mix with my water. I brought Mountain House chicken stew and some freeze-dried green peas, some peanut butter and honey, lots of dried apricots, coffee and Carnation instant breakfast for morning.

Jackson stood very still while I adjusted his backpack. He carries the dog food and enough water for all of us. He takes himself very seriously when he's got his pack on. He won't step off the trail for any reason, not even to chase rabbits, and he gets nervous and angry if I do. That morning he was impatient with me. "Miles to go, Mom," he said over his shoulder. I snapped my boots into my skis and we were off.

There are not too many good things you can say about temperatures that dip past twenty below zero, except this: They turn the landscape into a crystal palace and they turn your vision into Superman's. In the cold thin morning air the trees and mountains, even the twigs and shadows, seemed to leap out of the background like a 3-D movie, only it was better than 3-D because I could feel the sharpness of the air.

I have a friend in Moab who swears that Utah is the center of the fourth dimension, and although I know he has in mind something much different and more complicated than subzero weather, it was there, on that ice-edged morning, that I felt on the verge of seeing something more than depth perception in the brutal clarity of the morning sun.

As I kicked along the first couple of miles, I notice the sun crawling higher in the sky and yet the day wasn't really warming, and I wondered if I should have brought another vest, another layer to put between me and the cold night ahead.

It was utterly quiet out there, and what minimal noise we made intruded on the   20 morning like a brass band: the squeaking of my bindings, the slosh of the water in Jackson's pack, the whoosh of nylon, the jangle of dog tags. It was the bass line and percussion to some primal song, and I kept wanting to sing to it, but I didn't know the words.

Jackson and I crested the top of a hill and stopped to wait for Hailey. The trail stretched out as far as we could see into the meadow below us and beyond, a double track and pole plants carving through softer trails of rabbit and deer.

"Nice place," I said to Jackson, and his tail thumped the snow underneath him without sound.

We stopped for lunch near something that looked like it could be a lake in its other life, or maybe just a womb-shaped meadow. I made peanut butter and honey sandwiches for all of us, and we opened the apricots.

"It's fabulous here," I told the dogs. "But so far it's not working."

25   There had never been anything wrong with my life that a few good days in the wilderness wouldn't cure, but there I sat in the middle of all those crystal-coated trees, all that diamond-studded sunshine, and I didn't feel any better. Apparently clinical depression was not like having a bad day, it wasn't even like having a lot of bad days, it was more like a house of mirrors, it was like being in a room full of one-way glass.

"Come on, Mom," Jackson said. "Ski harder, go faster, climb higher."

Hailey turned her belly to the sun and groaned.

"He's right," I told her. "It's all we can do."

After lunch the sun had moved behind our backs, throwing a whole different light on the path ahead of us. The snow we moved through stopped being simply white and became translucent, hinting at other colors, reflections of blues and purples and grays. I thought of Moby Dick, you know, the whiteness of the whale, where white is really the absence of all color, and whiteness equals truth, and Ahab's search is finally futile, as he finds nothing but his own reflection.

30   "Put your mind where your skis are," Jackson said, and we made considerably better time after that.

The sun was getting quite low in the sky when I asked Jackson if he thought we should stop to build the snow cave, and he said he'd look for the next good bank. About one hundred yards down the trail we found it, a gentle slope with eastern exposure that didn't look like it would cave in under any circumstances. Jackson started to dig first.

Let me make one thing clear. I knew only slightly more about building snow caves than Jackson, having never built one, and all my knowledge coming from disaster tales of winter camping fatalities. I knew several things *not* to do when building a snow cave, but I was having a hard time knowing what exactly to do. But Jackson helped, and Hailey supervised, and before too long we had a little cave built, just big enough for three. We ate dinner quite pleased with our accomplishments and set the bivvy sack up inside the cave just as the sun slipped away and dusk came over Beaver Creek.

The temperature, which hadn't exactly soared during the day, dropped twenty degrees in as many minutes, and suddenly it didn't seem like such a great idea to change my long underwear. The original plan was to sleep with the dogs inside the bivvy sack but outside the sleeping bag, which was okay with Jackson the super-metabolizer, but not so with Hailey, the couch potato. She whined and wriggled and managed to stuff her entire fat body down inside my mummy bag, and Jackson stretched out full-length on top.

One of the unfortunate things about winter camping is that it has to happen when the days are so short. Fourteen hours is a long time to lie in a snow cave under the most perfect of circumstances. And when it's thirty-two below, or forty, fourteen hours seems like weeks.

35   I wish I could tell you I dropped right off to sleep. In truth, fear crept into my spine with the cold and I never closed my eyes. Cuddled there, amid my dogs and water bottles, I spent half of the night chastising myself for thinking I was Wonder Woman,

not only risking my own life but the lives of my dogs, and the other half trying to keep the numbness in my feet from crawling up to my knees. When I did doze off, which was actually more like blacking out than dozing off, I'd come back to my senses wondering if I had frozen to death, but the alternating pain and numbness that started in my extremities and worked its way into my bones convinced me I must still be alive.

It was a clear night, and every now and again I would poke my head out of its nest of down and nylon to watch the progress of the moon across the sky. There is no doubt that it was the longest and most uncomfortable night of my life.

But then the sky began to get gray, and then it began to get pink, and before too long the sun was on my bivvy sack, not warm, exactly, but holding the promise of warmth later in the day. And I ate apricots and drank Kool-Aid-flavored coffee and celebrated the rebirth of my fingers and toes, and the survival of many more important parts of my body. I sang "Rocky Mountain High" and "If I Had a Hammer," and yodeled and whistled, and even danced the two-step with Jackson and let him lick my face. And when Hailey finally emerged from the sleeping bag a full hour after I did, we shared a peanut butter and honey sandwich and she said nothing ever tasted so good.

We broke camp and packed up and kicked in the snow cave with something resembling glee.

I was five miles down the trail before I realized what had happened. Not once in that fourteen-hour night did I think about deadlines, or bills, or the man in the desert. For the first time in many months I was happy to see a day beginning. The morning sunshine was like a present from the gods. What really happened, of course, is that I remembered about joy.

I know that one night out at thirty-two below doesn't sound like much to those   40
of you who have climbed Everest or run the Iditarod or kayaked to Antarctica, and I won't try to convince you that my life was like the movies where depression goes away in one weekend, and all of life's problems vanish with a moment's clear sight. The simple truth of the matter is this: On Sunday I had a glimpse outside of the house of mirrors, on Saturday I couldn't have seen my way out of a paper bag. And while I was skiing back toward the truck that morning, a wind came up behind us and swirled the snow around our bodies like a blizzard under blue sky. And I was struck by the simple perfection of the snowflakes, and startled by the hopefulness of sun on frozen trees.

CRITICAL THINKING QUESTIONS

1. Write a *claim of policy* that this story suggests for an individual who is battling depression. Does the claim have merit?

2. In the closing paragraph, the narrator anticipates and attempts to rebut readers' objections. How effective is this strategy?

WRITING TOPIC

Compare and contrast Houston's narrator and the man in London's "To Build a Fire" (page 295). Specifically, examine their value assumptions about their place in nature and their relationship to their canine companions. Which character's assumptions do you think are generally representative of many people today? On what evidence—observations, examples—do you base your conclusion?

Sarah Orne Jewett (1849–1909)

A White Heron

I

The woods were already filled with shadows one June evening, just before eight o'clock, though a bright sunset still glimmered faintly among the trunks of the trees. A little girl was driving home her cow, a plodding, dilatory, provoking creature in her behavior, but a valued companion for all that. They were going away from whatever light there was, and striking deep into the woods, but their feet were familiar with the path, and it was no matter whether their eyes could see it or not.

There was hardly a night the summer through when the old cow could be found waiting at the pasture bars; on the contrary, it was her greatest pleasure to hide herself away among the huckleberry bushes, and though she wore a loud bell she had made the discovery that if one stood perfectly still it would not ring. So Sylvia had to hunt for her until she found her, and call Co'! Co'! with never an answering Moo, until her childish patience was quite spent. If the creature had not given good milk and plenty of it, the case would have seemed very different to her owners. Besides, Sylvia had all the time there was, and very little use to make of it. Sometimes in pleasant weather it was a consolation to look upon the cow's pranks as an intelligent attempt to play hide and seek, and as the child had no playmates she lent herself to this amusement with a good deal of zest. Though this chase had been so long that the wary animal herself had given an unusual signal of her whereabouts, Sylvia had only laughed when she came upon Mistress Moolly at the swampside, and urged her affectionately homeward with a twig of birch leaves. The old cow was not inclined to wander farther, she even turned in the right direction for once as they left the pasture, and stepped along the road at a good pace. She was quite ready to be milked now, and seldom stopped to browse. Sylvia wondered what her grandmother would say because they were so late. It was a great while since she had left home at half-past five o'clock, but everybody knew the difficulty of making this errand a short one.

Mrs. Tilley had chased the hornéd torment too many summer evenings herself to blame any one else for lingering, and was only thankful as she waited that she had Sylvia, nowadays, to give such valuable assistance. The good woman suspected that Sylvia loitered occasionally on her own account; there never was such a child for straying about out-of-doors since the world was made! Everybody said that it was a good change for a little maid who had tried to grow for eight years in a crowded manufacturing town, but as for Sylvia herself, it seemed as if she never had been alive at all before she came to live at the farm. She thought often with wistful compassion of a wretched geranium that belonged to a town neighbor.

"'Afraid of folks,'" old Mrs. Tilley said to herself, with a smile, after she had made the unlikely choice of Sylvia from her daughter's houseful of children, and was returning to the farm. "'Afraid of folks,' they said! I guess she won't be troubled no great with 'em up to the old place!" When they reached the door of the lonely house and stopped to unlock it, and the cat came to purr loudly, and rub against them, a deserted pussy, indeed, but fat with young robins, Sylvia whispered that this was a beautiful place to live in, and she never should wish to go home.

The companions followed the shady woodroad, the cow taking slow steps and the child very fast ones. The cow stopped long at the brook to drink, as if the pasture were not half a swamp, and Sylvia stood still and waited, letting her bare feet cool themselves in the shoal water, while the great twilight moths struck softly against her. She waded on through the brook as the cow moved away, and listened to the thrushes with a heart that beat fast with pleasure. There was a stirring in the great boughs overhead. They were full of little birds and beasts that seemed to be wide awake, and going about their world, or else saying goodnight to each other in sleepy twitters. Sylvia herself felt sleepy as she walked along. However, it was not much farther to the house, and the air was soft and sweet. She was not often in the woods so late as this, and it made her feel as if she were a part of the gray shadows and the moving leaves. She was just thinking how long it seemed since she first came to the farm a year ago, and wondering if everything went on in the noisy town just the same as when she was there; the thought of the great red-faced boy who used to chase and frighten her made her hurry along the path to escape from the shadow of the trees.

Suddenly this little woods-girl is horror-stricken to hear a clear whistle not very far away. Not a bird's-whistle, which would have a sort of friendliness, but a boy's whistle, determined, and somewhat aggressive. Sylvia left the cow to whatever sad fate might await her, and stepped discreetly aside into the brushes, but she was just too late. The enemy had discovered her, and called out in a very cheerful and persuasive tone, "Halloa, little girl, how far is it to the road?" and trembling Sylvia answered almost inaudibly, "A good ways."   5

She did not dare to look boldly at the tall young man, who carried a gun over his shoulder, but she came out of her bush and again followed the cow, while he walked alongside.

"I have been hunting for some birds," the stranger said kindly, "and I have lost my way, and need a friend very much. Don't be afraid," he added gallantly. "Speak up and tell me what your name is, and whether you think I can spend the night at your house, and go out gunning early in the morning."

Sylvia was more alarmed than before. Would not her grandmother consider her much to blame? But who could have foreseen such an accident as this? It did not seem to be her fault, and she hung her head as if the stem of it were broken, but managed to answer "Sylvy," with much effort when her companion again asked her name.

Mrs. Tilley was standing in the doorway when the trio came into view. The cow gave a loud moo by way of explanation.

10   "Yes, you'd better speak up for yourself, you old trial! Where'd she tucked herself away this time, Sylvy?" But Sylvia kept an awed silence; she knew by instinct that her grandmother did not comprehend the gravity of the situation. She must be mistaking the stranger for one of the farmer-lads of the region.

The young man stood his gun beside the door, and dropped a lumpy game-bag beside it; then he bade Mrs. Tilley good-evening, and repeated his wayfarer's story, and asked if he could have a night's lodging.

"Put me anywhere you like," he said. "I must be off early in the morning, before day; but I am very hungry, indeed. You can give me some milk at any rate, that's plain."

"Dear sakes, yes," responded the hostess, whose long slumbering hospitality seemed to be easily awakened. "You might fare better if you went out to the main road a mile or so, but you're welcome to what we've got. I'll milk right off, and you make yourself at home. You can sleep on husks or feathers," she proffered graciously. "I raised them all myself. There's good pasturing for geese just below here towards the ma'sh. Now step round and set a plate for the gentleman, Sylvy!" And Sylvia promptly stepped. She was glad to have something to do, and she was hungry herself.

It was a surprise to find so clean and comfortable a little dwelling in this New England wilderness. The young man had known the horrors of its most primitive housekeeping, and the dreary squalor of that level of society which does not rebel at the companionship of hens. This was the best thrift of an old-fashioned farmstead, though on such a small scale that it seemed like a hermitage. He listened eagerly to the old woman's quaint talk, he watched Sylvia's pale face and shining gray eyes with ever growing enthusiasm, and insisted that this was the best supper he had eaten for a month, and afterward the new-made friends sat down in the door-way together while the moon came up.

15   Soon it would be berry-time, and Sylvia was a great help at picking. The cow was a good milker, though a plaguy thing to keep track of, the hostess gossiped frankly, adding presently that she had buried four children, so Sylvia's mother, and a son (who might be dead) in California were all the children she had left. "Dan, my boy, was a great hand to go gunning," she explained sadly. "I never wanted for pa'tridges or gray squer'ls while he was to home. He's been a great wand'rer, I expect, and he's no hand to write letters. There, I don't blame him, I'd ha' seen the world myself if it had been so I could."

"Sylvy takes after him," the grandmother continued affectionately, after a minute's pause. "There ain't a foot o' ground she don't know her way over, and the wild creatures counts her one o' themselves. Squer'ls she'll tame to come an' feed right out o' her hands, and all sorts o' birds. Last winter she got the jay-birds to bangeing here, and I believe she'd 'a' scanted herself of her own meals to have plenty to throw out amongst 'em, if I had n't kep' watch. Anything but crows, I tell her, I'm willin' to help support—though Dan he had a tamed one o' them that did seem to have reason same as folks. It was round here a good spell after he went away. Dan an' his father they didn't hitch,—but he never held up his head ag'in after Dan had dared him an' gone off."

The guest did not notice this hint of family sorrows in his eager interest in something else.

"So Sylvy knows all about birds, does she?" he exclaimed, as he looked round at the little girl who sat, very demure but increasingly sleepy, in the moonlight. "I am making a collection of birds myself. I have been at it ever since I was a boy." (Mrs. Tilley smiled.) "There are two or three very rare ones I have been hunting for these five years. I mean to get them on my own ground if they can be found."

"Do you cage 'em up?" asked Mrs. Tilley doubtfully, in response to this enthusiastic announcement.

"Oh no, they're stuffed and preserved, dozens and dozens of them," said the ornithologist, "and I have shot or snared every one myself. I caught a glimpse of a white heron a few miles from here on Saturday, and I have followed it in this direction. They have never been found in this district at all. The little white heron, it is," and he turned again to look at Sylvia with the hope of discovering that the rare bird was one of her acquaintances. 20

But Sylvia was watching a hop-toad in the narrow footpath.

"You would know the heron if you saw it," the stranger continued eagerly. "A queer tall white bird with soft feathers and long thin legs. And it would have a nest perhaps in the top of a high tree, made of sticks, something like a hawk's nest."

Sylvia's heart gave a wild beat; she knew that strange white bird, and had once stolen softly near where it stood in some bright green swamp grass, away over at the other side of the woods. There was an open place where the sunshine always seemed strangely yellow and hot, where tall, nodding rushes grew, and her grandmother had warned her that she might sink in the soft black mud underneath and never be heard of more. Not far beyond were the salt marshes just this side the sea itself, which Sylvia wondered and dreamed much about, but never had seen, whose great voice could sometimes be heard above the noise of the woods on storm nights.

"I can't think of anything I should like so much as to find that heron's nest," the handsome stranger was saying. "I would give ten dollars to anybody who could show it to me," he added desperately, "and I mean to spend my whole vacation hunting for it if need be. Perhaps it was only migrating, or had been chased out of its own region by some bird of prey."

Mrs. Tilley gave amazed attention to all this, but Sylvia still watched the toad, not divining, as she might have done at some calmer time, that the creature wished to get 25 to its hole under the door-step, and was much hindered by the unusual spectators at that hour of the evening. No amount of thought, that night, could decide how many wished-for treasures the ten dollars, so lightly spoken of, would buy.

The next day the young sportsman hovered about the woods, and Sylvia kept him company, having lost her first fear of the friendly lad, who proved to be most kind and sympathetic. He told her many things about the birds and what they knew and where they lived and what they did with themselves. And he gave her a jack-knife, which she thought as great a treasure as if she were a desert-islander. All day long he did not once make her troubled or afraid except when he brought down some unsuspecting singing creature from its bough. Sylvia would have liked him vastly better without his gun; she could not understand why he killed the very birds he seemed to like so much. But as the day waned, Sylvia still watched the young man with loving admiration. She had never seen anybody so charming and delightful; the woman's heart, asleep in the child, was vaguely thrilled by a dream of love. Some premonition of that great power stirred and swayed these young creatures who traversed the solemn woodlands with soft-footed silent care. They stopped to listen to a bird's song; they pressed forward again eagerly, parting the branches—speaking to each other rarely and in whispers; the young man going first and Sylvia following, fascinated, a few steps behind, with her gray eyes dark with excitement.

She grieved because the longed-for white heron was elusive, but she did not lead the guest, she only followed, and there was no such thing as speaking first. The sound of her own unquestioned voice would have terrified her—it was hard enough to answer yes or no when there was need of that. At last evening began to fall, and they drove the cow home together, and Sylvia smiled with pleasure when they came to the place where she heard the whistle and was afraid only the night before.

II

Half a mile from home, at the farther edge of the woods, where the land was highest, a great pine-tree stood, the last of its generation. Whether it was left for a boundary mark, or for what reason, no one could say; the woodchoppers who had felled its mates were dead and gone long ago, and a whole forest of sturdy trees, pines and oaks and maples, had grown again. But the stately head of this old pine towered above them all and made a landmark for sea and shore miles and miles away. Sylvia knew it well. She had always believed that whoever climbed to the top of it could see the ocean; and the little girl had often laid her hand on the great rough trunk and looked up wistfully at those dark boughs that the wind always stirred, no matter how hot and still the air might be below. Now she thought of the tree with a new excitement, for why, if one climbed it at break of day could not one see all the world, and easily discover from whence the white heron flew, and mark the place, and find the hidden nest?

What a spirit of adventure, what wild ambition! What fancied triumph and delight and glory for the later morning when she could make known the secret! It was almost too real and too great for the childish heart to bear.

All night the door of the little house stood open and the whippoorwills came   30
and sang upon the very step. The young sportsman and his old hostess were sound
asleep, but Sylvia's great design kept her broad awake and watching. She forgot to
think of sleep. The short summer night seemed as long as the winter darkness, and at
last when the whippoorwills ceased, and she was afraid the morning would after all
come too soon, she stole out of the house and followed the pasture path through the
woods, hastening toward the open ground beyond, listening with a sense of comfort
and companionship to the drowsy twitter of a half-awakened bird, whose perch she
had jarred in passing. Alas, if the great wave of human interest which flooded for the
first time this dull little life should sweep away the satisfactions of an existence heart
to heart with nature and the dumb life of the forest!

There was the huge tree asleep yet in the paling moonlight, and small and silly
Sylvia began with utmost bravery to mount to the top of it, with tingling, eager blood
coursing the channels of her whole frame, with her bare feet and fingers, that pinched
and held like bird's claws to the monstrous ladder reaching up, up, almost to the sky
itself. First she must mount the white oak tree that grew alongside, where she was almost lost among the dark branches and the green leaves heavy and wet with dew; a
bird fluttered off its nest, and a red squirrel ran to and fro and scolded pettishly at the
harmless housebreaker. Sylvia felt her way easily. She had often climbed there, and
knew that higher still one of the oak's upper branches chafed against the pine trunk,
just where its lower boughs were set close together. There, when she made the dangerous pass from one tree to the other, the great enterprise would really begin.

She crept out along the swaying oak limb at last, and took the daring step across
into the old pine-tree. The way was harder than she thought; she must reach far and
hold fast, the sharp dry twigs caught and held her and scratched her like angry talons,
the pitch made her thin little fingers clumsy and stiff as she went round and round the
tree's great stem, higher and higher upward. The sparrows and robins in the woods
below were beginning to wake and twitter to the dawn, yet it seemed much lighter there
aloft in the pine-tree, and the child knew she must hurry if her project were to be of
any use.

The tree seemed to lengthen itself out as she went up, and to reach farther and
farther upward. It was like a great main-mast to the voyaging earth; it must truly have
been amazed that morning though all its ponderous frame as it felt this determined
spark of human spirit wending its way from higher branch to branch. Who knows how
steadily the least twigs held themselves to advantage this light, weak creature on her
way! The old pine must have loved his new dependent. More than all the hawks, and
bats, and moths, and even the sweet voiced thrushes, was the brave, beating heart of
the solitary gray-eyed child. And the tree stood still and frowned away the winds that
June morning while the dawn grew bright in the east.

Sylvia's face was like a pale star, if one had seen it from the ground, when the last
thorny bough was past, she stood trembling and tired but wholly triumphant,
high in the treetop. Yes, there was the sea with the dawning sun making a golden daz-
zle over it, and toward that glorious east flew two hawks with slow-moving pinions.

How low they looked in the air from that height when one had only seen them before far up, and dark against the blue sky. Their gray feathers were as soft as moths; they seemed only a little way from the tree, and Sylvia felt as if she too could go flying away among the clouds. Westward, the woodlands and farms reached miles and miles into the distance; here and there were church steeples, and white villages, truly it was a vast and awesome world!

35   The birds sang louder and louder. At last the sun came up bewilderingly bright. Sylvia could see the white sails of ships out at sea, and the clouds that were purple and rose-colored and yellow at first began to fade away. Where was the white heron's nest in the sea of green branches, and was this wonderful sight and pageant of the world the only reward for having climbed to such a giddy height? Now look down again, Sylvia, where the green marsh is set among the shining birches and dark hemlocks; there where you saw the white heron once you will see him again; look, look! a white spot of him like a single floating feather comes up from the dead hemlock and grows larger, and rises, and comes close at last, and goes by the landmark pine with steady sweep of wing and outstretched slender neck and crested head. And wait! wait! do not move a foot or a finger, little girl, do not send an arrow of light and consciousness from your two eager eyes, for the heron has perched on a pine bough not far beyond yours, and cries back to his mate on the nest and plumes his feathers for the new day!

The child gives a long sigh a minute later when a company of shouting cat-birds comes also to the tree, and vexed by their fluttering and lawlessness the solemn heron goes away. She knows his secret now, the wild, light, slender bird that floats and wavers, and goes back like an arrow presently to his home in the green world beneath. Then Sylvia, well satisfied, makes her perilous way down again, not daring to look far below the branch she stands on, ready to cry sometimes because her fingers ache and her lamed feet slip. Wondering over and over again what the stranger would say to her, and what he would think when she told him how to find his way straight to the heron's nest.

"Sylvy, Sylvy!" called the busy old grandmother again and again, but nobody answered, and the small husk bed was empty and Sylvia had disappeared.

The guest waked from a dream, and remembering his day's pleasure hurried to dress himself that might it sooner begin. He was sure from the way the shy little girl looked once or twice yesterday that she had at least seen the white heron, and now she must really be made to tell. Here she comes now, paler than ever, and her worn old frock is torn and tattered, and smeared with pine pitch. The grandmother and the sportsman stand in the door together and question her, and the splendid moment has come to speak of the dead hemlock-tree by the green marsh.

But Sylvia does not speak after all, though the old grandmother fretfully rebukes her, and the young man's kind, appealing eyes are looking straight in her own. He can make them rich with money; he has promised it, and they are poor now. He is so well worth making happy, and he waits to hear the story she can tell.

40   No, she must keep silence! What is it that suddenly forbids her and makes her dumb? Has she been nine years growing and now, when the great world for the first time puts out a hand to her, must she thrust it aside for a bird's sake? The murmur of the pine's green branches is in her ears, she remembers how the white heron came flying through

the golden air and how they watched the sea and the morning together, and Sylvia cannot speak; she cannot tell the heron's secret and give its life away.

Dear loyalty, that suffered a sharp pang as the guest went away disappointed later in the day, that could have served and followed him and loved him as a dog loves! Many a night Sylvia heard the echo of his whistle haunting the pasture path as she came home with the loitering cow. She forgot even her sorrow at the sharp report of his gun and the sight of thrushes and sparrow's dropping silent to the ground, their songs hushed and their pretty feathers stained and wet with blood. Were the birds better friends than their hunter might have been,—who can tell? Whatever treasures were lost to her, woodlands and summer-time, remember! Bring your gifts and graces and tell your secrets to this lonely country child!

CRITICAL THINKING QUESTIONS

1. In the predawn, Sylvia slips out of her grandmother's home to locate the white heron's nesting place so she can tell the young man and earn his gratitude and a monetary reward. But when the moment arrives for her to reveal the heron's nest location, she decides "she must keep silence." What *value assumptions* about nature enter into Sylvia's decision?

2. Like Sylvia, the young man seems to regard the natural world with reverence. However, carrying a gun, "the ornithologist" has a distinctly different purpose. What values motivate the young man's pursuit of nature?

3. In the depiction of the two opposing views toward nature, represented by Sylvia and the young man, does the author seem to favor one or the other? Find specific passages that may reveal the author's underlying *bias*. Is the language primarily emotional (*pathos* appeal) or logical (*logos* appeal)?

4. What is the author's *implied claim* about the value of wilderness? How does the closing paragraph qualify the claim?

Ursula K. Le Guin (b. 1929)

May's Lion

Jim remembers it as a bobcat, and he was May's nephew, and ought to know. It probably was a bobcat. I don't think May would have changed her story, though you can't trust a good story-teller not to make the story suit herself, or get the facts to fit the story better. Anyhow she told it to us more than once, because my mother and I would ask for it; and the way I remember it, it was a mountain lion. And the way I remember May telling it is sitting on the edge of the irrigation tank we used to swim in, cement rough as a lava flow and hot in the sun, the long cracks tarred over. She was an old lady then with a long Irish upper lip, kind and wary and balky. She liked to come sit and talk with my mother while I swam; she didn't have all that many people to talk to. She always had chickens, in the chickenhouse very near the back door of the farmhouse, so the whole place smelled pretty strong of chickens, and as long as she could she kept a cow or two down in the old barn by the creek. The first of May's cows I remember was Pearl, a big handsome Holstein who gave fourteen or twenty-four or forty gallons or quarts of milk at a milking, whichever is right for a prize milker. Pearl was beautiful in my eyes when I was four or five years old; I loved and admired her. I remember how excited I was, how I reached upward to them, when Pearl or the workhorse Prince, for whom my love amounted to worship, would put an immense and sensitive muzzle through the three-strand fence to whisk a cornhusk from my fearful hand; and then the munching and the sweet breath and the big nose would be at the barbed wire again: the offering is acceptable.... After Pearl there was Rosie, a purebred Jersey. May got her either cheap or free because she was a runt calf, so tiny that May brought her home on her lap in the back of the car, like a fawn. And Rosie always looked like she had some deer in her. She was a lovely, clever little cow and even more willful than old May. She often chose not to come in to be milked. We would hear May calling and then see her trudging across our lower pasture with the bucket, going to find Rosie wherever Rosie had decided to be milked today on the wild hills she had to roam in, a hundred acres of our and Old Jim's land. Then May had a fox terrier named Pinky, who yipped and nipped and turned me against fox terriers for life, but he was long gone when the mountain lion came; and the black cats who lived in the barn kept discreetly out of the story. As a matter of fact now I think of it the chickens weren't in it either. It might have been quite different if they had been. May had quit keeping chickens after old Mrs. Walter died. It was just her all alone there, and Rosie and the cats down in the barn, and nobody else within sight or sound of the old farm. We were in our house up the hill only in the summer, and Jim lived in town, those years. What time of year it was I don't know, but I imagine the grass still green or just turning gold. And May was in the house, in the kitchen, where she lived entirely unless she was asleep or outdoors, when she heard this noise.

Now you need May herself, sitting skinny on the edge of the irrigation tank, seventy or eighty or ninety years old, nobody knew how old May was and she had made sure they couldn't find out, opening her pleated lips and letting out this noise—a huge, awful yowl, starting soft with a nasal hum and rising slowly into a snarling gargle that sank away into a sobbing purr. . . . It got better every time she told the story.

"It was some meow," she said.

So she went to the kitchen door, opened it, and looked out. Then she shut the kitchen door and went to the kitchen window to look out, because there was a mountain lion under the fig tree.

Puma, cougar, catamount; *Felis concolor,* the shy, secret, shadowy lion of the New   5
World, four or five feet long plus a yard of black-tipped tail, weighs about what a woman weighs, lives where the deer live from Canada to Chile, but always shyer, always fewer, the color of dry leaves, dry grass.

There were plenty of deer in the Valley in the forties, but no mountain lion had been seen for decades anywhere near where people lived. Maybe way back up in the canyons; but Jim, who hunted, and knew every deer-trail in the hills, had never seen a lion. Nobody had, except May, now, alone in her kitchen.

"I thought maybe it was sick," she told us. "It wasn't acting right. I don't think a lion would walk right into the yard like that if it was feeling well. If I'd still had the chickens it'd be a different story maybe! But it just walked around some, and then it lay down there," and she points between the fig tree and the decrepit garage. "And then after a while it kind of meowed again, and got up and come into the shade right there." The fig tree, planted when the house was built, about the time May was born, makes a great, green, sweet-smelling shade. "It just laid there looking around. It wasn't well," says May.

She had lived with and looked after animals all her life; she had also earned her living for years as a nurse.

"Well, I didn't know exactly what to do for it. So I put out some water for it. It didn't even get up when I come out the door. I put the water down there, not so close to it that we'd scare each other, see, and it kept watching me, but it didn't move. After I went back in it did get up and tried to drink some water. Then it made that kind of meowowow. I do believe it come here because it was looking for help. Or just for company, maybe."

The afternoon went on, May in the kitchen, the lion under the fig tree.   10

But down in the barnyard by the creek was Rosie the cow. Fortunately the grate was shut, so she could not come wandering up to the house and meet the lion; but she would be needing to be milked, come six or seven o'clock, and that got to worrying May. She also worried how long a sick mountain lion might hang around, keeping her shut in the house. May didn't like being shut in.

"I went out a time or two, and went shoo!"

Eyes shining amidst fine wrinkles, she flaps her thin arms at the lion. "Shoo! Go on home now!"

But the silent wild creature watches her with yellow eyes and does not stir.

"So when I was talking to Miss Macy on the telephone, she said it might have   15
rabies, and I ought to call the sheriff. I was uneasy then. So finally I did that, and they come out, those county police, you know. Two carloads."

Her voice is dry and quiet.

"I guess there was nothing else they knew how to do. So they shot it."

She looks off across the field Old Jim, her brother, used to plow with Prince the horse and irrigate with the water from this tank. Now wild oats and blackberry grow there. In another thirty years it will be a rich man's vineyard, a tax write-off.

"He was seven feet long, all stretched out, before they took him off. And so thin! They all said, 'Well, Aunt May, I guess you were scared there! I guess you were some scared!' But I wasn't. I didn't want him shot. But I didn't know what to do for him. And I did need to get to Rosie."

20   I have told this true story which May gave to us as truly as I could, and now I want to tell it as fiction, yet without taking it from her: rather to give it back to her, if I can do so. It is a tiny part of the history of the Valley, and I want to make it part of the Valley outside history. Now the field that the poor man plowed and the rich man harvested lies on the edge of a little town, houses and workshops of timber and fieldstone standing among almond, oak, and eucalyptus trees; and now May is an old woman with a name that means the month of May: Rains End. An old woman with a long, wrinkled-pleated upper lip, she is living alone for the summer in her summer place, a meadow a mile or so up in the hills above the little town. Sinshan. She took her cow Rose with her, and since Rose tends to wander she keeps her on a long tether down by the tiny creek, and moves her into fresh grass now and then. The summerhouse is what they call a nine-pole house, a mere frame of poles stuck in the ground—one of them is a live digger-pine sapling—with stick and matting walls, and mat roof and floors. It doesn't rain in the dry season, and the roof is just for shade. But the house and its little front yard where Rains End has her camp stove and clay oven and matting loom are well shaded by a fig tree that was planted there a hundred years or so ago by her grandmother.

Rains End herself has no grandchildren; she never bore a child, and her one or two marriages were brief and very long ago. She has a nephew and two grandnieces, and feels herself an aunt to all children, even when they are afraid of her and rude to her because she has got so ugly with old age, smelling as musty as a chickenhouse. She considers it natural for children to shrink away from somebody part way dead, and knows that when they're a little older and have got used to her they'll ask her for stories. She was for sixty years a member of the Doctors Lodge, and though she doesn't do curing any more people still ask her to help with nursing sick children, and the children come to long for the kind, authoritative touch of her hands when she bathes them to bring a fever down, or changes a dressing, or combs out bed-tangled hair with witch hazel and great patience.

So Rains End was just waking up from an early afternoon nap in the heat of the day, under the matting roof, when she heard a noise, a huge, awful yowl that started soft with a nasal hum and rose slowly into a snarling gargle that sank away into a sobbing purr. . . . And she got up and looked out from the open side of the house of sticks and matting, and saw a mountain lion under the fig tree. She looked at him from her house; he looked at her from his.

And this part of the story is much the same: the old woman; the lion; and, down by the creek, the cow.

It was hot. Crickets sang shrill in the yellow grass on all the hills and canyons, in all the chaparral. Rains End filled a bowl with water from an unglazed jug and came slowly out of the house. Halfway between the house and the lion she set the bowl down on the dirt. She turned and went back to the house.

The lion got up after a while and came and sniffed at the water. He lay down again 25 with a soft, querulous groan, almost like a sick child, and looked at Rains End with the yellow eyes that saw her in a different way than she had ever been seen before.

She sat on the matting in the shade of the open part of her house and did some mending. When she looked up at the lion she sang under her breath, tunelessly; she wanted to remember the Puma Dance Song but could only remember bits of it, so she made a song for the occasion:
You are there, lion.
You are there, lion. . . .

As the afternoon wore on she began to worry about going down to milk Rose. Un-milked, the cow would start tugging at her tether and making a commotion. That was likely to upset the lion. He lay so close to the house now that if she came out that too might upset him, and she did not want to frighten him or to become frightened of him. He had evidently come for some reason, and it behooved her to find out what the reason was. Probably he was sick; his coming so close to a human person was strange, and people who behave strangely are usually sick or in some kind of pain. Sometimes, though, they are spiritually moved to act strangely. The lion might be a messenger, or might have some message of his own for her or her townspeople. She was more used to seeing birds as messengers; the four-footed people go about their own business. But the lion, dweller in the Seventh House, comes from the place dreams come from. Maybe she did not understand. Maybe someone else would understand. She could go over and tell Valiant and her family, whose summerhouse was in Gahheya meadow, farther up the creek; or she could go over to Buck's, on Baldy Knoll. But there were four or five adolescents there, and one of them might come and shoot the lion, to boast that he'd saved old Rains End from getting clawed to bits and eaten.

Mooooooo! said Rose, down by the creek, reproachfully.

The sun was still above the southwest ridge, but the branches of pines were across it and the heavy heat was out of it, and shadows were welling up in the low fields of wild oats and blackberry.

Moooooo! said Rose again, louder. 30

The lion lifted up his square, heavy head, the color of dry wild oats, and gazed down across the pastures. Rains End knew from that weary movement that he was very ill. He had come for company in dying, that was all.

"I'll come back, lion," Rains End sang tunelessly. "Lie still. Be quiet. I'll come back soon." Moving softly and easily, as she would move in a room with a sick child, she got her milking pail and stool, slung the stool on her back with a woven strap so as to leave a hand free, and came out of the house. The lion watched her at first very tense, the yellow eyes firing up for a moment, but then put his head down again with that little grudging, groaning sound. "I'll come back, lion," Rains End said. She went down to the creekside and milked a nervous and indignant cow. Rose could smell lion, and demanded in several ways, all eloquent, just what Rains End intended to *do?* Rains End ignored her questions and sang milking songs to her: "Su bonny, su bonny, be still my grand cow. . . ." Once she had to slap her hard on the hip. "Quit that, you old fool! Get over! I am *not* going to untie you and have you walking into trouble! I won't let him come down this way."

She did not say how she planned to stop him.

She retethered Rose where she could stand down in the creek if she liked. When she came back up the rise with the pail of milk in hand, the lion had not moved. The sun was down, the air above the ridges turning clear gold. The yellow eyes watched her, no light in them. She came to pour milk into the lion's bowl. As she did so, he all at once half rose up. Rains End started, and spilled some of the milk she was pouring. "Shoo! Stop that!" she whispered fiercely, waving her skinny arm at the lion. "Lie down now! I'm afraid of you when you get up, can't you see that, stupid? Lie down now, lion. There you are. Here I am. It's all right. You know what you're doing." Talking softly as she went, she returned to her house of stick and matting. There she sat down as before, in the open porch, on the grass mats.

35   The mountain lion made the grumbling sound, ending with a long sigh, and let his head sink back down on his paws.

Rains End got some cornbread and a tomato from the pantry box while there was still daylight left to see by, and ate slowly and neatly. She did not offer the lion food. He had not touched the milk, and she thought he would eat no more in the House of Earth.

From time to time as the quiet evening darkened and stars gathered thicker overhead she sang to the lion. She sang the five songs of *Going Westward to the Sunrise,* which are sung to human beings dying. She did not know if it was proper and appropriate to sing these songs to a dying mountain lion, but she did not know his songs.

Twice he also sang: once a quavering moan, like a house cat challenging another tom to battle, and once a long, sighing purr.

Before the Scorpion had swung clear of Sinshan Mountain, Rains End had pulled her heavy shawl around herself in case the fog came in, and had gone sound asleep in the porch of her house.

40   She woke with the grey light before sunrise. The lion was a motionless shadow, a little farther from the trunk of the fig tree than he had been the night before. As the light grew, she saw that he had stretched himself out full length. She knew he had finished his dying, and sang the fifth song, the last song, in a whisper, for him:

The doors of the Four Houses are open.

Surely they are open.

Near sunrise she went to milk Rose, and to wash in the creek. When she came back up to the house she went closer to the lion, though not so close as to crowd him, and stood for a long time looking at him stretched out in the long, tawny, delicate light. "As thin as I am!" she said to Valiant, when she went up to Gahheya later in the morning to tell the story and to ask help carrying the body of the lion off where the buzzards and coyotes could clean it.

It's still your story, Aunt May; it was your lion. He came to you. He brought his death to you, a gift; but the men with the guns won't take gifts, they think they own death already. And so they took from you the honor he did you, and you felt that loss. I wanted to restore it. But you don't need it. You followed the lion where he went, years ago now.

CRITICAL THINKING QUESTION

In the closing paragraph, Le Guin's narrator is fairly explicit in condemning the county police, "the men with guns," who shoot the lion. May, however, says, "I guess there was nothing else for them to do." Do you side with May's or the narrator's assessment of the situation?

WRITING TOPIC

Consider the saying, "Fiction is a lie that tells the truth." In Le Guin's story, the narrator says, "I have told this true story which May gave to us as truly as I could, and now I want to tell it as fiction, yet without taking it from her: rather to give it back to her, if I can do so. It is a tiny part of the history of the Valley, and I want to make it part of the Valley outside history." By retelling May's story as "fiction," what "truth" is the narrator attempting to express? Do you agree with the narrator that the fictionalized version of this tiny part of the Valley's history contains more truth than the factual account?

Jack London (1876–1916)

To Build a Fire

Day had broken cold and grey, exceedingly cold and grey, when the man turned aside from the main Yukon trail and climbed the high earthbank, where a dim and little-travelled trail led eastward through the fat spruce timberland. It was a steep bank, and he paused for breath at the top, excusing the act to himself by looking at his watch. It was nine o'clock. There was no sun nor hint of sun, though there was not a cloud in the sky. It was a clear day, and yet there seemed an intangible pall over the face of things, a subtle gloom that made the day dark, and that was due to the absence of sun. This fact did not worry the man. He was used to the lack of sun. It had been days since he had seen the sun, and he knew that a few more days must pass before that cheerful orb, due south, would just peep above the skyline and dip immediately from view.

The man flung a look back along the way he had come. The Yukon lay a mile wide and hidden under three feet of ice. On top of this ice were as many feet of snow. It was all pure white, rolling in gentle undulations where the ice jams of the freeze-up had formed. North and south, as far as his eye could see, it was unbroken white, save for a dark hairline that curved and twisted from around the spruce-covered island to the south, and that curved and twisted away into the north, where it disappeared behind another spruce-covered island. This dark hairline was the trail—the main trail—that led south five hundred miles to the Chilcoot Pass, Dyea, and salt water; and that led north seventy miles to Dawson, and still on to the north a thousand miles to Nulato, and finally to St. Michael, on Bering Sea, a thousand miles and half a thousand more.

But all this—the mysterious, far-reaching hairline trail, the absence of sun from the sky, the tremendous cold, and the strangeness and weirdness of it all—made no impression on the man. It was not because he was long used to it. He was a newcomer in the land, a *chechaquo*, and this was his first winter. The trouble with him was that he was without imagination. He was quick and alert in the things of life, but only in the things, and not in the significances. Fifty degrees below zero meant eighty-odd degrees of frost. Such fact impressed him as being cold and uncomfortable, and that was all. It did not lead him to meditate upon his frailty as a creature of temperature, and upon man's frailty in general, able only to live within certain narrow limits of heat and cold; and from there on it did not lead him to the conjectural field of immortality and man's place in the universe. Fifty degrees below zero stood for a bite of frost that hurt and that must be guarded against by the use of mittens, ear flaps, warm moccasins, and thick socks. Fifty degrees below zero. That there should be anything more to it than that was a thought that never entered his head.

As he turned to go on, he spat speculatively. There was a sharp explosive crackle that startled him. He spat again. And again, in the air, before it could fall to the snow, the spittle crackled. He knew that at fifty below spittle crackled on the snow, but this spittle had crackled in the air. Undoubtedly it was colder than fifty below—how much colder he did not know. But the temperature did not matter. He was bound for the old claim on the left fork of Henderson Creek, where the boys were already. They had come over across the divide from the Indian Creek country, while he had come the roundabout way to take a look at the possibilities of getting out logs in the spring from the islands in the Yukon. He would be in to camp by six o'clock; a bit after dark, it was true, but the boys would be there, a fire would be going, and a hot supper would be ready. As for lunch, he pressed his hand against the protruding bundle under his jacket. It was also under his shirt, wrapped up in a handkerchief and lying against the naked skin. It was the only way to keep the biscuits from freezing. He smiled agreeably to himself as he thought of those biscuits, each cut open and sopped in bacon grease, and each enclosing a generous slice of fried bacon.

5   He plunged in among the big spruce trees. The trail was faint. A foot of snow had fallen since the last sled had passed over, and he was glad he was without a sled,

travelling light. In fact, he carried nothing but the lunch wrapped in the handkerchief. He was surprised, however, at the cold. It certainly was cold, he concluded, as he rubbed his numb nose and cheekbones with his mittened hand. He was a warm-whiskered man, but the hair on his face did not protect the high cheekbones and the eager nose that thrust itself aggressively into the frosty air.

At the man's heels trotted a dog, a big native husky, the proper wolfdog, grey-coated and without any visible or temperamental difference from its brother, the wild wolf. The animal was depressed by the tremendous cold. It knew that it was no time for travelling. Its instinct told it a truer tale than was told to the man by the man's judgment. In reality, it was not merely colder than fifty below zero; it was colder than sixty below, than seventy below. It was seventy-five below zero. Since the freezing point is thirty-two above zero, it meant that one hundred and seven degrees of frost obtained. The dog did not know anything about thermometers. Possibly in its brain there was no sharp consciousness of a condition of very cold such as was in the man's brain. But the brute had its instinct. It experienced a vague but menacing apprehension that subdued it and made it slink along at the man's heels, and that made it question eagerly every unwonted movement of the man as if expecting him to go into camp or to seek shelter somewhere and build a fire. The dog had learned fire, and it wanted fire, or else to burrow under the snow and cuddle its warmth away from the air.

The frozen moisture of its breathing had settled on its fur in a fine powder of frost, and especially were its jowls, muzzle, and eyelashes whitened by its crystal breath. The man's red beard and moustache were likewise frosted, but more solidly, the deposit taking the form of ice and increasing with every warm, moist breath he exhaled. Also, the man was chewing tobacco, and the muzzle of ice held his lips so rigidly that he was unable to clear his chin when he expelled the juice. The result was a crystal beard of the color and solidity of amber that was increasing its length on his chin. If he fell down it would shatter itself, like glass, into brittle fragments. But he did not mind the appendage. It was the penalty all tobacco chewers paid in that country, and he had been out before in two cold snaps. They had not been so cold as this, he knew, but by the spirit thermometer at Sixty Mile he knew they had been registered at fifty below and at fifty-five.

He held on through the level stretch of woods for several miles, crossed a wide flat of nigger heads, and dropped down a bank to the frozen bed of a small stream. This was Henderson Creek, and he knew he was ten miles from the forks. He looked at his watch. It was ten o'clock. He was making four miles an hour, and he calculated that he would arrive at the forks at half-past twelve. He decided to celebrate that event by eating his lunch there.

The dog dropped in again at his heels, with a tail drooping discouragement, as the man swung along the creek bed. The furrow of the old sled trail was plainly visible, but a dozen inches of snow covered up the marks of the last runners. In a month no man had come up or down that silent creek. The man held steadily on. He was not much given to thinking, and just then particularly he had nothing to think about save that he would eat lunch at the forks and that at six o'clock he would be in camp with the boys. There was nobody to talk to; and, had there been, speech would have been impossible because of the ice muzzle on his mouth. So he continued monotonously to chew tobacco and to increase the length of his amber beard.

10   Once in a while the thought reiterated itself that it was very cold and that he had never experienced such cold. As he walked along he rubbed his cheekbones and nose with the back of his mittened hand. He did this automatically, now and again changing hands. But, rub as he would, the instant he stopped his cheekbones went numb, and the following instant the end of his nose went numb. He was sure to frost his cheeks; he knew that, and experienced a pang of regret that he had not devised a nose strap of the sort Bud wore in cold snaps. Such a strap passed across the cheeks, as well, and saved them. But it didn't matter much, after all. What were frosted cheeks? A bit painful, that was all; they were never serious.

Empty as the man's mind was of thoughts, he was keenly observant, and he noticed the changes in the creeks, the curves and bends and timber jams, and always he sharply noted where he placed his feet. Once, coming round a bend, he shied abruptly, like a startled horse, curved away from the place where he had been walking, and retreated several places back along the trail. The creek he knew was frozen clear to the bottom—no creek could contain water in that arctic winter—but he knew also that there were springs that bubbled out from the hillsides and ran along under the snow and on top of the ice of the creek. He knew that the coldest snaps never froze these springs, and he knew likewise their danger. They were traps. They hid pools of water under the snow that might be three inches deep, or three feet. Sometimes a skin of ice half an inch thick covered them, and in turn was covered by the snow. Sometimes there were alternate layers of water and ice skin, so that when one broke through he kept on breaking through for a while, sometimes wetting himself to the waist.

That was why he had shied in such a panic. He had felt the give under his feet and heard the crackle of a snow-hidden ice skin. And to get his feet wet in such a temperature meant trouble and danger. At the very least it meant delay, for he would be forced to stop and build a fire, and under its protection to bare his feet while he dried his socks and moccasins. He stood and studied the creek bed and its banks, and decided that the flow of water came from the right. He reflected awhile, rubbing his nose and cheeks, then skirted to the left, stepping gingerly and testing the footing for each step. Once clear of the danger, he took a fresh chew of tobacco and swung along at his four-mile gait.

In the course of the next two hours he came upon several similar traps. Usually the snow above the hidden pools had a sunken, candied appearance that advertised the danger. Once again, however, he had a close call; and once, suspecting danger, he compelled the dog to go on in front. The dog did not want to go. It hung back until the man shoved it forward, and then it went quickly across the white, unbroken surface. Suddenly it broke through, floundered to one side, and got away to firmer footing. It had wet its forefeet and legs, and almost immediately the water that clung to it turned to ice. It made quick efforts to lick the ice off its legs, then dropped down in the snow and began to bite out the ice that had formed between the toes. This was a matter of instinct. To permit the ice to remain would mean sore feet. It did not know this. It merely obeyed the mysterious prompting that arose from the deep crypts of its being.

But the man knew, having achieved a judgment on the subject, and he removed the mitten from his right hand and helped to tear out the ice particles. He did not expose his fingers more than a minute, and was astonished at the swift numbness that smote them. It certainly was cold. He pulled on the mitten hastily, and beat the hand savagely across his chest.

At twelve o'clock the day was at its brightest. Yet the sun was too far south on its winter journey to clear the horizon. The bulge of the earth intervened between it and Henderson Creek, where the man walked under a clear sky at noon and cast no shadow. At half-past twelve, to the minute, he arrived at the forks of the creek. He was pleased at the speed he had made. If he kept it up, he would certainly be with the boys by six. He unbuttoned his jacket and shirt and drew forth his lunch. The action consumed no more than a quarter of a minute, yet in that brief moment the numbness laid hold of the exposed fingers. He did not put the mitten on, but, instead, struck the fingers a dozen sharp smashes against his leg. Then he sat down on a snow-covered log to eat. The sting that followed upon the striking of his fingers against his leg ceased so quickly that he was startled. He had had no chance to take a bite of biscuit. He struck the fingers repeatedly and returned them to the mitten, baring the other hand for the purpose of eating. He tried to take a mouthful, but the ice muzzle prevented. He had forgotten to build a fire and thaw out. He chuckled at his foolishness, and as he chuckled he noted the numbness creeping into the exposed fingers. Also, he noted that the stinging which had first come to his toes when he sat down was already passing away. He wondered whether the toes were warm or numb. He moved them inside the moccasins and decided that they were numb.

He pulled the mitten on hurriedly and stood up. He was a bit frightened. He 15 stamped up and down until the stinging returned into the feet. It certainly was cold, was his thought. That man from Sulphur Creek had spoken the truth when telling how cold it sometimes got in the country. And he had laughed at him at the time! That showed one must not be too sure of things. There was no mistake about it, it *was* cold. He strode up and down, stamping his feet and threshing his arms, until reassured by the returning warmth. Then he got out matches and proceeded to make a fire. From the undergrowth, where high water of the previous spring had lodged a supply of seasoned twigs, he got his firewood. Working carefully from a small beginning, he soon had a roaring fire, over which he thawed the ice from his face and in the protection of which he ate his biscuits. For the moment the cold of space was outwitted. The dog took satisfaction in the fire, stretching out close enough for warmth and far enough away to escape being singed.

When the man had finished, he filled his pipe and took his comfortable time over a smoke. Then he pulled on his mittens, settled the ear flaps of his cap firmly about his ears, and took the creek trail up the left fork. The dog was disappointed and yearned back towards the fire. This man did not know cold. Possibly all the generations of his ancestry had been ignorant of cold, of real cold, of cold one hundred and seven degrees below freezing point. But the dog knew; all its ancestry knew, and it had inherited the knowledge. And it knew that it was not good to walk abroad in such fearful cold. It was the time to lie snug in a hole in the snow and wait for a curtain of cloud to be drawn across the face of outer space whence this cold came. On the other hand, there was no keen intimacy between the dog and the man. The one was the toil slave of the other, and the only caresses it had ever received were the caresses of the whip lash and of harsh and menacing throat sounds that threatened the whip lash. So the dog made no effort to communicate its apprehension to the man. It was not concerned in the welfare of the man; it was for its own sake that it yearned back towards the fire. But the man whistled, and spoke to it with the sound of whip lashes, and the dog swung in at the man's heels and followed after.

The man took a chew of tobacco and proceeded to start a new amber beard. Also, his moist breath quickly powdered with white his moustache, eyebrows, and lashes. There did not seem to be so many springs on the left fork of the Henderson, and for half an hour the man saw no signs of any. And then it happened. At a place where there were no signs, where the soft, unbroken snow seemed to advertise solidity beneath, the man broke through. It was not deep. He wet himself half-way to the knees before he floundered out of the firm crust.

He was angry, and cursed his luck aloud. He had hoped to get into camp with the boys at six o'clock, and this would delay him an hour, for he would have to build a fire and dry out his footgear. This was imperative at that low temperature—he knew that much; and he turned aside to the bank, which he climbed. On top, tangled in the underbrush about the trunks of several small spruce trees, was a high-water deposit of dry firewood—sticks and twigs, principally, but also larger portions of seasoned branches and fine, dry, last year's grasses. He threw down several large pieces on top of the snow. This served for a foundation and prevented the young flame from drowning itself in the snow it otherwise would melt. The flame he got by touching a match to a small shred of birch bark that he took from his pocket. This burned even more readily than paper. Placing it on the foundation, he fed the young flame with wisps of dry grass and with the tiniest dry twigs.

He worked slowly and carefully, keenly aware of his danger. Gradually, as the flame grew stronger, he increased the size of the twigs with which he fed it. He squatted in the snow pulling the twigs out from their entanglement in the brush and feeding directly to the flame. He knew there must be no failure. When it is seventy-five below zero, a man must not fail in his first attempt to build a fire—that is, if his feet are wet. If his feet are dry, and he fails, he can run along the trail for half a mile and restore his circulation. But the circulation of wet and freezing feet cannot be restored by running when it is seventy-five below. No matter how fast he runs, the wet feet will freeze the harder.

20   All this the man knew. The old-timer on Sulphur Creek had told him about it the previous fall, and now he was appreciating the advice. Already all sensation had gone out of his feet. To build the fire he had been forced to remove his mittens, and the fingers had quickly gone numb. His pace of four miles an hour had kept his heart pumping blood to the surface of his body and to all the extremities. But the instant he stopped, the action of the pump eased down. The cold of space smote the unprotected tip of the planet, and he, being on that unprotected tip, received the full force of the blow. The blood of his body recoiled before it. The blood was alive, like the dog,

and like the dog it wanted to hide away and cover itself up from the fearful cold. So long as he walked four miles an hour, he pumped that blood, willy-nilly, to the surfaces; but not it ebbed away and sank down into the recesses of his body. The extremities were the first to feel its absence. His wet feet froze the faster, and his exposed fingers numbed the faster, though they had not yet begun to freeze. Nose and cheeks were already freezing, while the skin of all his body chilled as it lost its blood.

But he was safe. Toes and nose and cheeks would be only touched by the frost, for the fire was beginning to burn with strength. He was feeding it with twigs the size of his finger. In another minute he would be able to feed it with branches the size of his wrist, and then he could remove his wet footgear, and, while it dried, he could keep his naked feet warm by the fire, rubbing them at first, of course, with snow. The fire was a success. He was safe. He remembered the advice of the old-timer on Sulphur Creek, and smiled. The old-timer had been very serious in laying down the law that no man must travel alone in the Klondike after fifty below. Well, here he was; he had had the accident; he was alone; and he had saved himself. Those old-timers were rather womanish, some of them, he thought. All a man had to do was to keep his head, and he was all right. Any man who was a man could travel alone. But it was surprising, the rapidity with which his cheeks and nose were freezing. And he had not thought his fingers could go lifeless in so short a time. Lifeless they were, for he could scarcely make them move together to grip a twig, and they seemed remote from his body and from him. When he touched a twig, he had to look and see whether or not he had hold of it. The wires were pretty well down between him and his finger ends.

All of which counted for little. There was the fire, snapping and crackling and promising life with every dancing flame. He started to untie his moccasins. They were coated with ice; the thick German socks were like sheaths of iron halfway to the knees; and the moccasin strings were like rods of steel all twisted and knotted as by some conflagration. For a moment he tugged with his numb fingers, then, realizing the folly of it, he drew his sheath knife.

But before he could cut the strings, it happened. It was his own fault or, rather, his mistake. He should not have built the fire under the spruce tree. He should have built it in the open. But it had been easier to pull the twigs from the brush and drop them directly on the fire. Now the tree under which he had done this carried a weight of snow on its boughs. No wind had blown for weeks, and each bough was fully freighted. Each time he had pulled a twig he had communicated a slight agitation to the tree—an imperceptible agitation, so far as he was concerned, but an agitation sufficient to bring about the disaster. High up in the tree one bough capsized its load of snow. This fell on the boughs beneath, capsizing them. This process continued, spreading out and involving the whole tree. It grew like an avalanche, and it descended without warning upon the man and the fire, and the fire was blotted out! Where it had burned was a mantle of fresh and disordered snow.

The man was shocked. It was as though he had just heard his own sentence of death. For a moment he sat and stared at the spot where the fire had been. Then he grew very calm. Perhaps the old-timer on Sulphur Creek was right. If he had only had a trail mate he would have been in no danger now. The trail mate could have built the fire. Well, it was up to him to build the fire over again, and this second time there must be no failure. Even if he succeeded, he would most likely lose some toes. His feet must be badly frozen by now, and there would be some time before the second fire was ready.

25   Such were his thoughts, but he did not sit and think them. He was busy all the time they were passing through his mind. He made a new foundation for a fire, this time in the open, where no treacherous tree could blot it out. Next he gathered dry grasses and tiny twigs from the high-water flotsam. He could not bring his fingers together to pull them out, but he was able to gather them by the handful. In this way he got many rotten twigs and bits of green moss that were undesirable, but it was the best he could do. He worked methodically, even collecting an armful of the larger branches to be used later when the fire gathered strength. And all the while the dog sat and watched him, a certain yearning wistfulness in its eyes, for it looked upon him as the fire provider, and the fire was slow in coming.

When all was ready, the man reached in his pocket for a second piece of birch bark. He knew the bark was there, and, though he could not feel it with his fingers, he could hear its crisp rustling as he fumbled for it. Try as he would, he could not clutch hold of it. And all the time, in his consciousness, was the knowledge that each instant his feet were freezing. This thought tended to put him in a panic, but he fought against it and kept calm. He pulled on his mittens with his teeth, and threshed his arms back and forth, beating his hands with all his might against his sides. He did this sitting down, and he stood up to do it; and all the while the dog sat in the snow, its wolf brush of a tail curled around warmly over its forefront, its sharp wolf ears pricked forward intently as it watched the man. And the man, as he beat and threshed with his arms and hands, felt a great surge of envy as he regarded the creature that was warm and secure in its natural covering.

After a time he was aware of the first faraway signals of sensation in his beaten fingers. The faint tingling grew stronger till it evolved into a stinging ache that was excruciating, but which the man hailed with satisfaction. He stripped the mitten from his right hand and fetched forth the birch bark. The exposed fingers were quickly going numb again. Next he brought out his bunch of sulphur matches. But the tremendous cold had already driven the life out of his fingers. In his effort to separate one match from the others, the whole bunch fell in the snow. He tried to pick it out of the snow, but failed. The dead fingers could neither touch nor clutch. He was very careful. He drove the thought of his freezing feet, and nose, and cheeks, out of his mind, devoting his whole soul to the matches. He watched, using the sense of vision in place of that touch, and when he saw his fingers on each side of the bunch, he closed them— that is, he willed to close them, for the wires were down, and the fingers did not obey. He pulled the mitten on the right hand, and beat it fiercely against his knee. Then with both mittened hands, he scooped the bunch of matches, along with much snow, into his lap. Yet he was no better off.

After some manipulation he managed to get the bunch between the heels of his mittened hands. In his fashion he carried it to his mouth. The ice crackled and snapped when by a violent effort he opened his mouth. He drew the lower jaw in, curled the upper lip out of the way, and scraped the bunch with his upper teeth in order to sep-arate a match. He succeeded in getting one, which he dropped on his lap. He was no better off. He could not pick it up. Then he devised a way. He picked it up in his teeth and scratched it on his leg. Twenty times he scratched before he succeeded in light-ing it. As it flamed he held it with his teeth to the birch bark. But the burning brim-stone went up his nostrils and into his lungs, causing him to cough spasmodically. The match fell into the snow and went out.

The old-timer on Sulphur Creek was right, he thought in the moment of con-trolled despair that ensued: after fifty below, a man should travel with a partner. He beat his hands, but failed in exciting any sensation. Suddenly he bared both hands, re-moving the mittens with his teeth. He caught the whole bunch between the heels of his hands. His arm muscles not being frozen enabled him to press the hand heels tightly against the matches. Then he scratched the bunch along his leg. It flared into flame, seventy sulphur matches at once! There was no wind to blow them out. He kept his head to one side to escape the strangling fumes, and held the blazing bunch to the birch bark. As he so held it, he became aware of sensation in his hand. His flesh was burning. He could smell it. Deep down below the surface he could feel it. The sensation developed into pain that grew acute. And still he endured it, holding the flame of the matches clumsily to the bark that would not light readily because his own burning hands were in the way, absorbing most of the flame.

At last, when he could endure no more, he jerked his hands apart. The blazing matches fell sizzling into the snow, but the birch bark was alight. He began laying dry grasses and the tiniest twigs on the flame. He could not pick and choose, for he had to lift the fuel between the heels of his hands. Small pieces of rotten wood and green moss clung to the twigs, and he bit them off as well as he could with his teeth. He cherished the flame carefully and awkwardly. It meant life, and it must not per-ish. The withdrawal of blood from the surface of his body now made him begin to shiver, and he grew more awkward. A large piece of green moss fell squarely on the little fire. He tried to poke it out with his fingers, but his shivering frame made him poke too far, and he disrupted the nucleus of the little fire, the burning grasses and tiny twigs separating and scattering. He tried to poke them together again, but in spite of the tenseness of the effort, his shivering got away with him, and the twigs were hope-lessly scattered. Each twig gushed a puff of smoke and went out. The fire provider had failed. As he looked apathetically about him, his eyes chanced on the dog, sitting across the ruins of the fire from him, in the snow, making restless, hunching move-ments, slightly lifting one forefoot and then the other, shifting its weight back and forth on them with wistful eagerness.

The sight of the dog put a wild idea into his head. He remembered the tale of the man, caught in a blizzard, who killed a steer and crawled inside the carcass, and so was saved. He would kill the dog and bury his hands in the warm body until the numbness went out of them. Then he could build another fire. He spoke to the dog, calling it to him; but in his voice was a strange note of fear that frightened the animal, who had never known the man to speak in such a way before. Something was the matter, and its sus-picious nature sensed danger—it knew not what danger, but somewhere, somehow, in its brain arose an apprehension of the man. It flattened its ears down at the sound of the man's voice, and its restless, hunching movements and the liftings and shiftings of its forefeet became more pronounced; but it would not come to the man. He got on his hands and knees and crawled towards the dog. This unusual posture again excited suspicion, and the animal sidled mincingly away.

The man sat up in the snow for a moment and struggled for calmness. Then he pulled on his mittens, by means of his teeth, and got upon his feet. He glanced down at first in order to assure himself that he was really standing up, for the absence of sensation in his feet left him unrelated to the earth. His erect position in itself started to drive the webs of suspicion from the dog's mind; and when he spoke peremptorily, with the sound of whip lashes in his voice, the dog rendered its customary allegiance and came to him. As it came within reaching distance, the man lost his control. His arms flashed out to the dog, and he experienced genuine surprise when he discovered that his hands could not clutch, that there was neither bend nor feeling in the fingers. He had forgotten for the moment that they were frozen and that they were freezing more and more. All this happened quickly, and before the animal could get away, he encircled its body with his arms. He sat down in the snow, and in this fashion held the dog, while it snarled and whined and struggled.

But it was all he could do, hold its body encircled in his arms and sit there. He realized he could not kill the dog. There was no way to do it. With his helpless hands he could neither draw nor hold his sheath knife nor throttle the animal. He released it, and it plunged wildly away, with tail between its legs, and still snarling. It halted forty feet away and surveyed him curiously, with ears sharply pricked forward.

The man looked down at his hands in order to locate them, and found them hanging on the ends of his arms. It struck him as curious that one should have to use his eyes in order to find out where his hands were. He began threshing his arms back and forth, beating the mittened hands against his sides. He did this for five minutes, violently, and his heart pumped enough blood up to the surface to put a stop to his shivering. But no sensation was aroused in the hands. He had an impression that they hung like weights on the ends of his arms, but when he tried to run the impression down, he could not find it.

35   A certain fear of death, dull and oppressive, came to him. This fear quickly became poignant as he realized that it was no longer a mere matter of freezing his fingers and toes, or of losing his hands and feet, but that it was a matter of life and death with the chances against him. This threw him into a panic, and he turned and ran up the creek bed along the old, dim trail. The dog joined in behind him and kept up with him. He ran blindly, without intention, in fear such as he had never known in his life. Slowly, as be ploughed and floundered through the snow, he began to see things again—the banks of the creek, the old timber jams, the leafless aspens, and the sky. The running made him feel better. He did not shiver. Maybe, if he ran on, his feet would thaw out; and, anyway, if he ran far enough, he would reach camp and the boys. Without doubt he would lose some fingers and toes and some of his face; but the boys would take care of him, and save the rest of him when he got there. And at the same time there was another thought in his mind that said he would never get to the camp

and the boys; that it was too many miles away, that the freezing had too great a start on him, and that he would soon be stiff and dead. This thought he kept in the background and refused to consider. Sometimes it pushed itself forward and demanded to be heard, but he thrust it back and strove to think of other things.

It struck him as curious that he could run at all on feet so frozen that he could not feel them when they struck the earth and took the weight of his body. He seemed to himself to skim along above the surface, and to have no connection with the earth. Somewhere he had once seen a winged Mercury, and he wondered if Mercury felt as he felt when skimming over the earth.

His theory of running until he reached camp and the boys had one flaw in it: he lacked the endurance. Several times he stumbled, and finally he tottered, crumpled up, and fell. When he tried to rise, he failed. He must sit and rest, he decided, and next time he would merely walk and keep on going. As he sat and regained his breath, he noted that he was feeling quite warm and comfortable. He was not shivering, and it even seemed that a warm glow had come to his chest and trunk. And yet, when he touched his nose or cheeks, there was no sensation. Running would not thaw them out. Nor would it thaw out his hands and feet. Then the thought came to him that the frozen portions of his body must be extending. He tried to keep this thought down, to forget it, to think of something else; he was aware of the panicky feeling that it caused, and he was afraid of the panic. But the thought asserted itself, and persisted, until it produced a vision of his body totally frozen. This was too much, and he made another wild run along the trail. Once he slowed down to a walk, but the thought of the freezing extending itself made him run again.

And all the time the dog ran with him, at his heels. When he fell down a second time, it curled its tail over its forefeet and sat in front of him, facing him, curiously eager and intent. The warmth and security of the animal angered him, and he cursed it till it flattened down its ears appeasingly. This time the shivering came more quickly upon the man. He was losing in his battle with the frost. It was creeping into his body from all sides. The thought of it drove him on, but he ran no more than a hundred feet, when he staggered and pitched headlong. It was his last panic. When he had recovered his breath and control, he sat up and entertained in his mind the conception of meeting death with dignity. However, the conception did not come to him in such terms. His idea of it was that he had been making a fool of himself, running around like a chicken with its head cut off—such was the simile that occurred to him. Well, he was bound to freeze anyway, and he might as well take it decently. With this new-found peace of mind came the first glimmerings of drowsiness. A good idea, he thought, to sleep off to death. It was like taking an anaesthetic. Freezing was not so bad as people thought. There were lots worse ways to die.

He pictured the boys finding his body next day. Suddenly he found himself with them, coming along the trail looking for himself. And, still with them, he came around a turn in the trail and found himself lying in the snow. He did not belong with himself any more, for even then he was out of himself, standing with the boys and looking at himself in the snow. It certainly was cold, was his thought. When he got back to the States he could tell the folks what real cold was. He drifted on from this to a vision of the old-timer on Sulphur Creek. He could see him quite clearly, warm and comfortable, and smoking a pipe.

40   "You were right, old hoss; you were right," the man mumbled to the old-timer of Sulfur Creek.

Then the man drowsed off into what seemed to him the most comfortable and satisfying sleep he had ever known. The dog sat facing him and waiting. The brief day drew to a close in a long, slow twilight. There were no signs of a fire to be made, and, besides, never in the dog's experience had it known a man to sit like that in the snow and make no fire. As the twilight drew on, its eager yearning for the fire mastered it, and with a great lifting and shifting of forefeet, it whined softly, then flattened its ears down in anticipation of being chidden by the man. But the man remained silent. Later the dog whined loudly. And still later it crept close to the man and caught the scent of death. This made the animal bristle and back away. A little longer it delayed, howling under the stars that leaped and danced and shone brightly in the cold sky. Then it turned and trotted up the trail in the direction of the camp it knew, where were the other food providers and fire providers.

CRITICAL THINKING QUESTIONS

1. Dismissing the old-timer's warning—"no man must travel alone in the Klondike below fifty degrees"—the man sets out alone on his journey along the Yukon. Later, after his "accident" of breaking through some ice and then saving himself, the man thought, "Those old-timers were rather womanish, some of them. . . . Any man who was a man could travel alone." Evaluate the man's reasoning in *jumping to the conclusion* that the old-timer was wrong:

   a. On what *evidence* does he base his conclusion? How do logic and emotion influence his reasoning?

   b. What *warrant* informs his definition of a man?

2. What *value assumptions* about animals underlie the man's interaction with the dog? How does the story's plot challenge those assumptions?

WRITING TOPIC

What is London's *claim* about the individual person and nature? Can you think of evidence—examples from your own experience and knowledge—that supports this claim? In what ways have we attempted to alter the relationship between humans and nature? What is your perspective on these topics? Do you think there is a natural order among living things that should be respected by science and technology? Is there a middle-ground (*Rogerian*) position?

Leslie Marmon Silko (b. 1948)

The Man to Send Rain Clouds

One

They found him under a big cottonwood tree. His Levi jacket and pants were faded light blue so that he had been easy to find. The big cottonwood tree stood apart from a small grove of winterbare cottonwoods which grew in the wide, sandy arroyo. He had been dead for a day or more, and the sheep had wandered and scattered up and down the arroyo. Leon and his brother-in-law, Ken, gathered the sheep and left them in the pen at the sheep camp before they returned to the cottonwood tree. Leon waited under the tree while Ken drove the truck through the deep sand to the edge of the arroyo. He squinted up at the sun and unzipped his jacket—it sure was hot for this time of year. But high and northwest the blue mountains were still deep in snow. Ken came sliding down the low, crumbling bank about fifty yards down, and he was bringing the red blanket.

Before they wrapped the old man, Leon took a piece of string out of his pocket and tied a small gray feather in the old man's long white hair. Ken gave him the paint. Across the brown wrinkled forehead he drew a streak of white, and along the high cheekbones he drew a strip of blue paint. He paused and watched Ken throw pinches of corn meal and pollen into the wind that fluttered the small gray feather. Then Leon painted with yellow under the old man's broad nose; and finally, when he had painted green across the chin, he smiled.

"Send us rain clouds, Grandfather." They laid the bundle in the back of the pickup and covered it with a heavy tarp before they started back to the pueblo.

They turned off the highway onto the sandy pueblo road. Not long after they passed the store and post office they saw Father Paul's car coming toward them. When he recognized their faces he slowed his car and waved for them to stop. The young priest rolled down the car window.

"Did you find old Teofilo?" he asked loudly.   5

Leon stopped the truck. "Good morning, Father. We were just out to the sheep camp. Everything is O.K. now."

"Thank God for that. Teofilo is a very old man. You really shouldn't allow him to stay at the sheep camp alone."

"No, he won't do that any more now."

"Well, I'm glad you understand. I hope I'll be seeing you at Mass this week—we missed you last Sunday. See if you can get old Teofilo to come with you." The priest smiled and waved at them as they drove away.

Two

10   Louise and Teresa were waiting. The table was set for lunch, and the coffee was boiling on the black iron stove. Leon looked at Louise and then at Teresa.

"We found him under a cottonwood tree in the big arroyo near sheep camp. I guess he sat down to rest in the shade and never got up again." Leon walked toward the old man's bed. The red plaid shawl had been shaken and spread carefully over the bed, and a new brown flannel shirt and pair of stiff new Levis were arranged neatly beside the pillow. Louise held the screen door open while Leon and Ken carried in the red blanket. He looked small and shriveled, and after they dressed him in the new shirt and pants he seemed more shrunken.

It was noontime now because the church bells rang the Angelus. They ate the beans with hot bread, and nobody said anything until after Teresa poured the coffee.

Ken stood up and put on his jacket. "I'll see about the gravediggers. Only the top layer of soil is frozen. I think it can be ready before dark."

Leon nodded his head and finished his coffee. After Ken had been gone for a while, the neighbors and clanspeople came quietly to embrace Teofilo's family and to leave food on the table because the gravediggers would come to eat when they were finished.

Three

15   The sky in the west was full of pale-yellow light. Louise stood outside with her hands in the pockets of Leon's green army jacket that was too big for her. The funeral was over, and the old men had taken their candles and medicine bags and were gone. She waited until the body was laid into the pickup before she said anything to Leon. She touched his arm, and he noticed that her hands were still dusty from the corn meal that she had sprinkled around the old man. When she spoke, Leon could not hear her.

"What did you say? I didn't hear you."

"I said that I had been thinking about something."

"About what?"

"About the priest sprinkling holy water for Grandpa. So he won't be thirsty."

20   Leon stared at the new moccasins that Teofilo had made for the ceremonial dances in the summer. They were nearly hidden by the red blanket. It was getting colder, and the wind pushed gray dust down the narrow pueblo road. The sun was approaching the long mesa where it disappeared during the winter. Louise stood there shivering and watching his face. Then he zipped up his jacket and opened the truck door. "I'll see if he's there."

Four

Ken stopped the pickup at the church, and Leon got out; and then Ken drove down the hill to the graveyard where people were waiting. Leon knocked at the old carved door with its symbols of the Lamb. While he waited he looked up at the twin bells from the king of Spain with the last sunlight pouring around them in their tower.

The priest opened the door and smiled when he saw who it was. "Come in! What brings you here this evening?"

The priest walked toward the kitchen, and Leon stood with his cap in his hand, playing with the earflaps and examining the living room—the brown sofa, the green armchair, and the brass lamp that hung down from the ceiling by links of chain. The priest dragged a chair out of the kitchen and offered it to Leon.

"No thank you, Father. I only came to ask you if you would bring your holy water to the graveyard."

The priest turned away from Leon and looked out the window at the patio full   25 of shadows and the dining-room windows of the nuns' cloister across the patio. The curtains were heavy, and the light from within faintly penetrated; it was impossible to see the nuns inside eating supper. "Why didn't you tell me he was dead? I could have brought the Last Rites anyway."

Leon smiled. "It wasn't necessary, Father."

The priest stared down at his scuffed brown loafers and the worn hem of his cassock. "For a Christian burial it was necessary."

His voice was distant, and Leon thought that his blue eyes looked tired.

"It's O.K. Father, we just want him to have plenty of water."

The priest sank down into the green chair and picked up a glossy missionary mag-   30 azine. He turned the colored pages full of lepers and pagans without looking at them.

"You know I can't do that, Leon. There should have been the Last Rites and a funeral Mass at the very least."

Leon put on his green cap and pulled the flaps down over his ears. "It's getting late, Father. I've got to go."

When Leon opened the door Father Paul stood up and said, "Wait." He left the room and came back wearing a long brown overcoat. He followed Leon out the door and across the dim churchyard to the adobe steps in front of the church. They both stooped to fit through the low adobe entrance. And when they started down the hill to the graveyard only half of the sun was visible above the mesa.

The priest approached the grave slowly, wondering how they had managed to dig into the frozen ground; and then he remembered that this was New Mexico, and saw the pile of cold loose sand beside the hole. The people stood close to each other with little clouds of steam puffing from their faces. The priest looked at them and saw a pile of jackets, gloves, and scarves in the yellow, dry tumbleweeds that grew in the graveyard. He looked at the red blanket, not sure that Teofilo was so small, wondering if it wasn't some perverse Indian trick—something they did in March to ensure a good harvest—wondering if maybe old Teofilo was actually at sheep camp corralling the sheep for the night. But there he was, facing into a cold dry wind and squinting at the last sunlight, ready to bury a red wool blanket while the faces of his parishioners were in shadow with the last warmth of the sun on their backs.

His fingers were stiff, and it took him a long time to twist the lid off the holy   35 water. Drops of water fell on the red blanket and soaked into dark icy spots. He sprinkled the grave and the water disappeared almost before it touched the dim, cold sand;

it reminded him of something—he tried to remember what it was, because he thought if he could remember he might understand this. He sprinkled more water; he shook the container until it was empty, and the water fell through the light from sundown like August rain that fell while the sun was still shining, almost evaporating before it touched the wilted squash flowers.

The wind pulled at the priest's brown Franciscan robe and swirled away the corn meal and pollen that had been sprinkled on the blanket. They lowered the bundle into the ground, and they didn't bother to untie the stiff pieces of new rope that were tied around the ends of the blanket. The sun was gone, and over on the highway the eastbound lane was full of headlights. The priest walked away slowly. Leon watched him climb the hill, and when he had disappeared within the tall, thick walls, Leon turned to look up at the high blue mountains in the deep snow that reflected a faint red light from the west. He felt good because it was finished, and he was happy about the sprinkling of the holy water; now the old man could send them big thunderclouds for sure.

CRITICAL THINKING QUESTIONS

1. In this story, the author notes specific colors and lighting frequently in depicting characters and setting. List details that include color or lighting and speculate on their thematic significance.

2. Explain how this story leaves you feeling.

3. What is Silko's *implied claim* about Native Americans' spiritual heritage in late twentieth-century America? What evidence in the story supports your interpretation of her claim?

WRITING TOPIC

Why do you think Father Paul decides to bend the rules of his religion and accompany Leon to the graveyard to sprinkle holy water for Teofilo? Another mystery in Father Paul's character is suggested in the next to last paragraph: "He sprinkled the grave and the water disappeared almost before it touched the dim, cold sand; it reminded him of something—he tried to remember what it was, because he thought if he could remember he might understand this." Using evidence from the story and your own ideas and speculation, write a brief character sketch of Father Paul.

Eudora Welty (1909–2001)

A Worn Path

It was December—a bright frozen day in the early morning. Far out in the country there was an old Negro woman with her head tied in a red rag, coming along a path through the pinewoods. Her name was Phoenix Jackson. She was very old and small and she walked slowly in the dark pine shadows, moving a little from side to side in her steps, with the balanced heaviness and lightness of a pendulum in a grandfather clock. She carried a thin, small cane made from an umbrella, and with this she kept tapping the frozen earth in front of her. This made a grave and persistent noise in the still air, that seemed meditative like the chirping of a solitary little bird.

She wore a dark striped dress reaching down to her shoe tops, and an equally long apron of bleached sugar sacks, with a full pocket: all neat and tidy, but every time she took a step she might have fallen over her shoe-laces, which dragged from her unlaced shoes. She looked straight ahead. Her eyes were blue with age. Her skin had a pattern all its own of numberless branching wrinkles and as though a whole little tree stood in the middle of her forehead, but a golden color ran underneath, and the two knobs of her cheeks were illuminated by a yellow burning under the dark. Under the red rag her hair came down on her neck in the frailest of ringlets, still black, and with an odor like copper.

Now and then there was a quivering in the thicket. Old Phoenix said, "Out of my way, all you foxes, owls, beetles, jack rabbits, coons, and wild animals! . . . Keep out from under these feet, little bob-whites. . . . Keep the big wild hogs out of my path. Don't let none of those come running my direction. I got a long way." Under her small black-freckled hand her cane, limber as a buggy whip, would switch at the brush as if to rouse up any hiding things.

On she went. The woods were deep and still. The sun made the pine needles almost too bright to look at, up where the wind rocked. The cones dropped as light as feathers. Down in the hollow was the mourning dove—it was not too late for him.

The path ran up a hill. "Seem like there is chains about my feet, time I get this far," she said, in the voice of argument old people keep to use with themselves. "Something always takes a hold of me on this hill—pleads I should stay."   5

After she got to the top she turned and gave a full, severe look behind her where she had come. "Up through pines," she said at length. "Now down through oaks."

Her eyes opened their widest, and she started down gently. But before she got to the bottom of the hill a bush caught her dress.

Her fingers were busy and intent, but her skirts were full and long, so that before she could pull them free in one place they were caught in another. It was not possible to allow the dress to tear. "I in the thorny bush," she said. "Thorns, you doing your appointed work. Never want to let folks pass—no sir. Old eyes thought you was a pretty little *green* bush."

Finally, trembling all over, she stood free, and after a moment dared to stoop for her cane.

10   "Sun so high!" she cried, leaning back and looking, while the thick tears went over her eyes. "The time getting all gone here."

At the foot of this hill was a place where a log was laid across the creek.

"Now comes the trial," said Phoenix.

Putting her right foot out, she mounted the log and shut her eyes. Lifting her skirt, levelling her cane fiercely before her, like a festival figure in some parade, she began to march across. Then she opened her eyes and she was safe on the other side.

"I wasn't as old as I thought," she said.

15   But she sat down to rest. She spread her skirts on the bank around her and folded her hands over her knees. Up above her was a tree in a pearly cloud of mistletoe. She did not dare to close her eyes, and when a little boy brought her a little plate with a slice of marble-cake on it she spoke to him. "That would be acceptable," she said. But when she went to take it there was just her own hand in the air.

So she left that tree, and had to go through a barbed-wire fence. There she had to creep and crawl, spreading her knees and stretching her fingers like a baby trying to climb the steps. But she talked loudly to herself: she could not let her dress be torn now, so late in the day, and she could not pay for having her arm or her leg sawed off if she got caught fast where she was.

At last she was safe through the fence and risen up out in the clearing. Big dead trees, like black men with one arm, were standing in the purple stalks of the withered cotton field. There sat a buzzard.

"Who you watching?"

In the furrow she made her way along.

20   "Glad this not the season for bulls," she said, looking sideways, "and the good Lord made his snakes to curl up and sleep in the winter. A pleasure I don't see no two-headed snake coming around that tree, where it come once. It took a while to get by him, back in the summer."

She passed through the old cotton and went into a field of dead corn. It whispered and shook and was taller than her head. "Through the maze now," she said, for there was no path.

Then there was something tall, black, and skinny there, moving before her.

At first she took it for a man. It could have been a man dancing in the field. But she stood still and listened, and it did not make a sound. It was as silent as a ghost.

"Ghost," she said sharply, "who be you the ghost of? For I have heard of nary death close by."

25   But there was no answer—only the ragged dancing in the wind.

She shut her eyes, reached out her hand, and touched a sleeve. She found a coat and inside that an emptiness, cold as ice.

"You scarecrow," she said. Her face lighted. "I ought to be shut up for good," she said with laughter. "My senses is gone. I too old. I the oldest people I ever know. Dance, old scarecrow," she said, "while I dancing with you."

She kicked her foot over the furrow, and with mouth drawn down, shook her head once or twice in a little strutting way. Some husks blew down and whirled in streamers about her skirts.

Then she went on, parting her way from side to side with the cane, through the whispering field. At last she came to the end, to a wagon track where the silver grass blew between the red ruts. The quail were walking around like pullets, seeming all dainty and unseen.

"Walk pretty," she said. "This the easy place. This the easy going."   30

She followed the track, swaying through the quiet bare fields, through the little strings of tree silver in their dead leaves, past cabins silver from weather, with the doors and windows boarded shut, all like old women under a spell sitting there. "I walking in their sleep," she said, nodding her head vigorously.

In a ravine she went where a spring was silently flowing through a hollow log. Old Phoenix bent and drank. "Sweet-gum makes the water sweet," she said, and drank more. "Nobody know who made this well, for it was here when I was born."

The track crossed a swampy part where the moss hung as white as lace from every limb. "Sleep on, alligators, and blow your bubbles." Then the track went into the road.

Deep, deep the road went down between the high green-colored banks. Overhead the live-oaks met, and it was as dark as a cave.

A black dog with a lolling tongue came up out of the weeds by the ditch. She was   35
meditating, and not ready, and when he came at her she only hit him a little with her cane. Over she went in the ditch, like a little puff of milk-weed.

Down there, her senses drifted away. A dream visited her, and she reached her hand up, but nothing reached down and gave her a pull. So she lay there and presently went to talking. "Old woman," she said to herself, "that black dog came up out of the weeds to stall you off, and now there he sitting on his fine tail, smiling at you."

A white man finally came along and found her—a hunter, a young man, with his dog on a chain.

"Well, Granny!" he laughed. "What are you doing there?"

"Lying on my back like a June-bug waiting to be turned over, mister," she said, reaching up her hand.

He lifted her up, gave her a swing in the air, and set her down, "Anything bro-   40
ken, Granny?"

"No sir, them old dead weeds is springy enough," said Phoenix, when she had got her breath. "I thank you for your trouble."

"Where do you live, Granny?" he asked, while the two dogs were growling at each other.

"Away back yonder, sir, behind the ridge. You can't even see it from here."

"On your way home?"

"No, sir, I going to town."   45

"Why, that's too far! That's as far as I walk when I come out myself, and I get something for my trouble." He patted the stuffed bag he carried, and there hung down a little closed claw. It was one of the bob-whites, with its beak hooked bitterly to show it was dead. "Now you go on home, Granny!"

"I bound to go to town, mister," said Phoenix. "The time come around."

He gave another laugh, filling the whole landscape. "I know you old colored people! Wouldn't miss going to town to see Santa Claus!"

But something held Old Phoenix very still. The deep lines in her face went into a fierce and different radiation. Without warning, she had seen with her own eyes a flashing nickel fall out of the man's pocket onto the ground.

50   "How old are you, Granny?" he was saying.

"There is no telling, mister," she said, "no telling."

Then she gave a little cry and clapped her hands and said, "Git on away from here, dog! Look! Look at that dog!" She laughed as if in admiration. "He ain't scared of nobody. He a big black dog." She whispered, "Sic him!"

"Watch me get rid of that cur," said the man. "Sic him, Pete! Sic him!"

Phoenix heard the dogs fighting, and heard the man running and throwing sticks. She even heard a gunshot. But she was slowly bending forward by that time, further and further forward, the lids stretched down over her eyes, as if she were doing this in her sleep. Her chin was lowered almost to her knees. The yellow palm of her hand came out from the fold of her apron. Her fingers slid down and along the ground under the piece of money with the grace and care they would have in lifting an egg from under a sitting hen. Then she slowly straightened up, she stood erect, and the nickel was in her apron pocket. A bird flew by. Her lips moved. "God watching me the whole time. I come to stealing."

55   The man came back, and his own dog panted about them. "Well, I scared him off that time," he said, and then he laughed and lifted his gun and pointed it at Phoenix.

She stood straight and faced him.

"Doesn't the gun scare you?" he said, still pointing it.

"No, sir, I seen plenty go off closer by, in my day, and for less than what I done," she said, holding utterly still.

He smiled, and shouldered the gun. "Well, Granny," he said, "you must be a hundred years old, and scared of nothing. I'd give you a dime if I had any money with me. But you take my advice and stay home, and nothing will happen to you."

60   "I bound to go on my way, mister," said Phoenix. She inclined her head in the red rag. Then they went in different directions, but she could hear the gun shooting again and again over the hill.

She walked on. The shadows hung from the oak trees to the road like curtains. Then she smelled wood-smoke, and smelled the river, and she saw a steeple and the cabins on their steep steps. Dozens of little black children whirled around her. There ahead was Natchez shining. Bells were ringing. She walked on.

In the paved city it was Christmas time. There were red and green electric lights strung and crisscrossed everywhere, and all turned on in the daytime. Old Phoenix would have been lost if she had not distrusted her eyesight and depended on her feet to know where to take her.

She paused quietly on the sidewalk where people were passing by. A lady came along in the crowd, carrying an armful of red-, green-, and silver-wrapped presents; she gave off perfume like the red roses in hot summer, and Phoenix stopped her.

"Please, missy, will you lace up my shoe?" She held up her foot.

"What do you want, Grandma?"   65

"See my shoe," said Phoenix. "Do all right for out in the country, but wouldn't look right to go in a big building."

"Stand still then, Grandma," said the lady. She put her packages down on the sidewalk beside her and laced and tied both shoes tightly.

"Can't lace 'em with a cane," said Phoenix. "Thank you, missy. I doesn't mind asking a nice lady to tie up my shoe, when I gets out on the street."

Moving slowly and from side to side, she went into the big building and into a tower of steps, where she walked up and around and around until her feet knew to stop.

She entered a door, and there she saw nailed up on the wall the document that   70
had been stamped with the gold seal and framed in the gold frame, which matched the dream that was hung up in her head.

"Here I be," she said. There was a fixed and ceremonial stiffness over her body.

"A charity case, I suppose," said an attendant who sat at the desk before her.

But Phoenix only looked above her head. There was sweat on her face, the wrinkles in her skin shone like a bright net.

"Speak up, Grandma," the woman said. "What's your name? We must have your history, you know. Have you been here before? What seems to be the trouble with you?"

Old Phoenix only gave a twitch to her face as if a fly were bothering her.   75

"Are you deaf?" cried the attendant.

But then the nurse came in.

"Oh, that's just old Aunt Phoenix," she said. "She doesn't come for herself—she has a little grandson. She makes these trips just as regular as clockwork. She lives away back off the Old Natchez Trace." She bent down. "Well, Aunt Phoenix, why don't you just take a seat? We won't keep you standing after your long trip." She pointed.

The old woman sat down, bolt upright in the chair.

"Now, how is the boy?" asked the nurse.   80

Old Phoenix did not speak.

"I said, how is the boy?"

But Phoenix only waited and stared straight ahead, her face very solemn and withdrawn into rigidity.

"Is his throat any better?" asked the nurse. "Aunt Phoenix, don't you hear me? Is your grandson's throat any better since the last time you came for the medicine?"

With her hands on her knees, the old woman waited, silent, erect and motion-   85
less, just as if she were in amour.

"You mustn't take up our time this way, Aunt Phoenix," the nurse said. "Tell us quickly about your grandson, and get it over with. He isn't dead, is he?"

At last there came a flicker and then a flame of comprehension across her face, and she spoke.

"My grandson. It was my memory had left me. There I sat and forgot why I made my long trip."

"Forgot?" The nurse frowned. "After you came so far?"

90 Then Phoenix was like an old woman begging a dignified forgiveness for waking up frightened in the night. "I never did go to school, I was too old at the Surrender," she said in a soft voice. "I'm an old woman without an education. It was my memory fail me. My little grandson, he is just the same, and I forgot it in the coming."

"Throat never heals, does it?" said the nurse, speaking in a loud, sure voice to Old Phoenix. By now she had a card with something written on it, a little list. "Yes. Swallowed lye. When was it—January—two-three years ago—"

Phoenix spoke unasked now. "No, missy, he not dead, he just the same. Every little while his throat begin to close up again, and he not able to swallow. He not get his breath. He not able to help himself. So the time come around, and I go on another trip for the soothing medicine."

"All right. The doctor said as long as you came to get it, you could have it," said the nurse. "But it's an obstinate case."

"My little grandson, he sit up there in the house all wrapped up, waiting by himself," Phoenix went on. "We is the only two left in the world. He suffer and it don't seem to put him back at all. He got a sweet look. He going to last. He wear a little patch quilt and peep out holding his mouth open like a little bird. I remembers so plain now. I not going to forget him again, no, the whole enduring time. I could tell him from all the others in creation."

95 "All right." The nurse was trying to hush her now. She brought her a bottle of medicine. "Charity," she said, making a check mark in a book.

Old Phoenix held the bottle close to her eyes and then carefully put it into her pocket.

"I thank you," she said.

"It's Christmas time, Grandma," said the attendant. "Could I give you a few pennies out of my purse?"

"Five pennies is a nickel," said Phoenix stiffly.

100 "Here's a nickel," said the attendant.

Phoenix rose carefully and held out her hand. She received the nickel and then fished the other nickel out of her pocket and laid it beside the new one. She stared at her palm closely, with her head on one side.

Then she gave a tap with her cane on the floor.

"That is what come to me to do," she said. "I going to the store and buy my child a little windmill they sells, made out of paper. He going to find it hard to believe there such a thing in the world. I'll march myself back where he waiting, holding it straight up in this hand."

She lifted her free hand, gave a little nod, turned round, and walked out of the doctor's office. Then her slow step began on the stairs, going down.

CRITICAL THINKING QUESTIONS

1. a. When Phoenix arrives at the clinic, the attendant makes the *inference* that she is "a charity case." On what evidence is her inference based?
    b. What value assumptions underlie her inference?
    c. Do you think the attendant has "jumped to a conclusion," or is her conclusion valid?
    d. Later, when Phoenix is leaving, what do you think is the attendant's motive in offering Phoenix a few pennies?

2. Phoenix chats amiably with all she encounters along her path. Arriving at the clinic, she announces, "Here I be," and then she seems to become temporarily mute. Why this sudden loss of speech?

3. What is the significance of the title?

WRITING TOPIC

What is wisdom? Write a claim statement that defines wisdom, and use evidence from this story and your own experience to illustrate and support your definition.

Virginia Woolf (1882–1941)
Kew Gardens

From the oval-shaped flower-bed there rose perhaps a hundred stalks spreading into heart-shaped or tongue-shaped leaves halfway up and unfurling at the tip red or blue or yellow petals marked with spots of colour raised upon the surface; and from the red, blue or yellow gloom of the throat emerged a straight bar, rough with gold dust and slightly clubbed at the end. The petals were voluminous enough to be stirred by the summer breeze, and when they moved, the red, blue and yellow lights passed one over the other, staining an inch of the brown earth beneath with a spot of the most intricate colour. The light fell either upon the smooth, grey back of a pebble, or, the shell of a snail with its brown, circular veins, or falling into a raindrop, it expanded with such intensity of red, blue and yellow the thin walls of water that one expected them to burst and disappear. Instead, the drop was left in a second silver grey once more, and the light now settled upon the flesh of a leaf, revealing the branching thread of fibre beneath the surface, and again it moved on and spread its illumination in the vast green spaces beneath the dome of the heart-shaped and tongue-shaped leaves. Then the breeze stirred rather more briskly overhead and the colour was flashed into the air above, into the eyes of the men and women who walk in Kew Gardens in July.

The figures of these men and women straggled past the flower-bed with a curiously irregular movement not unlike that of the white and blue butterflies who crossed the turf in zig-zag flights from bed to bed. The man was about six inches in front of the woman, strolling carelessly, while she bore on with greater purpose, only turning her head now and then to see that the children were not too far behind. The man kept this distance in front of the woman purposely, though perhaps unconsciously, for he wished to go on with his thoughts.

"Fifteen years ago I came here with Lily," he thought. "We sat somewhere over there by a lake and I begged her to marry me all through the hot afternoon. How the dragonfly kept circling round us: how clearly I see the dragonfly and her shoe with the square silver buckle at the toe. All the time I spoke I saw her shoe and when it moved impatiently I knew without looking up what she was going to say: the whole of her seemed to be in her shoe. And my love, my desire, were in the dragonfly; for some reason I thought that if it settled there, on that leaf, the broad one with the red flower in the middle of it, if the dragonfly settled on the leaf she would say 'Yes' at once. But the dragonfly went round and round: it never settled anywhere—of course not, happily not, or I shouldn't be walking here with Eleanor and the children. Tell me, Eleanor. D'you ever think of the past?"

"Why do you ask, Simon?"

5   "Because I've been thinking of the past. I've been thinking of Lily, the woman I might have married. . . . Well, why are you silent? Do you mind my thinking of the past?"

"Why should I mind, Simon? Doesn't one always think of the past, in a garden with men and women lying under the trees. Aren't they one's past, all that remains of it, those men and women, those ghosts lying under the trees . . . one's happiness, one's reality?"

"For me, a square silver shoe buckle and a dragonfly—"

"For me, a kiss. Imagine six little girls sitting before their easels twenty years ago, down by the side of a lake, painting the water-lilies, the first red water-lilies I'd ever seen. And suddenly a kiss, there on the back of my neck. And my hand shook all the afternoon so that I couldn't paint. I took out my watch and marked the hour when I would allow myself to think of the kiss for five minutes only—it was so precious—the kiss of an old grey-haired woman with a wart on her nose, the mother of all my kisses all my life. Come, Caroline, come, Hubert."

They walked on past the flower-bed, now walking four abreast, and soon diminished in size among the trees and looked half transparent as the sunlight and shade swam over their backs in large trembling irregular patches.

10   In the oval flower-bed the snail, whose shell had been stained red, blue and yellow for the space of two minutes or so, now appeared to be moving very slightly in its shell, and next began to labour over the crumbs of loose earth which broke away and rolled down as it passed over them. It appeared to have a definite goal in front of it, differing in this respect from the singular high stepping angular green insect who

attempted to cross in front of it, and waited for a second with its antennae trembling as if in deliberation, and then stepped off as rapidly and strangely in the opposite direction. Brown cliffs with deep green lakes in the hollows, flat, blade-like trees that waved from root to tip, round boulders of grey stone, vast crumpled surfaces of a thin crackling texture—all these objects lay across the snail's progress between one stalk and another to his goal. Before he had decided whether to circumvent the arched tent of a dead leaf or to breast it there came past the bed the feet of other human beings.

This time they were both men. The younger of the two wore an expression of perhaps unnatural calm; he raised his eyes and fixed them very steadily in front of him while his companion spoke, and directly his companion had done speaking he looked on the ground again and sometimes opened his lips only after a long pause and sometimes did not open them at all. The elder man had a curiously uneven and shaky method of walking, jerking his hand forward and throwing up his head abruptly, rather in the manner of an impatient carriage horse tired of waiting outside a house; but in the man these gestures were irresolute and pointless. He talked almost incessantly; he smiled to himself and again began to talk, as if the smile had been an answer. He was talking about spirits—the spirits of the dead, who, according to him, were even now telling him all sorts of odd things about their experiences in Heaven.

"Heaven was known to the ancients as Thessaly, William, and now, with this war, the spirit matter is rolling between the hills like thunder." He paused, seemed to listen, smiled, jerked his head and continued:

"You have a small electric battery and a piece of rubber to insulate the wire—isolate?—insulate?—well, we'll skip the details, no good going into details that wouldn't be understood—and in short the little machine stands in any convenient position by the head of the bed, we will say, on a neat mahogany stand. All arrangements being properly fixed by workmen under my direction, the widow applies her ear and summons the spirit by sign as agreed. Women! Widows! Women in black—"

Here he seemed to have caught sight of a woman's dress in the distance, which in the shade looked a purple black. He took off his hat, placed his hand upon his heart, and hurried towards her muttering and gesticulating feverishly. But William caught him by the sleeve and touched a flower with the tip of his walking-stick in order to divert the old man's attention. After looking at it for a moment in some confusion the old man bent his ear to it and seemed to answer a voice speaking from it, for he began talking about the forests of Uruguay which he had visited hundreds of years ago in company with the most beautiful young woman in Europe. He could be heard murmuring about forests of Uruguay blanketed with the wax petals of tropical roses, nightingales, sea beaches, mermaids, and women drowned at sea, as he suffered himself to be moved on by William, upon whose face the look of stoical patience grew slowly deeper and deeper.

Following his steps so closely as to be slightly puzzled by his gestures came two 15 elderly women of the lower middle class, one stout and ponderous, the other rosy cheeked and nimble. Like most people of their station they were frankly fascinated by other signs of eccentricity betokening a disordered brain, especially in the well-to-do; but they were too far off to be certain whether the gestures were merely eccentric or genuinely mad. After they had scrutinized the old man's back in silence for a moment and given each other a queer, sly look, they went on energetically piecing together their very complicated dialogue:

"Nell, Bert, Lot, Cess, Phil, Pa, he says, I says, she says, I says, I says—"

"My Bert, Sis, Bill, Grandad, the old man, sugar,

Sugar, flour, kippers, greens,

Sugar, sugar, sugar."

The ponderous woman looked through the pattern of falling words at the flowers standing cool, firm, and upright in the earth, with a curious expression. She saw them as a sleeper waking from a heavy sleep sees a brass candlestick reflecting the light in an unfamiliar way, and closes his eyes and opens them, and seeing the brass candlestick again, finally starts broad awake and stares at the candlestick with all his powers. So the heavy woman came to a standstill opposite the oval-shaped flower-bed, and ceased even to pretend to listen to what the other woman was saying. She stood there letting the words fall over her, swaying the top part of her body slowly backwards and forwards, looking at the flowers. Then she suggested that they should find a seat and have their tea.

The snail had now considered every possible method of reaching his goal without going round the dead leaf or climbing over it. Let alone the effort needed for climbing a leaf, he was doubtful whether the thin texture which vibrated with such an alarming crackle when touched even by the tips of his horns would bear his weight; and this determined him finally to creep beneath it, for there was a point where the leaf curved high enough from the ground to admit him. He had just inserted his head in the opening and was taking stock of the high brown roof and was getting used to the cool brown light when two other people came past outside on the turf. This time they were both young, a young man and a young woman. They were both in the prime of youth, the season before the smooth pink folds of the flower have burst their gummy case, when the wings of the butterfly, though fully grown, are motionless in the sun.

"Lucky it isn't Friday," he observed.

"Why? D'you believe in luck?"

20 "They make you pay sixpence on Friday."

"What's a sixpence anyway? Isn't it worth sixpence?"

"What's 'it'—what do you mean by 'it'?"

"O, anything—I mean—you know what I mean."

Long pauses came between each of these remarks: they were uttered in toneless and monotonous voices. The couple stood still on the edge of the flower-bed, and together pressed the end of her parasol deep down into the soft earth. The action and the fact that his hand rested on the top of hers expressed their feelings in a strange way, as these short insignificant words also expressed something, words with short wings for their heavy body of meaning, inadequate to carry them far and thus alighting awkwardly upon the very common objects that surrounded them, and were to their inexperienced touch so massive; but who knows (so they thought as they pressed the parasol into the earth) what precipices aren't concealed in them, or what slopes of ice don't shine in the sun on the other side? Who knows? Who has ever seen this before?

Even when she wondered what sort of tea they gave you at Kew, he felt that something loomed up behind her words, and stood vast and solid behind them; and the mist very slowly rose and uncovered—O, Heavens, what were those shapes?—little white tables, and waitresses who looked first at her and then at him; and there was a bill that he would pay with a real two-shilling piece, and it was real, all real, he assured himself, fingering the coin in his pocket, real to everyone except to him and to her; even to him it began to seem real; and then—but it was too exciting to stand and think any longer, and he pulled the parasol out of the earth with a jerk and was impatient to find the place where one had tea with other people, like other people.

"Come along, Trissie; it's time we had our tea."　　　　　　　　　　　　25

"Wherever *does* one have one's tea?" she asked with the oddest thrill of excitement in her voice, looking vaguely round and letting herself be drawn on down the grass path, trailing her parasol; turning her head this way and that way forgetting her tea, wishing to go down there and then down there, remembering orchids and cranes among wild flowers, a Chinese pagoda and a crimson crested bird; but he bore her on.

Thus one couple after another with much the same irregular and aimless movement passed the flower-bed and were enveloped in layer after layer of green-blue vapour, in which at first their bodies had substance and a dash of colour, but later both substance and colour dissolved in the green-blue atmosphere. How hot it was! So hot that even the thrush chose to hop, like a mechanical bird, in the shadow of the flowers, with long pauses between one movement and the next; instead of rambling vaguely the white butterflies danced one above another, making with their white shifting flakes the outline of a shattered marble column above the tallest flowers; the glass roofs of the palm house shone as if a whole market full of shiny green umbrellas had opened in the sun; and in the drone of the aeroplane the voice of the summer sky murmured its fierce soul. Yellow and black, pink and snow white, shapes of all these colours, men, women, and children were spotted for a second upon the horizon, and then, seeing the breadth of yellow that lay upon the grass, they wavered and sought shade beneath the trees, dissolving like drops of water in the yellow and green atmosphere, staining it faintly with red and blue. It seemed as if all gross and heavy bodies had sunk down in the heat motionless and lay huddled upon the ground, but their voices went wavering from them as if they were flames lolling from the thick waxen bodies of candles. Voices. Yes, voices. Wordless voices, breaking the silence suddenly with such depth of contentment, such passion of desire, or, in the voices of children, such freshness of surprise; breaking the silence? But there was no silence; all the time the motor omnibuses were turning their wheels and changing their gear; like a vast nest of Chinese boxes all of wrought steel turning ceaselessly one within another the city murmured; on the top of which the voices cried aloud and the petals of myriads of flowers flashed their colours into the air.

CRITICAL THINKING QUESTIONS

1. Who are the characters, nonhuman and human, in this story? Does one character seem more significant than others?

2. Examine the story's dialogue, which includes snippets of conversation involving four separate pairs of human visitors. What does each conversation reveal?

3. What do the nonhuman characters—the flowers, the snail, the dragonfly, and butterflies—contribute to the story?

WRITING TOPIC

This story records the minute details of a particular time in a particular place, Kew Gardens—from the progress of a snail with "a definite goal in front of it" to the remarks and actions of a young couple who "together pressed the end of her parasol deep down into the soft earth." With its symphony of sights and sounds, the classic plot question—what happens next?—seems to play second string to setting. However, turning to theme questions—Why? For what purpose?—construct a response. What does this story imply about reality, the meaning of lives in a time and place? What evidence supports your response? To what extent do you accept this conception of reality?

POETRY

∧∧

Lucille Clifton (b. 1936)

For deLawd

people say they have a hard time
understanding how I
go on about my business
playing my Ray Charles
hollering at my kids—   5
seem like my Afro
cut off in some old image
would show I got a long memory
and I come from a line
of black and going on women   10
who got used to making it through murdered sons
and who kept on pushing
who fried chicken
ironed
swept off the back steps   15
who grief kept
for their still alive sons
for their sons coming
for their sons gone
just pushing   20
in the inner city
or
like we call it
home
we think a lot about uptown   25
and the silent nights
and the houses straight as
dead men
and the pastel lights
and we hang on to our no place   30
happy to be alive
and in the inner city
or
like we call it
home

CRITICAL THINKING QUESTIONS

1. Has the speaker persuaded you that the inner city is a home where one can feel "happy to be alive"? Why or why not?

2. What is Clifton's implied claim about life in the suburbs? How does the cartoon on p. 21 support Clifton's claim?

RESEARCH/WRITING TOPIC—Sustainable Cities and Egalitarianism

"The rich are getting richer and the poor are getting poorer"—This aphorism refers to a perceived widening gap in economic well-being among members of society. Some claim that this gap is most evident in our cities, for example, images of stranded New Orleans residents, following the flooding of New Orleans after Hurricane Katrina in 2005. Meanwhile, looking back to the second half of the twentieth century, we saw a phenomenon called urban flight, as city dwellers (with the economic means to do so) escaped the danger and dirt of the cities and settled in suburbs. However, this century is marked by clear efforts to revive cities—to make them both safer and "greener." Indeed, many young adult professionals are choosing to locate in large cities, not only for the professional but also the cultural/entertainment options—the fast-paced lifestyle. As cities reinvent themselves, are the long-term (and often poorer) residents being left behind, priced out of their homes and neighborhoods? Can a sustainable city model be created that supports the needs and promotes the well-being of all its residents? (See also Linda Hogan's poem, "Heartland," and Carl Sandburg's, "Chicago.")

James Dickey (1923–1997)

Deer among Cattle

Here and there in the searing beam
Of my hand going through the night meadow
They all are grazing

5   With pins of human light in their eyes.
A wild one also is eating
The human grass,

Slender, graceful, domesticated
By darkness, among the bredfor-slaughter,

Having bounded their paralyzed fence
And inclined his branched forehead onto   10
Their green frosted table,
The only live thing in this flashlight

Who can leave whenever he wishes,
Turn grass into forest,   15

Foreclose inhuman brightness from his eyes
But stands here still, unperturbed,
In their wide-open country,

The sparks from my hand in his pupils
Unmatched anywhere among cattle,

Grazing with them the night of the hammer   20
As one of their own who shall rise.

CRITICAL THINKING QUESTIONS

1. What *value assumptions* about animals does Dickey's poem address?

2. Make an *inference* about the claim of value implicit in the poem's last four lines. What evidence in the poem supports your conclusion?

Carolyn Forché (b. 1950)

Dulcimer Maker

Calf-deep in spruce dust
wood curls off his knife
blade wet bare bulb light.

The finish of his hands
shows oil, grain, knots   5
where his growth scarred him.

Planing black oak
thin to flow sounds.
Tones of wind filling
bottle lips.   10

It is his work tying strings
across fresh-cut pine.

He sings into wood, listens:
tree rings, water!

15   The wood drinks his cloth,
its roots going to the depths of him,
spreading.

He wants to build a lute for music
carved on Sumerian stones, a music
20   no one has heard for three thousand years.

For this he will work
the oldest wood he can find.
It will not be as far away,
as unfamiliar.

CRITICAL THINKING QUESTIONS

1. What values does the dulcimer maker's work represent?

2. What do you think the last two lines may mean?

WRITING TOPIC

Do you know any artisans such as this dulcimer maker? How does our society value artisans and their work?

Robert Frost (1874–1963)

A Young Birch

The birch begins to crack its outer sheath
Of baby green and show the white beneath,
As whosoever likes the young and slight
May well have noticed. Soon entirely white
5   To double day and cut in half the dark
It will stand forth, entirely white in bark,
And nothing but the top a leafy green—
The only native tree that dares to lean,

Relying on its beauty, to the air.
(Less brave perhaps than trusting are the fair.)   10
And someone reminiscent will recall
How once in cutting brush along the wall
He spared it from the number of the slain,
At first to be no bigger than a cane,
And then no bigger than a fishing pole,   15
But now at last so obvious a bole
The most efficient help you ever hired
Would know that it was there to be admired,

And zeal would not be thanked that cut it down
When you were reading books or out of town.   20
It was a thing of beauty and was sent
To live its life out as an ornament.

CRITICAL THINKING QUESTIONS

1. Read and compare Forché's "Dulcimer Maker" and Frost's "A Young Birch."

    a. Presumably, the "oldest wood" that the dulcimer maker desires for building his instrument would require cutting down a tree, possibly from a virgin forest. What *warrant/value assumption* justifies this action?
    b. What is Frost's *claim* about the value of trees?
    c. Are the values you articulated above consistent and complementary or incompatible and contradictory? Why?

Linda Hogan (b. 1947)

Heartland

There are few moments of silence
but it comes
through little pores in the skin.
Between traffic and voices
it comes   5
and I begin to understand those city poems,
small prayers
where we place our palms together

and feel the heart
10   beating in a handful of nothing.

City poems
about yellow hard hats
and brotherly beggars
Wasn't Lazarus one of these?
15   And now Saint Pigeon of the Railroad Tracks
paces across a child's small handprint,
human acids etching themselves into metal.

We are all the least of these,
beggars, almsmen,
20   listening hard to the underground language
of the wrist.
Through the old leather of our feet
city earth with fossils and roots
breathes the heart of soil upward,
25   the voice of our gods beneath concrete.

CRITICAL THINKING QUESTIONS

1. What do you think the poet means by "city poems"?

2. In stanza 3, what is the "underground language" we all are "listening hard to"?

WRITING TOPIC

Read the prose piece, "Time and the Machine," by Aldous Huxley, written in the first half of the twentieth century (page 370). Huxley claims that urbanism and industrialism have changed our consciousness of time; we are "inhabitant[s] of an artificial universe that is, to a great extent, walled off from the world of nature." Hogan's poem, written in the latter part of the twentieth century, presents an implicit argument for us to penetrate this wall of separation. In a sense, the poet offers a solution to the problem Huxley presents. Are you convinced by Hogan's argument? Why or why not?

Galway Kinnell (b. 1927)

Saint Francis and the Sow

The bud
stands for all things,
even for those things that don't flower,
for everything flowers, from within, of self-blessing;
though sometimes it is necessary   5
to reteach a thing its loveliness,
to put a hand on its brow
of the flower
and retell it in words and in touch
it is lovely   10
until it flowers again from within, of self-blessing;
as Saint Francis
put his hand on the creased forehead
of the sow, and told her in words and in touch
blessings of earth on the sow, and the sow   15
began remembering all down her thick length,
from the earthen snout all the way
through the fodder and slops to the spiritual curl of the tail,
from the hard spininess spiked out from the spine
down through the great broken heart   20
to the sheer blue milken dreaminess spurting and shuddering
from the fourteen teats into the fourteen mouths sucking and
blowing beneath them:
the long, perfect loveliness of sow.

CRITICAL THINKING QUESTIONS

1. In one or two sentences, summarize Kinnell's claim.

2. On which rhetorical appeal does the poet rely? Point out and evaluate specific examples of this appeal.

3. Examine the *diction* in the second half of the poem. How does language contribute to the persuasive effect of the poet's argument?

Denise Levertov (1923–1997)

The Victors

In June the bush we call
alder was heavy, listless,
its leaves studded with galls,

growing wherever we didn't
5   want it. We cut it
savagely, hunted it from the pasture, chopped it

away from the edge of the wood.
In July, still everywhere, it appeared
wearing green berries.
Anyway it must go. It takes
the light and air and the good of the earth
from flowers and young trees.

But now in August
its berries are red. Do the birds
eat them? Swinging

clusters of red, the hedges are full of them,
red-currant red, a graceful
ornament or a merry smile.

CRITICAL THINKING QUESTIONS

1. In the last line, the poet says the berries can be "a merry smile"? How do you interpret the metaphor?

2. Who or what are the victors?

3. Describe the poet's tone. How does tone influence your assessment of her *ethos?*

——————————————

Rainer Maria Rilke (1875–1926)

The Panther

TRANSLATED BY STEPHEN MITCHELL

His vision, from the constantly passing bars,
has grown so weary that it cannot hold
anything else. It seems to him there are
a thousand bars; and behind the bars, no world.

As he paces in cramped circles, over and over,   5
the movement of his powerful soft strides
is like a ritual dance around a center
in which a mighty will stands paralyzed.

Only at times, the curtain of the pupils
lifts, quietly—. An image enters in,   10
rushes down through the tensed, arrested muscles,
plunges into the heart and is gone.

CRITICAL THINKING QUESTIONS

1. On which of the rhetorical appeals does the poet rely?

2. What value assumptions about animals are suggested? How would these values
   factor into the debate over the use of animals for medical research?

3. Articulate a claim for the poem. Extend or qualify the claim to apply to today's
   zoos.

Theodore Roethke (1908–1963)

Meditation at Oyster River

1

Over the low, barnacled, elephant-colored rocks,
Come the first tide-ripples, moving, almost without sound, toward me,
Running along the narrow furrows of the shore, the rows of dead clam shells;
Then a runnel behind me, creeping closer,
5   Alive with tiny striped fish, and young crabs climbing in and out of the water.

No sound from the bay. No violence.
Even the gulls quiet on the far rocks,
Silent, in the deepening light,
Their cat-mewing over,
10   Their child-whimpering.

At last one long undulant ripple,
Blue-black from where I am sitting,
Makes almost a wave over a barrier of small stones,
Slapping lightly against a sunken log.
15   I dabble my toes in the brackish foam sliding forward,
Then retire to a rock higher up on the cliff-side.
The wind slackens, light as a moth fanning a stone:
A twilight wind, light as a child's breath
Turning not a leaf, not a ripple.
20   The dew revives on the beach-grass;
The salt-soaked wood of a fire crackles;
A fish raven turns on its perch (a dead tree in the rivermouth),
Its wings catching a last glint of the reflected sunlight.

2

The self persists like a dying star,
25   In sleep, afraid. Death's face rises afresh,
Among the shy beasts, the deer at the salt-lick,
The doe with its sloped shoulders loping across the highway,
The young snake, poised in green leaves, waiting for its fly,
The hummingbird, whirring from quince-blossom to morning-glory—
30   With these I would be.

And with water: the waves coming forward, without cessation,
The waves, altered by sand-bars, beds of kelp, miscellaneous driftwood,
Topped by cross-winds, tugged at by sinuous undercurrents
The tide rustling in, sliding between the ridges of stone,
The tongues of water, creeping in, quietly.   35

3

In this hour,
In this first heaven of knowing,
The flesh takes on the pure poise of the spirit,
Acquires, for a time, the sandpiper's insouciance,
The hummingbird's surety, the kingfisher's cunning—   40
I shift on my rock, and I think:
Of the first trembling of a Michigan brook in April,
Over a lip of stone, the tiny rivulet;
And that wrist-thick cascade tumbling from a cleft rock,
Its spray holding a double rain-bow in early morning,   45
Small enough to be taken in, embraced, by two arms,—
Or the Tittebawasee, in the time between winter and spring,
When the ice melts along the edges in early afternoon.
And the midchannel begins cracking and heaving from the pressure beneath,
The ice piling high against the iron-bound spiles,   50
Gleaming, freezing hard again, creaking at midnight—
And I long for the blast of dynamite,
The sudden sucking roar as the culvert loosens its debris of branches and sticks,
Welter of tin cans, pails, old bird nests, a child's shoe riding a log,
As the piled ice breaks away from the battered spiles,   55
And the whole river begins to move forward, its bridges shaking.

4

Now, in this waning of light,
I rock with the motion of morning;
In the cradle of all that is,
I'm lulled into half-sleep   60
By the lapping of water,
Cries of the sandpiper.
Water's my will, and my way,
And the spirit runs, intermittently,
In and out of the small waves,   65

Runs with the intrepid shorebirds—
How graceful the small before danger!

In the first of the moon,
All's a scattering,
70   A shining.

WRITING TOPIC

Roethke's poem implies that a natural world setting is vital to *his* meditative experience. In the debate over public funding for preserving nature areas, some persons might generalize from Roethke's experience to make a case for preserving these areas. Others, however, might reject such a generalization, arguing that only small numbers of people seek out nature areas for meditation. Based on your experience and observation, which side of the debate do you support?

Pattiann Rogers (b. 1940)

Rolling Naked in the Morning Dew

Out among the wet grasses and wild barley-covered
Meadows, backside, frontside, through the white clover
And feather peabush, over spongy tussocks
And shaggy-mane mushrooms, the abandoned nests
5   Of larks and bobolinks, face to face
With vole trails, snail niches, jelly
Slug eggs; or in a stone-walled garden, level
With the stemmed bulbs of orange and scarlet tulips,
Cricket carcasses, the bent blossoms of sweet william,
10   Shoulder over shoulder, leg over leg, clear
To the ferny edge of the goldfish pond—some people
Believe in the rejuvenating powers of this act—naked
As a toad in the forest, belly and hips, thighs
And ankles drenched in the dew-filled gulches

15   Of oak leaves, in the soft fall beneath yellow birches,
All of the skin exposed directly to the *killy* cry
Of the kingbird, the buzzing of grasshopper sparrows,
Those calls merging with the dawn-red mists
Of crimson steeplebush, entering the bare body then
20   Not merely through the ears but through the skin
Of every naked person willing every event and potentiality

Of a damp transforming dawn to enter.

Lillie Langtry practiced it, when weather permitted,
Lying down naked every morning in the dew,
With all of her beauty believing the single petal   25
Of her white skin could absorb and assume
That radiating purity of liquid and light.
And I admit to believing myself, without question,
In the magical powers of dew on the cheeks
And breasts of Lillie Langtry believing devotedly   30
In the magical powers of early morning dew on the skin
Of her body lolling in purple beds of bird's-foot violets,
Pink prairie mimosa. And I believe, without doubt,
In the mystery of the healing energy coming
From that wholehearted belief in the beneficent results   35
Of the good delights of the naked body rolling
And rolling through all the silked and sun-filled,
Dusky-winged, sheathed and sparkled, looped
And dizzied effluences of each dawn
Of the rolling earth.   40

Just consider how the mere idea of it alone
Has already caused me to sing and sing
This whole morning long.

CRITICAL THINKING QUESTIONS

1. a. What is Rogers attempting to persuade her readers to do?
   b. How do the last lines *qualify* her claim? Does this qualifier strengthen or weaken the persuasive effect of her claim?

2. a. List the evidence Rogers provides for her claim. On which *rhetorical appeal* does she rely, and how effective is this strategy?
   b. What *testimonial evidence* does Rogers provide?

WRITING TOPIC

What value appeals are implicit in Rogers's argument? In a broader context, Rogers seems to advocate that an individual adopt an outlook on his or her daily living experience. How would you articulate this outlook? Do many people you know endorse this outlook and attitude towards their lives? How does it compare and contrast with your personal outlook on your daily experience?

Carl Sandburg (1878–1967)

Chicago

Hog Butcher for the World,
Tool Maker, Stacker of Wheat,
Player with Railroads and the Nation's Freight Handler;
Stormy, husky, brawling,
5   City of the Big Shoulders:

They tell me you are wicked and I believe them, for I have seen your painted
women under the gas lamps luring the farm boys.
And they tell me you are crooked and I answer: Yes, it is true I have seen the
gunman kill and go free to kill again.
And they tell me you are brutal and my reply is: On the faces of women and
children I have seen the marks of wanton hunger.
And having answered so I turn once more to those who sneer at this my city,
and I give them back the sneer and say to them:
10   Come and show me another city with lifted head singing so proud to be alive
and coarse and strong and cunning.
Flinging magnetic curses amid the toil of piling job on job, here is a tall bold
slugger set vivid against the little soft cities;
Fierce as a dog with tongue lapping for action, cunning as a savage pitted
against the wilderness,
Bareheaded,
Shoveling,
15   Wrecking,
Planning,
Building, breaking, rebuilding,
Under the smoke, dust all over his mouth, laughing with white teeth,
Under the terrible burden of destiny laughing as a young man laughs,
20   Laughing even as an ignorant fighter laughs who has never lost a battle,
Bragging and laughing that under his wrist is the pulse, and under his
ribs the heart of the people,
Laughing!
Laughing the stormy, husky, brawling laughter of Youth, half-naked,
sweating, proud to be Hog butcher, Tool Maker, Stacker of Wheat,
Player with Railroads and Freight Handler to the Nation.

CRITICAL THINKING QUESTIONS

1. In personifying Chicago as "Youth," what values or characteristics does the poet attribute to youth? Do you agree or disagree with the poet's generalizations about the nature of youth?

2. Based on the poet's depiction of Chicago in the early twentieth century, articulate a *claim of value* about the city at that time. How would you modify this claim to apply to today's larger metropolitan cities? Or, write a *claim of value* that specifies a city you know firsthand, either as a resident or a visitor.

Anne Sexton (1928–1974)

The Fury of Flowers and Worms

Let the flowers make a journey
on Monday so that I can see
ten daisies in a blue vase
with perhaps one red ant
crawling to the gold center.   5
A bit of the field on my table,
close to the worms
who struggle blindly,
moving deep into their slime,
moving deep into God's abdomen,   10
moving like oil through water,
sliding through the good brown.

The daisies grow wild
like popcorn.
They are God's promise to the field.   15
How happy I am, daisies, to love you.
How happy you are to be loved
and found magical, like a secret
from the sluggish field.
If all the world picked daisies   20

wars would end, the common cold would stop,
unemployment would end, the monetary market
would hold steady and no money would float.

Listen world,
25   if you'd just take the time to pick
the white fingers, the penny heart,
all would be well.
They are so unexpected.
They are as good as salt.
30   If someone had brought them
to van Gogh's room daily
his ear would have stayed on.
I would like to think that no one would die anymore
if we all believed in daisies
35   but the worms know better, don't they?
They slide into the ear of a corpse
and listen to his great sigh.

CRITICAL THINKING QUESTIONS

1. Examining the poem stanza by stanza, describe the poet's varying tone. How do these shifts affect your assessment of the poet's *ethos* appeal?

2. Do the flowers or the worms dominate? What do you think is this poem's implied claim? Do you agree or disagree?

Gary Snyder (b. 1930)

The Call of the Wild

The heavy old man in his bed at night
Hears the Coyote singing
in the back meadow.
All the years he ranched and mined and logged.
A Catholic.
A native Californian.   5
and the Coyotes howl in his
Eightieth year.

He will call the Government
Trapper   10
Who uses iron leg-traps on Coyotes,
Tomorrow.
My sons will lose this
Music they have just started
To love.   15

The ex acid-heads from the cities
Converted to Guru or Swami,
Do penance with shiny
Dopey eyes, and quit eating meat.
In the forests of North America,   20
The land of Coyote and Eagle,
They dream of India, of
forever blissful sexless highs.
And sleep in oil-heated
Geodesic domes, that   25
Were stuck like warts
In the woods.

And the Coyote singing
is shut away
for they fear   30
the call
of the wild.
And they sold their virgin cedar trees,
the tallest trees in miles,
To a logger   35
Who told them,

"Trees are full of bugs."
The Government finally decided
To wage the war all-out. Defeat is Un-American.
And they took to the air,   40
Their women beside them
in bouffant hairdos
putting nail-polish on the
gunship cannon-buttons.
And they never came down,   45
for they found,
the ground
is pro-Communist. And dirty.
And the insects side with the Viet Cong.

50   So they bomb and they bomb
      Day after day, across the planet
      blinding sparrows
      breaking the ear-drums of owls
      splintering trunks of cherries
55   twining and looping
      deer intestines
      in the shaken, dusty, rocks.
      All these Americans up in special cities in the sky
      Dumping poisons and explosives
60   Across Asia first,
      And next North America,
      A war against earth.
      When it's done there'll be
      no place
65   A Coyote could hide.

      envoy

      I would like to say
      Coyote is forever
      Inside you.

70   But it's not true.

CRITICAL THINKING QUESTIONS

1. According to Snyder, who is responsible for "a war against earth"?

2. Give examples of the poet's use of *pathos* appeal. Are some examples more effective than others in persuading you to accept the poet's viewpoint?

WRITING TOPIC

Reading the poem's last nine lines from today's perspective, what is your viewpoint of Snyder's foreboding statement? Defend or refute his assertion that the Coyote is *not* "forever/Inside you."

William Stafford (1914–1992)

Traveling through the Dark

Traveling through the dark I found a deer
dead on the edge of the Wilson River road.
It is usually best to roll them into the canyon:
that road is narrow; to swerve might make more dead.

By glow of the tail-light I stumbled back of the car   5
and stood by the heap, a doe, a recent killing;
she had stiffened already, almost cold.
I dragged her off; she was large in the belly.

My fingers touching her side brought me the reason—
her side was warm; her fawn lay there waiting,   10
alive, still, never to be born.
Beside that mountain road I hesitated.

The car aimed ahead its lowered parking lights;
under the hood purred the steady engine.
I stood in the glare of the warm exhaust turning red;   15
around our group I could hear the wilderness listen.

I thought hard for us all—my only swerving—,
then pushed her over the edge into the river.

CRITICAL THINKING QUESTIONS

1. Use the rhetorical triangle to examine this poem.

   a. How does the poet create *ethos* appeal?
   b. How does the poet use *logos* appeal?
   c. How does the poet use *pathos* appeal?

2. Evaluate the persuasive effect of each rhetorical appeal. In your view, is one more effective (or less effective) than the other two appeals? Why?

WRITING TOPIC

We generally agree that freedom is inextricably linked to an individual's right to choose. And we generally agree that the freedom to make choices carries with it the mantle of responsibility for the consequences of one's choices. Also, other persons judge us—assess our character or *ethos*—by the choices we make. Examine this poem in the context of these ethical principles. What choice confronts the speaker? Does he accept or shirk the mantle of responsibility? Finally, how do you judge him?

Robert Penn Warren (1905–1989)

from *Audubon*

I. Was Not the Lost Dauphin

[A]

Was not the lost dauphin, though handsome was only
Base-born and not even able
To make a decent living, was only
Himself, Jean Jacques, and his passion—what
Is man but his passion?

                        Saw,
5   Eastward and over the cypress swamp, the dawn,
Redder than meat, break;
And the large bird,
Long neck outthrust, wings crooked to scull air, moved
In a slow calligraphy, crank, flat, and black against
10   The color of God's blood spilt, as though
Pulled by a string.

                        Saw
It proceed across the inflamed distance.
Moccasins set in hoar frost, eyes fixed on the bird,
15   Thought: "On that sky it is black."
Thought: "In my mind it is white."
Thinking: "*Ardea occidentalis,* heron, the great one."

[B]

October: and the bear,   20
Daft in the honey-light, yawns.

The bear's tongue, pink as a baby's, out-crisps to the curled tip,
It bleeds the black blood of the blueberry.

The teeth are more importantly white
Than has ever been imagined.   25
The bear feels his own fat
Sweeten, like a drowse, deep to the bone.

Bemused, above the fume of ruined blueberries,
The last bee hums.

The wings, like mica, glint   30
In the sunlight.

He leans on his gun. Thinks
How thin is the membrane between himself and the world.

VI. Love and Knowledge

Their footless dance
Is of the beautiful liability of their nature.
Their eyes are round, boldly convex, bright as a jewel,
And merciless. They do not know
Compassion, and if they did,   5
We should not be worthy of it. They fly
In air that glitters like fluent crystal
And is hard as perfectly transparent iron, they cleave it
With no effort. They cry
In a tongue multitudinous, often like music.   10

He slew them, at surprising distances, with his gun.
Over a body held in his hand, his head was bowed low,
But not in grief.

He put them where they are, and there we see them:
In our imagination.   15

What is love?

Our name for it is knowledge.

Dawn: his heart shook in the tension of the world.

Dawn: and what is your passion?

VII. Tell Me a Story

[A]

Long ago, in Kentucky, I, a boy, stood
By a dirt road, in first dark, and heard
The great geese hoot northward.

5   I could not see them, there being no moon
And the stars sparse. I heard them.

I did not know what was happening in my heart.

It was the season before the elderberry blooms,
Therefore they were going north.

The sound was passing northward.

[B]

10   Tell me a story.

In this century, and moment, of mania,
Tell me a story.

Make it a story of great distances, and starlight.

The name of the story will be Time,
15   But you must not pronounce its name.

Tell me a story of deep delight.

CRITICAL THINKING QUESTIONS

1. John James Audubon (1785–1851), an ornithologist, is famous for his paintings of North American birds. In these excerpts, the poet shows Audubon shooting those birds he would later represent in masterful paintings. In "VI. Love and

Knowledge," how does the poet explain Audubon's actions? How do you judge Audubon?

2. Hunters and wildlife preservationists often have much more in common than their emotions allow them to acknowledge. What value assumptions (*warrants*) might the two factions share?

Walt Whitman (1819–1892)

from *Song of Myself*

14

The wild gander leads his flock through the cool night,
Ya-honk he says, and sounds it down to me like an invitation,
The pert may suppose it meaningless, but I listening close,
Find its purpose and place up there toward the wintry sky.

The sharp-hoof'd moose of the north, the cat on the house-sill,
the chickadee, the prairie-dog,   5
The litter of the grunting sow as they tug at her teats,
The brood of the turkey-hen and she with her half-spread wings,
I see in them and myself the same old law.

The press of my foot to the earth springs a hundred affections,
They scorn the best I can do to relate them.   10

I am enamour'd of growing out-doors.

Of men that live among cattle or taste of the ocean or woods,
Of the builders and steerers of ships and the wielders of axes and
mauls, and the drivers of horses,
I can eat and sleep with them week in and week out.

What is commonest, cheapest, nearest, easiest, is Me,   15
Me going in for my chances, spending for vast returns,
Adorning myself to bestow myself on the first that will take me,
Not asking the sky to come down to my good will,
Scattering it freely forever.

CRITICAL THINKING QUESTIONS

1. Describe the *ethos* Whitman creates. Point out evidence from the poem that suggests those character qualities.

2. What values does Whitman assign to "growing out-doors"? From your perspective as a twenty-first-century reader, are the values Whitman, a late nineteenth-century poet, celebrates still valid?

Walt Whitman

from *Song of Myself*

31

I believe a leaf of grass is no less than the journey-work of the stars,
And the pismire is equally perfect, and a grain of sand, and the egg of the wren,
And the tree-toad is a chief-d'œuvre for the highest,
And the running blackberry would adorn the parlors of heaven,
5   And the narrowest hinge in my hand puts to scorn all machinery,
And the cow crunching with depress'd head surpasses any statue,
And a mouse is miracle enough to stagger sextillions of infidels.

I find I incorporate gneiss, coal, long-threaded moss, fruits, grains, esculent roots,
And am stucco'd with quadrupeds and birds all over,
10 And have distanced what is behind me for good reasons,
But call any thing back again when I desire it.

In vain the speeding or shyness,
In vain the plutonic rocks send their old heat against my approach,
In vain the mastodon retreats beneath its powder'd bones,
15 In vain objects stand leagues off and assume manifold shapes,
In vain the ocean settling in hollows and the great monsters lying low,
In vain the buzzard houses herself with the sky,
In vain the snake slides through the creepers and logs,
In vain the elk takes to the inner passes of the woods,
20 In vain the razor-bill'd auk sails far north to Labrador,
I follow quickly, I ascend to the nest in the fissure of the cliff.

CRITICAL THINKING QUESTIONS

1. Articulate a *claim of value* for stanza one.

2. How does stanza one support and/or qualify Whitman's implied argument for an enlarged sense of self?

3. What is your attitude toward the *ethos* the poet creates?

William Wordsworth (1770–1850)

To My Sister

It is the first mild day of March:
Each minute sweeter than before,
The redbreast sings from the tall larch
that stands beside our door.

There is a blessing in the air,   5
Which seems a sense of joy to yield
To the bare trees, and mountains bare,
And grass in the green field.

My sister! ('tis a wish of mine)
Now that our morning meal is done,   10
Make haste, your morning task resign;
Come forth and feel the sun.

Edward will come with you;—and, pray,
Put on with speed your woodland dress;
And bring no book: for this one day   15
We'll give to idleness.

No joyless forms shall regulate
Our living calendar:
We from to-day, my Friend, will date
The opening of the year.   20

Love, now a universal birth,
From heart to heart is stealing,
From earth to man, from man to earth:
—It is the hour of feeling.

25   One moment now may give us more
        Than years of toiling reason:
        Our minds shall drink at every pore
        The spirit of the season.

        Some silent laws our hearts will make,
30   Which they shall long obey:
        We for the year to come may take
        Our temper from to-day.

        And from the blessed power that rolls
        About, below, above,
35   We'll frame the measure of our souls:
        They shall be tuned to love.

        Then come, my Sister! come, I pray,
        With speed put on your woodland dress;
        And bring no book: for this one day
40   We'll give to idleness.

CRITICAL THINKING QUESTIONS

1. The poet is making a direct argument to his sister. What is his claim?

2. Examine the supporting evidence—his reasoning. How persuasive is it?

3. Has the poet convinced you to "give to idleness"? Why or why not?

James Wright (1927–1980)

A Blessing

    Just off the highway to Rochester, Minnesota,
    Twilight bounds softly forth on the grass.
    And the eyes of those two Indian ponies
    Darken with kindness.
5   They have come gladly out of the willows
    To welcome my friend and me.
    We step over the barbed wire into the pasture
    Where they have been grazing all day, alone.
    They ripple tensely, they can hardly contain their happiness

That we have come.   10
They bow shyly as wet swans. They love each other.
There is no loneliness like theirs.
At home once more,
They begin munching the young tufts of spring in the darkness.
I would like to hold the slenderer one in my arms,   15
For she has walked over to me
And nuzzled my left hand.
She is black and white,
Her mane falls wild on her forehead,
And the light breeze moves me to caress her long ear   20
That is delicate as the skin over a girl's wrist.
Suddenly I realize
That if I stepped out of my body I would break
Into blossom.

WRITING TOPIC

Read and compare Wright's poem with Rogers's "Rolling Naked in the Morning Dew" (page 333). Drawing on these poems and your own imagination and experience, write an argument targeting older adults that gives vitality to the cliché, "take time to stop and smell the roses."

NONFICTION

∿∿

Edward Abbey (1927–1989)
Eco-Defense

If a stranger batters your door down with an axe, threatens your family and yourself with deadly weapons, and proceeds to loot your home of whatever he wants, he is committing what is universally recognized—by law and in common morality—as a crime. In such a situation the householder has both the right and the obligation to defend himself, his family, and his property by whatever means are necessary. This right and this obligation is universally recognized, justified, and praised by all civilized human communities. Self-defense against attack is one of the basic laws not only of human society but of life itself, not only of human life but of all life.

The American wilderness, what little remains, is now undergoing exactly such an assault. With bulldozer, earth mover, chainsaw, and dynamite the international timber, mining, and beef industries are invading our public lands—property of all Americans—bashing their way into our forests, mountains, and rangelands and looting them for everything they can get away with. This for the sake of short-term profits in the corporate sector and multimillion-dollar annual salaries for the three-piece-suited gangsters (MBA—Harvard, Yale, University of Tokyo, et alia) who control and manage these bandit enterprises. Cheered on, naturally, by *Time, Newsweek,* and *The Wall Street Journal,* actively encouraged, inevitably, by those jellyfish government agencies that are supposed to *protect* the public lands, and as always aided and abetted in every way possible by the compliant politicians of our Western states, such as Babbitt, DeConcini, Goldwater, McCain, Hatch, Garn, Simms, Hansen, Andrus, Wallop, Domenici and Co. Inc.—who would sell the graves of their mothers if there's a quick buck in the deal, over or under the table, what do they care.

Representative government in the United States has broken down. Our legislators do not represent the public, the voters, or even those who voted for them but rather the commercial industrial interests that finance their political campaigns and control the organs of communication—the TV, the newspapers, the billboards, the radio. Politics is a game for the rich only. Representative government in the USA represents money, not people, and therefore has forfeited our allegiance and moral support. We owe it nothing but the taxation it extorts from us under threats of seizure of property, imprisonment, or in some cases already, when resisted, a violent death by gunfire.

Such is the nature and structure of the industrial megamachine (in Lewis Mumford's term) which is now attacking the American wilderness. That wilderness is our ancestral home, the primordial homeland of all living creatures including the human, and the present final dwelling place of such noble beings as the grizzly bear, the mountain lion, the eagle and the condor, the moose and the elk and the pronghorn antelope, the redwood tree, the yellow pine, the bristlecone pine, and yes, why not say it?—the streams, waterfalls, rivers, the very bedrock itself of our hills, canyons, deserts, mountains. For many of us, perhaps for most of us, the wilderness is more our home than the little stucco boxes, wallboard apartments, plywood trailer-houses, and cinderblock condominiums in which the majority are now confined by the poverty of an overcrowded industrial culture.

And if the wilderness is our true home, and if it is threatened with invasion, pillage, and destruction—as it certainly is—then we have the right to defend that home, as we would our private quarters, by whatever means are necessary. (An Englishman's home is his castle; the American's home is his favorite forest, river, fishing stream, her favorite mountain or desert canyon, his favorite swamp or woods or lake.) We have the right to resist and we have the obligation; not to defend that which we love would be dishonorable. The majority of the American people have demonstrated on every possible occasion that they support the ideal of wilderness preservation; even our politicians are forced by popular opinion to *pretend* to support the idea; as they have learned, a vote against wilderness is a vote against their own reelection. We are justified then in defending our homes—our private home and our public home—not only by common law and common morality but also by common belief. We are the majority; they—the powerful—are in the minority.

How best defend our homes? Well, that is a matter of the strategy, tactics, and technique which eco-defense is all about.

What is eco-defense? Eco-defense means fighting back. Eco-defense means sabotage. Eco-defense is risky but sporting; unauthorized but fun; illegal but ethically imperative. Next time you enter a public forest scheduled for chainsaw massacre by some timber corporation and its flunkies in the US Forest Service, carry a hammer and a few pounds of 60-penny nails in your creel, saddlebag, game bag, backpack, or picnic basket. Spike those trees; you won't hurt them; they'll be grateful for the protection; and you may save the forest. Loggers hate nails. My Aunt Emma back in West Virginia has been enjoying this pleasant exercise for years. She swears by it. It's good for the trees, it's good for the woods, and it's good for the human soul. Spread the word.

CRITICAL THINKING QUESTION

Edward Abbey sets up an enemy who threatens the environment: "three-piece-suited gangsters," he calls them. Compare his use of this enemy with the enemy Jane Martin creates in her dramatic monologue, *Rodeo,* on page 56.

WRITING TOPIC

Abbey openly calls for spiking trees, a practice that can lead to injury among loggers and is illegal. He asks you, the reader, to willfully violate the law in an act of civil disobedience. Similarly, a number of environmental organizations today practice and sometimes advocate civil disobedience. For example, Greenpeace boats illegally disrupt whaling and fishing activities, PETA members block hunters, Sea Shepherd followers sometimes intervene in the legal capture of dolphins, and the Animal Liberation Front has burned veterinary labs. Is there an environmental cause for which you would consider breaking the law? Argue with evidence that this particular cause would justify civil disobedience.

Rachel Carson (1907–1964)

The Obligation to Endure

from *Silent Spring*

The history of life on earth has been a history of interaction between living things and their surroundings. To a large extent, the physical form and the habits of the earth's vegetation and its animal life have been molded by the environment. Considering the whole span of earthly time, the opposite effect, in which life actually modifies its surroundings, has been relatively slight. Only within the moment of time represented by the present century has one species—man—acquired significant power to alter the nature of his world.

During the past quarter century this power has not only increased to one of disturbing magnitude but it has changed in character. The most alarming of all man's assaults upon the environment is the contamination of air, earth, rivers, and sea with dangerous and even lethal materials. This pollution is for the most part irrecoverable; the chain of evil it initiates not only in the world that must support life but in living tissues is for the most part irreversible. In this now universal contamination of the environment, chemicals are the sinister and little-recognized partners of radiation in changing the very nature of the world—the very nature of its life. Strontium 90, released through nuclear explosions into the air, comes to earth in rain or drifts down as fallout, lodges in soil, enters into the grass or corn or wheat grown there, and in time takes up its abode in the bones of a human being, there to remain until his death. Similarly, chemicals sprayed on croplands or forests or gardens lie long in soil, entering into living organisms, passing from one to another in a chain of poisoning and death. Or they pass mysteriously by underground streams until they emerge and, through the alchemy of air and sunlight, combine into new forms that kill vegetation, sicken cattle, and work unknown harm on those who drink from once pure wells. As Albert Schweitzer has said, "Man can hardly even recognize the devils of his own creation."

It took hundreds of millions of years to produce the life that now inhabits the earth—eons of time in which that developing and evolving and diversifying life reached a state of adjustment and balance with its surroundings. The environment, rigorously shaping and directing the life it supported, contained elements that were hostile as well as supporting. Certain rocks gave out dangerous radiation; even within the light of the sun, from which all life draws its energy, there were shortwave radiations with power to injure. Given time—time not in years but in millennia—life adjusts, and a balance has been reached. For time is the essential ingredient; but in the modern world there is no time.

The rapidity of change and the speed with which new situations are created follow the impetuous and heedless pace of man rather than the deliberate pace of nature. Radiation is no longer merely the background radiation of rocks, the bombardment of cosmic rays, the ultraviolet of the sun that have existed before there was any life on earth; radiation is now the unnatural creation of man's tampering with the atom. The chemicals to which life is asked to make its adjustment are no longer merely the calcium and silica and copper and all the rest of the minerals washed out of the rocks and carried in rivers to the sea; they are the synthetic creations of man's inventive mind, brewed in his laboratories, and having no counterparts in nature.

To adjust to these chemicals would require time on the scale that is nature's; it would require not merely the years of a man's life but the life of generations. And even this, were it by some miracle possible, would be futile, for the new chemicals come from our laboratories in an endless stream; almost 500 annually find their way into actual use in the United States alone. The figure is staggering and its implications are not easily grasped—500 new chemicals to which the bodies of men and animals are required somehow to adapt each year, chemicals totally outside the limits of biologic experience. 5

Among them are many that are used in man's war against nature. Since the mid-1940s over 200 basic chemicals have been created for use in killing insects, weeds, rodents, and other organisms described in the modern vernacular as "pests"; and they are sold under several thousand different brand names.

These sprays, dusts, and aerosols are now applied almost universally to farms, gardens, forests, and homes—nonselective chemicals that have the power to kill every insect, the "good" and the "bad," to still the song of birds and the leaping of fish in the streams, to coat the leaves with a deadly film, and to linger on in soil—all this though the intended target may be only a few weeds or insects. Can anyone believe it is possible to lay down such a barrage of poisons on the surface of the earth without making it unfit for all life? They should not be called "insecticides," but "biocides."

The whole process of spraying seems caught up in an endless spiral. Since DDT was released for civilian use, a process of escalation has been going on in which ever more toxic materials must be found. This has happened because insects, in a triumphant vindication of Darwin's principle of the survival of the fittest, have evolved super races immune to the particular insecticide used, hence a deadlier one has always to be developed—and then a deadlier one than that. It has happened also because, for reasons to be described later, destructive insects often undergo a "flareback," or resurgence, after spraying, in numbers greater than before. Thus the chemical war is never won, and all life is caught in its violent crossfire.

Along with the possibility of the extinction of mankind by nuclear war, the central problem of our age has therefore become the contamination of man's total environment with such substances of incredible potential for harm—substances that accumulate in the tissues of plants and animals and even penetrate the germ cells to shatter or alter the very material of heredity upon which the shape of the future depends.

10   Some would-be architects of our future look toward a time when it will be possible to alter the human germ plasm by design. But we may easily be doing so now by inadvertence, for many chemicals, like radiation, bring about gene mutations. It is ironic to think that man might determine his own future by something so seemingly trivial as the choice of an insect spray.

All this has been risked—for what? Future historians may well be amazed by our distorted sense of proportion. How could intelligent beings seek to control a few unwanted species by a method that contaminated the entire environment and brought the threat of disease and death even to their own kind? Yet this is precisely what we have done. We have done it, moreover, for reasons that collapse the moment we examine them. We are told that the enormous and expanding use of pesticides is necessary to maintain farm production. Yet is our real problem not one of *overproduction?* Our farms, despite measures to remove acreages from production and to pay farmers *not* to produce, have yielded such a staggering excess of crops that the American taxpayer in 1962 is paying out more than one billion dollars a year as the total carrying cost of the surplus-food storage program. And is the situation helped when one branch of the Agriculture Department tries to reduce production while another states, as it did in 1958, "It is believed generally that reduction of crop acreages under provisions of the Soil Bank will stimulate interest in use of chemicals to obtain maximum production on the land retained in crops."

All this is not to say there is no insect problem and no need of control. I am saying, rather, that control must be geared to realities, not to mythical situations, and that the methods employed must be such that they do not destroy us along with the insects.

The problem whose attempted solution has brought such a train of disaster in its wake is an accompaniment of our modern way of life. Long before the age of man, insects inhabited the earth—a group of extraordinarily varied and adaptable beings. Over the course of time since man's advent, a small percentage of the more than half a million species of insects have come into conflict with human welfare in two principal ways: as competitors for the food supply and as carriers of human disease.

Disease-carrying insects become important where human beings are crowded together, especially under conditions where sanitation is poor, as in time of natural disaster or war or in situations of extreme poverty and deprivation. Then control of some sort becomes necessary. It is a sobering fact, however . . . that the method of massive chemical control has had only limited success, and also threatens to worsen the very conditions it is intended to curb.

Under primitive agricultural conditions the farmer had few insect problems.   15 These arose with the intensification of agriculture—the devotion of immense acreages to a single crop. Such a system set the stage for explosive increases in specific insect populations. Single-crop farming does not take advantage of the principles by which nature works; it is agriculture as an engineer might conceive it to be. Nature has introduced great variety into the landscape, but man has displayed a passion for simplifying it. Thus he undoes the built-in checks and balances by which nature holds the species within bounds. One important natural check is a limit on the amount of suitable habitat for each species. Obviously then, an insect that lives on wheat can build up its population to much higher levels on a farm devoted to wheat than on one in which wheat is intermingled with other crops to which the insect is not adapted.

The same thing happens in other situations. A generation or more ago, the towns of large areas of the United States lined their streets with the noble elm tree. Now the beauty they hopefully created is threatened with complete destruction as disease sweeps through the elms, carried by a beetle that would have only limited chance to build up large populations and to spread from tree to tree if the elms were only occasional trees in a richly diversified planting.

Another factor in the modern insect problem is one that must be viewed against a background of geologic and human history: the spreading of thousands of different kinds of organisms from their native homes to invade new territories. This worldwide migration has been studied and graphically described by the British ecologist Charles Elton in his recent book *The Ecology of Invasions.* During the Cretaceous Period, some hundred million years ago, flooding seas cut many land bridges between continents and living things found themselves confined in what Elton calls "colossal separate nature reserves." There, isolated from others of their kind, they developed many new species. When some of the land masses were joined again, about fifteen million years ago, these species began to move out into new territories—a movement that is not only still in progress but is now receiving considerable assistance from man.

The importation of plants is the primary agent in the modern spread of species, for animals have almost invariably gone along with the plants, quarantine being a comparatively recent and not completely effective innovation. The United States Office of Plant Introduction alone has introduced almost 200,000 species and varieties of plants from all over the world. Nearly half of the 180 or so major insect enemies of plants in the United States are accidental imports from abroad, and most of them have come as hitchhikers on plants.

In new territory, out of reach of the restraining hand of the natural enemies that kept down its numbers in its native land, an invading plant or animal is able to become enormously abundant. Thus it is no accident that our most troublesome insects are introduced species.

20   These invasions, both the naturally occurring and those dependent on human assistance, are likely to continue indefinitely. Quarantine and massive chemical campaigns are only extremely expensive ways of buying time. We are faced, according to Dr. Elton, "with a life-and-death need not just to find new technological means of suppressing this plant or that animal"; instead we need the basic knowledge of animal populations and their relations to their surroundings that will "promote an even balance and damp down the explosive power of outbreaks and new invasions."

Much of the necessary knowledge is now available but we do not use it. We train ecologists in our universities and even employ them in our governmental agencies but we seldom take their advice. We allow the chemical death rain to fall as though there were no alternative, whereas in fact there are many, and our ingenuity could soon discover many more if given opportunity.

Have we fallen into a mesmerized state that makes us accept as inevitable that which is inferior or detrimental, as though having lost the will or the vision to demand that which is good? Such thinking, in the words of the ecologist Paul Shepard, "idealizes life with only its head out of water, inches above the limits of toleration of the corruption of its own environment. . . . Why should we tolerate a diet of weak poisons, a home in insipid surroundings, a circle of acquaintances who are not quite our enemies, the noise of motors with just enough relief to prevent insanity? Who would want to live in a world which is just not quite fatal?"

Yet such a world is pressed upon us. The crusade to create a chemically sterile, insect-free world seems to have engendered a fanatic zeal on the part of many specialists and most of the so-called control agencies. On every hand there is evidence that those engaged in spraying operations exercise a ruthless power. "The regulatory entomologists . . . function as prosecutor, judge and jury, tax assessor and collector and sheriff to enforce their own orders," said Connecticut entomologist Neely Turner. The most flagrant abuses go unchecked in both state and federal agencies.

It is not my contention that chemical insecticides must never be used. I do contend that we have put poisonous and biologically potent chemicals indiscriminately into the hands of persons largely or wholly ignorant of their potentials for harm. We have subjected enormous numbers of people to contact with these poisons, without their consent and often without their knowledge. If the Bill of Rights contains no guarantee that a citizen shall be secure against lethal poisons distributed either by private individuals or by public officials, it is surely only because our forefathers, despite their considerable wisdom and foresight, could conceive of no such problem.

25   I contend, furthermore, that we have allowed these chemicals to be used with little or no advance investigation of their effect on soil, water, wildlife, and man himself. Future generations are unlikely to condone our lack of prudent concern for the integrity of the natural world that supports all life.

There is still very limited awareness of the nature of the threat. This is an era of specialists, each of whom sees his own problem and is unaware of or intolerant of the larger frame into which it fits. It is also an era dominated by industry, in which the right to make a dollar at whatever cost is seldom challenged. When the public protests, confronted with some obvious evidence of damaging results of pesticide applications, it is fed little tranquilizing pills of half truth. We urgently need an end to these false assurances, to the sugar coating of unpalatable facts. It is the public that is being asked to assume the risks that the insect controllers calculate. The public must decide whether it wishes to continue on the present road, and it can do so only when in full possession of the facts. In the words of Jean Rostand, "The obligation to endure gives us the right to know."

CRITICAL THINKING QUESTIONS

1. What is Carson's claim?

2. What types of evidence does the author provide to support her claim? Does she rely more heavily on *logos* or *pathos* appeal?

3. This essay is from her 1962 book, *Silent Spring.* How does the author build *ethos* appeal with her audience?

RESEARCH/WRITING TOPIC—Citizen Power and Environmental Policy

Reread this essay's closing paragraph. From your perspective as a reader today, consider the implications of Carson's warnings and call to action, "The public must decide. . . ." Choose a specific issue area to research—for example, genetically modified foods, mercury levels in fish, alternative fuels such as ethanol. Are we demanding and are we receiving the facts we need to make choices about the short- and long-term health and environmental impacts of (*specific issue*), or are we being "fed little tranquilizing pills of half truth"?

Annie Dillard (b. 1945)

from "The Present"
in *Pilgrim at Tinker Creek*

III

Live water heals memories. I look up the creek and here it comes, the future, being borne aloft as on a winding succession of laden trays. You may wake and look from the window and breathe the real air, and say, with satisfaction or with longing, "This is it." But if you look up the creek, if you look up the creek in any weather, your spirit fills, and you are saying, with an exulting rise of the lungs, "Here it comes!"

Here it comes. In the far distance I can see the concrete bridge where the road crosses the creek. Under that bridge and beyond it the water is flat and silent, blued by distance and stilled by depth. It is so much sky, a fallen shred caught in the cleft of banks. But it pours. The channel here is straight as an arrow; grace itself is an archer. Between the dangling wands of bankside willows, beneath the overarching limbs of tulip, walnut, and Osage orange, I see the creek pour down. It spills toward me streaming over a series of sandstone tiers, down, and down, and down. I feel as though I stand at the foot of an infinitely high staircase, down which some exuberant spirit is flinging tennis ball after tennis ball, eternally, and the one thing I want in the world is a tennis ball.

There must be something wrong with a creekside person who, all things being equal, chooses to face downstream. It's like fouling your own nest. For this and a leather couch they pay fifty dollars an hour? Tinker Creek doesn't back up, pushed up its own craw, from the Roanoke River; it flows down, easing, from the northern, unseen side of Tinker Mountain. "Gravity, to Copernicus, is the nostalgia of things to become spheres." This is a curious, tugged version of the great chain of being. Ease is the way of perfection, letting fall. But, as in the classic version of the great chain, the pure trickle that leaks from the unfathomable heart of Tinker Mountain, this Tinker Creek, widens, taking shape and cleaving banks, weighted with the live and intricate impurities of time, as it descends to me, to where I happen to find myself, in this intermediate spot, halfway between here and there. Look upstream. Just simply turn around; have you no will? The future is a spirit, or a distillation *of the* spirit, heading my way. It is north. The future is the light on the water; it comes, mediated, only on the skin of the real and present creek. My eyes can stand no brighter light than this; nor can they see without it, if only the undersides of leaves.

Trees are tough. They last, taproot and bark, and we soften at their feet. "For we are strangers before thee, and sojourners, as were all our fathers: our days on the earth are as a shadow, and there is none abiding." We can't take the lightning, the scourge of high places and rare airs. But we can take the light, the reflected light that shines up the valleys on creeks. Trees stir memories; live waters heal them. The creek is the mediator, benevolent, impartial, subsuming my shabbiest evils and dissolving them, transforming them into live moles, and shiners, and sycamore leaves. It is a place even my faithlessness hasn't offended; it still flashes for me, now and tomorrow, that intricate, innocent face. It waters an undeserving world, saturating cells with lodes of light. I stand by the creek over rock under trees.

5   It is sheer coincidence that my hunk of the creek is strewn with boulders. I never merited this grace, that when I face upstream I scent the virgin breath of mountains, I feel a spray of mist on my cheeks and lips, I hear a ceaseless splash and susurrus, a sound of water not merely poured smoothly down air to fill a steady pool, but tumbling live about, over, under, around, between, through an intricate speckling of rock. It is sheer coincidence that upstream from me the creek's bed is ridged in horizontal croppings of sandstone. I never merited this grace, that when I face upstream I see the

light on the water careening towards me, inevitably, freely, down a graded series of ter-races like the balanced winged platforms on an infinite, inexhaustible font. "Ho, if you are thirsty, come down to the water; ho, if you are hungry, come and sit and eat." This is the present, at last. I can pat the puppy any time I want. This is the now, this flickering, broken light, this air that the wind of the future presses down my throat, pumping me buoyant and giddy with praise.

My God, I look at the creek. It is the answer to Merton's prayer, "Give us time!" It never stops. If I seek the senses and skill of children, the information of a thousand books, the innocence of puppies, even the insights of my own city past, I do so only, solely, and entirely that I might look well at the creek. You don't run down the pre-sent, pursue it with baited hooks and nets. You wait for it, empty-handed, and you are filled. You'll have fish left over. The creek is the one great giver. It is, by definition, Christmas, the incarnation. This old rock planet gets the present for a present on its birthday every day.

Here is the word from a subatomic physicist: "Everything that has already hap-pened is particles, everything in the future is waves." Let me twist his meaning. Here it comes. The particles are broken; the waves are translucent, laving, roiling with beauty like sharks. The present is the wave that explodes over my head, flinging the air with particles at the height of its breathless unroll; it is the live water and light that bears from undisclosed sources the freshest news, renewed and renewing, world without end.

WRITING TOPIC

We know that water is vital to life, and we generally acknowledge its value as an energy source and appreciate its recreational values. However, Dillard's ex-cerpt from *Pilgrim at Tinker Creek* and Roethke's poem, "Meditation at Oyster River," (page 332) celebrate an intangible and less obvious value of water—mov-ing water as a source of reflection and for rejuvenation. Would our quality of life be diminished without places where we can observe freely moving water? Must these places be private or, at least, conducive to solitary visitations? Using Roethke's poem, Dillard's prose selection, and your own experiences and ideas, write an essay that examines and assesses the intangible value of water.

Ralph Waldo Emerson (1803–1882)

from *Nature*

To go into solitude, a man needs to retire as much from his chamber as from society. I am not solitary whilst I read and write, though nobody is with me. But if a man would be alone, let him look at the stars. The rays that come from those heavenly worlds, will separate between him and vulgar things. One might think the atmosphere was made transparent with this design, to give man, in the heavenly bodies, the perpetual presence of the sublime. Seen in the streets of cities, how great they are! If the stars should appear one night in a thousand years, how would men believe and adore; and preserve for many generations the remembrance of the city of God which had been shown! But every night come out these preachers of beauty, and light the universe with their admonishing smile.

The stars awaken a certain reverence, because though always present, they are always inaccessible; but all natural objects make a kindred impression, when the mind is open to their influence. Nature never wears a mean appearance. Neither does the wisest man extort all her secret, and lose his curiosity by finding out all her perfection. Nature never became a toy to a wise spirit. The flowers, the animals, the mountains, reflected all the wisdom of his best hour, as much as they had delighted the simplicity of his childhood.

When we speak of nature in this manner, we have a distinct but most poetical sense in the mind. We mean the integrity of impression made by manifold natural objects. It is this which distinguishes the stick of timber of the woodcutter, from the tree of the poet. The charming landscape which I saw this morning, is indubitably made up of some twenty or thirty farms. Miller owns this field, Locke that, and Manning the woodland beyond. But none of them owns the landscape. There is a property in the horizon which no man has but he whose eye can integrate all the parts, that is, the poet. This is the best part of these men's farms, yet to this their land-deeds give them no title.

To speak truly, few adult persons can see nature. Most persons do not see the sun. At least they have a very superficial seeing. The sun illuminates only the eye of the man, but shines into the eye and the heart of the child. The lover of nature is he whose inward and outward senses are still truly adjusted to each other; who has retained the spirit of infancy even into the era of manhood. His intercourse with heaven and earth, becomes part of his daily food. In the presence of nature, a wild delight runs through the man, in spite of real sorrows. Nature says,—he is my creature, and maugre all his impertinent griefs, he shall be glad with me. Not the sun or the summer alone, but every hour and season yields its tribute of delight; for every hour and change corresponds to and authorizes a different state of the mind, from breathless noon to grimmest midnight. Nature is a setting that fits equally well a comic or a mourning piece. In good health, the air is a cordial of incredible virtue. Crossing a bare common, in snow puddles, at twilight, under a clouded sky, without unaffecting, the landscape which they compose, is round and symmetrical. And as the eye is the best composer, so light is the first of painters. There is no object so foul that intense light will not make beautiful. And the stimulus it affords to the sense, and a sort of infinitude which it hath, like space and time, make all matter gay. Even the corpse hath its own beauty. But beside this general grace diffused over nature, almost all the individual forms are agreeable to the eye, as is proved by our endless imitations of some of them, as the acorn, the grape, the pine-cone, the wheat-ear, the egg, the wings and forms of most birds, the lion's claw, the serpent, the butterfly, sea-shells, flames, clouds, buds, leaves, and the forms of many trees, as the palm.

For better consideration, we may distribute the aspects of Beauty in a threefold manner.   5

1. First, the simple perception of natural forms is a delight. The influence of the forms and actions in nature, is so needful to man, that, in its lowest functions, it seems to lie on the confines of commodity and beauty. To the body and mind which have been cramped by noxious work or company, nature is medicinal and restores their tone. The tradesman, the attorney comes out of the din and craft of the street, and sees the sky and the woods, and is a man again. In their eternal calm, he finds himself. The health of the eye seems to demand a horizon. We are never tired, so long as we can see far enough.

But in other hours, Nature satisfies the soul purely by its loveliness, and without any mixture of corporeal benefit. I have seen the spectacle of morning from the hill-top over against my house, from day-break to sun-rise, with emotions which an angel might share. The long slender bars of cloud float like fishes in the sea of crimson light. From the earth, as a shore, I look out into that silent sea. I seem to partake its rapid transformations: the active enchantment reaches my dust, and I dilate and conspire with the morning wind. How does Nature deify us with a few and cheap elements! Give me health and a day, and I will make the pomp of emperors ridiculous. The dawn is my Assyria; the sun-set and moon-rise my Paphos, and unimaginable realms of faerie, broad noon shall be my England of the senses and the understanding; the night shall be my Germany of mystic philosophy and dreams.

Not less excellent, except for our less susceptibility in the afternoon, was the charm, last evening, of a January sunset. The western clouds divided and subdivided themselves into pink flakes modulated with tints of unspeakable softness; and the air had so much life and sweetness, that it was a pain to come within doors. What was it that nature would say? Was there no meaning in the live repose of the valley behind the mill, and which Homer or Shakespeare could not re-form for me in words? The leafless trees become spires of flame in the sunset, with the blue east for their background, and the stars of the dead calices of flowers, and every withered stem and stubble rimmed with frost, contribute something to the mute music.

The inhabitants of cities suppose that the country landscape is pleasant only half the year. I please myself with observing the graces of the winter scenery, and believe that we are as much touched by it as by the genial influences of summer. To the attentive eye, each moment of the year has its own beauty, and in the same field, it beholds, every hour, a picture which was never seen before, and which shall never be seen again. The heavens change every moment, and reflect their glory or gloom on the plains beneath. The state of the crop in the surrounding farms alters the expression of the earth from week to week. The succession of native plants in the pastures and roadsides, which make the silent clock by which time tells the summer hours, will make even the divisions of the day sensible to a keen observer. The tribes of birds and insects, like the plants punctual to their time, follow each other, and the year has room for all. By water-courses, the variety is greater. In July, the blue pontederia or pickerel-weed blooms in large beds in the shallow parts of our pleasant river, and swarms with yellow butterflies in continual motion. Art cannot rival this pomp of purple and gold. Indeed the river is a perpetual gala, and boasts each month a new ornament.

10   But this beauty of Nature which is seen and felt as beauty, is the least part. The shows of day, the dewy morning, the rainbow, mountains, orchards in blossom, stars, moonlight, shadows in still water, and the like, if too eagerly hunted, become shows merely, and mock us with their unreality. Go out of the house to see the moon, and 't is mere tinsel; it will not please as when its light shines upon your necessary journey. The beauty that shimmers in the yellow afternoons of October, who ever could clutch it? Go forth to find it, and it is gone: 't is only a mirage as you look from the windows of the diligence.

        2. The presence of a higher, namely, of the spiritual element is essential to its perfection. The high and divine beauty which can be loved without effeminacy, is that which is found in combination with the human will, and never separate. Beauty is the mark God sets upon virtue. Every natural action is graceful. Every heroic act is also decent, and causes the place and the bystanders to shine. We are taught by great actions that the universe is the property of every individual in it. Every rational creature has all nature for his dowry and estate. It is his, if he will. He may divest himself of it; he may creep into a corner, and abdicate his kingdom, as most men do, but he is entitled to the world by his constitution. In proportion to the energy of his thought and will, he takes up the world into himself. "All those things for which men plough, build, or sail, obey virtue;" said an ancient historian. "The winds and waves," said Gibbon, "are always on the side of the ablest navigators." So are the sun and moon and all the stars of heaven. When a noble act is done,—perchance in a scene of great natural beauty; when Leonidas and his three hundred martyrs consume one day in dying, and the sun and moon come each and look at them once in the steep defile of Thermopylæ; when Arnold Winkelried, in the high Alps, under the shadow of the avalanche, gathers in his side a sheaf of Austrian spears to break the line for his comrades; are not these heroes entitled to add the beauty of the scene to the beauty of the deed? When the bark of Columbus nears the shore of America;—before it, the beach lined with savages, fleeing out of all their huts of cane; the sea behind; and the purple mountains of the Indian Archipelago around, can we separate the man from the living picture? Does not the New World clothe his form with her palm-groves and savannahs as fit drapery? Ever does natural beauty steal in like air, and envelope great actions. When Sir Harry Vane was dragged up the Tower-hill, sitting on a sled, to suffer death, as the champion of the English laws, one of the multitude cried out to him,

"You never sate on so glorious a seat." Charles II, to intimidate the citizens of London, caused the patriot Lord Russel to be drawn in an open coach, through the principal streets of the city, on his way to the scaffold. "But," to use the simple narrative of his biographer, "the multitude imagined they saw liberty and virtue sitting by his side." In private places, among sordid objects, an act of truth or heroism seems at once to draw to itself the sky as its temple, the sun as its candle. Nature stretcheth out her arms to embrace man, only let his thoughts be of equal greatness. Willingly does she follow his steps with the rose and the violet, and bend her lines of grandeur and grace to the decoration of her darling child. Only let his thoughts be of equal scope, and the frame will suit the picture. A virtuous man, is in unison with her works, and makes the central figure of the visible sphere. Homer, Pindar, Socrates, Phocion, associate themselves fitly in our memory with the whole geography and climate of Greece. The visible heavens and earth sympathize with Jesus. And in common life, whosoever has seen a person of powerful character and happy genius, will have remarked how easily he took all things along with him,—the persons, the opinions, and the day, and nature became ancillary to a man.

3. There is still another aspect under which the beauty of the world may be viewed, namely, as it becomes an object of the intellect. Beside the relation of things to virtue, they have a relation to thought. The intellect searches out the absolute order of things as they stand in the mind of God, and without the colors of affection. The intellectual and the active powers seem to succeed each other in man, and the exclusive activity of the one, generates the exclusive activity of the other. There is something unfriendly in each to the other, but they are like the alternate periods of feeding and working in animals; each prepares and certainly will be followed by the other. Therefore does beauty, which, in relation to actions, as we have seen comes unsought, and comes because it is unsought, remain for the apprehension and pursuit of the intellect; and then again, in its turn, of the active power. Nothing divine dies. All good is eternally reproductive. The beauty of nature reforms itself in the mind, and not for barren contemplation, but for new creation.

All men are in some degree impressed by the face of the world. Some men even to delight. This love of beauty is Taste. Others have the same love in such excess, that, not content with admiring, they seek to embody it in new forms. The creation of beauty is Art.

The production of a work of art throws a light upon the mystery of humanity. A work of art is an abstract or epitome of the world. It is the result or expression of nature, in miniature. For although the works of nature are innumerable and all different, the result or the expression of them all is similar and single. Nature is a sea of forms radically alike and even unique. A leaf, a sunbeam, a landscape, the ocean, make an analogous impression on the mind. What is common to them all,—that perfectness and harmony, is beauty. Therefore the standard of beauty, is the entire circuit of natural forms,—the totality of nature; which the Italians expressed by defining beauty "il piu nell' uno." Nothing is quite beautiful alone: nothing but is beautiful in the whole. A single object is only so far beautiful as it suggests this universal grace. The poet, the painter, the sculptor, the musician, the architect seek each to concentrate this radiance of the world on one point, and each in his several work to satisfy the love of beauty which stimulates him to produce. Thus is Art, a nature passed through the alembic of man. Thus in art, does nature work through the will of a man filled with the beauty of her first works.

15   The world thus exists to the soul to satisfy the desire of beauty. Extend this element to the uttermost, and I call it an ultimate end. No reason can be asked or given why the soul seeks beauty. Beauty, in its largest and profoundest sense, is one expression for the universe. God is the all-fair. Truth, and goodness, and beauty, are but different faces of the same All. But beauty in nature is not ultimate. It is the herald of inward and eternal beauty, and is not alone a solid and satisfactory good. It must therefore stand as a part and not as yet the last or highest expression of the final cause of Nature.

CRITICAL THINKING QUESTION

Does Emerson's prose have stronger *logos* or *pathos* appeal? Can you find examples of each?

WRITING TOPIC

Copy five or six passages from the *Nature* excerpt that seem important or interesting to you. Select two or three and freewrite about each for five or ten minutes; record your personal reflection and reaction, questions or confusions. Be prepared to share your writings with a small group in class.

Jane Goodall (b. 1934)

A Plea for the Chimpanzees

The chimpanzee is more like us, genetically, than any other animal. It is because of similarities in physiology, in biochemistry, and in the immune system that medical science makes use of the living bodies of chimpanzees in its search for cures and vaccines for a variety of human diseases.

There are also behavioral, psychological, and emotional similarities between chimpanzees and humans, resemblances so striking that they raise a serious ethical question: Are we justified in using an animal so close to us—an animal, moreover, that is highly endangered in its African forest home—as a human substitute in medical experimentation?

In the long run, we can hope that scientists will find ways of exploring human physiology and disease, and of testing cures and vaccines, that do not depend on the use of living animals of any sort. A number of steps in this direction already have been taken, prompted in large part by a growing public awareness of the suffering that is being inflicted on millions of animals. More and more people are beginning to realize that nonhuman animals—even rats and guinea pigs—are not just unfeeling machines but are capable of enjoying their lives, and of feeling fear, pain, and despair.

But until alternatives have been found, medical science will continue to use animals in the battle against human disease and suffering. And some of those animals will continue to be chimpanzees.

Because they share with us 99 percent of their genetic material, chimpanzees can   5
be infected with some human diseases that do not infect other animals. They are currently being used in research on the nature of hepatitis non-A non-B, for example, and they continue to play a major role in the development of vaccines against hepatitis B.

Many biomedical laboratories are looking to the chimpanzee to help them in the race to find a vaccine against acquired immune deficiency syndrome. Chimpanzees are not good models for AIDS research; although the AIDS virus stays alive and replicates within the chimpanzee's bloodstream, no chimp has yet come down with the disease itself. Nevertheless, many of the scientists involved argue that only by using chimpanzees can potential vaccines be safely tested.

Given the scientists' professed need for animals in research, let us turn aside from the sensitive ethical issue of whether chimpanzees *should* be used in medical research, and consider a more immediate issue: How are we treating the chimpanzees that are actually being used?

Just after Christmas I watched, with shock, anger, and anguish, a videotape— made by an animal rights group during a raid—revealing the conditions in a large biomedical research laboratory, under contract to the National Institutes of Health, in which various primates, including chimpanzees, are maintained. In late March, I was given permission to visit the facility.

It was a visit I shall never forget. Room after room was lined with small, bare cages, stacked one above the other, in which monkeys circled round and round and chimpanzees sat huddled, far gone in depression and despair.

Young chimpanzees, three or four years old, were crammed, two together, into tiny   10
cages measuring 57 cm by 57 cm and only 61 cm high. They could hardly turn around. Not yet part of any experiment, they had been confined in these cages for more than three months.

The chimps had each other for comfort, but they would not remain together for long. Once they are infected, probably with hepatitis, they will be separated and placed in another cage. And there they will remain, living in conditions of severe sensory deprivation, for the next several years. During that time, they will become insane.

A juvenile female rocked from side to side, sealed off from the outside world behind the glass doors of her metal isolation chamber. She was in semidarkness. All she could hear was the incessant roar of air rushing through vents into her prison.

In order to demonstrate the "good" relationship the lab's caretaker had with this chimpanzee, one of the scientists told him to lift her from the cage. The caretaker opened the door. She sat, unmoving. He reached in. She did not greet him—nor did he greet her. As if drugged, she allowed him to take her out. She sat motionless in his arms. He did not speak to her, she did not look at him. He touched her lips briefly. He returned her to her cage. She sat again on the bars of the floor. The door closed.

I shall be haunted forever by her eyes, and by the eyes of the other infant chimpanzees I saw that day. Have you ever looked into the eyes of a person who, stressed beyond endurance, has given up, succumbed utterly to the crippling helplessness of despair? I once saw a little African boy whose whole family had been killed during the fighting in Burundi. He too looked out at the world, unseeing, from dull, blank eyes.

15   Though this particular laboratory may be one of the worst, from what I have learned, most of the other biomedical animal-research facilities are not much better. Yet only when one has some understanding of the true nature of the chimpanzee can the cruelty of these captive conditions be fully understood.

An Isolating Cage

Chimpanzees are very social by nature. Bonds between individuals, particularly between family members and close friends, can be affectionate and supportive, and can endure throughout their lives. The accidental separation of two friendly individuals can cause them intense distress. Indeed, the death of a mother may be such a psychological blow to her child that even if the child is five years old and no longer dependent on its mother's milk, it may pine away and die.

It is impossible to overemphasize the importance of friendly physical contact for the well-being of the chimpanzee. Again and again one can watch a frightened or tense individual relax if she is patted, kissed, or embraced reassuringly by a companion. Social grooming, which provides hours of close contact, is undoubtedly the single most important social activity.

Chimpanzees in their natural habitat are active for much of the day. They travel extensively within their territory, which can be as large as 50 km^2 for a community of about 50 individuals. If they hear other chimpanzees calling as they move through the forest, or anticipate arriving at a good food source, they typically break into excited charging displays, racing along the ground, hurling sticks and rocks and shaking the vegetation. Youngsters, particularly, are full of energy, and spend long hours playing with one another or by themselves, leaping through the branches and gamboling along the ground. Adults sometimes join these games. Bunches of fruit, twigs, and rocks may be used as toys.

Chimpanzees enjoy comfort. They construct sleeping platforms each night, using a multitude of leafy twigs to make their beds soft. Often, too, they make little "pillows" on which to rest during a midday siesta.

20   Chimps are highly intelligent. They display cognitive abilities that were, until recently, thought to be unique to humans. They are capable of cross-modal transfer of information—that is, they can identify by touch an object they have previously only

seen, and vice versa. They are capable of reasoned thought, generalization, abstraction, and symbolic representation. They have some concept of self. They have excellent memories and can, to some extent, plan for the future. They show a capacity for intentional communication that depends, in part, on their ability to understand the motives of the individuals with whom they are communicating.

Chimpanzees are capable of empathy and altruistic behavior. They show emotions that are undoubtedly similar, if not identical, to human emotions—joy, pleasure, contentment, anxiety, fear, and rage. They even have a sense of humor.

The chimpanzee child and the human child are alike in many ways: in their capacity for endless romping and fun; their curiosity; their ability to learn by observation, imitation, and practice; and, above all, their need for reassurance and love. When young chimpanzees are brought up in a human home and treated like human children, they learn to eat at the table, to help themselves to snacks from the refrigerator, to sort and put away cutlery, to brush their teeth, to play with dolls, to switch on the television and select a program that interests them and watch it.

Young chimpanzees can easily learn over 200 signs of the American language of the deaf and use these signs to communicate meaningfully with humans and with one another. One youngster in the laboratory of Roger S. Fouts, a psychologist at Central Washington University, has picked up 68 signs from four older signing chimpanzee companions, with no coaching from humans. The chimp uses the signs in communication with other chimpanzees and with humans.

The chimpanzee facilities in most biomedical research laboratories allow for the expression of almost none of these activities and behaviors. They provide little—if anything—more than the warmth, food and water, and veterinary care required to sustain life. The psychological and emotional needs of these creatures are rarely catered to, and often not even acknowledged.

In most labs the chimpanzees are housed individually, one chimp to a cage, unless they are part of a breeding program. The standard size of each cage is about 7.6 m^2 and about 1.8 m high. In one facility, a cage described in the catalogue as "large," designed for a chimpanzee of up to 25 kg, measures 0.76 by 1.1 m, with a height of 1.6 m. Federal requirements for cage size are dependent on body size; infant chimpanzees, who are the most active, are often imprisoned in the smallest cages. 25

In most labs, the chimpanzees cannot even lie with their arms and legs outstretched. They are not let out to exercise. There is seldom anything for them to do other than eat, and then only when food is brought. The caretakers are usually too busy to pay attention to individual chimpanzees. The cages are bleak and sterile, with bars above, bars below, bars on every side. There is no comfort in them, no bedding. The chimps, infected with human disease, will often feel sick and miserable.

A Harmful System

What of the human beings who administer these facilities—the caretakers, veterinarians, and scientists who work at them? If they are decent, compassionate people, how can they condone, or even tolerate, the kind of conditions I have described?

They are, I believe, victims of a system that was set up long before the cognitive abilities and emotional needs of chimpanzees were understood. Newly employed staff members, equipped with a normal measure of compassion, may well be sickened by what they see. And, in fact, many of them do quit their jobs, unable to endure the suffering they see inflicted on the animals yet feeling powerless to help.

But others stay on and gradually come to accept the cruelty, believing (or forcing themselves to believe) that it is an inevitable part of the struggle to reduce human suffering. Some become hard and callous in the process, in Shakespeare's words, "all pity choked with custom of fell deeds."

30   A handful of compassionate and dedicated caretakers and veterinarians are fighting to improve the lot of the animals in their care. Veterinarians are often in a particularly difficult position, for if they stand firm and try to uphold high standards of humane care, they will not always be welcome in the lab.

Many of the scientists believe that a bleak, sterile, and restricting environment is necessary for their research. The cages must be small, the scientists maintain, because otherwise it is too difficult to treat the chimpanzees—to inject them, to draw their blood, or to anesthetize them. Moreover, they are less likely to hurt themselves in small cages.

The cages must also be barren, with no bedding or toys, say the scientists. This way, the chimpanzees are less likely to pick up diseases or parasites. Also, if things are lying about, the cages are harder to clean.

And the chimpanzees must be kept in isolation, the scientists believe, to avoid the risk of cross-infection, particularly in hepatitis research.

Finally, of course, bigger cages, social groups, and elaborate furnishings require more space, more caretakers—and more money. Perhaps, then, if we are to believe these researchers, it is not possible to improve conditions for chimpanzees imprisoned in biomedical research laboratories.

35   I believe not only that it *is* possible, but that improvements are absolutely necessary. If we do not do something to help these creatures, we make a mockery of the whole concept of justice.

Quality of Life in the Laboratory

Perhaps the most important way we can improve the quality of life of the laboratory chimps is to increase the number of carefully trained caretakers. These people should be selected for their understanding of animal behavior and their compassion and respect for, and dedication to, their charges. Each caretaker, having established a relationship of trust with the chimpanzees in his care, should be allowed to spend time with the animals over and above that required for cleaning the cages and providing the animals with food and water.

It has been shown that a chimpanzee who has a good relationship with his caretaker will cooperate calmly during experimental procedures, rather than react with fear or anger. At the Dutch Primate Center in Rijswijk, for example, some chimpanzees have been trained to leave their group cage on command and move into small, single cages for treatment. At the Stanford Primate Center in California, a number of chimpanzees were taught to extend their arms for the drawing of blood. In return they were given a food reward.

Much can be done to alleviate the pain and distress felt by younger chimpanzees during experimental procedures. A youngster, for example, can be treated when in the presence of a trusted human friend. Experiments have shown that young chimps react with high levels of distress if subjected to mild electric shocks when alone, but show almost no fear or pain when held by a sympathetic caretaker.

What about cage size? Here we should emulate the animal-protection regulations that already exist in Switzerland. These laws stipulate that a cage must be, at minimum, about 20 m^2 and 3 m high for pairs of chimpanzees.

The chimpanzees should never be housed alone unless this is an essential part of   40 the experimental procedure. For chimps in solitary confinement, particularly youngsters, three to four hours of friendly interaction with a caretaker should be mandatory. A chimp taking part in hepatitis research, in which the risk of cross-infection is, I am told, great, can be provided with a companion of a compatible species if it doesn't infringe on existing regulations—a rhesus monkey, for example, which cannot catch or pass on the disease.

For healthy chimpanzees there should be little risk of infection from bedding and toys. Stress and depression, however, can have deleterious effects on their health. It is known that clinically depressed humans are more prone to a variety of physiological disorders, and heightened stress can interfere with immune function. Given the chimpanzee's similarities to humans, it is not surprising that the chimp in a typical laboratory, alone in his bleak cage, is an easy prey to infections and parasites.

Thus, the chimpanzees also should be provided with a rich and stimulating environment. Climbing apparatus should be obligatory. There should be many objects for them to play with or otherwise manipulate. A variety of simple devices designed to alleviate boredom could be produced quite cheaply. Unexpected food items will elicit great pleasure. If a few simple buttons in each cage were connected to a computer terminal, it would be possible for the chimpanzees to feel they at least have some control over their world—if one button produced a grape when pressed, another a drink, another a video picture. (The Canadian Council on Animal Care recommends the provision of television for primates in solitary confinement, or other means of enriching their environment.)

Without doubt, it will be considerable more costly to maintain chimpanzees in the manner I have outlined. Should we begrudge them the extra dollars? We take from them their freedom, their health, and often their lives. Surely, the least we can do is try to provide them with some of the things that could make their imprisonment more bearable.

There are hopeful signs. I was immensely grateful to officials of the National Institutes of Health for allowing me to visit the primate facility, enabling me to see the conditions there and judge them for myself. And I was even more grateful for the fact that they gave me a great deal of time for serious discussions of the problem. Doors were opened and a dialogue begun. All who were present at the meetings agreed that, in light of present knowledge, it is indeed necessary to give chimpanzees a better deal in the labs.

45   I have had the privilege of working among wild, free chimpanzees for more than 26 years. I have gained a deep understanding of chimpanzee nature. Chimpanzees have given me so much in my life. The least I can do is to speak out for the hundreds of chimpanzees who, right now, sit hunched, miserable and without hope, staring out with dead eyes from their metal prisons. They cannot speak for themselves.

CRITICAL THINKING QUESTIONS

1. Examine Goodall's argument for its appeal to *logos*. List the factual evidence she offers in support of her claim that the chimpanzees deserve humane treatment.

2. Examine Goodall's argument for its appeal to *pathos*. List the words and phrases, such as "mental prisons," which Goodall has selected for their emotional impact.

3. Examine Goodall's argument for its appeal to *ethos*. List words and phrases that create this appeal.

4. Which appeal do you believe to be the most powerful in this argument?

5. Review the discussion of Rogerian argument in Chapter One. How does Goodall's essay reflect the characteristics of a Rogerian argument?

Aldous Huxley (1894–1963)

Time and the Machine

from *The Olive Tree*

Time, as we know it, is a very recent invention. The modern time-sense is hardly older than the United States. It is a by-product of industrialism—a sort of psychological analogue of synthetic perfumes and aniline dyes.

   Time is our tyrant. We are chronically aware of the moving minute hand, even of the moving second hand. We have to be. There are trains to be caught, clocks to be punched, tasks to be done in specified periods, records to be broken by fractions of a second, machines that set the pace and have to be kept up with. Our consciousness of the smallest units of time is now acute. To us, for example, the moment 8:17 A.M. means something—something very important, if it happens to be the starting time of our daily train. To our ancestors, such an odd eccentric instant was without significance—did not even exist. In inventing the locomotive, Watt and Stevenson were part inventors of time.

Another time-emphasizing entity is the factory and its dependent, the office. Factories exist for the purpose of getting certain quantities of goods made in a certain time. The old artisan worked as it suited him with the result that consumers generally had to wait for the goods they had ordered from him. The factory is a device for making workmen hurry. The machine revolves so often each minute; so many movements have to be made, so many pieces produced each hour. Result: the factory worker (and the same is true, *mutatis mutandis,* of the office worker) is compelled to know time in its smallest fractions. In the hand-work age there was no such compulsion to be aware of minutes and seconds.

Our awareness of time has reached such a pitch of intensity that we suffer acutely whenever our travels take us into some corner of the world where people are not interested in minutes and seconds. The unpunctuality of the Orient, for example, is appalling to those who come freshly from a land of fixed meal-times and regular train services. For a modern American or Englishman, waiting is a psychological torture. An Indian accepts the blank hours with resignation, even with satisfaction. He has not lost the fine art of doing nothing. Our notion of time as a collection of minutes, each of which must be filled with some business or amusement, is wholly alien to the Oriental, just as it was wholly alien to the Greek. For the man who lives in a pre-industrial world, time moves at a slow and easy pace; he does not care about each minute, for the good reason that he has not been made conscious of the existence of minutes.

This brings us to a seeming paradox. Acutely aware of the smallest constituent   5
particles of time—of time, as measured by clock-work and train arrivals and the revolutions of machines—industrialized man has to a great extent lost the old awareness of time in its larger divisions. The time of which we have knowledge is artificial, machine-made time. Of natural, cosmic time, as it is measured out by sun and moon, we are for the most part almost wholly unconscious. Pre-industrial people know time in its daily, monthly and seasonal rhythms. They are aware of sunrise, noon and sunset; of the full moon and the new; of equinox and solstice; of spring and summer, autumn and winter. All the old religions, including Catholic Christianity, have insisted on this daily and seasonal rhythm. Pre-industrial man, was never allowed to forget the majestic movement of cosmic time.

Industrialism and urbanism have changed all this. One can live and work in a town without being aware of the daily march of the sun across the sky; without ever seeing the moon and stars. Broadway and Piccadilly are our Milky Way; our constellations are outlined in neon tubes. Even changes of season affect the townsman very little. He is the inhabitant of an artificial universe that is, to a great extent, walled off from the world of nature. Outside the walls, time is cosmic and moves with the motion of sun and stars. Within, it is an affair of revolving wheels and is measured in seconds and minutes—at its longest, in eight-hour days and six-day weeks.

We have a new consciousness; but it has been purchased at the expense of the old consciousness.

CRITICAL THINKING QUESTION

Huxley explicitly blames industrialism and urbanism for our loss of awareness of cosmic time and our separation from the world of nature. Is Huxley's indictment valid? For debate purposes, be prepared to defend or to refute Huxley's claim.

WRITING TOPIC

Today's computer technology has given us digital time and virtual reality. Has this technology created yet a "new consciousness"? How would you explain this twenty-first-century consciousness? Do you agree or disagree that (like Huxley's townsman) we are "inhabitant[s] of an artificial universe that is, to a great extent, walled off from the world of nature"?

Verlyn Klinkenborg (b. 1952)

At the Edge of the Visible

Darkness seems to collect at this time of year, as though it had trickled downhill from late June's solstice into the sump of November. Fog settles onto damp leaves in the woods—not Prufrock's yellow fog or the amber fog of the suburbs, but a gray-white hanging mist that feels like the down or underfur of some pervasive beast.

White birches line the slopes beyond the pasture as if they were there to fence in the fog, to keep it from inundating the house in a weightless avalanche. The day stays warm, but even at noon it feels as though dusk has already set in. The chickens roost early. The horses linger by the gate, ready for supper.

Usually I feel starved for light about now. But this year I've reveled in these damp, dark November days. It's a kind of waking hibernation, I suppose, a desire to live enclosed, for a while at least, in a world defined by the vaporous edges of our small farm.

My ambition extends all the way to feeding the woodstove and sitting with the Border terrier, Tavish, in my lap, which perfectly suits his ambitions. The frenzy of the spring garden has long since faded. My plans to refence the place, to make it sheep-proof, have been put on hold for another year. We're just sitting around waiting for the ground to freeze.

5   This is not how it's supposed to be, I know. I keep an endless mental list of the things that need to be done. But when a gray day comes, when the horses stand over their hay as though there were all the time in the world to eat it, one of the things that needs to be done is to sit still.

The ducks and geese are especially good at that. They come out of their yard in a rush in the mornings and forage ravenously across the pastures and into the garden debris. But an hour or two later they lie quietly on the lawn, like ships on a green sea, some gazing intently at the world around them, some with their heads tucked into their wings. I consider myself a student of their stillness.

On a gray November day, it's surprising how long it takes the light to finally fade. Not long ago I visited a friend on her ranch in eastern Colorado. She wanted to work her sheepdog, Wiz, in an enclosure set among the cottonwoods in a sandy draw. The very edge of darkness had already come. My friend drove a small flock of Katahdin sheep, scattering, out of their pen. At the sight of Wiz darting back and forth, they bunched.

There is not much luminosity in a sheep's fleece, but there was enough to rest my eyes upon. After a while, the sheep returned to their pen, and we walked down a path under the cottonwoods to the edge of a meadow. We stood in full night. But out in the shortgrass, dusk still lingered as though it might never go out.

WRITING TOPIC

Klinkenborg tells us on days such as the one he describes, "one of the things that needs to be done is to sit still." Rewrite this idea as a general claim about life and then make a list of evidence drawn from your personal experience and observation that might support such a claim.

RESEARCH/WRITING TOPIC—The Future of the Family Farm

Klinkenborg comes from a family of Iowa farmers and lives on a small farm in upstate New York. As such, Klinkenborg's essays for the *New York Times* and his books, such as *Rural Life*, celebrate the values of rural living. Meanwhile, during the latter part of the twentieth century, large corporate farms (agribusiness) began to muscle small farms, quite literally, off the land. However, small farm owners have begun fighting back, mobilizing their support through groups such as Farm Aid and the National Family Farm Coalition. Their message of healthy and fresh food from family farms is resonating with growing numbers of the public. In 2006, singer and writer Willie Nelson, one of the founders of Farm Aid, appealed directly to individuals to take action: "If you value good food from family farms, call your legislator and demand a Farm Bill. . . ."[2] Do you know any small farm owners? Is there a farmers' market in your community? Meanwhile, the "green" or "good food" movement seems to be catching on among corporate food producers. Who are their suppliers, small farms or agribusiness? After researching this topic, compose a letter that you might send to your legislator to demand a Farm Bill.

---

[2]Willie Nelson, "Save Family Farms, Save America," *AlterNet* 27 April 2006, 10 June 2006 <http://www.alternet.org/module/printversion/35404>.

Aldo Leopold (1876–1944)

Thinking Like a Mountain

A deep chesty bawl echoes from rimrock to rimrock, rolls down the mountain, and fades into the far blackness of the night. It is an outburst of wild defiant sorrow, and of contempt for all the adversities of the world.

Every living thing (and perhaps many a dead one as well) pays heed to that call. To the deer it is a reminder of the way of all flesh, to the pine a forecast of midnight scuffles and of blood upon the snow, to the coyote a promise of gleanings to come, to the cowman a threat of red ink at the bank, to the hunter a challenge of fang against bullet. Yet behind these obvious and immediate hopes and fears there lies a deeper meaning, known only to the mountain itself. Only the mountain has lived long enough to listen objectively to the howl of a wolf.

Those unable to decipher the hidden meaning know nevertheless that it is there, for it is felt in all wolf country, and distinguishes that country from all other land. It tingles in the spine of all who hear wolves by night, or who scan their tracks by day. Even without sight or sound of wolf, it is implicit in a hundred small events: the midnight whinny of a pack horse, the rattle of rolling rocks, the bound of a fleeing deer, the way shadows lie under the spruces. Only the ineducable tyro can fail to sense the presence or absence of wolves, or the fact that mountains have a secret opinion about them.

My own conviction on this score dates from the day I saw a wolf die. We were eating lunch on a high rimrock, at the foot of which a turbulent river elbowed its way. We saw what we thought was a doe fording the torrent, her breast awash in white water. When she climbed the bank toward us and shook out her tail, we realized our error: it was a wolf. A half-dozen others, evidently grown pups, sprang from the willows and all joined in a welcoming mêlée of wagging tails and playful maulings. What was literally a pile of wolves writhed and tumbled in the center of an open flat at the foot of our rimrock.

5   In those days we had never heard of passing up a chance to kill a wolf. In a second we were pumping lead into the pack, but with more excitement than accuracy: how to aim a steep downhill shot is always confusing. When our rifles were empty, the old wolf was down, and a pup was dragging a leg into impassable slide-rocks.

We reached the old wolf in time to watch a fierce green fire dying in her eyes. I realized then, and have known ever since, that there was something new to me in those eyes—something known only to her and to the mountain. I was young then, and full of trigger-itch; I thought that because fewer wolves meant more deer, that no wolves would mean hunters' paradise. But after seeing the green fire die, I sensed that neither the wolf nor the mountain agreed with such a view.

*   *   *

Since then I have lived to see state after state extirpate its wolves. I have watched the face of many a newly wolfless mountain, and seen the south-facing slopes wrinkle with a maze of new deer trails. I have seen every edible bush and seedling browsed, first to anaemic desuetude, and then to death. I have seen every edible tree defoliated to the height of a saddlehorn. Such a mountain looks as if someone had given God new pruning shears, and forbidden Him all other exercise. In the end the starved bones of the hoped-for deer herd, dead of its own too-much, bleach with the bones of the dead sage, or molder under the high-lined junipers.

I now suspect that just as a deer herd lives in mortal fear of its wolves, so does a mountain live in mortal fear of its deer. And perhaps with better cause, for while a buck pulled down by wolves can be replaced in two or three years, a range pulled down by too many deer may fail of replacement in as many decades.

So also with cows. The cowman who cleans his range of wolves does not realize   10
that he is taking over the wolf's job of trimming the herd to fit the range. He has not learned to think like a mountain. Hence we have dust-bowls, and rivers washing the future into the sea.

*   *   *

We all strive for safety, prosperity, comfort, long life, and dullness. The deer strives with his supple legs, the cowman with trap and poison, the statesman with pen, the most of us with machines, votes, and dollars, but it all comes to the same thing: peace in our time. A measure of success in this is all well enough, and perhaps is a requisite to objective thinking, but too much safety seems to yield only danger in the long run. Perhaps this is behind Thoreau's dictum: In wildness is the salvation of the world. Perhaps this is the hidden meaning in the howl of the wolf, long known among mountains, but seldom perceived among men.

CRITICAL THINKING QUESTION

Use the three rhetorical appeals—*ethos, logos, pathos*—to analyze and evaluate Leopold's argument for preserving wolves.

WRITING TOPIC

In his closing paragraph, Leopold warns that "too much safety seems to yield only danger in the long run," a statement that would seem to be contradictory and counterintuitive. What does his warning mean to you? Do you agree or disagree?

RESEARCH/WRITING TOPIC—Hunting Controversy: To Hunt or Not to Hunt

Recounting the day he saw a wolf die, Leopold expresses clear censure of his participation in the shootings, his young man's "trigger-itch . . . pumping lead into the pack" of wolves. Unfortunately, events such as those prompt many persons to label hunters as wanton killers. Yet hunters number among the most staunch conservationists, working to preserve native habitats to sustain diverse populations of animals and birds. Meanwhile, development has swallowed up large chunks of natural habitat. Increasingly, deer, alligators, bears, wolves, to name a few, are wandering into neighborhoods and even cities, damaging personal property and posing threats to humans. Thus, hunters claim that by thinning their populations, they are, in a sense, "thinking like a mountain." Also, many hunters say they kill only what they will eat—meat that is, arguably, far healthier than that which is packaged and sold in grocery stores. But, animal rights advocates argue, the solution is not to slaughter more animals but to limit development and its concurrent destruction of habitat. Finally, according to some, killing an animal is outright unethical. Clearly, compelling arguments exist in this controversy. Is hunting a defensible sport and an ethical practice? (See also Rick Bass's story, "Antlers.")

Joyce Carol Oates (b. 1938)

Against Nature

We soon get through with Nature. She excites an expectation which she cannot satisfy.

—THOREAU, *JOURNAL*, 1854

Sir, if a man has experienced the inexpressible, he is under no obligation to attempt to express it.

—SAMUEL JOHNSON

The writer's resistance to Nature.

It has no sense of humor: in its beauty, as in its ugliness, or its neutrality, there is no laughter.

It lacks a moral purpose.

It lacks a satiric dimension, registers no irony.

Its pleasures lack resonance, being accidental; its horrors, even when premedi-   5
tated, are equally perfunctory, "red in tooth and claw," et cetera.

It lacks a symbolic subtext—excepting that provided by man.

It has no (verbal) language.

It has no interest in ours.

It inspires a painfully limited set of responses in "nature writers"—
REVERENCE, AWE, PIETY, MYSTICAL ONENESS.

It eludes us even as it prepares to swallow us up, books and all.   10

I was lying on my back in the dirt gravel of the towpath beside the Delaware and
Raritan Canal, Titusville, New Jersey, staring up at the sky and trying, with no success, to overcome a sudden attack of tachycardia that had come upon me out of
nowhere—such attacks are always "out of nowhere," that's their charm—and all around
me Nature thrummed with life, the air smelling of moisture and sunlight, the canal
reflecting the sky, red-winged blackbirds testing their spring calls; the usual. I'd become
the jar in Tennessee, a fictitious center, or parenthesis, aware beyond my erratic heartbeat of the numberless heartbeats of the earth, its pulsing, pumping life, sheer life, incalculable. Struck down in the midst of motion—I'd been jogging a minute before—I
was "out of time" like a fallen, stunned boxer, privileged (in an abstract manner of
speaking) to be an involuntary witness to the random, wayward, nameless motion on
all sides of me.

Paroxysmal tachycardia can be fatal, but rarely; if the heartbeat accelerates to
250–270 beats a minute you're in trouble, but the average attack is about 100–150
beats and mine seemed about average; the trick now was to prevent it from getting
worse. Brainy people try brainy strategies, such as thinking calming thoughts, pseudo-
mystic thoughts, *If I die now it's a good death,* that sort of thing, *if I die this is a good
place and good time;* the idea is to deceive the frenzied heartbeat that, really, you don't
care: you hadn't any other plans for the afternoon. The important thing with tachycardia is to prevent panic! you must prevent panic! otherwise you'll have to be taken
by ambulance to the closest emergency room, which is not so very nice a way to
spend the afternoon, really. So I contemplated the blue sky overhead. The earth beneath my head. Nature surrounding me on all sides; I couldn't quite see it but I could
hear it, smell it, sense it, there is something *there,* no mistake about it. Completely
oblivious to the predicament of the individual but that's only "natural," after all, one
hardly expects otherwise.

When you discover yourself lying on the ground, limp and unresisting, head in
the dirt, and, let's face it, helpless, the earth seems to shift forward as a presence; hard,
emphatic, not mere surface but a genuine force—there is no other word for it but
presence. To keep in motion is to keep in time, and to be stopped, stilled, is to be
abruptly out of time, in another time dimension perhaps, an alien one, where human
language has no resonance. Nothing to be said about it expresses it, nothing touches
it, it's an absolute against which nothing human can be measured. . . . Moving through

space and time by way of your own volition you inhabit an interior consciousness, a hallucinatory consciousness, it might be said, so long as breath, heartbeat, the body's autonomy hold; when motion is stopped you are jarred out of it. The interior is invaded by the exterior. The outside wants to come in, and only the self's fragile membrane prevents it.

The fly buzzing at Emily's death.

15   Still, the earth *is* your place. A tidy grave site measured to your size. Or, from another angle of vision, one vast democratic grave.

Let's contemplate the sky. Forget the crazy hammering heartbeat, don't listen to it, don't start counting, remember that there is a clever way of breathing that conserves oxygen as if you're lying below the surface of a body of water breathing through a very thin straw but you *can* breathe through it if you're careful, if you don't panic; one breath and then another and then another, isn't that the story of all lives? careers? Just a matter of breathing. Of course it is. But contemplate the sky, it's there to be contemplated. A mild shock to see it so blank, blue, a thin airy ghostly blue, no clouds to disguise its emptiness. You are beginning to feel not only weightless but near-bodiless, lying on the earth like a scrap of paper about to be blown off. Two dimensions and you'd imagined you were three! And there's the sky rolling away forever, into infinity—if "infinity" can be "rolled into"—and the forlorn truth is, that's where you're going too. And the lovely blue isn't even blue, is it? isn't even there, is it? a mere optical illusion, isn't it? no matter what art has urged you to believe.

Early Nature memories. Which it's best not to suppress.

. . . Wading, as a small child, in Tonawanda Creek near our house, and afterward trying to tear off, in a frenzy of terror and revulsion, the sticky fat black bloodsuckers that had attached themselves to my feet, particularly between my toes.

. . . Coming upon a friend's dog in a drainage ditch, dead for several days, evidently the poor creature had been shot by a hunter and left to die, bleeding to death, and we're stupefied with grief and horror but can't resist sliding down to where he's lying on his belly, and we can't resist squatting over him, turning the body over.

20   . . . The raccoon, mad with rabies, frothing at the mouth and tearing at his own belly with his teeth, so that his intestines spill out onto the ground . . . a sight I seem to remember though in fact I did not see. I've been told I did not see.

Consequently, my chronic uneasiness with Nature mysticism; Nature adoration; Nature-as-(moral)-instruction-for-mankind. My doubt that one can, with philosophical validity, address "Nature" as a single coherent noun, anything other than a Platonic, hence discredited, is-ness. My resistance to "Nature writing" as a genre, except when it is brilliantly fictionalized in the service of a writer's individual vision—Thoreau's books and *Journal;* of course, but also, less known in this country, the miniaturist prose poems of Colette (*Flowers and Fruit*) and Ponge (*Taking the Side of Things*)—in which case it becomes yet another, and ingenious, form of storytelling. The subject is *there* only by the grace of the author's language.

Nature has no instructions for mankind except that our poor beleaguered humanist-democratic way of life, our fantasies of the individual's high worth, our sense that the weak, no less than the strong, have a right to survive, are absurd. When Edmund of *King Lear* said excitedly, "Nature, be thou my goddess!" he knew whereof he spoke.

In any case, where *is* Nature, one might (skeptically) inquire. Who has looked upon her/its face and survived?

But isn't this all exaggeration, in the spirit of rhetorical contentiousness? Surely Nature is, for you, as for most reasonably intelligent people, a "perennial" source of beauty, comfort, peace, escape from the delirium of civilized life; a respite from the ego's ever-frantic strategies of self-promotion, as a way of ensuring (at least in fantasy) some small measure of immortality? Surely Nature, as it is understood in the usual slap-dash way, as human, if not dilettante, *experience* (hiking in a national park, jogging on the beach at dawn, even tending, with the usual comical frustrations, a suburban garden), is wonderfully consoling; a place where, when you go there, it has to take you in?—a palimpsest of sorts you choose to read, layer by layer, always with care, always cautiously, in proportion to your psychological strength?

Nature: as in Thoreau's upbeat Transcendentalist mode ("The indescribable in-   25 nocence and beneficence of Nature,—such health, such cheer, they afford forever! and such sympathy have they ever with our race, that all Nature would be affected . . . if any man should ever for a just cause grieve"), and not in Thoreau's grim mode ("Nature is hard to be overcome but she must be overcome").

Another way of saying, not *Nature-in-itself* but *Nature-as-experience.*

The former, Nature-in-itself, is, to allude slantwise to Melville, a blankness ten times blank; the latter is what we commonly, or perhaps always, mean, when we speak of Nature as a noun, a single entity—something of *ours.* Most of the time it's just an activity, a sort of hobby, a weekend, a few days, perhaps a few hours, staring out the window at the mind-dazzling autumn foliage of, say, northern Michigan, being rendered speechless—temporarily—at the sight of Mr. Shasta, the Grand Canyon, Ansel Adams's West. Or Nature writ small, contained in the back yard. Nature filtered through our optical nerves, our "senses," our fiercely romantic expectations. Nature that pleases us because it mirrors our souls, or gives the comforting illusion of doing so.

Nature as the self's (flattering) mirror, but not ever, no, never, Nature-in-itself.

Nature is mouths, or maybe a single mouth. Why glamorize it, romanticize it?—well, yes, but we must, we're writers, poets, mystics (of a sort) aren't we, precisely what else are we to do but glamorize and romanticize and generally exaggerate the significance of anything we focus the white heat of our "creativity" upon? And why not Nature, since it's there, common property, mute, can't talk back, allows us the possibility of transcending the human condition for a while, writing prettily of mountain ranges, white-tailed deer, the purple crocuses outside this very window, the thrumming dazzling "life force" we imagine we all support. Why not?

Nature *is* more than a mouth—it's a dazzling variety of mouths. And it pleases   30 the senses, in any case, as the physicists' chill universe of numbers certainly does not.

Oscar Wilde, on our subject:

Nature is no great mother who has borne us. She is our creation. It is in our brain that she quickens to life. Things are because we see them, and what we see, and how we see it, depends on the Arts that have influenced us. To look at a thing is very different from seeing a thing. . . . At present, people see fogs, not because there are fogs, but because poets and painters have taught them the mysterious loveliness of such effects. There may have been fogs for centuries in London. I dare say there were. But no one saw them. They did not exist until Art had invented them. . . . Yesterday evening Mrs. Arundel insisted on my going to the window and looking at the glorious sky, as she called it. And so I had to look at it. . . . And what was it? It was simply a very second-rate Turner, a Turner of a bad period, with all the painter's worst faults exaggerated and over-emphasized.

"The Decay of Lying," 1889

(If we were to put it to Oscar Wilde that he exaggerates, his reply might well be, "Exaggeration? I don't know the meaning of the word.")

Walden, that most artfully composed of prose fictions, concludes, in the rhapsodic chapter "Spring," with Henry David Thoreau's contemplation of death, decay, and regeneration as it is suggested to him, or to his protagonist, by the spectacle of vultures feeding off carrion. There is a dead horse close by his cabin, and the stench of its decomposition, in certain winds, is daunting. Yet "the assurance it gave me of the strong appetite and inviolable health of Nature was my compensation for this. I love to see that Nature is so rife with life that myriads can be afforded to be sacrificed and suffered to prey upon one another; that tender organizations can be so serenely squashed out of existence like pulp,—tadpoles which herons gobble up, and tortoises and toads run over in the road; and that sometimes it has rained flesh and blood! . . . The impression made on a wise man is that of universal innocence."

Come off it, Henry David. You've grieved these many years for your elder brother, John, who died a ghastly death of lockjaw; you've never wholly recovered from the experience of watching him die. And you know, or must know, that you're fated too to die young of consumption. . . . But this doctrinaire Transcendentalist passage ends *Walden* on just the right note. It's as impersonal, as coolly detached, as the Oversoul itself: a "wise man" filters his emotions through his brain.

Or through his prose.

35   Nietzsche: "We all pretend to ourselves that we are more simpleminded than we are: that is how we get a rest from our fellow men."

> Once out of nature I shall never take
> My bodily form from any natural thing,
> But such a form as Grecian goldsmiths make
> Of hammered gold and gold enamelling
> To keep a drowsy Emperor awake;
> Or set upon a golden bough to sing
> To lords and ladies of Byzantium
> Of what is past, or passing, or to come.

William Butler Yeats, "Sailing to Byzantium"

Yet even the golden bird is a "bodily form [taken from a] natural thing." No, it's impossible to escape!

The writer's resistance to Nature.

Wallace Stevens: "In the presence of extraordinary actuality, consciousness takes the place of imagination."

Once, years ago, in 1972 to be precise, when I seemed to have been another person, related to the person I am now as one is related, tangentially, sometimes embarrassingly, to cousins not seen for decades—once, when we were living in London, and I was very sick, I had a mystical vision. That is, I "had" a "mystical vision"—the heart sinks: such pretension—or something resembling one. A fever dream, let's call it. It impressed me enormously and impresses me still, though I've long since lost the capacity to see it with my mind's eye, or even, I suppose, to believe in it. There is a statute of limitations on "mystical visions," as on romantic love.

I was very sick, and I imagined my life as a thread, a thread of breath, or heartbeat, or pulse, or light—yes, it was light, radiant light; I was burning with fever and I ascended to that plane of serenity that might be mistaken for (or *is*, in fact) Nirvana, where I had a waking dream of uncanny lucidity:

> My body is a tall column of light and heat.
> My body is not "I" but "it."
> My body is not one but many.

My body, which "I" inhabit is inhabited as well by other creatures, unknown to   40
me, imperceptible—the smallest of them mere sparks of light.

My body, which I perceive as substance, is in fact an organization of infinitely complex, overlapping, imbricated structures, radiant light their manifestation, the "body" a tall column of light and blood heat, a temporary agreement among atoms, like a high-rise building with numberless rooms, corridors, corners, elevator shafts, windows. . . . In this fantastical structure the "I" is deluded as to its sovereignty, let alone its autonomy in the (outside) world; the most astonishing secret is that the "I" doesn't exist!—but it behaves as if it does, as if it were one and not many.

In any case, without the "I" the tall column of light and heat would die, and the microscopic life particles would die with it . . . will die with it. The "I," which doesn't exist, is everything.

> But Dr. Johnson is right, the inexpressible need not be expressed.
> And what resistance, finally? There is none.

This morning, an invasion of tiny black ants. One by one they appear, out of nowhere—that's their charm too!—moving single file across the white Parsons table where I am sitting, trying without much success to write a poem. A poem of only three or four lines is what I want, something short, tight, mean; I want it to hurt like a white-hot wire up the nostrils, small and compact and turned in upon itself with the density of a hunk of rock from the planet Jupiter. . . .

But here come the black ants: harbingers, you might say, of spring. One by one by one they appear on the dazzling white table and one by one I kill them with a forefinger, my deft right forefinger, mashing each against the surface of the table and then dropping it into a wastebasket at my side. Idle labor, mesmerizing, effortless, and I'm curious as to how long I can do it—sit here in the brilliant March sunshine killing ants with my right forefinger—how long I, and the ants, can keep it up.

45   After a while I realize that I can do it a long time. And that I've written my poem.

CRITICAL THINKING QUESTION

Describe the author's tone. How do you assess her *ethos* appeal?

WRITING TOPIC

Using selections in this chapter, defend, refute, and/or qualify Oates's argument against nature and nature writers.

N. Scott Momaday (b. 1934)

from *The Way to Rainy Mountain*

Headwaters

Noon in the intermountain plain:
There is scant telling of the marsh—
A log, hollow and weather-stained,
An insect at the mouth, and moss—
Yet waters rise against the roots,
Stand brimming to the stalks. What moves?
What moves on this archaic force
Was wild and welling at the source.

Introduction

A single knoll rises out of the plain in Oklahoma, north and west of the Wichita Range. For my people, the Kiowas, it is an old landmark, and they gave it the name Rainy Mountain. The hardest weather in the world is there. Winter brings blizzards, hot tornadic winds arise in the spring, and in summer the prairie is an anvil's edge. The grass turns brittle and brown, and it cracks beneath your feet. There are green belts along the rivers and creeks, linear groves of hickory and pecan, willow and witch hazel. At a distance in July or August the steaming foliage seems almost to writhe in fire. Great green and yellow grasshoppers are everywhere in the tall grass, popping up like corn to string the flesh, and tortoises crawl about on the red earth, going nowhere in the plenty of time. Loneliness is an aspect of the land. All things in the plain are isolate; there is no confusion of objects in the eye, but *one* hill or *one* tree or *one* man. To look upon that landscape in the early morning, with the sun at your back, is to lose the sense of proportion. Your imagination comes to life, and this, you think, is where Creation was begun.

I returned to Rainy Mountain in July. My grandmother had died in the spring, and I wanted to be at her grave. She had lived to be very old and at last infirm. Her only living daughter was with her when she died, and I was told that in death her face was that of a child.

I like to think of her as a child. When she was born, the Kiowas were living the last great moment of their history. For more than a hundred years they had controlled the open range from the Smoky Hill River to the Red, from the headwaters of the Canadian to the fork of the Arkansas and Cimarron. In alliance with the Comanches, they had ruled the whole of the southern Plains. War was their sacred business, and they were among the finest horsemen the world has ever known. But warfare for the Kiowas was preeminently a matter of disposition rather than of survival, and they never understood the grim, unrelenting advance of the U.S. Cavalry. When at last, divided and ill-provisioned, they were driven onto the Staked Plains in the cold rains of autumn, they fell into panic. In Palo Duro Canyon they abandoned their crucial stores to pillage and had nothing then but their lives. In order to save themselves, they surrendered to the soldiers at Fort Sill and were imprisoned in the old stone corral that now stands as a military museum. My grandmother was spared the humiliation of those high gray walls by eight or ten years, but she must have known from birth the affliction of defeat, the dark brooding of old warriors.

Her name was *Aho*, and she belonged to the last culture to evolve in North America. Her forebears came down from the high country in western Montana nearly three centuries ago. They were a mountain people, a mysterious tribe of hunters whose language has never been positively classified in any major group. In the late seventeenth century they began a long migration to the south and east. It was a journey toward the dawn, and it led to a golden age. Along the way the Kiowas were befriended by the Crows, who gave them the culture and religion of the Plains. They acquired horses, and their ancient nomadic spirit was suddenly free of the ground. They acquired Tai-me, the sacred Sun Dance doll, from that moment the object and symbol of their worship, and so shared in the divinity of the sun. Not least, they acquired the sense of destiny, therefore courage and pride. When they entered upon the southern Plains they had been transformed. No longer were they slaves to the simple necessity of survival; they were a lordly and dangerous society of fighters and thieves, hunters and priests of the sun. According to their origin myth, they entered the world through a hollow log. From one point of view, their migration was the fruit of an old prophecy, for indeed they emerged from a sunless world.

5   Although my grandmother lived out her long life in the shadow of Rainy Mountain, the immense landscape of the continental interior lay like memory in her blood. She could tell of the Crows, whom she had never seen, and of the Black Hills, where she had never been. I wanted to see in reality what she had seen more perfectly in the mind's eye, and traveled fifteen hundred miles to begin my pilgrimage.

Yellowstone, it seemed to me, was the top of the world, a region of deep lakes and dark timber, canyons and waterfalls. But, beautiful as it is, one might have the sense of confinement there. The skyline in all directions is close at hand, the high wall of the woods and deep cleavages of shade. There is a perfect freedom in the mountains, but it belongs to the eagle and the elk, the badger and the bear. The Kiowas reckoned their stature by the distance they could see, and they were bent and blind in the wilderness.

Descending eastward, the highland meadows are a stairway to the plain. In July the inland slope of the Rockies is luxuriant with flax and buckwheat, stonecrop and larkspur. The earth unfolds and the limit of the land recedes. Clusters of trees, and animals grazing far in the distance, cause the vision to reach away and wonder to build upon the mind. The sun follows a longer course in the day, and the sky is immense beyond all comparison. The great billowing clouds that sail upon it are shadows that move upon the grain like water, dividing light. Farther down, in the land of the Crows and Blackfeet, the plain is yellow. Sweet clover takes hold of the hills and bends upon itself to cover and seal the soil. There the Kiowas paused on their way; they had come to the place where they must change their lives. The sun is at home on the plains. Precisely there does it have the certain character of a god. When the Kiowas came to the land of the Crows, they could see the dark lees of the hills at dawn across the Bighorn River, the profusion of light on the grain shelves, the oldest deity ranging after the solstices. Not yet would they veer southward to the caldron of the land that lay below; they must wean their blood from the northern winter and hold the mountains a while longer in their view. They bore Tai-me in procession to the east.

A dark mist lay over the Black Hills, and the land was like iron. At the top of a ridge I caught sight of Devil's Tower upthrust against the gray sky as if in the birth of time the core of the earth had broken through its crust and the motion of the world was begun. There are things in nature that engender an awful quiet in the heart of man; Devil's Tower is one of them. Two centuries ago, because they could not do otherwise, the Kiowas made a legend at the base of the rock. My grandmother said:

> Eight children were there at play, seven sisters and their brother. Suddenly the boy was struck dumb; he trembled and began to run upon his hands and feet. His fingers became claws, and his body was covered with fur. Directly there was a bear where the

boy had been. The sisters were terrified; they ran, and the bear after them. They came to the stump of a great tree, and the tree spoke to them. It bade them climb upon it, and as they did so it began to rise into the air. The bear came to kill them, but they were just beyond its reach. It reared against the tree and scored the bark all around with its claws. The seven sisters were borne into the sky, and they became the stars of the Big Dipper.

From that moment, and so long as the legend lives, the Kiowas have kinsmen in the night sky. Whatever they were in the mountains, they could be no more. However tenuous their well-being, however much they had suffered and would suffer again, they had found a way out of the wilderness.

My grandmother had a reverence for the sun, a holy regard that now is all but gone out of mankind. There was a wariness in her, and an ancient awe. She was a Christian in her later years, but she had come a long way about, and she never forgot her birthright. As a child she had been to the Sun Dances, she had taken part in those annual rites, and by them she had learned the restoration of her people in the presence of Tai-me. She was about seven when the last Kiowa Sun Dance was held in 1887 on the Washita River above Rainy Mountain Creek. The buffalo were gone. In order to consummate the ancient sacrifice—to impale the head of a buffalo bull upon the medicine tree—delegation of old men journeyed into Texas, there to beg and barter for an animal from the Goodnight herd. She was ten when the Kiowas came together for the last time as a living Sun Dance culture. They could find no buffalo; they had to hang an old hide from the sacred tree. Before the dance could begin, a company of soldiers rode out from Fort Sill under orders to disperse the tribe. Forbidden without cause the essential act of their faith, having seen the wild herds slaughtered and left to rot upon the ground, the Kiowas backed away forever from the medicine tree. That was July 20, 1890, at the great bend of the Washita. My grandmother was there. Without bitterness, and for as long as she lived, she bore a vision of deicide.

Now that I can have her only in memory, I see my grandmother in the several postures that were peculiar to her: standing at the wood stove on a winter morning and turning meat in a great iron skillet; sitting at the south window, bent above her beadwork, and afterwards, when her vision failed, looking down for a long time into the fold of her hands; going out upon a cane, very slowly as she did when the weight of age came upon her; praying. I remember her most often at prayer. She made long, rambling prayers out of suffering and hope, having seen many things. I was never sure that I had the right to hear, so exclusive were they of all mere custom and company. The last time I saw her she prayed standing by the side of her bed at night, naked to the waist, the light of a kerosene lamp moving upon her dark skin. Her long, black hair, always drawn and braided in the day, lay upon her shoulders and against her breasts like a shawl. I do not speak Kiowa, and I never understood her prayers, but there was something inherently sad in the sound, some merest hesitation upon the syllables of sorrow. She began in a high and descending pitch, exhausting her breath to silence; then again and again—and always the same intensity of effort, of something that is, and is not, like urgency in the human voice. Transported so in the dancing light among the shadows of her room, she seemed beyond the reach of time. But that was illusion; I think I knew then that I should not see her again.

Houses are like sentinels in the plain, old keepers of the weather watch. There, in a very little while, wood takes on the appearance of great age. All colors wear soon away in the wind and rain, and then the wood is burned gray and the grain appears and the nails turn red with rust. The windowpanes are black and opaque; you imagine there is nothing within, and indeed there are many ghosts, bones given up to the land. They stand here and there against the sky, and you approach them for a longer time than you expect. They belong in the distance; it is their domain.

Once there was a lot of sound in my grandmother's house, a lot of coming and going, feasting and talk. The summers there were full of excitement and reunion. The Kiowas are a summer people; they abide the cold and keep to themselves, but when the season turns and the land becomes warm and vital they cannot hold still; an old love of going returns upon them. The aged visitors who came to my grandmother's house when I was a child were made of lean and leather, and they bore themselves upright. They wore great black hats and bright ample shirts that shook in the wind. They rubbed fat upon their hair and wound their braids with strips of colored cloth. Some of them painted their faces and carried the scars of old and cherished enmities. They were an old council of warlords, come to remind and be reminded of who they were. Their wives and daughters served them well. The women might indulge themselves; gossip was at once the mark and compensation of their servitude. They made loud and elaborate talk among themselves, full of jest and gesture, fright and false alarm. They went abroad in fringed and flowered shawls, bright beadwork and German silver. They were at home in the kitchen, and they prepared meals that were banquets.

There were frequent prayer meetings, and great nocturnal feasts. When I was a child I played with my cousins outside, where the lamplight fell upon the ground and the singing of the old people rose up around us and carried away into the darkness. There were a lot of good things to eat, a lot of laughter and surprise. And afterwards, when the quiet returned, I lay down with my grandmother and could hear the frogs away by the river and feel the motion of the air.

Now there is a funeral silence in the rooms, the endless wake of some final word. The walls have closed in upon my grandmother's house. When I returned to it in mourning, I saw for the first time in my life how small it was. It was late at night, and there was a white moon, nearly full. I sat for a long time on the stone steps by the kitchen door. From there I could see out across the land; I could see the long row of trees by the creek, the low light upon the rolling plains, and the stars of the Big Dipper. Once I looked at the moon and caught sight of a strange thing. A cricket had perched upon the handrail, only a few inches away from me. My line of vision was such that the creature filled the moon like a fossil. It had gone there, I thought, to live and die, for there, of all places, was its small definition made whole and eternal. A warm wind rose up and purled like the longing within me.

15   The next morning I awoke at dawn and went out on the dirt road to Rainy Mountain. It was already hot, and the grasshoppers began to fill the air. Still, it was early in

the morning, and the birds sang out of the shadows. The long yellow grass on the mountain shone in the bright light, and a scissortail hied above the land. There, where it ought to be, at the end of a long and legendary way, was my grandmother's grave. Here and there on the dark stones were ancestral names. Looking back once, I saw the mountain and came away.

WRITING TOPIC

After reading this excerpt, how are you left feeling about Native American cultural heritage? To extend your exploration, you can also read Leslie Marmon Silko's story, "The Man to Send the Rain Clouds," (page 307) and Sherman Alexie's poem, "The Reservation Cab Driver," (page 176).

Janisse Ray (b. 1962)

Forest Beloved

from *Ecology of a Cracker Childhood*

Maybe a vision of the original longleaf pine flatwoods has been endowed to me through genes, because I seem to remember their endlessness. I seem to recollect when these coastal plains were one big, brown-and-tan, daybreak-to-dark longleaf forest. It was a monotony one learned to love, for this is a place that, like a friend, offers multiplied loyally with the passing years. A forest never tells its secrets but reveals them slowly over time, and a longleaf forest is full of secrets.

I know a few of them.

Longleaf pines are long-lived, reaching ages over five hundred years. As trees mature, their heartwood becomes so heavy and thick with resins that saw blades bounce away from it, and if saw teeth manage to enter the grain, they quickly gum up and dull. Heartwood mills a strong everlasting timber the color of ripe amber that earned longleaf the name "heart pine." Parcels of the tree, especially stumps and the area of the heart, are more heavily tamped with resin, and that wood is called "fat lightered," though people use the two names interchangeably, "heart pine" and "fat lightered," and sometimes they say only "fat," as in "Put another piece of that fat on the fire." It is so rich with concentrated, cured sap that it burns like a flare and has long been used, in very small pieces, as kindling; the resinous knots were early lanterns.

In the heart rests both the tree's strength and its weakness. After about ninety years, pines often are infected with red heart, a nonmortal fungus that makes the heartwood softer, more porous, and more flammable, and that often hollows out the pine and makes of it a refuge.

5   You don't think about diversity when you look at longleaf. In a fully functioning longleaf woodland, tree diversity is low. A single species of pine reigns in an open monologue of tall timbers (except on sandhills where occurs an understory of turkey, post, and bluejack oak). The trees grow spaced so far apart in pine savannas, sunshine bathing the ground, that you can see forever; they are as much grassland as forest. The limbs of longleaf pine are gray and scaly and drape as the tree matures, and its needles are very long, up to seventeen inches, like a piano player's fingers, and held upright at ends of the limbs, like a bride holds her bouquet. In 1791, naturalist and explorer William Bartram, in his *Travels,* called the Southern pinelands a "vast forest of the most stately pine trees that can be imagined."

The ground cover, a comforter laid on the land, contains the diversity. *Wiregrass* dominates—it's a flammable, thin-leaved, yellowish bunchgrass that grows calf-high and so thick it resembles a mop head. From this sinewy matrix of wiregrass all manner of forbs, grasses, and low shrubs poke up. At every step, another leaf shape or petal form begs examination and documentation.

Meadow beauty. Liatris. Greeneyes. Summer farewell. Bracken fern. Golden aster. Sandhill blazing star. Goat's rue. Yellow-eyed grass. Purple balduina. Beautiful pawpaw. Pineland hoary pea. Wireleaf dropseed. Hair grass. Little bluestem. Lopside Indian grass. Toothache grass. Britton's beargrass. Gopher apple. Dwarf live oak. Low-bush blueberry. Blackberry. Runner oaks. Splitbeard bluestem. Honeycomb head. Croton. Clammey weed. Dog tongue. Rayless goldenrod. Narrow-leaf sunflower. Black-eyed Susan. Dwarf wax myrtle. New Jersey tea. Inkberry. Dwarf chinquapin. Cooley's meadowrue. Chaffseed. Sandhills milkvetch. Spurge ipecac. Wireweed. Sandwort. Blue lupine. Winter-flowering pixie-moss. Clasping warea. Pigeon wing. Toothed savory. Hairy wild indigo.

One hundred ninety-one species of rare vascular plants are associated with longleaf/wiregrass, 122 of these endangered or threatened.

When John Muir conducted what he termed his "floral pilgrimage" to the Gulf in 1867, somewhere on the fall line between Thomson and Augusta, Georgia, he described "the northern limit of the remarkable longleafed pine, a tree from sixty to seventy feet in height, from twenty to thirty inches in diameter, with leaves ten to fifteen inches long in dense radiant masses at the ends of the naked branches.

10   "The wood is strong, hard and very resinous," he wrote. "It makes excellent ship spars, bridge timbers, and flooring." Later he added, "I thank the Lord with all my heart for his goodness in granting me admission to this magnificent realm."

What thrills me most about longleaf forests is how the pine trees sing. The horizontal limbs of flattened crowns hold the wind as if they are vessels, singing bowls, and air stirs in them like a whistling kettle. I lie in thick grasses covered with sun and listen to the music made there.

This music cannot be heard anywhere else on the earth.

Rustle, whisper, shiver, whinny. Aria, chorus, ballad, chant. Lullaby. In the choirs of the original groves, the music must have resounded for hundreds of miles in a single note of rise and fall, lift and wane, and stirred the red-cockaded woodpeckers nesting in the hearts of these pines, where I also nest, child of soft heart. Now we strain to hear the music; anachronous, it has an edge. It falters, a great tongue chopped in pieces.

Something happens to you in an old-growth forest. At first you are curious to see the tremendous girth and height of the trees, and you sally forth, eager. You start to saunter, then amble, slower and slower, first like a fox and then an armadillo and then a tortoise, until you are trudging at the pace of an earthworm, and then even slower, the pace of a sassafras leaf's turning. The blood begins to languish in your veins, until you think it has turned to sap. You hanker to touch the trees and embrace them and lean your face against their bark, and you do. You smell them. You look up at leaves so high their shapes are beyond focus, into far branches with circumferences as thick as most trees.

Every limb of your body becomes weighted, and you have to prop yourself up. There's this strange current of energy running skyward, like a thousand tiny bells tied to your capillaries, ringing with your heartbeat. You sit and lean against one trunk— it's like leaning against a house or a mountain. The trunk is your spine, the nerve centers reaching into other worlds below ground and above. You stand and press your body into the ancestral and enduring arms wide and your fingers do not touch. You wonder how big the unseen gap.

If you stay in one place too long, you know you'll root.   15

I drink old-growth forest in like water. This is the homeland that built us. Here I walk shoulder to shoulder with history—my history. I am in the presence of something ancient and venerable, perhaps of time itself, its unhurried passing marked by immensity and stolidity, each year purged by fire, cinched by a ring. Here mortality's roving hands grapple with air. I can see my place as human in a natural order more grand whole and functional than I've ever witnessed, and I am humbled, not frightened, by it. Comforted. It is as if a round table springs up in the cathedral of pines and God graciously pulls out a chair for me, and I no longer have to worry about what happens to souls.

CRITICAL THINKING QUESTIONS

1. "Forest Beloved," a chapter from Janisse Ray's book, *Ecology of a Cracker Childhood*, is not overtly an argumentative piece. Even so, it implies an argument. Write out one (or more) *claim*(s) that you can infer for the essay.

2. What type of *evidence* does the implied argument use? Find and write out specific examples of the evidence that supports the claim(s) you identified above.

3. Describe the *tone* of Ray's voice. Point out specific language from the text of her essay that depicts the qualities of tone you identify.

4. Of the three rhetorical appeals—*ethos, pathos, logos*—which one or ones stand out? Point out examples and discuss their appeal.

WRITING TOPIC

Modeling a Master: Model Ray's implied argument and build an argument based on descriptive and sensory details.

- First, think about a place that for you is "beloved," a place in which a part of you is "rooted." As noted in the chapter introduction, this place need not be a place of nature, as Ray describes; it could be an urban setting, such as Clifton describes in "For deLawd." Or use your imagination and create a place that you would consider "beloved."

- Begin by modeling, almost *verbatim*, Ray's opening sentence: "Maybe a vision of _____ has been endowed to me through genes, because I seem to remember _____." Now immerse yourself in seeing, smelling, tasting, touching, hearing this "vision." Write out phrases and sentences with the goal of making this vision come to life in language. For now, do not concern yourself with creating an argument.

- Next, read over what you have written with the goal of creating an argument. Formulate a claim, a personal perspective about this place that you would like to impress upon your readers.

- To follow Ray's model, write your essay as *implied argument;* that is, do not state your claim outright. Use the type of evidence and appeals you identified in responding to question 2 above. All in all, "show, don't tell."

Henry David Thoreau (1817–1862)

Solitude

from *Walden, or Life in the Woods*

This is a delicious evening, when the whole body is one sense, and imbibes delight through every pore. I go and come with a strange liberty in Nature, a part of herself. As I walk along the stony shore of the pond in my shirt-sleeves, though it is cool as well as cloudy and windy, and I see nothing special to attract me, all the elements are unusually congenial to me. The bullfrogs trump to usher in the night, and the note of the whip-poor-will is borne on the rippling wind from over the water. Sympathy with the fluttering alder and poplar leaves almost takes away my breath; yet, like the lake, my serenity is rippled but not ruffled. These small waves raised by the evening wind are as remote from storm as the smooth reflecting surface. Though it is now dark, the wind blows and roars in the wood, the waves still dash, and some creatures lull the rest with their notes. The repose is never complete. The wildest animals do not repose, but seek their prey now; the fox, and skunk, and rabbit, now roam the fields and woods without fear. They are Nature's watchmen—links which connect the days of animated life.

When I return to my house I find that visitors have been there and left their cards, either a bunch of flowers, or a wreath of evergreen, or a name in pencil on a yellow walnut leaf or a chip. They who come rarely to the woods take some little piece of the forest into their hands to play with by the way, which they leave, either intentionally or accidentally. One has peeled a willow wand, woven it into a ring, and dropped it on my table. I could always tell if visitors had called in my absence, either by the bended twigs or grass, or the print of their shoes, and generally of what sex or age or quality they were by some slight trace left, as a flower dropped, or a bunch of grass plucked and thrown away, even as far off as the railroad, half a mile distant, or by the lingering odor of a cigar or pipe. Nay, I was frequently notified of the passage of a traveller along the highway sixty rods off by the scent of his pipe.

There is commonly sufficient space about us. Our horizon is never quite at our elbows. The thick wood is not just at our door, nor the pond, but somewhat is always clearing, familiar and worn by us, appropriated and fenced in some way, and reclaimed from Nature. For what reason have I this vast range and circuit, some square miles of unfrequented forest, for my privacy, abandoned to me by men? My nearest neighbor is a mile distant, and no house is visible from any place but the hill-tops within half a mile of my own. I have my horizon bounded by woods all to myself; a distant view of the railroad where it touches the pond on the one hand, and of the fence which skirts the woodland road on the other. But for the most part it is as solitary where I live as on the prairies. It is as much Asia or Africa as New England. I have, as it were, my own sun and moon and stars, and a little world all to myself. At night there was never a traveller passed my house, or knocked at my door, more than if I were the first or last man; unless it were in the spring, when at long intervals some came from the village to fish for pouts—they plainly fished much more in the Walden Pond of their own natures, and baited their hooks with darkness—but they soon retreated, usually with light baskets, and left "the world to darkness and to me," and the black kernel of the night was never profaned by any human neighborhood. I believe that men are generally still a little afraid of the dark, though the witches are all hung, and Christianity and candles have been introduced.

Yet I experienced sometimes that the most sweet and tender, the most innocent and encouraging society may be found in any natural object, even for the poor misanthrope and most melancholy man. There can be no very black melancholy to him who lives in the midst of nature and has his senses still. There was never yet such a storm but it was Æolian music to a healthy and innocent ear. Nothing can rightly compel a simple and brave man to a vulgar sadness. While I enjoy the friendship of the seasons I trust that nothing can make life a burden to me. The gentle rain which waters my beans and keeps me in the house today is not drear and melancholy, but good for me too. Though it prevents my hoeing them, it is of far more worth than my hoeing. If it should continue so long as to cause the seeds to rot in the ground and destroy the potatoes in the low lands, it would still be good for the grass on the uplands, and, being good for the grass, it would be good for me. Sometimes, when I compare myself with other men, it seems as if I were more favored by the gods than they, beyond any deserts that I am conscious of; as if I had a warrant and surety at their hands which my fellows have not, and were especially guided and guarded. I do not flatter myself, but if it be possible they flatter me. I have never felt lonesome, or in the least oppressed by a sense of solitude, but once, and that was a few weeks after I came to the woods, when, for an hour, I doubted if the near neighborhood of man was not essential to a serene and healthy life. To be alone was something unpleasant. But I was at the same time conscious of a slight insanity in my mood, and seemed to foresee my recovery. In the midst of a gentle rain while these thoughts prevailed, I was suddenly sensible of such sweet and beneficent society in Nature, in the very pattering of the drops, and in every sound and sight around my house, an infinite and unaccountable friendliness all at once like an atmosphere sustaining me, as made the fancied advantages of human neighborhood insignificant, and I have never thought of them since. Every little pine needle expanded and swelled with sympathy and befriended me. I was so distinctly made aware of the presence of something kindred to me, even in scenes which we are accustomed to call wild and dreary, and also that the nearest of blood to me and humanest was not a person nor a villager, that I thought no place could ever be strange to me again.

> Mourning untimely consumes the sad;
> Few are their days in the land of the living,
> Beautiful daughter of Toscar.

5   Some of my pleasantest hours were during the long rain-storms in the spring or fall, which confined me to the house for the afternoon as well as the forenoon, soothed by their ceaseless roar and pelting; when an early twilight ushered in a long evening in which many thoughts had time to take root and unfold themselves. In those driving northeast rains which tried the village houses so, when the maids stood ready with mop and pail in front entries to keep the deluge out, I sat behind my door in my little house, which was all entry, and thoroughly enjoyed its protection. In one heavy thunder-shower the lightning struck a large pitch pine across the pond, making a very conspicuous and perfectly regular spiral groove from top to bottom, an inch or more deep, and four or five inches wide, as you would groove a walking-stick. I passed it again the other day, and was struck with awe on looking up and beholding that mark, now more distinct than ever, where a terrific and resistless bolt came down out of the harmless sky eight years ago. Men frequently say to me, "I should think you would feel lonesome down there, and want to be nearer to folks, rainy and snowy days and nights especially." I am tempted to reply to such—This whole earth which we inhabit is but a point in space. How far apart, think you, dwell the two most distant inhabitants of yonder star, the breadth of whose disk cannot be appreciated by our instruments? Why should I feel lonely? is not our planet in the Milky Way? This which you put

seems to me not to be the most important question. What sort of space is that which separates a man from his fellows and makes him solitary? I have found that no exertion of the legs can bring two minds much nearer to one another. What do we want most to dwell near to? Not to many men surely, the depot, the post-office, the barroom, the meeting-house, the school-house, the grocery, Beacon Hill, or the Five Points, where men most congregate, but to the perennial source of our life, whence in all our experience we have found that to issue, as the willow stands near the water and sends out its roots in that direction. This will vary with different natures, but this is the place where a wise man will dig his cellar. . . . I one evening overtook one of my towns-men, who has accumulated what is called "a handsome property"—though I never got a *fair* view of it—on the Walden road, driving a pair of cattle to market, who inquired of me how I could bring my mind to give up so many of the comforts of life. I answered that I was very sure I liked it passably well; I was not joking. And so I went home to my bed, and left him to pick his way through the darkness and the mud to Brighton—or Bright-town—which place he would reach some time in the morning.

Any prospect of awakening or coming to life to a dead man makes indifferent all times and places. The place where that may occur is always the same, and indescribably pleasant to all our senses. For the most part we allow only outlying and transient circumstances to make our occasions. They are, in fact, the cause of our distraction. Nearest to all things is that power which fashions their being. *Next* to us the grandest laws are continually being executed. *Next* to us is not the workman whom we have hired, with whom we love so well to talk, but the workman whose work we are.

"How vast and profound is the influence of the subtile powers of Heaven and of Earth!"

"We seek to perceive them, and we do not see them; we seek to hear them, and we do not hear them; identified with the substance of things, they cannot be separated from them."

"They cause that in all the universe men purify and sanctify their hearts, and clothe themselves in their holiday garments to offer sacrifices and oblations to their ancestors. It is an ocean of subtile intelligences. They are everywhere, above us, on our left, on our right; they environ us on all sides."

We are the subjects of an experiment which is not a little interesting to me. Can 10 we not do without the society of our gossips a little while under these circumstances— have our own thoughts to cheer us? Confucius says truly, "Virtue does not remain as an abandoned orphan; it must of necessity have neighbors."

With thinking we may be beside ourselves in a sane sense. By a conscious effort of the mind we can stand aloof from actions and their consequences; and all things, good and bad, go by us like a torrent. We are not wholly involved in Nature. I may be either the driftwood in the stream, or Indra in the sky looking down on it. I *may* be affected by a theatrical exhibition; on the other hand, I *may not* be affected by an actual event which appears to concern me much more. I only know myself as a human entity; the scene, so to speak, of thoughts and affections; and am sensible of a certain doubleness by which I can stand as remote from myself as from another. However intense my experience, I am conscious of the presence and criticism of a part of me, which, as it were, is not a part of me, but spectator, sharing no experience, but taking note of it, and that is no more I than it is you. When the play, it may be the tragedy, of life is over, the spectator goes his way. It was a kind of fiction, a work of the imagination only, so far as he was concerned. This doubleness may easily make us poor neighbors and friends sometimes.

I find it wholesome to be alone the greater part of the time. To be in company, even with the best, is soon wearisome and dissipating. I love to be alone. I never found the companion that was so companionable as solitude. We are for the most part more lonely when we go abroad among men than when we stay in our chambers. A man thinking or working is always alone, let him be where he will. Solitude is not measured by the miles of space that intervene between a man and his fellows. The really diligent student in one of the crowded hives of Cambridge College is as solitary as a dervis in the desert. The farmer can work alone in the field or the woods all day, hoeing or chopping, and not feel lonesome, because he is employed; but when he comes home at night he cannot sit down in a room alone, at the mercy of his thoughts, but must be where he can "see the folks," and recreate, and, as he thinks, remunerate himself for his day's solitude; and hence he wonders how the student can sit alone in the house all night and most of the day without ennui and "the blues"; but he does not realize that the student, though in the house, is still at work in *his* field, and chopping in *his* woods, as the farmer in his, and in turn seeks the same recreation and society that the latter does, though it may be a more condensed form of it.

Society is commonly too cheap. We meet at very short intervals, not having had time to acquire any new value for each other. We meet at meals three times a day, and give each other a new taste of that old musty cheese that we are. We have had to agree on a certain set of rules, called etiquette and politeness, to make this frequent meeting tolerable and that we need not come to open war. We meet at the post-office, and at the sociable, and about the fireside every night; we live thick and are in each other's way, and stumble over one another, and I think that we thus lose some respect for one another. Certainly less frequency would suffice for all important and hearty communications. Consider the girls in a factory—never alone, hardly in their dreams. It would be better if there were but one inhabitant to a square mile, as where I live. The value of a man is not in his skin, that we should touch him.

I have heard of a man lost in the woods and dying of famine and exhaustion at the foot of a tree, whose loneliness was relieved by the grotesque visions with which, owing to bodily weakness, his diseased imagination surrounded him, and which he believed to be real. So also, owing to bodily and mental health and strength, we may be continually cheered by a like but more normal and natural society, and come to know that we are never alone.

15   I have a great deal of company in my house; especially in the morning, when nobody calls. Let me suggest a few comparisons, that some one may convey an idea of my situation. I am no more lonely than the loon in the pond that laughs so loud, or than Walden Pond itself. What company has that lonely lake, I pray? And yet it has not the blue devils, but the blue angels in it, in the azure tint of its waters. The sun is

alone, except in thick weather, when there sometimes appear to be two, but one is a mock sun. God is alone—but the devil, he is far from being alone; he sees a great deal of company; he is legion. I am no more lonely than a single mullein or dandelion in a pasture, or a bean leaf, or sorrel, or a horse-fly, or a humblebee. I am no more lonely than the Mill Brook, or a weathercock, or the north star, or the southwind, or an April shower, or a January thaw, or the first spider in a new house.

I have occasional visits in the long winter evenings, when the snow falls fast and the wind howls in the wood, from an old settler and original proprietor, who is reported to have dug Walden Pond, and stoned it, and fringed it with pine woods; who tells me stories of old time and of new eternity; and between us we manage to pass a cheerful evening with social mirth and pleasant views of things, even without apples or cider—a most wise and humorous friend, whom I love much, who keeps himself more secret than ever did Goffe or Whalley; and though he is thought to be dead, none can show where he is buried. An elderly dame, too, dwells in my neighborhood, invisible to most persons, in whose odorous herb garden I love to stroll sometimes, gathering simples and listening to her fables; for she has a genius of unequalled fertility, and her memory runs back farther than mythology, and she can tell me the original of every fable, and on what fact every one is founded, for the incidents occurred when she was young. A ruddy and lusty old dame, who delights in all weathers and seasons, and is likely to outlive all her children yet.

The indescribable innocence and beneficence of Nature—of sun and wind and rain, of summer and winter—such health, such cheer, they afford forever! and such sympathy have they ever with our race, that all Nature would be affected, and the sun's brightness fade, and the winds would sigh humanely, and the clouds rain tears, and the woods shed their leaves and put on mourning in midsummer, if any man should ever for a just cause grieve. Shall I not have intelligence with the earth? Am I not partly leaves and vegetable mould myself?

What is the pill which will keep us well, serene, contented? Not my or thy great-grandfather's, but our great-grandmother Nature's universal, vegetable, botanic medicines, by which she has kept herself young always, outlived so many old Parrs in her day, and fed her health with their decaying fatness. For my panacea, instead of one of those quack vials of a mixture dipped from Acheron and the Dead Sea, which come out of those long shallow black-schooner looking wagons which we sometimes see made to carry bottles, let me have a draught of undiluted morning air. Morning air! If men will not drink of this at the fountainhead of the day, why, then, we must even bottle up some and sell it in the shops, for the benefit of those who have lost their subscription ticket to morning time in this world. But remember, it will not keep quite till noonday even in the coolest cellar, but drive out the stopples long ere that and follow westward the steps of Aurora. I am no worshipper of Hygeia, who was the daughter of that old herb-doctor Æsculapius, and who is represented on monuments holding a serpent in one hand, and in the other a cup out of which the serpent sometimes drinks; but rather of Hebe, cup-bearer to Jupiter, who was the daughter of Juno and wild lettuce, and who had the power of restoring gods and men to the vigor of youth. She was probably the only thoroughly sound-conditioned, healthy, and robust young lady that ever walked the globe, and wherever she came it was spring.

CRITICAL THINKING QUESTION

"I find it wholesome to be alone the greater part of the time," Thoreau declares. List some reasons the author provides in arguing for the virtue of solitude. How does Nature contribute to his argument?

WRITING TOPICS

1. Write an essay that defends, refutes, and/or qualifies Thoreau's argument for solitude.
2. Read Oates's essay, "Against Nature" (page 376). Acting as Thoreau's spokesperson, write a response to Oates's critique.

CHAPTER ACTIVITIES
AND TOPICS FOR WRITING ARGUMENTS

1. What makes a place a home? How does an individual form a connection with a geographic location or physical environment that marks this place as his or her home? Also, why do some places, despite years of one's residence, never feel like a home? Based on your reading of several literature selections and your own experience and observations, write a personal perspective argument about place and home (literature suggestions: Bass's "Antlers" and Clifton's "For deLawd").

2. a. What is the value of a tree? Read several literature selections to explore various perspectives on the issue question, and write a Rogerian argument that addresses the issue (literature suggestions: Forché's "The Dulcimer Maker," Frost's "A Young Birch," Oliver's "A Black Walnut Tree," Ray's "Forest Beloved").

   b. For this research-based writing project, examine land management policies involving America's woodlands and national forests. Wildfires, especially in Florida and Western regions, regularly ravage thousands of acres of woodland and often threaten, if not also destroy, human habitations. National Interagency Coordination Center data, compiled on year-to-date large fires (January to May, 2000–2006), show a dramatic increase in wildfire activity: the average number of fires for the seven-year period was 29,884, compared with 39,350 fires for 2006. Certainly, draught conditions are significant factors in this increase. However, foresters and conservationists also point their fingers at conflicting land management policies—from the extreme of clear-cutting, on the one hand, to the extreme of "zero-cutting," on the other hand. Meanwhile, foresters, commercial enterprises, and conservation groups are debating how policies can be designed to promote what some have called "compatible forestry." Some groups advocate "prescribed burns" as a means of controlling rampant wildfires and sustaining ecosystems, while others question the logic of setting a fire to control fire. Do some research on the issue of forest management and write a claim of policy Rogerian argument.

3. In her book, *The Perfect Vehicle: What It Is About Motorcycles*, Melissa Holbrook Pierson says,

   Our aim . . . it seems [is] to accumulate goods. At the end of this metaphoric road stands the non-metaphoric Kmart, glistening like Oz and filled to the rafters with a hundred cheap mementos of wildflowers, in forms of candle, air freshener, sachet, cologne, bath bead, potpourri, and incense stick. In its prior life, of course, the ground under the big store bloomed with wildflowers.[3]

---

[3]Melissa Holbrook Pierson, *The Perfect Vehicle: What It Is about Motorcycles* (New York: W. W. Norton, 1997), p. 153.

What is our personal responsibility toward the natural world, toward what we term our *natural resources?* What power do we have to influence events? Of course, the word *resources* implies something to be used, yet how far do we go? Read about the conflicts between jobs and the environment that have been prominent in this country. Does the need to preserve age-old redwood forests outweigh loggers' need for paychecks in California? Are fish in the Gulf of Mexico more important than jobs for the commercial fishermen living along that coast? Conflicts such as these are usually settled in the courts. Read about one of these or a similar conflict, and, as you read, create a list of emotionally charged *diction* used by both sides. (literature suggestions: Le Guin's "May's Lion," Abbey's "Eco-Defense," Dillard's "The Present," Huxley's "Time and the Machine")

4. What value do zoos serve? Today's zoos do not enclose animals in small cages such as Rainer Maria Rilke's poem, "The Panther," describes. Animals are provided with habitats, modeled after their native habitats. From the zoo visitor's perspective, the animals appear to roam freely. Yet some animal welfare groups claim that it is unethical to remove an animal from its native habitat. Regardless of the aesthetic qualities of the zoo's environment, the animal is still captive—denied its right to freedom. Also, zoo critics contend that efforts to breed animals in captivity are both costly and unsuccessful. In contrast, advocates argue that zoos provide opportunities for important research that contributes to species' viability. Moreover, zoos bring the general public in direct contact with wild and exotic animals, therefore, fostering public support for preserving endangered species. Conduct research on the economic, ethical, and scientific issues in the debate over zoos. Based on some readings in this chapter and your research findings, write a *claim of value* argument about zoos (literature suggestions: Bass's "Antlers," Jewett's "A White Heron," Le Guin's "May's Lion," Rilke's "The Panther").

5. What efforts should we make to maintain wild animal populations? In making his argument for the preservation of wolves in "Thinking Like a Mountain," Aldo Leopold concludes with a reference to "Thoreau's dictum: In wildness is the salvation of the world." Two symbols of "wildness," popularized by environmental groups, have been the wolf and the grizzly, species whose numbers were greatly diminished throughout the twentieth century. Ongoing efforts to restore wolf populations in the lower forty-eight states have been highly controversial. More recently, proposed experimental programs to restore grizzly populations in some wilderness areas in the western mountain states have engendered an emotional debate. Research the issue of wolf and/or grizzly habitat restoration efforts. Based on your research, take a position on the issue and defend it.

6. Unlike Thoreau in the mid-nineteenth century, most of us cannot walk out our back doors and into a wilderness area, yet many of us continue to seek out some kind of wilderness experience. Meanwhile, the millions of visitors to national parks and wilderness areas "run the risk of loving them to death," according to a

Nature Conservancy article.[4] Granted, the national parks and nature preserves exist for the enjoyment of their human visitors; after all, public funding (tax revenue) contributes to their maintenance. But the value of these parks and preserves resides in their integrity as natural resources—in their wildness and pristine qualities. Meanwhile, biologists, park officials, and conservation groups are struggling to balance the demands of the human population and the demands of resource protection.

Research this issue area and write a claim of policy argument. You probably will need to narrow this issue. For example, you can research management policies at a specific national park, perhaps one you have visited; or you can research the guidelines or restrictions on the use of automobiles, helicopters, horses, or snowmobiles in national forests or parks (related literature selections: Houston's "A Blizzard under Blue Sky," Snyder's "The Call of the Wild," Emerson's excerpt from *Nature*).

COLLABORATION ACTIVITY: CREATING A ROGERIAN ARGUMENT

For this activity, you will work in teams of four to research, write, and present a Rogerian argument on a contemporary issue that has emerged from your exploration of readings in this chapter. The Writing Topics following many of the selections can help you identify an issue. For a discussion of the Rogerian Argument and a suggested organizational approach to the assignment, please see Chapter Three.

Following are guidelines for this collaboration activity:

- Identify an *issue*.
- Divide the research/writing responsibilities as follows:
  - Student one: introduction section
  - Student two: body section, affirmative position
  - Student three: body section, opposing position
  - Student four: conclusion, summation and middle-ground position

Following are characteristics of effective collaboration. The team member should:

- *Contribute* by collecting information related to the issue;
- *Take responsibility* by completing his or her assigned work on time;
- *Engage* with team members by listening to and considering other viewpoints.

Sample Issue: Energy Exploration

Over a half century ago, Aldo Leopold noted that "conservation is a state of harmony between men and nature."[5] Since the national tragedy of the September 11, 2001, terrorist attacks and the ongoing Iraq War, debate over energy resources—how to protect our nation from terrorists, sustain a robust economy, and yet preserve

---

[4]"Whose Woods These Are?" *Nature Conservancy* (July/Aug 1998): 3.
[5]qtd. in Steven J. McCormick, "Building on a Tradition of Innovation," *Nature Conservancy* (fall 2003): 4.

fragile ecosystems—has taken a central position on the national forum. In 2005, by a narrow vote, Congress voted to open previously protected areas in the Arctic National Wildlife Refuge to oil exploration; Congress also has been considering loosening restrictions on drilling in offshore areas of the Southwest Gulf region. Meanwhile, coal is an abundant natural resource, yet extracting and burning this material also raises environmental and health concerns. What energy policies should be promoted to ensure that the nation's energy needs are met?

Literature suggestions: "New World" and "A Short History of America" in Chapter One; "Heartland" and "Chicago" in Chapter Five; "Apostrophe to Man" in Chapter Seven.

MAKING CONNECTIONS

Chapter Four: Nature and Place

The ethics of hunting
Bass, "Antlers"; Cooper, "The Slaughter of the Pigeons"; Jewett, "A White Heron"; Warren, from *Audubon;* Leopold, "Thinking Like a Mountain"

The individual and nature
London, "To Build a Fire"; Welty, "A Worn Path"; Whitman, *Song of Myself, 14* and *31;* Emerson, from *Nature;* Klinkenborg, "At the Edge of the Visible"

Place and identity
Clifton, "For deLawd"; Hogan, "Heartland"; Momaday, "The Way to Rainy Mountain"; Ray, "Forest Beloved"

Humans and animals
Le Guin, "May's Lion"; Dickey, "Deer Among Cattle"; Rilke, "The Panther"; Stafford, "Traveling through the Dark"; Goodall, "A Plea for the Chimpanzees"

Wilderness and environmental policy
Snyder, "The Call of the Wild"; Abbey, "Eco-Defense"; Carson, "The Obligation to Endure"; Leopold, "Thinking Like a Mountain"

Nature as therapy
Houston, "A Blizzard under Blue Sky"; Roethke, "Meditation at Oyster River"; Dillard, "The Present"; Thoreau, "Solitude"; Oates (as "devil's advocate"), "Against Nature"

Cross-Chapter Connections

The value of urban spaces
Momaday, "New World" and Crumb, "A Short History of America" (Chapter One); Setterberg, "The Usual Stuff: (Chapter Four); Woolf, "Kew Gardens," Hogan, "Heartland," Sandburg, "Chicago" (Chapter Five); Brooks, "The Boy Died in My Alley" (Chapter Seven)

ᴧᴧ CHAPTER 6 ᴧᴧ

Family and Identity

"Mickey and Minnie sitting in a tree, k-i-s-s-i-n-g; first comes love, then comes marriage, then comes baby in the baby carriage." And then the house, the car, the dog, and we have The Family. This schoolyard jingle taunts the young girl or boy who dares to smile at a child of the opposite sex. Though childhood play, it reflects a long-standing cultural ideal: You fall in love, you get married, you have children . . . you "live happily ever after." Of course, the well-documented reality is that many couples neither live happily together nor ever after. In fact, couples are choosing cohabitation without marriage and, increasingly, without children. Meanwhile, a parent may be pushing the baby in the stroller without a partner or, perhaps, with a partner of the same sex. Some applaud these variations on The Family; after all, they argue, a loving family is a healthy one, and neither laws nor social custom should attempt to dictate the bonds of love. Equally passionate are those who decry these variations. They claim that the collapse of the traditional (heterosexual, two-parent) family structure has eroded "family values," instigated a contagion of social illnesses, and fed into a moral decrepitude that threatens to bring down the country. Clearly, no single definition of The Family can be agreed upon; however, most of us do agree upon the primary importance of family in our individual lives and, as adults, aspire to create a family of our own—however different that family may be.

Looking back to the first half of the twentieth century, we see the model of the family evolve from the extended family to the nuclear family as people abandoned the working farm and moved to the city. By the end of the twentieth century, however, extended families were reemerging, although in an updated guise from earlier times: divorced parents were remarrying and creating families made up of step-siblings and step-parents. And crossing into the twenty-first century, we witness more and more young adults choosing to postpone (or reject) marriage and children. As an alternative to the traditional family centered on a husband and wife, they are forging families of friends, peer groups of individuals, who may or may not share living space, but who do share emotional intimacies and traditional family rituals and holidays such as Thanksgiving and birthday celebrations.

Not surprisingly, TV programs, notably sitcoms, reflect the metamorphosis of the family. In the early 1960s, shows such as *Father Knows Best* and *Leave It to Beaver* featured the then, so-called ideal family: the wise, bread-winner Dad (always smiling); the docile, homemaker Mom (also smiling); and a pair of mischievous but dutiful children. The post–civil rights movement and Vietnam War generation of the 1970s, however, added the image of the perfect family of the 60s sitcom to its list of grievances. In response, TV unleashed sitcoms featuring the likes of the hapless and gratingly flawed Archie Bunker family. In place of ingratiating smiles and niceties, they berated each other relentlessly. Also, in keeping with the women's equal rights movement of the 1970s, *The Mary Tyler Moore Show* validated the presence of women in the working world; women had moved out of the home and into the workplace. Then in the 1980s with the inauguration of Ronald Reagan as president, the pendulum of family sentiment swung back toward the right: Mom and Dad and children, the nuclear family, again took center stage on the TV sitcom (*Family Ties*), although with a dose of diversity on *The Cosby Show.* Even though the Cosby family seemed to represent a feel-good return to the "perfect" family of the 60s, the show featured an African-American (upper-middle-class) family and the new Superwoman, Clair Huxtable, a loving and nurturing mom and wife who also was a well-respected, successful attorney. On the other hand, shows such as *Roseanne* and *The Simpsons* featured working-class families, a refreshing antidote to the near-perfect Cosby family. And in the 1990s, TV sitcoms introduced the hyperextended family of friends, adults forming families with their peers, in shows such as *Seinfeld* and *Friends.* Even though the friends in Monica's apartment don't live together, they drop in on each other spontaneously and regularly, somewhat like college students in a dormitory. Living independently, these characters, however, are sustained by an emotional interdependency—a sort of family "on call." More recently, bringing homosexuality out of the closet and onto major network TV, *Will & Grace* features two best friends who share living quarters and emotional intimacy but have distinctly different sexual orientations.

Suggesting that TV sitcoms depicting single adult lifestyles reflect reality, one newspaper declared, "Married couples are the new endangered species."[1] Meanwhile, recent data show a reversal in the rising divorce rate of the 1990s: Divorce rates have fallen below the 50 percent marker—perhaps, in part, due to young adults' choosing to delay the nuptial proclamation, "till death do us part." Regardless of statistics, every June, the fashion industry's self-proclaimed wedding month, advertisers saturate the market with images of the perfect wedding. Clearly these advertisers are not playing to an unreceptive audience. The ideal of marriage and family seems to reign supreme, in our dreams if not in reality.

Looking to the past and to our future, how do we assess the "state" of the family? And how does each of us shape our personal identity as an individual in response to

---

[1]Martha Irvine, "Married Couples Are the New Endangered Species," *Tallahassee Democrat,* November 25, 1999, sec. B, p. 6.

our experiences and our attitudes about family? As suggested earlier, popular culture, in particular, the TV sitcom, tends to reflect current trends or fads. Authors of literature, however, for the most part, are less beholden to commercial interests than TV producers; they need not please a projected audience—or keep up with Nielsen ratings.

Rather than reinforcing socially popular attitudes and assumptions, the stories, poems, plays, and essays in this chapter are more likely to shake up our sensibilities and provoke us to question assumptions and examine underlying values and beliefs. For example, in the poem, "Cinderella," Anne Sexton playfully lampoons the happily-ever-after myth. Kate Chopin's story, "The Storm," dares to suggest that a wife's moment of spontaneous infidelity may rejuvenate rather than wreck her marriage. Although statistics suggest that divorce is fairly commonplace, John Updike's story, "Separating," reminds us that the emotional reality of a marital breakup still stuns its family members. Meanwhile, Harvey Fierstein's play, *On Tidy Endings*, brings to center stage a homosexual relationship and family dynamics. One of the play's characters, Marion, says she married right after college and "settled down for a nice quiet life of Kids and Careers. . . . Talk about life's little surprises!" Reading Fierstein's play, we hear the voices of individuals who, despite differences in sexual preferences, share a basic human need for love.

In our search for answers to the question, who am I?, we can look to our parents and grandparents and ask, who were they? A number of authors' works present the perspective of the adult looking back on his or her parents or forebears to ponder the identity question. In a retrospective poem, "I Go Back to May, 1937," Sharon Olds's speaker arrives at a somewhat grim conclusion; however, in "Mothers," Nikki Giovanni's reflections lead her to celebrate the bond among generations. Essayist Scott Russell Sanders focuses on his father's role in shaping his values and personal identity. And Pauli Murray's chapter from her memoir about growing up in the first part of the twentieth century testifies to the value of family stories and the protective bond of the extended family.

Seeking love and approval, we may "look homeward" to our family. And what if the family roots have been stretched across national borders or halfway around the globe? When children grow up in a nation that is not their parents' homeland, what are the effects on the family members' identities and their sense of home? In "Safe," Cherylene Lee shows how Chinese immigrants endure and prevail as a family living in San Francisco. Describing her parents' perspective, Lee's narrator says, "Only the family home felt safe to them and this is what they tried to impart on both my brother and me." Crossing cultural and ethnic lines is the assumption that the "family home" provides a refuge, a safe haven from the dangers beyond its (locked) doors. Several works in this chapter prompt us to ask if this notion is based on reality or wishful thinking.

In the story, "A Red Sweater," Fae Myenne Ng's narrator says, "Family exists only because somebody has a story, and knowing that story connects us to a history." As we read the works that follow, we may ask ourselves what story we have to tell and how it "connects us to a history" that informs our identity.

PREWRITING AND DISCUSSION

1. Write about your concept of family. Describe specific experiences, observations, or ideas that inform your definition.

2. Describe your role as a member of a family. How is your sense of self-identity defined by your experiences with family? What personal values do you attribute directly to your experience with family?

FICTION

∧∧∧

Kate Chopin (1851–1904)
The Storm

I

The leaves were so still that even Bibi thought it was going to rain. Bobinôt, who was accustomed to converse on terms of perfect equality with his little son, called the child's attention to certain sombre clouds that were rolling with sinister intention from the west, accompanied by a sullen, threatening roar. They were at Friedheimer's store and decided to remain there till the storm had passed. They sat within the door on two empty kegs. Bibi was four years old and looked very wise.

"Mama'll be 'fraid, yes," he suggested with blinking eyes.

"She'll shut the house. Maybe she got Sylvie helpin' her this evening," Bobinôt responded reassuringly.

"No; she ent got Sylvie. Sylvie was helpin' her yistiday," piped Bibi.

Bobinôt arose and going across to the counter purchased a can of shrimps, of 5
which Calixta was very fond. Then he returned to his perch on the keg and sat stolidly holding the can of shrimps while the storm burst. It shook the wooden store and seemed to be ripping great furrows in the distant field. Bibi laid his little hand on his father's knee and was not afraid.

II

Calixta, at home, felt no uneasiness for their safety. She sat at a side window sewing furiously on a sewing machine. She was greatly occupied and did not notice the approaching storm. But she felt very warm and often stopped to mop her face on which the perspiration gathered in beads. She unfastened her white sacque at the throat. It began to grow dark, and suddenly realizing the situation she got up hurriedly and went about closing windows and doors.

Out on the small front gallery she had hung Bobinôt's Sunday clothes to air and she hastened out to gather them before the rain fell. As she stepped outside, Alcée Laballière rode in at the gate. She had not seen him very often since her marriage, and never alone. She stood there with Bobinôt's coat in her hands, and the big rain drops began to fall. Alcée rode his horse under the shelter of a side projection where the chickens had huddled and there were plows and a harrow piled up in the corner.

"May I come and wait on your gallery till the storm is over, Calixta?" he asked.

"Come 'long in, M'sieur Alcée."

10   His voice and her own startled her as if from a trance, and she seized Bobinôt's vest. Alcée, mounting to the porch, grabbed the trousers and snatched Bibi's braided jacket that was about to be carried away by a sudden gust of wind. He expressed an intention to remain outside, but it was soon apparent that he might as well have been out in the open: the water beat in upon the boards in driving sheets, and he went inside, closing the door after him. It was even necessary to put something beneath the door to keep the water out.

"My! what a rain! It's good two years since it rain' like that," exclaimed Calixta as she rolled up a piece of bagging and Alcée helped her to thrust it beneath the crack.

She was a little fuller of figure than five years before when she married; but she had lost nothing of her vivacity. Her blue eyes still retained their melting quality; and her yellow hair, dishevelled by the wind and rain, kinked more stubbornly than ever about her ears and temples.

The rain beat upon the low, shingled roof with a force and clatter that threatened to break an entrance and deluge them there. They were in the dining room—the sitting room—the general utility room. Adjoining was her bed room, with Bibi's couch along side her own. The door stood open, and the room with its white, monumental bed, its closed shutters, looked dim and mysterious.

Alcée flung himself into a rocker and Calixta nervously began to gather up from the floor the lengths of a cotton sheet which she had been sewing.

15   "If this keeps up, *Dieu sait* if the levees goin' to stan' it!" she exclaimed.

"What have you got to do with the levees?"

"I got enough to do! An' there's Bobinôt with Bibi out in that storm—if he only didn' left Friedheimer's!"

"Let us hope, Calixta, that Bobinôt's got sense enough to come in out of a cyclone."

She went and stood at the window with a greatly disturbed look on her face. She wiped the frame that was clouded with moisture. It was stiflingly hot. Alcée got up and joined her at the window, looking over her shoulder. The rain was coming down in sheets obscuring the view of far-off cabins and enveloping the distant wood in a gray mist. The playing of the lighting was incessant. A bolt struck a tall chinaberry tree at the edge of the field. It filled all visible space with a blinding glare and the crash seemed to invade the very boards they stood upon.

20   Calixta put her hands to her eyes, and with a cry, staggered backward. Alcée's arm encircled her, and for an instant he drew her close and spasmodically to him.

"*Bonté!*" she cried, releasing herself from his encircling arm and retreating from the window, "the house'll go next! If I only knew w'ere Bibi was!" She would not compose herself; she would not be seated. Alcée clasped her shoulders and looked into her face. The contact of her warm, palpitating body when he had unthinkingly drawn her into his arms, had aroused all the old-time infatuation and desire for her flesh.

"Calixta," he said, "don't be frightened. Nothing can happen. The house is too low to be struck, with so many tall trees standing about. There! aren't you going to be quiet? say, aren't you?" He pushed her hair back from her face that was warm and steaming. Her lips were as red and moist as pomegranate seed. Her white neck and a glimpse of her full, firm bosom disturbed him powerfully. As she glanced up at him the fear in her liquid blue eyes had given place to a drowsy gleam that unconsciously betrayed a sensuous desire. He looked down into her eyes and there was nothing for him to do but to gather her lips in a kiss. It reminded him of Assumption.

"Do you remember—in Assumption, Calixta?" he asked in a low voice broken by passion. Oh! she remembered; for in Assumption he had kissed her and kissed and kissed her; until his senses would well nigh fail, and to save her he would resort to a desperate flight. If she was not an immaculate dove in those days, she was still inviolate; a passionate creature whose very defenselessness had made her defense, against which his honor forbade him to prevail. Now—well, now—her lips seemed in a manner free to be tasted, as well as her round, white throat and her whiter breasts.

They did not heed the crashing torrents, and the roar of the elements made her laugh as she lay in his arms. She was a revelation in that dim, mysterious chamber; as white as the couch she lay upon. Her firm, elastic flesh that was knowing for the first time its birthright, was like a creamy lily that the sun invites to contribute its breath and perfume to the undying life of the world.

The generous abundance of her passion, without guile or trickery, was like a white   25
flame which penetrated and found response in depths of his own sensuous nature that had never yet been reached.

When he touched her breasts they gave themselves up in quivering ecstasy, inviting his lips. Her mouth was a fountain of delight. And when he possessed her, they seemed to swoon together at the very borderland of life's mystery.

He stayed cushioned upon her, breathless, dazed, enervated, with his heart beating like a hammer upon her. With one hand she clasped his head, her lips lightly touching his forehead. The other hand stroked with a soothing rhythm his muscular shoulders.

The growl of the thunder was distant and passing away. The rain beat softly upon the shingles, inviting them to drowsiness and sleep. But they dared not yield.

The rain was over; and the sun was turning the glistening green world into a palace of gems. Calixta, on the gallery, watched Alcée ride away. He turned and smiled at her with a beaming face; and she lifted her pretty chin in the air and laughed aloud.

III

Bobinôt and Bibi, trudging home, stopped without at the cistern to make them-   30
selves presentable.

"My! Bibi, w'at will yo' mama say! You ought to be ashame'. You oughtn' put on those good pants. Look at 'em! An' that mud on yo' collar! How you got that mud on yo' collar, Bibi? I never saw such a boy!" Bibi was the picture of pathetic resignation. Bobinôt was the embodiment of serious solicitude as he strove to remove from his own person and his son's the signs of their tramp over heavy roads and through wet fields. He scraped the mud off Bibi's bare legs and feet with a stick and carefully removed all traces from his heavy brogans. Then, prepared for the worst—the meeting with an over-scrupulous housewife, they entered cautiously at the back door.

Calixta was preparing supper. She had set the table and was dripping coffee at the hearth. She sprang up as they came in.

"Oh! Bobinôt! You back! My! but I was uneasy. W'ere you been during the rain? An' Bibi? he ain't wet? he ain't hurt?" She had clasped Bibi and was kissing him effusively. Bobinôt's explanations and apologies which he had been composing all along the way, died on his lips as Calixta felt him to see if he were dry, and seemed to express nothing but satisfaction at their safe return.

"I brought you some shrimps, Calixta," offered Bobinôt, hauling the can from his ample side pocket and laying it on the table.

35   "Shrimps! Oh, Bobinôt! you too good fo' anything!" and she gave him a smacking kiss on the cheek that resounded. "*J'vous réponds,* we'll have a feas' to night! umph-umph!"

Bobinôt and Bibi began to relax and enjoy themselves, and when the three seated themselves at table they laughed much and so loud that anyone might have heard them as far away as Laballière's.

IV

Alcée Laballière wrote to his wife, Clarisse, that night. It was a loving letter, full of tender solicitude. He told her not to hurry back, but if she and the babies liked it at Biloxi, to stay a month longer. He was getting on nicely; and though he missed them, he was willing to bear the separation a while longer—realizing that their health and pleasure were the first things to be considered.

V

As for Clarisse, she was charmed upon receiving her husband's letter. She and the babies were doing well. The society was agreeable; many of her old friends and acquaintances were at the bay. And the first free breath since her marriage seemed to restore the pleasant liberty of her maiden days. Devoted as she was to her husband, their intimate conjugal life was something which she was more than willing to forego for a while.

So the storm passed and everyone was happy.

CRITICAL THINKING QUESTIONS

1. How does Bobinôt's role as a husband inform his self-identity? How does Calixta's role as a wife inform hers?

2. What *claim* about marriage does "The Storm" imply? Point to specific evidence in the story that supports this claim? Are you convinced? Why or why not?

WRITING TOPIC

The closing line asserts, "So the storm passed and everyone was happy." Is this a "happy" ending? What assumptions about happiness underlie the narrator's assertion? Do you accept or reject those assumptions? Why?

Lydia Davis (b. 1947)

Break It Down

He's sitting there staring at a piece of paper in front of him. He's trying to break it down. He says:

I'm breaking it all down. The ticket was $600 and then after that there was more for the hotel and food and so on, for just ten days. Say $80 a day, no, more like $100 a day. And we made love, say, once a day on the average. That's $100 a shot. And each time it lasted maybe two or three hours so that would be anywhere from $33 to $50 an hour, which is expensive.

Though of course that wasn't all that went on, because we were together almost all day long. She would keep looking at me and every time she looked at me it was worth something, and she smiled at me and didn't stop talking and singing, something I said, she would sail into it, a snatch, for me, she would be gone from me a little ways but smiling too, and tell me jokes, and I loved it but didn't exactly know what to do about it and just smiled back at her and felt slow next to her, just not quick enough. So she talked and touched me on the shoulder and the arm, she kept touching and stayed close to me. You're with each other all day long and it keeps happening, the touches and smiles, and it adds up, it builds up, and you know where you'll be that night, you're talking and every now and then you think about it, no, you don't think, you just feel it as a kind of destination, what's coming up after you leave wherever you are all evening, and you're happy about it and you're planning it all, not in your head, really, somewhere inside your body, or all through your body, it's all mounting up and coming together so that when you get in bed you can't help it, it's a real performance, it all pours out, but slowly, you go easy until you can't anymore, or you hold back the whole time, you hold back and touch the edges of everything, you edge around until you have to plunge in and finish it off, and when you're finished, you're too weak to stand but after a while you have to go to the bathroom and you stand, your legs are trembling, you hold on to the door frames, there's a little light coming in through the window, you can see your way in and out, but you can't really see the bed.

So it's not really $100 a shot because it goes on all day, from the start when you wake up and feel her body next to you, and you don't miss a thing, not a thing of what's next to you, her arm, her leg, her shoulder, her face, that good skin, I have felt other good skin, but this skin is just the edge of something else, and you're going to start going, and no matter how much you crawl all over each other it won't be enough, and when your hunger dies down a little then you think how much you love her and that starts you off again, and her face, you look over at her face and can't believe how you got there and how lucky and it's still all a surprise and it never stops, even after it's over, it never stops being a surprise.

It's more like you have a good sixteen or eighteen hours a day of this going on, even when you're not with her it's going on, it's good to be away because it's going to be so good to go back to her, so it's still here, and you can't go off and look at some old street or some old painting without still feeling it in your body and a few things that   5 happened the day before that don't mean much by themselves or wouldn't mean much if you weren't having this thing together, but you can't forget and it's all inside you all the time, so that's more like, say, sixteen into a hundred would be $6 an hour, which isn't too much.

And then it really keeps going on while you're asleep, though you're probably dreaming about something else, a building, maybe, I kept dreaming, every night, almost, about this building, because I would spend a lot of every morning in this old stone building and when I closed my eyes I would see these cool spaces and have this peace inside me, I would see the bricks of the floor and the stone arches and the space, the emptiness between, like a kind of dark frame around what I could see beyond, a garden, and this space was like stone too because of the coolness of it and the gray shadow, that kind of luminous shade, that was glowing with the light of the sun falling beyond the arches, and there was also the great height of the ceiling, all this was in my mind all the time though I didn't know it until I closed my eyes, I'm asleep and I'm not dreaming about her but she's lying next to me and I wake up enough times in the night to remember she's there, and notice, say, once she was lying on her back but now she's curled around me, I look at her closed eyes, I want to kiss her eyelids, I want to feel that soft skin under my lips, but I don't want to disturb her, I don't want to see her frown as though in her sleep she has forgotten who I am and feels just that something is bothering her and so I just look at her and hold on to it all, these times when I'm watching over her sleep and she's next to me and isn't away from me the way she will be later, I want to stay awake all night just to go on feeling that, but I can't, I fall asleep again, though I'm sleeping lightly, still trying to hold on to it.

But it isn't over when it ends, it goes on after it's all over, she's still inside you like a sweet liquor, you are filled with her, everything about her has kind of bled into you, her smell, her voice, the way her body moves, it's all inside you, at least for a while after, then you begin to lose it, and I'm beginning to lose it, you're afraid of how weak you are, that you can't get her all back into you again and now the whole thing is going out of your body and it's more in your mind than your body, the pictures come to you one by one and you look at them, some of them last longer than others, you were together in a very white clean place, a coffeehouse, having breakfast together, and the place is so white that against it you can see her clearly, her blue eyes, her smile, the colors of her clothes, even the print of the newspaper she's reading when she's not looking up at you, the light brown and red and gold of her hair when she's got her head down reading, the brown coffee, the brown rolls, all against that white table and those white plates and silver urns and silver knives and spoons, and against that quiet of the sleepy people in that room sitting alone at their tables with just some chinking and clattering of spoons and cups in saucers and some hushed voices her voice now and then rising and falling. The pictures come to you and you have to hope they won't lose their life too fast and dry up though you know they will and that you'll also forget some of what happened, because already you're turning up little things that you nearly forgot.

We were in bed and she asked me, Do I seem fat to you? and I was surprised because she didn't seem to worry about herself at all in that way and I guess I was reading into it that she did worry about herself so I answered what I was thinking and said stupidly that she had a very beautiful body, that her body was perfect, and I really meant it as an answer, but she said kind of sharply, That's not what I asked, and so I had to try to answer her again, exactly what she had asked.

And once she lay over against me late in the night and she started talking, her breath in my ear, and she just went on and on, and talked faster and faster, she couldn't stop, and I loved it, I just felt that all that life in her was running into me too, I had so little life in me, her life, her fire, was coming into me, in that hot breath in my ear, and I just wanted her to go on talking forever right there next to me, and I would go on living, like that, I would be able to go on living, but without her I don't know.

Then you forget some of it all, maybe most of it all, almost all of it, in the end, and you work hard at remembering everything now so you won't ever forget, but you can kill it too even by thinking about it too much, though you can't help thinking about it nearly all the time.   10

And then when the pictures start to go you start asking some questions, just little questions, that sit in your mind without any answers, like why did she have the light on when you came in to bed one night, but it was off the next, but she had it on the night after that and she had it off the last night, why, and other questions, little questions that nag at you like that.

And finally the pictures go and these dry little questions just sit there without any answers and you're left with this large heavy pain in you that you try to numb by reading, or you try to ease it by getting out into public places where there will be people around you, but no matter how good you are at pushing that pain away, just when you think you're going to be all right for a while, that you're safe, you're kind of holding it off with all your strength and you're staying in some little bare numb spot of ground, then suddenly it will all come back, you'll hear a noise, maybe it's a cat crying or a baby, or something else like her cry, you hear it and make that connection in a part of you you have no control over and the pain comes back so hard that you're afraid, afraid of how you're falling back into it again and you wonder, no, you're terrified to ask how you're ever going to climb out of it.

And so it's not only every hour of the day while it's happening, but it's really for hours and hours every day after that, for weeks, though less and less, so that you could work out the ratio if you wanted, maybe after six weeks you're only thinking about it an hour or so in the day altogether, a few minutes here and there spread over, or a few minutes here and there and half an hour before you go to sleep, or sometimes it all comes back and you stay awake with it half the night.

So when you add up all that, you've only spent maybe $3 an hour on it.

If you have to figure in the bad times too, I don't know. There weren't any bad times   15 with her, though maybe there was one bad time, when I told her I loved her. I couldn't help it, this was the first time this had happened with her, now I was half falling in love with her or maybe completely if she had let me but she couldn't or I couldn't completely because it was all going to be so short and other things too, and so I told her, and didn't know of any way to tell her first that she didn't have to feel this was a burden, the fact that I loved her, or that she didn't have to feel the same about me, or say the same back, that it was just that I had to tell her, that's all, because it was bursting inside me, and saying it wouldn't even begin to take care of what I was feeling, really I couldn't say anything of what I was feeling because there was so much, words couldn't handle it, and making love only made it worse because then I wanted words badly but they were no good, no good at all, but I told her anyway, I was lying on top of her and her hands were up by her head and my hands were on hers and our fingers were locked and there was a little light on her face from the window but I couldn't really see her and I was afraid to say it but I had to say it because I wanted her to know, it was the last night, I had to tell her then or I'd never have another chance, I just said, Before you go to sleep, I have to tell you before you go to sleep that I love you, and immediately, right away after, she said, I love you too, and it sounded to me as if she didn't mean it, a little flat, but then it usually sounds a little flat when someone says, I love you too, because they're just saying it back even if they do mean it, and the problem is that I'll never know if she meant it, or maybe someday she'll tell me whether she meant it or not, but there's no way to know now, and I'm sorry I did that, it was a trap I didn't mean to put her in, I can see it was a trap, because if she hadn't said anything at all I know that would have hurt too, as though she were taking something from me and just accepting it and not giving anything back, so she really had to, even just to be kind to me, she had to say it, and I don't really know now if she meant it.

Another bad time, or it wasn't exactly bad, but it wasn't easy either, was when I had to leave, the time was coming, and I was beginning to tremble and feel empty, nothing in the middle of me, nothing inside, and nothing to hold me up on my legs, and then it came, everything was ready, and I had to go, and so it was just a kiss, a quick one, as though we were afraid of what might happen after a kiss, and she was almost wild then, she reached up to a hook by the door and took an old shirt, a green and blue shirt from the hook, and put it in my arms, for me to take away, the soft cloth was full of her smell, and then we stood there close together looking at a piece of paper she had in her hand and I didn't lose any of it, I was holding it tight, that last minute or two, because this was it, we'd come to the end of it, things always change, so this was really it, over.

Maybe it works out all right, maybe you haven't lost for doing it, I don't know, no, really, sometimes when you think of it you feel like a prince really, you feel just like a king, and then other times you're afraid, you're afraid, not all the time but now and then, of what it's going to do to you, and it's hard to know what to do with it now.

Walking away I looked back once and the door was still open, I could see her standing far back in the dark of the room, I could only really see her white face still looking out at me, and her white arms.

I guess you get to a point where you look at that pain as if it were there in front of you three feet away lying in a box, an open box, in a window somewhere. It's hard and cold, like a bar of metal. You just look at it there and say, All right, I'll take it, I'll buy it. That's what it is. Because you know all about it before you even go into this thing. You know the pain is part of the whole thing. And it isn't that you can say afterwards the pleasure was greater than the pain and that's why you would do it again. That has nothing to do with it. You can't measure it, because the pain comes after and it lasts longer. So the question really is, Why doesn't that pain make you say, I won't do it again? When the pain is so bad that you have to say that, but you don't.

So I'm just thinking about it, how you can go in with $600, more like $1,000,   20
and how you can come out with an old shirt.

CRITICAL THINKING QUESTIONS

1. By examining the writing style, you will see the author breaks all the rules for sentence construction, sometimes creating long run-on or fused sentences. How does this style contribute to the author's purpose? Hint: First identify what you believe to be the author's purpose.

2. Compare the writing style in this story to the style in the story, "A Blizzard under Blue Sky" by Pam Houston (Chapter Five). In either or both cases, does the style contribute to the *ethos* appeal of the narrator?

3. "Break It Down" is an example of a story told only from the narrator's perspective. Is that perspective accurate? How would the story differ if it were told from the woman's point of view?

> **RESEARCH/WRITING TOPIC—Cohabitation: "Shacking Up" or "Playing It Safe"?**
>
> Many young adults have muted the wedding bells. According to the U.S. Census Bureau (2000), the number of unmarried couples living together between 1990 and 2000 increased by 72 percent. Is this a selfish, if not an immoral choice, a way to enjoy sexual intimacy without the legal constraints and social refinements of marriage? Or is it a reasonable prelude to marriage, a way to share domesticity and build the foundations of a lifelong relationship? To examine diverse perspectives, do some firsthand research by interviewing friends and relatives.

Genaro González (b. 1949)

Too Much His Father's Son

In the middle of the argument, without warning, Arturo's mother confronted her husband point-blank: "Is it another woman?"

"For heaven's sake, Carmela, not in front of—"

"Nine is old enough to know. You owe both of us that much."

Sitting in the room, Arturo could not help but overhear. Usually he could dissimulate with little effort—being a constant chaperone on his cousin Anita's dates had made him a master at fading into the background. But at that moment he was struggling hard to control a discomfort even more trying than those his cousin and her boyfriends put him through.

5   The argument had already lasted an hour and, emotionally, his mother had carried its brunt. Trying to keep her voice in check was taking more out of her than if she had simply vented her tension.

His father, though, lay fully clothed in bed, shirt half-buttoned and hands locked under his head. From his closed eyes and placid breathing, one would have thought that her frustration was simply lulling him into a more profound relaxation. Only an occasional gleam from those perfect, white teeth told Arturo he was still listening, and even then with bemused detachment.

"Is it another woman, Raúl?"

His father batted open his eyes only to look away, as though the accusation did not even merit the dignity of a defense. His gaze caught Arturo and tried to lock him into the masculine intimacy they often shared, an unspoken complicity between father and son. But at that instant it simply aggravated Arturo's shame.

"Who is she, Raúl?"

10   His smile made it clear that if there were another woman, he was not saying. "You tell me. You're the one who made her up."

Arturo had seen that smile in all its shadings—sometimes with disarming candor, but more often full of arrogance. When his father wished, his smile could become a gift of pearls, invigorating all who saw his teeth shining with their special luster.

Yet other times his father needed only to curl his lips, and those same teeth turned into a sadistic show of strength. Well aware of his power over others, the father seemed indifferent to whether the end effect exalted or belittled.

Out of nowhere, perhaps to add to the confusion he ordered, "Bring *abuelo*'s belt, Arturo."

Instead of strapping it on, he pretended to admire what had once been his own father's gun belt. The holster was gone, but a bullet that had remained rusted inside a middle clasp added a certain authority. The hand-tooled leather, a rich dark brown, had delicate etchings now too smooth to decipher. His grandfather Edelmiro had been a large, mean-looking man in life, and Arturo still remembered the day his father received the belt. He had strapped it on for only a moment, over his own belt. Later that day Arturo opened the closet for a closer inspection and had come upon his father, piercing another notch for his smaller waist.

15   His mother continued to confront his father, who idly looped the belt, grabbed it at opposite ends and began whipping it with a solemn force. At first the rhythmic slaps disconcerted her, until she turned their tension into punctuations for her own argument. Suddenly the belt cracked so violently that Arturo thought the ancient cartridge had fired. He was startled, as much from the noise as from

the discovery that his father's legendary control had snapped. For an instant both parents, suddenly realizing how far things had gone, appeared paralyzed.

No, his father would never strike her, he was sure of that. But nobody had ever pushed him that far, least of all his mother, whose own strength had always been her patience.

He wondered why his eyes were suddenly brimming. Perhaps trespassing into the unknown terrified him, or perhaps he was ashamed of his father's indifference. That confusion—crying without knowing why—frightened him even more.

"See, Carmela? Now you've got the boy blubbering."

He was hoping to hide his weakness from his father, and the unmasking only added to the disgrace. Desperate to save face, he yelled, "I'm leaving!"

As always his father turned the threat in his favor. "That's good, son. Wait out-   20 side and let me handle this."

"I'm going to *papá grande's* house!"

Arturo had never been that close to his mother's family, and that made his decision all the more surprising. But if his father felt betrayed he did not show it. "Fine, then. You're on your own."

It took him a while to catch his father's sarcasm and his own unthinking blunder; he did not know the way to his grandparents' house. He had walked there only once—last Sunday—and that time his mother had disoriented him with a different route from the one his father took.

But now, standing there facing his father, he had no choice. Rushing out the kitchen door, he ran across the back yard, expecting at any moment to be stopped in his tracks. When his arms brushed against a clothesline, he almost tripped as if his father had lassoed him with his belt. Not until he reached the alley did he realize he had been hoping his father would indeed stop him, even with a word.

He crossed the alley into an abandoned lot. There he matted a patch of grass and   25 weeds reaching his waist and settled in, so as to give his heart time to hush. He sat for a long time, wondering whether to gather his thoughts or let them scramble until nothing mattered.

From Doña Chole's house came the blare of a Mexican radio station. Two announcers were sandwiching every song with a frenzied assault. Farther away David's father continued working on his pet project—a coop and flypen for his game cocks: four or five swift whacks into wood . . . silence . . . then another volley. For a while he lost himself in the hammering. If he listened closer he could hear the cursing and singing that gave the neighborhood life. Only his own home remained absolutely still.

Soon the sun began to get in his eyes whenever he looked homeward. A cool breeze was blowing at his back, and as he waited in the weeds a sun-toasted aroma penetrated his corduroy shirt.

Someone was coming up the path, making soft lashing sounds in the weeds. His intuition told him that the person was Fela the *curandera* and when he finally dared peek he immediately dove back into his hiding place, wondering whether to congratulate or curse himself.

A part of him scrambled for a rational explanation: who else could it be? Fela the healer was the only grown-up unconcerned about snakes in the undergrowth. In her daily forages for herbs she was used to cutting swaths through the weeds. Yet another side of him was forced to side with the barrio lore—that she had special powers, that she appeared and disappeared at will, that she could think your thoughts before they occurred to you.

30   The brushing got closer, so he lay very still, trying to imitate his father's self-discipline. When the rustling suddenly stopped, he swore the waft of his corduroy shirt had given him away.

A voice called out: "Since when do little boys live in the wild?"

His heart began beating wildly, but her tone carried enough teasing that he half-raised his head.

"You're hiding from someone?"

All at once, he had a clear image of his father sprawled across the bed, amused, almost bored. Arturo answered her question with a nod, afraid that if he spoke, his rage might leap out and injure them both.

35   "You did something bad?"

He managed a hoarse, determined vow: "I'm going to smash my father's teeth."

He expected the violence in his words to stun her, but instead she disarmed him with a kind smile. "Whatever for? He has such nice teeth. Some day yours will look just like his."

For a moment, in place of the familiar habit of his own body, he experienced an undefined numbness, followed by the fascinated terror of someone who has inherited a gleaming crown with awesome responsibilities. He stood speechless, repulsed yet tempted by the thought of turning into his father.

"Anyway," she added, "before you know it he'll be old and toothless like me."

40   She picked a row of burrs clinging to her faded dress, then said as she left, "And tell your mother she's in my thoughts and prayers." Watching her walk away, he tried without success to retrace the route he and his mother had taken to her father's house at the time of their secret visit last Sunday.

That Sunday morning, while his mother talked to Fela in the living room, he had sat on a wicker chair on Fela's porch, entertained by Cuco, an ancient caged parrot with colorful semi-circles under his eyes. Arturo was feeding him chile from a nearby plant to make him talk. "Say it," he urged between bribes: *"Chinga tu madre."* But the chile only agitated Cuco's whistling.

"Come on, you stupid bird. *Chinga tu madre.* Screw your mother."

Suddenly there was a raucous squawk. "Screw your *padre* instead!"

As he wheeled about and felt the blood rush to his face, Fela was already raising her arms in innocence. "Who says he's stupid? That's an exotic, bilingual bird you're talking to."

From there, he and his mother had gone to his grandparents' house. Her route through alleys and unfenced back yards led him to ask, "How do you know all these shortcuts?"

She had paused to dry her forehead on her sleeve, and for the first time in days   45
he had seen her smile. "I grew up in this barrio. This is where I used to play."

Trying to imagine her at the same age he now was, he had to smile to himself.

When they got to his grandfather's house, they had to wait until his grandfather
Marcelo finished his *radionovela*. Then, after hearing where they had been and why,
his grandfather shook his head. "I knew your marriage would come to this. But going
to Fela was a mistake. If he finds out he'll claim you're trying to win him back through
witchcraft."

"I had to know if he's seeing another woman."

"And what if he is?"   50

Arturo had never seen her as serene and as serious when she answered, "Then he's
not worth winning back."

"But a *curandera* . . . Why not see a priest?"

Arturo's grandmother took her side. "What for, Marcelo? He'd only give her your
advice: accept him as your cross in life."

"I wouldn't in this case. An unfaithful husband is one thing, an arrogant s.o.b. is
another. Still, a priest could say a few prayers in your behalf."

"Fela offered to do that herself."   55

"And no doubt offered good advice," his grandmother added.

His mother's fist clenched his own. "Yes," she said, and her firmness made it
obvious that was the last word.

His grandfather, deep in thought, held his breath without taking his eyes off him.
Then he closed them and exhaled a stale rush of cigarette smoke, as if unclouding his
thoughts. "I've always said your father was a *cabrón*."

"Now, Marcelo. Don't turn him against his own father," his grandmother interjected.

"Mamá's right. None of this is Arturo's fault. He's going through enough as   60
it is."

"True. But I still wouldn't give a kilo of crap for the whole de la O family, starting with Edelmiro."

"May he rest in peace," said his grandmother.

His grandfather stood up. "Not if there's a devil down below."

"Marcelo! He was your *compadre*."

"I had as much choice in the matter as the boy had in being his grandson." He   65
turned to Arturo's mother. "Remember, if there's a falling out, don't ask that family for
anything. Your place is here."

His grandmother added, "And of course that includes Arturo. He's as much a
part of the family as the rest of us."

His grandfather had simply said, "Let's hope he's not too much his father's
son."

By now the late afternoon sun was slanting long, slender shadows his way, but he
was determined to spend the night there if need be. He began counting in cycles of
hundreds to keep his uncertainty in check.

Suddenly the rear screen door opened and his father leaned against it, his belt slung over his chest and shoulder like a bandoliered and battle-weary warrior.

70   "Arturo, come inside." Whenever he wanted to conceal something from the neighbors, he used that phrase.

Arturo slowly stood up but held his ground, as much from stubbornness as dread.

"It's all right, son." His father sounded final yet forgiving, like a king who had put down a castle uprising, regained control and had decided to pardon the traitors.

Arturo blinked but once, but his pounding heart made even something that small seem a life-and-death concession.

Then his mother appeared alongside his father, and for an instant, framed by the doorway, their pose reminded him of their newlywed portrait in the living room: his hands at his sides, her own clasped in front, both heads slightly tilted as if about to rest on each other's shoulder. In that eye blink of an interval before she stepped outside, he felt like an outsider looking in.

75   She was halfway between him and the house when his father said, "Your mother's bringing you back."

He could not believe her betrayal. After all that, she had surrendered and was bringing him in as well. He wanted to cry out at her for having put him through so much. But another part of him understood he shared the blame, for not helping her, for being too much his father's son.

"I forgot the way," he said. Although she was quite close he could not tell whether she heard—much less accepted—his timid apology. He managed his first step homeward when she blocked his path, gently took his hand and guided him in the opposite direction.

He heard, or perhaps only imagined, his father: "Come back." He tugged her arm in case she had not heard. She tightened her grasp to show that she had. Then, intuiting his dilemma, she paused, saying nothing but still gazing away from the house. He realized then and there that the decision was for him alone to make. Hers had already been made.

Unable to walk back or away, he felt like the only living thing in the open. Then his father called out, "Son," and he knew it was his last call. His spine shivered as though a weapon had been sighted at his back, and he imagined his father removing from his belt the cartridge reserved for the family traitor.

80   There was no way of telling how long he braced himself for whatever was coming, until he finally realized that the moment of reckoning was already behind him. It was then that he felt his father's defeat in his own blood. With it came the glorious fear of a fugitive burning his bridges into the unknown, or a believer orphaned from a false faith. And in that all-or-nothing instant that took so little doing and needed even less understanding, his all-powerful father evaporated into the myth he had always been.

He felt a flesh-and-blood grasp that both offered and drew strength. He began to walk away, knowing there was no turning back.

CRITICAL THINKING QUESTIONS

1. When Arturo chooses his mother over his father, he acknowledges that "his all-powerful father" had been a "myth." Describe this myth and its ideals and values. Do you agree or disagree with Arturo's rejection of those values?

2. Disregarding your personal opinion, make a case for Arturo's mother to stay with her husband. What *warrant* about marriage informs this argument? In anticipating the opposing argument, what *warrant* informs that argument?

Ernest Hemingway (1899–1961)

Hills Like White Elephants

The hills across the valley of the Ebro were long and white. On this side there was no shade and no trees and the station was between two lines of rails in the sun. Close against the side of the station there was the warm shadow of the building and a curtain, made of strings of bamboo beads, hung across the open door into the bar, to keep out flies. The American and the girl with him sat at a table in the shade, outside the building. It was very hot and the express from Barcelona would come in forty minutes. It stopped at this junction for two minutes and went on to Madrid.

"What should we drink?" the girl asked. She had taken off her hat and put it on the table.

"It's pretty hot," the man said.

"Let's drink beer."

"Dos cervezas," the man said into the curtain.   5

"Big ones?" a woman asked from the doorway.

"Yes. Two big ones."

The woman brought two glasses of beer and two felt pads. She put the felt pads and the beer glasses on the table and looked at the man and the girl. The girl was looking off at the line of hills. They were white in the sun and the country was brown and dry.

"They look like white elephants," she said.

"I've never seen one," the man drank his beer.   10

"No, you wouldn't have."

"I might have," the man said. "Just because you say I wouldn't have doesn't prove anything."

The girl looked at the bead curtain. "They've painted something on it," she said. "What does it say?"

"Anis del Toro. It's a drink."

"Could we try it?"   15

The man called "Listen" through the curtain. The woman came out from the bar.
"Four reales."
"We want two Anis del Toro."
"With water?"
20 "Do you want it with water?"
"I don't know," the girl said. "Is it good with water?"
"It's all right."
"You want them with water?" asked the woman.
"Yes, with water."
25 "It tastes like licorice," the girl said and put the glass down.
"That's the way with everything."
"Yes," said the girl. "Everything tastes of licorice. Especially all the things you've waited so long for, like absinthe."
"Oh, cut it out."
"You started it," the girl said. "I was being amused. I was having a fine time."
30 "Well, let's try and have a fine time."
"All right. I was trying. I said the mountains looked like white elephants. Wasn't that bright?"
"That was bright."
"I wanted to try this new drink. That's all we do, isn't it—look at things and try new drinks?"
"I guess so."
35 The girl looked across at the hills.
"They're lovely hills," she said. "They don't really look like white elephants. I just meant the coloring of their skin through the trees."
"Should we have another drink?"
"All right."
The warm wind blew the bead curtain against the table.
"The beer's nice and cool," the man said.
40 "It's lovely," the girl said.
"It's really an awfully simple operation, Jig," the man said. "It's not really an operation at all."
The girl looked at the ground the table legs rested on.
"I know you wouldn't mind it, Jig. It's really not anything. It's just to let the air in."
45 "The girl did not say anything."
"I'll go with you and I'll stay with you all the time. They just let the air in and then it's all perfectly natural."
"Then what will we do afterward?"
"We'll be fine afterward. Just like we were before."
"What makes you think so?"
50 "That's the only thing that bothers us. It's the only thing that's made us unhappy."
The girl looked at the bead curtain, put her hand out and took hold of two of the strings of beads.
"And you think then we'll be all right and be happy."

"I know we will. You don't have to be afraid. I've known lots of people that have done it."

"So have I," said the girl. "And afterward they were all so happy."

"Well," the man said, "if you don't want to you don't have to. I wouldn't have you   55
do it if you didn't want to. But I know it's perfectly simple."

"And you really want to?"

"I think it's the best thing to do. But I don't want you to do it if you don't really want to."

"And if I do it you'll be happy and things will be like they were and you'll love me?"

"I love you now. You know I love you."

"I know. But if I do it, then it will be nice again if I say things are like white ele-   60
phants, and you'll like it?"

"I'll love it. I love it now but I just can't think about it. You know how I get when I worry."

"If I do it you won't ever worry?"

"I won't worry about that because it's perfectly simple."

"Then I'll do it. Because I don't care about me."

"What do you mean?"   65

"I don't care about me."

"Well, I care about you."

"Oh, yes. But I don't care about me. And I'll do it and then everything will be fine."

"I don't want you to do it if you feel that way."

The girl stood up and walked to the end of the station. Across, on the other side,   70
were fields of grain and trees along the banks of the Ebro. Far away, beyond the river, were mountains. The shadow of a cloud moved across the field of grain and she saw the river through the trees.

"And we could have all this," she said. "And we could have everything and every day we make it more impossible."

"What did you say?"

"I said we could have everything."

"We can have everything."

"No, we can't."   75

"We can have the whole world."

"No, we can't."

"We can go everywhere."

"No, we can't. It isn't ours any more."

"It's ours."   80

"No, it isn't. And once they take it away, you never get it back."

"But they haven't taken it away."

"We'll wait and see."

"Come on back in the shade," he said. "You mustn't feel that way."

"I don't feel any way," the girl said. "I just know things."   85

"I don't want you to do anything that you don't want to do—"

"Nor that isn't good for me," she said. "I know. Could we have another beer?"

"All right. But you've got to realize—"

"I realize," the girl said. "Can't we maybe stop talking?"

90   They sat down at the table and the girl looked across at the hills on the dry side of the valley and the man looked at her and at the table.

"You've got to realize," he said, "that I don't want you to do it if you don't want to. I'm perfectly willing to go through with it if it means anything to you."

"Doesn't it mean anything to you? We could get along."

"Of course it does. But I don't want anybody but you. I don't want anyone else. And I know it's perfectly simple."

"Yes, you know it's perfectly simple."

95   "It's all right for you to say that, but I do know it."

"Would you do something for me now?"

"I'd do anything for you."

"Would you please please please please please please please stop talking?"

He did not say anything but looked at the bags against the wall of the station. There were labels on them from all the hotels where they had spent nights.

100   "But I don't want you to," he said. "I don't care anything about it."

"I'll scream," the girl said.

The woman came out through the curtains with two glasses of beer and put them down on the damp felt pads. "The train comes in five minutes," she said.

"What did she say?" asked the girl.

"That the train is coming in five minutes."

105   The girl smiled brightly at the woman, to thank her.

"I'd better take the bags over to the other side of the station," the man said. She smiled at him.

"All right. Then come back and we'll finish the beer."

He picked up the two heavy bags and carried them around the station to the other tracks. He looked up the tracks but could not see the train. Coming back, he walked through the barroom, where people waiting for the train were drinking. He drank an Anis at the bar and looked at the people. They were all waiting reasonably for the train. He went out through the bead curtain. She was sitting at the table and smiled at him.

"Do you feel better?" he asked.

110   "I feel fine," she said. "There's nothing wrong with me. I feel fine."

CRITICAL THINKING QUESTIONS

1. Do the "man" and "girl" mean what they say? Does he really want what is best for her as he proclaims? Does she really believe she is just "fine"? Point to specific passages to support your judgment.

2. The man is persistent in his effort to persuade his partner to go through with "it." Write out his reasons. In paragraph 60, the girl says, "But if I do it, then it

will be nice again if I say things like white elephants, and you'll like it?" All in all, do you think the man has convinced her to go through with it?

3. Both the man and girl regularly use the pronoun "it," for example, as noted in the above question. For another instance of their use of this pronoun, reread their exchange in paragraphs 70–94. List both characters' uses of "it," and write out the noun or noun phrases to which you think the pronoun refers. Based on this analysis, make an *inference* (see Glossary) about the couple's relationship.

4. At the end of the story, who has control of the situation—the man or the girl? Why? Point to textural evidence to support your conclusion.

WRITING TOPIC

Read Anne Sexton's poem, "Cinderella," later in this chapter. How do the couple in Hemingway's story illustrate "That story"?

Cherylene Lee (b. 1953)

Safe

My brother sets himself on fire every summer. He's not a pyromaniac and it's not a political statement. He does it in front of people at Worlds of Water, U.S.A. My brother is a flame diver—a stuntman on a high diving platform who douses himself in flammable liquid, has someone light a torch to him, then launches himself into a cool blue pool, toes pointed, form correct—though that is hard to make out through all the flame and smoke. He says the crowds go wild because they feel afraid. He makes them feel safe.

Safe. That is the most important consideration for our family. Perhaps there is a Chinese gene encoded with a protein for caution. Or perhaps it's because my father's tailor shop is not doing so well or because of my mother's blindness. Perhaps it's because my mother and father married late in life and weren't sure how to protect their children.

We try to take precautions. My mother won't go out at night for fear of what the darkness holds. She doesn't like me to take a shower after dinner for fear I might get a cramp and somehow drown in the shower's spray. She doesn't like me to walk home from school alone, nor does she like me to walk home with boys. She'd rather I walked home with girls, at least three for maximum protection so one can always run for help. I've tried to explain to her, I like walking alone, it's not always possible to walk in female threes, I don't even have that many girlfriends. "You have to watch out at your age, you can't be too safe," she warns, "but don't hang around with the fast ones."

My father is just as bad. He's so afraid someone will dent his car, he won't park in a lot that doesn't have two spaces side by side for his ten-year-old station wagon. He refuses to go into a grocery store if he could be the first or last customer—"That's when the robbers are most likely to come." He won't eat in restaurants without first wiping the chopsticks, rice bowl, tea cup, or plate, silverware, and glass—"So many germs everywhere." He has more locks and alarms on his tailor shop door than the bank that's two doors down. It takes him ten minutes to open them up each day, turn off the alarms, before calling my mother to let her know that he has arrived safely.

5   We live in San Francisco—a city with its share of dangers though my parents have done their best to shield my brother and me from having to face most of them. More than from just physical harm, they've tried to protect us from loss—loss of face, loss of happiness, loss of innocence. So far we have been protected by their constant vigilance. Not that I have been sheltered so much I can't go places on my own or do things without my parents' consent, but their warnings, cautions, and dire predictions have had an effect. While I have always felt safe and have never wanted for anything, neither can I say that I've ever wanted at all. I have never been in danger, never known a need for risk. That's why I was so shocked when my brother announced he wanted to become a flame diver.

It isn't as risky as it seems, at least according to my brother who claims he could do the dive in his sleep. He wears a special flame-retardant suit. It protects him head to foot from the flames that consume him three times a day, six days a week, three months of the year. His summer job—his only job—hasn't changed him much except that he has no facial hair. The suit shields him from burns, but the wind sometimes blows flames under his protective helmet, singeing the hair off his face. The first summer he started doing this work, it took me awhile to recognize what was different about him when he sat down to dinner. He had no eyebrows, no eye lashes, just eyes, big brown eyes that seemed too large for the rest of his face. Since then he's taken to drawing in eyebrows with an eyebrow pencil because he doesn't want people to worry. Otherwise he's normal, though for a while I admit I was afraid of my brother. Who was this guy who grew up with me and suddenly became a flame diver? I thought maybe he would turn into some awful monster with scarred flesh and a swollen head from the fire and adulation. But my brother remains the same—shy, soft-spoken, introverted. Maybe he's happier these days or maybe I just think that because I am relieved. After hearing so much about danger, all he's lost are his eyebrows.

I've never seen my brother actually do his stunt though our father has many pictures of his dives hanging on the walls of his tailor shop. My brother won't let any of us watch him. He thinks we'll jinx him and we don't want to do that. He hasn't let us watch him since a high school diving meet three years ago when he made the varsity swim team. On his final and hardest dive of that meet, his foot slipped during his preparation jump causing him to start his backward twist out of control and his head to nick the edge of the platform. Our mother, already nearly blind, became hysterical even before the blood began oozing up in the water. By instinct she started screaming, "My boy, my boy!" the instant his head made contact, before anyone else knew something was wrong. Her screams echoed like a wailing gull inside the indoor swim gym. Luckily my brother wasn't badly hurt, ten stitches closed him up, but he was so embarrassed by our mother's shrieking that he asked us not to attend anymore, our presence brought him bad luck. That's why we all stay away now and only look at the pictures of his dives after he's already done them. When we know he's safe.

According to my mother, her eyesight started going bad because my father's eyes wandered. Years ago, when his tailor shop was in Chinatown, his clients were mostly women. He made cheongsams, the tight-fitting Chinese dresses the girls in the Miss Chinatown contest wear. He also did special occasion clothes, Chinese jackets, western-style wedding dresses, men's suits and such, but his busiest time of the year used to be the months before Chinese New Year when the Miss Chinatown contest was held. He would carefully take the measurements of each eager contestant, help her choose material that brought out her best coloring—mostly variations on fire-engine red—and cut the gowns so that they showed off each girl to her best advantage. My mother used to help my father by doing the embroidery on the dresses. Dragons and phoenixes were her favorite and my mother's embroidery was beautiful, small stitches of metallic thread, so fine they looked like brush strokes. She never needed a pattern, the dragons and phoenixes appeared in her head, she saw their outlines, their wings outstretched, their images flying on satin or silk which guided her hands as if by magic.

Her embroidery made my father's work much sought after, but one day she claimed her husband of 12 years was taking too much time getting the measurements of a young girl. His hands lingered a bit too long over the tape encircling her hips. After that my mother refused to do any more embroidery. She said her eyesight was failing, though she saw with bitter sharpness all the times my father's eyes seem to pause over a young girl's figure. My mother refused to see a doctor. She claimed her vision was a gift of the gods, just like her dragons and phoenixes, and my father must be up to something very bad to make it become so blurry. She became so enraged at women entering the shop, she insisted on taking their measurements herself, though indeed her eyesight was very poor and she often mistook the numbers on the tape causing much grief during the fitting sessions. Without her special embroidery and because of her mistaken measurements, my father's business suffered. He became just another tailor, his prices were considered high, his patterns a bit old-fashioned. My father decided to move his shop away from Chinatown, to a neighborhood where he would have more men for clients, not young girls seeking the Miss Chinatown crown, and thereby give my mother some peace.

But the neighborhood he chose did not give them peace. The taquerias and salsa music, the easy gatherings of young men at street corners, the rapid Spanish spoken in shops made both my father and mother feel out of place. My mother stopped going to work with my father and preferred to stay at home. She spent her time making "frogs"—Chinese buttons of thin braid twisted into three circles forming the bulges of a frog's head and eyes. She didn't have to see in order to make these buttons, she could feel her way along. She knew by instinct the exact place where stitches were needed to hold the button's shape. But Chinese buttons were not popular items in my father's new location. My parents' caution toward the outside world increased with my father's diminishing income. Only the family home felt safe to them and this is what they tried to impart to both my brother and me.

Of course my parents didn't want my brother to become a flame diver. They didn't even want him to join the swim team in high school—"too many accidents happen in pools"—but my brother didn't tell them he joined until after he'd already done it. I helped

10

him forge our parents' signatures on the school release form, as he had done for me whenever I cut class. He didn't tell them the truth until after his first competition when he won first place for the platform swan dive. That gave them something to brag about and brag my father did. None of his customers could ever leave his shop without some comment on the first-place ribbon hanging on my father's wall. Our parents didn't like that my brother had gone behind their backs—my father never mentioned that part or my role in the conspiracy—but their pride in my brother's accomplishment did mollify some of their fear. I suppose the possibility of a college scholarship also helped. My father couldn't afford to send my brother to college—he'd used his life savings moving his shop—and since my brother wasn't too academic, his talent for diving, risky as it was, seemed the best path toward the safety of college. My father thought my brother would get a diving scholarship, learn a risk-free well-paying profession, give up his high diving ways after graduation, and live a safe life ever after.

My brother didn't get a scholarship. Although he had a spectacular swan dive, he couldn't seem to master any other. Something happened to his orientation when he tried to perform twists and somersaults. Maybe that time he hit his head made him fearful of hitting the platform again. He couldn't seem to get the spin of going head over heels quite right. When he tried a half twist or a backward gainer, his body went over too far or sometimes not far enough. He suffered spectacular belly flops. He was such a perfectionist though, he practiced diving for hours, but usually only his favorite one—the elegant and beautiful swan dive. A repertory of one dive wasn't enough to impress college recruiters, who thought my brother odd in his singular passion for swan dives. He was looked at and passed over many times during his senior year. Our parents were crushed that my brother wasn't asked to try out for any college team, but my brother didn't seem to mind. He told me one night he thought he could perform swan dives for a living.

"Look at these guys," he showed me a magazine that advertised tours to Mexico displaying muscular men in skimpy bathing suits diving off impossibly high cliffs. "Nothing but swan dives. People pay to see this."

"But you're not Mexican. And those cliffs are so high."

15 "It doesn't matter, I'm not going to do cliffs. There are other ways to make dives exciting. Look at this." He pulled out another magazine showing tours to Puerto Rico. This ad pictured tourists outside a fancy hotel looking entranced at the sight of a man, encased in flames, diving into a deep blue pool. The tourists clutched at their drinks, their mouths and eyes open in amazement. The caption read: "Thrills everywhere, with comfort you can't compare. Come to the island that has it all—Puerto Rico."

"This is more what I had in mind."

"Puerto Rico?"

"No, I'm going to become a flame diver. I can do it better than this guy. Look, he's not even vertical going in."

"But how can you, where can you—" I could hardly ask a question. None of us had ever been out of state, let alone leave home for such far off lands as Mexico or unimaginably, Puerto Rico.

20 "I can do it here."

"We don't have a swimming pool."

"God you're so dumb. I'm talking about Worlds of Water, U.S.A. It's only 30 miles from here. It's the perfect place. People are tired of watching animals do tricks for them. They feel guilty about it. They would rather see a man on fire than dolphins going through flaming hoops."

"Wait till mom and dad hear this." I could already imagine their torrents of protests. They hated candles on birthday cakes, their fear of fire was so great.

"They'll come around," my brother assured me. "It's what I want to do."

When I was thirteen, my mother asked for her embroidery basket to see if I possessed her talent. She sat me down with scraps of cloth, a packet of needles, and spools of thread though her eyesight was so poor by then, she could no longer thread the needles. She told me to close my eyes and picture a mighty dragon. She told me to feel its power, feel the flames shooting from the mouth. "Let this image guide your hands, the needle will follow the flames."

I closed my eyes and tried to see her dragon. I tried to feel its heat and let the needle follow. But I was constantly pricking myself, the thread tangled, the cloth bunched up. When I looked at my clumsy stitches all I saw were chicken scratches, uneven threads, unraveling patterns, my mother's nerves frayed at the edge. I had no dragons and phoenixes in me. My mother told me to go wash my hands and be careful putting away the scissors. She knew I hadn't inherited her gift, but she protected me just the same. She said such embroidery was not in fashion, not important anymore. We never tried again.

"I didn't raise my son to perform silly tricks for strangers," was my father's first reaction. "You are not a trained animal."

"I'm not a caged one either," I'd never heard my brother use that tone, especially in front of our father. "I can do it, dad. I've been practicing diving for years."

"High school meets, this is different."

"What's wrong with going to city college?" mother asked. "You can learn a trade, meet a nice girl. Who will you meet at this water world? Nobody there but fish."

"Ma, I have learned a trade. I know how to dive."

"Trying to kill yourself is no way for my son to make a living."

"Diving isn't trying to kill myself, dad. It feels like flying to me."

"Didn't you hear how many people were killed in that plane crash over Mexico? Flying isn't safe anymore." Our mother knew how to change the subject.

"I'm talking about diving, Ma. Swan dives."

"So why do you have to set yourself on fire?"

"Because I need a gimmick to make it look exciting. Dangerous."

There it was—the D-word. They'll never go for it, I thought. How could he expect their support when he played on their worst fears? I felt sorry for my brother then. All his diving dreams and he had to choose the wrong word.

"But it only has to look dangerous, dad. Really it's very safe."

I don't think my father was always so cautious. He was quite the gambler once. He used to go to weekly poker games in Chinatown before he moved his shop. He used to talk about opening a factory or a specialty store featuring mom's embroidery. But that was before the trouble began, before she started accusing him.

When I look at my father now, sighing as he hems a pair of trousers, replaces a zipper, or watches my mother making her buttons, I don't think he ever had a wandering eye. I think my mother must have made it up because her vision was blurred. I think she was afraid without her embroidery, my father would no longer need her. She thought he would find a younger woman, leave her with two children, middle-aged, blind, and alone.

But that never happened. I think my father felt embarrassed that he had no dragon in his head. My mother was the one with the gift. She had the visions that spread to his cloth. She had the instinct that knew just how to hold buttons and things together. He was afraid he would lose her. They didn't know how to reassure themselves, so they moved the shop to a new location and tried to shield my brother and me from further loss in a dangerous world.

Three nights after my brother made his announcement that he was going to become a flame diver, my father brought home this special material—something like rubber only more flexible—and spent hours gluing it together with a special flame retardant glue. He placed a glued piece over our kitchen stove testing to see if it melted, putting his hand on the burner to see how hot it grew. He timed how long it took before the material grew too hot for his hand. He glued squares of it together to see if he could take more heat. My mother insisted my father not risk his sewing hands and stuck her own into the makeshift glove holding it over the gas flame, turning the stove to high, staring with unseeing eyes at the blue circle of heat, patiently daring it to burn her. My parents experimented for a month with different materials, different glues, different thicknesses, different flames before deciding a suit could indeed be made that would protect their flesh and blood. Engulfed by my brother's passion, only they could make him safe.

I haven't told my parents yet, not even my brother though maybe he would understand. I see a man after school. He lives two blocks from the school and I go to his house everyday before I walk home alone. He is an older white man, not as old as my father. He called to me from his window one day as I was walking home and asked if I could bring in his paper and check his mail box for him. When I brought in his paper and mail, he was very polite and apologized for troubling me, but he couldn't get out of bed. He asked if I had a few minutes and would I mind reading something to him, he wanted to hear another voice. He asked me to read Ann Landers' column. I think he was very lonely. I read to him and he thanked me and that's how it began. Now I read to him for 15 minutes everyday, sometimes things from the newspaper, sometimes things from magazines, mostly magazines about sex that he gets delivered in the mail. The magazines are the type my parents would never approve of me reading. I sit at the foot of his bed and read and he listens to me with closed eyes. Sometimes his body tenses and I see sweat break out on his forehead. He listens so intently, I feel heat coming off his body. He's always very polite to me. He says that I am a gift. He says that when he hears my voice, it helps him to feel alive.

45   My brother tells me what a rush it is to be a sponge for everyone's fear. To be so focused on what he does, he only hears his own heart beat. He's vaguely aware of the ladder he climbs to the platform hanging above the pool. He doesn't hear the roll of the drum, he doesn't hear his name announced, he doesn't hear the height of the platform

called out, he doesn't see the water. Encased in his protective suit, glued with familial pride, he feels which way the wind blows by the way it buffets his body. He tells me the exact routine. The number of deep breaths he takes, the number of sprays of butane needed to coat him from head to foot, the sound of the torch which explodes with a roar, the moment he holds his flaming hands outstretched before closing his eyes and flying. He tells me he opens his eyes at the peak of his arch—a dragon sailing through pure blue silk before tucking his head and splashing into the satin smooth mouth of the pool.

And I have imagined the crowd's awe building up with the flames, the tightening nerves with the drum roll, the fearful split second of silence, the collective breath for this human torch against blue sky, the lesser sun god, this crazy kid. And then I've imagined the plunge, a blurred arch of orange and smoke, a curve straightening to a lightning shaft, a sizzling hiss as he breaks the water, the cheers welling up like ocean waves sweeping aside stunned silence. I imagine when my brother surfaces and swims to the side of the pool, the audience sees a phoenix rising, their fears melt, the smiles grow, the celebration is complete. And as he doffs his helmet, waving his arms and smiling broadly, he reassures the crowd that all is well, nothing bad has happened, no loss has occurred. He dove through fire and survived. He lives to dive again. Everything is normal.

CRITICAL THINKING QUESTIONS

1. a. Expressing shock over her brother's wanting to be a flame diver, the narrator says, "I've never been in danger, never known a need for risk." Later in the story, however, she tells about her daily reading sessions with "an older white man, not as old as my father." She says she reads from newspapers and magazines, "mostly magazines about sex. . . . He's always very polite to me. He says that I am a gift." How have reason and emotion factored into the narrator's decision to read to this man?

    b. The narrator says she has not even told her brother that she is seeing this man after school, "though maybe he would understand." What is it she thinks he might understand? Do you think she should continue her visits?

2. Read Peter D. Kramer's essay, "Divorce and Our National Values," included later in this chapter. How does this story suggest a different cultural perspective on Kramer's claim about the divorce rate and American values?

WRITING TOPICS

1. Early on, the narrator says, "Safe. That is the most important consideration for our family. Perhaps there is a Chinese gene encoded with a protein for caution." The narrator suggests that the focus on the safety of one's family members may be particularly strong for her Chinese family, especially when the family has transplanted itself in a foreign culture. An assumption held by the narrator's parents is that family must provide a safe haven, a barrier from the destructive influence

of outsiders. What do your experiences and observations suggest about the concept of family as protection, a safeguard for its members?

2. Does family provide a safety net that protects its members or a net that entraps them? As you formulate a claim for this family issue, you could choose to construct a Rogerian argument that posits middle-ground perspective (other literature suggestions: Fierstein's play, *On Tidy Endings*, page 483.

Fae Myenne Ng (b. 1957)

A Red Sweater

I chose red for my sister. Fierce, dark red. Made in Hong Kong. Hand Wash Only because it's got that skin of fuzz. She'll look happy. That's good. Everything's perfect, for a minute. That seems enough.

Red. For Good Luck. Of course. This fire-red sweater is swollen with good cheer. Wear it, I will tell her. You'll look lucky.

We're a family of three girls. By Chinese standards, that's not lucky. "Too bad," outsiders whisper, ". . . nothing but daughters. A failed family."

First, Middle, and End girl. Our order of birth marked us. That came to tell more than our given names.

5   My eldest sister, Lisa, lives at home. She quit San Francisco State, one semester short of a psychology degree. One day she said, "Forget about it, I'm tired." She's working full time at Pacific Telephone now. Nine hundred a month with benefits. Mah and Deh think it's a great deal. They tell everybody, "Yes, our Number One makes good pay, but that's not even counting the discount. If we call Hong Kong, China even, there's forty percent off!" As if anyone in their part of China had a telephone.

Number Two, the in-between, jumped off the 'M' floor three years ago. Not true! What happened? Why? Too sad! All we say about that is, "It was her choice."

We sent Mah to Hong Kong. When she left Hong Kong thirty years ago, she was the envy of all: "Lucky girl! You'll never have to work." To marry a sojourner was to have a future. Thirty years in the land of gold and good fortune, and then she returned to tell the story: three daughters, one dead, one unmarried, another who-cares-where, the thirty years in sweatshops, and the prince of the Golden Mountain turned into a toad. I'm glad I didn't have to go with her. I felt her shame and regret. To return, seeking solace and comfort, instead of offering banquets and stories of the good life.

I'm the youngest. I started flying with Pan Am the year Mah returned to Hong Kong, so I got her a good discount. She thought I was good for something then. But when she returned, I was pregnant.

"Get an abortion," she said. "Drop the baby," she screamed.

"No."   10

"Then get married."

"No. I don't want to."

I was going to get an abortion all along. I just didn't like the way they talked about the whole thing. They made me feel like dirt, that I was a disgrace. Now I can see how I used it as an opportunity. Sometimes I wonder if there wasn't another way. Everything about those years was so steamy and angry. There didn't seem to be any answers.

"I have no eyes for you," Mah said.

"Don't call us," Deh said.   15

They wouldn't talk to me. They ranted idioms to each other for days. The apartment was filled with images and curses I couldn't perceive. I got the general idea: I was a rotten, no-good, dead thing. I would die in a gutter without rice in my belly. My spirit—if I had one—wouldn't be fed. I wouldn't see good days in this life or the next.

My parents always had a special way of saying things.

Now I'm based in Honolulu. When our middle sister jumped, she kind of closed the world. The family just sort of fell apart. I left. Now, I try to make up for it, but the folks still won't see me, but I try to keep in touch with them through Lisa. Flying cuts up your life, hits hardest during the holidays. I'm always sensitive then. I feel like I'm missing something, that people are doing something really important while I'm up in the sky, flying through time zones.

So I like to see Lisa around the beginning of the year. January, New Year's, and February, New Year's again, double luckiness with our birthdays in between. With so much going on, there's always something to talk about.

"You pick the place this year," I tell her.   20

"Around here?"

"No," I say. 'Around here' means the food is good and the living hard. You eat a steaming rice plate, and then you feel like rushing home to sew garments or assemble radio parts or something. We eat together only once a year, so I feel we should splurge. Besides, at the Chinatown places, you have nothing to talk about except the bare issues. In American restaurants, the atmosphere helps you along. I want nice light and a view and handsome waiters.

"Let's go somewhere with a view," I say.

We decide to go to FOLLOWING SEA, a new place on the Pier 39 track. We're early, the restaurant isn't crowded. It's been clear all day, so I think the sunset will be nice. I ask for a window table. I turn to talk to my sister, but she's already talking to a waiter. He's got that dark island tone that she likes. He's looking her up and down. My sister does not blink at it. She holds his look and orders two Johnny Walkers. I pick up a fork, turn it around in my hand. I seldom use chopsticks now. At home, I eat my rice in a plate, with a fork. The only chopsticks I own, I wear in my hair. For a moment, I feel strange sitting here at this unfamiliar table. I don't know this tablecloth, this linen, these candles. Everything seems foreign. It feels like we should be different people. But each time I look up, she's the same. I know this person. She's my sister. We sat together with chopsticks, mismatched bowls, braids, and braces, across the formica tabletop.

25   "I like three pronged forks," I say, pressing my thumb against the sharp points.
My sister rolls her eyes. She lights a cigarette.

I ask for one.

I finally say, "So, what's new?"

"Not much." Her voice is sullen. She doesn't look at me. Once a year, I come in, asking questions. She's got the answers, but she hates them. For me, I think she's got the peace of heart, knowing that she's done her share for Mah and Deh. She thinks I have the peace, not caring. Her life is full of questions, too, but I have no answers.

30   I look around the restaurant. The sunset is not spectacular and we don't comment on it. The waiters are lighting candles. Ours is bringing the drinks. He stops very close to my sister, seems to breathe her in. She raises her face toward him. "Ready?" he asks. My sister orders for us. The waiter struts off.

"Tight ass," I say.

"The best," she says.

My scotch tastes good. It reminds me of Deh. Johnny Walker or Seagrams 7, that's what they served at Chinese banquets. Nine courses and a bottle. No ice. We learned to drink it Chinese style, in teacups. Deh drank from his rice bowl, sipping it like hot soup. By the end of the meal, he took it like cool tea, in bold mouthfuls. We sat watching, our teacups of scotch in our laps, his three giggly girls.

Relaxed, I'm thinking there's a connection. Johnny Walker then and Johnny Walker now. I ask for another cigarette and this one I enjoy. Now my Johnny Walker pops with ice. I twirl the glass to make the ice tinkle.

35   We clink glasses. Three times for good luck. She giggles. I feel better.

"Nice sweater," I say.

"Michael Owyang," she says. She laughs. The light from the candle makes her eyes shimmer. She's got Mah's eyes. Eyes that make you want to talk. Lisa is reed-thin and tall. She's got a body that clothes look good on. My sister slips something on and it wraps her like skin. Fabric has pulse on her.

"Happy birthday, soon," I say.

"Thanks, and to yours too, just as soon."

40   "Here's to Johnny Walker in shark's fin soup," I say.

"And squab dinners."

"I LOVE LUCY," I say.

We laugh. It makes us feel like children again. We remember how to be sisters.

I raise my glass. "To I LOVE LUCY, squab dinners, and brown bags."

45   "To bones," she says.

"Bones," I repeat. This is a funny that gets sad, and knowing it, I keep laughing. I am surprised how much memory there is in one word. Pigeons. Only recently did I learn they're called squab. Our word for them was pigeon—on a plate or flying over Portsmouth Square. A good meal at 40 cents a bird. In line by dawn, we waited at the butcher's listening for the slow, churning motor of the trucks. We watched the live fish flushing out of the tanks into the garbage pails. We smelled the honey-brushed cha sui bows baking. When the white laundry truck turned onto Wentworth, there was a puffing tail of feathers following it. A stench filled the alley. The crowd squeezed in around the truck. Old ladies reached into the crates, squeezing and tugging for the plumpest pigeons.

My sister and I picked the white ones, those with the most expressive eyes. Dove birds, we called them. We fed them leftover rice in water, and as long as they stayed plump, they were our pets, our baby dove birds. And then one day we'd come home from school and find them cooked. They were a special, nutritious treat. Mah let us fill our bowls high with little pigeon parts: legs, breasts, and wings, and take them out to the front room to watch I LOVE LUCY. We took brown bags for the bones. We balanced our bowls on our laps and laughed at Lucy. We leaned forward, our chopsticks crossed in mid-air, and called out, "Mah! Mah! Come watch! Watch Lucy cry!"

But she always sat alone in the kitchen sucking out the sweetness of the lesser parts: necks, backs, and the head. "Bones are sweeter than you know," she always said. She came out to check the bags. "Clean bones," she said, shaking the bags. "No waste," she said.

Our dinners come with a warning. "Plate's hot. Don't touch." My sister orders a carafe of house white. "Enjoy," he says, smiling at my sister. She doesn't look up.

I can't remember how to say scallops in Chinese. I ask my sister, she doesn't 50
know either. The food isn't great. Or maybe we just don't have the taste buds in us to go crazy over it. Sometimes I get very hungry for Chinese flavors: black beans, garlic and ginger, shrimp paste and sesame oil. These are tastes we grew up with, still dream about. Crave. Run around town after. Duck liver sausage, beancurd, jook, salted fish, and fried dace with black beans. Western flavors don't stand out, the surroundings do. Three pronged forks. Pink tablecloths. Fresh flowers. Cute waiters. An odd difference.

"Maybe we should have gone to Sun Hung Heung. At least the vegetables are real," I say.

"Hung toh-vee-foo-won-tun!" she says.

"Yeah, yum!" I say.

I remember Deh teaching us how to pick bok choy, his favorite vegetable. "Stick your fingernail into the stem. Juicy and firm, good. Limp and tough, no good." The three of us followed Deh, punching our thumbnails into every stem of bok choy we saw.

"Deh still eating bok choy?" 55

"Breakfast, lunch and dinner." My sister throws her head back, and laughs. It is Deh's motion. She recites in a mimic tone. "Your Deh, all he needs is a good hot bowl of rice and a plate full of greens. A good monk."

There was always bok choy. Even though it was nonstop for Mah—rushing to the sweatshop in the morning, out to shop on break, and then home to cook by evening—she did this for him. A plate of bok choy, steaming with the taste of ginger and garlic. He said she made good rice. Timed full-fire until the first boil, medium until the grains formed a crust along the sides of the pot, and then low-flammed to let the rice steam. Firm, that's how Deh liked his rice.

The waiter brings the wine, asks if everything is alright.

"Everything," my sister says.

60   There's something else about this meeting. I can hear it in the edge of her voice. She doesn't say anything and I don't ask. Her lips make a contorting line; her face looks sour. She lets out a breath. It sounds like she's been holding it in too long.

"Another fight. The bank line," she says. "He waited four times in the bank line. Mah ran around outside shopping. He was doing her a favor. She was doing him a favor. Mah wouldn't stop yelling. 'Get out and go die! Useless Thing! Stinking Corpse!'"

I know he answered. His voice must have had that fortune teller's tone to it. You listened because you knew it was a warning.

He always threatened to disappear, jump off the Golden Gate. His thousand-year-old threat. I've heard it all before. "I will go. Even when dead, I won't be far enough away. Curse the good will that blinded me into taking you as wife!"

I give Lisa some of my scallops. "Eat," I tell her.

65   She keeps talking. "Of course, you know how Mah thinks, that nobody should complain because she's been the one working all these years."

I nod. I start eating, hoping she'll follow.

One bite and she's talking again. "You know what shopping with Mah is like, either you stand outside with the bags like a servant, or inside like a marker, holding a place in line. You know how she gets into being frugal—saving time because it's the one free thing in her life. Well, they're at the bank and she had him hold her place in line while she runs up and down Stockton doing her quick shopping maneuvers. So he's in line, and it's his turn, but she's not back. So he has to start all over at the back again. Then it's his turn but she's still not back. When she finally comes in, she's got bags in both hands, and he's going through the line for the fourth time. Of course she doesn't say sorry or anything."

I interrupt. "How do you know all this?" I tell myself not to come back next year. I tell myself to apply for another transfer, to the East Coast.

"She told me. Word for word." Lisa spears the scallops, puts it in her mouth. I know it's cold by now. "Word for word," she repeats. She cuts a piece of chicken. "Try," she says.

70   I think about how we're sisters. We eat slowly, chewing carefully, like old people. A way to make things last, to fool the stomach.

Mah and Deh both worked too hard; it's as if their marriage was a marriage of toil—of toiling together. The idea is that the next generation can marry for love.

In the old country, matches were made, strangers were wedded, and that was fate. Those days, sojourners like Deh were considered princes. To become the wife to such a man was to be saved from the war-torn villages.

Saved to work. After dinner, with the rice still in between her teeth, Mah sat down at her Singer. When we pulled out the wall-bed, she was still there, sewing. The street noises stopped long before she did. The hot lamp made all the stitches blur together. And in the mornings, long before any of us awoke, she was already there, sewing again.

His work was hard, too. He ran a laundry on Polk Street. He sailed with the American President Lines. Things started to look up when he owned the take-out place in Vallejo, and then his partner ran off. So he went to Alaska and worked the canneries.

75   She was good to him too. We remember. How else would we have known him all those years he worked in Guam, in the Fiji islands, in Alaska? Mah always gave him majestic welcomes home. It was her excitement that made us remember him.

I look around. The restaurant is full. The waiters move quickly.

I know Deh. His words are ugly. I've heard him. I've listened. And I've always wished for the street noises, as if in the traffic of sound, I believe I can escape. I know the hard color of his eyes and the tightness in his jaw. I can almost hear his teeth grind. I know this. Years of it.

Their lives weren't easy. So is their discontent without reason?

What about the first one? You didn't even think to come to the hospital. The first one, I say! Son or daughter, dead or alive, you didn't even come!

What about living or dying? Which did you want for me that time you pushed me back   80
to work before my back brace was off?

Money! Money!! Money to eat with, to buy clothes with, to pass this life with!

Don't start that again! Everything I make at that dead place I hand . . .

How come . . .

What about . . .

So . . .   85

It was obvious. The stories themselves meant little. It was how hot and furious they could become.

Is there no end to it? What makes their ugliness so alive, so thick and impossible to let go of?

"I don't want to think about it anymore." The way she says it surprises me. This time I listen. I imagine what it would be like to take her place. It will be my turn one day.

"Ron," she says, wiggling her fingers above the candle. "A fun thing."

The opal flickers above the flame. I tell her that I want to get her something spe-   90
cial for her birthday, ". . . next trip I get abroad." She looks up at me, smiles.

For a minute, my sister seems happy. But she won't be able to hold onto it. She grabs at things out of despair, out of fear. Gifts grow old for her. Emotions never ripen, they sour. Everything slips away from her. Nothing sustains her. Her beauty has made her fragile.

We should have eaten in Chinatown. We could have gone for coffee in North Beach, then for jook at Sam Wo's.

"No work, it's been like that for months, just odd jobs," she says.

I'm thinking, it's not like I haven't done my share. I was a kid once, I did things because I felt I should. I helped fill out forms at the Chinatown employment agencies. I went with him to the Seaman's Union. I waited too, listening and hoping for those calls: "Busboy! Presser! Prep Man!" His bags were packed, he was always ready to go. "On standby," he said.

Every week. All the same. Quitting and looking to start all over again. In the   95
end, it was like never having gone anywhere. It was like the bank line, waiting for nothing.

How many times did my sister and I have to hold them apart? The flat *ting!* sound as the blade slapped onto the linoleum floors, the wooden handle of the knife slamming into the corner. Was it she or I who screamed, repeating all their ugliest words? Who shook them? Who made them stop?

The waiter comes to take the plates. He stands by my sister for a moment. I raise my glass to the waiter.

"You two Chinese?" he asks.

"No," I say, finishing off my wine. I roll my eyes. I wish I had another Johnny Walker. Suddenly I don't care.

100   "We're two sisters," I say. I laugh. I ask for the check, leave a good tip. I see him slip my sister a box of matches.

Outside, the air is cool and brisk. My sister links her arm into mine. We walk up Bay onto Chestnut. We pass Galileo High School and then turn down Van Ness to head toward the pier. The bay is black. The foghorns sound far away. We walk the whole length of the pier without talking.

The water is white where it slaps against the wooden stakes. For a long time Lisa's wanted out. She can stay at that point of endurance forever. Desire that becomes old feels too good, it's seductive. I know how hard it is to go.

The heart never travels. You have to be heartless. My sister holds that heart, too close and for too long. This is her weakness, and I like to think, used to be mine. Lisa endures too much.

We're lucky, not like the bondmaids growing up in service, or the new-born daughters whose mouths were stuffed with ashes. Courtesans with the three-inch foot, beardless, soft-shouldered eunuchs, and the frightened child-brides, they're all stories to us. We're the lucky generation. Our parents forced themselves to live through the humiliation in this country so that we could have it better. We know so little of the old country. We repeat the names of Grandmothers and Uncles, but they will always be strangers to us. Family exists only because somebody has a story, and knowing the story connects us to a history. To us, the deformed man is oddly compelling, the forgotten man is a good story. A beautiful woman suffers.

105   I want her beauty to buy her out.

The sweater cost two weeks' pay. Like the 40-cent birds that are now a delicacy, this is a special treat. The money doesn't mean anything. It is, if anything, time. Time is what I would like to give her.

A red sweater. 100%. The skin of fuzz will be a fierce rouge on her naked breasts.

Red. Lucky. Wear it. Find that man. The new one. Wrap yourself around him. Feel the pulsing between you. Fuck him and think about it. 100% angora. Hand Wash Only. Worn Once.

CRITICAL THINKING QUESTIONS

1.   What *claim of value* about family does this story suggest to you?

2.   List *evidence* from the story that supports this claim.

WRITING TOPICS

Select one of the following quotations from Ng's story. First, discuss its significance within the dramatic context of the story. Next, extend your reflections beyond the boundaries of the story and discuss its broader implications.

a. "Desire that becomes old feels too good, it's seductive."
b. "The heart never travels. You have to be heartless."
c. "Family exists only because somebody has a story to tell, and knowing that story connects us to a history."

Grace Paley (b. 1922)

A Conversation with My Father

My father is eighty-six years old and in bed. His heart, that bloody motor, is equally old and will not do certain jobs any more. It still floods his head with brainy light. But it won't let his legs carry the weight of his body around the house. Despite my metaphors, this muscle failure is not due to his old heart, he says, but to a potassium shortage. Sitting on one pillow, leaning on three, he offers last-minute advice and makes a request.

"I would like you to write a simple story just once more," he says, "the kind de Maupassant wrote, or Chekhov, the kind you used to write. Just recognizable people and then write down what happened to them next."

I say, "Yes, why not? That's possible." I want to please him, though I don't remember writing that way. I *would* like to try to tell such a story, if he means the kind that begins: "There was a woman . . ." followed by plot, the absolute line between two points which I've always despised. Not for literary reasons, but because it takes all hope away. Everyone, real or invented, deserves the open destiny of life.

Finally I thought of a story that had been happening for a couple of years right across the street. I wrote it down, then read it aloud. "Pa," I said, "how about this? Do you mean something like this?"

> Once in my time there was a woman and she had a son. They lived nicely, in a small apartment in Manhattan. This boy at about fifteen became a junkie, which is not unusual in our neighborhood. In order to maintain her close friendship with him, she became a junkie too. She said it was part of the youth culture, with which she felt very much at home. After a while, for a number of reasons, the boy gave it all up and left the city and his mother in disgust. Hopeless and alone, she grieved. We all visit her.

"O.K., Pa, that's it," I said. "An unadorned and miserable tale."   5

"But that's not what I mean," my father said. "You misunderstood me on purpose. You know there's a lot more to it. You know that. You left everything out. Turgenev wouldn't do that. Chekhov wouldn't do that. There are in fact Russian writers you never heard of, you don't have an inkling of, as good as anyone, who can write a plain ordinary story, who would not leave out what you have left out. I object not to facts but to people sitting in trees talking senselessly, voices from who knows where. . . ."

"Forget that one, Pa, what have I left out now? In this one?"

"Her looks, for instance."

"Oh. Quite handsome, I think. Yes."

10   "Her hair?"

"Dark, with heavy braids, as though she were a girl or a foreigner."

"What were her parents like, her stock? That she became such a person. It's interesting, you know."

"From out of town. Professional people. The first to be divorced in their country. How's that? Enough?" I asked.

15   "With you, it's all a joke," he said. "What about the boy's father? Why didn't you mention him? Who was he? Or was the boy born out of wedlock?"

"Yes," I said. "He was born out of wedlock."

"For Godsakes, doesn't anyone in your stories get married? Doesn't anyone have the time to run down to City Hall before they jump into bed?"

"No," I said. "In real life, yes. But in my stories, no."

"Why do you answer me like that?"

"Oh, Pa, this is a simple story about a smart woman who came to N.Y.C. full of interest love trust excitement very up to date, and about her son, what a hard time she had in this world. Married or not, it's of small consequence."

20   "It is of great consequence," he said.

"O.K.," I said.

"O.K. O.K. yourself," he said, "but listen. I believe you that she's good-looking, but I don't think she was so smart."

"That's true," I said. "Actually that's the trouble with stories. People start out fantastic. You think they're extraordinary, but it turns out as the work goes along, they're just average with a good education. Sometimes the other way around, the person's kind of dumb innocent, but he outwits you and you can't even think of an ending good enough."

"What do you do then?" he asked. He had been a doctor for a couple of decades and he's still interested in details, craft, technique.

25   "Well, you just have to let the story lie around till some agreement can be reached between you and the stubborn hero."

"Aren't you talking silly now?" he asked. "Start again," he said. "It so happens I'm not going out this evening. Tell the story again. See what you can do this time."

"O.K.," I said. "But it's not a five-minute job." Second attempt:

Once, across the street from us, there was a fine handsome woman, our neighbor. She had a son whom she loved because she'd known him since birth (in helpless chubby infancy, and in the wrestling, hugging ages, seven to ten, as well as earlier and later). This boy, when he fell into the fist of adolescence, became a junkie. He was not a hopeless one. He was in fact hopeful, an ideologue and successful converter. With his busy brilliance, he wrote persuasive articles for his high-school newspaper. Seeking a wide audience, using important connections, he drummed into Lower Manhattan newsstand distribution a periodical called *Oh! Golden Horse!*

In order to keep him from feeling guilty (because guilt is the stony heart of nine tenths of all clinically diagnosed cancers in America today, she said), and because she had always believed in giving bad habits room at home where one could keep an eye on them, she too became a junkie. Her kitchen was famous for a while—a center for intellectual addicts who knew what they were doing. A few felt artistic like Coleridge and others were scientific and revolutionary like Leary. Although she was often high herself, certain good mothering reflexes remained, and she saw to it that there was lots of orange juice around and honey and milk and vitamin pills. However, she never cooked anything but chili, and that no more than once a week. She explained, when we talked to her, seriously, with neighborly concern, that it was her part in the youth culture and she would rather be with the young, it was an honor, than with her own generation.

One week, while nodding through an Antonioni film, this boy was severely jabbed by the elbow of a stern and proselytizing girl, sitting beside him. She offered immediate apricots and nuts for his sugar level, spoke to him sharply, and took him home.

She had heard of him and his work and she herself published, edited, and wrote a competitive journal called *Man Does Live by Bread Alone*. In the organic heat of her continuous presence he could not help but become interested once more in his muscles, his arteries, and nerve connections. In fact he began to love them, treasure them, praise them with funny little songs in *Man Does Live. . . .*

> the fingers of my flesh transcend
> my transcendental soul
> the tightness in my shoulders end
> my teeth have made me whole

To the mouth of his head (that glory of will and determination) he brought hard apples, nuts, wheat germ, and soybean oil. He said to his old friends, From now on, I guess I'll keep my wits about me. I'm going on the natch. He said he was about to begin a spiritual deep-breathing journey. How about you too, Mom? he asked kindly.

His conversion was so radiant, splendid, that neighborhood kids his age began to say that he had never been a real addict at all, only a journalist along for the smell of the story. The mother tried several times to give up what had become without her son and his friends a lonely habit. This effort only brought it to supportable levels. The boy and his girl took their electronic mimeograph and moved to the bushy edge of another borough. They were very strict. They said they would not see her again until she had been off drugs for sixty days.

At home alone in the evening, weeping, the mother read and reread the seven issues of *Oh! Golden Horse!* They seemed to her as truthful as ever. We often crossed the street to visit and console. But if we mentioned any of our children who were at college or in the hospital or dropouts at home, she would cry out, My baby! My baby! and burst into terrible, face-scarring, time-consuming tears. The End.

First my father was silent, then he said, "Number One: You have a nice sense of humor. Number Two: I see you can't tell a plain story. So don't waste time." Then he said sadly, "Number Three: I suppose that means she was alone, she was left like that, his mother. Alone. Probably sick?"

30   I said, "Yes."

"Poor woman. Poor girl, to be born in a time of fools, to live among fools, The end. The end. Your were right to put that down. The end."

I didn't want to argue, but I had to say, "Well, it is not necessarily the end, Pa."

Yes," he said, "what a tragedy. The end of a person."

"No, Pa," I begged him. "It doesn't have to be. She's only about forty. She could be a hundred different things in this world as time goes on. A teacher or a social worker. An ex-junkie! Sometimes it's better than having a master's in education."

35   "Jokes," he said. "As a writer that's your main trouble. You don't want to recognize it. Tragedy! Plain tragedy? Historical tragedy? No hope. The end."

"Oh, Pa," I said. "She could change."

"In your own life, too, you have to look it in the face." He took a couple of nitroglycerin. "Turn to five," he said, pointing to the dial on the oxygen tank. He inserted the tubes into his nostrils and breathed deep. He closed his eyes and said, "No."

I had promised the family to always let him have the last word when arguing, but in this case I had a different responsibility. That woman lives across the street. She's my knowledge and my invention. I'm sorry for her. I'm not going to leave her there in that house crying. (Actually neither would Life, which unlike me has no pity.)

Therefore: She did change. Of course her son never came home again. But right now, she's the receptionist in a storefront community clinic in the East Village. Most of the customers are young people, some old friends. The head doctor has said to her, "If we only had three people in this clinic with your experiences. . . ."

40   "The doctor said that?" My father took the oxygen tubes out of his nostrils and said, "Jokes. Jokes again."

"No, Pa, it could really happen that way, it's a funny world nowadays."

"No," he said. "Truth first. She will slide back. A person must have character. She does not."

"No, Pa," I said. "That's it. She's got a job. Forget it. She's in that storefront working."

"How long will it be?" he asked. "Tragedy! You too. When will you look it in the face?"

CRITICAL THINKING QUESTIONS

1. To analyze this "conversation" as an argument, identify at least two *issues.* Choose the issue that seems most significant or interesting to you and write out the *position* that each character, the father and the daughter, argues.

2. In evaluating the argument, would you declare a winner? If so, who? And if not, why? Do you support the father's or the daughter's viewpoint? Why?

WRITING TOPIC

How do you define character? What *value assumptions* influence your perspective on character and individual identity? What evidence—personal experiences, observations, specific individuals (family members, peers, teachers, coaches, etc.)—has contributed to your value assumptions about character? Based on your reflections on Paley's story and your own experience, write an argument about the significance of character as a factor in shaping an individual's identity.

John Updike (b. 1932)

Separating

The day was fair. Brilliant. All that June the weather had mocked the Maples' internal misery with solid sunlight—golden shafts and cascades of green in which their conversations had wormed unseeing, their sad murmuring selves the only stain in Nature. Usually by this time of the year they had acquired tans; but when they met their elder daughter's plane on her return from a year in England they were almost as pale as she, though Judith was too dazzled by the sunny opulent jumble of her native land to notice. They did not spoil her homecoming by telling her immediately. Wait a few days, let her recover from jet lag, had been one of their formulations, in that string of gray dialogues—over coffee, over cocktails, over Cointreau—that had shaped the strategy of their dissolution, while the earth performed its annual stunt of renewal unnoticed beyond their closed windows. Richard had thought to leave at Easter; Joan had insisted they wait until the four children were at last assembled, with all exams passed and ceremonies attended, and the bauble of summer to console them. So he had drudged away, in love, in dread, repairing screens, getting the mowers sharpened, rolling and patching their new tennis court.

The court, clay, had come through its first winter pitted and windswept bare of redcoat. Years ago the Maples had observed how often, among their friends, divorce followed a dramatic home improvement, as if the marriage were making one last twitchy effort to live; their own worst crisis had come amid the plaster dust and exposed plumbing of a kitchen renovation. Yet, a summer ago, as canary-yellow bulldozers gaily churned a grassy, daisy-dotted knoll into a muddy plateau, and a crew of pigtailed young men raked and tamped clay into a plane, this transformation did not strike them as ominous, but festive in its impudence; their marriage could rend the earth for fun. The next spring, waking each day at dawn to a sliding sensation as if the bed were being tipped, Richard found the barren tennis court, its net and tapes still rolled in the barn, an environment congruous with his mood of purposeful desolation, and the crumbling of handfuls of clay into cracks and holes (dogs had frolicked on the court in a thaw; rivulets had evolved trenches) an activity suitably elemental and interminable. In his sealed heart he hoped the day would never come.

Now it was here. A Friday. Judith was reacclimated; all four children were assembled, before jobs and camps and visits again scattered them. Joan thought they should be told one by one. Richard was for making an announcement at the table. She said, "I think just making an announcement is a cop-out. They'll start quarrelling and playing to each other instead of focusing. They're each individuals, you know, not just some corporate obstacle to your freedom."

"O.K., O.K. I agree." Joan's plan was exact. That evening, they were giving Judith a belated welcome-home dinner, of lobster and champagne. Then, the party over, they, the two of them, who nineteen years before would push her in a baby carriage along Tenth Street to Washington Square, were to walk her out of the house, to the bridge across the salt creek, and tell her, swearing her to secrecy. Then Richard Jr., who was going directly from work to a rock concert in Boston, would be told, either late when he returned on the train or early Saturday morning before he went off to his job; he was seventeen and employed as one of a golf-course maintenance crew. Then the two younger children, John and Margaret, could, as the morning wore on, be informed.

5   "Mopped up, as it were," Richard said.

"Do you have any better plan? That leaves you the rest of Saturday to answer any questions, pack, and make your wonderful departure."

"No," he said, meaning he had no better plan, and agreed to hers, though it had an edge of false order, a plea for control in the semblance of its achievement, like Joan's long chore lists and financial accountings and, in the days when he first knew her, her too copious lecture notes. Her plan turned one hurdle for him into four—four knife-sharp walls, each with a sheer blind drop on the other side.

All spring he had been morbidly conscious of insides and outsides, of barriers and partitions. He and Joan stood as a thin barrier between the children and the truth. Each moment was a partition, with the past on one side and the future on the other, a future containing this unthinkable *now*. Beyond four knifelike walls a new life for him waited vaguely. His skull cupped a secret, a white face, a face both frightened and soothing, both strange and known, that he wanted to shield from tears, which he felt all about him, solid as the sunlight. So haunted, he had become obsessed with battening down the house against his absence, replacing screens and sash cords, hinges and latches—a Houdini making things snug before his escape.

The lock. He had still to replace a lock on one of the doors of the screened porch. The task, like most such, proved more difficult than he had imagined. The old lock, aluminum frozen by corrosion, had been deliberately rendered obsolete by manufacturers. Three hardware stores had nothing that even approximately matched the mortised hole its removal (surprisingly easy) left. Another hole had to be gouged, with bits too small and saws too big, and the old hole fitted with a block of wood—the chisels dull, the saw rusty, his fingers thick with lack of sleep. The sun poured down, beyond the porch, on a world of neglect. The bushes already needed pruning, the windward side of the house was shedding flakes of paint, rain would get in when he was gone, insects, rot, death. His family, all those he would lose, filtered through the edges of his awareness as he struggled with screw holes, splinters, opaque instructions, minutiae of metal.

10   Judith sat on the porch, a princess returned from exile. She regaled them with stories of fuel shortages, of bomb scares in the Underground, of Pakistani workmen loudly lusting after her as she walked past on her way to dance school. Joan came and went,

in and out of the house, calmer than she should have been, praising his struggles with the lock as if this were one more and not the last of their chain of shared chores. The younger of his sons, John, now at fifteen suddenly, unwittingly handsome, for a few minutes held the rickety screen door while his father clumsily hammered and chiseled, each blow a kind of sob in Richard's ears. His younger daughter, having been at a slumber party, slept on the porch hammock through all the noise—heavy and pink, trusting and forsaken. Time, like the sunlight, continued relentlessly; the sunlight slowly slanted. Today was one of the longest days. The lock clicked, worked. He was through. He had a drink; he drank it on the porch, listening to his daughter. "It was so sweet," she was saying, "during the worst of it, how all the butcher's and bakery shops kept open by candlelight. They're all so plucky and cute. From the papers, things sounded so much worse here—people shooting people in gas lines, and everybody freezing."

Richard asked her, "Do you still want to live in England forever?" *Forever:* the concept, now a reality upon him, pressed and scratched at the back of his throat.

"No," Judith confessed, turning her oval face to him, its eyes still childishly far apart, but the lips set as over something succulent and satisfactory. "I was anxious to come home. I'm an American." She was a woman. They had raised her; he and Joan had endured together to raise her, alone of the four. The others had still some raising left in them. Yet it was the thought of telling Judith—the image of her, their first baby, walking between them arm in arm to the bridge—that broke him. The partition between himself and the tears broke. Richard sat down to the celebratory meal with the back of his throat aching; the champagne, the lobster seemed phases of sunshine; he saw them and tasted them through tears. He blinked, swallowed, croakily joked about hay fever. The tears would not stop leaking through; they came not through a hole that could be plugged but through a permeable spot in a membrane, steadily, purely, endlessly, fruitfully. They became, his tears, a shield for himself against these others—their faces, the fact of their assembly, a last time as innocents, at a table where he sat the last time as head. Tears dropped from his nose as he broke the lobster's back; salt flavored his champagne as he sipped it; the raw clench at the back of his throat was delicious. He could not help himself.

His children tried to ignore his tears. Judith on his right, lit a cigarette, gazed upward in the direction of her too energetic, too sophisticated exhalation; on her other side, John earnestly bent his face to the extraction of the last morsels—legs, tail segments—from the scarlet corpse. Joan, at the opposite end of the table, glanced at him surprised, her reproach displaced by a quick grimace, of forgiveness, or of salute to his superior gift of strategy. Between them, Margaret, no longer called Bean, thirteen and large for her age, gazed from the other side of his pane of tears as if into a shopwindow at something she coveted—at her father, a crystalline heap of splinters and memories. It was not she, however, but John who, in the kitchen, as they cleared the plates and carapaces away, asked Joan the question: *"Why is Daddy crying?"*

Richard heard the question but not the murmured answer. Then he heard Bean cry, "Oh, no-oh!"—the faintly dramatized exclamation of one who had long expected it.

John returned to the table carrying a bowl of salad. He nodded tersely at his father and his lips shaped the conspiratorial words "She told." 15

"Told what?" Richard asked aloud, insanely.

The boy sat down as if to rebuke his father's distraction with the example of his own good manners and said quietly, "The separation."

Joan and Margaret returned; the child, in Richard's twisted vision, seemed diminished in size, and relieved, relieved to have had the boogeyman at last proved real. He called out to her—the distances at the table had grown immense—"You knew, you always knew," but the clenching at the back of his throat prevented him from making sense of it. From afar he heard Joan talking, levelly, sensibly, reciting what they had prepared: it was a separation for the summer, an experiment. She and Daddy both agreed it would be good for them; they needed space and time to think; they liked each other but did not make each other happy enough, somehow.

Judith, imitating her mother's factual tone, but in her youth off-key, too cool, said, "I think it's silly. You should either live together or get divorced."

20   Richard's crying, like a wave that has crested and crashed, had become tumultuous; but it was overtopped by another tumult, for John, who had been so reserved, now grew larger and larger at the table. Perhaps his younger sister's being credited with knowing set him off. "Why didn't you *tell* us?" he asked, in a large round voice quite unlike his own. "You should have *told* us you weren't getting along."

Richard was startled into attempting to force words through his tears. "We *do* get along, that's the trouble, so it doesn't show even to us—" "That we do not love each other" was the rest of the sentence; he couldn't finish it.

Joan finished for him, in her style. "And we've always, *especially,* loved our children."

John was not mollified. "What do you care about *us?*" he boomed. "We're just little things you *had.*" His sisters' laughing forced a laugh from him, which he turned hard and parodistic: "Ha ha *ha.*" Richard and Joan realized simultaneously that the child was drunk, on Judith's homecoming champagne. Feeling bound to keep the center of the stage, John took a cigarette from Judith's pack, poked it into his mouth, let it hang from his lower lip, and squinted like a gangster.

"You're not little things we had," Richard called to him. "You're the whole point. But you're grown. Or almost."

25   The boy was lighting matches. Instead of holding them to his cigarette (for they had never seen him smoke; being "good" had been his way of setting himself apart), he held them to his mother's face, closer and closer, for her to blow out. Then he lit the whole folder—a hiss and then a torch, held against his mother's face. Prismed by tears, the flame filled Richard's vision; he didn't know how it was extinguished. He heard Margaret say, "Oh stop showing off," and saw John, in response, break the cigarette in two and put the halves entirely into his mouth and chew, sticking out his tongue to display the shreds to his sister.

Joan talked to him, reasoning—a fountain of reason, unintelligible. "Talked about it for years . . . our children must help us . . . Daddy and I both want . . ." As the boy listened, he carefully wadded a paper napkin into the leaves of his salad, fashioned a ball of paper and lettuce, and popped it into his mouth, looking around the table for the expected laughter. None came. Judith said, "Be mature," and dismissed a plume of smoke.

Richard got up from this stifling table and led the boy outside. Though the house was in twilight, the outdoors still brimmed with light, the long waste light of high

summer. Both laughing, he supervised John's spitting out the lettuce and paper and tobacco into the pachysandra. He took him by the hand—a square gritty hand, but for
its softness a man's. Yet, it held on. They ran together up into the field, past the tennis court. The raw banking left by the bulldozers was dotted with daisies. Past the
court and a flat stretch where they used to play family baseball stood a soft green rise
glorious in the sun, each weed and species of grass distinct as illumination on parchment. "I'm sorry, so sorry." Richard cried. "You were the only one who ever tried to help
me with all the goddam jobs around this place."

Sobbing, safe within his tears and the champagne, John explained, "It's not just
the separation, it's the whole crummy year, I *hate* that school, you can't make any
friends, the history teacher's a scud."

They sat on the crest of the rise, shaking and warm from their tears but easier in
their voices, and Richard tried to focus on the child's sad year—the weekdays long with
homework, the weekends spent in his room with model airplanes, while his parents
murmured down below, nursing their separation. How selfish, how blind, Richard
thought; his eyes felt scoured. He told his son, "We'll think about getting you trans-
ferred. Life's too short to be miserable."

They had said what they could, but did not want the moment to heal, and talked   30
on, about the school, about the tennis court, whether it would ever again be as good
as it had been that first summer. They walked to inspect it and pressed a few more tapes
more firmly down. A little stiltedly, perhaps trying to make too much of the moment,
to prolong it, Richard led the boy to the spot in the field where the view was best, of
the metallic blue river, the emerald marsh, the scattered islands velvet with shadow in
the low light, the white bits of beach far away. "See," he said. "It goes on being beautiful. It'll be here tomorrow."

"I know," John answered, impatiently. The moment had closed.

Back in the house, the others had opened some white wine, the champagne
being drunk, and still sat at the table, the three females, gossiping. Where Joan sat
had become the head. She turned, showing him a tearless face, and asked, "All
right?"

"We're fine," he said, resenting it, though relieved, that the party went on without
him.

In bed she explained, "I couldn't cry I guess because I cried so much all spring. It
really wasn't fair. It's your idea, and you made it look as though I was kicking you out."

"I'm sorry," he said. "I couldn't stop. I wanted to but couldn't."   35

"You *didn't* want to. You loved it. You were having your way, making a general
announcement."

"I love having it over," he admitted. "God, those kids were great. So brave and
funny," John, returned to the house, had settled to a model airplane in his room, and
kept shouting down to them, "I'm O.K. No sweat." "And the way," Richard went on,
cozy in his relief, "they never questioned the reasons we gave. No thought of a third
person. Not even Judith."

"That *was* touching," Joan said.

He gave her a hug. "You were great too. Thank you." Guiltily, he realized he did not feel separated.

40   "You still have Dickie to do," she told him. These words set before him a black mountain in the darkness; its cold breath, its near weight affected his chest. Of the four children Dickie was most nearly his conscience. Joan did not need to add, "That's one piece of your dirty work I won't do for you."

"I know. I'll do it. You go to sleep."

Within minutes, her breathing slowed, became oblivious and deep. It was quarter to midnight. Dickie's train from the concert would come in at one-fourteen. Richard set the alarm for one. He had slept atrociously for weeks. But whenever he closed his lids some glimpse of the last hours scorched them—Judith exhaling toward the ceiling in a kind of aversion, Bean's mute staring, the sunstruck growth of the field where he and John had rested. The mountain before him moved closer, moved within him; he was huge, momentous. The ache at the back of his throat felt stale. His wife slept as if slain beside him. When, exasperated by his hot lids, his crowded heart, he rose from bed and dressed, she awoke enough to turn over. He told her then, "If I could undo it all, I would."

"Where would you begin?" she asked. There was no place. Giving him courage, she was always giving him courage. He put on shoes without socks in the dark. The children were breathing in their rooms, the downstairs was hollow. In their confusion they had left lights burning. He turned off all but one, the kitchen overhead. The car started. He had hoped it wouldn't. He met only moonlight on the road; it seemed a diaphanous companion, flickering in the leaves along the roadside, haunting his rearview mirror like a pursuer, melting under his headlights. The center of town, not quite deserted, was eerie at this hour. A young cop in uniform kept company with a gang of T-shirted kids on the steps of the bank. Across from the railroad station, several bars kept open. Customers, mostly young, passed in and out of the warm night, savoring summer's novelty. Voices shouted from cars as they passed; an immense conversation seemed in progress. Richard parked and in his weariness put his head on the passenger seat, out of the commotion and wheeling lights. It was as when, in the movies, an assassin grimly carries his mission through the jostle of a carnival—except the movies cannot show the precipitous, palpable slope you cling to within. You cannot climb back down; you can only fall. The synthetic fabric of the car seat, warmed by his cheek, confided to him an ancient, distant scent of vanilla.

A train whistle caused him to lift his head. It was on time; he had hoped it would be late. The slender drawgates descended. The bell of approach tingled happily. The great metal body, horizontally fluted, rocked to a stop, and sleepy teen-agers disembarked, his son among them. Dickie did not show surprise that his father was meeting him at this terrible hour. He sauntered to the car with two friends, both taller than he. He said "Hi" to his father and took the passenger's seat with an exhausted promptness that expressed gratitude. The friends got into the back, and Richard was grateful; a few more minutes' postponement would be won by driving them home.

45   He asked. "How was the concert?"

"Groovy," one boy said from the back seat.

"It bit," the other said.

"It was O.K.," Dickie said, moderate by nature, so reasonable that in his childhood the unreason of the world had given him headaches, stomach aches, nausea. When the second friend had been dropped off at his dark house, the boy blurted, "Dad, my eyes are killing me with hay fever! I'm out there cutting that mothering grass all day!"

"Do we still have those drops?"

"They didn't do any good last summer."   50

"They might this." Richard swung a U-turn on the empty street. The drive home took a few minutes. The mountain was here, in his throat. "Richard," he said, and felt the boy, slumped and rubbing his eyes, go tense at his tone, "I didn't come to meet you just to make your life easier. I came because your mother and I have some news for you, and you're a hard man to get ahold of these days. It's sad news."

"That's O.K." The reassurance came out soft, but quick, as if released from the tip of a spring.

Richard had feared that his tears would return and choke him, but the boy's manliness set an example, and his voice issued forth steady and dry. "It's sad news, but it needn't be tragic news, at least for you. It should have no practical effect on your life, though it's bound to have an emotional effect. You'll work at your job, and go back to school in September. Your mother and I are really proud of what you're making of your life; we don't want that to change at all."

"Yeah," the boy said lightly, on the intake of his breath, holding himself up. They turned the corner; the church they went to loomed like a gutted fort. The home of the woman Richard hoped to marry stood across the green. Her bedroom light burned.

"Your mother and I," he said, "have decided to separate. For the summer. Noth- 55
ing legal, no divorce yet. We want to see how it feels. For some years now, we haven't been doing enough for each other, making each other as happy as we should be. Have you sensed that?"

"No," the boy said. It was an honest, unemotional answer: true or false in a quiz.

Glad for the factual basis, Richard pursued, even garrulously, the details. His apartment across town, his utter accessibility, the split vacation arrangements, the advantages to the children, the added mobility and variety of the summer. Dickie listened, absorbing. "Do the others know?"

Richard described how they had been told.

"How did they take it?"

"The girls pretty calmly. John flipped out; he shouted and ate a cigarette and 60
made a salad out of his napkin and told us how much he hated school."

His brother chuckled. "He did?"

"Yeah. The school issue was more upsetting for him than Mom and me. He seemed to feel better for having exploded."

"He did?" The repetition was the first sign that he was stunned.

"Yes. Dickie, I want to tell you something. This last hour, waiting for your train to get in, has been about the worst of my life. I hate this. *Hate* it. My father would have died before doing it to me." He felt immensely lighter, saying this. He had dumped the mountain on the boy. They were home. Moving swiftly as a shadow, Dickie was out of the car, through the bright kitchen. Richard called after him, "Want a glass of milk or anything?"

65 "No thanks."

"Want us to call the course tomorrow and say you're too sick to work?"

"No, that's all right." The answer was faint, delivered at the door to his room; Richard listened for the slam of a tantrum. The door closed normally. The sound was sickening.

Joan had sunk into that first deep trough of sleep and was slow to awake. Richard had to repeat, "I told him."

"What did he say?"

70 "Nothing much. Could you go say good night to him? Please."

She left their room, without putting on a bathrobe. He sluggishly changed back into his pajamas and walked down the hall. Dickie was already in bed, Joan was sitting beside him, and the boy's bedside clock radio was murmuring music. When she stood, an inexplicable light—the moon?—outlined her body through the nightie. Richard sat on the warm place she had indented on the child's narrow mattress. He asked him, "Do you want the radio on like that?"

"It always is."

"Doesn't it keep you awake? It would me."

"No."

75 "Are you sleepy?"

"Yeah."

"Good. Sure you want to get up and go to work? You've had a big night."

"I want to."

Away at school this winter he had learned for the first time that you can go short of sleep and live. As an infant he had slept with an immobile, sweating intensity that had alarmed his babysitters. As the children aged, he became the first to go to bed, earlier for a time than his younger brother and sister. Even now, he would go slack in the middle of a television show, his sprawled legs hairy and brown. "O.K. Good boy. Dickie, listen. I love you so much, I never knew how much until now. No matter how this works out, I'll always be with you. Really."

80 Richard bent to kiss an averted face but his son, sinewy, turned and with wet cheeks embraced him and gave him a kiss, on the lips, passionate as a woman's. In his father's ear he moaned one word, the crucial, intelligent word: *"Why?"*

Why. It was a whistle of wind in a crack, a knife thrust, a window thrown open on emptiness. The white face was gone, the darkness was featureless. Richard had forgotten why.

CRITICAL THINKING QUESTIONS

1. Explaining the separation to the children, Joan recites her and Richard's prepared lines: "it was a separation for the summer, an experiment; . . . they liked each other but did not make each other happy enough, somehow." What *warrant* about happiness in a marriage underlies Joan's explanation? Discuss why you accept or do not accept this warrant.

2. List gender stereotypes regarding emotions and expressiveness that are associated with boys/men and girls/women. How do the characters in this story support or challenge those stereotypes?

WRITING TOPIC

In telling the children about their separation, Richard and Joan have agreed to call it "an experiment . . . for the summer." Are they protecting the children or themselves? Is withholding the full truth the same as a lie, and if so, can a lie be justified (see also Chopin's "The Storm," page 405)?

Alice Walker (b. 1944)

Everyday Use
for your grandmama

I will wait for her in the yard that Maggie and I made so clean and wavy yesterday afternoon. A yard like this is more comfortable than most people know. It is not just a yard. It is like an extended living room. When the hard clay is swept clean as a floor and the fine sand around the edges lined with tiny, irregular grooves, anyone can come and sit and look up into the elm tree and wait for the breezes that never come inside the house.

Maggie will be nervous until after her sister goes: she will stand hopelessly in corners, homely and ashamed of the burn scars down her arms and legs, eyeing her sister with a mixture of envy and awe. She thinks her sister has held life always in the palm of one hand, that "no" is a word the world never learned to say to her.

You've no doubt seen those TV shows where the child who has "made it" is confronted, as a surprise, by her own mother and father, tottering in weakly from backstage. (A pleasant surprise, of course: What would they do if parent and child came on the show only to curse out and insult each other?) On TV mother and child embrace and smile into each other's faces. Sometimes the mother and father weep, the child wraps them in her arms and leans across the table to tell how she would not have made it without their help. I have seen these programs.

Sometimes I dream a dream in which Dee and I are suddenly brought together on a TV program of this sort. Out of a dark and soft-seated limousine I am ushered into a bright room filled with many people. There I meet a smiling, gray, sporty man like Johnny Carson who shakes my hand and tells me what a fine girl I have. Then we are on the stage and Dee is embracing me with tears in her eyes. She pins on my dress a large orchid, even though she has told me once that she thinks orchids are tacky flowers.

5   In real life I am a large, big-boned woman with rough, man-working hands. In the winter I wear flannel nightgowns to bed and overalls during the day. I can kill and clean a hog as mercilessly as a man. My fat keeps me hot in zero weather. I can work outside all day, breaking ice to get water for washing; I can eat pork liver cooked over the open fire minutes after it comes steaming from the hog. One winter I knocked a bull calf straight in the brain between the eyes with a sledge hammer and had the meat hung up to chill before nightfall. But of course all this does not show on television. I am the way my daughter would want me to be: a hundred pounds lighter, my skin like an uncooked barley pancake. My hair glistens in the hot bright lights. Johnny Carson has much to do to keep up with my quick and witty tongue.

But that is a mistake. I know even before I wake up. Who ever knew a Johnson with a quick tongue? Who can even imagine me looking a strange white man in the eye? It seems to me I have talked to them always with one foot raised in flight, with my head turned in whichever way is farthest from them. Dee, though. She would always look anyone in the eye. Hesitation was no part of her nature.

"How do I look, Mama?" Maggie says, showing just enough of her thin body enveloped in pink skirt and red blouse for me to know she's there, almost hidden by the door.

"Come out into the yard," I say.

Have you ever seen a lame animal, perhaps a dog run over by some careless person rich enough to own a car, sidle up to someone who is ignorant enough to be kind to him? That is the way my Maggie walks. She has been like this, chin on chest, eyes on ground, feet in shuffle, ever since the fire that burned the other house to the ground.

10   Dee is lighter than Maggie, with nicer hair and a fuller figure. She's a woman now, though sometimes I forget. How long ago was it that the other house burned? Ten, twelve years? Sometimes I can still hear the flames and feel Maggie's arms sticking to me, her hair smoking and her dress falling off her in little black papery flakes. Her eyes seemed stretched open, blazed open by the flames reflected in them. And Dee. I see her standing off under the sweet gum tree she used to dig gum out of; a look of concentration on her face as she watched the last dingy gray board of the house fall in toward the red-hot brick chimney. Why don't you do a dance around the ashes? I'd wanted to ask her. She had hated the house that much.

I used to think she hated Maggie, too. But that was before we raised the money, the church and me, to send her to Augusta to school. She used to read to us without pity; forcing words, lies, other folks' habits, whole lives upon us two, sitting trapped and ignorant underneath her voice. She washed us in a river of make-believe, burned us with a lot of knowledge we didn't necessarily need to know. Pressed us to her with the serious way she read, to shove us away at just the moment, like dimwits, we seemed about to understand.

Dee wanted nice things. A yellow organdy dress to wear to her graduation from high school; black pumps to match a green suit she'd made from an old suit somebody gave me. She was determined to stare down any disaster in her efforts. Her eyelids would not flicker for minutes at a time. Often I fought off the temptation to shake her. At sixteen she had a style of her own: and knew what style was.

I never had an education myself. After second grade the school was closed down. Don't ask me why: in 1927 colored asked fewer questions than they do now. Sometimes Maggie reads to me. She stumbles along good-naturedly but can't see well. She knows she is not bright. Like good looks and money, quickness passed her by. She will marry John Thomas (who has mossy teeth in an earnest face) and then I'll be free to sit here and I guess just sing church songs to myself. Although I never was a good singer. Never could carry a tune. I was always better at a man's job. I used to love to milk till I was hooked in the side in '49. Cows are soothing and slow and don't bother you, unless you try to milk them the wrong way.

I have deliberately turned my back on the house. It is three rooms, just like the one that burned, except the roof is tin; they don't make shingle roofs any more. There are no real windows, just some holes cut in the sides, like the portholes in a ship, but not round and not square, with rawhide holding the shutters up on the outside. This house is in a pasture, too, like the other one. No doubt when Dee sees it she will want to tear it down. She wrote me once that no matter where we "choose" to live, she will manage to come see us. But she will never bring her friends. Maggie and I thought about this and Maggie asked me, "Mama, when did Dee ever *have* any friends?"

She had a few. Furtive boys in pink shirts hanging about on washday after 15 school. Nervous girls who never laughed. Impressed with her they worshiped the well-turned phrase, the cute shape, the scalding humor that erupted like bubbles in lye. She read to them.

When she was courting Jimmy T she didn't have much time to pay to us, but turned all her fault finding power on him. He *flew* to marry a cheap city girl from a family of ignorant flashy people. She hardly had time to recompose herself.

When she comes I will meet—but there they are!

Maggie attempts to make a dash for the house, in her shuffling way, but I stay her with my hand. "Come back here," I say. And she stops and tries to dig a well in the sand with her toe.

It is hard to see them clearly through the strong sun. But even the first glimpse of leg out of the car tells me it is Dee. Her feet were always neat-looking, as if God himself had shaped them with a certain style. From the other side of the car comes a short, stocky man. Hair is all over his head a foot long and hanging from his chin like a kinky mule tail. I hear Maggie suck in her breath. "Uhnnnh," is what it sounds like. Like when you see the wriggling end of a snake just in front of your foot on the road. "Uhnnnh."

Dee next. A dress down to the ground, in this hot weather. A dress so loud it 20 hurts my eyes. There are yellows and oranges enough to throw back the light of the sun. I feel my whole face warming from the heat waves it throws out. Earrings gold, too, and hanging down to her shoulders. Bracelets dangling and making noises when she moves her arm up to shake the folds of the dress out of her armpits. The dress is loose and flows, and as she walks closer, I like it. I hear Maggie go "Uhnnnh" again.

It is her sister's hair. It stands straight up like the wool on a sheep. It is black as night and around the edges are two long pigtails that rope about like small lizards disappearing behind her ears.

"Wa-su-zo-Tean-o!" she says, coming on in that gilding way the dress makes her move. The short stocky fellow with the hair to his navel is all grinning and he follows up with "Asalamalakim, my mother and sister!" He moves to hug Maggie but she falls back, right up against the back of my chair. I feel her trembling there and when I look up I see the perspiration falling off her chin.

"Don't get up," says Dee. Since I am stout it takes something of a push. You can see me trying to move a second or two before I make it. She turns, showing white heels through her sandals, and goes back to the car. Out she peeks next with a Polaroid. She stoops down quickly and lines up picture after picture of me sitting there in front of the house with Maggie cowering behind me. She never takes a shot without making sure the house is included. When a cow comes nibbling around the edge of the yard she snaps it and me and Maggie *and* the house. Then she puts the Polaroid in the back seat of the car, and comes up and kisses me on the forehead.

Meanwhile Asalamalakim is going through motions with Maggie's hand. Maggie's hand is as limp as a fish, and probably as cold, despite the sweat, and she keeps trying to pull it back. It looks like Asalamalakim wants to shake hands but wants to do it fancy. Or maybe he don't know how people shake hands. Anyhow, he soon gives up on Maggie.

"Well," I say. "Dee."

25   "No, Mama," she says. "Not 'Dee,' Wangero Leewanika Kemanjo!"

"What happened to 'Dee'?" I wanted to know.

"She's dead," Wangero said. "I couldn't bear it any longer, being named after the people who oppress me."

"You know as well as me you was named after your aunt Dicie," I said. Dicie is my sister. She named Dee. We called her "Big Dee" after Dee was born.

"But who was *she* named after?" asked Wangero.

30   "I guess after Grandma Dee," I said.

"And who was she named after?" asked Wangero.

"Her mother," I said, and saw Wangero was getting tired. "That's about as far back as I can trace it," I said. Though, in fact, I probably could have carried it back beyond the Civil War through the branches.

"Well," said Asalamalakim, "there you are."

"Uhnnnh," I heard Maggie say.

35   "There I was not," I said, "before 'Dicie' cropped up in our family, so why should I try to trace it that far back?"

He just stood there grinning, looking down on me like somebody inspecting a Model A car. Every once in a while he and Wangero sent eye signals over my head.

"How do you pronounce this name?" I asked.

"You don't have to call me by it if you don't want to," said Wangero.

"Why shouldn't I?" I asked. "If that's what you want us to call you, we'll call you."

40   "I know it might sound awkward at first," said Wangero.

"I'll get used to it," I said. "Ream it out again."

Well, soon we got the name out of the way. Asalamalakim had a name twice as long and three times as hard. After I tripped over it two or three times he told me to just call him Hakim-a-barber. I wanted to ask him was he a barber, but I didn't really think he was, so I didn't ask.

"You must belong to those beef-cattle peoples down the road," I said. They said "Asalamalakim" when they met you, too, but they didn't shake hands. Always too busy: feeding the cattle, fixing the fences, putting up salt-lick shelters, throwing down hay. When the white folks poisoned some of the herd the men stayed up all night with rifles in their hands. I walked a mile and a half just to see the sight.

Hakim-a-barber said, "I accept some of their doctrines, but farming and raising cattle is not my style." (They didn't tell me, and I didn't ask, whether Wangero (Dee) had really gone and married him.)

We sat down to eat and right away he said he didn't eat collards and pork was un-   45
clean. Wangero, though, went on through the chitlins and corn bread, the greens and everything else. She talked a blue streak over the sweet potatoes. Everything delighted her. Even the fact that we still used the benches her daddy made for the table when we couldn't afford to buy chairs.

"Oh, Mama!" she cried. Then turned to Hakim-a-barber. "I never knew how lovely these benches are. You can feel the rump prints," she said, running her hands underneath her and along the bench. Then she gave a sigh and her hand closed over Grandma Dee's butter dish. "That's it!" she said. "I knew there was something I wanted to ask you if I could have." She jumped up from the table and went over in the corner where the churn stood, the milk in it clabber by now. She looked at the churn and looked at it.

"This churn top is what I need," she said. "Didn't Uncle Buddy whittle it out of a tree you all used to have?"

"Yes," I said.

"Uh huh," she said happily. "And I want the dasher, too."

"Uncle Buddy whittle that, too?" asked the barber.   50

Dee (Wangero) looked up at me.

"Aunt Dee's first husband whittled the dash," said Maggie so low you almost couldn't hear her. "His name was Henry, but they called him Stash."

"Maggie's brain is like an elephant's," Wangero said, laughing. "I can use the churn top as a centerpiece for the alcove table," she said, sliding a plate over the churn, "and I'll think of something artistic to do with the dasher."

When she finished wrapping the dasher the handle stuck out. I took it for a moment in my hands. You didn't even have to look close to see where hands pushing the dasher up and down to make butter had left a kind of sink in the wood. In fact, there were a lot of small sinks; you could see where thumbs and fingers had sunk into the wood. It was beautiful light yellow wood, from a tree that grew in the yard where Big Dee and Stash had lived.

After dinner Dee (Wangero) went to the trunk at the foot of my bed and started   55
rifling through it. Maggie hung back in the kitchen over the dishpan. Out came Wangero

with two quilts. They had been pieced by Grandma Dee and then Big Dee and me had hung them on the quilt frames on the front porch and quilted them. One was in the Lone Star pattern. The other was Walk Around the Mountain. In both of them were scraps of dresses Grandma Dee had worn fifty and more years ago. Bits and pieces of Grandpa Jarrell's Paisley shirts. And one teeny faded blue piece, about the size of a penny match-box, that was from Great Grandpa Ezra's uniform that he wore in the Civil War.

"Mama," Wangero said sweet as a bird. "Can I have these old quilts?"

I heard something fall in the kitchen, and a minute later the kitchen door slammed.

"Why don't you take one or two of the others?" I asked. "These old things was just done by me and Big Dee from some tops your grandma pieced before she died."

"No," said Wangero. "I don't want those. They are stitched around the borders by machine."

60   "That'll make them last better," I said.

"That's not the point," said Wangero. "These are all pieces of dresses Grandma used to wear. She did all this stitching by hand. Imagine!" She held the quilts securely in her arms, stroking them.

"Some of the pieces, like those lavender ones, come from old clothes her mother handed down to her," I said, moving up to touch the quilts. Dee (Wangero) moved back just enough so that I couldn't reach the quilts. They already belonged to her.

"Imagine!" she breathed again, clutching them closely to her bosom.

"The truth is," I said, "I promised to give them quilts to Maggie, for when she marries John Thomas."

65   She gasped like a bee had stung her.

"Maggie can't appreciate these quilts!" she said. "She'd probably be backward enough to put them to everyday use."

"I reckon she would," I said. "God knows I been saving 'em for long enough with nobody using 'em. I hope she will!" I didn't want to bring up how I had offered Dee (Wangero) a quilt when she went away to college. Then she had told me they were old-fashioned, out of style.

"But they're *priceless!*" she was saying now, furiously; for she has a temper. "Maggie would put them on the bed and in five years they'd be in rags. Less than that!"

"She can always make some more," I said. "Maggie knows how to quilt."

70   Dee (Wangero) looked at me with hatred. "You just will not understand. The point is these quilts, *these* quilts!"

"Well," I said, stumped. "What would *you* do with them?"

"Hang them," she said. As if that was the only thing you *could* do with quilts.

Maggie by now was standing in the door. I could almost hear the sound her feet made as they scraped over each other.

"She can have them, Mama," she said, like somebody used to never winning anything, or having anything reserved for her. "I can 'member Grandma Dee without the quilts."

75   I looked at her hard. She had filled her bottom lip with checkerberry snuff and it gave her face a kind of dopey, hangdog look. It was Grandma Dee and Big Dee who taught her how to quilt herself. She stood there with her scarred hands hidden

in the folds of her skirt. She looked at her sister with something like fear but she wasn't mad at her. This was Maggie's portion. This was the way she knew God to work.

When I looked at her like that something hit me in the top of my head and ran down to the soles of my feet. Just like when I'm in church and the spirit of God touches me and I get happy and shout. I did something I never had done before: hugged Maggie to me, then dragged her on into the room, snatched the quilts out of Miss Wangero's hands and dumped them into Maggie's lap. Maggie just sat there on my bed with her mouth open.

"Take one or two of the others," I said to Dee.

But she turned without a word and went out to Hakim-a-barber.

"You just don't understand," she said, as Maggie and I came out to the car.

"What don't I understand?" I wanted to know.   80

"Your heritage," she said. And then she turned to Maggie, kissed her, and said, "You ought to try to make something of yourself, too, Maggie. It's really a new day for us. But from the way you and Mama still live you'd never know it."

She put on some sunglasses that hid everything above the tip of her nose and her chin.

Maggie smiled; maybe at the sunglasses. But a real smile, not scared. After we watched the car dust settle I asked Maggie to bring me a dip of snuff. And then the two of us sat there just enjoying, until it was time to go in the house and go to bed.

CRITICAL THINKING QUESTIONS

1. What is Walker's implied *claim of value* about family heritage? What evidence in the story supports this claim? Do you agree or disagree with this claim?

2. When the mother refuses Dee's demand for the quilts and hands them over to Maggie, how did you react? What values informed your reaction?

3. In the closing scene, how is the author using *pathos* appeal?

WRITING TOPIC

In a classic rock song, the Rolling Stones sing, "You can't always get what you want, but if you try sometimes, you just might find you get what you need." Relating this quote to Walker's "Everyday Use" and your personal experience/observations, develop your own claim about getting what you *want* . . . trying, and finding what you *need*. Using evidence from the story and your experience, write an essay defending your claim.

POETRY

Anne Bradstreet (1612?–1672)

To My Dear and Loving Husband

If ever two were one, then surely we.
If ever man were loved by wife, then thee;
If ever wife was happy in a man,
Compare with me, ye women, if you can.
5   I prize thy love more than whole mines of gold
Or all the riches that the East doth hold.
Nor ought but love from thee, give recompense.
My love is such that rivers cannot quench,
Thy love is such I can no way repay,
10   The heavens reward thee manifold, I pray.
Then while we live, in love let's so persevere
That when we live no more, we may live ever.

WRITING TOPIC

You might be tempted to *jump to the conclusion* that the poet had been only recently married, thus, is still in the "honeymoon" frame of mind. Read about Anne Bradstreet in the "Authors' Biographical Notes" at the back of the book. Based on these facts, you can reasonably assume that Bradstreet's married life was one of daily, arduous physical toil, and constant danger—hardly a recipe for a "happy" marriage. Yet her poem is an eloquent tribute to marital love. To what degree does the poem reflect love in today's marriages? Does the poem describe marital love as it is—or as it *should* be? Relate specific personal observations and examples to support your viewpoint. For a different perspective on marital love, read Kate Chopin's story "The Storm" (page 405).

Gwendolyn Brooks (1917–2000)

The Mother

Abortions will not let you forget.
You remember the children you got that you did not get,
The damp small pulps with a little or with no hair,
The singers and workers that never handled the air.
You will never neglect or beat   5
Them, or silence or buy with a sweet.
You will never wind up the sucking-thumb
Or scuttle off ghosts that come.
You will never leave them, controlling your luscious sigh,
Return for a snack of them, with gobbling mother-eye.   10

I have heard in the voices of the wind the voices of my dim killed children.
I have contracted. I have eased
My dim dears at the breasts they could never suck.
I have said, Sweets, if I sinned, if I seized
Your luck   15
And your lives from your unfinished reach,
If I stole your births and your names,
Your straight baby tears and your games,
Your stilted or lovely loves, your tumults, your marriages, aches, and your deaths,
If I poisoned the beginnings of your breaths,   20
Believe that even in my deliberateness I was not deliberate.
Though why should I whine,
Whine that the crime was other than mine?—
Since anyhow you are dead.
Or rather, or instead,   25
You were never made.

But that too, I am afraid,
Is faulty: oh, what shall I say, how is the truth to be said?
You were born, you had body, you died.
It is just that you never giggled or planned or cried.   30
Believe me, I loved you all.
Believe me, I knew you, though faintly, and I loved, I loved you
All.

CRITICAL THINKING QUESTIONS

1. Beginning with line 21, when the speaker says, "Believe . . .," she seems to be sorting
   through her conscience in trying to articulate "the truth." How do you interpret lines

21 to 30? How do you think she is judging herself, assessing herself as "the mother"? Working with three or four classmates, read and compare your interpretations, and then collaborate on a statement that your group will present to the rest of the class. Be prepared to point to specific evidence from the poem to defend your interpretation.

2. What is the effect of repetition in the poem's closing stanza? Who is the speaker, the mother, trying to convince?

3. Examining this poem as an implied argument, what is its *issue question?* What is its *claim?* What *evidence* in the poem supports your statement of the claim?

4. Assess the speaker's *ethos.*

Gwendolyn Brooks

Ulysses

Religion

At home we pray every morning, we
get down on our knees in a circle,
holding hands, holding Love,
5   and we sing Hallelujah.

Then we go into the World.

Daddy *speeds,* to break bread with his Girl Friend.
Mommy's a Boss. And a lesbian.
(She too has a nice Girl Friend.)

My brothers and sisters and I come to school.
10   We bring knives pistols bottles, little boxes, and cans.

We talk to the man who's cool at the playground gate.
Nobody Sees us, nobody stops our sin.

Our teachers feed us geography.
We spit it out in a hurry.

15   Now we are coming home.

At home, we pray every evening, we
get down on our knees in a circle,
holding hands, holding Love.

And we sing Hallelujah.

CRITICAL THINKING QUESTIONS

1. Note the specific nouns the poet capitalizes, as well as the verb "Sees" in line 12. The immediate visual effect is to call attention to these words, as though they were proper nouns. Speculate as to why these particular nouns are capitalized. (For another example of unconventional capitalization in a poem, read Emily Dickinson's "Much madness is divinest sense," page 179.)

2. Who are the "we" the speaker refers to throughout the poem? Are they "family"? Which cultural norms about the family do they represent, and which ones do they refute?

3. Create your own *claim of value* about the family depicted in Brooks's poem.

WRITING TOPIC

The poem's title alludes explicitly to the hero of Homer's epic narrative verse, *The Odyssey*. In this ancient Greek epic, following the fall of his homeland Troy, Ulysses (or Odysseus) wanders for ten years before he finally can return to his wife and son. During his wandering, he faces seemingly insurmountable obstacles created by the ancient Greek gods. Defend, refute, or qualify the following claim: The family in Brooks's poem is heroic. Use evidence from the poem and your own observations to support your position.

Michael Cleary (b. 1945)

Boss's Son

The first weeks were the worst.
They were all full-timers
half a generation older at least,
and me headed for college, pegged for sure
among beer drinking, beer trucking men.   5
And they let me know it,
their muscle cars and pick-ups more real
than jock glory and SAT's.

Whatever I'd done, they stuck
a big fat "but" on its skinny ass: 10
I was football captain, but I was quarterback—
just another name for bossing guys around.

I was strong enough, *but* I liked books.
I had a pretty girl, *but* I was pussywhipped.
15   My pride unraveled like a baseball's snarled insides.
So I did twice my share, blisters
torn til calluses covered my hands like shells.

Gradually, they taught me their secrets:
let your legs do the lifting and save your back.
20   Load last things first so pints, quarts, cans, kegs
come undone top to bottom, back to front,
first stop to last and handle everything just once.
Snugging the load, making it stay that way all day
so corners and dumbshit drivers don't tumble it away
25   in explosions of foam soaking up half a day's pay.

After work we hung around and drank for free.
I salvaged bottles from the cooler's breakage bin,
hosing off scum and bits of glass.
I guzzled, smoked, swore with the best of them.
30   Playing the boy at night, I played the man
next morning, showed up early
and tried not to puke on company time.

Paydays we went to sour-smelling hangouts
of touchy pride and easy violence. Once
35   I saw a logger bite off a chunk
of a guy's cheek like an apple, then promise
to wait til he got back from the emergency room.
We waited, too, and they went at it again
for what seemed a good half hour.
40   Blood splattered all over the alley.

Those summers I changed
into that life easy as T-shirts and steel-toed boots,
doing the grunt work and putting down salesmen
like my father with their soft hands and ties,
45   gloried in sweat and sore muscles and hangovers
like nobody's goddamn boss's son.
After four years I was out of college
and out of there forever. Three months later,
the artery that burst inside my father's head
50   dropped him to the warehouse floor and he was gone.

What did he wonder about me living so hard,
trying to prove myself to everyone but him?
It was one more thing between us

I couldn't explain and he wouldn't understand.
I wanted the world to love me, I suppose, 55
on its own rough terms,
but I wanted him to love me, too,
for whatever man I was or was trying to be,
for the first time not in the name of the father
but some pilgrim who could be any man's son. 60

CRITICAL THINKING QUESTIONS

1. Write about what you see as the *connotations* (see Glossary) of the word "pride" in line 15 and then again about its *connotations* in line 34.

2. How does pride prompt a young adult to establish his or her own independence and identity?

WRITING TOPIC

Read Scott Russell Sanders's essay on page 510. Both Sanders's essay and Cleary's poem address issues of class differences. While we like to think of the United States as an egalitarian society, both Sanders's essay and Cleary's poem suggest otherwise. In what ways do they challenge the notion of egalitarianism? Do you agree or disagree with the writers? Use evidence to support your opinion.

———————

Gregory Corso (b. 1930)

Marriage

Should I get married? Should I be good?
Astound the girl next door with my velvet suit and faustus hood?
Don't take her to movies but to cemeteries
tell all about werewolf bathtubs and forked clarinets
then desire her and kiss her and all the preliminaries 5
and she going just so far and I understanding why
not getting angry saying You must feel! It's beautiful to feel!
Instead take her in my arms lean against an old crooked tombstone
and woo her the entire night the constellations in the sky—

When she introduces me to her parents 10
back straightened, hair finally combed, strangled by a tie,
should I sit knees together on their 3rd degree sofa

and not ask Where's the bathroom?
How else to feel other than I am,
15   often thinking Flash Gordon soap—
O how terrible it must be for a young man
seated before a family and the family thinking
We never saw him before! He wants our Mary Lou!
After tea and homemade cookies they ask What do you do for a living?

20   Should I tell them? Would they like me then?
Say All right get married, we're losing a daughter
but we're gaining a son—
And should I then ask Where's the bathroom?

O God, and the wedding! All her family and her friends
25   and only a handful of mine all scroungy and bearded
just wait to get at the drinks and food—
And the priest! he looking at me as if I masturbated
asking me Do you take this woman for your lawful wedded wife?
And I trembling what to say say Pie Glue!
30   I kiss the bride all those corny men slapping me on the back
She's all yours, boy! Ha-ha-ha!
And in their eyes you could see some obscene honeymoon going on—
Then all that absurd rice and clanky cans and shoes
Niagara Falls! Hordes of us! Husbands! Wives! Flowers! Chocolates!
All streaming into cozy hotels
35   All going to do the same thing tonight

The indifferent clerk he knowing what was going to happen
The lobby zombies they knowing what
The whistling elevator man he knowing
The winking bellboy knowing
40   Everybody knowing! I'd be almost inclined not to do anything!
Stay up all night! Stare that hotel clerk in the eye!
Screaming: I deny honeymoon! I deny honeymoon!
running rampant into those almost climactic suites
45   yelling Radio belly! Cat shovel!
O I'd live in Niagara forever! in a dark cave beneath the Falls
I'd sit there the Mad Honeymooner
devising ways to break marriages, a scourge of bigamy
a saint of divorce—

50   But I should get married I should be good
How nice it'd be to come home to her
and sit by the fireplace and she in the kitchen
aproned young and lovely wanting my baby

and so happy about me she burns the roast beef
and comes crying to me and I get up from my big papa chair   55
saying Christmas teeth! Radiant brains! Apple deaf!
God what a husband I'd make! Yes, I should get married!
So much to do! like sneaking into Mr Jones' house late at night
and cover his golf clubs with 1920 Norwegian books

Like hanging a picture of Rimbaud on the lawnmower   60
like pasting Tannu Tuva postage stamps all over the picket fence
like when Mrs Kindhead comes to collect for the Community Chest
grab her and tell her There are unfavorable omens in the sky!
And when the mayor comes to get my vote tell him
When are you going to stop people killing whales!   65
And when the milkman comes leave him a note in the bottle
Penguin dust, bring me penguin dust, I want penguin dust—

Yet if I should get married and it's Connecticut and snow
and she gives birth to a child and I am sleepless, worn,
up for nights, head bowed against a quiet window, the past behind me,   70
finding myself in the most common of situations a trembling man
knowledged with responsibility not twig-smear nor Roman coin soup—
O what would that be like!
Surely I'd give it for a nipple a rubber Tacitus
For a rattle a bag of broken Bach records   75
Tack Della Francesca all over its crib
Sew the Greek alphabet on its bib
And build for its playpen a roofless Parthenon

No, I doubt I'd be that kind of father
Not rural not snow no quiet window   80
but hot smelly tight New York City
seven flights up, roaches and rats in the walls
a fat Reichian wife screeching over potatoes Get a job!
And five nose running brats in love with Batman
And the neighbors all toothless and dry haired   85
like those hag masses of the 18th century
all wanting to come in and watch TV

The landlord wants his rent
Grocery store Blue Cross Gas & Electric Knights of Columbus
Impossible to lie back and dream Telephone snow, ghost parking—   90
No! I should not get married I should never get married!
But—imagine if I were married to a beautiful sophisticated woman
tall and pale wearing an elegant black dress and long black gloves
holding a cigarette holder in one hand and a highball in the other

95   and we lived high up in a penthouse with a huge window
from which we could see all of New York and ever farther on clearer days
No, can't imagine myself married to that pleasant prison dream—

O but what about love? I forget love
not that I am incapable of love
100   it's just that I see love as odd as wearing shoes—
I never wanted to marry a girl who was like my mother
And Ingrid Bergman was always impossible
And there's maybe a girl now but she's already married
And I don't like men and—
105   but there's got to be somebody!
Because what if I'm 60 years old and not married,
all alone in a furnished room with pee stains on my underwear
and everybody else is married! All the universe married but me!

Ah, yet well I know that were a woman possible as I am possible
110   then marriage would be possible—
Like SHE in her lonely alien gaud waiting her Egyptian lover
so I wait—bereft of 2,000 years and the bath of life.

CRITICAL THINKING QUESTIONS

1. The poet poses the question, "Should I get married?" List the evidence he provides for both sides of the argument under the headings, Marry . . . Don't Marry.

2. From your own perspective, make your own list of evidence under the headings, Marry . . . Don't Marry.

Nikki Giovanni (b. 1943)

Mothers

the last time i was home
to see my mother we kissed
exchanged pleasantries
and unpleasantries pulled a warm
comforting silence around
5   us and read separate books

i remember the first time
i consciously saw her
we were living in a three room
apartment on burns avenue

mommy always sat in the dark
i don't know how i knew that but she did

that night i stumbled into the kitchen
maybe because i've always been
a night person or perhaps because i had wet the bed   15
she was sitting on a chair
the room was bathed in moonlight diffused through
those thousands of panes landlords who rented
to people with children were prone to put in windows

she may have been smoking but maybe not   20
her hair was three-quarters her height
which made me a strong believer in the samson myth
and very black

i'm sure i just hung there by the door
i remember thinking: what a beautiful lady   25

she was very deliberately waiting
perhaps for my father to come home
from his night job or maybe for a dream
that had promised to come by
"come here" she said "i'll teach you   30
a poem: *i see the moon*
    the moon sees me
    god bless the moon
    and god bless me"
i taught it to my son
who recited it for her
just to say we must learn
to bear the pleasures   35
as we have borne the pains

CRITICAL THINKING QUESTIONS

1. Examine the details of the speaker's depiction of her childhood memory, and draw some inferences about the mother's life at this time.

2. In teaching the poem, what message is the mother imparting to her daughter?

3. The speaker also has taught the poem to her son, and it is he who now recites it for his grandmother. In light of the poem's title, how is this detail significant?

WRITING TOPIC

Some social critics argue that the failure of parents (and some add, schools) to teach values to children is a primary cause for increasing problems among youth—

from rude and boorish behavior to drug use and violence. What is the poet's implied claim about the teaching of values? Reflecting on your childhood, can you recall a moment when you learned a lesson about values? How do you think children should be taught values?

Thomas Hardy (1840–1928)

The Ruined Maid

"O 'Melia, my dear, this does everything crown!
Who could have supposed I should meet you in Town?
And whence such fair garments, such prosperi-ty?"
"O didn't you know I'd been ruined?" said she.

5   "You left us in tatters, without shoes or socks,
Tired of digging potatoes, and spudding up docks;
And now you've gay bracelets and bright feathers three!"
"Yes: that's how we dress when we're ruined," said she.

"At home in the barton you said 'thee' and 'thou,'
10   And 'thik oon,' and 'theäs oon,' and 't'other'; but now
Your talking quite fits 'ee for high compa-ny!"
"Some polish is gained with one's ruin," said she.

"Your hands were like paws then, your face blue and bleak
15   But now I'm bewitched by your delicate cheek,
And your little gloves fit as on any la-dy!"
"We never do work when we're ruined," said she.

"You used to call home-life a hag-ridden dream,
And you'd sigh, and you'd sock; but at present you seem
To know not of megrims or melancho-ly!"
20   "True. One's pretty lively when ruined," said she.

"I wish I had feathers, a fine sweeping gown,
And a delicate face, and could strut about Town!"
"My dear—a raw country girl, such as you be,
Cannot quite expect that. You ain't ruined," said she.

CRITICAL THINKING QUESTIONS

1. By leaving her home life on the farm, what has 'Melia left behind? What has she gained in her new life in Town?

2. Compare and contrast the values associated with her previous lifestyle and with her present one.

3. Her former acquaintance, who still lives in the country, seems to think that 'Melia has found prosperity and happiness in Town. How does this *inference* represent flawed reasoning?

Seamus Heaney (b. 1939)

Digging

Between my finger and my thumb
The squat pen rests; snug as a gun.

Under my window, a clean rasping sound
When the spade sinks into gravelly ground:
My father, digging. I look down   5

Till his straining rump among the flowerbeds
Bends low, comes up twenty years away
Stooping in rhythm through potato drills
Where he was digging.

The coarse boot nestled on the lug, the shaft   10
Against the inside knee was levered firmly.
He rooted out tall tops, buried the bright edge deep
To scatter new potatoes that we picked
Loving their cool hardness in our hands.

By God, the old man could handle a spade.   15
Just like his old man.

My grandfather cut more turf in a day
Than any other man on Toner's bog.
Once I carried him milk in a bottle
Corked sloppily with paper. He straightened up   20
To drink it, then fell to right away

Nicking and slicing neatly, heaving sods
Over his shoulder, going down and down
For the good turf. Digging.

The cold smell of potato mould, the squelch and slap   25
Of soggy peat, the curt cuts of an edge
Through living roots awaken in my head.

But I've no spade to follow men like them.
Between my finger and my thumb
30   The squat pen rests.
I'll dig with it.

CRITICAL THINKING QUESTIONS

1. What common assumptions about the differences between mental labor and physical labor are challenged in this poem?

2. What is the poet's claim about the relationship between his work as a writer and his father's and grandfather's work as farmers?

3. List the evidence Heaney provides for his claim. On which rhetorical appeal does he rely?

WRITING TOPIC

Reflecting on your own experience and observations, how important is family heritage today?

Peter Meinke (b. 1932)

Advice to My Son

—FOR TIM

The trick is, to live your days
as if each one may be your last
(for they go fast, and young men lose their lives
in strange and unimaginable ways)
5   but at the same time, plan long range
(for they go slow: if you survive
the shattered windshield and the bursting shell
you will arrive
at our approximation here below
10   of heaven or hell).
To be specific, between the peony and the rose
plant squash and spinach, turnips and tomatoes;
beauty is nectar
and nectar, in a desert, saves—

but the stomach craves stronger sustenance   15
than the honied vine.
Therefore, marry a pretty girl
after seeing her mother;
speak truth to one man,
work with another;   20
and always serve bread with your wine.
But, son,
always serve wine.

CRITICAL THINKING QUESTIONS

In lines 17 to 18, the speaker makes the claim, "Therefore, marry a pretty girl,"
with this *qualifier* phrase, "after seeing her mother." What *warrants* or *value assumptions* underlie that statement? Are they valid?

COLLABORATION WRITING TOPIC

Meinke is giving advice to his son, "—FOR TIM." Working with several other students (preferably in mixed gender groups), create a female version of Meinke's poem, "Advice to My Daughter." Be prepared to present your poem to the rest of the class.

Naomi Shihab Nye (b. 1952)

Arabic Coffee

It was never too strong for us:
make it blacker, Papa,
thick in the bottom,
tell again how the years will gather
in small white cups,   5
how luck lives in a spot of grounds.
Leaning over the stove, he let it
boil to the top, and down again.
Two times. No sugar in his pot.
And the place where men and women   10
break off from one another
was not present in that room.
The hundred disappointments,
fire swallowing olive-wood beads

15   at the warehouse, and the dreams
        tucked like pocket handkerchiefs
        into each day, took their places
        on the table, near the half-empty
        dish of corn. And none was
20   more important than the others,
        and all were guests. When
        he carried the tray into the room,
        high and balanced in his hands,
        it was an offering to all of them,
25   stay, be seated, follow the talk
        wherever it goes. The coffee was
        the center of the flower.
        Like clothes on a line saying
        you will live long enough to wear me,
30   a motion of faith. There is this,
        and there is more.

WRITING TOPIC

Compare this poem to Mark Strand's "The Continuous Life" (page 479). Both poems reflect on the meaning of human life. Compare and contrast the two poets' viewpoints. Articulate each poet's central claim. Which claim do you support? Drawing on evidence from the poems and your own experience, defend your position.

Sharon Olds (b. 1942)

I Go Back to May, 1937

I see them standing at the formal gates of their colleges,
I see my father strolling out
under the ochre sandstone arch, the
red tiles glinting like bent
5   plates of blood behind his head, I
see my mother with a few light books at her hip
standing at the pillar made of tiny bricks with the
wrought-iron gate still open behind her, its
sword-tips black in the May air,
10   they are about to graduate, they are about to get married,
they are kids, they are dumb, all they know is they are
innocent, they would never hurt anybody.

I want to go up to them and say Stop,
don't do it—she's the wrong woman,
he's the wrong man, you are going to do things   15
you cannot imagine you would ever do,
you are going to do bad things to children,
you are going to suffer in ways you never heard of,
you are going to want to die. I want to go
up to them there in the late May sunlight and say it,   20
her hungry pretty blank face turning to me,
her pitiful beautiful untouched body,
his arrogant handsome blind face turning to me,
his pitiful beautiful untouched body,
but I don't do it. I want to live. I   25
take them up like the male and female
paper dolls and bang them together
at the hips like chips of flint as if to
strike sparks from them, I say
Do what you are going to do, and I will tell about it.   30

CRITICAL THINKING QUESTIONS

1. Olds's poem addresses the *issue question*—should the daughter try to stop her parents from marrying each other?

2. List the evidence the speaker provides in examining the question. Why does she decide not to stop her parents from marrying?

RESEARCH/WRITING TOPIC—Genetic Research: Unethical Tampering or Human Progress?

Consider Olds's poem from a broad perspective: What if we could see into the future—how our lives will play out? Would this be a good thing? You can expand your thinking on this topic by researching biotechnology (the Human Genome Project) which may open the door—or, many critics say, Pandora's box—for us to program our genes and, thus, "predict" and presumably improve our lives. To what degree, if any, is experimenting with human DNA acceptable? [The 1997 film *Gattaca* focuses on this topic.]

Mary Oliver (b. 1935)

The Black Walnut Tree

My mother and I debate:
we could sell
the black walnut tree
to the lumberman,
5   and pay off the mortgage.
Likely some storm anyway
will churn down its dark boughs,
smashing the house. We talk
slowly, two women trying
10   in a difficult time to be wise.
Roots in the cellar drains,
I say, and she replies
that the leaves are getting heavier
every year, and the fruit
15   harder to gather away.
But something brighter than money
moves in our blood—an edge
sharp and quick as a trowel
that wants us to dig and sow.
20   So we talk, but we don't do
anything. That night I dream
of my fathers out of Bohemia
filling the blue fields
of fresh and generous Ohio
25   with leaves and vines and orchards.
What my mother and I both know
is that we'd crawl with shame
in the emptiness we'd made
in our own and our fathers' backyard.
30   So the black walnut tree
swings through another year
of sun and leaping winds,
of leaves and bounding fruit,
and, month after month, the whip-
35   crack of the mortgage.

CRITICAL THINKING QUESTIONS

1. In debating the sale of the black walnut tree, how does the speaker appeal to *pathos*?

2. How does she appeal to *logos?*

3. What *warrant* supports the women's decision to preserve the tree? Is it valid? Can you think of issues you have debated where this warrant entered into the argument?

WRITING TOPIC

Do you think the mother's and daughter's fathers would agree or disagree with the women's decision? Why?

Dudley Randall (1914–2000)

Ballad of Birmingham

(On the Bombing of a Church in Birmingham, Alabama, 1963)

"Mother dear, may I go downtown
Instead of out to play,
And march the streets of Birmingham
In a Freedom March today?"

"No, baby, no, you may not go,   5
For the dogs are fierce and wild,
And clubs and hoses, guns and jails
Aren't good for a little child."

"But, mother, I won't be alone.
Other children will go with me,   10
And march the streets of Birmingham
To make our country free."

"No, baby, no, you may not go,
For I fear those guns will fire.
But you may go to church instead   15
And sing in the children's choir."

She has combed and brushed her night-dark hair.
And bathed rose petal sweet.
And drawn white gloves on her small brown hands,
And white shoes on her feet.   20

The mother smiled to know her child
Was in the sacred place,

But that smile was the last smile
To come upon her face.

25 For when she heard the explosion,
Her eyes grew wet and wild.
She raced through the streets of Birmingham
Calling for her child.

She clawed through bits of glass and brick.
30 Then lifted out a shoe.
"Oh, here's the shoe my baby wore,
But, baby, where are you?"

CRITICAL THINKING QUESTIONS

1. Working in small groups, write out at least two *implied claims* for this poem. List *evidence* for each claim.

2. In committing an act of terrorism, what *value assumption* does the terrorist use to justify his or her act?

3. How does Randall's poem refute the terrorist's assumption?

WRITING TOPIC

Both Randall's poem and Giovanni's poem, "Mothers" (page 464) feature the depth and power of maternal love. Compare and contast the perspectives that each piece of literature presents. Based on your study, write a *Rogerian argument* about the conflicting powers of maternal love.

Adrienne Rich (b. 1929)

Aunt Jennifer's Tigers

Aunt Jennifer's tigers prance across a screen,
Bright topaz denizens of a world of green.
They do not fear the men beneath the tree;
They pace in sleek chivalric certainty.

Aunt Jennifer's fingers fluttering through her wool
Find even the ivory needle hard to pull.
5 The massive weight of Uncle's wedding band

Sits heavily upon Aunt Jennifer's hand.

When Aunt is dead, her terrified hands will lie
Still ringed with ordeals she was mastered by.   10
The tigers in the panel that she made
Will go on prancing, proud and unafraid.

Adrienne Rich

Delta

If you have taken this rubble for my past
raking through it for fragments you could sell
know that I long ago moved on
deeper into the heart of the matter

If you think you can grasp me, think again: 5
my story flows in more than one direction
a delta springing from the riverbed
with its five fingers spread

Anne Sexton (1928–1974)

Cinderella

You always read about it:
the plumber with twelve children
who wins the Irish Sweepstakes.
From toilets to riches.
That story.   5

Or the nursemaid,
some luscious sweet from Denmark
who captures the oldest son's heart.
From diapers to Dior.
That story.   10

Or a milkman who serves the wealthy,
eggs, cream, butter, yogurt, milk,
the white truck like an ambulance

15 who goes into real estate
and makes a pile.
From homogenized to martinis at lunch.

Or the charwoman
who is on the bus when it cracks up
and collects enough from the insurance.
20 From mops to Bonwit Teller.
That story.

Once
the wife of a rich man was on her deathbed
and she said to her daughter Cinderella:
25 Be devout. Be good. Then I will smile
down from heaven in the seam of a cloud.
The man took another wife who had
two daughters, pretty enough
but with hearts like blackjacks.
30 Cinderella was their maid.
She slept on the sooty hearth each night
and walked around looking like Al Jolson.
Her father brought presents home from town,
jewels and gowns for the other women
35 but the twig of a tree for Cinderella.
She planted that twig on her mother's grave
and it grew to a tree where a white dove sat.
Whenever she wished for anything the dove
would drop it like an egg upon the ground.
40 The bird is important, my dears, so heed him.

Next came the ball, as you all know.
It was a marriage market.
The prince was looking for a wife.
All but Cinderella were preparing
45 and gussying up for the big event.
Cinderella begged to go too.
Her stepmother threw a dish of lentils
into the cinders and said: Pick them
up in an hour and you shall go.
50 The white dove brought all his friends;
all the warm wings of the fatherland came,
and picked up the lentils in a jiffy.
No, Cinderella, said the stepmother,
you have no clothes and cannot dance.
55 That's the way with stepmothers.

Cinderella went to the tree at the grave
and cried forth like a gospel singer:
Mama! Mama! My turtledove,
send me to the prince's ball!
The bird dropped down a golden dress   60
and delicate little gold slippers.
Rather a large package for a simple bird.
So she went. Which is no surprise.
Her stepmother and sisters didn't
recognize her without her cinder face   65
and the prince took her hand on the spot
and danced with no other the whole day.

As nightfall came she thought she'd better
get home. The prince walked her home
and she disappeared into the pigeon house   70
and although the prince took an axe and broke
it open she was gone. Back to her cinders.
These events repeated themselves for three days.
However on the third day the prince
covered the palace steps with cobbler's wax   75
and Cinderella's gold shoe stuck upon it.
Now he would find whom the shoe fit
and find his strange dancing girl for keeps.
He went to their house and the two sisters
were delighted because they had lovely feet.   80
The eldest went into a room to try the slipper on
but her big toe got in the way so she simply
sliced it off and put on the slipper.
The prince rode away with her until the white dove
told him to look at the blood pouring forth.   85
That is the way with amputations.
They don't just heal up like a wish.
The other sister cut off her heel
but the blood told as blood will.
The prince was getting tired.   90
He began to feel like a shoe salesman.
But he gave it one last try.
This time Cinderella fit into the shoe
like a love letter into its envelope.
At the wedding ceremony   95
the two sisters came to curry favor
and the white dove pecked their eyes out.
Two hollow spots were left
like soup spoons.

100   Cinderella and the prince
         lived, they say, happily ever after,
         like two dolls in a museum case
         never bothered by diapers or dust,
         never arguing over the timing of an egg,
105   never telling the same story twice,
         never getting a middle-aged spread,
         their darling smiles pasted on for eternity
         Regular Bobbsey Twins.
         That story.

CRITICAL THINKING QUESTIONS

1. Sexton's poem mocks the fantasy of happiness forever. Besides fairy tales, which by definition are fantasies, how do popular culture and the media feed our fantasies of the "happily-ever-after" life?

2. Related to the myth of the happily-ever-after life is the quest for eternal youth and beauty. In the Walt Disney version of *Cinderella,* Cinderella is beautiful, and the prince, handsome. What *value assumption* is reinforced by their physical perfection?

WRITING TOPIC

Defend the place of the myth of happily-ever-after in our culture. In what ways might the fantasy of everlasting happiness be a positive force?

Gary Snyder (b. 1930)

Not Leaving the House

When Kai is born
I quit going out

Hang around the kitchen—make cornbread
Let nobody in.
5   Mail is flat.
Masa lies on her side, Kai sighs,
Non washes and sweeps
We sit and watch
Masa nurse, and drink green tea.

10   Navajo turquoise beads over the bed
       A peacock tail feather at the head

A badger pelt from Nagano-ken
For a mattress; under the sheet;
A pot of yogurt setting
Under the blankets, at his feet.   15

Masa, Kai,
And Non, our friend
In the green garden light reflected in
Not leaving the house.
From dawn til late at night   20
making a new world of ourselves
around this life.

CRITICAL THINKING QUESTION

What view of a father does this poem present?

WRITING TOPIC

Some career women are choosing single motherhood by using sperm donors to conceive a child. Implicit in this choice is a *warrant* or value assumption about the father's role and the family. What is this warrant? How does Snyder's poem implicitly refute this warrant? Using this poem and other literature selections in this chapter, as well as your own primary evidence (personal experience and observations), write and defend a *claim of value* about the father's role in a family. (See Chapter Activity #3, for a longer, research-based paper on this topic.)

Mark Strand (b. 1934)

The Continuous Life

What of the neighborhood homes awash
In a silver light, of children hunched in the bushes,
Watching the grownups for signs of surrender,
Signs the irregular pleasures of moving
From day to day, of being adrift on the swell of duty   5
Have run their course? O parents, confess
To your little ones the night is a long way off
And your taste for the mundane grows; tell them
Your worship of household chores has barely begun;
Describe the beauty of shovels and rakes, brooms and mops;0   10
Say there will always be cooking and cleaning to do,

That one thing leads to another, which leads to another;
Explain that you live between two great darks, the first
With an ending, the second without one, that the luckiest
15   Thing is having been born, that you live in a blur
Of hours and days, months and years, and believe
It has meaning, despite the occasional fear
You are slipping away with nothing completed, nothing
To prove you existed. Tell the children to come inside,
20   That your search goes on for something you lost: a name,
A book of the family that fell from its own small matter
Into another, a piece of the dark that might have been yours—
You don't really know. Say that each of you tries
To keep busy, learning to lean down close and hear
25   The careless breathing of earth and feel its available
Languor come over you, wave after wave, sending
Small tremors of love through your brief,
Undeniable selves, into your days, and beyond.

CRITICAL THINKING QUESTIONS

1. Analyze this poem as a *Rogerian argument:*
   a. State the *issue question* that is implied in the poem's first six lines.
   b. Examine the evidence in lines 6 to 22. Describe the speaker's tone as he postulates responses to the issue question. What words or phrases contribute to a Rogerian tone?
   c. Reading the last six lines (23 to 28) as the conclusion to the poet's argument, write out a Rogerian argument claim statement—a *qualified position* in response to the issue question.

2. Reflecting on your experiences and your observations of the lives of parents, defend or refute the claim you articulated in **1c**.

Margaret Walker (1915–1998)

Lineage

My grandmothers were strong.
They followed plows and bent to toil.
They moved through fields sowing seed.
They touched earth and grain grew.
5   They were full of sturdiness and singing.
My grandmothers were strong.

My grandmothers are full of memories.
Smelling of soap and onions and wet clay
With veins rolling roughly over quick hands
They have many clean words to say.   10
My grandmothers were strong.
Why am I not as they?

CRITICAL THINKING QUESTIONS

1. What qualities does the speaker imply she has lost that her grandmothers possessed?

2. How does this poem define "strong"?

3. What value assumptions does the speaker make about the rewards of physical toil? Do you accept them?

WRITING TOPIC

Compare and contrast Heaney's "Digging" and Walker's "Lineage." Although both poems examine similar situations and share the warrant—family heritage is valuable, the poems' two speakers arrive at opposing claims about their "lineage." Do you think Heaney's or Walker's speaker is more representative of people today when they assess their role in continuing the family lineage? Develop a claim and support it with your analyses of the poems, as well as your own personal experience and observations.

Richard Wilbur (b. 1921)

The Writer

In her room at the prow of the house
Where light breaks, and the windows are tossed with linden,
My daughter is writing a story.

I pause in the stairwell, hearing
From her shut door a commotion of typewriter-keys   5
Like a chain hauled over a gunwale.

Young as she is, the stuff
Of her life is a great cargo, and some of it heavy:
I wish her a lucky passage.

10
But now it is she who pauses,
As if to reject my thought and its easy figure.
A stillness greatens, in which

The whole house seems to be thinking,
And then she is at it again with a bunched clamor
15
Of strokes, and again is silent.

I remember the dazed starling
Which was trapped in that very room, two years ago,
How we stole in, lifted a sash

And retreated, not to affright it;
20
And how for a helpless hour, through the crack of the door,
We watched the sleek, wild, dark

And iridescent creature
Batter against the brilliance, drop like a glove
To the hard floor, or the desk-top,

25
And wait then, humped and bloody,
For the wits to try it again; and how our spirits
Rose when, suddenly sure,
It lifted off from a chair-back,
Beating a smooth course for the right window
30
And clearing the sill of the world.

It is always a matter, my darling,
Of life or death, as I had forgotten. I wish
What I wished you before, but harder.

CRITICAL THINKING QUESTIONS

1. Who is the teacher, and who is the learner in this poem?

2. What claim does this poem imply about the process of learning?

3. Compare and contrast this poem and Meinke's "Advice to My Son" (page 468). How do the two fathers illustrate different styles of parental counseling?

WRITING TOPIC

Do you think a child's gender influences a father's parenting style and techniques? What specific experiences and observations inform your conclusion?

DRAMA

∧∧∧

Harvey Fierstein (b. 1954)
On Tidy Endings

Scene

The curtain rises on a deserted, modern Upper West Side apartment. In the bright daylight that pours in through the windows we can see the living room of the apartment. Far Stage Right is the galley kitchen, next to it the multilocked front door with intercom. Stage Left reveals a hallway that leads to the two bedrooms and baths.

Though the room is still fully furnished (couch, coffee table, etc.), there are boxes stacked against the wall and several photographs and paintings are on the floor leaving shadows on the wall where they once hung. Obviously someone is moving out. From the way the boxes are neatly labeled and stacked, we know that this is an organized person.

From the hallway just outside the door we hear the rattling of keys and two arguing voices:

Jim (*Offstage*): I've got to be home by four. I've got practice.
Marion (*Offstage*): I'll get you to practice, don't worry.
Jim (*Offstage*): I don't want to go in there.
Marion (*Offstage*): Jimmy, don't make Mommy crazy, alright? We'll go inside, I'll call Aunt Helen and see if you can go down and play with Robbie.

(The door opens. MARION is a handsome woman of forty. Dressed in a business suit, her hair conservatively combed, she appears to be going to a business meeting. JIM is a boy of eleven. His playclothes are typical, but someone has obviously just combed his hair. MARION recovers the key from the lock.)

Jim: Why can't I just go down and ring the bell?
Marion: Because I said so.

(As MARION steps into the room she is struck by some unexpected emotion. She freezes in her path and stares at the empty apartment. JIM lingers by the door.)

Jim: I'm going downstairs.
Marion: Jimmy, please
Jim: This place gives me the creeps.
Marion: This was your father's apartment. There's nothing creepy about it.
Jim: Says you.
Marion: You want to close the door, please?

*(*Jim *reluctantly obeys.)*

Marion: Now, why don't you go check your room and make sure you didn't leave anything.
Jim: It's empty.
Marion: Go look.
Jim: I looked last time.
Marion (*Trying to be patient*): Honey, we sold the apartment. You're never going to be here again. Go make sure you have everything you want.
Jim: But Uncle Arthur packed everything.
Marion (*Less patiently*): Go make sure.
Jim: There's nothing in there.
Marion (*Exploding*): I said make sure!

*(*Jim *jumps, then realizing that she's not kidding, obeys.)*

Marion: Everything's an argument with that one. (*She looks around the room and breathes deeply. There is sadness here. Under her breath:*) I can still smell you. (*Suddenly not wanting to be alone*) Jimmy? Are you okay?
Jim (*Returning*): Nothing. Told you so.
Marion: Uncle Arthur must have worked very hard. Make sure you thank him.
Jim: What for? Robbie says, (*Fey mannerisms*) "They love to clean up things!"
Marion: Sometimes you can be a real joy.
Jim: Did you call Aunt Helen?
Marion: Do I get a break here? (*Approaching the boy understandingly*) Wouldn't you like to say good-bye?
Jim: To who?
Marion: To the apartment. You and your daddy spent a lot of time here together. Don't you want to take one last look around?
Jim: Ma, get a real life.
Marion: "Get a real life." (*Going for the phone*) Nice. Very nice.
Jim: Could you call already?
Marion (*Dialing*): Jimmy, what does this look like I'm doing?
*(*Jim *kicks at the floor impatiently. Someone answers the hone at the other end.)*
Marion (*Into the phone*): Helen? Hi, we're upstairs. . . . No, we just walked in the door. Jimmy wants to know if he can come down. . . . Oh, thanks.

(Hearing that, Jim *breaks for the door.)*

Marion (*Yelling after him*): Don't run in the halls! And don't play with the elevator buttons!

(The door slams shut behind him.)

Marion (*Back to the phone*): Hi. . . . No, I'm okay. It's a little weird being here. . . . No. Not since the funeral, and then there were so many people. Jimmy told me to get "a real life." I don't think I could handle anything realer. . . . No, please. Stay where you are. I'm fine. The doorman said Arthur would be right back and my lawyer should have been here already. . . . Well, we've got the papers to sign and a few other odds and ends to clean up. Shouldn't take long.

(The intercom buzzer rings.)

Marion: Hang on, that must be her.
(MARION *goes to the intercom and speaks*) Yes? . . . Thank you.
(*Back to the phone*) Helen? Yeah, it's the lawyer. I'd better go. . . . Well, I could use a stiff drink, but I drove down. Listen, I'll stop by on my way out. Okay? Okay. 'Bye.

(She hangs up the phone, looks around the room. That uncomfortable feeling returns to her quickly. She gets up and goes to the front door; opens it and looks out. No one there yet. She closes the door, shakes her head knowing that she's being silly and starts back into the room. She looks around, can't make it and retreats to the door. She opens it, looks out, closes it, but stays right there, her hand on the doorknob.
The bell rings. She throws open the door.)

Marion: That was quick.

(JUNE LOWELL *still has her finger on the bell. Her arms are loaded with contracts.* MARION'S *contemporary,* JUNE *is less formal in appearance and more hyper in her manner.)*

June: That was quicker. What, were you waiting by the door?
Marion (*Embarrassed*): No. I was just passing it. Come on in.
June: Have you got your notary seal?
Marion: I think so.
June: Great. Then you can witness. I left mine at the office and thanks to gentrification I'm double-parked downstairs. (*Looking for a place to dump her load*) Where?
Marion (*Definitely pointing to the coffee table*): Anywhere. You mean you're not staying?
June: If you really think you need me I can go down and find a parking lot. I think there's one over on Columbus. So, I can go down, park the car in the lot and take a cab back if you really think you need me.
Marion: Well . . . ?
June: But you shouldn't have any problems. The papers are about as straightforward as papers get. Arthur is giving you power of attorney to sell the apartment and you're giving him a check for half the purchase price. Everything else is just signing papers that state that you know that you signed the other papers. Anyway, he knows the deal, his lawyers have been over it all with him, it's just a matter of signatures.
Marion (*Not fine*): Oh, fine.
June: Unless you just don't want to be alone with him . . . . ?
Marion: With Arthur? Don't be silly.
June (*Laying out the papers*): Then you'll handle it solo? Great. My car thanks you, the parking lot thanks you, and the cab driver that wouldn't have gotten a tip thanks you. Come have a quick look-see.

Marion (*Joining her on the couch*): There are a lot of papers here.

June. Copies. Not to worry. Start here.

(MARION *starts to read.*)

June: I ran into Jimmy playing Elevator Operator.

(MARION *jumps.*)

June: I got him off at the sixth floor. Read on.

Marion: This is definitely not my day for dealing with him.

(JUNE *gets up and has a look around.*)

June: I don't believe what's happening in this neighborhood. You made quite an investment when you bought this place.

Marion: Collin was always very good at figuring out those things.

June: Well, he sure figured this place right. What, have you tripled your money in ten years?

Marion: More.

June: It's a shame to let it go.

Marion: We're not ready to be a two-dwelling family.

June: So, sublet it again.

Marion: Arthur needs the money from the sale.

June: Arthur got plenty already. I'm not crying for Arthur.

Marion: I don't hear you starting in again, do I?

June: Your interests and your wishes are my only concern.

Marion: Fine.

June: I still say we should contest Collin's will.

Marion: June! . . .

June: You've got a child to support.

Marion: And a great job, and a husband with a great job. Tell me what Arthur's got.

June: To my thinking, half of everything that should have gone to you. And more. All of Collin's personal effects, his record collection. . . .

Marion: And I suppose their three years together meant nothing.

June: When you compare them to your sixteen-year marriage? Not nothing, but not half of everything.

Marion (*Trying to change the subject*): June, who gets which copies?

June: Two of each to Arthur. One you keep. The originals and anything else come back to me. (*Looking around*) I still say you should've sublet the apartment for a year and then sold it. You would've gotten an even better price. Who wants to buy an apartment when they know someone died in it. No one. And certainly no one wants to buy an apartment when they know the person died of AIDS.

Marion (*Snapping*): June. Enough!

June (*Catching herself*): Sorry. That was out of line. Sometimes my mouth does that to me. Hey, that's why I'm a lawyer. If my brain worked as fast as my mouth I would have gotten a real job.

Marion (*Holding out a stray paper*): What's this?

June: I forgot. Arthur's lawyer sent that over yesterday. He found it in Collin's safety-deposit box. It's an insurance policy that came along with some consulting job he did in Japan. He either forgot about it when he made out his will or else he wanted you to get the full payment. Either way, it's yours.

Marion: Are you sure we don't split this?

June: Positive.

Marion: But everything else . . . ?

June: Hey, Arthur found it, his lawyer sent it to me. Relax, it's all yours. Minus my commission, of course. Go out and buy yourself something. Anything else before I have to use my cut to pay the towing bill?

Marion: I guess not.

June (*Starting to leave*): Great. Call me when you get home. (*Stopping at the door and looking back*) Look, I know that I'm attacking this a little coldly. I am aware that someone you loved has just died. But there's a time and place for everything. This is about tidying up loose ends, not holding hands. I hope you'll remember that when Arthur gets here. Call me.

(And she's gone.

MARION looks ill at ease to be alone again. She nervously straightens the papers into neat little piles, looks at them and then remembers:)

Marion: Pens. We're going to need pens.

(At last a chore to be done. She looks in her purse and finds only one. She goes to the kitchen and opens a drawer where she finds two more. She starts back to the table with them but suddenly remembers something else. She returns to the kitchen and begins going through the cabinets until she finds what she's looking for: a blue Art Deco teapot. Excited to find it, she takes it back to the couch.

Guilt strikes. She stops, considers putting it back, wavers, then:)

Marion(*to herself*): Oh, he won't care. One less thing to pack.

(She takes the teapot and places it on the couch next to her purse. She is happier. Now she searches the room with her eyes for any other treasures she may have overlooked. Nothing here. She wanders off into the bedroom.

We hear keys outside the front. ARTHUR lets himself into the apartment carrying a load of empty cartons and a large shopping bag.

ARTHUR is in his mid-thirties, pleasant looking though sloppily dressed in work clothes and slightly overweight.

ARTHUR enters the apartment just as MARION comes out of the bedroom carrying a framed watercolor painting. They jump at the sight of each other.)

Marion: Oh, hi, Arthur. I didn't hear the door.

Arthur (*Staring at the painting*): Well hello, Marion.

Marion (*Guiltily*): I was going to ask you if you were thinking of taking this painting because if you're not going to then I'll take it. Unless, of course, you want it.

Arthur: No. You can have it.

Marion: I never really liked it, actually. I hate cats. I didn't even like the show. I needed something for my college dorm room. I was never the rock star poster type. I kept it in the back of a closet for years until Collin moved in here and took it. He said he liked it.

Arthur: I do too.

Marion: Well, then you keep it.

Arthur: No. Take it.

Marion: We've really got no room for it. You keep it.

Arthur: I don't want it.

Marion: Well, if you're sure.

Arthur *(Seeing the teapot)*: You want the teapot?

Marion: If you don't mind.

Arthur: One less thing to pack.

Marion: Funny, but that's exactly what I thought. One less thing to pack. You know, my mother gave it to Collin and me when we moved in to our first apartment. Silly sentimental piece of junk, but you know.

Arthur: That's not the one.

Marion: Sure it is. Hall used to make them for Westinghouse back in the thirties. I see them all the time at antiques shows and I always wanted to buy another, but they ask such a fortune for them.

Arthur: We broke the one your mother gave you a couple of years ago. That's a reproduction. You can get them almost anywhere in the Village for eighteen bucks.

Marion: Really? I'll have to pick one up.

Arthur: Take this one. I'll get another.

Marion: No, it's yours. You bought it.

Arthur: One less thing to pack.

Marion: Don't be silly. I didn't come here to raid the place.

Arthur: Well, was there anything else of Collin's that you thought you might like to have?

Marion: Now I feel so stupid, but actually I made a list. Not for me. But I started thinking about different people; friends, relatives, you know, that might want to have something of Collin's to remember him by. I wasn't sure just what you were taking and what you were throwing out. Anyway, I brought the list. (*Gets it from her purse*) Of course these are only suggestions. You probably thought of a few of these people yourself. But I figured it couldn't hurt to write it all down. Like I said, I don't know what you are planning on keeping.

Arthur (*Taking the list*): I was planning on keeping it all.

Marion: Oh, I know. But most of these things are silly. Like his high school yearbooks. What would you want with them?

Arthur: Sure. I'm only interested in his Gay period.

Marion: I didn't mean it that way. Anyway, you look it over. They're only suggestions. Whatever you decide to do is fine with me.

Arthur (*Folding the list*): It would have to be, wouldn't it. I mean, it's all mine now. He did leave this all to me.

(MARION *is becoming increasingly nervous, but tries to keep a light approach as she takes a small bundle of papers from her bag.*)

Marion: While we're on the subject of what's yours. I brought a batch of condolence cards that were sent to you care of me. Relatives mostly.

Arthur (*Taking them*): More cards? I'm going to have to have another printing of thank-you notes done.

Marion: I answered these last week, so you don't have to bother. Unless you want to.

Arthur: Forge my signature?

Marion: Of course not. They were addressed to both of us and they're mostly distant relatives or friends we haven't seen in years. No one important.

Arthur: If they've got my name on them, then I'll answer them myself.

Marion: I wasn't telling you not to, I was only saying that you don't have to.

Arthur: I understand.

(MARION *picks up the teapot and brings it to the kitchen.*)

Marion: Let me put this back.

Arthur: I ran into Jimmy in the lobby.

Marion: Tell me you're joking.

Arthur: I got him to Helen's.

Marion: He's really racking up the points today.

Arthur: You know, he still can't look me in the face.

Marion: He's reacting to all of this in strange ways. Give him time. He'll come around. He's really very fond of you.

Arthur: I know. But he's at that awkward age: under thirty. I'm sure in twenty years we'll be the best of friends.

Marion: It's not what you think.

Arthur: What do you mean?

Marion: Well, you know.

Arthur: No I don't know. Tell me.

Marion: I thought that you were intimating something about his blaming you for Collin's illness and I was just letting you know that it's not true. (*Foot in mouth, she braves on.*) We discussed it a lot and . . . uh . . . he understands that his father was sick before you two ever met.

Arthur: I don't believe this.

Marion: I'm just trying to say that he doesn't blame you.

Arthur: First of all, who asked you? Second of all, that's between him and me. And third and most importantly, of course he blames me. Marion, he's eleven years old. You can discuss all you want, but the fact is that his father died of a "fag" disease and I'm the only fag around to finger.

Marion: My son doesn't use that kind of language.

Arthur: Forget the language. I'm talking about what he's been through. Can you imagine the kind of crap he's taken from his friends? That poor kid's been chased and chastised from one end of town to the other. He's got to have someone to blame just to survive. He can't blame you, you're all he's got. He can't blame his father; he's dead. So, Uncle Arthur gets the shaft. Fine, I can handle it.

Marion: You are so wrong, Arthur. I know my son and that is not the way his mind works.

Arthur: I don't know what you know. I only know what I know. And all I know is what I hear and see. The snide remarks, the little smirks . . . And it's not just the illness. He's been looking for a scapegoat since the day you and Collin first split up. Finally he has one.

Marion (*Getting very angry now*): Wait. Are you saying that if he's going to blame someone it should be me?

Arthur: I think you should try to see things from his point of view.

Marion: Where do you get off thinking you're privy to my son's point of view?

Arthur: It's not that hard to imagine. Life's rolling right along, he's having a happy little childhood, when suddenly one day his father's moving out. No explanations, no reasons, none of the fights that usually accompany such things. Divorce is hard enough for a kid to understand when he's listened to years of battles, but yours?

Marion: So what should we have done? Faked a few months' worth of fights before Collin moved out?

Arthur: You could have told him the truth, plain and simple.

Marion: He was seven years old at the time. How the hell do you tell a seven-year-old that his father is leaving his mother to go sleep with other men?

Arthur: Well, not like that.

Marion: You know, Arthur, I'm going to say this as nicely as I can: Butt out. You're not his mother and you're not his father.

Arthur: Thank you. I wasn't acutely aware of that fact. I will certainly keep that in mind from now on.

Marion: There's only so much information a child that age can handle.

Arthur: So it's best that he reach his capacity on the street.

Marion: He knew about the two of you. We talked about it.

Arthur: Believe me, he knew before you talked about it. He's young, not stupid.

Marion: It's very easy for you to stand here and criticize, but there are aspects that you will just never be able to understand. You weren't there. You have no idea what it was like for me. You're talking to someone who thought that a girl went to college to meet a husband. I went to protest rallies because I liked the music. I bought a guitar because I thought it looked good on the bed! This lifestyle, this knowledge that you take for granted, was all a little out of left field for me.

Arthur: I can imagine.

Marion: No. I don't think you can. I met Collin in college, married him right after graduation and settled down for a nice quiet life of Kids and Careers. You think I had any idea about this? Talk about life's little surprises. You live with someone for sixteen years, you share your life, your bed, and have a child together, and then you wake up one day and he tells you that to him it's all been a lie. A lie. Try that on for size. Here you are the happiest couple you know, fulfilling your every life fantasy and he tells you he's living a lie.

Arthur: I'm sure he never said that.

Marion: Don't be so sure. There was a lot of new ground being broken back then and plenty of it was muddy.

Arthur: You know that he loved you.

Marion: What's that supposed to do, make things easier? It doesn't. I was brought up to believe, among other things, that if you had love that was enough. So what if I wasn't everything he wanted. Maybe he wasn't exactly everything I wanted either. So, you know what? You count your blessings and you settle.

Arthur: No one has to settle. Not him. Not you.

Marion: Of course not. You can say, "Up yours!" to everything and everyone who depends on and needs you, and go off to make yourself happy.

Arthur: It's not that simple.

Marion: No. This is simpler. Death is simpler. (*Yelling out*) Happy now?

(*They stare at each other.* MARION *calms the rage and catches her breath.* ARTHUR *holds his emotions in check.*)

Arthur: How about a nice hot cup of coffee? Tea with lemon? Hot cocoa with a marshmallow floating in it?

Marion (*Laughs*): I was wrong. You *are* a mother.

(ARTHUR *goes into the kitchen and starts preparing things.* MARION *loafs by the doorway.*)

Marion: I lied before. He *was* everything I ever wanted.

(ARTHUR *stops, looks at her, and then changes the subject as he goes on with his work.*)

Arthur: When I came into the building and saw Jimmy in the lobby I absolutely freaked for a second. It's amazing how much they look alike. It was like seeing a little miniature Collin standing there.

Marion: I know. He's like Collin's clone. There's nothing of me in him.

Arthur: I always kinda hoped that when he grew up he'd take after me. Not much chance, I guess.

Marion: Don't do anything fancy in there.

Arthur: Please. Anything we can consume is one less thing to pack.

Marion: So you've said.

Arthur: So *we've* said.

Marion: I want to keep seeing you and I want you to see Jim. You're still part of this family. No one's looking to cut you out.

Arthur: Ah, who'd want a kid to grow up looking like me anyway. I had enough trouble looking like this. Why pass on the misery?

Marion: You're adorable.

Arthur: Is that like saying I have a good personality?

Marion: I think you are one of the most naturally handsome men I know.

Arthur: Natural is right, and the bloom is fading.

Marion: All you need is a few good nights' sleep to kill those rings under your eyes.

Arthur: Forget the rings under my eyes, (*Grabbing his middle*) . . . how about the rings around my moon?

Marion: I like you like this.

Arthur: From the time that Collin started using the wheelchair until he died, about six months, I lost twenty-three pounds. No gym, no diet. In the last seven weeks I've gained close to fifty.

Marion: You're exaggerating.

Arthur: I'd prove it on the bathroom scale, but I sold it in working order.

Marion: You'd never know.

Arthur: Marion, *you'd* never know, but ask my belt. Ask my pants. Ask my underwear. Even my stretch socks have stretch marks. I called the ambulance at five A.M., he was gone at nine and by nine-thirty, I was on a first-name basis with Sara Lee. I can quote the business hours of every ice-cream parlor, pizzeria and bakery on the island of Manhattan. I know the location of every twenty-four-hour grocery in the greater New York area, and I have memorized the phone numbers of every Mandarin, Szechuan and Hunan restaurant with free delivery.

Marion: At least you haven't wasted your time on useless hobbies.

Arthur: Are you kidding? I'm opening my own Overeater's Hotline. We'll have to start small, but expansion is guaranteed.

Marion: You're the best, you know that? If I couldn't be everything that Collin wanted then I'm grateful that he found someone like you.

Arthur (*Turning on her without missing a beat*): Keep your goddamned gratitude to yourself. I didn't go through any of this for you. So your thanks are out of line. And he didn't find "someone like" me. It was me.

Marion (*Frightened*): I didn't mean. . . .

Arthur: And I wish you'd remember one thing more: He died in my arms, not yours.

(*MARION is totally caught off guard. She stares disbelieving, openmouthed. ARTHUR walks past her as he leaves the kitchen with place mats. He puts them on the coffee table. As he arranges the papers and place mats he speaks, never looking at her.*)

Arthur: Look, I know you were trying to say something supportive. Don't waste your breath. There's nothing you can say that will make any of this easier for me. There's no way for you to help me get through this. And that's your fault. After three years you still have no idea or understanding of who I am. Or maybe you do know but refuse to accept it. I don't know and I don't care. But at least understand, from my point of view, who you are: You are my husband's *ex*-wife. If you like, the mother of *my* stepson. Don't flatter yourself into thinking you're any more than that. And whatever you are, you're certainly not my friend.

(*He stops, looks up at her; then passes her again as he goes back to the kitchen. MARION is shaken, working hard to control herself. She moves toward the couch.*)

Marion: Why don't we just sign these papers and I'll be out of your way.

Arthur: Shouldn't you say *I'll* be out of *your* way? After all, I'm not just signing papers. I'm signing away my home.

Marion (*Resolved not to fight, she gets her purse*): I'll leave the papers here. Please have them notarized and returned to my lawyer.

Arthur: Don't forget my painting.

Marion (*Exploding*): What do you want from me, Arthur?

Arthur (*Yelling back*): I want you the hell out of my apartment! I want you out of my life! And I want you to leave Collin alone!

Marion: The man's dead. I don't know how much more alone I can leave him.

(ARTHUR *laughs at the irony, but behind the laughter is something much more desperate.*)

Arthur: Lots more, Marion. You've got to let him go.

Marion: For the life of me, I don't know what I did, or what you think I did, for you to treat me like this. But you're not going to get away with it. You will not take your anger out on me. I will not stand here and be badgered and insulted by you. I know you've been hurt and I know you're hurting but you're not the only one who lost someone here.

Arthur (*Topping her*): Yes I am! You didn't just lose him. I did! You lost him five years ago when he divorced you. This is not your moment of grief and loss, it's mine! (*Picking up the bundle of cards and throwing it toward her*) These condolences do not belong to you, they're mine. (*Tossing her list back to her*) His things are not yours to give away, they're mine! This death does not belong to you, it's mine! Bought and paid for outright. I suffered for it, I bled for it. I was the one who cooked his meals. I was the one who spoon-fed them. I pushed his wheelchair. I carried and bathed him. I wiped his backside and changed his diapers. I breathed life into and wrestled fear out of his heart. I kept him alive for two years longer than any doctor thought possible and when it was time I was the one who prepared him for death.

I paid in full for my place in his life and I will *not* share it with you. We are not the two widows of Collin Redding. Your life was not here. Your husband didn't just die. You've got a son and a life somewhere else. Your husband's sitting, waiting for you at home, wondering, as I am, what the hell you're doing here and why you can't let go.

(MARION *leans back against the couch. She's blown away.* ARTHUR *stands staring at her.*)

Arthur (*Quietly*): Let him go, Marion. He's mine. Dead or alive; mine.

(*The teakettle whistles.* ARTHUR *leaves the room, goes to the kitchen and pours the water as* MARION *pulls herself together.*

ARTHUR *carries the loaded tray back into the living room and sets it down on the coffee table. He sits and pours a cup.*)

Arthur: One marshmallow or two?

(MARION *stares, unsure as to whether the attack is really over or not.*)

Arthur: (*Placing them in her cup*). Take three, they're small.

(MARION *smiles and takes the offered cup.*)

Arthur: (*Campily*). Now let me tell you how I *really* feel.

(MARION *jumps slightly, then they share a small laugh. Silence as they each gather themselves and sip their refreshments.*)

Marion (*Calmly*): Do you think that I sold the apartment just to throw you out?

Arthur: I don't care about the apartment . . .

Marion: . . . Because I really didn't. Believe me.

Arthur: I know.

Marion: I knew the expenses here were too much for you, and I knew you couldn't afford to buy out my half . . . I figured if we sold it, that you'd at least have a nice chunk of money to start over with.

Arthur: You could've given me a little more time.

Marion: Maybe. But I thought the sooner you were out of here, the sooner you could go on with your life.

Arthur: Or the sooner you could go on with yours.

Marion: Maybe. (*Pauses to gather her thoughts*) Anyway, I'm not going to tell you that I have no idea what you're talking about. I'd have to be worse than deaf and blind not to have seen the way you've been treated. Or mistreated. When I read Collin's obituary in the newspaper and saw my name and Jimmy's name and no mention of you . . . (*Shakes her head, not knowing what to say*) You know that his secretary was the one who wrote that up and sent it in. Not me. But I should have done something about it and I didn't. I know.

Arthur: Wouldn't have made a difference. I wrote my own obituary for him and sent it to the smaller papers. They edited me out.

Marion: I'm sorry. I remember, at the funeral, I was surrounded by all of Collin's family and business associates while you were left with your friends. I knew it was wrong. I knew I should have said something but it felt good to have them around me and you looked like you were holding up . . . Wrong. But saying that it's all my fault for not letting go? . . . There were other people involved.

Arthur: Who took their cue from you.

Marion: Arthur, you don't understand. Most people that we knew as a couple had no idea that Collin was Gay right up to his death. And even those that did know only found out when he got sick and the word leaked out that it was AIDS. I don't think I have to tell you how stupid and ill-informed most people are about homosexuality. And AIDS. . . ? The kinds of insane behavior that word inspires? . . .

Those people at the funeral, how many times did they call to see how he was doing over these years? How many of them ever went to see him in the hospital? Did any of them even come here? So, why would you expect them to act any differently after his death?

So, maybe that helps to explain their behavior, but what about mine, right? Well, maybe there is no explanation. Only excuses. And excuse number one is that you're right, I have never really let go of him. And I am jealous of you. Hell, I was jealous of anyone that Collin ever talked to, let alone slept with . . . let alone loved.

The first year, after he moved out, we talked all the time about the different men he was seeing. And I always listened and advised. It was kind of fun. It kept us close. It kept me a part of his intimate life. And the bottom line was always that he wasn't happy with the men he was meeting. So, I was always allowed to hang on to the hope that one day he'd give it all up and come home. Then he got sick.

He called me, told me he was in the hospital and asked if I'd come see him. I ran. When I got to his door there was a sign, INSTRUCTIONS FOR VISITORS OF AN AIDS PATIENT. I nearly died.

Arthur: He hadn't told you?

Marion: No. And believe me, a sign is not the way to find these things out. I was so angry . . . And he was so sick . . . I was sure that he'd die right then. If not from the illness then from the hospital staff's neglect. No one wanted to go near him and I didn't bother fighting with them because I understood that they were scared. I was scared. That whole month in the hospital I didn't let Jimmy visit him once.

You learn.

Well, as you know, he didn't die. And he asked if he could come stay with me until he was well. And I said yes. Of course, yes. Now, here's something I never thought I'd ever admit to anyone: had he asked to stay with me for a few weeks I would have said no. But he asked to stay with me until he was well and knowing there was no cure I said yes. In my craziness I said yes because to me that meant forever. That he was coming back to me forever. Not that I wanted him to die, but I assumed from everything I'd read . . . And we'd be back together for whatever time he had left. Can you understand that?

*(*ARTHUR *nods.)*

Marion (*Gathers her thoughts again*): Two weeks later he left. He moved in here. Into this apartment that we had bought as an investment. Never to live in. Certainly never to live apart in. Next thing I knew, the name Arthur starts appearing in every phone call, every dinner conversation.

"Did you see the doctor?"

"Yes. Arthur made sure I kept the appointment."

"Are you going to your folks for Thanksgiving?"

"No. Arthur and I are having some friends over."

I don't know which one of us was more of a coward, he for not telling or me for not asking about you. But eventually you became a given. Then, of course, we met and became what I had always thought of as friends.

*(*ARTHUR *winces in guilt.)*

Marion: I don't care what you say, how could we not be friends with something so great in common: love for one of the most special human beings there ever was. And don't try and tell me there weren't times when you enjoyed my being around as an ally. I can think of a dozen occasions when we ganged up on him, teasing him with our intimate knowledge of his personal habits.

(ARTHUR has to laugh.)

Marion: Blanket stealing? Snoring? Excess gas, no less? (*Takes a moment to enjoy this truce*) I don't think that my loving him threatened your relationship. Maybe I'm not being truthful with myself. But I don't. I never tried to step between you. Not that I ever had the opportunity. Talk about being joined at the hip! And that's not to say I wasn't jealous. I was. Terribly. Hatefully. But always lovingly. I was happy for Collin because there was no way to deny that he was happy. With everything he was facing, he was happy. Love did that. You did that.

He lit up with you. He came to life. I envied that and all the time you spent together, but more, I watched you care for him (sometimes *overcare* for him), and I was in awe. I could never have done what you did. I never would have survived. I really don't know how you did.

Arthur: Who said I survived?

Marion: Don't tease. You did an absolutely incredible thing. It's not as if you met him before he got sick. You entered a relationship that you knew in all probability would end this way and you never wavered.

Arthur: Of course I did. Don't have me sainted, Marion. But sometimes you have no choice. Believe me, if I could've gotten away from him I would've. But I was a prisoner of love.

(He makes a campy gesture and pose.)

Marion: Stop.

Arthur: And there were lots of pluses. I got to quit a job I hated, stay home all day and watch game shows. I met a lot of doctors and learned a lot of big words. (ARTHUR *jumps up and goes to the pile of boxes where he extracts one and brings it back to the couch.*) And then there was all the exciting traveling I got to do. This box has a souvenir from each one of our trips. Wanna see?

*(*MARION *nods. He opens the box and pulls things out one by one.)*

Arthur (*Continues*) (*Holding up an old bottle*): This from the house we rented in Reno when we went to clear out his lungs. (*Holding handmade potholders*) This is from the hospital in Reno. Collin made them. They had a great arts and crafts program. (*Copper bracelets*) These are from a faith healer in Philly. They don't do much for a fever, but they look great with a green sweater. (*Glass ashtrays*) These are from our first visit to the clinic in France. Such lovely people. (*A Bible*) This is from our second visit to the clinic in France. (*A bead necklace*) A Voodoo doctor in New Orleans. Next time we'll have to get there earlier in the year. I think he sold all the pretty ones at Mardi Gras. (*A tiny piñata*) Then there was Mexico. Black market drugs and empty wallets. (*Now pulling things out at random*) L.A., San Francisco, Houston, Boston . . . We traveled everywhere they offered hope for sale and came home with souvenirs.

(ARTHUR *quietly pulls a few more things out and then begins to put them all back into the box slowly. Softly as he works:*)

Marion, I would have done anything, traveled anywhere to avoid . . . or delay . . . Not just because I loved him so desperately, but when you've lived the way we did for three years . . . the battle becomes your life. (*He looks at her and then away.*)

His last few hours were beyond any scenario I had imagined. He hadn't walked in nearly six months. He was totally incontinent. If he spoke two words in a week I was thankful. Days went by without his eyes ever focusing on me. He just stared out at I don't know what. Not the meals as I fed him. Not the TV I played constantly for company. Just out. Or maybe in.

It was the middle of the night when I heard his breathing become labored. His lungs were filling with fluid again. I knew the sound. I'd heard it a hundred times before. So, I called the ambulance and got him to the hospital. They hooked him up to the machines, the oxygen, shot him with morphine and told me that they would do what they could to keep him alive.

But, Marion, it wasn't the machines that kept him breathing. He did it himself. It was that incredible will and strength inside him. Whether it came from his love of life or fear of death, who knows. But he'd been counted out a hundred times and a hundred times he fought his way back.

I got a magazine to read him, pulled a chair up to the side of his bed and holding his hand, I wondered whether I should call Helen to let the cleaning lady in or if he'd fall asleep and I could sneak home for an hour. I looked up from the page and he was looking at me. Really looking right into my eyes. I patted his cheek and said, "Don't worry, honey, you're going to be fine."

But there was something else in his eyes. He wasn't satisfied with that. And I don't know why, I have no idea where it came from, I just heard the words coming out of my mouth, "Collin, do you want to die?" His eyes filled and closed, he nodded his head.

I can't tell you what I was thinking, I'm not sure I was. I slipped off my shoes, lifted his blanket and climbed into bed next to him. I helped him to put his arms around me, and mine around him, and whispered as gently as I could into his ear, "It's alright to let go now. It's time to go on." And he did.

Marion, you've got your life and his son. All I have is an intangible place in a man's history. Leave me that. Respect that.

Marion: I understand.

(ARTHUR *suddenly comes to life, running to get the shopping bag that he'd left at the front door.*)

Arthur: Jeez! With all the screamin' and sad storytelling I forget something. (*He extracts a bouquet of flowers from the bag.*) I brung you flowers and everything.

Marion: You brought *me* flowers?

Arthur: Well, I knew you'd never think to bring me flowers and I felt that on an occasion such as this somebody oughta get flowers from somebody.

Marion: You know, Arthur, you're really making me feel like a worthless piece of garbage.

Arthur: So what else is new? (*He presents the flowers.*) Just promise me one thing: Don't press one in a book. Just stick them in a vase and when they fade just toss them out. No more memorabilia.

Marion: Arthur, I want to do something for you and I don't know what. Tell me what you want.

Arthur: I want little things. Not much. I want to be remembered. If you get a Christmas card from Collin's mother, make sure she sent me one too. If his friends call to see how you are, ask if they've called me. Have me to dinner so I can see Jimmy. Let me take him out now and then. Invite me to his wedding.

(They both laugh.)

Marion: You've got it.

Arthur (*Clearing the table*): Let me get all this cold cocoa out of the way. We still have the deed to do.

Marion (*Checking her watch*): And I've got to get Jimmy home in time for practice.

Arthur: Band practice?

Marion: Baseball. (*Picking her list off the floor*) About this list, you do what you want.

Arthur: Believe me, I will. But I promise to consider your suggestions. Just don't rush me. I'm not ready to give it all away. (ARTHUR *is off to the kitchen with his tray and the phone rings. He answers it in the kitchen.*) Hello? . . . Just a minute. (*Calling out*) It's your eager Little Leaguer.

*(*MARION *picks up the living room extension and* ARTHUR *hangs his up.)*

Marion (*Into the phone*): Hello, honey. . . . I'll be down in five minutes. No. You know what? You come up here and get me. . . . NO, I said you should come up here. . . . I said I want you to come up here. . . . Because I said so. . . . Thank you.

(She hangs up the receiver.)

Arthur (*Rushing to the papers*): Alright, where do we start on these?

Marion (*Getting out her seal*): I guess you should just start signing everything and I'll stamp along with you. Keep one of everything on the side for yourself.

Arthur: Now I feel so rushed. What am I signing?

Marion: You want to do this another time?

Arthur: No. Let's get it over with. I wouldn't survive another session like this.

(He starts to sign and she starts her job.)

Marion: I keep meaning to ask you; how are you?

Arthur (*At first puzzled and then*): Oh, you mean my health? Fine. No, I'm fine. I've been tested, and nothing. We were very careful. We took many precautions. Collin used to make jokes about how we should invest in rubber futures.

Marion: I'll bet.

Arthur (*Stops what he's doing*): It never occurred to me until now. How about you?

Marion: (*Not stopping*). Well, we never had sex after he got sick.

Arthur: But before?

Marion (*Stopping but not looking up*): I have the antibodies in my blood. No signs that it will ever develop into anything else. And it's been five years so my chances are pretty good that I'm just a carrier.

Arthur: I'm so sorry. Collin never told me.

Marion: He didn't know. In fact, other than my husband and the doctors, you're the only one I've told.

Arthur: You and your husband. . . ?

Marion: Have invested in rubber futures. There'd only be a problem if we wanted to have a child. Which we do. But we'll wait. Miracles happen every day.

Arthur: I don't know what to say.

Marion: Tell me you'll be there if I ever need you.

(ARTHUR gets up, goes to her and puts his arms around her. They hold each other. He gently pushes her away to make a joke.)

Arthur: Sure! Take something else that should have been mine.

Marion: Don't even joke about things like that.

(The doorbell rings. They pull themselves together.)

Arthur: You know we'll never get these done today.

Marion: So, tomorrow.

(ARTHUR goes to open the door as MARION gathers her things. He opens the door and JIMMY is standing in the hall.)

Jim: C'mon, Ma. I'm gonna be late.

Arthur: Would you like to come inside?

Jim: We've gotta go.

Marion: Jimmy, come on.

Jim: Ma!

(She glares. He comes in. ARTHUR closes the door.)

Marion (*Holding out the flowers*): Take these for Mommy.

Jim (*Taking them*): Can we go?

Marion (*Picking up the painting*): Say good-bye to your Uncle Arthur.

Jim: 'Bye, Arthur. Come on.

Marion: Give him a kiss.

Arthur: Marion, don't.

Marion: Give your uncle a kiss good-bye.

Jim: He's not my uncle.

Marion: No. He's a hell of a lot more than your uncle.

Arthur (*Offering his hand*): A handshake will do.

Marion: Tell Uncle Arthur what your daddy told you.

Jim: About what?

Marion: Stop playing dumb. You know.

Arthur: Don't embarrass him.

Marion: Jimmy, please.

Jim (*He regards his* mother's *softer tone and then speaks*): He said that after me and Mommy he loved you the most.

Marion (*Standing behind him*): Go on.

Jim: And that I should love you too. And make sure that you're not lonely or very sad.

Arthur: Thank you.

(ARTHUR *reaches down to the boy and they hug.* JIM *gives him a little peck on the cheek and then breaks away.*)

Marion (*Going to open the door*): Alright, kid, you done good. Now let's blow this joint before you muck it up.

(JIM *rushes out the door.* MARION *turns to* ARTHUR)

Marion: A child's kiss is magic. Why else would they be so stingy with them. I'll call you.

(ARTHUR *nods understanding.* MARION *pulls the door closed behind her.* ARTHUR *stands quietly as the lights fade to black.*)

The End

NOTE: *If being performed on film, the final image should be of* ARTHUR *leaning his back against the closed door on the inside of the apartment and* MARION *leaning on the outside of the door. A moment of thought and then they both move on.*

CRITICAL THINKING QUESTIONS

1. a. Speaking for Arthur, define "family."
    b. Speaking for Marion, define "family."

2. What *connotative* meanings (see Glossary) are associated with "tidy"? Explain the significance of the play's title. Does *On Tidy Endings* present a "happy ending"? Have Arthur and Marion given into a temporary truce between eternal rivals or found the roots for nurturing family bonds? Use evidence from the play to justify your viewpoint.

WRITING TOPIC

What claim about the definition of family does *On Tidy Endings* imply? Write an essay that explains the play's claim about family and then, using evidence from other literature selections and your own experience and observations, defend, refute, and/or qualify the claim. As you clarify your thinking, consider the fact that despite his hard work and care for Collin, Arthur is denied the rights associated with a legally sanctioned civil union.

NONFICTION

∧∧∧

Major Sullivan Ballou's Last Letter to His Wife

A week before the Civil War Battle of Bull Run, Sullivan Ballou, a Major in the Second Rhode Island Volunteers, wrote home to his wife in Smithfield.

July 14, 1861
Sara Ballou
Washington, D.C.

Dear Sara,
The indications are very strong that we shall move in a few days, perhaps tomorrow. Less I shall not be able to write you again, I feel compelled to write a few lines that may fall under your eye when I am no more.

Our movement may be one of a few days duration and full of pleasure—and it may be one of severe conflict and death to me. Not my will, but thine O God, be done. If it is necessary that I should fall on the battlefield for my country, I am ready. I have no misgivings about or lack of confidence in the cause in which I am engaged, and my courage does not halt or falter. I know how American civilization now leans upon the triumph of the government and how great a debt we owe to those who went before us through the blood and suffering of the revolution. I am willing, perfectly willing, to lay down all my joys in this life to help maintain this government and to pay that debt.

But, my dear wife, when I know that with my own joys I lay down nearly all of yours, and replace them in this life with cares and sorrows—when, after having eaten for long years the bitter fruit of orphanage myself, I must offer it as their only sustenance to my dear little children—is it weak or dishonorable, while the banner of my purpose floats calmly and proudly in the breeze, that my unbounded love for you, my darling wife and children, should struggle in fierce, though useless, contest with my love of country?

I cannot describe to you my feelings on this calm summer night, when two thousand men are sleeping around me, many of them enjoying the last, perhaps, before that of death—and I, suspicious that Death is creeping behind me with his fatal dart, am communing with God, my country, and thee.

I have sought most closely and diligently, and often in my breast, for a wrong 5 motive in thus hazarding the happiness of those I loved and I could not find one. A pure love of my country and of the principles have often advocated before the people and "the name of honor that I love more than I fear death" have called upon me, and I have obeyed.

Sara, my love for you is depthless. It seems to bind me with mighty cables that nothing but omnipotence can break. Yet my love of country comes over me like a strong wind and bears me irresistibly with all those chains to the battlefield. The memory of all the blissful moments I have enjoyed with you come crowding over me. I feel most deeply grateful to God and you that I have enjoyed them for so long. How hard it is for me to give them up and burn to ashes our hopes and future years when, God willing, we might still have lived and loved together and seen our boys grown up to honorable manhood around us. I have, I know, but few and small claims upon Divine Providence, but something whispers to me—perhaps it is the wafted prayer of my little Edgar—that I shall return to my loved ones unharmed. If I do not, my dear Sara, never forget how much I love you, and when my last breath escapes me on the battlefield, it will whisper your name.

Forgive my many faults and the many pains I have caused you. How thoughtless, how foolish I have sometimes been. How gladly would I wash out with my tears every little spot upon your happiness, and struggle with all the misfortune of this world, to shield you and my children from harm. But I cannot. I must watch you from the spirit land and hover near you, while you buffet the storms with your precious little freight, and wait with sad patience till we meet to part no more. But, oh Sara, if the dead can come back to this earth and fly unseen around those they love, I shall always be with you on the brightest day and the darkest night. Always. Always. When the soft breeze fans your cheek, it shall be my breath. When the cool air caresses your throbbing temple, it shall be my spirit passing by. Sara, do not mourn me dead. Think I am gone and wait for me. We shall meet again.

As for my little boys, they will grow as I have done, and never know a father's love and care. Little Willie is too young to remember me long, and my blue-eyed Edgar will keep my frolics with him among the dimmest memories of his childhood. Sara, I have unlimited confidence in your maternal care and your development of their characters. Tell my two mothers his and hers I call God's blessing upon them. O Sara, I wait for you there! Come to me, and lead thither my children.

Your loving husband,

Sullivan Ballou

A week after writing this letter, Major Ballou was killed at the first Battle of Bull Run.

CRITICAL THINKING QUESTIONS

1. Ballou's letter is not only a poignant expression of his love for his family—his wife Sara and his two young sons—but also an articulate description of his conflict centered on this love and his love of country. Write out the passages that depict this conflict. Examine the *figurative language* (see Glossary). In what specific ways does this language reveal this husband/father/soldier's conflict? How has he resolved his conflict?

2. Analyze this letter as a *Rogerian argument* on the personal conflict the war creates for Ballou. What is Ballou's compromise or middle-ground position? You may want to refer to Chapter 1, "Rogerian Argument Strategy," page 17.

MODELING A MASTER/WRITING TOPIC

Examine paragraph 7 for its rhetorical strategies—for example, sentence rhythm, patterns, and lengths; use of figurative language and repetition. Try modeling the paragraph. Cast yourself in the role of one who is writing a letter to an intimate friend to explain to him or her your feelings about a difficult choice—for example, you must leave your hometown to go away to college, or you must leave the country in order to avoid military service for a war you believe is immoral.

Peter D. Kramer (b. 1948)

Divorce and Our National Values

How shall we resolve a marital crisis? Consider an example from the advice column of Ann Landers. An "Iowa Wife" wrote to ask what she should do about her husband's habit, after 30 years of marriage, of reading magazines at table when the couple dined out. Ann Landers advised the wife to engage her husband by studying subjects of interest to him.

Readers from around the country protested. A "14-Year-Old Girl in Pennsylvania" crystallized the objections: "You told the wife to read up on sports or business, whatever he was interested in, even though it might be boring to her. Doesn't that defeat the basic idea of being your own self?" Chastened, Ann Landers changed course, updated her stance: Reading at table is a hostile act, perhaps even grounds for divorce.

When it comes to marriage, Ann Landers seems a reasonable barometer of our values. In practical terms, reading the sports pages might work for some Iowa wife—but we do not believe that is how spouses ought to behave. Only the second response, consider divorce, expresses our overriding respect for autonomy, for the unique and separate self.

Look south now from Iowa and Pennsylvania to Louisiana, where a new law allows couples to opt for a "covenant marriage"—terminable only after a lengthy separation or because of adultery, abandonment, abuse or imprisonment. The law has been praised by many as an expedient against the epidemic of divorce and an incarnation of our "traditional values."

Whether the law will lower the divorce rate is an empirical question to be decided   5
in the future, but it is not too soon to ask: Does covenant marriage express the values we live by?

History seems to say no. American literature's one great self-help book is "Walden," a paean to self-reliance and an homage to Henry David Thoreau's favorite preacher, Ralph Waldo Emerson, who declaimed: "Say to them, O father, O mother, O wife, O brother, O friend, I have lived with you after appearances hitherto. Henceforward, I am the truth's. . . . I must be myself. I cannot break my self any longer for you, or you."

The economic philosophy we proudly export, fundamentalist capitalism, says that society functions best when members act in a self-interested manner. The nation's founding document is a bill of divorcement. Autonomy is the characteristic American virtue.

As a psychiatrist, I see this value embedded in our psychotherapy, the craft that both shapes and expresses the prevailing common sense. In the early 1970's, Carl Rogers, known as the "Psychologist of America," encapsulated the post–World War II version of our ideals: A successful marriage is one that increases the "self-actualization" of each member. Of a failed union, he wrote: "If Jennifer had from the first insisted on being her true self, the marriage would have had much more strife and much more hope."

Rogers was expressing the predominant viewpoint; for most of the past 50 years, enhanced autonomy has been a goal of psychotherapy. Erik Erikson began the trend by boldly proclaiming that the search for identity had become as important in his time as the study of sexuality was in Freud's. Later, Murray Bowen, a founder of family therapy, invoked a scale of maturity whose measure is a person's ability to maintain his or her beliefs in the face of family pressures. The useful response to crises within couples, Bowen suggested, is to hold fast to your values and challenge your partner to rise to meet your level of maturity.

10   But autonomy was a value for men only, and largely it was pseudoautonomy, the successful man propped up by the indentured wife and overburdened mother. (No doubt Thoreau sent his clothes home for laundering.)

The self-help movement, beginning in the 1970's, extended this American ideal to women. Once both partners are allowed to be autonomous, the continuation of marriage becomes more truly voluntary. In this sense, an increase in divorce signals social progress.

It signals social progress, except that divorce is itself destructive. So it seems to me the question is whether any other compelling value counterbalances the siren song of self-improvement.

Turning again to psychotherapy, we do hear arguments for a different type of American value. Answering Erikson's call for individual identity, Helen Merrell Lynd, a sociologist at Sarah Lawrence College, wrote, "Nor must complete finding of one-self . . . precede finding oneself in and through other persons."

Her belief entered psychiatry through the writings of her pupil, Jean Baker Miller. A professor of psychiatry at Boston University, Dr. Miller faults most psychotherapy for elevating autonomy at the expense of qualities important to women, such as mutuality. To feel connected (when there is genuine give-and-take) is to feel worth. Miller wants a transformed culture in which mutuality "is valued as highly as, or more highly than, self-enhancement."

Mutuality is an ideal the culture believes it should honor but does not quite. Ours 15 is a society that does a half-hearted job of inculcating compromise, which is to say that we still teach these skills mainly to women. Much of psychotherapy addresses the troubles of those who make great efforts at compromise only to be taken advantage of by selfish partners.

Often the more vulnerable spouse requires rescue through the sort of move Ann Landers recommends, vigorous self-assertion, and even divorce.

Mutuality is a worthy ideal, one that might serve as a fit complement and counterbalance to our celebration of the self. But if we do not reward it elsewhere—if in the school and office and marketplace, we celebrate self-assertion—it seems worrisome to ask the institution of marriage to play by different rules.

What is insidious about Louisiana's covenant marriage is that, contrary to claims on its behalf, it is out of touch with our traditional values: self-expression, selffulfillment, self-reliance.

The Louisiana law invites couples to lash themselves to a morality the broader culture does not support, an arrangement that creates a potential for terrible tensions.

Though we profess abhorrence of divorce, I suspect that the divorce rate reflects 20 our national values with great exactness, and that conventional modern marriage—an eternal commitment with loopholes galore—expresses precisely the degree of loss of autonomy that we are able to tolerate.

WRITING TOPICS

1. Kramer suggests that, on the one hand, we Americans celebrate the individual, autonomy, and self-fulfillment, and, on the other hand, we honor marriage as the centerpiece of social stability. Must these values be competitive and destructive, or can they be complementary and empowering? Why?

2. Read Updike's "Separating" (page 441) in the context of Kramer's discussion of values and the marital crisis. How does Richard's and Joan's impending separation provide evidence for Kramer's claim?

Pauli Murray (1910–1985)

The Inheritance of Values

There was pride on both sides of the Fitzgerald family, but my greatest inheritance, perhaps, was a dogged persistence, a granite quality of endurance in the face of calamity. There was pride in family background, of course, but my folks took greater pride in doing any kind of honest work to earn a living and remain independent. Some people thought this trait was peculiarly Grandfather's, that Grandmother was flighty and contentious.

They did not know the inside story: how she had struggled to keep her home together and bring up six children with her husband going blind and losing ground most of the way. Her tenacity, like that of Grandfather, sprang partly from her deep religious faith and partly from a mulishness which refused to countenance despair.

"There's more ways to kill a dog beside choking him on butter," she used to say.

She was remembering those uncertain years when the children were growing up and Grandfather was fighting for his pension while trying to build a home. He had bought an acre of ground in Durham, planned his house on the edge of his line and used the rest of the land to dig clay for his brickyard. He made bricks by hand, the hard kind used for outer walls and guaranteed to withstand all kinds of weather. It was a slow and costly process full of setbacks and failures. His hired men were often careless and took advantage of his blindness. They'd fire the kilns with raw green wood or go to sleep on the job in the middle of a burning and let the fires go out. Grandfather's bricks would come out crumbling and useless and he'd have to start all over again.

Then there were his lonely pilgrimages from place to place, guided only by his cane and a kind passerby, in search of old army comrades to help reconstruct his war record twenty years after his discharge. His search frequently ended in disappointment and he'd come home discouraged to make bricks for a while before starting out again. It took him almost ten years to prove his eligibility for pension payments.

5   During those years Grandmother was trying to educate their children. Fortunately, she came into a small inheritance when Mary Ruffin Smith died around 1885. Miss Mary had not forgotten the four Smith daughters. She left each of them one hundred acres of land with provision that a house be built upon it not to cost more than $150. To ensure that the land remained free from their husbands' debts or control, she gave them only a life interest in it and provided that it should pass to their children when they died. She also left her household goods and furnishings to be divided equally among the four.

Grandmother's hundred acres came out of the old Smith plantation near Chapel Hill. She was never entirely satisfied with this bequest; she felt Miss Mary had robbed her of the full inheritance her father had intended for her, and the restrictions of "heir property" which she did not own outright rankled. It served, however, as vindication of her own claims and was Miss Mary's backhanded recognition of their relationship. Aside from a twenty-five-acre gift to their half-brother, Julius, who was not of Smith blood, and a few small cash bequests, the four Smith daughters and their children were the only individuals remembered in Mary Ruffin Smith's will.

Whatever Grandmother's dissatisfactions, which increased as years passed, she made the most of her farm. She lived there with the children and worked the land while Grandfather was building his house in Durham. From time to time she sold off timber to help him in his brick business. She used whatever cash she could raise from her crops and fruit to send the children off to school. When she had no crops or fruit, she'd sell the chickens, the hogs or whatever else she could lay her hands on.

Aunt Sallie would never forget the time Grandmother sent Aunt Maria to Hampton Institute to take up the tailoring trade. When time came for tuition, Grandmother had no money so she decided to sell her cow. Grandfather was away from home working on his pension, Aunt Pauline was off teaching and Uncle Tommie was away at school. Grandmother had no one to send to market except Sallie and Agnes, who were about twelve and eleven years old at the time, but she was not dismayed.

"Children," she told them, "I want you to drive this cow down to Durham and take her to Schwartz' market. Tell Mr. Schwartz that Cornelia Smith sent her and that she's a fine milk cow. I want a good price on her and I'm depending on you to get it."

It was a huge undertaking for two little girls—Durham was fifteen miles away and   10
the cow was none too manageable—but it would never have occurred to them that they could not deliver the cow. They started out early in the morning on a trip which took all day. The cow strayed off the road from time to time to graze in the meadows or lie down to rest and they had to pull and tug at her to get her started again. They arrived at the market in Durham near nightfall, somewhat frightened, their clothes torn and spattered with mud. When Mr. Schwartz heard all the commotion outside and came to find two bedraggled little girls standing guard over a huge cow, he listened to their story in disbelief.

"You don't mean to tell me you drove that cow all the way from Chapel Hill?" he asked.

"Yes sir, we did."

"Well, I never. And you say you're Robert Fitzgerald's daughters?"

"Yes sir, we are."

"How do I know you didn't steal that cow?"   15

The little girls stood their ground.

"If you doubt our word, you send for our Uncle Richard Fitzgerald."

Mr. Schwartz finally sent for Uncle Richard, who came, took one look at them and laughed.

"They're my brother's children all right, and if they say their mother sent the cow to market, you can take their word for it," he told Mr. Schwartz. So the butcher bought the cow on the spot and Aunt Maria stayed in school another few months.

It was also part of Grandfather's creed not to coddle his daughters. He expected   20
them to make their way in life as he had done. I found a letter he had written to Aunt Maria on September 25, 1895. She had finished her work at Hampton and gone to Philadelphia to find employment as a dressmaker, without success. She wrote to Grandfather for money to come home. He replied.

> You must not depend upon sewing. I'd go into service. You can get $12 to $15 per month and stick to work for two months without taking up your money, and you can come home independent. . . . I find many a fine mechanic tramping through the state because he cannot work at his trade. Too many people make this great mistake. You must do as I did when I first went to Philadelphia, then a boy 16. I couldn't get the kind of employment I sought so I took whatever I could get to do and stuck at it until I had accumulated enough to carry me where I wanted to go with money in my pocket. Now you are young and as able as you ever will be. You can live anywhere on the face of the earth as other people can. Take my advice, getting your board and lodging and $15 per month and you will soon be able to come home.

Thrift was another household god in Grandfather's home. It was not only a strong ingredient of his own children's training but it was expected of all prospective sons-in-law. When young Leon B. Jeffers wrote my grandparents for consent to marry Aunt Maria in 1901, they replied in the affirmative, saying, "From earliest acquaintance with you, you have been held in highest esteem by us. Although you may not have money and riches to bestow upon her now, if you have that pure and undefiled love to present to her, with thrift and good management you can soon accumulate some property."

Only three of my grandparents' children were still living when I was coming along—Aunt Pauline, Aunt Maria (who preferred to be called Marie) and Aunt Sallie—all schoolteachers and all having a hand in my upbringing. Their brother, Uncle Tommie, had left home before he was twenty and was never heard from again. Some thought he was lost at sea and others that he died of smallpox during the Spanish-American War. The youngest sister, Roberta, succumbed to typhoid fever when she was barely nineteen. My own mother, Agnes, who had departed from the teaching tradition to become a registered nurse, died suddenly when I was three, leaving six children and my father, who was ill. I saw him only once after that before he died.

Having no parents of my own, I had in effect three mothers, each trying to impress upon me those traits of character expected of a Fitzgerald—stern devotion to duty, capacity for hard work, industry and thrift, and above all honor and courage in all things. Grandfather, of course, was their standard bearer for most of the virtues, but sometimes they talked of my own mother, who was a woman of beauty and courage and whose spirit became a guiding force in my own life although I was too young to remember her.

What happened on my mother's wedding night seemed typical of her courage. Her wedding to William H. Murray, a brilliant young schoolteacher from Baltimore, was scheduled for nine o'clock on the evening of July 1, 1903, at Emanuel A.M.E. Church on Chapel Hill Road in Durham, after which the reception was to be held at Grandfather's house. Engraved invitations were sent out to numerous relatives and friends and the five Fitzgerald daughters were as excited as if all of them were brides. Will Murray was the most popular of their brothers-in-law. He had come down from Baltimore in grand style, flanked by a troupe of young men to attend him.

25   Preparations were in full swing; everybody was scurrying about all day long. There had never been such a big wedding in the Fitzgerald household. Aunt Marie Jeffers, who was expecting a child, was putting the finishing touches on my mother's wedding gown. As family modiste, she wouldn't think of letting Aggie get married until her skillful fingers had supervised each tuck and fold.

It had been a stiflingly hot day and toward evening a thunderstorm threatened. The bride was almost ready and Aunt Marie stepped back to survey her handiwork when her face went deadly pale, she screamed and fell upon her knees in her first sharp labor pains. The wedding preparations were thrown into bedlam; everything came to a standstill. People gathered at the church and the groom was waiting impatiently, but there was no bride.

At Grandfather's house Aunt Marie's screams could be heard all over the neighborhood. To add to the confusion the thunderstorm struck with terrifying intensity. It was the worst of all times for a child to be born in the Fitzgerald home, but if my mother was frightened she gave no sign. She slipped quietly out of her wedding clothes, put on her uniform and took her place beside the doctor who came to attend Aunt Marie. She was all nurse, coolheaded and composed. Childbirth was hazardous in those days and for a while it looked as if Aunt Marie would not make it. At the height of the storm, between sharp flashes of lightning and rolls of thunder which shook the house, the baby came. My mother's trained eye saw that the doctor's forceps were askew in the emergency and she quickly readjusted them, saving the baby's life. Even so, his head and neck were severely bruised and cut in the delivery and nobody expected him to live. He was thrown aside while doctor and nurse worked frantically to save the mother's life.

Somebody suggested that Agnes call off her wedding, but she shook her head and stuck to her post. When it finally appeared that Aunt Marie would survive the crisis, my mother turned to the neglected infant, bathed and bandaged him, treated his wounds, hovered over him, smacked him and almost breathed life into him. She did not turn him loose until he let out a lusty cry and she felt that he would live. She then calmly washed her hands, put on her wedding dress once more and went out into a downpour to meet her groom. Everything went off as planned, except that it was several hours later and very much subdued. The reception was switched to Uncle Richard's house and the bride received her guests as graciously as if nothing untoward had happened. The baby, Gerald, celebrated his fifty-second birthday not long ago and Aunt Marie reached eighty-one before she died.

It was through these homespun stories, each with its own moral, that my elders sought to build their family traditions. In later years I realized how very much their wealth had consisted of intangibles. They had little of the world's goods and less of its recognition but they had forged enduring values for themselves which they tried to pass on to me. I would have need of these resources when I left the rugged security of Grandfather's house and found myself in a maze of terrifying forces which I could neither understand nor cope with. While my folks could not shield me from the impact of these forces, through their own courage and strength they could teach me to withstand them. My first experience with this outer world came the summer I was nearly seven.

CRITICAL THINKING QUESTIONS

1. What is Murray's *claim* about the definition of wealth?

2. What *evidence* does she offer in support?

3. What is your viewpoint about Murray's definition?

Scott Russell Sanders (b. 1945)

The Men We Carry in Our Minds

This must be a hard time for women," I say to my friend Anneke. "They have so many paths to choose from, and so many voices calling them."

"I think it's a lot harder for men," she replies.

"How do you figure that?"

"The women I know feel excited, innocent, like crusaders in a just cause. The men I know are eaten up with guilt."

5   We are sitting at the kitchen table drinking sassafras tea, our hands wrapped around the mugs because this April morning is cool and drizzly. "Like a Dutch morning," Anneke told me earlier. She is Dutch herself, a writer and midwife and peacemaker, with the round face and sad eyes of a woman in a Vermeer painting who might be waiting for the rain to stop, for a door to open. She leans over to sniff a sprig of lilac, pale lavender, that rises from a vase of cobalt blue.

"Women feel such pressure to be everything, do everything," I say. "Career, kids, art, politics. Have their babies and get back to the office a week later. It's as if they're trying to overcome a million years' worth of evolution in one lifetime."

"But we help one another. We don't try to lumber on alone, like so many wounded grizzly bears, the way men do." Anneke sips her tea. I gave her the mug with owls on it, for wisdom. "And we have this deep-down sense that we're in the *right*—we've been held back, passed over, used—while men feel they're in the wrong. Men are the ones who've been discredited, who have to search their souls."

I search my soul. I discover guilty feelings aplenty—toward the poor, the Vietnamese, Native Americans, the whales, an endless list of debts—a guilt in each case that is as bright and unambiguous as a neon sign. But toward women I feel something more confused, a snarl of shame, envy, wary tenderness, and amazement. This muddle troubles me. To hide my unease I say, "You're right, it's tough being a man these days."

"Don't laugh." Anneke frowns at me, mournful-eyed, through the sassafras steam. "I wouldn't be a man for anything. It's much easier being the victim. All the victim has to do is break free. The persecutor has to live with his past."

10   How deep is that past? I find myself wondering after Anneke has left. How much of an inheritance do I have to throw off? Is it just the beliefs I breathed in as a child? Do I have to scour memory back through father and grandfather? Through St. Paul? Beyond Stonehenge and into the twilit caves? I'm convinced the past we must contend with is deeper even than speech. When I think back on my childhood, on how I learned to see men and women, I have a sense of ancient, dizzying depths. The back roads of Tennessee and Ohio where I grew up were probably closer, in their sexual patterns, to the campsites of Stone Age hunters than to the genderless cities of the future into which we are rushing.

The first men, besides my father, I remember seeing were black convicts and white guards, in the cottonfield across the road from our farm on the outskirts of

Memphis. I must have been three or four. The prisoners wore dingy gray-and-black zebra suits, heavy as canvas, sodden with sweat. Hatless, stooped, they chopped weeds in the fierce heat, row after row, breathing the acrid dust of boll-weevil poison. The overseers wore dazzling white shirts and broad shadowy hats. The oiled barrels of their shotguns flashed in the sunlight. Their faces in memory are utterly blank. Of course those men, white and black, have become for me an emblem of racial hatred. But they have also come to stand for the twin poles of my early vision of manhood—the brute toiling animal and the boss.

When I was a boy, the men I knew labored with their bodies. They were marginal farmers, just scraping by, or welders, steelworkers, carpenters; they swept floors, dug ditches, mined coal, or drove trucks, their forearms ropy with muscle; they trained horses, stoked furnaces, built tires, stood on assembly lines wrestling parts onto cars and refrigerators. They got up before light, worked all day long whatever the weather, and when they came home at night they looked as though somebody had been whipping them. In the evenings and on weekends they worked on their own places, tilling gardens that were lumpy with clay, fixing broken-down cars, hammering on houses that were always too drafty, too leaky, too small.

The bodies of the men I knew were twisted and maimed in ways visible and invisible. The nails of their hands were black and split, the hands tattooed with scars. Some had lost fingers. Heavy lifting had given many of them finicky backs and guts weak from hernias. Racing against conveyor belts had given them ulcers. Their ankles and knees ached from years of standing on concrete. Anyone who had worked for long around machines was hard of hearing. They squinted, and the skin of their faces was creased like the leather of old work gloves. There were times, studying them, when I dreaded growing up. Most of them coughed, from dust or cigarettes, and most of them drank cheap wine or whiskey, so their eyes looked bloodshot and bruised. The fathers of my friends always seemed older than the mothers. Men wore out sooner. Only women lived into old age.

As a boy I also knew another sort of men, who did not sweat and break down like mules. They were soldiers, and so far as I could tell they scarcely worked at all. During my early school years we lived on a military base, an arsenal in Ohio, and every day I saw GIs in the guardshacks, on the stoops of barracks, at the wheels of olive drab Chevrolets. The chief fact of their lives was boredom. Long after I left the Arsenal I came to recognize the sour smell the soldiers gave off as that of souls in limbo. They were all waiting—for wars, for transfers, for leaves, for promotions, for the end of their hitch—like so many braves waiting for the hunt to begin. Unlike the warriors of older tribes, however, they would have no say about when the battle would start or how it would be waged. Their waiting was broken only when they practiced for war. They fired guns at targets, drove tanks across the churned-up fields of the military reservation, set off bombs in the wrecks of old fighter planes. I knew this was all play. But I also felt certain that when the hour for killing arrived, they would kill. When the real shooting started, many of them would die. This was what soldiers were *for,* just as a hammer was for driving nails.

Warriors and toilers: those seemed, in my boyhood vision, to be the chief destinies   15
for men. They weren't the only destinies, as I learned from having a few male teachers,

from reading books, and from watching television. But the men on television—the politicians, the astronauts, the generals, the savvy lawyers, the philosophical doctors, the bosses who gave orders to both soldiers and laborers—seemed as remote and unreal to me as the figures in tapestries. I could no more imagine growing up to become one of these cool, potent creatures than I could imagine becoming a prince.

A nearer and more hopeful example was that of my father, who had escaped from a red-dirt farm to a tire factory, and from the assembly line to the front office. Eventually he dressed in a white shirt and tie. He carried himself as if he had been born to work with his mind. But his body, remembering the earlier years of slogging work, began to give out on him in his fifties, and it quit on him entirely before he turned sixty-five. Even such a partial escape from man's fate as he had accomplished did not seem possible for most of the boys I knew. They joined the Army, stood in line for jobs in the smoky plants, helped build highways. They were bound to work as their fathers had worked, killing themselves or preparing to kill others.

A scholarship enabled me not only to attend college, a rare enough feat in my circle, but even to study in a university meant for the children of the rich. Here I met for the first time young men who had assumed from birth that they would lead lives of comfort and power. And for the first time I met women who told me that men were guilty of having kept all the joys and privileges of the earth for themselves. I was baffled. What privileges? What joys? I thought about the maimed, dismal lives of most of the men back home. What had they stolen from their wives and daughters? The right to go five days a week, twelve months a year, for thirty or forty years to a steel mill or a coal mine? The right to drop bombs and die in war? The right to feel every leak in the roof, every gap in the fence, every cough in the engine, as a wound they must mend? The right to feel, when the lay-off comes or the plant shuts down, not only afraid but ashamed?

I was slow to understand the deep grievances of women. This was because, as a boy, I had envied them. Before college, the only people I had ever known who were interested in art or music or literature, the only ones who read books, the only ones who ever seemed to enjoy a sense of ease and grace were the mothers and daughters. Like the menfolk, they fretted about money, they scrimped and made-do. But, when the pay stopped coming in, they were not the ones who had failed. Nor did they have to go to war, and that seemed to me a blessed fact. By comparison with the narrow, ironclad days of fathers, there was an expansiveness, I thought, in the days of mothers. They went to see neighbors, to shop in town, to run errands at school, at the library, at church. No doubt, had I looked harder at their lives, I would have envied them less. It was not my fate to become a woman, so it was easier for me to see the graces. Few of them held jobs outside the home, and those who did filled thankless roles as clerks and waitresses. I didn't see, then, what a prison a house could be, since houses seemed to me brighter, handsomer places than any factory. I did not realize—because such things were never spoken of—how often women suffered from men's bullying. I did learn about the wretchedness of abandoned wives, single mothers, widows; but I also learned about the wretchedness of lone men. Even then I could see how exhausting it was for a mother to cater all day to the needs of young children. But if I had been asked, as a boy, to choose between tending a baby and tending a machine, I think I would have chosen the baby. (Having now tended both, I know I would choose the baby.)

So I was baffled when the women at college accused me and my sex of having cornered the world's pleasures. I think something like my bafflement has been felt by other boys (and by girls as well) who grew up in dirt-poor farm country, in mining country, in black ghettos, in Hispanic barrios, in the shadows of factories, in Third World nations—any place where the fate of men is as grim and bleak as the fate of women. Toilers and warriors. I realize now how ancient these identities are, how deep the tug they exert on men, the undertow of a thousand generations. The miseries I saw, as a boy, in the lives of nearly all men I continue to see in the lives of many—the body-breaking toil, the tedium, the call to be tough, the humiliating powerlessness, the battle for a living and for territory.

When the women I met at college thought about the joys and privileges of men, they   20
did not carry in their minds the sort of men I had known in my childhood. They thought of their fathers, who were bankers, physicians, architects, stockbrokers, the big wheels of the big cities. These fathers rode the train to work or drove cars that cost more than any of my childhood houses. They were attended from morning to night by female helpers, wives and nurses and secretaries. They were never laid off, never short of cash at month's end, never lined up for welfare. These fathers made decisions that mattered. They ran the world.

The daughters of such men wanted to share in this power, this glory. So did I. They yearned for a say over their future, for jobs worthy of their abilities, for the right to live at peace, unmolested, whole. Yes, I thought, yes yes. The difference between me and these daughters was that they saw me, because of my sex, as destined from birth to become like their fathers, and therefore as an enemy to their desires. But I knew better. I wasn't an enemy, in fact or in feeling. I was an ally. If I had known, then, how to tell them so, would they have believed me? Would they now?

CRITICAL THINKING QUESTIONS

1. Rewrite Sanders's first paragraph (the essay's first two sentences) as a *claim statement,* followed by *because: Women must have . . . because they. . . .*

2. What *warrant* links the support clause (*because . . .*) to the claim? Do you accept the warrant?

WRITING TOPIC

Sanders concludes that the women he met at college should have regarded him as an ally rather than an enemy. How does Sanders's assertion reframe the issue question—who has it better, men or women? Write out the question that frames the argument for Sanders's assertion. Based on the images of men and women that you carry in your mind, which issue question has more relevance and validity? Write an essay defending your claim.

CHAPTER ACTIVITIES
AND TOPICS FOR WRITING ARGUMENTS

1. What is "marital bliss"? Should you expect to experience self-development and equality within a marriage? What does it mean to choose a marriage partner in the twenty-first century? Should engaged couples create and sign a prenuptial contract? Do some background research on prenuptial contracts. Then conduct primary research on the state of marriage in the twenty-first century: Interview peers, friends, and family members and ask them their views on the above questions. (For a representative sample, be sure to talk with persons representing different age groups and to include an even gender mix in your sample.) Based on your research findings and several chapter readings, write an argument that advocates or disputes prenuptial contracts. Or write a Rogerian argument that advocates a rethinking of the conventional concept of marriage (literature suggestions: Chopin's "The Storm," Updike's "Separating," Bradstreet's "To, My Dear and Loving Husband," Corso's "Marriage," Fierstein's *On Tidy Endings,* Kramer's "Divorce and Our National Values").

2. The nineteenth-century Russian writer Leo Tolstoy opens Chapter One of his novel, *Anna Karenina,* with this two-part assertion: "All happy families are like one another; each unhappy family is unhappy in its own way."[2] What assumptions or warrants are implied in his assertion about "happy families"? What assumptions are implied about "unhappy" families? Extend your thinking beyond Tolstoy's assertions to your own experience, observations, and several readings in this chapter. Write an essay that defends, refutes, and/or qualifies Tolstoy's assertions about happy and unhappy families (literature suggestions: Updike's Separating Snyder's "Not Leaving the House," Murray's "The Inheritance of Values").

3. What is the role of a father? Is a father's participation in a child's growing up more significant in a son's or in a daughter's long-term well-being? If a parent's personal income is sufficient, can a single parent (mom or dad) be "good enough" for child-rearing? How important is it for a child to have regular daily contact with both his or her mom and dad? Conduct research to find out what family therapists and sociologists are saying about these parenting issues; also, ask friends for their viewpoints. Based on your research findings and several literature selections, argue a position on an aspect of parenting (literature suggestions: González's "Too Much His Father's Son," Paley's "A Conversation with My Father," Updike's "Separating," Cleary's "Boss's Son," Wilbur's "The Writer").

---

[2]Leo Tolstoy, *Anna Karenina* (New York: Signet Classics, 1961), p. 17.

4. How do family traditions and cultural legacies contribute to and/or inhibit an individual's self-identity? What do you know about your family history? How is this history shared, and how is it valued among individual family members? Beyond its literal meaning, what are the broader implications of the cliché, "keeping the family name alive"? Or has this cliché outlived its validity? A number of readings in this chapter address an aspect of family tradition/cultural heritage and individual identity and fulfillment—for example, Lee's "Safe," Ng's "A Red Sweater," Walker's "Everyday Use," Heaney's "Digging," Rich's, "Delta," Walker's "Lineage." Drawing on evidence from several readings and your own experience and observations, write a claim of value argument about an aspect of family heritage and individual identity.

5. What are the long-term effects of divorce on children? According to Census Bureau statistics, the divorce rate peaked in the late 1970s and early 1980s, and even though the rate has been declining for the past twenty years, the United States' divorce rate still stands at 49 percent of all marriages.[3] Now that the children of the recent divorce boom are adults themselves, some are speaking out about the lasting effects of their parents' divorces. In a *Time* magazine cover story, Walter Kirn reported the research findings and conclusions of therapist Judith Wallerstein. Wallerstein's research, based on interviews with adult children of divorce, suggests that divorce has significant and lasting negative impacts on children. And most significantly, Wallerstein argues that parents should stick it out and stay married for their children's sake. However, other experts vigorously dispute Wallerstein's conclusions. Author Katha Pollitt, for example, contends, "America doesn't need more 'good enough' marriages full of depressed and bitter people. . . . The 'good enough' divorce—why isn't that ever the cover story?"[4] Conduct some research on the issue of children and divorce, and reflect on several readings in this chapter. Based on your findings, take a stand on Wallerstein's claim that parents should stay together for their children's long-term welfare (literature suggestions: González's "Too Much His Father's Son," Updike's "Separating," Olds's "I Go Back to May, 1937").

6. Why get married? As noted in the chapter introduction, couples increasingly are choosing to form intimate relationships and cohabitate without getting married. As such, these couples side-step the legal constraints—and benefits—of the marriage bond. Moreover, social attitudes seem to be softening. This lifestyle option, once wholly rejected, is now tolerated by many and applauded by some. Write an argument in response to the question, why get married? (literature suggestions: Davis's "Break It Down," Hemingway's "Hills Like White Elephants," Corso's "Marriage," Hardy's "The Ruined Maid")

---

[3]Walter Kirn, "Should You Stay Together for the Kids?" *Time,* September 25, 2000, pp. 75–82.
[4]Katha Pollitt, "Is Divorce Getting a Bum Rap?" *Time,* September 25, 2000, p. 82.

COLLABORATION ACTIVITY: CREATING
A ROGERIAN ARGUMENT

For this activity, you will work in small teams to research, write, and present a Rogerian argument on a contemporary issue that has emerged from your exploration of readings in this chapter. The "Writing Topics," following many of the selections, can help you identify an issue. For a discussion of the Rogerian Argument and a suggested organizational approach to the assignment, please see Chapter Three.

Following are guidelines for this collaboration activity:

* Identify an *issue.*
* Divide the research/writing responsibilities as follows:
  * Student one: introduction section
  * Student two: body section, affirmative position
  * Student three: body section, opposing position
  * Student four: conclusion, summation and middle-ground position.

Following are characteristics of effective collaboration. The team member should:

* *Contribute* by collecting information related to the issue.
* *Take responsibility* by completing his or her assigned work on time.
* *Engage* with team members by listening to and considering other viewpoints.

Sample Issue: Same-Sex Marriage

In May 2004, Massachusetts became the first state to legalize marriage between members of the same sex. This action followed from a November 2003 decision by the state's highest court that denying gay and lesbian couples the right to marry violated the state's constitution. As of summer 2004, five states (California, New York, Rhode Island, Vermont, and Wisconsin) have introduced legislation that would permit same-sex couples to marry; meanwhile, more than thirty-five states have introduced legislation to preserve the traditional definition of marriage as a union between a man and a woman. Opponents argue that sanctioning marriage between same-sex couples undermines the institution of marriage; advocates, on the other hand, claim that no couple, regardless of sex, can be denied the civil rights associated with marriage. Should same-sex marriages be legalized?

Literature suggestions: Kenan's "The Foundations of the Earth" in Chapter Four; Bradstreet's "To My Dear and Loving Husband," Snyder's "Not Leaving the House," Tsui's "A Chinese Banquet," and Fierstein's *Tidy Endings* in Chapter Six

MAKING CONNECTIONS

Chapter Six: Family and Identity

"I now pronounce you man and wife 'til. . . .
Chopin, "The Storm"; Updike, "Separating"; Bradstreet, "To My Dear and Loving Husband"; Corso, "Marriage"; Rich, "Aunt Jennifer's Tigers"; Ballou, "Major Sullivan Ballou's Last Letter to His Wife"; Fierstein, *On Tidy Endings*

Family and the home as shelter
Lee, "Safe"; Ng, "A Red Sweater"; Olds, "I Go Back to May, 1937"; Snyder, "Not Leaving the House"

The role of mother
Brooks, "The Mother"; Giovanni, "Mothers"; Randall, "Ballad of Birmingham"

The role of father
Paley, "A Conversation with My Father"; Updike, "Separating"; Meinke, "Advice to My Son"; Snyder, "Not Leaving the House"; Wilbur, "The Writer"

Family heritage and identity
Walker, "Everyday Use"; Heaney, "Digging"; Oliver, "The Black Walnut Tree"; Walker, "Lineage" Murray, "The Inheritance of Values"

Cross-Chapter Connections

Love and commitment
Hayden, "Those Winter Sundays" (Chapter One); Chopin, "Désireé's Baby" (Chapter Four); Welty, "A Worn Path" (Chapter Five); Hemingway, "Hills Like White Elephants," Wilbur, "The Writer" (Chapter Six)

᭞᭞ CHAPTER 7 ᭞᭞

Power and Responsibility

Do you recall a playground bully from your childhood, that child whose strength and physical power made him intimidating? What was frightening was not merely his strength but how he chose to use that strength. He was threatening because sometimes he did not act responsibly and, thus, could hurt you. On the other hand, not all threatening children were physically powerful; some gained control through manipulation. They, too, could exert a power over you, potentially harming you by irresponsibly starting rumors and exploiting gossip to achieve their goals.

As adults, we continue to witness the abuse of power by individuals who seek to influence and control others for their own gain. In our eyes, such individuals act irresponsibly when they buy votes in our government, create insider-stock deals on Wall Street, or merely forget to consider the feelings of others as they pursue their goals. The hard truth is that with power comes responsibility, for we are all answerable, eventually accountable, for our actions.

Are you familiar with Shakespeare's play *Macbeth*? Lady Macbeth and her husband are ruthless in their acquisition of power and become intoxicated with it once they have it. The price for their irresponsibility is death, and for four hundred years now the world has found the story of their downfall instructive. Literature has examined this relationship between power and responsibility since the earliest time. The Greeks understood it well, as can be seen in the plays of Sophocles, Aristophanes, and Euripedes. The Roman playwrights Plautus and Terrence clearly understood it, as later did the poets Dante and Milton. The modern novelist F. Scott Fitzgerald explored this idea in his famous novel *The Great Gatsby,* as the fabulously wealthy Gatsby eventually pays dearly for his cavalier treatment of others.

But it is not only the rich and famous among us who struggle with the relationship between power and responsibility. At all levels of society, the theme of power and responsibility is reflected in our literature. Look at this poem by Maxine Kumin:

Woodchucks

Gassing the woodchucks didn't turn out right.
The knockout bomb from the Feed and Grain Exchange
was featured as merciful, quick at the bone
and the case we had against them was airtight,
5   both exits shoehorned shut with puddingstone,
but they had a sub-sub-basement out of range.

Next morning they turned up again, no worse
for the cyanide than we for our cigarettes
and state-store Scotch, all of us up to scratch.
10   They brought down the marigolds as a matter of course
and then took over the vegetable patch
nipping the broccoli shoots, beheading the carrots.

The food from our mouths, I said, righteously thrilling
to the feel of the .22, the bullets' neat noses.
15   I, a lapsed pacifist fallen from grace
puffed with Darwinian pieties for killing,
now drew a bead on the littlest woodchuck's face.
He died down in the everbearing roses.

Ten minutes later I dropped the mother. She
20   flipflopped in the air and fell, her needle teeth
still hooked in a leaf of Swiss chard.
Another baby next. O one-two-three
the murderer inside me rose up hard,
the hawkeye killer came on stage forthwith.

25   There's one chuck left. Old wily fellow, he keeps
me cocked and ready day after day after day.
All night I hunt his humped-up form. I dream
I sight along the barrel in my sleep.
If only they'd all consented to die unseen
30   Gassed underground the quiet Nazi way.

The poet certainly understands the conflicts surrounding the use of power. With the .22 in hand, the speaker is able to deal out death to these creatures who are merely pursuing their natural instincts and mean no personal harm. Notice line 16, "puffed with Darwinian pieties for killing." *The survival of the fittest* is the phrase from Darwin everyone knows, and in this case what qualifies the speaker as the *fittest?* The ability to use the .22, of course. In fact, Darwin's ideas about evolution and the hierarchy of living things have been used to justify many exertions of power in recent history; some of these instances you may deem abusive. Obviously, the Holocaust comes to mind, but acts of genocide continue today. Later in this chapter, you can read the essay, "Religion and Animal Rights" by Tom Regan, in which he discusses the issue of power and responsibility as it relates to our treatment of animals as a food source.

Saying, "I thought the time had come when a few boundaries ought to be moved," Henrik Ibsen, a Norwegian playwright, wrote *The Doll's House* in 1879 and certainly ignited some controversies that continue to resonate in our contemporary world. In this play, which has seen several modern revivals on Broadway, a lawyer's wife named Nora chafes against the reins of power held firmly in the hands of her husband. As a result, she rebels, at first in small ways, but eventually as scandal threatens to destroy their social position, Nora sees the reality of her situation:

Nora: . . . when I lived at home with Papa, he used to tell me his opinion about everything, and so I had the same opinion. If I thought differently, I had to hide it from him, or he wouldn't have liked it. He called me his little doll, and he used to play with me just as I played with my dolls. Then I came to live in your house—

Helmer: That's no way to talk about our marriage!

Nora (*Undisturbed*): I mean when I passed out of Papa's hands into yours. You arranged everything to suit your own tastes, and so I came to have the same tastes as yours . . .

* * *

[Briefly, they discuss the idea of happiness.]

Helmer (*Nora's husband*): Haven't you been happy here?

Nora: No, that's something I've never been. I thought I had, but really I've never been happy.

Helmer: Never . . . happy?

Nora: No, only gay. And you've always been so kind to me. But our home has been nothing but a play-room. I've been your doll-wife here, just as at home I was Papa's doll-child . . .

You can be certain that in 1879 this play, focusing as it does on the acquisition and use of power within a marriage, "moved a few boundaries," as Ibsen said. Since Nora's unwillingness to bend to her husband's influence so obviously conflicted with traditional gender roles, many people in the original audience were outraged. Yet that is what literature so often does: It prods us to look beyond the status quo, beyond those values and social configurations we so readily accept.

In the 1970s and 1980s, *A Doll's House* found great favor among the members of the women's movement. The late 1990s saw yet another successful Broadway revival of this play, not because the idea of a woman demanding independence was any longer so shocking but because its theme of power and responsibility continues to appeal to audiences. In a reversal of roles, the 1999 film *American Beauty* portrays a husband rebelling against the powerless situation in which he finds himself, first quitting his job in advertising and then completely altering his marriage. The struggle over power and the consequences of responsibility for the use of that power are themes we continue to see played out in the literature of the twenty-first century. For example, in this chapter, Iraqi veteran and writer John Crawford provides an on-the-ground view of the burden of responsibility soldiers bear when they are, literally, armed with the power to kill.

As you read, you will have the opportunity to examine this theme in the works of early American writer Nathaniel Hawthorne, who was quite ready to teach his readers about the use and abuse of power. In his story, "The Birth-Mark," Hawthorne's character, Aylmer, wields power over his wife, Georgiana. In a modern setting, Nadine Gordimer centers her short story, "Terminal," on the promises and responsibilities two people share when one is stricken with illness. In this instance, no one is acting selfishly or for personal gain; however, an important choice must be made, and the decision tests the boundaries of commitment. In the contemporary story, "He Becomes Deeply and Famously Drunk," Brady Udall creates the character, Archie, who discovers his long-awaited moment of power is far from what he had envisioned. As we read literature, we continually see characters struggle with the issues of power and responsibility and, in some cases, learn from their mistakes. As readers, we watch, consider, and learn.

PREWRITING AND DISCUSSION

1. What do people mean when they talk about *power?* Focus on a particular context, such as state government, the family, the schools, or the community. Who has power and who does not—and why? Is power related to money? To respect?

2. Consider the saying, "Power corrupts, and absolute power corrupts absolutely." Can you think of examples where that phrase has proven to be true? Can you think of examples of powerful people who are above corruption, people who forego personal benefits in order to work for the good of others?

3. Write for a few minutes about *responsibility*. What responsibility do we as individuals have to our families, communities, or nation? In small groups, discuss your ideas of power and responsibility.

FICTION

∿

Toni Cade Bambara (b. 1939)
The Lesson

Back in the days when everyone was old and stupid or young and foolish and me and Sugar were the only ones just right, this lady moved on our block with nappy hair and proper speech and no makeup. And quite naturally we laughed at her, laughed the way we did at the junk man who went about his business like he was some big-time president and his sorry-ass horse his secretary. And we kinda hated her too, hated the way we did the winos who cluttered up our parks and pissed on our handball walls and stank up our hallways and stairs so you couldn't halfway play hide-and-seek without a goddamn gas mask. Miss Moore was her name. The only woman on the block with no first name. And she was black as hell, cept for her feet, which were fish-white and spooky. And she was always planning these boring-ass things for us to do, us being my cousin, mostly, who lived on the block cause we all moved North the same time and to the same apartment then spread out gradual to breathe. And our parents would yank our heads into some kinda shape and crisp up our clothes so we'd be presentable for travel with Miss Moore, who always looked like she was going to church, though she never did. Which is just one of the things the grownups talked about when they talked behind her back like a dog. But when she came calling with some sachet she'd sewed up or some gingerbread she'd made or some book, why then they'd all be too embarrassed to turn her down and we'd get handed over all spruced up. She'd been to college and said it was only right that she should take responsibility for the young ones' education, and she not even related by marriage or blood. So they'd go for it. Specially Aunt Gretchen. She was the main gofer in the family. You got some ole dumb shit foolishness you want somebody to go for, you send for Aunt Gretchen. She been screwed into the go-along for so long, it's a blood-deep natural thing with her. Which is how she got saddled with me and Sugar and Junior in the first place while our mothers were in a la-de-da apartment up the block having a good ole time.

So this one day Miss Moore rounds us all up at the mailbox and it's puredee hot and she's knockin herself out about arithmetic. And school suppose to let up in summer I heard, but she don't never let up. And the starch in my pinafore scratching the shit outta me and I'm really hating this nappy-head bitch and her goddamn college degree. I'd much rather go to the pool or to the show where it's cool. So me and Sugar leaning on the mailbox being surly, which is a Miss Moore word. And Flyboy checking out what everybody brought for lunch. And Fat Butt already wasting his peanut-butter-and-jelly sandwhich like the pig he is. And Junebug punching on Q.T.'s arm for potato chips. And Rosie Giraffe shifting from one hip to the other waiting for somebody to step on her foot or ask her if she from Georgia so she can kick ass, preferably Mercedes'. And Miss Moore asking us do we know what money is, like we a bunch of retards. I mean real money, she say, like it's only poker chips or monopoly papers we lay on the grocer. So right away I'm tired of this and say so. And would much rather snatch Sugar and go to the Sunset and terrorize the West Indian kids and take their hair ribbons and their money too. And Miss Moore files that remark away for next week's lesson on brotherhood, I can tell. And finally I say we oughta get to the subway cause it's cooler and besides we might meet some cute boys. Sugar done swiped her mama's lipstick, so we ready.

So we heading down the street and she's boring us silly about what things cost and what our parents make and how much goes for rent and how money ain't divided up right in this country. And then she gets to the part about we all poor and live in the slums, which I don't feature. And I'm ready to speak on that, but she steps out in the street and hails two cabs just like that. Then she hustles half the crew in with her and hands me a five-dollar bill and tells me to calculate 10 percent tip for the driver. And we're off. Me and Sugar and Junebug and Flyboy hangin' out the window and hollering to everybody, putting lipstick on each other cause Flyboy a faggot anyway, and making farts with our sweaty armpits. But I'm mostly trying to figure how to spend this money. But they all fascinated with the meter ticking and Junebug starts laying bets as to how much it'll read when Flyboy can't hold his breath no more. Then Sugar lays bets as to how much it'll be when we get there. So I'm stuck. Don't nobody want to go for my plan, which is to jump out at the next light and run off to the first bar-b-que we can find. Then the driver tells us to get the hell out cause we there already. And the meter reads eighty-five cents. And I'm stalling to figure out the tip and Sugar say give him a dime. And I decide he don't need it bad as I do, so later for him. But then he tries to take off with Junebug foot still in the door so we talk about his mama something ferocious. Then we check out that we on Fifth Avenue and everybody dressed up in stockings. One lady in a fur coat, hot as it is. White folks crazy.

"This is the place," Miss Moore say, presenting it to us in the voice she uses at the museum. "Let's look in the windows before we go in."

5   "Can we steal?" Sugar asks very serious like she's getting the ground rules squared away before she plays. "I beg your pardon," say Miss Moore, and we fall out. So she leads us around the windows of the toy store and me and Sugar screamin', "This is mine, that's mine, I gotta have that, that was made for me, I was born for that," till Big Butt drowns us out.

"Hey, I'm going to buy that there."

"That there? You don't even know what it is, stupid."

"I do so," he say punchin on Rosie Giraffe. "It's a microscope."

"Whatcha gonna do with a microscope, fool?"

10   "Look at things."

"Like what, Ronald?" ask Miss Moore. And Big Butt ain't got the first notion. So here go Miss Moore gabbing about the thousands of bacteria in a drop of water and the somethinorother in a speck of blood and the million and one living things in the air around us is invisible to the naked eye. And what she say that for? Junebug go to town on that "naked" and we rolling. Then Miss Moore ask what it cost. So we all jam into the window smudgin it up and the price tag say $300. So then she ask how long'd take for Big Butt and Junebug to save up their allowances. "Too long," I say. "Yeh," adds Sugar, "outgrown it by that time." And Miss Moore say no, you never outgrow learning instruments. "Why, even medical students and interns and," blah, blah, blah. And we ready to choke Big Butt for bringing it up in the first damn place.

"This here costs four hundred eighty dollars," say Rosie Giraffe. So we pile up all over her to see what she pointin out. My eyes tell me it's a chunk of glass cracked with something heavy, and different-color inks dripped into the splits, then the whole thing put into a oven or something. But for $480 it don't make sense.

"That's a paperweight made of semi-precious stones fused together under tremendous pressure," she explains slowly, with her hands doing the mining and all the factory work.

"So what's a paperweight?" asks Rosie Giraffe.

"To weigh paper with, dumbbell," say Flyboy, the wise man from the East. 15

"Not exactly," say Miss Moore, which is what she say when you warm or way off too. "It's to weigh paper down so it won't scatter and make your desk untidy." So right away me and Sugar curtsy to each other and then to Mercedes who is more the tidy type.

"We don't keep paper on top of the desk in my class," say Junebug, figuring Miss Moore crazy or lyin one.

"At home, then," she say. "Don't you have a calendar and a pencil case and a blotter and a letter-opener on your desk at home where you do your homework?" And she know damn well what our homes look like cause she nosys around in them every chance she gets.

"I don't even have a desk," say Junebug. "Do we?"

"No. And I don't get no homework neither," say Big Butt. 20

"And I don't even have a home," say Flyboy like he do at school to keep the white folks off his back and sorry for him. Send this poor kid to camp posters, is his specialty.

"I do," says Mercedes. "I have a box of stationery on my desk and a picture of my cat. My godmother bought the stationery and the desk. There's a big rose on each sheet and the envelopes smell like roses."

"Who wants to know about your smelly-ass stationery," say Rosie Giraffe fore I can get my two cents in.

"It's important to have a work area all your own so that . . . "

"Will you look at this sailboat, please," say Flyboy, cuttin her off and pointin 25 to the thing like it was his. So once again we tumble all over each other to gaze at this magnificent thing in the toy store which is just big enough to maybe sail two kittens across the pond if you strap them to the posts tight. We all start reciting the price tag like we in assembly. "Handcrafted sailboat of fiberglass at one thousand one hundred ninety-five dollars."

"Unbelievable," I hear myself say and am really stunned. I read it again for myself just in case the group recitation put me in a trance. Same thing. For some reason this pisses me off. We look at Miss Moore and she lookin at us, waiting for I dunno what.

"Who'd pay all that when you can buy a sailboat set for a quarter at Pop's, a tube of glue for a dime, and a ball of string for eight cents? It must have a motor and a whole lot else besides," I say. "My sailboat cost me about fifty cents."

"But will it take water?" say Mercedes with her smart ass.

"Took mine to Alley Pond Park once," say Flyboy. "String broke, Lost it. Pity."

30   "Sailed mine in Central Park and it keeled over and sank. Had to ask my father for another dollar."

"And you got the strap," laugh Big Butt. "The jerk didn't even have a string on it. My old man wailed on his behind."

Little Q.T. was staring hard at the sailboat and you could see he wanted it bad. But he too little and somebody'd just take it from him. So what the hell. "This boat for kids, Miss Moore?"

"Parents silly to buy something like that just to get all broke up," say Rosie Giraffe.

"That much money it should last forever," I figure.

35   "My father'd buy it for me if I wanted it.

"Your father, my ass," say Rosie Giraffe getting a chance to finally push Mercedes.

"Must be rich people shop here," say Q.T.

"You are a very bright boy," say Flyboy. "What was your first clue?" And he rap him on the head with the back of his knuckles, since Q.T. the only one he could get away with. Though Q.T. liable to come up behind you years later and get his licks in when you half expect it.

"What I want to know is," I says to Miss Moore though I never talk to her, I wouldn't give the bitch that satisfaction, "is how much a real boat costs? I figure a thousand'd get you a yacht any day."

40   "Why don't you check that out," she says, "and report back to the group?" Which really pains my ass. If you gonna mess up a perfectly good swim day least you could do is have some answers. "Let's go in," she say like she got something up her sleeve. Only she don't lead the way. So me and Sugar turn the corner to where the entrance is, but when we get there I kinda hang back. Not that I'm scared, what's there to be afraid of, just a toy store. But I feel funny, shame. But what I got to be shamed about? Got as much right to go in as anybody. But somehow I can't seem to get hold of the door, so I step away for Sugar to lead. But she hangs back too. And I look at her and she looks at me and this is ridiculous. I mean, damn, I have never ever been shy about doing nothing or going nowhere. But then Mercedes steps up and then Rosie Giraffe and Big Butt crowd in behind and shove, and next

thing we all stuffed into the doorway with only Mercedes squeezing past us, smoothing out her jumper and walking right down the aisle. Then the rest of us tumble in like a glued-together jigsaw done all wrong. And people lookin at us. And it's like the time me and Sugar crashed into the Catholic church on a dare. But once we got in there and everything so hushed and holy and the candles and the bowin and the handkerchiefs on all the drooping heads, I just couldn't go through with the plan. Which was for me to run up to the altar and do a tap dance while Sugar played the nose flute and messed around in the holy water. And Sugar kept givin me the elbow. Then later teased me so bad I tied her up in the shower and turned it on and locked her in. And she'd be there till this day if Aunt Gretchen hadn't finally figured I was lyin about the boarder takin a shower.

Same thing in the store. We all walkin on tiptoe and hardly touchin the games and puzzles and things. And I watched Miss Moore who is steady watchin us like she waitin for a sign. Like Mama Drewery watches the sky and sniffs the air and takes note of just how much slant is in the bird formation. Then me and Sugar bump smack into each other, so busy gazing at the toys, 'specially the sailboat. But we don't laugh and go into our fat-lady bump-stomach routine. We just stare at that price tag. Then Sugar run a finger over the whole boat. And I'm jealous and want to hit her. Maybe not her, but I sure want to punch somebody in the mouth.

"Watcha brings us here for, Miss Moore?"

"You sound angry, Sylvia. Are you mad about something?" Givin me one of them grins like she tellin a grown-up joke that never turns out to be funny. And she's lookin very closely at me like maybe she plannin to do my portrait from memory. I'm mad, but I won't give her that satisfaction. So I slouch around the store being very bored and say, "Let's go."

Me and Sugar at the back of the train watchin the tracks whizzin by large then small then gettin gobbled up in the dark. I'm thinkin about this tricky toy I saw in the store. A clown that somersaults on a bar then does chin-ups just cause you yank lightly at his leg. Cost $35. I could see me askin my mother for a $35 birthday clown. "You wanna who that costs what?" she'd say, cocking her head to the side to get a better view of the hole in my head. Thirty-five dollars could buy new bunk beds for Junior and Gretchen's boy. Thirty-five dollars and the whole household could go visit Granddaddy Nelson in the country. Thirty-five dollars would pay for the rent and the piano bill too. Who are these people that spend that much for performing clowns and $1,000 for toy sailboats? What kinda work they do and how they live and how come we ain't in on it? Where we are is who we are, Miss Moore always pointin out. But it don't necessarily have to be that way, she always adds then waits for somebody to say that poor people have to wake up and demand their share of the pie and don't none of us know what kind of pie she talkin about in the first damn place. But she ain't so smart cause I still got her four dollars from the taxi and she sure ain't gettin it. Messin up my day with this shit. Sugar nudges me in my pocket and winks.

45   Miss Moore lines us up in front of the mailbox where we started from, seem like years ago, and I got a headache for thinkin so hard. And we lean all over each other so we can hold up under the draggy-ass lecture she always finishes us off with at the end before we thank her for borin us to tears. But she just looks at us like she readin tea leaves. Finally she say, "Well, what did you think of F.A.O. Schwartz?"

Rosie Giraffe mumbles, "White folks crazy."

"I'd like to go there again when I get my birthday money," says Mercedes, and we shove her out the pack so she has to lean on the mailbox by herself.

"I'd like a shower. Tiring day," say Flyboy.

Then Sugar surprises me by sayin, "You know, Miss Moore, I don't think all of us here put together eat in a year what that sailboat costs." And Miss Moore lights up like somebody goosed her. "And?" she say, urging Sugar on. Only I'm standin on her foot so she don't continue.

50   "Imagine for a minute what kind of society it is in which some people can spend on a toy what it would cost to feed a family of six or seven. What do you think?"

"I think," say Sugar pushing me off her feet like she never done before, cause I whip her ass in a minute, "that this is not much of a democracy if you ask me. Equal chance to pursue happiness means an equal crack at the dough, don't it?" Miss Moore is besides herself and I am disgusted with Sugar's treachery. So I stand on her foot one more time to see if she'll shove me. She shuts up, and Miss Moore looks at me, sorrowfully I'm thinkin. And somethin weird is going on, I can feel it in my chest.

"Anybody else learn anything today?" lookin dead at me. I walk away and Sugar has to run to catch up and don't even seem to notice when I shrug her arm off my shoulder.

55   "Well, we got four dollars anyway," she says.

"Uh hunh."

"We could go to Hascombs and get half a chocolate layer and then go to the Sunset and still have plenty money for potato chips and ice-cream sodas."

"Uh hunh."

"Race you to Hascombs," she say.

We start down the block and she gets ahead which is O.K. by me cause I'm goin to the West End and then over the Drive to think this day through. She can run if she want to and even run faster. But ain't nobody gonna beat me at nuthin.

CRITICAL THINKING QUESTIONS

1. What is the lesson Miss Moore is teaching the children?

2. Is the author also teaching the reader a lesson? If so, what is the larger *issue* here?

3. Based on her closing comment, "But ain't nobody beat me at nuthin," what lesson has Sylvia learned?

WRITING TOPIC

Think of a young person to whom you would like to teach a lesson. Describe that person in a paragraph, and then create a "lesson plan" for instruction.

Objective: To teach _____ to

_____

_____

Instructional Plan: _____

_____

_____

_____

_____

Outcomes (what thinking or behavior do you want to see in this person as a result of your lesson?): _____

_____

_____

_____

Raymond Carver (1938–1988)

Cathedral

This blind man, an old friend of my wife's, he was on his way to spend the night. His wife had died. So he was visiting the dead wife's relatives in Connecticut. He called my wife from his in-laws'. Arrangements were made. He would come by train, a five-hour trip, and my wife would meet him at the station. She hadn't seen him since she worked for him one summer in Seattle ten yeas ago. But she and the blind man had kept in touch. They made tapes and mailed them back and forth. I wasn't enthusiastic about his visit. He was no one I knew. And his being blind bothered me. My idea of blindness came from the movies. In the movies, the blind moved slowly and never laughed. Sometimes they were led by seeing-eye dogs. A blind man in my house was not something I looked forward to.

That summer in Seattle she had needed a job. She didn't have any money. The man she was going to marry at the end of the summer was in officers' training school. He didn't have any money, either. But she was in love with the guy, and he was in love with her, etc. She'd seen something in the paper: HELP WANTED—*Reading to Blind Man,* and a telephone number. She phoned and went over, was hired on the spot. She'd worked with this blind man all summer. She read stuff to him, case studies, reports, that sort of thing. She helped him organize his little office in the county social-service department. They'd become good friends, my wife and the blind man. How do I know these things? She told me. And she told me something else. On her last day in the office, the blind man asked if he could touch her face. She agreed to this. She told me he touched his fingers to every part of her face, her nose—even her neck! She never forgot it. She even tried to write a poem about it. She was always trying to write a poem. She wrote a poem or two every year, usually after something really important had happened to her.

When we first started going out together, she showed me the poem. In the poem, she recalled his fingers and the way they had moved around over her face. In the poem, she talked about what she had felt at the time, about what went through her mind when the blind man touched her nose and lips. I can remember I didn't think much of the poem. Of course, I didn't tell her that. Maybe I just don't understand poetry. I admit it's not the first thing I reach for when I pick up something to read.

Anyway, this man who'd first enjoyed her favors, the officer-to-be, he'd been her childhood sweetheart. So okay. I'm saying that at the end of the summer she let the blind man run his hands over her face, said goodbye to him, married her childhood etc., who was now a commissioned officer, and she moved away from Seattle. But they'd kept in touch, she and the blind man. She made the first contact after a year or so. She called him up one night from an Air Force base in Alabama. She wanted to talk. They talked. He asked her to send him a tape and tell him about her life. She did this. She sent the tape. On the tape, she told the blind man about her husband and about their life together in the military. She told the blind man she loved her husband but she didn't like it where they lived and she didn't like it that he was a part of the military-industrial thing. She told the blind man she'd written a poem and he was in it. She told him that she was writing a poem about what it was like to be an Air Force officer's wife. The poem wasn't finished yet. She was still writing it. The blind man made a tape. He sent her the tape. She made a tape. This went on for years. My wife's officer was posted to one base and then another. She sent tapes from Moody AFB, McGuire, McConnell, and finally Travis, near Sacramento, where one night she got to feeling lonely and cut off from people she kept losing in that moving-around life. She got to feeling she couldn't go it another step. She went in and swallowed all the pills and capsules in the medicine chest and washed them down with a bottle of gin. Then she got into a hot bath and passed out.

5   But instead of dying, she got sick. She threw up. Her officer—why should he have a name? he was the childhood sweetheart, and what more does he want?—came home from somewhere, found her, and called the ambulance. In time, she put it all on a tape and sent the tape to the blind man. Over the years, she put all kinds of stuff on tapes and sent the tapes off lickety-split. Next to writing a poem every year, I think it was her chief means of recreation. On one tape, she told the blind man she'd decided to live away from her officer for a time. On another tape, she told him about her divorce. She and I began going out, and of course she told her blind man about it. She told him everything, or so it seemed to me. Once she asked me if I'd like to hear the latest tape from the blind man. This was a year ago. I was on the tape, she said. So I said okay, I'd listen to it. I got us drinks and we settled down in the living room. We made ready to listen. First she inserted the tape into the player and adjusted a couple of dials. Then she pushed a lever. The tape squeaked and someone began to talk in this loud voice. She lowered the volume.

After a few minutes of harmless chitchat, I heard my own name in the mouth of this stranger, this blind man I didn't even know! And then this: "From all you've said about him, I can only conclude—" But we were interrupted, a knock at the door, something, and we didn't ever get back to the tape. Maybe it was just as well. I'd heard all I wanted to.

Now this same blind man was coming to sleep in my house.

"Maybe I could take him bowling," I said to my wife. She was at the draining board doing scalloped potatoes. She put down the knife she was using and turned around.

"If you love me," she said, "you can do this for me. If you don't love me, okay. But if you had a friend, any friend, and the friend came to visit, I'd make him feel comfortable." She wiped her hands with the dish towel.

"I don't have any blind friends," I said.

"You don't have *any* friends," she said. "Period. Besides," she said, "goddamn 10 it, his wife's just died! Don't you understand that? The man's lost his wife!"

I didn't answer. She'd told me a little about the blind man's wife. Her name was Beulah. Beulah! That's a name for a colored woman.

"Was his wife a Negro?" I asked.

"Are you crazy?" my wife said. "Have you just flipped or something?" She picked up a potato. I saw it hit the floor, then roll under the stove. "What's wrong with you?" she said. "Are you drunk?"

"I'm just asking," I said.

Right then my wife filled me in with more detail than I cared to know. I made a 15 drink and sat at the kitchen table to listen. Pieces of the story began to fall into place.

Beulah had gone to work for the blind man the summer after my wife had stopped working for him. Pretty soon Beulah and the blind man had themselves a church wedding. It was a little wedding—who'd want to go to such a wedding in the first place?—just the two of them, plus the minister and the minister's wife. But it was a church wedding just the same. It was what Beulah had wanted, he'd said. But even then Beulah must have been carrying the cancer in her glands. After they had been inseparable for eight years—my wife's word, *inseparable*—Beulah's health went into a rapid decline. She died in a Seattle hospital room, the blind man sitting beside the bed and holding on to her hand. They'd married, lived and worked together, slept together—had sex, sure—and then the blind man had to bury her. All this without his having ever seen what the goddamned woman looked like. It was beyond my understanding. Hearing this, I felt sorry for the blind man for a little bit. And then I found myself thinking what a pitiful life this woman must have led. Imagine a woman who could never see herself as she was seen in the eyes of her loved one. A woman who could go on day after day and never receive the smallest compliment from her beloved. A woman whose husband could never read the expression on her face, be it misery or something better. Someone who could wear makeup or not—what difference to him? She could, if she wanted, wear green eyeshadow around one eye, a straight pin in her nostril, yellow slacks and purple shoes, no matter. And then to slip off into death, the blind man's hand on her hand, his blind eyes streaming tears—I'm imagining now—her last thought maybe this: that he never even knew what she looked like, and she on an express to the grave. Robert was left with a small insurance policy and half of a twenty-peso Mexican coin. The other half of the coin went into the box with her. Pathetic.

So when the time rolled around, my wife went to the depot to pick him up. With nothing to do but wait—sure, I blamed him for that—I was having a drink and watching the TV when I heard the car pull into the drive. I got up from the sofa with my drink and went to the window to have a look.

I saw my wife laughing as she parked the car. I saw her get out of the car and shut the door. She was still wearing a smile. Just amazing. She went around to the other side of the car to where the blind man was already starting to get out. This blind man, feature this, he was wearing a full beard! A beard on a blind man! Too much, I say. The blind man reached into the back seat and dragged out a suitcase. My wife took his arm, shut the car door, and, talking all the way, moved him down the drive and then up the steps to the front porch. I turned off the TV. I finished my drink, rinsed the glass, dried my hands. Then I went to the door.

My wife said, "I want you meet Robert. Robert, this is my husband. I've told you all about him." She was beaming. She had this blind man by his coat sleeve.

20   The blind man let go of his suitcase and up came his hand. I took it. He squeezed hard, held my hand, and then he let it go.

"I feel like we've already met," he boomed.

"Likewise," I said. I didn't know what else to say. Then I said. "Welcome. I've heard a lot about you." We began to move then, a little group, from the porch into the living room, my wife guiding him by the arm. The blind man was carrying his suitcase in his other hand. My wife said things like, "To your left here, Robert. That's right. Now watch it, there's a chair. That's it. Sit down right here. This is the sofa. We just bought this sofa two weeks ago."

I started to say something about the old sofa. I'd like that old sofa. But I didn't say anything. Then I wanted to say something else, small-talk, about the scenic ride along the Hudson. How going *to* New York, you should sit on the right-hand side of the train, and coming *from* New York, the left-hand side.

"Did you have a good train ride?" I said, "Which side of the train did you sit on, by the way?"

25   "What a question, which side!" my wife said. "What's it matter which side?" she said.

"I just asked," I said.

"Right side," the blind man said. "I hadn't been on a train in nearly forty years. Not since I was a kid. With my folks. That's been a long time. I'd nearly forgotten the sensation. I have winter in my beard now," he said. "So I've been told, anyway. Do I look distinguished, my dear?" the blind man said to my wife.

"You look distinguished, Robert," she said. "Robert," she said. "Robert, it's just so good to see you."

My wife finally took her eyes off the blind man and looked at me. I had the feeling she didn't like what she saw. I shrugged.

I've never met, or personally known, anyone who was blind. This blind man was 30
late forties, a heavy-set, balding man with stooped shoulders, as if he carried a great
weight there. He wore brown slacks, brown shoes, a light-brown shirt, a tie, a sports
coat. Spiffy. He also had this full beard. But he didn't use a cane and he didn't wear
dark glasses. I'd always thought dark glasses were a must for the blind. Fact was, I
wished he had a pair. At first glance, his eyes looked like anyone else's eyes. But if
you looked close, there was something different about them. Too much white in the
iris, for one thing, and the pupils seemed to move round in the sockets without
his knowing it or being able to stop it. Creepy. As I stared at his face, I saw the left
pupil turn in toward his nose while the other made an effort to keep in one place.
But it was only an effort, for that eye was on the roam without knowing it or wanting it to be.

I said, "Let me get you a drink. What's your pleasure? We have a little of everything. It's one of our pastimes."

"Bub, I'm a Scotch man myself," he said fast enough in this big voice.

"Right," I said. Bub! "Sure you are. I knew it."

He let his fingers touch his suitcase, which was sitting alongside the sofa. He
was taking his bearings. I didn't blame him for that.

"I'll move that up to your room," my wife said.   35

"No, that's fine," the blind man said loudly. "It can go up when I go up."

"A little water with the Scotch?" I said.

"Very little," he said.

"I knew it," I said,

He said, "Just a tad. The Irish actor, Barry Fitzgerald? I'm like that fellow. 40
When I drink water, Fitzgerald said, I drink water. When I drink whiskey, I drink
whiskey." My wife laughed. The blind man brought his hand up under his beard.
He lifted his beard slowly and let it drop.

I did the drinks, three big glasses of Scotch with a splash of water in each.
Then we made ourselves comfortable and talked about Robert's travels. First the
long flight from the West Coast to Connecticut, we covered that. Then from Connecticut up here by train. We had another drink concerning that leg of the trip.

I remembered having read somewhere that the blind didn't smoke because, as
speculation had it, they couldn't see the smoke they exhaled. I thought I knew that
much and that much only about blind people. But this blind man smoked his cigarette down to the nubbin and then lit another one. This blind man filled his ashtray and my wife emptied it.

When we sat down at the table for dinner, we had another drink. My wife
heaped Robert's plate with cube steak, scalloped potatoes, green beans. I buttered
him up two slices of bread. I said, "Here's bread and butter for you." I swallowed
some of my drink. "Now let us pray," I said, and the blind man lowered his head.
My wife looked at me, her mouth agape. "Pray the phone won't ring and the food
doesn't get cold," I said.

We dug in. We ate everything there was to eat on the table. We ate like there
was no tomorrow. We didn't talk. We ate. We scarfed. We grazed that table. We

were into serious eating. The blind man had right away located his foods, he knew just where everything was on his plate. I watched with admiration as he used his knife and fork on the meat. He'd cut two pieces of meat, fork the meat into his mouth, and then go all out for the scalloped potatoes, the beans next, and then he'd tear off a hunk of buttered bread and eat that. He'd follow this up with a big drink of milk. It didn't seem to bother him to use his fingers once in a while, either.

45   We finished everything, including half a strawberry pie. For a few moments, we sat as if stunned. Sweat beaded on our faces. Finally, we got up from the table and left the dirty plates. We didn't look back. We took ourselves into the living room and sank into our places again. Robert and my wife sat on the sofa. I took the big chair. We had us two or three more drinks while they talked about the major things that had come to pass for them in the past ten years. For the most part, I just listened. Now and then I joined in. I didn't want him to think I'd left the room, and I didn't want her to think I was feeling left out. They talked of things that had happened to them—to them!—these past ten years. I waited in vain to hear my name on my wife's sweet lips: "And then my dear husband came into my life"—something like that. But I heard nothing of the sort. More talk of Robert. Robert had done a little of everything, it seemed, a regular blind jack-of-all trades. But most recently he and his wife had had an Amway distributorship, from which, I gathered, they'd earned their living, such as it was. The blind man was also a ham radio operator. He talked in his loud voice about conversations he'd had with fellow operators in Guam, in the Philippines, in Alaska, and even in Tahiti. He said he'd have a lot of friends there if he ever wanted to go visit those places. From time to time, he'd turn his blind face toward me, put his hand under his beard, ask me something. How long had I been in my present position? (Three years.) Did I like my work? (I didn't.) Was I going to stay with it? (What were the options?) Finally, when I thought he was beginning to run down, I got up and turned on the TV.

My wife looked at me with irritation. She was heading toward a boil. Then she looked at the blind man and sad, "Robert, do you have a TV?"

The blind man said, "My dear, I have two TVs. I have a color set and a black-and-white thing, an old relic. It's funny, but if I turn the TV on, and I'm always turning it on, I turn on the color set. It's funny, don't you think?"

I didn't know what to say to that. I had absolutely nothing to say to that. No opinion. So I watched the news program and tried to listen to what the announcer was saying.

"This is a color TV," the blind man said. "Don't ask me how, but I can tell."

50   "We traded up a while ago," I said.

The blind man had another taste of his drink. He lifted his beard, sniffed it, and let it fall. He leaned forward on the sofa. He positioned his ashtray on the coffee table, then put the lighter to his cigarette. He leaned back on the sofa and crossed his legs at the ankles.

My wife covered her mouth, and then she yawned. She stretched. She said, "I think I'll go upstairs and put on my robe. I think I'll change into something else. Robert, you make yourself comfortable," she said.

"I'm comfortable," the blind man said.

"I want you to feel comfortable in this house," she said.

"I am comfortable," the blind man said.   55

After she'd left the room, he and I listened to the weather report and then to the sports roundup. By that time, she'd been gone so long I didn't know if she was going to come back. I thought she might have gone to bed. I wished she'd come back downstairs. I didn't want to be left alone with a blind man. I asked him if he wanted another drink, and he said sure. Then I asked if he wanted to smoke some dope with me. I said I'd just rolled a number. I hadn't, but I planned to do so in about two shakes.

"I'll try some with you," he said.

"Damn right," I said. "That's the stuff."

I got our drinks and sat down on the sofa with him. Then I rolled us two fat numbers. I lit one and passed it. I brought it to his fingers. He took it and inhaled.

"Hold it as long as you can," I said. I could tell he didn't know the first thing.   60

My wife came back downstairs wearing her pink robe and her pink slippers.

"What do I smell?" she said.

"We thought we'd have us some cannabis," I said.

My wife gave me a savage look. Then she looked at the blind man and said, "Robert, I didn't know you smoked."

He said, "I do now, my dear. There's a first time for everything. But I don't   65 feel anything yet."

"This stuff is pretty mellow," I said. "This stuff is mild. It's dope you can reason with," I said. "It doesn't mess you up."

"Not much it doesn't, bub," he said, and laughed.

My wife sat on the sofa between the blind man and me. I passed her the number. She took it and toked and then passed it back to me. "Which way is this going?" she said. Then she said, "I shouldn't be smoking this. I can hardly keep my eyes open as it is. That dinner did me in. I shouldn't have eaten so much."

"It was the strawberry pie," the blind man said. "That's what did it," he said, and he laughed his big laugh. Then he shook his head

"There's more strawberry pie," I said.   70

"Do you want some more, Robert?" my wife said.

"Maybe in a little while," he said.

We gave out attention to the TV. My wife yawned again. She said, "Your bed is made up when you feel like going to bed, Robert. I know you must have had a long day. When you're ready to go to bed, say so." She pulled his arm. "Robert?"

He came to and said, "I've had a real nice time. This beats tapes, doesn't it?"

I said, "Coming at you," and I put the number between his fingers. He inhaled, held   75 the smoke, and then let it go. It was like he'd been doing it since he was nine years old.

"Thanks, bub," he said. "But I think this is all for me. I think I'm beginning to feel it," he said. He held the burning roach out for my wife.

"Same here," she said. "Ditto. Me, too." She took the roach and passed it to me. "I may just sit here for a while between you two guys with my eyes closed. But don't let me bother you, okay? Either one of you. If it bothers you, say so. Otherwise, I may just sit here with my eyes closed until you're ready to go to bed," she said. "Your bed's made up, Robert, when you're ready. It's right next to our room at the top of the stairs. We'll show you up when you're ready. You wake me up now, you guys, if I fall asleep." She said that and then she closed her eyes and went to sleep.

The news program ended. I got up and changed the channel. I sat back down on the sofa. I wished my wife hadn't pooped out. Her head lay across the back of the sofa, her mouth open. She'd turned so that her robe had slipped away from her legs, exposing a juicy thigh. I reached to draw her robe back over her, and it was then that I glanced at the blind man. What the hell! I flipped the robe open again.

"You say when you want some strawberry pie," I said.

80   "I will," he said.

I said, "Are you tired? Do you want me to take you up to your bed? Are you ready to hit the hay?"

"Not yet," he said. "No, I'll stay up with you, bub. If that's all right. I'll stay up until you're ready to turn in. We haven't had a chance to talk. Know what I mean? I feel like me and her monopolized the evening." He lifted his beard and he let it fall. He picked up his cigarettes and his lighter.

"That's all right," I said. Then I said, "I'm glad for the company."

And I guess I was. Every night I smoked dope and stayed up as long as I could before I fell asleep. My wife and I hardly ever went to bed at the same time. When I did go to sleep, I had these dreams. Sometimes I'd wake up from one of them, heart going crazy.

85   Something about the church and the Middle Ages was on the TV. Not your run-of-the-mill TV fare. I wanted to watch something else. I turned to the other channels. But there was nothing on them, either. So I turned back to the first channel and apologized.

"Bub, it's all right," the blind man said. "It's fine with me. Whatever you want to watch is okay. I'm always learning something. Learning never ends. It won't hurt me to learn something tonight. I got ears," he said.

We didn't say anything for a time. He was leaning forward with his head turned at me, his right ear aimed in the direction of the set. Very disconcerting. Now and then his eyelids drooped and then they snapped open again. Now and then he put his fingers into his beard and tugged, like he was thinking about something he was hearing on the television.

On the screen, a group of men wearing cowls was being set upon and tormented by men dressed in skeleton costumes and men dressed as devils. The men dressed as devils wore devil masks, horns, and long tails. This pageant was part of a procession. The Englishman who was narrating the thing said it took place in Spain once a year. I tried to explain to the blind man what was happening.

"Skeletons," he said. "I know about skeletons," he said, and he nodded.

90   The TV showed this one cathedral. Then there was a long, slow look at another one. Finally, the picture switched to the famous one in Paris, with its flying buttresses

and its spires reaching up to the clouds. The camera pulled away to show the whole of the cathedral rising above the skyline.

There were times when the Englishman who was telling the thing would shut up, would simply let the camera move around over the cathedrals. Or else the camera would tour the countryside, men in fields walking behind oxen. I waited as long as I could. Then I felt I had to say something. I said, "They're showing the outside of this cathedral now. Gargoyles. Little statues carved to look like monsters. Now I guess they're in Italy. Yeah, they're in Italy. There's paintings on the walls of this one church."

"Are those fresco paintings, bub?" he asked, and he sipped from his drink.

I reached for my glass. But it was empty. I tried to remember what I could remember. "You're asking me are those frescoes?" I said. "That's a good question. I don't know."

The camera moved to a cathedral outside Lisbon. The differences in the Portuguese cathedral compared with the French and Italian were not that great. But they were there. Mostly the interior stuff. Then something occurred to me, and I said, "Something has occurred to me. Do you have any idea what a cathedral is? What they look like, that is? Do you follow me? If somebody says cathedral to you, do you have any notion what they're talking about? Do you know the difference between that and a Baptist church, say?"

He let the smoke dribble from his mouth. "I know they took hundreds of work- 95 ers fifty or a hundred years to build," he said. "I just heard the man say that, of course. I know generations of the same families worked on a cathedral. I heard him say that, too. The men who began their life's work on them, they never lived to see the completion of their work. In that wise, bub, they're no different from the rest of us, right?" He laughed. Then his eyelids drooped again. His head nodded. He seemed to be snoozing. Maybe he was imagining himself in Portugal. The TV was showing another cathedral now. This one was in Germany. The Englishman's voice droned on. "Cathedrals," the blind man said. He sat up and rolled his head back and forth. "If you want the truth, bub, that's about all I know. What I just said. What I heard him say. But maybe you could describe one to me? I wish you'd do it. I'd like that. If you want to know, I really don't have a good idea."

I stared hard at the shot of the cathedral on the TV. How could I even begin to describe it? But say my life depended on it. Say my life was being threatened by an insane guy who said I had to do it or else.

I stared some more at the cathedral before the picture flipped off into the countryside. There was no use. I turned to the blind man and said, "To begin with, they're very tall." I was looking around the room for clues. "They reach way up. Up and up. Toward the sky. They're so big, some of them, they have to have these supports. To help hold them up, so to speak. These supports are called buttresses. They remind me of viaducts, for some reason. But maybe you don't know viaducts, either? Sometimes the cathedrals have devils and such carved into the front. Sometimes lords and ladies. Don't ask me why this is," I said.

He was nodding. The whole upper part of his body seemed to be moving back and forth.

"I'm not doing so good, am I?" I said.

100   He stopped nodding and leaned forward on the edge of the sofa. As he listened to me, he was running his fingers through his beard. I wasn't getting through to him, I could see that. But he waited for me to go on just the same. He nodded, like he was trying to encourage me. I tried to think what else to say. "They're really big," I said. "They're massive. They're built of stone. Marble, too, sometimes. In those olden days, when they built cathedrals, men wanted to be close to God. In those olden days, God was an important part of everyone's life. You could tell this from their cathedral-building. I'm sorry," I said, "but it looks like that's the best I can do for you. I'm just no good at it."

"That's all right, bub," the blind man said. "Hey, listen. I hope you don't mind my asking you. Can I ask you something? Let me ask you a simple question, yes or no. I'm just curious and there's no offense. You're my host. But let me ask if you are in any way religious? You don't mind my asking?"

I shook my head. He couldn't see that, though. A wink is the same as a nod to a blind man. "I guess I don't believe in it. In anything. Sometimes it's hard. You know what I'm saying?"

"Sure, I do," he said.

"Right," I said.

105   The Englishman was still holding forth. My wife sighed in her sleep. She drew a long breath and went on with her sleeping.

"You'll have to forgive me," I said. "But I can't tell you what a cathedral looks like. It just isn't in me to do it. I can't do any more than I've done."

The blind man sat very still, his head down, as he listened to me.

I said, "The truth is, cathedrals don't mean anything special to me. Nothing. Cathedrals. They're something to look at on late-night TV. That's all they are."

It was then that the blind man cleared his throat. He brought something up. He took a handkerchief from his back pocket. Then he said. "I get it, bub. It's okay. It happens. Don't worry about it," he said. "Hey, listen to me. Will you do me a favor? I got an idea. Why don't you find us some heavy paper? And a pen. We'll do something. We'll draw one together. Get us a pen and some heavy paper. Go on, bub, get the stuff," he said.

110   So I went upstairs. My legs felt like they didn't have any strength in them. They felt like they did after I'd done some running. In my wife's room, I looked around. I found some ballpoints in a little basket on her table. And then I tried to think where to look for the kind of paper he was talking about.

Downstairs, in the kitchen, I found a shopping bag with onion skins in the bottom of the bag. I emptied the bag and shook it. I brought it into the living room and sat down with it near his legs. I moved some things, smoothed the wrinkles from the bag, spread it out on the coffee table.

The blind man got down from the sofa and sat next to me on the carpet.

He ran his fingers over the paper. He went up and down the sides of the paper. The edges, even the edges. He fingered the corners.

"All right," he said. "All right, let's do her."

He found my hand, the hand with the pen. He closed his hand over my hand. 115
"Go ahead, bub, draw," he said. "Draw. You'll see. I'll follow along with you. It'll
be okay. Just begin now like I'm telling you. You'll see. Draw," the blind man
said.

So I began. First I drew a box that looked like a house. It could have been the
house I lived in. Then I put a roof on it. At either end of the roof, I drew spires.
Crazy.

"Swell," he said. "Terrific. You're doing fine," he said. "Never thought anything
like this could happen in your lifetime, did you, bub? Well, it's a strange life, we all
know that. Go on now. Keep it up."

I put in windows with arches. I drew flying buttresses. I hung great doors. I
couldn't stop. The TV station went off the air. I put down the pen and closed and
opened my fingers. The blind man felt around over the paper. He moved the tips
of his fingers over the paper, all over what I had drawn, and he nodded.

"Doing fine," the blind man said.

I took up the pen again, and he found my hand. I kept at it. I'm no artist. But 120
I kept drawing just the same.

My wife opened up her eyes and gazed at us. She sat up on the sofa, her robe
hanging open. She said, "What are you doing? Tell me, I want to know."

I didn't answer her.

The blind man said, "We're drawing a cathedral. Me and him are working on
it. Press hard," he said to me. "That's right. That's good," he said. "Sure. You got
it, bub. I can tell. You didn't think you could. But you can, can't you? You're cooking with gas now. You know what I'm saying? We're going to really have us something here in a minute. How's the old arm?" he said. "Put some people in there
now. What's a cathedral without people?"

My wife said, "What's going on? Robert, what are you doing? What's going
on?"

"It's all right," he said to her. "Close your eyes now," the blind man said to me. 125

I did it. I closed them just like he said.

"Are they closed?" he said. "Don't fudge."

"They're closed," I said.

"Keep them that way," he said. He said, "Don't stop now. Draw."

So we kept on with it. His fingers rode my fingers as my hand went over the 130
paper. It was like nothing else in my life up to now.

Then he said, "I think that's it. I think you got it," he said. "Take a look. What
do you think?"

But I had my eyes closed. I thought I'd keep them that way for a little longer.
I thought it was something I ought to do.

"Well?" he said. "Are you looking?"

My eyes were still closed. I was in my house. I knew that. But I didn't feel like
I was inside anything.

"It's really something," I said.   135

CRITICAL THINKING QUESTIONS

1. At the end of the story, the narrator and the blind man sit together and draw a cathedral on a shopping bag. The narrator seems to undergo some sort of transformation: "It's really something," he says. What does he mean? Do you think the narrator will be a changed man when he wakes up the next morning? Can people actually gain insight in an instant, or is such a change more likely to occur in fiction?

2. Although teachers like to think education helps make human beings more sensitive to the needs of others, is that always the case? From your *personal experience*, how do you think people learn compassion? Can it be taught?

WRITING TOPIC

Write a brief personal experience essay about a time in your life when you gained insight into something. What had your attitude been previously? What triggered the insight? How did your attitude change?

Nadine Gordimer (b. 1923)
Terminal

"Even the cat buries its dirt; I carry mine around with me." She thought of saying it aloud many times in the weeks after she came home from the hospital. She did not know if he would decide to laugh—whether they would go so far as to laugh. The only time the existence of such a contraption had ever been mentioned by them before the illness happened was a few years ago, when—exchanging sheets of newspaper as they usually did, lovely weekend mornings in bed—she had been reading some article about unemployment and teenage prostitutes, and had remarked to him, my God, the job the welfare people found for this girl was in a factory that makes those rubber bag things for people who have to have their stomachs cut out—no wonder she went on the streets, poor little wretch. . . .

She remembered that morning, that newspaper, clearly. More and more of their conversation kept coming back. They had drifted to talk about the dreariness of industrialization; how early Marxists had ascribed this to alienation, which would disappear when the means of production were owned by the workers, but the factories of the Soviet Union and China were surely just as dreary as those of the West? And she remembered she had reminded him (they had visited Peking together) that at least the Chinese factory workers had ten-minute breaks for compulsory calisthenics twice a day—and he had said, would you swap that for a tea break and a fag?

The rubber thing that went past on the assembly belt before the sixteen-year-old future prostitute was as remote from the two of them, laughing in bed on a Sunday morning, as the life of any factory worker.

Now the contraption was attached to her own body. It issued from her, from the small wound hidden under her clothing. She had moved from their shared bed and he understood without a word. She had been taught at the hospital how to deal with the thing, it was horribly private in a way natural functions were not, since natural functions were—had been—experienced by them both. She was alone with her dirt.

The doctors said the thing would be taken away in time. Six weeks, the first   5
one predicted, not more than three months was what the second one told her. They should have coordinated their fairy story. They said that (after six weeks or three months) everything would be reconnected inside her. The wound that was kept open would be sewn up. She would be whole again, repaired, everything would work. She would go back to her teaching at the music school. She could go back there now—why not?—if she wanted to, so long as she didn't tire herself. But she didn't want to, carrying that thing with her. She had to listen to more stories—from encouraging friends—about how wonderfully other people managed, lived perfectly normal lives. Even a member of the British royal family, it was said. She shut them up with the fairy story, saying, but for me it's only for six weeks (or three months), I don't have to manage. He bought her two beautiful caftans, choosing them himself, and so perfectly right for her, just her colors, her style— in her pleasure she forgot (which she knew later was exactly what he hoped) she would be wearing them to cover that thing. She put on one or the other when the friends came to visit, and her outfit was admired, they said she must be malingering, she looked so marvelous. He confirmed to them that she was making good progress.

They had talked, once, early on. They had talked before that, in their lives, in the skein of their mingled lives—but how impersonal it was, really, then! A childish pact, blood-brotherhood; on a par with that endlessly rhetorical question, d'you love me, will you always love me: if either of us were to be incurably ill, neither would let the other suffer, would they? But when it happens—well, it never happens. Not in that silly, dramatic, clear-cut abstraction. Who can say what is "incurable"? Who can be sure what suffering is terminal, not worth prolonging in order to survive it? This one had a breast off twenty years ago, and is still going to the races every week. That one lost his prostate, can be seen knocking back gin-and-tonics at any cocktail party, with his third wife.

But just before she went into the hospital for the exploratory operation she found the time and place to reaffirm. "If it turns out to be bad, if it gets very bad . . . at any time, you promise you'll help me out of it. I would do it for you." He couldn't speak. She was lying with him in the dark; he nodded so hard the pact was driven into her shoulder by his chin. The bone hurt her. Then he made love to her, entering her body in covenant.

After the operation she found the tube leading out of her, the contraption. They did not talk again; only of cheerful things, only of getting better. The thing—the wound it issued from, that, unlike any other wound, couldn't be allowed to close, was like a contingent love affair concealed in his life or hers whose weight would tear their integument if admitted. They smiled at each other at once, every time their eyes met. It couldn't be borne, after all. There had to be a fairy story. It was told over and over, every day, in every plan they made for next week or next month or next year, never blinking an eyelid; in every assumption of continuing daily life neither believed. There were no words that were not lies. *Did the groceries come. There's been another hijacking. Are you all right in that chair. They say the election's set for Spring. We need new wine glasses. I should write letters. Order coffee and matches. Another crisis in the Middle East. Draw the curtains, the sun's in your eyes. I must have my hair done, Thursday.* If she took his hand now, it was only in the lie of immortality. The flesh, therefore, was not real for them anymore.

There was only one thing left that could not, by its very nature, have become a lie. There was only one place where love could survive: life was betrayed, but the covenant was not with life.

10   He drove her to the hairdresser that Thursday afternoon and when he came to fetch her he told her she looked pretty. She thanked him awkwardly as a girl with her first compliment. Beneath it she was overcome—the first strong emotion except fear and disgust, for many months—by an overwhelming trust in him. That night, alone in the room that was now her bedroom she counted out the hoarded pills and, before she washed them down with plain water, set under the paperweight of her cigarette lighter her note for him. "Keep your promise. Don't have me revived."

Ever since she was a child she had understood it as a deep sleep, that's all. Ever since she saw the first bird, lying under a hedge, whose eyes hadn't opened when it was poked with a twig. But one can only be aware of a sleep as one awakens from it, and so one will never be aware of that deep sleep—she had no fear of death but now she had the terror of feeling herself waking from it, herself coming back from what was not death at all, then, could not be. Her eyelids were rosy blinds through which light glowed. She opened them on the glossy walls of a hospital room. There was a hand in hers; his.

CRITICAL THINKING QUESTIONS

1. The friend obviously does not fulfill his promise, his tacit covenant (par. 7). Is that a violation of the trust she placed in him?

2. Occasionally one reads of an elderly person who kills his or her spouse to end the spouse's suffering. Such an act conflicts with forces in our society that argue against it (the courts, religious teachings). Under what *premises* do individuals act who choose to ignore these forces?

WRITING TOPIC

How does the image of the story's closing sentence leave you feeling? What words would you use to describe the mood of the story's ending?

Nathaniel Hawthorne (1804–1864)

The Birth-Mark

In the latter part of the last century there lived a man of science, an eminent proficient in every branch of natural philosophy, who not long before our story opens had made experience of a spiritual affinity more attractive than any chemical one. He had left his laboratory to the care of an assistant, cleared his fine countenance from the furnace smoke, washed the stain of acids from his fingers, and persuaded a beautiful woman to become his wife. In those days when the comparatively recent discovery of electricity and other kindred mysteries of Nature seemed to open paths into the region of miracle, it was not unusual for the love of science to rival the love of woman in its depth and absorbing energy. The higher intellect, the imagination, the spirit, and even the heart might all find their congenial aliment in pursuits which, as some of their ardent votaries believed, would ascend from one step of powerful intelligence to another, until the philosopher should lay his hand on the secret of creative force and perhaps make new worlds for himself. We know not whether Aylmer possessed this degree of faith in man's ultimate control over Nature. He had devoted himself, however, too unreservedly to scientific studies ever to be weaned from them by any second passion. His love for his young wife might prove the stronger of the two; but it could only be by intertwining itself with his love of science, and uniting the strength of the latter to his own.

Such a union accordingly took place, and was attended with truly remarkable consequences and a deeply impressive moral. One day, very soon after their marriage, Aylmer sat gazing at his wife with a trouble in his countenance that grew stronger until he spoke.

"Georgiana," said he, "has it never occurred to you that the mark upon your cheek might be removed?"

"No, indeed," said she, smiling; but perceiving the seriousness of his manner, she blushed deeply. "To tell you the truth it has been so often called a charm that I was simple enough to imagine it might be so."

5   "Ah, upon another face perhaps it might," replied her husband; "but never on yours. No, dearest Georgiana, you came so nearly perfect from the hand of Nature that this slightest possible defect, which we hesitate whether to term a defect or a beauty, shocks me, as being the visible mark of earthly imperfection."

"Shocks you, my husband!" cried Georgiana, deeply hurt; at first reddening with momentary anger, but then bursting into tears. "Then why did you take me from my mother's side? You cannot love what shocks you!"

To explain this conversation it must be mentioned that in the centre of Georgiana's left cheek there was a singular mark, deeply interwoven, as it were, with the texture and substance of her face. In the usual state of her complexion—a healthy though delicate bloom—the mark wore a tint of deeper crimson, which imperfectly defined its shape amid the surrounding rosiness. When she blushed it gradually became more indistinct, and finally vanished amid the triumphant rush of blood that bathed the whole cheek with its brilliant glow. But if any shifting motion caused her to turn pale there was the mark again, a crimson stain upon the snow, in which Aylmer sometimes deemed an almost fearful distinctness. Its shape bore not a little similarity to the human hand, though of the smallest pygmy size. Georgiana's loves were wont to say that some fairy at her birth hour had laid her tiny hand upon the infant's cheek, and left this impress there in token of the magic endowments that were to give her such sway over all hearts. Many a desperate swain would have risked life for the privilege of pressing his lips to the mysterious hand. It must not be concealed, however, that the impression wrought by this fairy sign manual varied exceedingly, according to the difference of temperament in the beholders. Some fastidious persons—but they were exclusively of her own sex—affirmed that the bloody hand, as they chose to call it, quite destroyed the effect of Georgiana's beauty, and rendered her countenance even hideous. But it would be as reasonable to say that one of those small blue stains which sometimes occur in the purest statuary marble would convert the Eve of Powers to a monster. Masculine observers, if the birth-mark did not heighten their admiration, contented themselves with wishing it away, that the world might possess one living specimen of ideal loveliness without the semblance of a flaw. After his marriage—for he thought little or nothing of the matter before—Aylmer discovered that this was the case with himself.

Had she been less beautiful—if Envy's self could have found aught else to sneer at—he might have felt his affection heightened by the prettiness of this mimic hand, now vaguely portrayed, now lost, now stealing forth again and glimmering to and fro with every pulse of emotion that throbbed within her heart; but seeing her otherwise so perfect, he found this one defect grow more and more intolerable with every moment of their united lives. It was the fatal flaw of humanity which Nature, in one shape or another, stamps ineffaceably on all her productions, either to imply that they are temporary and finite, or that their perfection must be wrought by toil and pain. The crimson hand expressed the ineludible gripe in which mortality clutches the highest and purest of earthly mould, degrading them into kindred with the lowest, and even with the very brutes, like whom their visible frames return to the dust. In this manner, selecting it as the symbol of his wife's liability to sin, sorrow, decay, and death, Aylmer's sombre imagination was not long in rendering the birth-mark a frightful object, causing him more trouble and horror than ever Georgiana's beauty, whether of soul or sense, had given him delight.

At all the seasons which should have been their happiest, he invariably and without intending it, nay, in spite of a purpose to the contrary, reverted to this one disastrous topic. Trifling as it at first appeared, it so connected itself with innumerable trains of thought and modes of feeling that it became the central point of all. With the morning twilight Aylmer opened his eyes upon his wife's face and recognized the symbol of imperfection; and when they sat together at the evening hearth his eyes wandered stealthily to her cheek, and beheld, flickering with the blaze of the wood fire, the spectral hand that wrote mortality where he would fain have worshipped. Georgiana soon learned to shudder at his gaze. It needed but a glance with the peculiar expression that his face often wore to change the roses of her cheek into a deathlike paleness, amid which the crimson hand was brought strongly out, like bas-relief of ruby on the whitest marble.

Late one night when the lights were growing dim, so as hardly to betray the stain 10 on the poor wife's cheek, she herself, for the first time, voluntarily took up the subject.

"Do you remember, my dear Aylmer," said she, with a feeble attempt at a smile, "have you any recollection of a dream last night about this odious hand?"

"None! none whatever!" replied Aylmer, starting; but then he added, in a dry, cold tone, affected for the sake of concealing the real depth of his emotion, "I might well dream of it; for before I fell asleep it had taken a pretty firm hold of my fancy."

"And you did dream of it?" continued Georgiana, hastily; for she dreaded lest a gush of tears should interrupt what she had to say. "A terrible dream! I wonder that you can forget it. Is it possible to forget this one expression?—'It is in her heart now; we must have it out!' Reflect, my husband; for by all means I would have you recall that dream."

The mind is in a sad state when Sleep, the all-involving, cannot confine her spectres within the dim region of her sway, but suffers them to break forth, affrighting this actual life with secrets that perchance belong to a deeper one. Aylmer now remembered his dream. He had fancied himself with his servant Aminadab, attempting an operation for the removal of the birth-mark; but the deeper went the knife, the deeper sank the hand, until at length its tiny grasp appeared to have caught hold of Georgiana's heart; whence, however, her husband was inexorably resolved to cut or wrench it away

15   When the dream had shaped itself perfectly in his memory, Aylmer sat in his wife's presence with a guilty feeling. Truth often finds its way to the mind close muffled in robes of sleep, and then speaks with uncompromising directness of matters in regard to which we practise an unconscious self-deception during our waking moments. Until now he had not been aware of the tyrannizing influence acquired by one idea over his mind, and of the lengths which he might find in his heart to go for the sake of giving himself peace.

"Aylmer," resumed Georgiana, solemnly, "I know not what may be the cost to both of us to rid me of this fatal birth-mark. Perhaps its removal may cause cureless deformity; or it may be the stain goes as deep as life itself. Again: do we know that there is a possibility, on any terms, of unclasping the firm gripe of this little hand which was laid upon me before I came into the world?"

"Dearest Georgiana, I have spent much thought upon the subject," hastily interrupted Aylmer. "I am convinced of the perfect practicability of its removal."

"If there be the remotest possibility of it," continued Georgiana, "let the attempt be made at whatever risk. Danger is nothing to me; for life, while this hateful mark makes me the object of your horror and disgust—life is a burden which I would fling down with joy. Either remove this dreadful hand, or take my wretched life! You have deep science. All the world bears witness of it. You have achieved great wonders. Cannot you remove this little, little mark, which I cover with the tips of two small fingers? Is this beyond your power, for the sake of your own peace, and to save your poor wife from madness?"

"Noblest, dearest, tenderest wife," cried Aylmer, rapturously, "doubt not my power. I have already given this matter the deepest thought—thought which might almost have enlightened me to create a being less perfect than yourself. Georgiana, you have led deeper than ever into the heart of science. I feel myself fully competent to render this dear cheek as faultless as its fellow; and then, most beloved, what will be my triumph when I shall have corrected what Nature left imperfect in her fairest work! Even Pygmalion, when his sculptured woman assumed life, felt not greater ecstasy than mine will be."

20   "It is resolved, then," said Georgiana, faintly smiling. "And, Aylmer, spare me not, though you should find the birth-mark take refuge in my heart at last."

Her husband tenderly kissed her cheek—her right cheek—not that which bore the impress of the crimson hand.

The next day Aylmer apprised his wife of a plan that he had formed whereby he might have opportunity for the intense thought and constant watchfulness which the proposed operation would require; while Georgiana, likewise, would enjoy the perfect repose essential to its success. They were to seclude themselves in the extensive apartments occupied by Aylmer as a laboratory, and where, during his toilsome youth, he had made discoveries in the elemental powers of Nature that had roused the admiration of all the learned societies in Europe. Seated calmly in this laboratory, the pale philosopher had investigated the secrets of the highest cloud region and of the profoundest mines; he had satisfied himself of the causes that kindled and kept alive the fires of the volcano; and had explained the mystery of the fountains, and how it is that they gush forth, some so bright and pure, and others with such rich medicinal virtues, from the dark bosom of the earth. Here, too, at an earlier period, he had studied the wonders of the human frame, and attempted to fathom the very process by which Nature assimilates all her precious influences from earth and air, and from the spiritual world, to create and foster man, her masterpiece. The latter pursuit, however, Aylmer had long laid aside in unwilling recognition of the truth—against which all seekers sooner or later stumble—that our great creative Mother, while she amuses us with apparently working in the broadest sunshine, is yet severely careful to keep her own secrets, and, in spite of her pretended openness, shows us nothing but results. She permits us, indeed, to mar, but seldom to mend, and, like a jealous patentee, on no account to make. Now, however, Aylmer resumed these half-forgotten investigations; not, of course, with such hopes or wishes as first suggested them; but because they involved much physiological truth and lay in the path of his proposed scheme for the treatment of Georgiana.

As he led her over the threshold of the laboratory, Georgiana was cold tremulous. Aylmer looked cheerfully into her face, with intent to reassure her, but was so startled with the intense glow of the birth-mark upon the whiteness of her cheek that he could not restrain a strong convulsive shudder. His wife fainted.

"Aminadab! Aminadab!" shouted Aylmer, stamping violently on the floor.

Forthwith there issued from an inner apartment a man of low stature, but bulky frame, with shaggy hair hanging about his visage, which was grimed with the vapors of the furnace. This personage had been Aylmer's underworker during his whole scientific career, and was admirably fitted for that office by his great mechanical readiness, and the skill with which, while incapable of comprehending a single principle, he executed all the details of his master's experiments. With his vast strength, his shaggy hair, his smoky aspect, and the indescribable earthiness that incrusted him, he seemed to represent man's physical nature; while Aylmer's slender figure, and pale, intellectual face, were no less apt a type of the spiritual element.

"Throw open the door of the boudoir, Aminadab," said Aylmer, "and burn a pastil."

"Yes, master," answered Aminadab, looking intently at the lifeless form of Georgiana; and then he muttered to himself, "If she were my wife, I'd never part with that birthmark."

When Georgiana recovered consciousness she found herself breathing an atmosphere of penetrating fragrance, the gentle potency of which had recalled her from her deathlike faintness. The scene around her looked like enchantment. Aylmer had converted those smoky, dingy, sombre rooms, where he had spent his brightest years in recondite pursuits, into a series of beautiful apartments not unfit to be the secluded abode of a lovely woman. The walls were hung with gorgeous curtains, which imparted the combination of grandeur and grace that no other species of adornment can achieve; and as they fell from the ceiling to the floor, their rich and ponderous folds, concealing all angles and straight lines, appeared to shut in the scene from infinite space. For aught Georgiana knew, it might be a pavilion among the clouds. And Aylmer, excluding the sunshine, which would have interfered with his chemical processes, had supplied its place with perfumed lamps, emitting flames of various hue, but all uniting in a soft, impurpled radiance. He now knelt by his wife's side, watching her earnestly, but without alarm; for he was confident in his science, and felt that he could draw a magic circle round her within which no evil might intrude.

"Where am I? Ah, I remember," said Georgiana, faintly; and she placed her hand over her cheek to hide the terrible mark from her husband's eyes.

30   "Fear not, dearest!" exclaimed he. "Do not shrink from me! Believe me, Georgiana, I even rejoice in this single imperfection, since it will be such a rapture to remove it."

"Oh, spare me!" sadly replied his wife. "Pray do not look at it again. I never can forget that convulsive shudder."

In order to soothe Georgiana, and, as it were, to release her mind from the burden of actual things, Aylmer now put in practice some of the light and playful secrets which science had taught him among its profounder lore. Airy figures, absolutely bodiless ideas, and forms of unsubstantial beauty came and danced before her, imprinting their momentary footsteps on beams of light. Though she had some indistinct idea of the method of these optical phenomena, still the illusion was almost perfect enough to warrant the belief that her husband possessed sway over the spiritual world. Then again, when she felt a wish to look forth from her seclusion, immediately, as if her thoughts were answered, the procession of external existence flitted across a screen. The scenery and the figures of actual life were perfectly represented, but with that bewitching, yet indescribable difference which always makes a picture, an image, or a shadow so much more attractive than the original. When wearied of this Aylmer bade her cast her eyes upon a vessel containing a quantity of earth. She did so, with little interest at first; but was soon startled to perceive the germ of a plant shooting upward from the soil. Then came the slender stalk; the leaves gradually unfolded themselves; and amid them was a perfect and lovely flower.

"It is magical!" cried Georgiana. "I dare not touch it."

"Nay, pluck it," answered Aylmer—"pluck it, and inhale its brief perfume while you may. The flower will wither in a few moments and leave nothing save its brown seed vessels; but thence may be perpetuated a race as ephemeral as itself."

35   But Georgiana had no sooner touched the flower than the whole plant suffered a blight, its leaves turning coal-black as if by the agency of fire.

"There was too powerful a stimulus," said Aylmer, thoughtfully.

To make up for this abortive experiment, he proposed to take her portrait by a scientific process of his own invention. It was to be effected by rays of light striking upon a polished plate of metal. Georgiana assented; but, on looking at the result, was affrighted to find the features of the portrait blurred and indefinable;

while the minute figure of a hand appeared where the cheek should have been. Aylmer snatched the metallic plate and threw it into a jar of corrosive acid.

Soon, however, he forgot these mortifying failures. In the intervals of study and chemical experiment he came to her flushed and exhausted, but seemed invigorated by her presence, and spoke in glowing language of the resources of his art. He gave a history of the long dynasty of the alchemists, who spent so many ages in quest of the universal solvent by which the golden principle might be elicited from all things vile and base. Aylmer appeared to believe that, by the plainest scientific logic, it was altogether within the limits of possibility to discover this long-sought medium; "but," he added, "a philosopher who should go deep enough to acquire the power would attain too lofty a wisdom to stoop to the exercise of it." Not less singular were his opinions in regard to the elixir vitae. He more than intimated that it was at his option to concoct a liquid that should prolong life for years, perhaps interminably; but that it would produce a discord in Nature which all the world, and chiefly the quaffer of the immortal nostrum, would find cause to curse.

"Aylmer, are you in earnest?" asked Georgiana, looking at him with amazement and fear. "It is terrible to possess such power, or even to dream of possessing it."

"Oh, do not tremble, my love," said her husband. "I would not wrong either you   40 or myself by working such inharmonious effects upon our lives; but I would have you consider how trifling, in comparison, is the skill requisite to remove this little hand."

At the mention of the birth-mark, Georgiana, as usual, shrank as if a redhot iron had touched her cheek.

Again Aylmer applied himself to his labors. She could hear his voice in the distant furnace room giving directions to Aminadab, whose harsh, uncouth, mishapen tones were audible in response, more like the grunt or growl of a brute than human speech. After hours of absence, Aylmer reappeared and proposed that she should now examine his cabinet of chemical products and natural treasures of the earth. Among the former he showed her a small vial, in which, he remarked, was contained a gentle yet most powerful fragrance, capable of impregnating all the breezes that blow across a kingdom. They were of inestimable value, the contents of that little vial; and, as he said so, he threw some of the perfume into the air and filled the room with piercing and invigorating delight.

"And what is this?" asked Georgiana, pointing to a small crystal globe containing a gold-colored liquid. "It is so beautiful to the eye that I could imagine it the elixir of life."

"In one sense it is," replied Aylmer; "or, rather, the elixir of immortality. It is the most precious poison that ever was concocted in this world. By its aid I could apportion the lifetime of any mortal at whom you might point your finger. The strength of the dose would determine whether he were to linger out years, or drop dead in the midst of a breath. No king on his guarded throne could keep his life if I, in my private station, should deem that the welfare of millions justified me in depriving him of it."

45   "Why do you keep such a terrific drug?" inquired Georgiana in horror.

"Do not mistrust me, dearest," said her husband, smiling; "its virtuous potency is yet greater than its harmful one. But see! here is a powerful cosmetic. With a few drops of this in a vase of water, freckles may be washed away as easily as the hands are cleansed. A stronger infusion would take the blood out of the cheek, and leave the rosiest beauty a pale ghost."

"Is it with this lotion that you intend to bathe my cheek?" asked Georgiana anxiously.

"Oh, no," hastily replied her husband; "this is merely superficial. Your case demands a remedy that shall go deeper."

In his interviews with Georgiana, Aylmer generally made minute inquiries as to her sensations and whether the confinement of the rooms and the temperature of the atmosphere agreed with her. These questions had such a particular drift that Georgiana began to conjecture that she was already subjected to certain physical influences, either breathed in with the fragrant air or taken with her food. She fancied likewise, but it might be altogether fancy, that there was a stirring up of her system—a strange, indefinite sensation creeping through her veins, and tingling, half painfully, half pleasurably, at her heart. Still, whenever she dared to look into the mirror, there she beheld herself pale as a white rose and with the crimson birthmark stamped upon her cheek. Not even Aylmer now hated it so much as she.

50   To dispel the tedium of the hours which her husband found it necessary to devote to the processes of combination and analysis, Georgiana turned over the volumes of his scientific library. In many dark old tomes she met with chapters full of romance and poetry. They were the works of philosophers of the middle ages, such as Albertus Magnus, Cornelius Agrippa, Paracelsus, and the famous friar who created the prophetic Brazen Head. All these antique naturalists stood in advance of their centuries, yet were imbued with some of their credulity, and therefore were believed, and perhaps imagined themselves to have acquired from the investigation of Nature a power above Nature, and from physics a sway over the spiritual world. Hardly less curious and imaginative were the early volumes of the Transactions of the Royal Society, in which the members, knowing little of the limits of natural possibility, were continually recording wonders or proposing methods whereby wonders might be wrought.

But to Georgiana the most engrossing volume was a large folio from her husband's own hand, in which he had recorded every experiment of his scientific career, its original aim, the methods adopted for its development, and its final success or failure, with the circumstances to which either event was attributable. The book, in truth, was both the history and emblem of his ardent, ambitious, imaginative, yet practical and laborious life. He handled physical details as if there were nothing beyond them; yet spiritualized them all, and redeemed himself from materialism by his strong and eager aspiration towards the infinite. In his grasp the veriest clod of earth assumed a soul. Georgiana, as she read, reverenced Aylmer and loved him more profoundly than ever, but with a less entire dependence on his judgment than heretofore. Much as he had accomplished, she could not but observe that his most splendid successes were almost invariably failures, if compared with the ideal at which he aimed. His brightest diamonds were the merest pebbles, and felt to be so by himself, in comparison with the inestimable gems which lay hidden beyond his reach. The volume, rich with achievements that had won renown for its author, was yet as melancholy a record as ever mortal hand had penned. It was the sad confession and continual exemplification of the shortcomings of the composite man, the spirit burdened with clay and working in matter, and of the despair that assails the higher nature at finding itself so miserably thwarted by the earthly part. Perhaps every man of genius in whatever sphere might recognize the image of his own experience in Aylmer's journal.

So deeply did these reflections affect Georgiana that she laid her face upon the open volume and burst into the tears. In this situation she was found by her husband.

"It is dangerous to read in a sorcerer's books," said he with a smile, though his countenance was uneasy and displeased. "Georgiana, there are pages in that volume which I can scarcely glance over and keep my senses. Take heed lest it prove as detrimental to you."

"It has made me worship you more than ever," said she.

"Ah, wait for this one success," rejoined he, "then worship me if you will. I 55 shall deem myself hardly unworthy of it. But come, I have sought you for the luxury of your voice. Sing to me, dearest."

So she poured out the liquid music of her voice to quench the thirst of his spirit. He then took his leave with a boyish exuberance of gayety, assuring her that her seclusion would endure but a little longer, and that the result was already certain. Scarcely had he departed when Georgiana felt irresistibly impelled to follow him. She had forgotten to inform Aylmer of a symptom which for two or three hours past had begun to excite her attention. It was a sensation in the fatal birthmark, not painful, but which induced a restlessness throughout her system. Hastening after her husband, she intruded for the first time into the laboratory.

The first thing that struck her eye was the furnace, that hot and feverish worker, with the intense glow of its fire, which by the quantities of soot clustered above it seemed to have been burning for ages. There was a distilling apparatus in full operation. Around the room were retorts, tubes, cylinders, crucibles, and other apparatus of chemical research. An electrical machine stood ready for immediate use. The atmosphere felt oppressively close, and was tainted with gaseous odors which had been tormented forth by the processes of science. The severe and homely simplicity of the apartment, with its naked walls and brick pavement, looked strange, accustomed as Georgiana had become to the fantastic elegance of her boudoir. But what chiefly, indeed almost solely, drew her attention, was the aspect of Aylmer himself.

He was pale as death, anxious and absorbed, and hung over the furnace as if it depended upon his utmost watchfulness whether the liquid which it was distilling should be the draught of immortal happiness or misery. How different from the sanguine and joyous mien that he had assumed for Georgiana's encouragement!

"Carefully now, Aminadab; carefully, thou human machine; carefully, thou man of clay!" muttered Aylmer, more to himself than his assistant. "Now if there be a thought too much or too little, it is all over."

60   "Ho! ho!" mumbled Aminadab. "Look, master! look!"

Aylmer raised his eyes hastily, and at first reddened, then grew paler than ever, on beholding Georgiana. He rushed towards her and seized her arm with a grip that left the print of his fingers upon it.

"Why do you come hither? Have you no trust in your husband?" cried he, impetuously, "Would you throw the blight of that fatal birth-mark over my labors? It is not well done. Go, prying woman, go!"

"Nay, Aylmer," said Georgiana with the firmness of which she possessed no stinted endowment, "it is not you that have a right to complain. You mistrust your wife; you have concealed the anxiety with which you watch the development of this experiment. Think not so unworthily of me, my husband. Tell me all the risk we run, and fear not that I shall shrink; for my share in it is less than your own."

"No, no, Georgiana!" said Aylmer, impatiently; "it must not be."

65   "I submit," replied she calmly. "And, Aylmer, I shall quaff whatever draught you bring me; but it will be on the same principle that would induce me to take a dose of poison if offered by your hand."

"My noble wife," said Aylmer, deeply moved, "I knew not the height and depth of your nature until now. Nothing shall be concealed. Know, then, that this crimson hand, superficial as it seems, has clutched its grasp into your being with a strength of which I had no previous conception. I have already administered agents powerful enough to do aught except to change your entire physical system. Only one thing remains to be tried. If that fails us we are ruined."

"Why did you hesitate to tell me this?" asked she.

"Because, Georgiana," said Aylmer, in a low voice, "there is danger."

"Danger? There is but one danger—that this horrible stigma shall be left upon my cheek!" cried Georgiana. "Remove it, remove it, whatever be the cost, or we shall both go mad!"

70   "Heaven knows your words are too true," said Aylmer, sadly. "And now, dearest, return to your boudoir. In a little while all will be tested."

He conducted her back and took leave of her with a solemn tenderness which spoke far more than his words how much was now at stake. After his departure, Georgiana became rapt in musings. She considered the character of Aylmer, and did it completer justice than at any previous moment. Her heart exulted, while it trembled, at his honorable love—so pure and lofty that it would accept nothing less than perfection nor miserably make itself contented with an earthlier nature than he had dreamed of. She felt how much more precious was such a sentiment than that meaner kind which would have borne with the imperfection for her sake, and have been guilty of treason to holy love by degrading its perfect idea to the level of the actual; and with her whole spirit she prayed that, for a single moment, she might satisfy his highest and deepest conception. Longer than one moment she well knew it could not be; for his spirit was ever on the march, ever ascending, and each instant required something that was beyond the scope of the instant before.

The sound of her husband's footsteps aroused her. He bore a crystal goblet containing a liquor colorless as water, but bright enough to be the draught of immortality. Aylmer was pale; but it seemed rather the consequence of a highly wrought state of mind and tension of spirit than of fear or doubt.

"The concoction of the draught has been perfect," said he, in answer to Georgiana's look. "Unless all my science have deceived me, it cannot fail."

"Save on your account, my dearest Aylmer," observed his wife, "I might wish to put off this birth-mark of mortality by relinquishing mortality itself in preference to any other mode. Life is but a sad possession to those who have attained precisely the degree of moral advancement at which I stand. Were I weaker and blinder it might be happiness. Were I stronger, it might be endured hopefully. But being what I find myself, methinks I am of all mortals the most fit to die."

"You are fit for heaven without tasting death!" replied her husband. "But why 75 do we speak of dying? The draught cannot fail. Behold its effect upon this plant."

On the window seat there stood a geranium diseased with yellow blotches, which had overspread all its leaves. Aylmer poured a small quantity of the liquid upon the soil in which it grew. In a little time, when the roots of the plant had taken up the moisture, the unsightly blotches began to be extinguished in a living verdure.

"There needed no proof," said Georgiana, quietly. "Give me the goblet. I joyfully stake all upon your word."

"Drink, then, thou lofty creature!" exclaimed Aylmer, with fervid admiration. "There is no taint of imperfection on thy spirit. Thy sensible frame, too, shall soon be all perfect."

She quaffed the liquid and returned the goblet to his hand.

"It is grateful," said she with a placid smile. "Methinks it is like water from a 80 heavenly fountain; for it contains I know not what of unobtrusive fragrance and deliciousness. It allays a feverish thirst that had parched me for many days. Now, dearest, let me sleep. My earthly senses are closing over my spirit like the leaves around the heart of a rose at sunset."

She spoke the last words with a gentle reluctance, as if it required almost more energy than she could command to pronounce the faint and lingering syllables. Scarcely had they loitered through her lips ere she was lost in slumber. Aylmer sat by her side, watching her aspect with the emotions proper to a man the whole value of whose existence was involved in the process now to be tested. Mingled with this mood, however, was the philosophic investigation characteristic of the man of science. Not the minutest symptom escaped him. A heightened flush of the cheek, a slight irregularity of breath, a quiver of the eyelid, a hardly perceptible tremor through the frame—such were the details which, as the moments passed, he wrote down in his folio volume. Intense thought had set its stamp upon every previous page of that volume, but the thoughts of years were all concentrated upon the last.

While thus employed, he failed not to gaze often at the fatal hand, and not without a shudder. Yet once, by a strange and unaccountable impulse, he pressed it with his lips. His spirit recoiled, however, in the very act; and Georgiana, out of the midst of her deep sleep, moved uneasily and murmured as if in remonstrance. Again Aylmer resumed his watch. Nor was it without avail. The crimson hand, which at first had been strongly visible upon the marble paleness of Georgiana's cheek, now grew more faintly outlined. She remained not less pale than ever; but the birth-mark, with every breath that came and went, lost somewhat of its former distinctness. Its presence had been awful; its departure was more awful still. Watch the stain of the rainbow fading out the sky, and you will know how the mysterious symbol passed away.

"By Heaven! it is well-nigh gone!" said Aylmer to himself, in almost irrepressible ecstasy. "I can scarcely trace it now. Success! success! And now it is like the faintest rose color. The lightest flush of blood across her cheek would overcome it. But she is so pale!"

He drew aside the window curtain and suffered the light of natural day to fall into the room and rest upon her cheek. At the same time he heard a gross, hoarse chuckle, which he had long known as his servant Aminadab's expression of delight.

85 "Ah, clod! ah, earthly mass!" cried Aylmer, laughing in a sort of frenzy, "you have served me well! Matter and spirit—earth and heaven—have both done their part in this! Laugh, thing of the senses! You have earned the right to laugh."

These exclamations broke Georgiana's sleep. She slowly unclosed her eyes and gazed into the mirror which her husband had arranged for that purpose. A faint smile flitted over her lips when she recognized how barely perceptible was now that crimson hand which had once blazed forth with such disastrous brilliancy as to scare away all their happiness. But then her eyes sought Aylmer's face with a trouble and anxiety that he could by no means account for.

"My poor Aylmer!" murmured she.

"Poor? Nay, richest, happiest, and most favored!" exclaimed he. "My peerless bride, it is successful! You are perfect!"

"My poor Aylmer," she repeated, with a more than human tenderness, "you have aimed loftily; you have done nobly. Do not repent that with so high and pure a feeling, you have rejected the best the earth could offer. Aylmer, dearest Aylmer, I am dying!"

90 Alas! it was too true! the fatal hand had grappled with the mystery of life, and was the bond by which an angelic spirit kept itself in union with a mortal frame. As the last crimson tint of the birth-mark—that sole token of human imperfection—faded from her cheek, the parting breath of the now perfect woman passed into the atmosphere, and her soul, lingering a moment near her husband, took its heavenward flight. Then a hoarse, chuckling laugh was heard again! Thus ever does the gross fatality of earth exult in its invariable triumph over the immortal essence which, in this dim sphere of half development, demands the completeness of a higher state. Yet, had Aylmer reached a profounder wisdom, he need not thus have flung away the happiness which would have woven his mortal life of the selfsame texture with the celestial. The momentary circumstance was too strong for him; he failed to look beyond the shadowy scope of time, and, living once for all in eternity, to find the perfect future in the present.

CRITICAL THINKING QUESTIONS

1. In the story's closing sentence, the narrator tells us, "... he [Aylmer] failed to look beyond the shadowy scope of time, and living once for all in Eternity, to

find the perfect Future in the present." In what ways do people today fail to find the perfect future in the present? On the other hand, how do certain individuals succeed in doing so?

2. "The Birth-Mark" supports a fairly transparent claim about the role of the scientist. As a scientist, Aylmer believes in the unbridled power of his reasoning and the scientific method to solve problems and to achieve perfection. However, as a critical thinker, one must consider an opposing perspective: The human impulse to seek, not necessarily perfection but an improved quality of life, has led to significant scientific advances. What is the role of the scientist? In responding to this question, consider textual evidence from Hawthorne's story, as well as from your own direct observations and firsthand knowledge.

3. Hawthorne's story also implies claims related to gender, as revealed by the dynamics between Aylmer and Georgiana. Create a claim and support it with textual evidence, as well as your own firsthand information and experiences.

4. Similar to Aylmer's attempt to create magical potions with his chemicals, advertisers can use computer wizardry to create images of men and women with perfect skin, perfect hair, the perfect body. Find some examples of these advertisements of physical perfection. Identify the claims and appeals used by the ads' creators.

RESEARCH/WRITING TOPIC—Stem-Cell Research: An Ethical Dilemma

In 1998, researchers isolated and derived stem cells from human embryos. Since then, the issue of the ethics of stem-cell research has been vigorously debated among scientists, policy makers, and private citizens. Because stem cells have the capacity to develop into any type of cell or system, proponents of this research hail its promise for treating debilitating conditions, such as Alzheimer's, diabetes, and heart disease, and for rejuvenating paralyzed limbs. However, the technology for deriving the stem cells requires the use of human embryonic tissues, a procedure which presents ethical and moral concerns for many people. Not surprisingly, some opponents of stem-cell research have made allusions to Hawthorne's "The Birth-Mark," suggesting that it is human hubris to presume to solve "the mystery of life" (par. 90). On the other hand, advocates of the research question the moral qualms over the use of this tissue when a viable human being's quality and longevity of life hang in the balance. As is often the case, reasonable and compassionate persons disagree on this issue. After researching this issue, develop your own argument on the issue of the ethics of stem-cell research.

Tim O'Brien (b. 1946)

The Things They Carried

First Lieutenant Jimmy Cross carried letters from a girl named Martha, a junior at Mount Sebastian College in New Jersey. They were not love letters, but Lieutenant Cross was hoping, so he kept them folded in plastic at the bottom of his rucksack. In the late afternoon, after a day's march, he would dig his foxhole, wash his hands under a canteen, unwrap the letters, hold them with the tips of his fingers, and spend the last hour of light pretending. He would imagine romantic camping trips into the White Mountains in New Hampshire. He would sometimes taste the envelope flaps, knowing her tongue had been there. More than anything, he wanted Martha to love him as he loved her, but the letters were mostly chatty, elusive on the matter of love. She was a virgin, he was almost sure. She was an English major at Mount Sebastian, and she wrote beautifully about her professors and roommates and midterm exams, about her respect for Chaucer and her great affection for Virginia Woolf. She often quoted lines of poetry; she never mentioned the war, except to say, Jimmy, take care of yourself. The letters weighed 10 ounces. They were signed Love, Martha, but Lieutenant Cross understood that Love was only a way of signing and did not mean what he sometimes pretended it meant. At dusk, he would carefully return the letters to his rucksack. Slowly, a bit distracted, he would get up and move among his men, checking the perimeter, then at full dark he would return to his hole and watch the night and wonder if Martha was a virgin.

The things they carried were largely determined by necessity. Among the necessities or near-necessities were P-38 can openers, pocket knives, heat tabs, wrist-watches, dog tags, mosquito repellent, chewing gum, candy, cigarettes, salt tablets, packets of Kool-Aid, lighters, matches, sewing kits, Military Payment Certificates, C rations, and two or three canteens of water. Together, these items weighed between 15 and 20 pounds, depending upon a man's habits or rate of metabolism. Henry Dobbins, who was a big man, carried extra rations; he was especially fond of canned peaches in heavy syrup over pound cake. Dave Jensen, who practiced field hygiene, carried a toothbrush, dental floss, and several hotel-sized bars of soap he'd stolen on R&R in Sydney, Australia. Ted Lavender, who was scared, carried tranquilizers until he was shot in the head outside the village of Than Khe in mid-April. By necessity, and because it was SOP, they all carried steel helmets that weighed 5 pounds including the liner and camouflage cover. They carried the standard fatigue jackets and trousers. Very few carried underwear. On their feet they carried jungle boots—2.1 pounds—and Dave Jensen carried three pairs of socks and a can of Dr. Scholl's foot powder as a precaution against trench foot. Until he was shot, Ted Lavender carried six or seven ounces of premium dope, which for him was a necessity. Mitchell Sanders, the RTO, carried condoms. Norman

Bowker carried a diary. Rat Kiley carried comic books. Kiowa, a devout Baptist, carried an illustrated New Testament that had been presented to him by his father, who taught Sunday school in Oklahoma City, Oklahoma. As a hedge against bad times, however, Kiowa also carried his grandmother's distrust of the white man, his grandfather's old hunting hatchet. Necessity dictated. Because the land was mined and booby-trapped, it was SOP for each man to carry a steelcentered, nylon-covered flak jacket, which weighed 6.7 pounds, but which on hot days seemed much heavier. Because you could die so quickly, each man carried at least one large compress bandage, usually in the helmet band for easy access. Because the nights were cold, and because the monsoons were wet, each carried a green plastic poncho that could be used as a raincoat or groundsheet or makeshift tent. With its quilted liner, the poncho weighed almost two pounds, but it was worth every ounce. In April, for instance, when Ted Lavender was shot, they used his poncho to wrap him up, then to carry him across the paddy, then to lift him into the chopper that took him away.

To carry something was to hump it, as when Lieutenant Jimmy Cross humped his love for Martha up the hills and through the swamps. In its intransitive form, to hump meant to walk, or to march, but it implied burdens far beyond the intransitive.

Almost everyone humped photographs. In his wallet, Lieutenant Cross carried two photographs of Martha. The first was a Kodacolor snapshot signed Love, though he knew better. She stood against a brick wall. Her eyes were gray and neutral, her lips slightly open as she stared straight-on at the camera. At night, sometimes, Lieutenant Cross wondered who had taken the picture, because he knew she had boyfriends, because he loved her so much, and because he could see the shadow of the picture-taker spreading out against the brick wall. The second photograph had been clipped from the 1968 Mount Sebastian yearbook. It was an action shot—women's volleyball—and Martha was bent horizontal to the floor, reaching, the palms of her hands in sharp focus, the tongue taut, the expression frank and competitive. There was no visible sweat. She wore white gym shorts. Her legs, he thought, were almost certainly the legs of a virgin, dry and without hair, the left knee cocked and carrying her entire weight, which was just over one hundred pounds. Lieutenant Cross remembered touching that left knee. A dark theater, he remembered, and the movie was *Bonnie and Clyde,* and Martha wore a tweed skirt, and during the final scene, when he touched her knee, she turned and looked at him in a sad, sober way that made him pull his hand back, but he would always remember the feel of the tweed skirt and the knee beneath it and the sound of the gunfire that killed Bonnie and Clyde, how embarrassing it was, how slow and oppressive. He remembered kissing her good night at the dorm door. Right then, he thought, he should've done something brave. He should've carried her up the stairs to her room and tied her to the bed and touched that left knee all night long. He should've risked it. Whenever he looked at the photographs, he thought of new things he should've done.

5   What they carried was partly a function of rank, partly of field specialty.

As a first lieutenant and platoon leader, Jimmy Cross carried a compass, maps, code books, binoculars, and a .45-caliber pistol that weighed 2.9 pounds fully loaded. He carried a strobe light and the responsibility for the lives of his men.

As an RTO, Mitchell Sanders carried the PRC-25 radio, a killer, 26 pounds with its battery.

As a medic, Rat Kiley carried a canvas satchel filled with morphine and plasma and malaria tablets and surgical tape and comic books and all the things a medic must carry, including M&M's for especially bad wounds, for a total weight of nearly 20 pounds.

As a big man, therefore a machine gunner, Henry Dobbins carried the M-60 which weighed 23 pounds unloaded, but which was almost always loaded. In addition, Dobbins carried between 10 and 15 pounds of ammunition draped in belts across his chest and shoulders.

10   As PFCs or Spec 4s, most of them were common grunts and carried the standard M-16 gas-operated assault rifle. The weapon weighed 7.5 pounds unloaded, 8.2 pounds with its full 20-round magazine. Depending on numerous factors, such as topography and psychology, the riflemen carried anywhere from 12 to 20 magazines, usually in cloth bandoliers, adding on another 8.4 pounds at minimum, 14 pounds at maximum. When it was available, they also carried M-16 maintenance gear—rods and steel brushes and swabs and tubes of LSA oil—all of which weighed about a pound. Among the grunts, some carried the M-79 grenade launcher, 5.9 pounds unloaded, a reasonably light weapon except for the ammunition, which was heavy. A single round weighed 10 ounces. The typical load was 25 rounds. But Ted Lavender, who was scared, carried 34 rounds when he was shot and killed outside Than Khe, and he went down under an exceptional burden, more than 20 pounds of ammunition, plus the flak jacket and helmet and rations and water and toilet paper and tranquilizers and all the rest, plus the unweighed fear. He was dead weight. There was no twitching or flopping. Kiowa, who saw it happen, said it was like watching a rock fall, or a big sandbag or something—just boom, then down—not like the movies where the dead guy rolls around and does fancy spins and goes ass over teakettle—not like that, Kiowa said, the poor bastard just flat-fuck fell. Boom. Down. Nothing else. It was a bright morning in mid-April. Lieutenant Cross felt the pain. He blamed himself. They stripped off Lavender's canteens and ammo, all the heavy things, and Rat Kiley said the obvious, the guy's dead, and Mitchell Sanders used his radio to report one U.S. KIA and to request a chopper. Then they wrapped Lavender in his poncho. They carried him out to a dry paddy, established security, and sat smoking the dead man's dope until the chopper came. Lieutenant Cross kept to himself. He pictured Martha's smooth young face, thinking he loved her more than anything, more than his men, and now Ted Lavender was dead because he loved her so much and could not stop thinking about her. When the dustoff arrived, they carried Lavender aboard. Afterward they burned Than Khe. They marched until dusk, then dug their holes, and that

night Kiowa kept explaining how you had to be there, how fast it was, how the poor guy just dropped like so much concrete. Boom-down, he said. Like cement.

In addition to the three standard weapons—the M-60, M-16, and M-79—they carried whatever presented itself, or whatever seemed appropriate as a means of killing or staying alive. They carried catch-as-catch-can. At various times, in various situations, they carried M-14s and CAR-15s and Swedish Ks and grease guns and captured AK-47s and Chi-Coms and RPGs and Simonov carbines and black market Uzis and .38-caliber Smith & Wesson handguns and 66 mm LAWs and shotguns and silencers and blackjacks and boyonets and C-4 plastic explosives. Lee Strunk carried a slingshot; a weapon of last resort, he called it. Mitchell Sanders carried brass knuckles. Kiowa carried his grandfather's feathered hatchet. Every third or fourth man carried a Claymore antipersonnel mine—3.5 pounds with its firing device. They all carried fragmentation grenades—14 ounces each. They all carried at least one M-18 colored smoke grenade—24 ounces. Some carried CS or tear gas grenades. Some carried white phosphorus grenades. They carried all they could bear, and then some, including a silent awe for the terrible power of the things they carried.

In the first week of April, before Lavender died, Lieutenant Jimmy Cross received a good-luck charm from Martha. It was a simple pebble, an ounce at most. Smooth to the touch, it was a milky white color with flecks of orange and violet, oval-shaped, like a miniature egg. In the accompanying letter, Martha wrote that she had found the pebble on the Jersey shoreline, precisely where the land touched water at high tide, where things came together but also separated. It was this separate-but-together quality, she wrote, that had inspired her to pick up the pebble and to carry it in her breast pocket for several days, where it seemed weightless, and then to send it through the mail, by air, as a token of her truest feelings for him. Lieutenant Cross found this romantic. But he wondered what her truest feelings were, exactly, and what she meant by separate-but-together. He wondered how the tides and waves had come into play on that afternoon along the Jersey shoreline when Martha saw the pebble and bent down to rescue it from geology. He imagined bare feet. Martha was a poet, with the poet's sensibilities, and her feet would be brown and bare, the toenails unpainted, the eyes chilly and somber like the ocean in March, and though it was painful, he wondered who had been with her that afternoon. He imagined a pair of shadows moving along the strip of sand where things came together but also separated. It was phantom jealousy, he knew, but he couldn't help himself. He loved her so much. On the march, through the hot days of early April, he carried the pebble in his mouth, turning it with his tongue, tasting sea salt and moisture. His mind wandered. He had difficulty keeping his attention on the war. On occasion he would yell at his men to spread out the column, to keep their eyes open, but then he would slip away into daydreams, just pretending, walking barefoot along the Jersey shore, with Martha, carrying nothing. He would feel himself rising. Sun and waves and gentle winds, all love and lightness.

What they carried varied by mission.

When a mission took them to the mountains, they carried mosquito netting, machetes, canvas tarps, and extra bug juice.

15   If a mission seemed especially hazardous, or if it involved a place they knew to be bad, they carried everything they could. In certain heavily mined AOs, where the land was dense with Toe Poppers and Bouncing Betties, they took turns humping a 28-pound mine detector. With its headphones and big sensing plate, the equipment was a stress on the lower back and shoulders, awkward to handle, often useless because of the shrapnel in the earth, but they carried it anyway, partly for safety, partly for the illusion of safety.

On ambush, or other night missions, they carried peculiar little odds and ends. Kiowa always took along his New Testament and a pair of moccasins for silence. Dave Jensen carried night-sight vitamins high in carotene. Lee Strunk carried his slingshot; ammo, he claimed, would never be a problem. Rat Kiley carried brandy and M&M's candy. Until he was shot, Tel Lavender carried the starlight scope, which weighed 6.3 pounds with its aluminum carrying case. Henry Dobbins carried his girlfriend's pantyhose wrapped around his neck as a comforter. They all carried ghosts. When dark came, they would move out single file across the meadows and paddies to their ambush coordinates, where they would quietly set up the Claymores and lie down and spend the night waiting.

Other missions were more complicated and required special equipment. In mid-April, it was their mission to search out and destroy the elaborate tunnel complexes in the Than Khe area south of Chu Lai. To blow the tunnels, they carried one-pound blocks of pentrite high explosives, four blocks to a man, 68 pounds in all. They carried wiring, detonators, and battery-powered clackers. Dave Jensen carried earplugs. Most often, before blowing the tunnels, they were ordered by higher command to search them, which was considered bad news, but by and large they just shrugged and carried out orders. Because he was a big man, Henry Dobbins was excused from tunnel duty. The others would draw numbers. Before Lavender died there were 17 men in the platoon, and whoever drew the number 17 would strip off his gear and crawl in headfirst with a flashlight and Lieutenant Cross's .45-caliber pistol. The rest of them would fan out as security. They would sit down or kneel, not facing the hole, listening to the ground beneath them, imagining cobwebs and ghosts, whatever was down there—the tunnel walls squeezing in—how the flashlight seemed impossibly heavy in the hand and how it was tunnel vision in the very strictest sense, compression in all ways, even time, and how you had to wiggle in—ass and elbows—a swallowed-up feeling—and how you found yourself worrying about odd things: Will your flashlight go dead? Do rats carry rabies? If you screamed, how far would the sound carry? Would your buddies hear it? Would they have the courage to drag you out? In some respects, though not many, the waiting was worse than the tunnel itself. Imagination was a killer.

On April 16, when Lee Strunk drew the number 17, he laughed and muttered something and went down quickly. The morning was hot and very still. Not good,

Kiowa said. He looked at the tunnel opening, then out across a dry paddy toward the village of Than Khe. Nothing moved. No clouds or birds or people. As they waited, the men smoked and drank Kool-Aid, not talking much, feeling sympathy for Lee Strunk but also feeling the luck of the draw. You win some, you lose some, said Mitchell Sanders, and sometimes you settle for a rain check. It was a tired line and no one laughed.

Henry Dobbins ate a tropical chocolate bar. Ted Lavender popped a tranquilizer and went off to pee.

After five minutes, Lieutenant Jimmy Cross moved to the tunnel, leaned down, 20 and examined the darkness. Trouble, he thought—a cave-in maybe. And then suddenly, without willing it, he was thinking about Martha. The stresses and fractures, the quick collapse, the two of them buried alive under all that weight. Dense, crushing love. Kneeling, watching the hole, he tried to concentrate on Lee Strunk and the war, all the dangers, but his love was too much for him, he felt paralyzed, he wanted to sleep inside her lungs and breathe her blood and be smothered. He wanted her to be a virgin and not a virgin, all at once. He wanted to know her. Intimate secrets: Why poetry? Why so sad? Why that grayness in her eyes? Why so alone? Not lonely, just alone—riding her bike across campus or sitting off by herself in the cafeteria— even dancing, she danced alone—and it was the aloneness that filled him with love. He remembered telling her that one evening. How she nodded and looked away. And how, later, when he kissed her, she received the kiss without returning it, her eyes wide open, not afraid, not a virgin's eyes, just flat and uninvolved.

Lieutenant Cross gazed at the tunnel. But he was not there. He was buried with Martha under the white sand at the Jersey shore. They were pressed together, and the pebble in his mouth was her tongue. He was smiling. Vaguely, he was aware of how quiet the day was, the sullen paddies, yet he could not bring himself to worry about matters of security. He was beyond that. He was just a kid at war, in love. He was twenty-four years old. He couldn't help it.

A few moments later Lee Strunk crawled out of the tunnel. He came up grinning, filthy but alive. Lieutenant Cross nodded and closed his eyes while the others clapped Strunk on the back and made jokes about rising from the dead.

Worms, Rat Kiley said. Right out of the grave. Fuckin' zombie.

The men laughed. They all felt great relief.

Spook city, said Mitchell Sanders. 25

Lee Strunk made a funny ghost sound, a kind of moaning, yet very happy, and right then, when Strunk made that high happy moaning sound, when we went Ahhooooo, right then Ted Lavender was shot in the head on his way back from peeing. He lay with his mouth open. The teeth were broken. There was a swollen black bruise under his left eye. The cheekbone was gone. Oh shit, Rat Kiley said, the guy's dead. The guy's dead, he kept saying, which seemed profound—the guy's dead. I mean really.

The things they carried were determined to some extent by superstition. Lieutenant Cross carried his good-luck pebble. Dave Jensen carried a rabbit's foot. Norman

Bowker, otherwise a very gentle person, carried a thumb that had been presented to him as a gift by Mitchell Sanders. The thumb was dark brown, rubbery to the touch, and weighed four ounces at most. It had been cut from a VC corpse, a boy of fifteen or sixteen. They'd found him at the bottom of an irrigation ditch, badly burned, flies in his mouth and eyes. The boy wore black shorts and sandals. At the time of his death he had been carrying a pouch of rice, a rifle and three magazines of ammunition.

You want my opinion, Mitchell Sanders said, there's a definite moral here.

He put his hand on the dead boy's wrist. He was quiet for a time, as if counting a pulse, then he patted the stomach, almost affectionately, and used Kiowa's hunting hatchet to remove the thumb.

30   Henry Dobbins asked what the moral was.

Moral?

You know. *Moral.*

Sanders wrapped the thumb in toilet paper and handed it across to Norman Bowker. There was no blood. Smiling, he kicked the boy's head, watched the flies scatter, and said, It's like with that old TV show—Paladin. Have gun, will travel.

35   Henry Dobbins thought about it.

Yeah, well, he finally said. I don't see no moral.

There it *is*, man.

Fuck off.

They carried USO stationery and pencils and pens. They carried Sterno, safety pins, trip flares, signal flares, spools of wire, razor blades, chewing tobacco, liberated joss sticks and statuettes of the smiling Buddha, candles, grease pencils, *The Stars and Stripes,* fingernail clippers, Psy Ops leaflets, bush hats, bolos, and much more. Twice a week, when the resupply choppers came in, they carried hot chow in green mermite cans and large canvas bags filled with iced beer and soda pop. They carried plastic water containers, each with a two-gallon capacity. Mitchell Sanders carried a set of starched tiger fatigues for special occasions. Henry Dobbins carried Black Flag insecticide. Dave Jensen carried empty sandbags that could be filled at night for added protection. Lee Strunk carried tanning lotion. Some things they carried in common. Taking turns, they carried the big PRC-77 scrambler radio, which weighed 30 pounds with its battery. They shared the weight of memory. They took up what others could no longer bear. Often, they carried each other, the wounded or weak. They carried infections. They carried chess sets, basketballs, Vietnamese-English dictionaries, insignia of rank, Bronze Stars and Purple Hearts, plastic cards imprinted with the Code of Conduct. They carried diseases, among them malaria and dysentery. They carried lice and ringworm and leeches and paddy algae and various rots and molds. They carried the land itself—Vietnam, the place, the soil—a powdery orange-red dust that covered their boots and fatigues and faces. They carried the sky. The whole atmosphere, they carried it, the humidity, the monsoons, the stink of fungus and decay, all of it, they carried gravity. They moved like mules. By daylight they took sniper fire, at night they were mortared, but it was not battle, it was just the endless march, village to village, without purpose, nothing won or lost. They marched for the sake of the march. They plodded along slowly, dumbly, leaning forward against the heat, unthinking, all blood and bone, simple grunts, soldiering with their legs, toiling up the hills and down into the paddies and across the rivers and up again and down, just humping, one step and then the next and then another, but no volition, no will, because it was automatic, it was anatomy, and the war was entirely a matter of posture and carriage, the hump was everything, a kind of inertia, a kind of emptiness, a dullness of desire and intellect and conscience and hope and human sensibility. Their principles were in their feet. Their calculations were biological. They had no sense of strategy or mission. They searched the villages without knowing what to look for, not caring, kicking over jars of rice, frisking children and old men, blowing tunnels, sometimes setting fires and sometimes not, then forming up and moving on to the next village, then other villages, where it would always be the same. They carried their own lives. The pressures were enormous. In the heat of early afternoon, they would remove their helmets and flak jackets, walking bare, which was dangerous but which helped ease the strain. They would often discard things along the route of march. Purely for comfort, they would throw away rations, blow their Claymores and grenades, no matter, because by nightfall the resupply choppers would arrive with more of the same, then a day or two later still more, fresh watermelons and crates of ammunition and sunglasses and woolen sweaters—the resources were stunning—sparklers for the Fourth of July, colored eggs for Easter—it was the great American war chest—the fruits of science, the smokestacks, the canneries, the arsenals at Hartford, the Minnesota forests, the machine shops, the vast fields of corn and wheat—they carried like freight trains; they carried it on their backs and shoulders—and for all the ambiguities of Vietnam, all the mysteries and unknowns, there was at least the single abiding certainty that they would never be at a loss for things to carry.

After the chopper took Lavender away, Lieutenant Jimmy Cross led his men   40
into the village of Than Khe. They burned everything. They shot chickens and dogs, they trashed the village well, they called in artillery and watched the wreckage, then they marched for several hours through the hot afternoon, and then at dusk, while Kiowa explained how Lavender died, Lieutenant Cross found himself trembling.

He tried not to cry. With his entrenching tool, which weighed five pounds, he began digging a hole in the earth.

He felt shame. He hated himself. He had loved Martha more than his men, and as a consequence Lavender was now dead, and this was something he would have to carry like a stone in his stomach for the rest of the war.

All he could do was dig. He used his entrenching tool like an ax, slashing, feeling both love and hate, and then later, when it was full dark, he sat at the bottom of his foxhole and wept. It went on for a long while. In part, he was grieving for Ted Lavender, but mostly it was for Martha, and for himself, because she belonged to another world, which was not quite real, and because she was a junior at Mount Sebastian College in New Jersey, a poet and a virgin and uninvolved, and because he realized she did not love him and never would.

Like cement, Kiowa whispered in the dark. I swear to God—boom, down. Not a word.

45   I've heard this, said Norman Bowker.

A pisser, you know? Still zipping himself up. Zapped while zipping.

All right, fine. That's enough.

Yeah, but you had to see it, the guy just—

I *heard*, man. Cement. So why not shut the fuck *up?*

50   Kiowa shook his head sadly and glanced over at the hole where Lieutenant Jimmy Cross sat watching the night. The air was thick and wet. A warm dense fog had settled over the paddies and there was the stillness that precedes rain.

After a time Kiowa sighed.

One thing for sure, he said. The lieutenant's in some deep hurt. I mean that crying jag—the way he was carrying on—it wasn't fake or anything, it was real heavy-duty hurt. The man cares.

Sure, Norman Bowker said.

Say what you want, the man does care.

55   We all got problems.

Not Lavender.

No, I guess not, Bowker said. Do me a favor, though.

Shut up?

That's a smart Indian. Shut up.

60   Shrugging, Kiowa pulled off his boots. He wanted to say more, just to lighten up his sleep, but instead he opened his New Testament and arranged it beneath his head as a pillow. The fog made things seem hollow and unattached. He tried not to think about Ted Lavender, but then he was thinking how fast it was, no drama, down and dead, and how it was hard to feel anything except surprise. It seemed unchristian. He wished he could find some great sadness, or even anger, but the emotion wasn't there and he couldn't make it happen. Mostly he felt pleased to be alive. He liked the smell of the New Testament under his cheek, the leather and ink and paper and glue, whatever the chemicals were. He liked hearing the sounds of night. Even his fatigue, it felt fine, the stiff muscles and the prickly awareness of his own body, a floating feeling. He enjoyed not being dead. Lying there, Kiowa admired Lieutenant Jimmy Cross's capacity for grief. He wanted to share the man's pain, he wanted to care as Jimmy Cross cared. And yet when he closed his eyes, all he could think was Boom-down, and all he could feel was the pleasure of having his boots off and the fog curling in around him and the damp soil and the Bible smells and the plush comfort of night.

After a moment Norman Bowker sat up in the dark.

What the hell, he said. You want to talk, *talk*. Tell it to me.

Forget it.

No, man, go on. One thing I hate, it's a silent Indian.

For the most part they carried themselves with poise, a kind of dignity. Now 65
and then, however, there were times of panic, when they squealed or wanted to
squeal but couldn't, when they twitched and made moaning sounds and covered
their heads and said Dear Jesus and flopped around on the earth and fired their
weapons blindly and cringed and sobbed and begged for the noise to stop and went
wild and made stupid promises to themselves and to God and to their mothers
and fathers, hoping not to die. In different ways, it happened to all of them. Afterward, when the firing ended, they would blink and peek up. They would touch
their bodies, feeling shame, then quickly hiding it. They would force themselves to
stand. As if in slow motion, frame by frame, the world would take on the old logic—
absolute silence, then the wind, then sunlight, then voices. It was the burden of
being alive. Awkwardly, the men would reassemble themselves, first in private, then
in groups, becoming soldiers again. They would repair the leaks in their eyes. They
would check for casualties, call in dust-offs, light cigarettes, try to smile, clear their
throats and spit and begin cleaning their weapons. After a time someone would
shake his head and say. No lie, I almost shit my pants, and someone else would
laugh, which meant it was bad, yes, but the guy had obviously not shit his pants,
it wasn't that bad, and in any case nobody would ever do such a thing and then go
ahead and talk about it. They would squint into the dense, oppressive sunlight. For
a few moments, perhaps, they would fall silent, lighting a joint and tracking its
passage from man to man, inhaling, holding in the humiliation. Scary stuff, one of
them might say. But then someone else would grin or flick his eyebrows and say,
Roger-dodger, almost cut me a new asshole, *almost*.

There were numerous such poses. Some carried themselves with a sort of wistful resignation, others with pride or stiff soldierly discipline or good humor or
macho zeal. They were afraid of dying but they were even more afraid to show it.

They found jokes to tell.

They used a hard vocabulary to contain the terrible softness. *Greased* they'd
say. *Offed, lit up, zapped while zipping.* It wasn't cruelty, just stage presence. They
were actors. When someone died, it wasn't quite dying, because in a curious way it
seemed scripted, and because they had their lines mostly memorized, irony mixed
with tragedy, and because they called it by other names, as if to encyst and destroy
the reality of death itself. They kicked corpses. They cut off thumbs. They talked
grunt lingo. They told stories about Ted Lavender's supply of tranquilizers, how the
poor guy didn't feel a thing, how incredibly tranquil he was.

There's a moral here, said Mitchell Sanders.

They were waiting for Lavender's chopper, smoking the dead man's dope. 70

The moral's pretty obvious, Sanders said, and winked. Stay away from drugs.
No joke, they'll ruin your day every time.

Cute, said Henry Dobbins.

Mind blower, get it? Talk about wiggy. Nothing left, just blood and brains.

They made themselves laugh.

75   There it is, they'd say. Over and over—there it is, my friend, there it is—as if the repetition itself were an act of poise, a balance between crazy and almost crazy, knowing without going, there it is, which meant be cool, let it ride, because Oh yeah man, you can't change what can't be changed, there it is, there it absolutely and positively and fucking well *is*.

They were tough.

They carried all the emotional baggage of men who might die. Grief, terror, love, longing—these were intangibles, but the intangibles had their own mass and specific gravity, they had tangible weight. They carried shameful memories. They carried the common secret of cowardice barely restrained, the instinct to run or freeze or hide, and in many respects this was the heaviest burden of all, for it could never be put down, it required perfect balance and perfect posture. They carried their reputations. They carried the soldier's greatest fear, which was the fear of blushing. Men killed, and died, because they were embarrassed not to. It was what had brought them to the war in the first place, nothing positive, no dream of glory or honor, just to avoid the blush of dishonor. They died so as not to die of embarrassment. They crawled into tunnels and walked point and advanced under fire. Each morning, despite the unknowns, they made their legs move. They endured. They kept humping. They did not submit to the obvious alternative, which was simply to close the eyes and fall. So easy, really. Go limp and tumble to the ground and let the muscles unwind and not speak and not bulge until your buddies picked you up and lifted you into the chopper that would roar and dip its nose and carry you off to the world. A mere matter of falling, yet no one ever fell. It was not courage, exactly; the object was not valor. Rather, they were too frightened to be cowards.

By and large they carried these things inside, maintaining the masks of composure. They sneered at sick call. They spoke bitterly about guys who had found release by shooting off their own toes or fingers. Pussies, they'd say. Candy-asses. It was fierce, mocking talk, with only a trace of envy or awe, but even so the image played itself out behind their eyes.

They imagined the muzzle against flesh. So easy: squeeze the trigger and blow away a toe. They imagined it. They imagined the quick, sweet pain, then the evacuation to Japan, then a hospital with warm beds and cute geisha nurses.

80   And they dreamed of freedom birds.

At night, on guard, staring into the dark, they were carried away by jumbo jets. They felt the rush of takeoff. *Gone!* they yelled. And then velocity—wings and engines—a smiling stewardess—but it was more than a plane, it was a real bird, a big sleek silver bird with feathers and talons and high screeching. They were flying. The weights fell off; there was nothing to bear. They laughed and held on tight, feeling the cold slap of wind and altitude, soaring, thinking *It's over, I'm gone!*—they were naked, they were light and free—it was all lightness, bright and fast and buoyant, light as light, a helium buzz in the brain, a giddy bubbling in the lungs as they were taken up over the clouds and the war, beyond duty, beyond gravity and mortification and global entanglements—*Sin loi!* they yelled. *I'm sorry, motherfuckers, but I'm out of it, I'm goofed, I'm on a space cruise, I'm gone!*—and it was a restful, unencumbered sensation, just riding the light waves, sailing that big silver freedom bird over the mountains and oceans, over America, over the farms and great sleeping cities and cemeteries and highways and the golden arches of McDonald's, it was flight, a kind of fleeing, a kind of falling, falling higher and higher, spinning off the edge of the earth and beyond the sun and through the vast, silent vacuum where there were no burdens and where everything weighed exactly nothing—*Gone!* they screamed. *I'm sorry but I'm gone!*—and so at night, not quite dreaming, they gave themselves over to lightness, they were carried, they were purely borne.

On the morning after Ted Lavender died, First Lieutenant Jimmy Cross crouched at the bottom of his foxhole and burned Martha's letters. Then he burned the two photographs. There was a steady rain falling, which made it difficult, but he used heat tabs and Sterno to build a small fire, screening it with his body, holding the photographs over the tight blue flame with the tips of his fingers.

He realized it was only a gesture. Stupid, he thought. Sentimental, too, but mostly just stupid.

Lavender was dead. You couldn't burn the blame.

Besides, the letters were in his head. And even now, without photographs, 85 Lieutenant Cross could see Martha playing volleyball in her white gym shorts and yellow T-shirt. He could see her moving in the rain.

When the fire died out, Lieutenant Cross pulled his poncho over his shoulders and ate breakfast from a can.

There was no great mystery, he decided.

In those burned letters Martha had never mentioned the war, except to say, Jimmy, take care of yourself. She wasn't involved. She signed the letters Love, but it wasn't love, and all the fine lines and technicalities did not matter. Virginity was no longer an issue. He hated her. Yes, he did. He hated her. Love, too, but it was a hard, hating kind of love.

The morning came up wet and blurry. Everything seemed part of everything else, the fog and Martha and the deepening rain.

He was a soldier, after all.   90

Half smiling, Lieutenant Jimmy Cross took out his maps. He shook his head hard, as if to clear it, then bent forward and began planning the day's march. In ten minutes, or maybe twenty, he would rouse the men and they would pack up and head west, where the maps showed the country to be green and inviting. They would do what they had always done. The rain might add some weight, but otherwise it would be one more day layered upon all the other days.

He was realistic about it. There was that new hardness in his stomach. He loved her but he hated her.

No more fantasies, he told himself.

Henceforth, when he thought about Martha, it would be only to think that she belonged elsewhere. He would shut down the daydreams. This was not Mount

Sebastian, it was another world, where there were no pretty poems or midterm exams, a place where men died because of carelessness and gross stupidity. Kiowa was right. Boomdown, and you were dead, never partly dead.

95 Briefly, in the rain, Lieutenant Cross saw Martha's gray eyes gazing back at him. He understood.

It was very sad, he thought. The things men carried inside. The things men did or felt they had to do.

He almost nodded at her, but didn't.

Instead he went back to his maps. He was now determined to perform his duties firmly and without negligence. It wouldn't help Lavender, he knew that, but from this point on he would comport himself as an officer. He would dispose of his good-luck pebble. Swallow it, maybe, or use Lee Strunk's slingshot, or just drop it along the trail. On the march he would impose strict field discipline. He would be careful to send out flank security, to prevent straggling or bunching up, to keep his troops moving at the proper pace and at the proper interval. He would insist on clean weapons. He would confiscate the remainder of Lavender's dope. Later in the day, perhaps, he would call the men together and speak to them plainly. He would accept the blame for what had happened to Ted Lavender. He would be a man about it. He would look them in the eyes, keeping his chin level, and he would issue the new SOPs in a calm, impersonal tone of voice, a lieutenant's voice, leaving no room for argument or discussion. Commencing immediately, he'd tell them, they would no longer abandon equipment along the route of march. They would police up their acts. They would get their shit together, and keep it together, and maintain it neatly and in good working order.

100 He would not tolerate laxity. He would show strength, distancing himself.

Among the men there would be grumbling, of course, and maybe worse, because their days would seem longer and their loads heavier, but Lieutenant Jimmy Cross reminded himself that his obligation was not to be loved but to lead. He would dispense with love; it was not now a factor. And if anyone quarreled or complained, he would simply tighten his lips and arrange his shoulders in the correct command posture. He might give a curt little nod. Or he might not. He might just shrug and say, Carry on, then they would saddle up and form into a column and move out toward the villages west of Than Khe.

CRITICAL THINKING QUESTIONS

1. As the leader of his platoon, the young Lieutenant Cross bears the heavy burden of power and responsibility. He blames himself for Ted Lavender's death. To what degree do you believe Cross is responsible?

2. Despite its terrible consequences, war is sometimes remembered as a time of bonding and friendship like no other. What is there in such a horrible situation that could make soldiers later miss it?

3. Sometimes the Vietnam War is portrayed to young people as the only war that fostered demonstrations and civil disobedience. Were there protests against

our involvement in World War I or II, or is the Hollywood image of happy, singing Army volunteers accurate?

WRITING TOPIC

Read Wilfred Owen's poem, "*Dulce Et Decorum Est*" (Chapter One, page 22). In O'Brien's story, find images which support Owen's **claim**. Substitute those images into the original poem.

Brady Udall (b. 1957)

He Becomes Deeply and Famously Drunk

I am a cowboy. There are others in this outfit who prefer to call themselves ranch hands or just "hands," maybe they think *cowboy* is a little too flamboyant for this day and age, who knows, but shit, I herd cows, I vaccinate, brand, dehorn and castrate cows, more often than not I smell exactly like a cow—I am a cowboy. I've been at this for nine months now and I figure I've earned the right to call myself whatever in God's name I please.

I am two months shy of eighteen years old, I'm covered with freckles and am quite good-looking if I can believe what the girls tell me. I am also a natural loud-mouth which has caused me no end of grief and misery. Pretty much all my life I've been hearing the same thing: take it easy, Archie, put a lid on it Archie, pipe the hell down. You hear this enough it gets on your nerves.

One of the good things about this kind of work: I can really let loose, talking and shouting and singing—at the top of my lungs if I want to and out in the brush there's no one to give a hooey but the cows. Something about my voice scares the cows, some of them are terrified of me, I swear it, when they hear me they get this rolling wild look in their eyes and start to running and climbing all over each other. My horse, Loaf, gets annoyed by all my talking and singing and every once in awhile she'll reach back and bite the hell out of my leg. I don't mind, I just hit her back, a good sock on the side of the head, and she won't try anything like that again for at least a couple weeks.

Before I came to work here I had this idea that A & C Ranch would be this big beautiful spread, full of rivers and green rolling hills, like that TV show *Big Valley*. I imagined myself as Heath Barkley, riding around on a shiny roan, wearing a vest and a silk scarf, smoking a long cigarillo and shooting bad guys lurking in the bushes. The actual ranch, I was sorry to learn, is plain and relatively small: fifteen hundred acres of overgrazed scrub land that can't support more than two hundred head at any one time. Mr. Platt, who is richer and more of a recluse than God, has his thousand-head herd spread out all over the place, on at least fourteen other pieces of land between here and the Navajo reservation, most of it government-owned. The sad truth is we spend more time zipping around in our pickup trucks than we do on our good and noble horses.

5   Today, for instance, we've got to go up around Sell's Pasture, a good forty-five-minute drive, to fix a busted windmill, a rickety fifty-footer that is a horror to climb. Of course it will be me, the new guy, climbing to the top of the damn thing, risking my neck and reputation. It's about five in the morning and I'm in the shower, singing the jingles to every TV commercial I can think of. Richard bangs on the bathroom door and shouts, "Archie, keep it down in there! Got-damn!"

     This is exactly what I'm talking about. I can't even take a shower without somebody having an opinion about it. Richard is one of the hands, he and I share a trailer out here on the ranch. He is the oldest of us, the veteran, and apparently his job is to keep an eye on me. Richard is short and middle-aged and one of these days I'm going to pick up his scrawny little body and break it over my knee if he is not careful. This morning Richard woke me up at five a.m. the way he does every morning, by shouting right in my ear, *Come to, you candy corn son of a bitch!* He learned this particular wake-up call in the Army and inflicts it on me each and every day. This kind of thing makes Richard feel like the big enchilada, so I let him get away with it.

     I yodel about six more jingles and then towel off and walk into the kitchen for a piece of toast, and Ted, the foreman, is there explaining to Richard how he wants to do things today. Ted lives in the old ranch house up on the hill with his wife and little girl. He had some serious childhood ailment and now he's got a lumpy over-sized head and hearing aids strapped to his big loose ears.

     "Change of plans," Ted says to me. "I'm taking Richard with me to help bring in the heifers from Copper Springs. I want you to pick up Jesus and get that windmill fixed. Take your time and fix it right. Take all day if you have to."

     "And put some pants on," Richard says. Richard absolutely hates my guts because I am bigger, younger, handsomer, and a hell of a lot smarter than he is.

10   I lift up the towel and show him my bare butt: one of the attributes women enjoy most about me. I sing a line from "Moon Over Georgia" in a girlish falsetto and do a few softshoe shuffles on the kitchen linoleum.

     Richard just sits there, red-faced, shoveling plain oatmeal into his mouth, unable to come up with anything to say. He is one of these literal types who simply cannot comprehend sarcasm or humor of any sort. He reaches over and grabs the Volume A encyclopedia from the kitchen counter and begins studying it, his nose inches from the page. About six months ago Richard decided that he was going to get himself educated. Instead of wasting all that time and money on a college education, he decided to read the entire Encyclopedia Brittanica, the whole blasted thing, from A to Z.

     Richard is terribly proud of himself for coming up with a way to become a genius and a scholar for only $99.95 in twelve easy monthly installments. Problem is, it's been over half a year now and Richard is only about a third of the way through the first volume. He is now an authority on aardvarks, acupuncture, and John Adams, but he'll be collecting social security before he could tell you what a zygote is.

I go back to the laundry room and take Doug off his perch. He acts happy to see me, bobs his head and hunches his shoulders. I get a piece of dog kibble from a bag in the cupboard and he snatches it out of my hand so quick you'd think he's dying of starvation.

Doug is an eight-year-old male turkey vulture. Because he doesn't get much exercise, he's a little overweight, but he is a good bird, and I've become attached to him; some nights when he has trouble sleeping, I'll take him to bed with me and hold him against my chest until he gets drowsy enough to go to sleep perched on my bedpost. He used to belong to one R. L. Ledbetter, who worked for Mr. Platt and lived in this trailer with Richard until one early morning a couple of years ago when R.L. got run over by a garbage truck crossing the road. R.L. had worked for a few years as a rodeo clown and used Doug (short for Douglas Fairbanks) in one of his acts. In this rodeo act, R.L. would act like he got shot by a villain, and Doug would come flying in out of nowhere, land on his chest and start picking at him. R.L. trained Doug to do this by hiding a Corn Nut somewhere on his person and Doug would go picking around until he found it, R.L. squirming and cringing whenever Doug got too near his crotch. Apparently rodeo crowds found this hilarious.

Even though Richard doesn't enjoy Doug's company all that much, he is convinced he can teach Doug to talk. Sometimes I'll come home and find Richard at the kitchen table, with Doug perched on the back of a chair and Richard saying something like, "Come on, Doug, say 'bazooka.' Ba-*zoo*-ka." And Doug sitting there mum as a fence post, watching barn swallows buzzing past the window. Richard says he read somewhere that vultures have the same vocal apparatus as parrots, and with enough persistence he thinks Doug could become a talking vulture. So far, Doug hasn't said a word.   15

I go back into my room where I put on jeans, a T-shirt—it's going to be a hot son of a bitch out there today—and a pair of workboots. I have to wear these run-of-the-mill clodhoppers because I've yet to find a pair of cowboy boots that will fit my splayed feet. When I go outside and fire up the old Ford the sun is just coming up and long shadows stretch out under the sage and creosote. I let the engine run for a minute, then I lay on the accelerator like Richard Petty in his prime, spraying dust and gravel everywhere, and head out on Witchicume Road, on my way to pick up Jesus.

I came out to the A & C to get my life turned around. My mother made the arrangements, did all the sweet-talking to get me out here and her theory goes something like this: you take your loudmouth juvenile delinquent with bad table manners, stick him out in the middle of nowhere, bust his balls with honest hard labor, and maybe, just maybe, he will turn out to be the upstanding citizen you hoped for all along. I'm pretty certain the folks out here weren't all that hot to hire a city kid with no ranch experience and a history with the law, but Ted was an old acquaintance of my father, and finally he gave in.

The truth is I've always wanted to come back, always harbored secret desires about strapping on the chaps and riding fences. I was born only forty miles from here, in Holbrook, and I lived on the ranch the first four and a half years of my life until my father was killed and my mother took me to live in Stillwater, Oklahoma, her hometown. My father was the ranch foreman and we lived in the old house where Ted and his family live now. Even though I can't remember anything at all about living here, I did some work on this ranch, in my own way, all those years ago. My mother told me that the winter I turned four, my father would take me out on the feed runs, put the old International into compound and let me steer, kneeling on the seat, while he stood in the back, breaking bales and pitching hay to the cows standing in the snow.

In Oklahoma I spent my energy talking too much, getting into fights, drinking booze, smashing mailboxes, pretty much being obnoxious however and wherever I could. I have something wrong with me, something bad inside that builds up until I have to let it out by talking, shouting, raging, letting it all loose, even if there is no one there to listen. (I even thrash and holler in my sleep sometimes—one more thing Richard holds against me.) But there are times when the only way I can get back to feeling normal again is by beating the shit out of someone who may not even deserve it, or by destroying something, it doesn't really matter what. When I feel this way, I get to punching or smashing or kicking and I can feel this blackness pouring out of me and I just keep going, it's a great feeling, just letting go, flailing away, until I feel empty and clean again. I've hurt some people and wrecked a lot of perfectly innocent cars, dishware, phone booths, electronic goods, what have you. Even though a lot of my teachers called me gifted (over and over again: unlimited potential! a diamond in the rough!), I never finished high school because they finally kicked me out once and for all. I've been arrested for battery, disorderly conduct, theft, vandalism, disturbing the peace, assaulting a police officer. I've been on probation since I was eleven years old.

20   I've seen therapists, psychiatrists, clergymen, even a hypnotist. My mother had high hopes for the hypnotist, but for some reason in my second session with the poor old guy I came out of my trance and sucker-punched him a good one right in the face. I don't remember doing it, only remember waking up and seeing him sitting on the carpet, his nose spattered on his face like a piece of rotten watermelon.

I have a probation officer, Ms. Condley, who calls Ted every week to make sure I haven't busted anyone's lip or committed an act of debauchery. Ms. Condley calls me every week, too, and asks me about my feelings, about my dreams and aspirations, it's all very sensitive, but she never says goodbye without reminding me that if I break my probation, if I slip up even a little, get even a little drunk or involve myself in some minor fisticuffs, I'll be sent off to boot camp and won't get out till I'm twenty-nine. So far I have been able to keep my ass clean. My only serious difficulty is keeping myself from beating the day-lights out of Richard.

A few weeks before I moved back out here I went to the public library and stole the only book I could find on cowboys. I wanted to get some general how-to information (how to put on a saddle, how to make a lasso, how to mount a horse) so that when I got here I wouldn't look like a complete fool. The book didn't give tips or anything like that, it was just a lot of quaint old bullshit about the cowboys of yore. I read the whole thing anyway. Under a pen and ink drawing of a couple of dirty cowpunchers weaving down Main Street, arm in arm, clutching half-empty whiskey bottles, was this caption:

After a mythic cattle drive or a bone-wearying spring roundup, the cowboy, looking for release and diversion, commonly finds his way to the nearest saloon where he becomes deeply and famously drunk.

I remember this because it describes to a T my father and the way he died. Like the cowboys in the picture, he liked to celebrate after a big job by getting himself good and hammered. It was his only vice and the one thing my mother could not stand about him. The day he died, they had finished getting the herd down off the mountain for the winter (nearly a two-week job) and he went into town to throw a few down with his crew at the Sure Seldom. He was two solid hours into his drinking when Calfred Pulsipher, a piece-of-shit well-digger with a lazy eyeball, came around to pick a fight. Calfred and my father had been good friends in their younger years, but Calfred had carried a grudge against my father ever since he lost his starting quarterback job to him on the Salado Wildcats eight-man football team. Apparently, Calfred said some terrible things about my mother, right there in front of my father's crew—sick, perverted things—and finally my father invited Calfred outside to settle it. Calfred went outside first and in the thirty seconds or so it took my drunk father to find the door, Calfred had time to pick up an industrial jack from the back of his pickup. When my father stepped out into the cold night air, ready to whip Calfred's sorry ass and be done with it, Calfred brought down the jack full force, right on top of his head. My father went down, stayed face down in the gravel for a minute or so, dead still, and suddenly got up punching with everything he had, as if the blow not only sobered him up but also lit a fire under his ass. He got some fine licks in on Calfred before one of the sheriff's deputies came and arrested them both.

Even though my father's head had stopped bleeding, the sheriff wanted to call   25 the ambulance in from Round Valley (there was no doctor in Salado in those days) but my father kept assuring everyone he was feeling fine, all he needed was a few more drinks to get rid of the headache he was having. In the end, the sheriff stuck them both in the same jail cell to sleep off their drunk. Some time that night in that puke-smelling cell full of drunks and no-goods and bums, my father died of bleeding in the brain, his head resting on the lap of Calfred Pulsipher, the man who killed him.

Out here in Arizona, Jesus is my only real friend. He is a tiny wetback, barely five feet tall with his boots on and even though he's lived on American soil for over two decades his English is as piss-poor as if he showed up here last Christmas. He has star-quality teeth and likes to keep his hair coifed and oiled with one curl hanging down on his forehead in the manner of old time movie actors. He's worked for Mr. Platt off and on for a good many years and while the others here resented me, pissed on me for being young and ignorant, enjoyed watching me make a fool of myself, Jesus helped me out from the start, taking time to show how to dally a rope, say, or throw a calf for branding.

Right now Jesus is explaining, in his own way, why he doesn't like people calling him a Mexican. He doesn't consider himself a Mexican at all, he says, because he is actually a full-blooded Yaqui Indian and very proud of it, a direct descendant of the Aztecs, who were, according to him, the most proud and powerful nation the world ever saw. And who, according to him, had it not been for malaria, typhoid and other white-man plagues, would have kicked some Spaniard ass.

"I'm not eh-Spanish," he says, thumping his chest like a little brown Tarzan. "I'm Yaqui."

"It's not *eh*-Spanish," I say. "That's not how you say it. You got to get your S's right. She sells seashells by the sea shore. Okay, I'm going to say a word and you repeat. Snoopy."

30   "Eh-Snoopy," Jesus says.

"Sssssnoopy," I say.

"Ehhhhh-snoopy," Jesus says.

"Ah shit," I say.

"Ah shit," says Jesus, proud of himself for making such great advancement in the language.

35   The guy truly is hopeless. Since he has done so much for me, I figured the least I could do was help him polish his English, but now, after nine months of correcting his pronunciation and word order, he hasn't improved a bit.

"Why don't you want to be an American?" I say. "All you have to do is get your green card, you've lived here long enough. Then you won't have to run from the border patrol any more."

"American?" Jesus says, a look of disgust twisting his wide brown face. "Americanos fat pigs, you know, honk honk."

"I'm fat, is that what you're saying?"

Jesus lifts up my T-shirt to have a look. He nods gravely. "Maybe," he says.

40   We stop for gas and coffee at Sud Baker's, a little eatery/truck stop. Once we've finished off our eggs and sausage, and with Jesus taking forever in the john, I pick up a loose copy of the local paper, *The Apache County Sentinel,* and there, right on the front page is that son of a bitch Calfred Pulsipher himself. It looks like an old wedding picture: Calfred's got these ridiculous lambchop sideburns and a thick polyester tie and one of his eyes, his left one, seems to be looking at the mole on his forehead while the other is pointed straight ahead. A fat woman, Calfred's wife, I guess, is sitting next to him, all dressed up. Underneath the picture it reads, *The Pulsipher children would like to congratulate Calfred and Erma on the occasion of their twenty-fifth wedding anniversary.*

A trembling starts in my stomach and moves out to my arms and hands. When I first got here I tried to look up Calfred's name in the phone book and when I couldn't find it, I convinced myself that he was dead or had moved away to Alaska. I thought I wouldn't have to worry about him anymore.

A secret: since I was five years old I have been a murderer in my heart. I've tortured, mutilated, torn, skewered, beaten, killed Calfred Pulsipher ten thousand times over. I've burned his house down, kidnapped his children, cut the head off his dog. I've dreamed, time and again, about being there that night at the Sure Seldom. In my dreams I've stopped him from killing my father in various ways, perforating him with an ice pick, shotgunning him in the gut, beating him bloody with a chain. I even made plans, back when I was twelve or thirteen and crazed with puberty, for stealing a car and a big-ass case of dynamite and coming all the way out here and blowing him into the outer reaches of space.

Growing up, I used to read a lot, mostly Zane Grey and Louis L'Amour, and in those books if someone killed a member of your family or even a friend, it was pretty much your *duty* to pay the son of a bitch back. It's what anyone who had any courage or sense of justice did; it's what cowboys did. It's what my father would have done.

My father's name was Quinn. He was a big man with a barrel chest, curly red hair, a missing front tooth—everybody loved him. He lost the tooth to the back hoof of an Appaloosa gelding and he never got it fixed because he thought the hole in his face made him look friendlier. He was an excellent golfer (ten handicap), liked old blues music, and had a deep-seated fear of bees. Although I was a kid, not much more than a toddler when he died, I know all kinds of things—facts, stories, anecdotes—about him. After my mother took me away to Stillwater, friends would call or sometimes stop in and they'd tell me things my father used to do, the kind of man he was. I remember a few of the visitors, usually it would be a man in Wranglers, alone, or maybe with a frizzy-haired woman with big earrings, and always they'd say things like, *Oh my God, he looks just like Quinn, doesn't he?* Or, *Listen there, he's even got Quinn's voice.* And without fail my mother would break down and have to leave the room.

My mother, I think, went certifiably crazy during the year after my father's death. Nobody really knows about this except me, because I was the only one who got to witness all the lunatic things she did. One of my clearest memories is of my mother, just a few days after we'd moved to Stillwater, running outside in only her underwear as a stranger's car pulled up to the curb, hysterical and shouting, "I knew he'd come back, oh my God, you're back! Look Archie, Daddy's home!" Or the time she ripped through the house, clearing out cupboards and cabinets, trashing the attic, sure my father was there because she could smell his English Leather cologne.

Finally, she went to see a doctor who introduced her to the wonderful world of pills. It's a world she's been living in ever since.

Now, out here on the ranch, I'm always finding reminders of him. A few weeks ago, I was down near the mud pond just south of the big house, mending fence with Richard when I found the letter Q carved deep into one of the anchor posts near the dam. It's kind of a tradition out here for the person that builds a fence to carve his initial into the final anchor post and I knew without a doubt it was my father that had done it. I imagined him there in the very spot I was standing, his shirt off, his big round shoulders covered with sweat, making cracks with his crew and grinning that gap-toothed grin while he cut his first initial into the thick cedar post with a buck knife.

By the time Jesus and I get to Sell's Pasture it is already upwards of ninety degrees and with the white sun burning into everything it feels like we're moving across the surface of Venus. After we pull off the highway, I have to guide the truck over three or four miles of a rutted two-track, me and Jesus bouncing all over the seat, the stiff sagebrush on the truck's underside like fingernails on a chalkboard. On our way over to the windmill Jesus notices a bad case of pinkeye on a Hereford calf. By the time he's got the medicine kit from the glove compartment, run the calf down on foot, lassoed it, thrown it to the ground and begun to doctor the eye, all the time keeping one eye on the calf's very pissed-off mother, I've climbed the ladder up to the platform and am doing my best to dismantle the windmill head and see what the problem is.

The windmill stopped working only a few days ago, so the galvanized holding tank is still half full of algae-green water and a few mangy cows are hanging around to check out what's going on. They don't have anything better to do, blinking those big dull eyes. I'll tell you one thing about cows: they're dumb-asses. They're so dumb it's hard to understand how stupid they really are.

50   Once in awhile I'll look down and see a metallic flash in the green water—huge shaggy goldfish and carp they put in the tanks to keep the algae down. These things grow to be as big as poodles and they swim around flapping their tails like they own the tank.

About a hundred yards away, over next to a juniper tree, Jesus struggles to keep the bawling calf down while performing the delicate work of injecting medicine directly into its eyeball with a syringe. I shout encouragements from up on my perch and Jesus grunts and hisses and calls the calf a bigtime donkey turd. By the time he's done he's sweating, covered with dust, the calf has crapped green pudding all over his pearl-buttoned shirt and what's worse, it's not even ten o'clock in the morning. He walks up to the holding tank, slings his hat like a Frisbee, sheds the rest of his clothes and steps in, the thick water closing around him. He slides down so that his head is just above water, still as a turtle on a rock.

I am banging away with my Vise-Grips at a stuck bolt, trying to loosen it, when I miss the bolt completely. My momentum throws me off balance, the whole windmill shifting underneath me, and I slip sideways off the side of the platform. I grab one of the supports to keep myself from falling, but my legs are dangling out from under me and with my White Mule work gloves on I can't get a good grip on the smooth, two-inch pipe. My hands begin to slide and my stomach curls up on itself and I look down past my feet and try to figure out the best way to fall without snapping my spine. Below me, Jesus leaps out of the tank, naked as a newborn, the huge fish writhing and bucking in the swampy water, and begins scrambling up the metal scaffolding, his wet hands and feet causing him to slip and flail and clutch.

I start bellowing, a loud panicked sound like a heifer giving birth, which causes all the cows in sight to spook and set off sprinting for the safety of the trees. Somehow I hold out, yelling the whole time, until Jesus reaches the platform from the other side and grabs my belt and with the strength of a man twice his size hauls me up.

I lie on my back for a minute staring at the blank sky and listening to my heart thumping so hard it sounds like bones are popping in my chest. Above me Jesus is standing there all goose-pimply with this huge grin on his face, as if my near-death experience has made his day. He keeps shaking his head; he just can't get over it. "Arshie hanging, feet kicking, help, help!" Jesus says, pantomiming the whole incident. "Arshie shouting like woman, oooooooha!, every cow runs away."

I get up and try to grab him but he ducks out of the way and cowers at the cor- 55 ner of the platform, mocking me, covering his head with his hands. "Big fat Americano scaring me. Oh boy," he says.

I stop going after him; I'm still a little nervous about one of us falling off this thing, and then I notice that Jesus has the biggest pecker I've ever seen. I get a good look at it and there's no doubt—I've been in a lot of locker rooms and seen quite a few, but this one takes the cake.

"That's a considerable pecker you've got there," I tell him, keeping a good grip on one of the supports.

He looks down at it, lifts it up with his hand like it's a vegetable he's considering purchasing at the supermarket. "Oh mama," he says.

He picks up the Vise-Grips, goes right to work on the stuck bolt, and starts lamenting that his wife took his kids to visit relatives down in Mexico and it's been two long weeks since his *pendejo* saw any action. He begins to croon some mournful Sonoran ballad, using the Vise-Grips like a microphone, and for some reason it seems perfectly appropriate that he is nude and fifty feet in the air.

We get the head dismantled and find that the windmill needs nothing more 60 than new suction leathers. In no time at all we've got the thing fixed, put back together, and I've joined Jesus down in the cow tank.

The inside of the tank is as slimy as frog innards and the huge fish curl around my stomach and legs and I still haven't decided whether the whole sensation is disgusting or kind of pleasant. We sit there for awhile and even though the windmill has been fixed, there is no wind to speak of and the big fan is completely still and useless as before. This kind of silence drives me crazy and I bear it for as long as I can until I ask the question I've been waiting to ask somebody for nine months: "You know who Calfred Pulsipher is?"

Jesus, who appeared to be falling asleep, sits up and looks right at me, but he only shrugs and mumbles something I can't understand.

"What?" I say.

"Nada, nada," he says.

"Do you know him?"   65

"Pool-see-fur," Jesus says, rolling the word across his tongue. I don't mind Jesus screwing around with me but sometimes he drives me nuts.

"Come on, you Mexican," I say. "Does he live around here?"

"Oh, he live around somewhere."

"Where?"

Now he's giving me that sly half grin that Latin males everywhere are famous 70 for. "Why you want to know?"

Since I've been here I haven't talked about Calfred Pulsipher or my father with anyone and now that I have, it feels like I've betrayed myself in some way. Even though I'm pretty sure everybody on the ranch knows my situation, not one of them has ever mentioned it, and that's the way I like it.

We look at each other across the tank, Jesus waiting for an answer and me not ready to give it.

Finally a mangy Hereford, either a very brave or a very stupid one, comes strolling right up to the tank to have a drink. Jesus hollers at the cow, calling it some of the most vile words in the English language and his pronunciation is absolutely perfect.

I didn't believe I could actually *enjoy* ranch work. I've heard some of the hands complain about certain kinds of work, mostly jobs that require getting down out of the saddle, but I pretty much love it all: branding, clearing ditches, building fence, irrigating. I love hauling hay, throwing those bales around as if they have *offended* me. I don't even mind getting up before the crack of dawn, even if I have to do it with Richard the army general barking in my ear. I like the way the world feels empty at that time of day; it seems as if you are the only one alive, early in the morning when you're up before everybody else and you can step out into the low light with your cup of coffee and hear a horse chewing grass from two hundred yards away.

75   Every day you get something new thrown at you; I mean, one thing I've never been around here is bored. You work all day, so busy sweating and busting your ass that you don't even have time to think; you go and go and go until you look up and notice the sun is nearly down and it's time to pack it in. There's nothing as nice as that ride home; the truck rumbling loosey-goosey down the road with a mind of its own, the radio hissing out Mexican trumpets, that sweet aching tiredness settling deep in your joints. You go home and fix yourself some dinner and even though it's nothing more than chili out of a can and a tube of instant biscuits it's the best damned meal you've ever had.

The only thing that will ruin a day like this is getting a call from my mother. My mother calls once or twice a week to make sure I'm caught up on all her problems. A few days ago she called me just as we were getting in from a day of calving out heifers to tell me that she had broken up with her boyfriend.

"Archie?" she said. "Archie? Are you there, honey?" Her voice was as high-pitched as a train whistle.

"I'm right here," I said.

Suddenly she began to weep and I knew immediately that she had taken too many of one pill or had mixed some up that weren't supposed to be mixed. She was speaking in that hysterical little-girl voice that I remember hearing so much after my father was killed.

80   "He left me, Arch, he's gone." She was practically shrieking. I didn't know who the hell she was talking about. I was able to piece together that her current boyfriend, a hot tub salesman named Chet, had decided to go back to his ex-wife in Florida. I told her I was sure she'd be able to find another boyfriend in a day or two.

"I miss you honey," she cried. "I want to see you. You're the only one left."

A number of times she's called me, trying to get me to come home, even though she herself is the one that did what was necessary to get me out here. One particularly bad night a couple of months ago she accused me of abandoning her, just as my father had done. Every time I talk to her it breaks the spell; I'm not Archie the cowboy anymore, but Archie the delinquent with his afflicted mother and dead father, with all his crimes against society. Honest, it makes me feel like crap.

Good thing that's a feeling that doesn't last long. I can hang up the phone, go to bed, sleep like a dead man, give Richard a hundred-watt smile when he rousts me out of bed, ready to get out on the open range and make those cows pay.

I've just come into town from shoveling about three tons of cowshit out at the loading corrals and now I'm here in a bar called Whirly Burly's (the guy at the door didn't card me; because of my six-four frame and five-o'clock shadow I haven't been carded since I was fourteen). I've decided to go through with it, I won't wait any longer: I'm going to locate Calfred Pulsipher and let him have it. I figured the natural place to look for him would be a bar; the man was a full-time drunk and I doubt he's changed his ways. But, I have to admit, this doesn't seem the kind of place you'd find somebody like Calfred Pulsipher, full as it is with a bunch of yahoos dressed up like they're waiting to audition for *Oklahoma!*

85

As I search the crowd, looking for something like the face I saw in the paper, I have this heavy, sick feeling in my gut. What if I do see him? What am I going to do? I've thought a lot about this, especially in the past few days, I've gone over and over it in my mind. My plan is simple and just: I'll do it to him the way he did it to my father: I'll pick a fight. I will *make* him fight me. The only difference is I won't need to use a forty-pound jack to finish him off.

But what about afterwards? Don't think I haven't considered that. Calfred Pulsipher killed my father and wasn't even given a trial. An autopsy was done and they said they could not infallibly trace the bleeding to any of the blows he received. Small town, bogus bullshit. My mother kept all the newspaper clippings and they tell the whole story; the way they saw it, two good old boys got drunk, had a bit of a scuffle, and one of them had the misfortune of getting killed. Sending somebody to jail wouldn't make anything better, would it? Why make a bad situation worse?

Just thinking about it makes my blood go lava-hot and I want to grab the chair I'm in and start smashing things and people. Even if I get thrown in the clink, *even* if they send me there forever, I've got to go through with it. I owe it to my father. I owe it to my mother and to myself. It's the one thing I want to get right in this fucked-up life of mine.

I sip my Dr Pepper and watch people pushing through the big swinging wooden doors and each time I get this needle-jab of dread in my chest, thinking it might be him, but it's only these assholes in their creased blue jeans. Honest, I'd like to line them up and whale the shit out of them, one by one, just for practice. And this music they all listen to. I may like the cowboy life but nobody says I have to listen to their music.

Everyone starts clearing chairs and lining up to do these ridiculous syncopated honky-tonk dance steps. Even though I smell like the end of civilization and I'm not wearing Tony Lamas and a shiny belt buckle the size of a dessert plate, a few of these swivel-hipped cowgirls with moisture in their cleavages come up and ask me to dance. I put on my best smile and politely decline; I have a lot on my mind.

90   I sit there and watch the clumps of young men crowded together, slamming beers and cat-calling the women, and for the first time since I've been in Arizona I feel lonely and a little homesick, sitting here by myself in a bar roaring with people having a good time.

Before going home I hit the remaining bars in Salado, all four of them, but there is not a sign of Calfred Pulsipher. When I drag my ass back to the trailer it's nearly one a.m. and I can see through the window that Richard, clad in camouflage-style long johns, has fallen asleep in his recliner with the Volume A encyclopedia nestled in his groin. I know he is waiting up for me; he wants to be the one to catch me when I slip up.

I'm tired but I don't feel like dealing with Richard, so I take a walk up the hill toward the ranch house. Though I hadn't meant to, I end up standing on the front lawn of the house, looking up at the dark windows, thinking: I used to live in this house. It is white, two-storied and has a wide covered porch with a built-in swinging love seat. In the nine months I've been here I've never stepped foot in this house, never really had any desire to, until now.

I walk around the place a couple of times, tripping over a Big Wheel, nearly falling into one of those plastic baby-pools, and finally I decide—what can it hurt?—to take a look inside. The only first-floor window I can find that doesn't have the shades drawn is back behind a thick mass of bushes. I use a breast-stroke swimming motion to claw my way in and find myself looking into what is probably the family room: pictures on the wall, a cowhide couch, a grandfather clock, a collection of old Coca-Cola bottles on the mantel. Everything is dark and shadowed, but I try to imagine what the room would look like in the light of day, what my mother—a young, pretty version—might have looked like sitting on the couch, or my father over in the corner, winding the clock.

I strain, I try, but nothing; I can't seem to jog a single memory. Then, just as I'm pulling myself out of the bushes, I hear something behind me and there's Ted in nothing but boxer shorts and unlaced running shoes holding a .22 pistol. His legs and chest are the color of mayonnaise.

95   "Hey," he says, squinting. He's not wearing his glasses and I can tell he doesn't know who I am—I think about making a break for it. Finally, I whisper, "Ted, it's Archie."

Ted fiddles with one of his hearing aids and says, "Archie?"

"Couldn't sleep," I say. "I'm out for a walk."

"Is there something wrong?" Ted says. "Something you need to talk about?"

I think of the questions I would love to ask Ted: *What was my father like when you knew him? Do we really have the same looks, the same way of talking? When you moved into the house did it smell like English Leather?* But I keep my mouth shut.

100   Ted looks at me for a minute, as if he's trying to make some kind of decision, and then he says, "That Miss Condley woman called tonight. She tried calling over to your place but you weren't there all night. She was pretty upset."

"Shit," I say. I'd completely forgotten it was Tuesday, the day Ms. Condley calls every week.

"Five o'clock's a bitch, Archie," Ted says, turning around to go inside. "I'd get to bed if I was you."

On my way to the trailer a wave of exhaustion hits me and I can barely put one foot in front of the other. Careful not to wake Richard, I check in on Doug who is pacing the floor of the laundry room like an expectant father, back and forth, back and forth, no doubt full of worries of his own—an insomniac if there ever was one. I pick him up and take him to bed with me. I lie under the covers and hold him tight against my chest—this kind of pressure calms him for some reason—and pretty soon he's making this gurgling noise in the back of his throat, almost like the purring of a cat. When he's good and relaxed I put him up on the bedpost where he hunkers right down and nods off. Crazy as it sounds, it comforts me to have him there, above me in the dark while I sleep.

Instead of lounging on the couch watching *Cheers* after work, I'm driving hell-bent-for-leather in a lavender Oldsmobile packed with illegal aliens. My blood is hopped up with adrenaline and I'm doing well over seventy with an old Mexican woman asleep in my lap.

This all started last night after surveying the bars and my little run-in with Ted. 105 I barely got to sleep and the next thing I knew there was Jesus, right in my bedroom, tugging on my big toe. "Arshie," he whispered. "Wake it up."

I could tell right away something was the matter; instead of that what-the-hell grin he always wears, his face was pinched and worried. And what's more, he'd once vowed never to step foot in a residence which housed a "big dirty-shit buzzard," as he put it. But here he was.

He jabbered in a mixture of English and Spanish and finally I got the gist of the problem; his family was stuck at the border. Jesus' wife and kids go down to visit family once or twice a year and they've always had someone, a contact, who would arrange for them to get across the border, bribe the right people, and drive them up to Salado. Now apparently, that contact had disappeared and the family was waiting at the border down near Nogales; Jesus had made arrangements for them to get across but there was nobody to pick them up. Jesus himself couldn't risk going; not only did he not have a driver's license (if he was stopped on the highway he'd end up on the other side of the border, too), he was supposed to go with Ted to the livestock auction in Albuquerque.

He pulled a fist-sized wad of money out of his pocket. "I pay big cash."

I pushed the wad away and told him he was insulting me with his money. What was a favor between friends? Jesus eyed me like he thought I was crazy, then began outlining what he wanted me to do.

My work today involved digging out several cattle guards and I worked like a 110 man on fire to get done early. I finished by four o'clock, drove the Ford home, and there was the '72 Oldsmobile sitting out in front of the trailer just as Jesus said it would be. He had borrowed the car from his Aunt Lourdes, and I figured it would be an inconspicuous looking vehicle, but this one looked like a pimp/drug pusher special. The damn thing was about as long as your average school bus and *purple.*

It drove like a champ, though. It's a four-hour drive down to Nogales but I made it in just under three, the huge rosary on the rearview mirror clacking against the windshield the whole way. By the time I got there it was just getting dark and starting to drizzle. I had no trouble finding the spot Jesus described to me; about eight miles west of Nogales a small utility road runs parallel to the twelve-foot border fence, which is intersected by some railroad tracks. Above the tracks two red warning lights cast their glow over everything, making you feel like you're in hell.

I had assumed that the family would be there, already across, but the place was as quiet and empty as the rest of the desert. I could hear coyotes shouting at each other off in the distance.

I sat there a good hour, seeing nothing, hearing nothing but the coyotes, getting more worried by the minute. With the racket the coyotes were making, and the perfect stillness of everything else, along with the red glow of the lights, I got paranoid. I was scared, I'll admit it. I wanted to fire up that long purple machine and get the hell away. On the way down I'd worried about getting back in time for Ms. Condley to call; since she missed me last night I knew she would be calling tonight, and being out of the house again would look suspicious. But now I was simply spooked about getting caught; it's not something I've checked on, but transporting illegal aliens is most likely a felony and would land me in some serious shit.

I got out of the car, pacing around in the mud, stopping to listen once in a while, until I heard what sounded like a car motor out in the dark. I strained my ears and after awhile I heard voices that sounded like they were coming from the other side of the fence. About a hundred yards off, in a shallow ravine, I saw movement. I crept closer and could just make out somebody working on the fence with what looked like a pair of wire-cutters.

115   I counted ten people coming under, a few of them children. When I agreed to pick up Jesus' family, I thought he meant his wife and kids, not the whole bunch. They all started off in the opposite direction from me, lugging shopping sacks full of belongings. It was obvious they could not see me so I flashed my headlights to let them know where I was. Immediately someone swore in Spanish and everyone began running towards the car, shouting and bumping into each other. About halfway to the car, one of the kids, apparently spooked and bewildered by this whole affair, peeled off to the left and began running helter-skelter through the brush. I went after him, using a little cowboy geometry; when going after a steer you don't pursue him directly, you estimate where his path will take him and you head out for that point. The kid, however, didn't cooperate, zigzagging like a rabbit under fire, with me high-stepping it through the mud behind him, clown-like.

By the time I was able to corral the kid and carry him back to the car, everyone had most of their belongings stuffed into the trunk, themselves jammed in the car, and some old lady was at the wheel, cranking the key and gunning the accelerator. I convinced her to scoot over and let me take the controls, and just as we started out, a pair of headlights with a search beam on top came over a hill about half a mile away. Who knows, it could have been some redneck out spot-lighting deer, but at that moment I was sure the border patrol, the FBI and CIA were all bearing down on us. Everyone shouted at once and the grandma put up a high-pitched wail, the kind you hear at third-world funerals. The car fishtailed in the mud and lumbered over clumps of cactus and mesquite; I kept the lights off so I had no idea where I was going. I'm a veteran of chases like these, but this time I was scared out of my mind, pretty much like everybody else in the car. Somebody in back prayed to the Virgin Mary, the kids screamed, Grandma wailed, and for once in my life I kept perfectly quiet.

It didn't take long for my eyes to adjust to the darkness and pretty soon I found myself on a washboard dirt road heading god-knows-where. A couple of times we saw headlights, way off in the distance, which made the Grandma start up her wail, inducing the kids in back to commence their crying again.

But now, after about a half hour of searching, we've got ourselves back on the highway and everybody seems to have calmed. Grandma is so relaxed she's snoring like a lumber-jack. By the time we make it to Salado, it's near midnight and pretty much everybody in the car except me is asleep. When I pull into Jesus' front yard, I can see him sitting under the old basketball hoop, his hands clamped together between his legs. I pull to a stop, shut off the engine and suddenly it's chaos again, people shouting and trying to untangle themselves, babies crying, Grandma giving orders.

As I help pull belongings out of the trunk I watch Jesus gather his two daughters and little son, hugging them, not willing to let go even though they are already squirming to get away. I know this is a common scene, a father being reunited with his kids, but for some reason, standing there in the dark on the other side of the car, I have to turn away. I look in the other direction, out at the lights of town, until Jesus comes up behind me and gives me a good whack on the back, saying, "Tank you, Arshie, very good," and holding a hand over his heart.

He invites me inside, but his tiny house is already overflowing with people, so   120 I ask him if I can take the Oldsmobile out for a drive. I've only had a couple hours of sleep in the last two days but I don't feel like going back to the trailer. Jesus says no problem, take the car to Las Vegas if you want.

I drive into Salado and stop at Burly's; I feel like talking to someone, blowing off a little steam, but the place is nearly empty tonight. Only a few old-timers sit at the bar, bending down to their shot glasses like birds drinking from a puddle. I take a table near the back and I sit there alone for a minute. I keep seeing that scene with Jesus and his kids and I feel so clenched and jumpy it's like I'm going to explode. So when the bartender calls over the bar, asking what do I want, without much hesitation I call back, "Shot of Jim Beam."

When the drink comes, I look at it for a minute before I lift it to my mouth. It's been less than a year since I had a drink, but the stuff scorches my throat like it's my first time ever. I sip the whiskey, swishing it around, and by the time I'm halfway finished with my second shot I've decided—it's almost like a revelation—that tonight is the night I'm going to take care of Calfred Pulsipher. I could wait around forever for him to come out of hiding, checking the bars, looking under every hat at the gas station and grocery store, or I could have some real-man balls and go directly to him.

Suddenly I can't stay a minute longer in that place, not even for a few more drinks, so I drop some money on the table, get into the car, and stop in at the Circle K for a six-pack. Then I'm on my way back to Jesus' house.

When I get there, the house is entirely dark. I figured everybody would still be up, celebrating or something, but the place is quiet as a tomb. Without meaning to I pound so hard on the door the whole house shakes.

125   I see a teenage girl—one of my passengers earlier tonight—peek through the window and then Jesus comes out, pants unzipped, shirt on inside-out. I can smell the damp scent of sex on him and there's no doubt I've just broken up the long-awaited reunion with his wife. He's in there putting that big pecker of his to good use and along comes Archie in the middle of the night to break things up.

I feel stupid and guilty, but I'm not going to let that stop me. "Jesus," I say, "I'm real sorry but I need you to tell me where Calfred Pulsipher lives."

"Ah?" Jesus says, peering out at me.

"I need to know where Calfred Pulsipher lives. Please."

"Now? You going there now?"

130   "Right now."

Jesus sighs, shouts back something inside to his wife, closes the door and steps outside next to me.

"Why you going there?" he says.

"All you have to do is tell me where."

"Come on," Jesus says, walking barefoot across the gravel and bullheads. He gets in his work truck and says, "I bring you."

135   I try to tell him that he only needs to give me directions, but he shakes his head, revs the engine, and says, "Come in."

I feel like cockroach shit for taking advantage of him like this, doing him a favor and then asking one in return right off the bat, ruining his night and everything. I try to tell him this on the way but he waves his hand at me without looking my way. I break one of the beers off the six-pack and hand it to him and he tosses it right out the window.

We're on the highway for a couple of miles before Jesus turns off on a tiny dirt road I've never noticed before. It's barely a cow track, full of mudholes and melon-sized boulders. Jesus keeps the truck on a straight course, heedless of the obstacles, and the truck jounces and rocks like a boat in high seas. I tear off one of the beers for myself; the whiskey I drank at Burly's hardly did a thing for me, and I know I'll need to be good and whacked-out to get through this whole thing, but the beer tastes sour and watery, and with all the bouncing around this truck is doing, I'm this close to throwing up all over the floor. So I chuck the remainder of the six-pack out the window, as far as it will go, and watch the cans jump and spray among the bushes. After what seems like miles of bump and rattle, Jesus turns again on another dirt road and suddenly stops.

"What's wrong?" I say.

"Here," he says.

I look around, seeing nothing but brush and slab-sided buttes, and then I no- 140 tice the shell of an old Buick sitting back off the road about thirty yards, and behind that, in the night-shadows of an old cottonwood, is a house no bigger than a rich man's bathroom. I look back at Jesus, who's staring out the windshield, and get out of the truck.

Walking toward that house it's like I'm a ghost, floating, nothing but air. I can't feel my feet touch the ground. I try not to think about what I'm doing, what I'm going to do. Once I'm within ten feet or so I can see that the house is a ramshackle adobe affair, mud showing through holes in the stucco. Somebody has done their best to make the place look nice, the tiny, half-dead lawn cluttered with ceramic elves, ducks whose wings spin when the wind blows, birdbaths and plastic sunflowers.

I step up on the porch and give the screen door three good raps. A long, sick minute passes before I hear someone shuffling along the floor. The porch light clicks on, the door opens toward me and somebody leans half into the light.

It takes me a moment to recognize Calfred Pulsipher. Instead of the young man in the newspaper picture, or the even younger man I've seen in my father's old yearbooks, this Calfred Pulsipher looks like he belongs in an old folk's home. His hair is thin and colorless, his back bowed, his skin papery and stained with coffee-colored blotches. An oxygen tube, strapped around his head, feeds into both his nostrils. He's pulling a wheeled tank behind him with one hand and in the other he's holding a rusty sawed-off shotgun, pointed at my stomach.

The light blinds him for a moment and he squints at me, bracing the screen door with his elbow. We stand there like that, two feet apart, staring at each other, until his eyes suddenly go wide, his mouth opens slowly, forming a circle, and he says, "Oh."

The gun slides out of his hand, bouncing off the threshold and clattering 145 against the oxygen tank.

I can't do anything but look from his right eye, which is locked on me, burning and wet, to his left, which is swiveling around in his head like a thing that's got a mind of its own. His brows are pushed up and together and his mouth is opening and closing without any sound.

He takes one stumbling step toward me, arms out. One of his knees buckles under him and he grabs my shirt, pulling himself back up, leaning into me, reaching up and putting his arms around my shoulders. I can feel his whiskers on my neck and I don't know if the strong, bitter smell of alcohol is coming from him or me. He holds his head against my collarbone, moving it back and forth, saying, "Oh, oh."

It would be so easy, all I would have to do is return his embrace, crush him in my arms until his bones cracked and his worthless lungs gave out. But I can't do it. I can't. My whole body feels numb and my hands are at my sides, as heavy and useless as hub caps.

He hangs on me like that, until Jesus steps out of the shadows and pulls me away. Jesus leads me back towards the truck and I make it only ten steps or so until I fall forward, my whole body gone limp with shame and relief. I catch myself with my hands and begin coughing into the dirt, it's like there are chunks of black matter dislodging themselves from deep inside, stuff that has been there forever is coming up, and I can't stop, my stomach heaving, and I begin to weep. I can't remember ever crying in my entire life, but I'm making up for it now, my sinuses burning with tears, my throat constricting on me, and I go like that, hacking and retching, unable to breathe, until I vomit violently into a clump of sagebrush.

150   Jesus stands over me, his hand on my back, and he says quietly, "Come on, Arshie. Get it up."

He wipes off my mouth with his shirt, helps me to my feet, and with his arm locked in mine, we start again for the truck. I look back and the last thing I see is Calfred Pulsipher still standing in the light, like a man caught in the bright beam of a spaceship.

The ride home is nothing more than a dense fog moving past, and when we get back to the trailer Doug is in the front room, waddling around in the dark like some deformed duck, picking crumbs off the carpet. Jesus kicks him out of the way, and Doug goes flapping toward the kitchen, a few black feathers coming loose. Jesus sits me down on the couch and asks me if I want him to stay with me. I tell him to get his ass on home where his wife is waiting for him to finish the job he'd started and he is out the door in a heartbeat.

Richard appears in his bedroom doorway, wearing his camo-pajamas, his hair smashed against one side of his head. "Hey, Ms. Condley called again," he says. "Sounds like you're in a little trouble."

"Ms. Condley can go to hell," I say, not caring whether Richard notices my puffy eyes or the thickness in my voice. "And so can you, for that matter."

155   Once Richard retreats to his room, I go and get Doug, who is sulking under the kitchen table, and take him outside. The sky has cleared and the stars are shining down and even though I've slept only a few minutes in the past few days, even though I'm exhausted and weak, there is still something inside me that needs to be released; I want to open up my lungs and shout like a maniac, wake everyone for miles. Instead, I take Doug in the crook of my arm and walk up the hill past the ranch house, which is glowing a faint, moonlit blue, all the way down to the mud pond where a few steers are standing around, rubbing their heads together. It's become such a bright night there's no difficulty at all in finding the anchor post, the one with my father's initial. I squat down next to that post and bite into it, hard, right near the Q. I bite so hard the muscles in my jaw begin to burn and I come away with a taste in my mouth of wood and salt and dust. I stand up, holding Doug close, looking down at the indentations my teeth made and a feeling of pride and certainty rises up in me. There is no doubt in my mind: this is my place, it's where I belong, and I'm here to stay.

CRITICAL THINKING QUESTIONS

1. This story centers on the concept of revenge. In the context of Archie's life, create a claim about vengeance. Point to specific details from the story that led you to this claim.

2. Given the facts of his life, Jesus might have been an angry character; however, he clearly is a positive force in Archie's life. Argue that Jesus is the hero in this story.

WRITING TOPIC

Archie's drive for revenge originates in a concept he gained from reading Westerns: "It's what anyone who had any courage or sense of justice did; it's what cowboys did" (par. 43). How is this quest admirable, and, at the same time, destructive?

Ed Vega (b. 1936)
Spanish Roulette

Sixto Andrade snapped the gun open and shut several times and then spun the cylinder, intrigued by the kaleidoscopic pattern made by the empty chambers. He was fascinated by the blue-black color of the metal, but more so by the almost toy-like quality of the small weapon. As the last rays of sunlight began their retreat from the four-room tenement flat, Sixto once again snapped the cylinder open and began loading the gun. It pleased him that each brass and lead projectile fit easily into each one of the chambers and yet would not fall out. When he had finished inserting the last of the bullets, he again closed the cylinder and, enjoying the increased weight of the gun, pointed it at the ceiling and pulled back the hammer.

"What's the piece for, man?"

Sixto had become so absorbed in the gun that he did not hear Willie Collazo, with whom he shared the apartment, come in. His friend's question came at him suddenly, the words intruding into the world he had created since the previous weekend.

"Nothing," he said, lowering the weapon.

"What do you mean, 'nothing'?" said Willie. "You looked like you were ready   5
to play Russian roulette when I came in, bro."

"No way, man," said Sixto, and as he had been shown by Tommy Ramos, he let the hammer fall back gently into place. "It's called Spanish roulette," he added, philosophically.

Willie's dark face broke into a wide grin and his eyes, just as if he were playing his congas, laughed before he did. "No kidding, man," he said. "You taking up a new line of work? I know things are rough but sticking up people and writing poetry don't go together."

Sixto put the gun on the table, tried to smile but couldn't, and recalled the last time he had read at the cafe on Sixth Street. Willie had played behind him, his hands making the drums sing a background to his words. "I gotta take care of some business, Willie," he said, solemnly, and, turning back to his friend, walked across the worn linoleum to the open window of the front room.

"Not like that, *panita*," Willie said as he followed him.

10   "Family stuff, bro."

"Who?"

"My sister," Sixto said without turning.

"Mandy?"

Sixto nodded, his small body taut with the anger he had felt when Mandy had finished telling him of the attack. He looked out over the street four flights below and fought an urge to jump. It was one solution but not *the* solution. Despairingly, he shook his head at the misery below: burned out buildings, torched by landlords because it was cheaper than fixing them; empty lots, overgrown with weeds and showing the ravages of life in the neighborhood. On the sidewalk, the discarded refrigerator still remained as a faceless sentinel standing guard over the lot, its door removed too late to save the little boy from Avenue B. He had been locked in it half the day while his mother, going crazy with worry, searched the streets so that by the time she saw the blue-faced child, she was too far gone to understand what it all meant.

15   He tried to cheer himself up by focusing his attention on the children playing in front of the open fire hydrant, but could not. The twilight rainbow within the stream of water, which they intermittently shot up in the air to make it cascade in a bright arc of white against the asphalt, was an illusion, *un engaño*, a poetic image of his childhood created solely to contrast his despair. He thought again of the crushed innocence on his sister's face and his blood felt like sand as it ran in his veins.

"You want to talk about it?" asked Willie.

"No, man," Sixto replied. "I don't."

Up the street, in front of the *bodega*, the old men were already playing dominoes and drinking beer. Sixto imagined them joking about each other's weaknesses, always, he thought ironically, with respect. They had no worries. Having lived a life of service to that which now beckoned him, they could afford to be light-hearted. It was as if he had been programmed early on for the task now facing him. He turned slowly, wiped an imaginary tear from his eyes and recalled his father's admonition about crying: "*Usted es un machito y los machos no lloran,* machos don't cry." How old had he been? Five or six, no more. He had fallen in the playground and cut his lip. His father's friends had laughed at the remark, but he couldn't stop crying and his father had shaken him. "*Le dije que usted no es una chancleta. ¡Apréndalo bien!*" "You are not a girl, understand that once and for all!"

Concerned with Sixto's mood, once again Willie tried drawing him out. "*Coño*, bro, she's only fifteen," he said. "*¿Qué pasó?*"

The gentleness and calm which Sixto so much admired had faded from Willie's 20
face and now mirrored his own anguish. It was wrong to involve his friend but perhaps that was part of it. Willie was there to test his resolve. He had been placed
there by fate to make sure the crime did not go unpunished. In the end, when it
came to act, he'd have only his wits and manhood.

"It's nothing, bro," Sixto replied, walking back into the kitchen. "I told you,
family business. Don't worry about it."

"Man, don't be like that."

There was no injury in Willie's voice and as if someone had suddenly punched
him in the stomach to obtain a confession, the words burst out of Sixto.

"*Un tipo la mangó en el rufo,* man. Some dude grabbed her. You happy now?"

"Where?" Willie asked, knowing that uttering the words was meaningless. "In 25
the projects?"

"Yeah, last week. She got let out of school early and he grabbed her in the elevator and brought her up to the roof."

"And you kept it all in since you came back from your Mom's Sunday night?"

"What was I supposed to do, man? Go around broadcasting that my sister got
took off?"

"I'm sorry, Sixto. You know I don't mean it like that."

"I know, man. I know." 30

"Did she know the guy? *Un cocolo,* right? A black dude. They're the ones that
go for that stuff."

"No, man. It wasn't no *cocolo.*"

"But she knew him."

"Yeah, you know. From seeing him around the block. *Un bonitillo,* man. Pretty
dude that deals coke and has a couple of women hustling for him. A dude named
Lino."

"*¿Bien blanco?* Pale dude with Indian hair like yours?" 35

"Yeah, that's the guy."

"Drives around in a gold Camaro, right?"

"Yeah, I think so." Willie nodded several times and then shook his head.

"He's Shorty Pardo's cousin, right?" Sixto knew about the family connection
but hadn't wanted to admit it until now.

"So?" he said, defiantly. 40

"Those people are crazy, bro," said Willie.

"I know."

"They've been dealing *tecata* up there in El Barrio since forever, man. Even
the Italians stay clear of them, they're so crazy."

"That doesn't mean nothing to me," said Sixto, feeling his street manhood,
the bravado which everyone develops growing up in the street, surfacing. Bad talk
was the antidote to fear and he wasn't immune to it. "I know how crazy they are,
but I'm gonna tell you something. I don't care who the dude is. I'm gonna burn him.
Gonna set his heart on fire with that piece."

"Hey, go easy, *panita,*" said Willie. "Be cool, bro. I know how you feel but that 45
ain't gonna solve nothing. You're an artist, man. You know that? A poet. And a

playwright. You're gonna light up Broadway one of these days." Willie was suddenly silent as he reflected on his words. He sat down on one of the kitchen chairs and lowered his head. After a few moments he looked up and said: "Forget what I said, man. I don't know what I'm talking about. I wouldn't know what to do if that happened to one of the women in my family. I probably would've done the dude in by now. I'm sorry I said anything. I just don't wanna see you messed up. And I'm not gonna tell you to go to the cops, either."

Sixto did not answer Willie. They both knew going to the police would serve no purpose. As soon as the old man found out, he'd beat her for not protecting herself. It would become a personal matter, as if it had been he who had submitted. He'd rant and rave about short skirts and lipstick and music and then compare everything to the way things were on the island and his precious hometown, his beloved Cacimar, like it was the center of the universe and the place where all the laws governing the human race had been created. But Sixto had nothing to worry about. He was different from his father. He was getting an education, had been enlightened to truth and beauty and knew about equality and justice. Hell, he was a new man, forged out of steel and concrete, not old banana leaves and coconuts. And yet, he wanted to strike back and was sick to his stomach because he wanted Lino Quintana in front of him, on his knees, begging for mercy. He'd smoke a couple of joints and float back uptown to the Pardo's turf and then blast away at all of them like he was the Lone Ranger.

He laughed sarcastically at himself and thought that in the end he'd probably back down, allow the matter to work itself out and let Mandy live with the scar for the rest of her life. And he'd tell himself that rape was a common thing, even in families, and that people went on living and working and making babies like a bunch of zombies, like somebody's puppets without ever realizing who was pulling the strings. It was all crazy. You were born and tagged with a name: Rodríguez, Mercado, Torres, Cartagena, Pantoja, Maldonado, Sandoval, Ballester, Nieves, Carmona. All of them, funny-ass Spanish names. And then you were told to speak English and be cool because it was important to try and get over by imitating the Anglo-Saxon crap, since that's where all the money and success were to be found. Nobody actually came out and said it, but it was written clearly in everything you saw, printed boldly between the lines of books, television, movies, advertising. And at the place where you got your love, your mother's milk, your rice and beans, you were told to speak Spanish and be respectful and defend your honor and that of the women around you.

"I'm gonna burn him, Willie," Sixto repeated. "Gonna burn him right in his *güevos*. Burn him right there in his balls so he can feel the pain before I blow him away and let God deal with him. He'll understand, man, because I don't." Sixto felt the dizzying anger blind him for a moment. "*Coño*, man, she was just fifteen," he pleaded, as if Willie could absolve him of his sin before it had been committed. "I have to do it, man. She was just a kid. *Una nena*, man. A little innocent girl who dug Latin music and danced only with her girlfriends at home and believed all the nonsense about purity and virginity, man. And now this son of a bitch went and did it to her. *Le hizo el daño.*"

That's what women called it. That damage. And it was true. Damaged goods. He didn't want to believe it but that's how he felt. In all his educated, enlightened splendor, that's how he felt. Like she had been rendered untouchable, her femaleness soiled and smeared forever. Like no man would want to love her, knowing what had happened. The whole thing was so devastating that he couldn't imagine what it was like to be a woman. If they felt even a little of what he was experiencing, it was too much. And he, her own brother, already talking as if she were dead. That's how bad it was. Like she was a memory.

"I'm gonna kill him, Willie," said Sixto once more, pounding on the wall. *¿Lo*   50
mato, coño! Lo mato, lo mato," he repeated the death threat over and over in a frenzy. Willie stood up and reached for his arm but Sixto pulled roughly away. "It's cool, man," he said, and put his opened hands in front of him. "I'm all right. Everything's cool."

"Slow down," Willie pleaded. "Slow down."

"You're right, man. I gotta slow down." Sixto sat down but before long was up again. "Man, I couldn't sleep the last couple of nights. I kept seeing myself wearing the shame the rest of my life. I gave myself every excuse in the book. I even prayed, Willie. Me, a spic from the streets of the Big Apple, hip and slick, writing my *jíbaro* poetry; *saliéndome las palabras de las entrañas; inventando foquin mundos like a god; like foquin* Juracán pitching lightning bolts at the people to wake them from their stupor, man. Wake them up from their lethargy and their four-hundred-year-old sleep of self-induced tyranny, you know?"

"I understand, man."

"Willie, man, I wanted my words to thunder, to shake the earth *pa' que la gente le pida a Yuquiyú que los salve.*"

"And it's gonna be that way, bro. You're the poet, man. The voice."   55

"And me praying. Praying, man. And not to Yuquiyú but to some distorted European idea. I'm messed up, bro. Really messed up. Writing all this jive poetry that's supposed to incite the people to take up arms against the oppressor and all the while my heart is dripping with feelings of love and brotherhood and peace like some programmed puppet, Willie."

"I hear you."

"I mean, I bought all that stuff, man. All that liberal American jive. I bought it. I marched against the war in Vietnam, against colonialism and capitalism, and for the Chicano brothers cracking their backs in the fields, marched till my feet were raw, and every time I saw lettuce or grapes, I saw poison. And man, it felt right, Willie."

"It was a righteous cause, man."

"And I marched for the independence of the island, *of Puerto Rico, Willie: de*   60
Portorro, de Borinquen, la buena, la sagrada, el terruño, madre de todos nosotros; bendita seas entre todas las mujeres y bendito sea el fruto de tu vientre pelú. I marched for the land of our people and it felt right."

"It is right, man."

"You know, once and for all I had overcome all the anger of being a colonized person without a country and my culture being swallowed up, digested and thrown back up so you can't even recognize what it's all about. I had overcome all the craziness and could stand above it; I could look down on the brothers and sisters who took up arms in '50 and '54 when I wasn't even a fantasy in my pop's mind, man. I could stand above all of them, even the ones with their bombs now. I could pay tribute to them with words but still judge them crazy. And it was okay. It felt right to wear two faces, to go back and forth from poetic fury to social condescension or whatever you wanna call it. I thought I had it beat with the education and the poetry and opening up my heart like some long-haired, brown-skinned hippy. And now this. I'm a hypocrite, man."

Like the water from the open fire hydrant, the words had rushed out of him. And yet he couldn't say exactly what it was that troubled him about the attack on his sister, couldn't pinpoint what it was that made his face hot and his blood race angrily in his veins. Willie, silenced by his own impotence, sat looking at him. He knew he could neither urge him on nor discourage him and inevitably he would have to stand aside and let whatever was to happen run its course. His voice almost a whisper, he said, "It's okay, Sixto. I know how it feels. Just let the pain come out, man. Just let it out. Cry if you have to."

But the pain would never leave him. Spics weren't Greeks and the word katharsis had no meaning in private tragedy. Sixto's mind raced back into time, searching for an answer, knowing, even as it fled like a wounded animal seeking refuge from its tormentors, that it was an aimless search. It was like running a maze. Like the rats in the psychology films and the puzzles in the children's section of weekend newspapers. One followed a path with a pencil until he came to a dead end, then retraced his steps. Thousands of years passed before him in a matter of minutes.

65   The Tainos: a peaceful people, some history books said. No way, he thought. They fought the Spaniards, drowned them to test their immortality. And their *caciques* were as fierce and as brave as Crazy Horse or Geronimo. Proud chiefs they were. Jumacao, Daguao, Yaureibo, Caguax, Agueybaná, Mabodamaca, Aymamán, Urayoán, Orocobix, Guarionex all fought the Spaniards with all they had ... *guasábara* ... *guasábara* ... *guasábara* ... their battle cry echoing through the hills like an eerie phantom; they fought their horses and dogs; they fought their swords and guns and when there was no other recourse, rather than submitting, they climbed sheer cliffs and, holding their children to their breasts, leapt into the sea.

And the blacks: *los negros,* whose blood and heritage he carried. They didn't submit to slavery but escaped and returned to conduct raids against the oppressors, so that the whole *negrito lindo* business, so readily accepted as a term of endearment, was a joke, an appeasement on the part of the Spaniards. The *bombas* and *bembas* and *ginganbó* and their all night dances and *oraciones* to Changó: warrior men of the Jelofe, Mandingo, Mende, Yoruba, Dahomey, Ashanti, Ibo, Fante, Baule and Congro tribes, choosing battle over slavery.

And the Spaniards: certainly not a peaceful people. For centuries they fought each other and then branched out to cross the sea and slaughter hundreds of thousands of Indians, leaving an indelible mark on entire civilizations, raping and pillaging and gutting the earth of its riches, so that when it was all done and they laid in a drunken stupor four hundred years later, their pockets empty, they rose again to fight themselves in civil war.

And way back, way back before El Cid Campeador began to wage war: The Moors. *Los moros . . . alhambra, alcázar, alcohol, almohada, alcade, alboroto* . . . NOISE . . . CRIES OF WAR . . . A thousand years the maze traveled and it led to a dead end with dark men atop fleet Arabian stallions, dark men, both in visage and intent, raising their scimitars against those dishonoring their house . . . they had invented algebra and Arabic numbers and it all added up to war . . . there was no other way . . .

"I gotta kill him, bro," Sixto heard himself say. "I gotta. Otherwise I'm as good as dead."

One had to live with himself and that was the worst part of it; he had to live with the knowledge and that particular brand of cowardice that eroded the mind and destroyed one's soul. And it wasn't so much that his sister had been wronged. He'd seen that. The injury came from not retaliating. He was back at the beginning. Banana leaves and coconuts and machete duels at sundown. Just like his father and his *jíbaro* values. For even if the aggressor never talked, even if he never mentioned his act to another soul for whatever reason, there was still another person, another member of the tribe, who could single him out in a crowd and say to himself: "That one belongs to me and so does his sister." 70

Sixto tried to recall other times when his manhood had been challenged, but it seemed as if everything had happened long ago and hadn't been important: kid fights over mention of his mother, rights of ownership of an object, a place in the hierarchy of the block, a word said of his person, a lie, a bump by a stranger on a crowded subway train—nothing ever going beyond words or at worst, a sudden shoving match quickly broken up by friends.

But this was different. His brain was not functioning properly, he thought. He tried watching himself, tried to become an observer, the impartial judge of his actions. Through a small opening in his consciousness, he watched the raging battle. His heart called for the blood of the enemy and his brain urged him to use caution. There was no thought of danger, for in that region of struggle, survival meant not so much escaping with his life, but conquering fear and regaining his honor.

Sixto picked up the gun and studied it once more. He pushed the safety to make sure it was locked and placed the gun between the waistband of his pants and the flesh of his stomach. The cold metal sent slivers of ice running down his legs. It was a pleasant sensation, much as if a woman he had desired for some time had suddenly let him know, in an unguarded moment, that intimacy was possible between them. Avoiding Willie's eyes, he walked around the kitchen, pulled out his shirt and let it hang out over his pants. It was important that he learn to walk naturally and reduce his self-consciousness about the weapon. But it was his mind working tricks again. Nobody would notice. The idea was to act calmly. That's what everyone said: the thieves, the cheap stickup men who mugged old people and taxi drivers; the burglars who, like vultures, watched the movement of a family until certain that they were gone, swooped down and cleaned out the apartment, even in the middle of the day; the check specialists, who studied mailboxes as if they were bank vaults so they could break them open and steal welfare checks or fat letters from the island on the chance they might contain money orders or cash. They all said it. Even the young gang kids said it. Don't act suspiciously. Act as if you were going about your business.

Going to shoot someone was like going to work. That was it. He'd carry his books and nobody would suspect that he was carrying death. He laughed inwardly at the immense joke. He'd once seen a film in which Robert Mitchum, posing as a preacher, had pulled a derringer out of a Bible in the final scene. Why not. He'd hollow out his Western Civilization text and place the gun in it. It was his duty. The act was a way of surviving, of earning what was truly his. Whether a pay check or an education, it meant nothing without self-respect.

75   But the pieces of the puzzle did not fit and Sixto sat down dejectedly. He let his head fall into his hands and for a moment thought he would cry. Willie said nothing and Sixto waited, listening, the void of silence becoming larger and larger, expanding so that the sounds of the street, a passing car, the excitement of a child, the rushing water from the open hydrant, a mother's window warning retreated, became fainter and seemed to trim the outer edges of the nothingness within the silence. He could hear his own breathing and the beating of his heart and still he waited.

And then slowly, as if waking from a refreshing sleep, Sixto felt himself grow calmer and a pleasant coldness entered his body as heart and mind finally merged and became tuned to his mission. He smiled at the feeling and knew he had gone through the barrier of doubt and fear which had been erected to protect him from himself, to make sure he did not panic at the last moment. War had to be similar. He had heard the older men, the ones who had survived Vietnam, talk about it. Sonny Maldonado with his plastic foot, limping everywhere he went, quiet and unassuming, talked about going through a doorway and into a quiet room where one died a little and then came out again, one's mind alive but the rest of the body already dead to the upcoming pain.

It had finally happened, he thought. There was no anger or regret, no rationalizations concerning future actions. No more justifications or talk about honor and dignity. Instead, Sixto perceived the single objective coldly. There was neither danger nor urgency in carrying out the sentence and avenging the wrong. It seemed almost too simple. If it took years he knew the task would be accomplished. He would study the habits of his quarry, chart his every movement, and one day he'd strike. He would wait in a deserted hallway some late night, calmly walk out of the shadows, only his right index finger and his brain connected and say: "How you doing, Lino?" and his voice alone would convey the terrible message. Sixto smiled to himself and saw, as in a slow motion cinematic shot, his mind's ghost delicately squeeze the trigger repeatedly, the small animal muzzle of the gun following Lino Quintana's body as it fell slowly and hit the floor, the muscles of his victim's face twitching and life ebbing away forever. It happened all the time and no one was ever discovered.

Sixto laughed, almost too loudly. He took the gun out from under his shirt and placed it resolutely on the table. "I gotta think some more, man," he said. "That's crazy rushing into the thing. You wanna beer, Willie?"

Willie was not convinced of his friend's newly found calm. Reluctantly, he accepted the beer. He watched Sixto and tried to measure the depth of his eyes. They had become strangely flat, the glint of trust in them absent. It was as if a thin, opaque veil had been sewn over the eyes to mask Sixto's emotions. He felt helpless but said nothing. He opened the beer and began mourning the loss. Sixto was right, he thought. It was Spanish roulette. Spics were born and the cylinder spun. When it stopped one was handed the gun and, without looking, had to bring it to one's head, squeeze the trigger and take his chances.

The belief was pumped into the bloodstream, carved into the flesh through   80
generations of strife, so that being was the enactment of a ritual rather than the beginning of a new life. One never knew his own reactions until faced with Sixto's dilemma. And yet the loss would be too great, the upcoming grief too profound and the ensuing suffering eternal. The violence would be passed on to another generation to be displayed as an invisible coat of arms, much as Sixto's answer had come to him as a relic. His friend would never again look at the world with wonder, and poetry would cease to spring from his heart. If he did write, the words would be guarded, careful, full of excuses and apologies for living. Willie started to raise the beer in a toast but thought better of it and set the can on the table.

"Whatever you do, bro," he said, "be careful."

"Don't worry, man," Sixto replied. "I got the thing under control." He laughed once again and suddenly his eyes were ablaze were hatred. He picked up the gun, stuck it back into his pants and stood up. "No good, man," he said, seemingly to himself, and rushed out, slamming the door of the apartment behind him.

Beyond the sound of the door, Willie could hear the whirring cylinder as it began to slow down, each minute click measuring the time before his friend had to raise the weapon to his head and kill part of himself.

CRITICAL THINKING QUESTIONS

1. There is a clear conflict in this story between the forces of learning and the forces of violence. Should Willie intervene? Which is the good side?

2. How do the main characters define the concept of justice?

WRITING TOPICS

1. Assuming Willie would argue for the poetic/learning side while Sixto would argue for the necessity for revenge, write a dialogue between the two men in which each states his side of the argument.

2. Acting as a third-party mediator, construct a Rogerian-style conclusion to the argument.

POETRY

Gwendolyn Brooks (1917–2000)
The Boy Died in My Alley

Without my having known.
Policeman said, next morning,
"Apparently died Alone."
"You heard a shot?" Policeman said.
5   Shots I hear and Shots I hear.
I never see the dead.

The Shot that killed him yes I heard
as I heard the Thousand shots before;
careening tinnily down the nights
10   across my years and arteries.

Policeman pounded on my door.
"Who is it?" "police!" Policeman yelled.
"A boy was dying in your alley.
A boy is dead, and in your alley.
15   And have you known this Boy before?"

I have known this Boy before.
I have known this Boy before, who
ornaments my alley.
I never saw his face at all.
20   I never saw his futurefall.
But I have known this Boy.

I have always heard him deal with death.
I have always heard the shout, the volley.
I have closed my heart-ears late and early.
25   And I have killed him ever.

I joined the Wild and killed him
with knowledgeable unknowing.
I saw where he was going.
I saw him Crossed. And seeing.
30   I did not take him down.

He cried not only "Father!"
but "Mother!
Sister!
Brother!"
The cry climbed up the alley.   35
It went up to the wind.
It hung upon the heaven
for a long
stretch-strain of Moment.

The red floor of my alley   40
is a special speech to me.

CRITICAL THINKING QUESTION

The speaker expresses concern for this dead boy. Why is she concerned?

WRITING TOPIC

Reread the last two lines of the poem. What does the narrator mean when she tells
us, "The red floor of my alley/is a special speech to me"? Write your version of this
"special speech."

Martín Espada (b. 1957)
Bully

Boston, Massachusetts, 1987
In the school auditorium,
the Theodore Roosevelt statue
is nostalgic
for the Spanish-American War,
each fist lonely for a saber   5
or the reins of anguish-eyed horses,
or a podium to clatter with speeches
glorying in the malaria of conquest.

But now the Roosevelt school
is pronounced *Hernández*.   10
Puerto Rico has invaded Roosevelt
with its army of Spanish-singing children
in the hallways,

15 brown children devouring
the stockpiles of the cafeteria,
children painting *Taíno* ancestors
that leap naked across murals.

Roosevelt is surrounded
by all the faces
20 he ever shoved in eugenic spite
and cursed as mongrels, skin of one race,
hair and cheekbones of another.

Once Marines tramped
from the newsreel of his imagination;
25 now children plot to spray graffiti
in parrot-brilliant colors
across the Victorian mustache
and monocle.

CRITICAL THINKING QUESTIONS

1. What is the poet's *claim of value* about Theodore Roosevelt?

2. On which rhetorical appeal does he base his argument?

3. Find examples of *connotative language* (see Glossary). Do these word usages contribute to or detract from the poet's argument?

RESEARCH/WRITING TOPIC—History and Presidential Legacies

Assume a role as Theodore Roosevelt's defender. Do some research and write a rebuttal to Espada's poem's argument. Or, using your research and Espada's poem as evidence, write a Rogerian argument that evaluates Roosevelt's legacy.

Carolyn Forché (b. 1950)
The Colonel

What you have heard is true. I was in his house. His wife carried a tray of coffee and sugar. His daughter filed her nails, his son went out for the night. There were daily papers, pet dogs, a pistol on the cushion beside him. The moon swung bare on its black cord over
5 the house. On the television was a cop show. It was in English. Broken

bottles were embedded in the walls around the house to scoop the kneecaps from a man's legs or cut his hands to lace. On the windows there were gratings like those in liquor stores. We had dinner, rack of lamb, good wine, a gold bell was on the table for calling the maid. The maid brought green mangoes, salt, a type of bread. I was asked how I enjoyed the country. There 10
was a brief commercial in Spanish. His wife took everything away. There was some talk then of how difficult it had become to govern. The parrot said hello on the terrace. The colonel told it to shut up, and pushed himself from the table. My friend said to me with his eyes: say nothing. The colonel returned with a sack used to bring groceries 15
home. He spilled many human ears on the table. They were like dried peach halves. There is no other way to say this. He took one of them in his hands, shook it in our faces, dropped it into a water glass. It came alive there. I am tired of fooling around, he said. As for the rights of anyone, tell your people they can go fuck them- 20
selves. He swept the ears to the floor with his arm and held the last of his wine in the air. Something for your poetry, no? he said. Some of the ears on the floor caught this scrap of his voice. Some of the ears on the floor were pressed to the ground.

CRITICAL THINKING QUESTIONS

1. In terms of persuasion, the colonel is not subtle. What is the by-product of his approach to persuasion? Think about what usually happens to dictators in the end.

2. Is there no way to argue with such a man as the colonel except through violence?

WRITING TOPIC

The colonel does not care about the rights of anyone, and in his situation he seems to be able to get away with this approach to governing and controlling people. Threatening people with physical violence creates an effective short-term argument; however, the by-product is anger and hostility which, in the long run, often is counterproductive. Using examples, argue that the carrot is more powerful than the stick.

Robert Frost (1874–1963)

Mending Wall

Something there is that doesn't love a wall,
That sends the frozen-ground-swell under it,
And spills the upper boulders in the sun;
And makes gaps even two can pass abreast.
5   The work of hunters is another thing:
I have come after them and made repair
Where they have left not one stone on a stone,
But they would have the rabbit out of hiding,
To please the yelping dogs. The gaps I mean,
10   No one has seen them made or heard them made,
But at spring mending-time we find them there.
I let my neighbor know beyond the hill;
And on a day we meet to walk the line
And set the wall between us once again.
15   We keep the wall between us as we go.
To each the boulders that have fallen to each.
And some are loaves and some so nearly balls
We have to use a spell to make them balance:
"Stay where you are until our backs are turned!"
20   We wear our fingers rough with handling them.
Oh, just another kind of outdoor game,
One on a side. It comes to little more:
There where it is we do not need the wall:
He is all pine and I am apple orchard.
25   My apple trees will never get across
And eat the cones under his pines, I tell him.
He only says, "Good fences make good neighbors."
Spring is the mischief in me, and I wonder
If I could put a notion in his head:
30   "*Why* do they make good neighbors? Isn't it
Where there are cows? But here there are no cows.
Before I built a wall I'd ask to know
What I was walling in or walling out,
And to whom I was like to give offense.
35   Something there is that doesn't love a wall,
That wants it down." I could say "Elves" to him,
But it's not elves exactly, and I'd rather
He said it for himself. I see him there
Bringing a stone grasped firmly by the top

In each hand, like an old-stone savage armed.   40
He moves in darkness as it seems to me,
Not of woods only and the shade of trees.
He will not go behind his father's saying,
And he likes having thought of it so well
He says again, "Good fences make good neighbors."   45

CRITICAL THINKING QUESTIONS

1. How does the speaker use *logos* appeal to argue against the fence between him and his neighbor?

2. In lines 32 and 33, the speaker says, "Before I built a wall I'd ask to know / What I was walling in or walling out." When fences are not walling in, what might they be walling out?

3. Whose viewpoint do you support, the speaker's—"Something there is that doesn't love a wall"—or the neighbor's—"Good fences make good neighbors"?

RESEARCH/WRITING TOPIC—Gated Communities: Havens or Fortresses?

Seeking security within a homogenous community, home owners are increasingly choosing to live in gated communities. While many champion this lifestyle choice as a way to revive the virtues and values of small towns—where you can go next door to borrow a cup of sugar, where your children can ride their bikes without your direct supervision—others claim these communities are widening the chasm between the haves and the have-nots, as well as creating barriers that segregate rather than integrate society. Is this a case of "good fences make good neighbors"? Or is there something in the urban environment that "doesn't love a wall"? Write an argument defending or rejecting the concept of the gated community.

Langston Hughes (1902–1967)

Democracy

Democracy will not come
Today, this year
Nor ever
Through compromise and fear.

5   I have as much right
As the other fellow has
To stand
On my two feet
And own the land.

10   I tire so of hearing people say,
Let things take their course.
Tomorrow is another day.
I do not need my freedom when I'm dead.
I cannot live on tomorrow's bread.

15   Freedom
Is a strong seed
Planted
In a great need.
I live here, too.
20   I want freedom
Just as you.

WRITING TOPIC

Write out the first four lines of the poem, "Democracy," as a prose statement. In the context of contemporary America, does the concept democracy remain "unrealized"? Argue that compared to fifty years ago, when Hughes wrote the poem, the country has made great strides toward democracy; *or* argue that compared to fifty years ago, while some aspects have changed, others remain much as they were. By using specific examples to support your claim, avoid merely making generalizations.

Langston Hughes
Theme for English B

The instructor said,

Go home and write
a page tonight.
And let that page come out of you—
5   *Then, it will be true.*

I wonder if it's that simple?
I am twenty-two, colored, born in Winston-Salem.

I went to school there, then Durham, then here
to this college on the hill above Harlem.
I am the only colored student in my class. 10
The steps from the hill lead down into Harlem,
through a park, then I cross St. Nicholas,
Eighth Avenue, Seventh, and I come to the Y,
the Harlem Branch Y, where I take the elevator
up to my room, sit down, and write this page: 15

It's not easy to know what is true for you or me
at twenty-two, my age. But I guess I'm what
I feel and see and hear, Harlem, I hear you:
hear you, hear me—we two—you, me, talk on this page.
(I hear New York, too.) Me—who? 20

Well, I like to eat, sleep, drink, and be in love.
I like to work, read, learn, and understand life.
I like a pipe for a Christmas present,
or records—Bessie, bop, or Bach.
I guess being colored doesn't make me not like 25
the same things other folks like who are other races.
So will my page be colored that I write?
Being me, it will not be white.
But it will be
a part of you, instructor. 30
You are white—
yet a part of me, as I am a part of you.
That's American.
Sometimes perhaps you don't want to be a part of me.
Nor do I often want to be a part of you. 35
But we are, that's true!
As I learn from you,
I guess you learn from me—
although you're older—and white—
and somewhat more free. 40

This is my page for English B.

CRITICAL THINKING QUESTIONS

1. What power issues is the poem's speaker addressing?

2. In resolving his power issues, what Rogerian position does the speaker articulate? What is your opinion of this position?

RESEARCH/WRITING TOPICS—Tradition and Multiculturalism

1. Writing in the first person, create an argument for preserving a tradition found within your family or community. After interviewing family members and friends, use anecdotes and narrative to make this tradition clear for the reader.

2. Read several articles about *multiculturalism* so you understand the term and some of the controversy surrounding it. Many colleges and universities have multicultural requirements; argue for or against maintaining a multicultural requirement on your campus.

Claude McKay (1890–1948)

America

Although she feeds me bread of bitterness,
And sinks into my throat her tiger's tooth,
Stealing my breath of life, I will confess
I love this cultured hell that tests my youth!
Her vigor flows like tides into my blood,
Giving me strength erect against her hate.
Her bigness sweeps my being like a flood.
Yet as a rebel fronts a king in state,
I stand within her walls with not a shred
Of terror, malice, not a word of jeer.
Darkly I gaze into the days ahead,
And see her might and granite wonders there,
Beneath the touch of Time's unerring hand,
Like priceless treasures sinking in the sand.

5

10

CRITICAL THINKING QUESTIONS

1. In line 4, the speaker proclaims, "I love this cultured hell that tests my youth!"
   a. List details from the poem that depict this love.
   b. Look up *ambiguity* in the Glossary. Which details create ambiguity, regarding this love?

2. Write out a claim of value about America that the speaker implies. To what degree do you agree or disagree with this claim?

James Merrill (1926–1995)
Casual Wear

Your average tourist: Fifty. 2.3
Times married. Dressed, this year, in Ferdi Plinthbower
Originals. Odds 1 to 9
Against her strolling past the Embassy

Today at noon. Your average terrorist: 5
Twenty-five. Celibate. No use for trends,
At least in clothing. Mark, though, where it ends.
People have come forth made of colored mist

Unsmiling on one hundred million screens
To tell of his prompt phone call to the station,   10
"Claiming responsibility"—devastation
Signed with a flourish, like the dead wife's jeans.

WRITING TOPIC

Read about a particular terrorist activity somewhere in the world. Then read further to gain some understanding of the group's motivation. First, write a letter
to the *New York Times* in which a leader of this group justifies its activities; then
write a letter to rebut the leader's argument.

Edna St. Vincent Millay (1892–1950)
Apostrophe to Man

(On reflecting that the world is ready to go to war again)

Detestable race, continue to expunge yourself, die out.
Breed faster, crowd, encroach, sing hymns, build bombing airplanes;
Make speeches, unveil statues, issue bonds, parade;
Convert again into explosives the bewildered ammonia and the distracted
    cellulose;
Convert again into putrescent matter drawing flies   5
The hopeful bodies of the young; exhort,
Pray, pull long faces, be earnest, be all but overcome, be photographed;
Confer, perfect your formulae, commercialize

Bacteria harmful to human tissue,
10   Put death on the market;
Breed, crowd, encroach, expand, expunge yourself, die out,
Homo called *sapiens*.

CRITICAL THINKING QUESTIONS

1. Much of this poem is a list, an enumeration of specifics. How is this strategy an effective organizational approach for Millay's subject?

2. Explain why the last line of the poem is an example of *irony* (see Glossary). You will need to look up *homo* and *sapiens* in a dictionary, if you are not absolutely certain you know what each means.

3. Judging by this poem, we might well describe the poet as *cynical.* Look up the meaning of *cynic.* Who were the cynics in Ancient Greece? Why do you believe Millay would or would not have fit in well with this group of philosophers?

WRITING TOPIC

Model the structure of this poem by creating your own version; however, begin your version with the words, "Admirable race," and continue by creating a positive list of attributes.

John Milton (1608–1674)

When I Consider How My Light Is Spent

When I consider how my light is spent,
    Ere half my days in this dark world and wide,
    And that one talent which is death to hide
Lodged with me useless, though my soul more bent
5   To serve therewith my Maker, and present
    My true account, lest He returning chide;
    "Doth God exact day-labor, light denied?"
I fondly ask. But Patience, to prevent
That murmur, soon replies, "God doth not need
10   Either man's work or His own gifts. Who best
Bear His mild yoke, they serve Him best. His state
Is kingly: thousands at His bidding speed,

And post o'er land and ocean without rest;
They also serve who only stand and wait."

CRITICAL THINKING QUESTIONS

1. According to Milton, in deciding how to use one's individual talents, what value assumption or *warrant* about the purpose of one's life underlies that choice? Do you accept this warrant?

2. In your opinion, what values should inform one's choice of a career or profession?

Naomi Shihab Nye (b. 1952)
Famous

The river is famous to the fish.
The loud voice is famous to silence,
which knew it would inherit the earth
before anybody said so.

The cat sleeping on the fence is famous to the birds   5
watching him from the birdhouse.

The tear is famous, briefly, to the cheek.
The idea you carry close to your bosom
is famous to your bosom.

The boot is famous to the earth,   10
more famous than the dress shoe,
which is famous only to floors.

The bent photograph is famous to the one who carries it
and not at all famous to the one who is pictured.

I want to be famous to shuffling men   15
who smile while crossing streets,
sticky children in grocery lines,
famous as the one who smiled back.

I want to be famous in the way a pulley is famous,
or a buttonhole, not because it did anything spectacular,   20
but because it never forgot what it could do.

CRITICAL THINKING QUESTIONS

1. What is Nye's *implied claim* for evaluating the concept of famous?

2. How does popular culture generally portray images of fame? What definition of "famous" do these images suggest?

WRITING TOPIC

Compare and contrast Nye's viewpoint on famous and the viewpoint projected by popular culture. What values do you think should be associated with famous? Based on your consideration of these perspectives, write your own argument for defining famous.

Sharon Olds (b. 1942)

The Promise

With the second drink, at the restaurant,
holding hands on the bare table
we are at it again, renewing our promise
to kill each other. You are drinking gin,
5   night-blue juniper berry
dissolving in your body, I am drinking Fumé,
chewing its fragrant dirt and smoke, we are
taking on earth, we are part soil already,
and always, wherever we are, we are also in our
10   bed, fitted naked closely
along each other, half passed out
after love, drifting back and
forth across the border of consciousness, our
bodies buoyant, clasped. Your hand
15   tightens on the table. You're a little afraid
I'll chicken out. What you do not want
is to lie in a hospital bed for a year
after a stroke, without being able to
think or die, you do not want
20   to be tied to a chair like my prim grandmother,
cursing. The room is dim around us,
ivory globes, pink curtains
bound at the waist, and outside
a weightless bright lifted-up

summer twilight. I tell you you don't   25
know me if you think I will not
kill you. Think how we have floated together
eye to eye, nipple to nipple,
sex to sex, the halves of a single creature
drifting up to the lip of matter   30
and over it—you know me from the bright, blood-flecked
delivery room, if a beast
had you in its jaws I would attack it, if the ropes
binding your soul are your own wrists I will cut them.

CRITICAL THINKING QUESTIONS

1. What is this poem's *implied claim* on the issue of active euthanasia or "mercy killing"?

2. What *evidence* does the speaker provide in making her case for keeping "our promise / to kill each other . . ."? On which *rhetorical appeal* does she rely?

3. How successful is the speaker in persuading you that she must keep the promise?

RESEARCH/WRITING TOPIC—Physician-Assisted Suicide: Merciful or Mercenary?

The poet's image of "lie[ing] in a hospital bed for a year/after a stroke without being able to/think or die" brings to mind difficult end of life issues for not only the stroke victim but also his or her family, friends, and doctors. When does life cease to have meaning? Certainly, this is a moral and ethical question with which individuals wrestle. But to what degree should laws intervene—either to allow or not to allow terminally ill individuals to choose to end their lives? At the time of this writing in 2006, only one state, Oregon, has such a law; the Death with Dignity Act was approved by Oregon voters in 1997. Research this issue, specifically, the consequences of Oregon's law. Should other states follow Oregon's lead, or should Oregon voters be persuaded to rescind the law?

Linda Pastan (b. 1932)

Ethics

In ethics class so many years ago
our teacher asked this question every fall:
if there were a fire in a museum
which would you save, a Rembrandt painting
5   or an old woman who hadn't many
years left anyhow? Restless on hard chairs
caring little for pictures or old age
we'd opt one year for life, the next for art
and always half-heartedly. Sometimes
10   the woman borrowed my grandmother's face
leaving her usual kitchen to wander
some drafty, half-imagined museum.
One year, feeling clever, I replied
why not let the woman decide herself?
15   Linda, the teacher would report, eschews
the burdens of responsibility.
This fall in a real museum I stand
before a real Rembrandt, old woman,
or nearly so, myself. The colors
20   within this frame are darker than autumn,
darker even than winter—the browns of earth,
though earth's most radiant elements burn
through the canvas. I know now that woman
and painting and season are almost one
25   and all beyond saving by children.

WRITING TOPIC

Pastan argues that we cannot expect children to make the kind of ethical decision her teacher posed. In contrast, however, many people argue that today, education does not teach values. Write a description of several times during your childhood, in school or out of school, when you received values instruction.

Public Enemy
Fight the Power

1989, the number, another summer (get down)
Sound of the funky drummer
Music hittin' your heart'cause I know you got soul
(Brothers and sisters, hey)
Listen if you're missin', y'all   5
Swingin' while I'm singin' (hey)
Givin' whatcha gettin'
Knowin' what I'm knowin'
While the black band's sweatin'
And the rhythm rhyme's rollin'   10
Gotta give us what we want (Uh!)
Gotta give us what we need (Hey!)
Our freedom of speech is freedom or death
We got to fight the powers that be
Lemme hear you say   15

FIGHT THE POWER
We got to fight the powers that be

As the rhythm's designed to bounce
What counts is that the rhyme's
Designed to fill your mind   20
Now that you've realized the pride's arrived
We got to pump the stuff to make us tough
From the heart
It's a start, a work of art
To revolutionize, make a change, nothin' strange   25
People people, we are the same
No we're not the same
'Cause we don't know the game
What we need is awareness, we can't get careless
You say what is this?   30
My beloved, let's go down to business
Mental self-defensive fitness
(Yo) Bum rush the show
You gotta go for what you know
To make everybody see, in order to fight the powers that be   35
Lemme hear you say

FIGHT THE POWER

We got to fight the powers that be

Elvis was a hero to most
40   But he never meant shit to me, you see
Straight up racist that sucker was simple and plain
Motherfuck him and John Wayne
'Cause I'm black and I'm proud
I'm ready and hyped plus I'm amped
45   Most of my heroes don't appear on no stamps
Sample a look back, you look and find
Nothin' but rednecks for 400 years if you check
"Don't Worry Be Happy"
Was a number one jam
50   Damn, if I say it you can slap me right here
(Get it) Let's get this party started right
Right on, c'mon
What we got to say (Yaaaah!)
Power to the people, no delay
55   To make everybody see
In order to fight the powers that be

FIGHT THE POWER
We got to fight the powers that be

CRITICAL THINKING QUESTIONS

1. Point out specific lines from the song where Public Enemy identifies the necessary steps in fighting the power.

2. Think about the word *fight* as it is used in this song. How do you think Public Enemy expects their listeners to respond to their command? List specific lines from the song that support your viewpoint.

3. Compare the use of repetition as a motivational strategy in these lyrics and in Walt Whitman's "Beat! Beat! Drums!"

WRITING TOPIC

Working together in small groups, convert John F. Kennedy's "Inaugural Address" (page 676) into a rap song. Use Public Enemy's "Fight the Power" as your model.

Walt Whitman (1819–1892)
Beat! Beat! Drums!

Beat! beat! drums!—blow! bugles! blow!
Through the windows—through doors—burst like a ruthless force,
Into the solemn church, and scatter the congregation,
Into the school where the scholar is studying;
Leave not the bridegroom quiet—no happiness must he have now
   with his bride,   5
Nor the peaceful farmer any peace, ploughing his field or gathering his grain,
So fierce you whirr and pound you drums—so shrill you bugles blow.

Beat! beat! drums!—blow! bugles! blow!
Over the traffic of cities—over the rumble of wheels in the streets;
Are beds prepared for sleepers at night in the houses? no sleepers must
   sleep in those beds,   10
No bargainers' bargains by day—no brokers or speculators—would
   they continue?
Would the talkers be talking? would the singer attempt to sing?
Would the lawyer rise in the court to state his case before the judge?
Then rattle quicker, heavier drums—you bugles wilder blow.

Beat! beat! drums!—blow! bugles! blow!   15
Make no parley—stop for no expostulation,
Mind not the timid—mind not the weeper or prayer,
Mind not the old man beseeching the young man,
Let not the child's voice be heard, nor the mother's entreaties,
Make even the trestles to shake the dead where they lie awaiting the hearses,   20
So strong you thump O terrible drums—so loud you bugles blow.

CRITICAL THINKING QUESTION

A primary rhetorical strategy in the poem is repetition. Look up *alliteration* in the Glossary and point out examples in the poem. How does this device reinforce the poet's message? What is Whitman's message?

WRITING TOPIC

Whitman wrote this poem in 1861, in an effort to rally the people behind the cause of the Union Army after its defeat in the first battle of Bull Run. Read Major Sullivan Ballou's "Last Letter to His Wife," written on the eve of this battle (page 501). Reading these two pieces side-by-side, what is your reaction?

DRAMA

ᴧᴧ

Aristophanes (c. 446 B.C.–c. 386 B.C.)

Lysistrata
Translated by Dudley Fitts

──────────── Persons Represented ────────────

LYSISTRATA,⎫
KALONIKE, ⎬ Athenian women
MYRRHINE, ⎭
LAMPITO, a Spartan woman
CHORUS
COMMISSIONER
KINESIAS, husband of Myrrhine

SPARTAN HERALD
SPARTAN AMBASSADOR
A SENTRY
[BABY SON OF KINESIAS
STRATYLLIS
SPARTANS
ATHENIANS]

Scene: Athens. First, a public square; later, beneath the walls of the Akropolis;* later, a courtyard within the Akropolis.

Prologue*

Athens; a public square; early morning; Lysistrata alone.

Lysistrata: If someone had invited them to a festival—
     of Bacchos,* say; or to Pan's* shrine, or to Aphrodite's *
     over at Kolias—, you couldn't get through the streets,
     what with the drums and the dancing. But now,
     not a woman in sight!
5   Except—oh, yes!

[*Enter* Kalonike.]

Here's one of my neighbors, at last. Good
     morning, Kalonike.

──────────

***Akropolis:** Fortress of Athens, sacred to the goddess Athena.
***Prologue:** Portion of the play explaining the background and current action.
***Bacchos:** (Bacchus) God of wine and the object of wild, orgiastic ritual and celebration; also called Dionysus.
***Pan:** God of nature, forests, flocks, and shepherds, depicted as half-man and half-goat. Pan was considered playful and lecherous.
***Aphrodite:** Goddess of love.

Kalonike: Good morning, Lysistrata.
                           Darling,
   don't frown so! You'll ruin your face!
Lysistrata: Never mind my face.   10
   Kalonike,
   the way we women behave! Really, I don't blame the men
   for what they say about us.
Kalonike: No; I imagine they're right.
Lysistrata: For example: I call a meeting
   to think out a most important matter—and what happens?
   The women all stay in bed!
Kalonike: Oh, they'll be along.
   It's hard to get away, you know: a husband, a cook,
   a child . . . Home life can be *so* demanding!
Lysistrata: What I have in mind is even more demanding.   15
Kalonike: Tell me: what is it?
Lysistrata: It's big.
Kalonike: Goodness! *How* big?
Lysistrata: Big enough for all of us.
Kalonike: But we're not all here!
Lysistrata: We would be, if *that's* what was up!   20
                      No, Kalonike,
   this is something I've been turning over for nights,
   long sleepless nights.
Kalonike: It must be getting worn down,
   then, if you've spent so much time on it.
Lysistrata: Worn down or not,
   it comes to this: Only we women can save Greece!
Kalonike: Only we women? Poor Greece!   25
Lysistrata: Just the same,
   it's up to us. First, we must liquidate
   the Peloponnesians—
Kalonike: Fun, fun!
Lysistrata: —and then the Boiotians.*
Kalonike: Oh! But not those heavenly eels!
Lysistrata: You needn't worry.   30
   I'm not talking about eels.—But here's the point:
   If we can get the women from those places—
   all those Boiotians and Peloponnesians—
   to join us women here, why, we can save
   all Greece!

*****Boiotians:** Crude-mannered inhabitants of Boiotia, which was noted for its seafood.

35   **Kalonike:** But dearest Lysistrata!
      How can women do a thing so austere, so
      political? We belong at home. Our only armor's
      our perfumes, our saffron dresses and
      our pretty little shoes!
      Lysistrata: Exactly. Those
      transparent dresses, the saffron, the
      perfume, those pretty shoes—
      Kalonike: Oh?
      Lysistrata: Not a single man would lift his spear—
40   **Kalonike:**   I'll send my dress to the dyer's tomorrow!
      Lysistrata: —or grab a shield—
      Kalonike: The sweetest little negligee—
      Lysistrata: —or haul out his sword.
      Kalonike: I know where
             I can buy the dreamiest sandals!
      Lysistrata: Well, so you see. Now, shouldn't
      the women have come?
45   **Kalonike:**   Come? They should have *flown!*
      Lysistrata: Athenians are always late.
                                     But imagine!
      There's no one here from the South Shore, or from Salamis.
      Kalonike: Things are hard over in Salamis, I swear.
             They have to get going at dawn.
      Lysistrata: And nobody from Acharnai.
             I thought they'd be here hours ago.
50   **Kalonike:**   Well, you'll get
      that awful Theagenes woman: she'll be
      a sheet or so in the wind.
                          But look!
      Someone at last! Can you see who they are?

      [*Enter* MYRRHINE *and other women.*]

      Lysistrata: They're from Anagyros.
      Kalonike: They certainly are.
             You'd know them anywhere, by the scent.
55   **Myrrhine:** Sorry to be late, Lysistrata.
                                     Oh come,
             don't scowl so. Say something!
      Lysistrata: My dear Myrrhine,
             what is there to say? After all,
             you've been pretty casual about the whole thing.
      Myrrhine: Couldn't find
             my girdle in the dark, that's all.

But what *is*
"the whole thing"?
Kalonike: No, we've got to wait   60
for those Boiotians and Peloponnesians.
Lysistrata: That's more like it.—But, look!
Here's Lampito!

[*Enter* LAMPITO *with women from Sparta.*]

Lysistrata: Darling Lampito,
how pretty you are today! What a nice color!
Goodness, you look as though you could strangle a bull!
Lampito: Ah think Ah could! It's the work-out   65
in the gym every day; and, of co'se that dance of ahs
where y' kick yo' own tail.
Kalonike: What an adorable figure!
Lampito: Lawdy, when y' touch me lahk that,
Ah feel lahk a heifer at the altar!
Lysistrata: And this young lady?   70
Where is she from?
Lampito: Boiotia. Social-Register type.
Lysistrata: Ah. "Boiotia of the fertile plain."
Kalonike: And if you look,
you'll find the fertile plain has just been mowed.
Lysistrata: And this lady?
Lampito: Hagh, wahd, handsome.
She comes from Korinth.
Kalonike: High and wide's the word for it.
Lampito: Which one of you   75
called this heah meeting, and why?
Lysistrata: I did.
Lampito: Well, then, tell us:
What's up?
Myrrhine: Yes, darling, what *is* on your mind, after all?
Lysistrata: I'll tell you.—But first, one little question.
Myrrhine: Well?
Lysistrata: It's your husbands. Fathers of your children. Doesn't it
    bother you
that they're always off with the Army? I'll stake my life,   80
not one of you has a man in the house this minute!
Kalonike: Mine's been in Thrace the last five months, keeping an eye
on that General.
Myrrhine: Mine's been in Pylos for seven.
Lampito: And mahn,

whenever he gets a *dis*charge, he goes raht back
85   with that li'l ole shield of his, and enlists again!
   Lysistrata: And not the ghost of a lover to be found!
      From the very day the war began—
                                          those Milesians!
      I could skin them alive!
                        —I've not seen so much, even,
      as one of those leather consolation prizes.—
90   But there! What's important is: If I've found a way
      to end the war, are you with me?
   Myrrhine: I should *say* so!
      Even if I have to pawn my best dress and
      drink up the proceeds.
   Kalonike: Me, too! Even if they split me
      right up the middle, like a flounder.
95 Lampito: Ah'm shorely with you.
      Ah'd crawl up Taygetos* on mah knees
      if that'd bring peace.
   Lysistrata: All right, then; here it is:
      Women! Sisters!
      If we really want our men to make peace,
      we must be ready to give up—
   Myrrhine: Give up what?
      Quick, tell us!
   Lysistrata: But *will* you?
   Myrrhine: We will, even if it kills us.
100 Lysistrata: Then we must give up going to bed with our men.

   [*Long silence.*]

      Oh? So now you're sorry? Won't look at me?
      Doubtful? Pale? All teary-eyed?
                              But come: be frank with me.
      Will you do it, or not? Well? Will you do it?
   Myrrhine: I couldn't. No.
105   Let the war go on.
   Kalonike: Nor I. Let the war go on.
   Lysistrata: You, you little flounder,
      ready to be split up the middle?
   Kalonike: Lysistrata, no!
      I'd walk through fire for you—you *know* I would!—but don't
      ask us to give up *that! Why, there's nothing like it!*
   Lysistrata: And you?

---

*Taygetos: A mountain range.

Boiotian:	No. I must say *I'd* rather walk through fire.	110

Lysistrata: What an *utterly perverted sex we women are!*
No wonder poets write tragedies about us.
There's only one thing we can think of.
                               But you from Sparta:
if you stand by me, we may win yet! Will you?
It means so much!

Lampito: Ah sweah, it means *too* much!   115
By the Two Goddesses,* it does! Asking a girl
to sleep—Heaven knows how long!—in a great big bed
with nobody there but herself! But Ah'll stay with you!
Peace comes first!

Lysistrata: Spoken like a true Spartan!

Kalonike: But if—
                     oh dear!   120
               —if we give up what you tell us to,
will there *be* any peace?

Lysistrata: Why, mercy, of course there will!
We'll just sit snug in our very thinnest gowns,
perfumed and powdered from top to bottom, and those men
simply won't stand still! And when we say No,
they'll go out of their minds! And there's your peace.   125
You can take my word for it.

Lampito: Ah seem to remember
that Colonel Menelaos threw his sword away
when he saw Helen's breast all bare.*

Kalonike: But, goodness me!
What if they just get up and leave us?

Lysistrata: In that case
we'll have to fall back on ourselves, I suppose.   130
But they won't.

Kalonike: I must say that's not much help. But
what if they drag us into the bedroom?

Lysistrata: Hang on to the door.

Kalonike: What if they slap us?

Lysistrata: If they do, you'd better give in.
But be sulky about it. Do I have to teach you how?   135
You know there's no fun for men when they have to force you.
There are millions of ways of getting them to see reason.

---

*Two Goddesses:** A woman's oath referring to Demeter, the earth goddess, and her daughter Persephone, who was associated with seasonal cycles of fertility.
*Colonel Menelaos . . . Helen's breast:** Helen, wife of King Menelaos of Sparta, was abducted by Paris and taken to Troy. The incident led to the Trojan War.

Don't you worry: a man
doesn't like it *unless the girl cooperates.*

140 **Kalonike:** I suppose so. Oh, all right. We'll go along.

Lampito: Ah imagine us Spahtans can arrange a peace. But you
Athenians! Why, you're just war-mongerers!

Lysistrata: Leave that to me.
I know how to make them listen.

Lampito: Ah don't see how.
After all, they've got their boats; and there's lots of money
piled up in the Akropolis.

145 **Lysistrata:**   The Akropolis? Darling,
we're taking over the Akropolis today!
That's the older women's job. All the rest of us
are going to the Citadel to sacrifice—you understand me?
And once there, we're in for good!

Lampito: Whee! Up the rebels!
Ah can see you're a good strat*ee*gist.

150 **Lysistrata:**   Well, then, Lampito,
what we have to do now is take a solemn oath.

Lampito: Say it. We'll sweah.

Lysistrata: This is it.
—But where's our Inner Guard?
                    —Look, Guard: you see this shield?
Put it down here. Now bring me the victim's entrails.

155 **Kalonike:** But the oath?

Lysistrata: You remember how in Aischylos' *Seven**
they killed a sheep and swore on a shield? Well, then?

Kalonike: But I don't see how you can swear for peace on a shield.

Lysistrata: What else do you suggest?

Kalonike: Why not a white horse?
We could swear by that.

Lysistrata: And where will you get a white horse?

160 **Kalonike:** I never thought of that. *What* can we do?

Lysistrata: I have it!
Let's set this big black wine-bowl on the ground
and pour in a gallon or so of Thasian,* and swear
not to add one drop of water.

Lampito: Ah lahk *that* oath!

Lysistrata: Bring the bowl and the wine-jug.

Kalonike: Oh, what a simply *huge* one!

---

*Seven: Aeschylus's *Seven Against Thebes*, which deals with the war between the sons of Oedipus for the throne of Thebes.
*Thasian: Wine from Thasos.

Lysistrata: Set it down. Girls, place your hands on the gift-offering.   165
    O *Goddess of Persuasion!* And *thou, O Loving-cup:*
    Look upon this our sacrifice, and
    be gracious!
Kalonike: See the blood spill out. How red and pretty it is!
Lampito: And Ah must say it smells good.
Myrrhine: Let me swear first!
Kalonike: No, by Aphrodite, we'll match for it!   170
Lysistrata: Lampito: all of you women: come, touch the bowl,
    and repeat after me—remember, this is an oath—:
    I WILL HAVE NOTHING TO DO WITH MY HUSBAND OR MY
        LOVER
Kalonike: *I will have nothing to do with my husband or my lover*
Lysistrata: THOUGH HE COME TO ME IN PITIABLE CONDITION   175
Kalonike: *Though he come to me in pitiable condition*
    (Oh Lysistrata! This is killing me!)
Lysistrata: IN MY HOUSE I WILL BE UNTOUCHABLE
Kalonike: *In my house I will be untouchable*
Lysistrata: IN MY THINNEST SAFFRON SILK   180
Kalonike: *In my thinnest saffron silk*
Lysistrata: AND MAKE HIM LONG FOR ME.
Kalonike: *And make him long for me.*
Lysistrata: I WILL NOT GIVE MYSELF
Kalonike: *I will not give myself*   185
Lysistrata: AND IF HE CONSTRAINS ME
Kalonike: *And if he constrains me*
Lysistrata: I WILL BE COLD AS ICE AND NEVER MOVE
Kalonike: *I will be cold as ice and never move*
Lysistrata: I WILL NOT LIFT MY SLIPPERS TOWARD THE   190
    CEILING
Kalonike: *I will not lift my slippers toward the ceiling*
Lysistrata: OR CROUCH ON ALL FOURS LIKE THE LIONESS IN
    THE CARVING
Kalonike: *Or crouch on all fours like the lioness in the carving*
Lysistrata: AND IF I KEEP THIS OATH LET ME DRINK FROM
    THIS BOWL
Kalonike: *And if I keep this oath let me drink from this bowl*   195
Lysistrata: IF NOT, LET MY OWN BOWL BE FILLED WITH
    WATER.
Kalonike: *If not, let my own bowl be filled with water.*
Lysistrata: You have all sworn?
Myrrhine: We have.

Lysistrata: Then thus
   I sacrifice the victim.

[Drinks largely.]

Kalonike: Save some for us!
200   Here's to you, darling, and to you, and to you!

[Loud cries offstage.]

Lampito: What's all *that* whoozy-goozy?
Lysistrata: Just what I told you.
   The older women have taken the Akropolis.
   Now you, Lampito,
   rush back to Sparta. We'll take care of things here. Leave
   these girls here for hostages.
205   The rest of you,
   up to the Citadel: and mind you push in the bolts.
Kalonike: But the men? Won't they be after us?
Lysistrata: Just you leave
   the men to me. There's not fire enough in the world,
   or threats either, to make me open these doors
   except on my own terms.
210 **Kalonike:**   I hope not, by Aphrodite!
   After all,
   we've got a *reputation for bitchiness to live up to.* [Exeunt.*]

Parodos:* **Choral Episode**

The hillside just under the Akropolis. Enter Chorus of Old Men with burning torches and braziers; much puffing and coughing.

Koryphaios(man)*: Forward march, Drakes, old friend: never you mind that
   damn big log banging hell down on your back.

Strophe 1*

Chorus(men): There's this to be said for longevity:
   You see things you thought that you'd never see.
      Look, Strymodoros, who would have thought it?
5   We've caught it—

---

    *Exeunt: Latin for "they go out."
    *Parodos: The song or ode chanted by the Chorus on their entry.
    *Koryphaios: Leader of the Chorus; also called Choragos. There are two Choruses and two Koryphaioi, one male and one female.
    *Strophe: Song sung by the Chorus as they danced from stage right to stage left.

the New Femininity!
The wives of our bosom, our board, our bed—
Now, by the gods, they've gone ahead
And taken the Citadel (Heaven knows why!),
Profanèd the sacred statuar-y,   10
                             And barred the doors,
                          The subversive whores!
Koryphaios[(m)]: Shake a leg there, Philurgos, man: The Akropolis or bust!
Put the kindling around here. We'll build one almighty big
bonfire for the whole bunch of bitches, every last one;   15
and the first we fry will be old Lykon's woman.

Antistrophe* 1

Chorus[(m)]:They're not going to give me the old horse-laugh!
No, by Demeter, they won't pull this off!
    Think of Kleomenes: even he
    Didn't go free   20
                    till he brought me his stuff.
A good man he was, all stinking and shaggy,
Bare as an eel except for the bag he
Covered his rear with. God, what a mess!
Never a bath in six years, I'd guess.
                        Pure Sparta, man!
                        He also ran.   25
Koryphaios[(m)]: That was a siege, friends! Seventeen ranks strong
we slept at the Gate. And shall we not do as much
against these women, whom God and Euripides hate?
If we don't, I'll turn in my medals from Marathon.   30

Strophe 2

Chorus[(m)]: Onward and upward! A little push,
    And we're there.
Ouch, my shoulders! I could wish
    For a pair
Of good strong oxen. Keep your eye   35
    On the fire there, it mustn't die.
                    Akh! Akh!
The smoke would make a cadaver cough!

***Antistrophe:** Song sung by the Chorus following the Strophe, as they danced back from stage left to stage right.

40   *Antistrophe 2*

Holy Herakles, a hot spark
  Bit my eye!
Damn this hellfire, damn this work!
  So say I.
Onward and upward just the same.
45   (Laches, remember the Goddess: for shame!)
                    Akh! Akh!
     The smoke would make a cadaver cough!
Koryphaios[(m)]: At last (and let us give suitable thanks to God
     for his infinite mercies) I have managed to bring
50   my personal flame to the common goal. It breathes, it lives.
     Now, gentlemen, let us consider. Shall we insert
     the torch, say, into the brazier, and thus extract
     a kindling brand? And shall we then, do you think,
     push on to the gate like valiant sheep? On the whole yes.
55   But I would have you consider this, too: if they—
     I refer to the women—should refuse to open,
     what then? Do we set the doors afire
     and smoke them out? At ease, men. Meditate.
     Akh, the smoke! Woof! What we really need
60   is the loan of a general or two from the Samos Command.*
     At least we've got this lumber off our backs.
     That's something. And now let's look to our fire.
     O Pot, brave Brazier, touch my torch with flame!
     Victory, Goddess, I invoke thy name!
65   Strike down these paradigms of female pride,
     And we shall hang our trophies up inside.

[*Enter* CHORUS OF OLD WOMEN *on the walls of the Akropolis, carrying jars of water.*]

Koryphaios[(woman)]: Smoke, girls, smoke! There's smoke all over the place!
     Probably fire, too. Hurry, girls! Fire! Fire!

Strophe 1

Chorus[(women)]: Nikodike, run!
  Or Kalyke's done
  To a turn, and poor Kritylla's
70   Smoked like a ham.
                    Damn
     These old men! Are we too late?

---

*Samos Command: Headquarters of the Athenian military.

I nearly died down at the place
Where we fill our jars:
   Slaves pushing and jostling—   75
   Such a hustling
I never saw in all my days.

Antistrophe 1

But here's water at last.
Haste, sisters, haste!
Slosh it on them, slosh it down,   80
the silly old wrecks!
                   Sex
Almighty! What they want's
A hot bath? Good. Send one down.
Athena of Athens town,
   Trito-born!* Helm of Gold!   85
   Cripple the old
Firemen! Help us help them drown!

[*The old men capture a woman,* STRATYLLIS.]

Stratyllis: Let me go! Let me go!
Koryphaios(w):   You walking corpses,
  have you no shame?
Koryphaios(m):   I wouldn't have believed it!
An army of women in the Akropolis!   90
Koryphaios(w):So we scare you, do we? Grandpa,
  you've seen only our pickets yet!
Koryphaios(m):   Hey, Phaidrias!
Help me with the necks of these jabbering hens!
Koryphaios(w): Down with your pots, girls! We'll need both hands
  if these antiques attack us!
Koryphaios(m): Want your face kicked in?   95
Koryphaios(w): Want your balls chewed off?
Koryphaios(m):   Look out! I've got a stick!
Koryphaios(w): You lay a half-inch of your stick on Stratyllis,
  and you'll never stick again!
Koryphaios(m): Fall apart!
Koryphaios(w):   I'll spit up your guts!
Koryphaios(m):   Euripides! Master!
  How well you knew women!

---

*Trito-born: Athena, goddess of wisdom, was said to have been born near Lake Tritonis, in Libya.

100 **Koryphaios**^(w):   Listen to him, Rhodippe,
    up with the pots!
Koryphaios^(m):   Demolition of God,
    what good are your pots?
Koryphaios^(w):   You refugee from the tomb,
    what good is your fire?
Koryphaios^(m):   Good enough to make a pyre
    to barbecue you!
Koryphaios^(w): We'll squizzle your kindling!
Koryphaios^(m): You think so?
105 **Koryphaios**^(w):   Yah! Just hang around a while!
Koryphaios^(m): Want a touch of my torch?
Koryphaios^(w):   It needs a good soaping.
Koryphaios^(m): How about you?
Koryphaios^(w):   Soap for a senile bridegroom!
Koryphaios^(m): Senile? Hold your trap
Koryphaios^(w):   Just *you* try to hold it!
Koryphaios^(m): The yammer of women!
KORYPHAIOS^(w):   Oh is that so?
110   You're not in the jury room now, you know.
Koryphaios^(m): Gentlemen, I beg you, burn off that woman's hair!
Koryphaios^(w): Let it come down!

[They empty their pots on the men.]

Koryphaios^(m): What a way to drown!
Koryphaios^(w):   Hot, hey?
Koryphaios^(m):   Say,
    enough!
Koryphaios^(w):   Dandruff
    needs watering. I'll make you
    nice and fresh.
Koryphaios^(m):   For God's sake, you,
    hold off!

Scene 1

[Enter a Commissioner accompanied by four constables.]

Commissioner: These degenerate women! What a racket of little drums,
    what a yapping for Adonis* on every house-top!
    It's like the time in the Assembly when I was listening
    to a speech—out of order, as usual—by that fool

---

*Adonis: Fertility god, loved by Aphrodite.

Demostratos,* all about troops for Sicily,*   5
that kind of nonsense—
                    and there was his wife
trotting around in circles howling
Alas for Adonis!—
                    and Demostratos insisting
we must draft every last Zakynthian that can walk—
and his wife up there on the roof,
drunk as an owl, yowling
Oh weep for Adonis!—
                    and that damned ox Demostratos
mooing away through the rumpus. That's what we get
for putting up with this wretched woman-business!

Koryphaios^(m): Sir, you haven't heard the half of it. They laughed at us!   15
Insulted us! They took pitchers of water
and nearly drowned us! We're still wringing out our clothes,
for all the world like unhousebroken brats.

Commissioner: Serves you right, by Poseidon!
Whose fault is it if these women-folk of ours
get out of hand? We coddle them,
we teach them to be wasteful and loose. You'll see a husband
go into a jeweler's. "Look," he'll say,
"jeweler," he'll say, "you remember that gold choker
you made for my wife? Well, she went to a dance last night   25
and broke the clasp. Now, I've got to go to Salamis,
and can't be bothered. Run over to my house tonight,
will you, and see if you can put it together for her."
Or another one
goes to a cobbler—a good strong workman, too,   30
with an awl that was never meant for child's play. "Here,"
he'll tell him, "one of my wife's shoes is pinching
her little toe. Could you come up about noon
and stretch it out for her?"
                    Well, what do you expect?
Look at me, for example, I'm a Public Officer,   35
and it's one of my duties to pay off the sailors.
And where's the money? Up there in the Akropolis!
And those blasted women slam the door in my face!
But what are we waiting for?
                    —Look here, constable,
stop sniffing around for a tavern, and get us   40

---

*Demostratos:** Athenian orator and politician.
*Sicily:** Reference to the Sicilian Expedition (415–413 B.C.) in which Athens was decisively defeated.

some crowbars. We'll force their gates! As a matter of fact,
I'll do a little forcing myself.

[*Enter* LYSISTRATA, *above, with* MYRRHINE, KALONIKE, *and the* BOIOTIAN.]

Lysistrata: No need of forcing.
Here I am, of my own accord. And all this talk
about locked doors—! We *don't need locked doors,*
45   but *just the least bit of common sense.*
Commissioner: Is that so, ma'am!
                            —Where's my constable?
                            —Constable,
arrest that woman, and tie her hands behind her.
LYSISTRATA: If he touches me, I swear by Artemis
there'll be one scamp dropped from the public pay-roll tomorrow!
50   **Commissioner:** Well, constable? You're not afraid, I suppose? Grab her,
two of you, around the middle!
KALONIKE: No, by Pandrosos!*
Lay a hand on her, and I'll jump on you so hard
your guts will come out the back door!
Commissioner: That's what *you* think!
Where's the sergeant?—Here, you: tie up that trollop first,
the one with the pretty talk!
55   **Myrrhine:**   By the Moon-Goddess,*
just try! They'll have to scoop you up with a spoon!
COMMISSIONER: Another one!
                        Officer, seize that woman!
                                    I swear
I'll put an end to this riot!
Boiotian: By the Taurian,*
one inch closer, you'll be one screaming bald-head!
60   **Commissioner:** Lord, what a mess! And my constables seem ineffective.
But—women get the best of us? By God, no!
                            —Skythians!*
Close ranks and forward march!
LYSISTRATA: "Forward," indeed!
By the Two Goddesses, what's the sense in *that?*
They're up against four companies of women
armed from top to bottom.
65   **Commissioner:**   Forward, my Skythians!
Lysistrata: Forward, yourselves, dear comrades!

***Pandrosos:** A woman's oath referring to one of the daughters of the founder of Athens.
***Moon**-Goddess: Artemis, goddess of the hunt and of fertility, daughter of Zeus.
***Taurian:** Reference to Artemis, who was said to have been worshiped in a cult at Taurica Chersonesos.
***Skythians:** Athenian archers.

You grainlettucebeanseedmarket girls!
You garlicandonionbreadbakery girls!
Give it to 'em! Knock 'em down! Scratch 'em!
Tell 'em what you think of 'em!

[*General melee, the* SKYTHIANS *yield.*]

—Ah, that's enough!

Sound a retreat: good soldiers don't rob the dead.   70
Commissioner: A nice day *this* has been for the police!
Lysistrata: Well, there you are.—Did you really think we women
  would be driven like slaves? Maybe now you'll admit
  that a woman knows something about spirit.
Commissioner: Spirit enough,   75
  especially spirits in bottles! Dear Lord Apollo!
Koryphaios[(m)]: Your Honor, there's no use talking to them. Words
  mean nothing whatever to wild animals like these.
  Think of the sousing they gave us! and the water
  was not, I believe, of the purest.   80
Koryphaios[(w)]: You shouldn't have come after us. And if you try it again,
  you'll be one eye short!—Although, as a matter of fact,
  what I like best is just to stay at home and read,
  like a sweet little bride: never hurting a soul, no,
  never going out. But if you *must* shake hornets' nests,   85
  look out for the hornets.

Strophe 1

Chorus[(m)]: Of all the beasts that God hath wrought
    What monster's worse than woman?
  Who shall encompass with his thought
    Their guile unending? No man.   90
  They've seized the Heights, the Rock, the Shrine—
    But to what end? I wot not.
  Sure there's some clue to their design!
    Have you the key? I thought not.
Koryphaios[(m)]: We might question them, I suppose. But I warn you, sir,   95
  don't believe anything you hear! It would be un-Athenian
  not to get to the bottom of this plot.
Commissioner: Very well.
  My first question is this: Why, so help you God,
  did you bar the gates of the Akropolis?
Lysistrata: Why?
  To keep the money, of course. No money, no war.   100
COMMISSIONER: You think that money's the cause of war?

Lysistrata: I do.
  Money brought about that Peisandros* business
  and all the other attacks on the State. Well and good!
  They'll not get another cent here!
Commissioner: And what will you do?
Lysistrata: What a question! From now on, we intend

105   to control the Treasury.
Commissioner: Control the Treasury!
Lysistrata: Why not? Does that seem strange? After all,
  we control our household budgets.
Commissioner: But that's different!
Lysistrata: "Different"? What do you mean?
Commissioner: I mean simply this:
  it's the Treasury that pays for National Defense.

110 **Lysistrata:** Unnecessary. We propose to abolish war.
Commissioner: Good God.—And National Security?
Lysistrata: Leave that to us.
Commissioner: You?
Lysistrata: Us.
Commissioner: We're done for, then!
Lysistrata: Never mind.
  We women will save you in spite of yourselves.
Commissioner: What nonsense!
Lysistrata: If you like. But you must accept it, like it or not.

115 **Commissioner:** Why, this is downright subversion!
Lysistrata: Maybe it is.
  But we're going to save you, Judge.
Commissioner: I don't *want* to be saved.
Lysistrata: Tut. The death-wish. All the more reason.
Commissioner: But the idea of women bothering
      themselves about peace and war!
Lysistrata: Will you listen to me?
Commissioner: Yes. But be brief, or I'll—

120 **Lysistrata:** This is no time for stupid threats.
Commissioner: By the gods,
  I can't stand any more!
An Old Woman: Can't stand? Well, well.
Commissioner: That's enough out of you, you old buzzard!
Now, Lysistrata: tell me what you're thinking.
Lysistrata: Glad to.
                   Ever since this war began

125   We women have been watching you men, agreeing with you,
  keeping our thoughts to ourselves. That doesn't mean

---

*__Peisandros:__ A politician who plotted against the Athenian democracy.

we were happy: we weren't, for we saw how things were going;
but we'd listen to you at dinner
arguing this way and that.

      —Oh you, and your big   130
Top Secrets!—
And then we'd grin *like little patriots*
(though goodness knows we didn't feel like grinning) and ask you:
"Dear, did the Armistice come up in Assembly today?"
    And you'd say, "None of your business! Pipe down!" you'd say.
And so we would.

An Old Woman: *I* wouldn't have, by God!   135
Commissioner: You'd have taken a beating, then!
      —Go on.
Lysistrata: Well, we'd be quiet. But then, you know, all at once
you men would think up something worse than ever.
Even *I* could see it was fatal. And, "Darling," I'd say,
"have you gone completely mad?" And my husband would look at me   140
and say, "Wife, you've got your weaving to attend to.
Mind your tongue, if you don't want a slap. 'War's
a man's affair!' "*
Commissioner: Good words, and well pronounced.
Lysistrata: You're a fool if you think so.
       It was hard enough
to put up with all this banquet-hall strategy.   145
But then we'd hear you out in the public square:
"Nobody left for the draft-quota here in Athens?"
you'd say; and, "No," someone else would say, "not a man!"
And so we women decided to rescue Greece.
You might as well listen to us now: you'll have to, later.   150
Commissioner: *You* rescue Greece? Absurd.
Lysistrata: You're the absurd one.
Commissioner: You expect me to take orders from a woman?
     I'd die first!
Lysistrata: Heavens, if that's what's bothering you, take my veil,
here, and wrap it around your poor head.
Kalonike: Yes,
and you can have my market-basket, too.   155
Go home, tighten your girdle, do the washing, mind
your beans! "War's a woman's affair!"
Koryphaios[(w)]:   Ground pitchers! Close ranks!

*****War's a man's affair!':** Quoted from Homer's *Iliad*, VI, 492, Hector's farewell to his wife, Andromache.

Antistrophe

Chorus[(w)]: This is a dance that I know well,
160   My knees shall never yield.
    Wobble and creak I may, but still
        I'll keep the well-fought field.
Valor and grace march on before,
    Love prods us from behind.
165   Our slogan is EXCELSIOR,
    Our watchword SAVE MANKIND.

Koryphaios[(w)]: Women, remember your grandmothers! Remember
    that little old mother of yours, what a stinger she was!
    On, on, never slacken. There's a strong wind astern!

170 **Lysistrata:** O Eros of delight! O Aphrodite! Kyprian!*
    If ever desire has drenched our breasts or dreamed
    in our thighs, let it work so now on the men of Hellas*
    that they shall tail us through the land, slaves, slaves
    to Woman, Breaker of Armies!

COMMISSIONER: And if we do?

175 **Lysistrata:** Well, for one thing, we shan't have to watch you
    going to market, a spear in one hand, and heaven knows
    what in the other.

Kalonike: Nicely said, by Aphrodite!

Lysistrata: As things stand now, you're neither men nor women.
    Armor clanking with kitchen pans and pots—
180   You sound like a pack of Korybantes!*

Commissioner: A man must do what a man must do.

Lysistrata: So I'm told.
    But to see a General, complete with Gorgon-shield,
    jingling along the dock to buy a couple of herrings!

Kalonike: *I* saw a Captain the other day—lovely fellow he was,
185   nice curly hair—sitting on his horse; and—can you believe it?—
    he'd just bought some soup, and was pouring it into his helmet!
    And there was a soldier from Thrace
    swishing his lance like something out of Euripides,
    and the poor fruit-store woman got so scared
190   that she ran away and let him have his figs free!

    ***Kyprian:** Reference to Aphrodite's association with Cyprus (Kyprus), a place sacred to her and a center
for her worship.
    ***Hellas:**
    ***Korybantes:** Priestesses of Cybele, a fertility goddess, who was celebrated in frenzied rituals accompanied
by the beating of cymbals.

Commissioner: All this is beside the point.
                              Will you be so kind
   as to tell me how you mean to save Greece?
Lysistrata: Of course.
   Nothing could be simpler.
Commissioner: I assure you, I'm all ears.
Lysistrata: Do you know anything about weaving?
   Say the yarn gets tangled: we thread it   195
   this way and that through the skein, up and down,
   until it's free. And it's like that with war.
   We'll send our envoys
   up and down, this way and that, all over Greece,
   until it's finished.
Commissioner: Yarn? Thread? Skein?   200
   Are you out of your mind? I tell you,
   war is a serious business.
Lysistrata: So serious
   that I'd like to go on talking about weaving.
Commissioner: All right. Go ahead.
Lysistrata: The first thing we have to do
   is to wash our yarn, get the dirt out of it.   205
   You see? Isn't there too much dirt here in Athens?
   You must wash those men away.
                              Then our spoiled wool—
   that's like your job-hunters, out for a life
   of no work and big pay. Back to the basket,
   citizens or not, allies or not,   210
   or friendly immigrants.
                              And your colonies?
   Hanks of wool lost in various places. Pull them
   together, weave them into one great whole,
   and our voters are clothed for ever.
Commissioner: It would take a woman
   to reduce state questions to a matter of carding and weaving.   215
Lysistrata: You fool! Who were the mothers whose sons sailed off
   to fight for Athens in Sicily?
Commissioner: Enough!
   I beg you, do not call back those memories.
Lysistrata: And then,
   instead of the love that every woman needs,
   we have only our single beds, where we can dream
   of our husbands off with the Army.   220

Bad enough for wives!
But what about our girls, getting older every day,
and older, and no kisses?

Commissioner: Men get older, too.

Lysistrata: Not in the same sense.

A soldier's discharged,
and he may be bald and toothless, yet he'll find

225   a pretty young thing to go to bed with.

But a woman!
Her beauty is gone with the first gray hair.
She can spend her time
consulting the oracles and the fortune-tellers,

230   but they'll never send her a husband.

Commissioner: Still, if a man can rise to the occasion—

Lysistrata: Rise? Rise, yourself!

[*Furiously*]

Go invest in a coffin!

You've money enough.

I'll bake you
a cake for the Underworld.

And here's your funeral
wreath!

[*She pours water upon him.*]

Myrrhine: And here's another!

[*More water.*]

Kalonike: And here's

235   my contribution!

[*More water.*]

Lysistrata: What are you waiting for?
All aboard Styx Ferry!

Charon's* calling for you!
It's sailing-time: don't disrupt the schedule!

Commissioner: The insolence of women! And to me!

240   No, by God, I'll go back to town and show
the rest of the Commission what might happen
        to them.   [*Exit* COMMISSIONER.]

Lysistrata: Really, I suppose we should have laid out his corpse
on the doorstep, in the usual way.

---

*Charon:** The god who ferried the souls of the newly dead across the river Styx to Hades.

But never mind.
We'll give him the rites of the dead tomorrow morning.
                    [*Exit* LYSISTRATA *with* MYRRHINE *and* KALONIKE.]

Parabasis:* Choral Episode

*Ode*1*

Koryphaios(m): Sons of Liberty, awake! The day of glory is at hand.
Chorus(m): I smell tyranny afoot, I smell it rising from the land.
I scent a trace of Hippias,* I sniff upon the breeze
A dismal Spartan hogo that suggests King Kleisthenes.*
   Strip, strip for action, brothers!   5
   Our wives, aunts, sisters, mothers
Have sold us out: the streets are full of godless female rages.
Shall we stand by and let our women confiscate our wages?
                              [Epirrhema* 1]
Koryphaios(m): Gentlemen, it's a disgrace to Athens, a disgrace
to all that Athens stands for, if we allow these grandmas   10
to jabber about spears and shields and making friends
with the Spartans. What's a Spartan? Give me a wild wolf
any day. No. They want the Tyranny back, I suppose.
Are we going to take that? No. Let us look like
the innocent serpent, but be the flower under it,   15
as the poet sings. And just to begin with,
I propose to poke a number of teeth
down the gullet of that harridan over there.

Antode 1*

Koryphaios(w): Oh, is that so? When you get home, your own mamma
    won't know you!
Chorus(w): Who do you think we are, you senile bravos? Well, I'll show you. 20
   I bore the sacred vessels in my eighth year,* and at ten

  ***Parabasis:** Section of the play in which the author presented his own views through the Koryphaios directly to the audience. The parabasis in *Lysistrata* is shorter than those in Aristophanes' other works and unusual in that the Koryphaios does not speak directly for the author.
  ***Ode:** Song sung by the Chorus.
  ***Hippias:** An Athenian tyrant.
  ***Kleisthenes:** A bisexual Athenian.
  ***Epirrhema:** A part of the parabasis spoken by the Koryphaios following an ode delivered by his or her half of the Chorus.
  ***Antode:** Lyric song sung by half of the Chorus in response to the Ode sung by the other half.
  ***eighth year:** Young girls between the ages of seven and eleven served in the temple of Athena in the Akropolis.

I was pounding out the barley for Athena Goddess;* then
   They made me Little Bear
   At the Brauronian Fair;*
25   I'd held the Holy Basket* by the time I was of age,
The Blessed Dry Figs had adorned my plump decolletage.

[Antepirrhema* 1]

Koryphaios^(w): A "disgrace to Athens," and I, just at the moment
I'm giving Athens the best advice she ever had?
Don't I pay taxes to the State? Yes, I pay them
30   in baby boys. And what do you contribute,
you impotent horrors? Nothing but waste: all
our Treasury,* dating back to the Persian Wars,
gone! rifled! And not a penny out of your pockets!
Well, then? Can you cough up an answer to that?
35   Look out for your own gullet, or you'll get a crack
from this old brogan that'll make your teeth see stars!

Ode 2

Chorus^(m):Oh insolence!
   Am I unmanned?
   Incontinence!
40   Shall my scarred hand
   Strike never a blow
   To curb this flowing
   female curse?
   Leipsydrion!*
45   Shall I betray
   The laurels won
   On that great day?
   Come, shake a leg;
   Shed old age, beg
50   The years reverse!

[Epirrhema 2]

Koryphaios^(m): Give them an inch, and we're done for! We'll have them
launching boats next and planning naval strategy,
sailing down on us like so many Artemisias.

---

*pounding out the barley for Athena Goddess: At age ten a girl could be chosen to grind the sacred grain of Athena.

*Brauronian Fair: A ritual in the cult of Artemis, who is associated with wild beasts, in which young girls dressed up as bears and danced for the goddess.

*Holy Basket: In one ritual to Athena, young girls carried baskets of objects sacred to the goddess.

*Antepirrhema: The speech delivered by the second Koryphaios after the second half of the Chorus had sung an ode.

*Treasury: Athenian politicians were raiding the funds that were collected by Athens to finance a war against Persia.

*Leipsydrion: A place where Athenian patriots had heroically fought.

Or maybe they have ideas about the cavalry.   55
That's fair enough, women are certainly good
in the saddle. Just look at Mikon's paintings,
vall those Amazons wrestling with all those men!
On the whole, a straitjacket's their best uniform.

Antode 2

Chorus(w):Tangle with me,   60
    And you'll get cramps.
    Ferocity
    's no use now, Gramps!
    By the Two,
    I'll get through
    To you wrecks yet!   65
    I'll scramble your eggs,
    I'll burn your beans,
    With my two legs.
    You'll see such scenes
    As never yet   70
    Your two eyes met.
    A curse? You bet!
                                            [Antepirrhema 2]
Koryphaios(w): If Lampito stands by me, and that delicious Theban girl,
    Ismenia—what good are *you?* You and your seven
    Resolutions! Resolutions? Rationing Boiotian eels   75
    and making our girls go without them at Hekate's* Feast!
    That was statesmanship! And we'll have to put up with it
    and all the rest of your decrepit legislation
    until some patriot—God give him strength!—
    grabs you by the neck and kicks you off the Rock.   80

Scene 2

[Reenter LYSISTRATA and her lieutenants.]

Koryphaios(w) (*tragic tone*): *Great Queen, fair Architect of our emprise,*
    Why lookst thou on us with foreboding eyes?
Lysistrata: The behavior of these idiotic women!
    There's something about the female temperament
    that I can't bear!
Koryphaios(w): What in the world do you mean?   5
Lysistrata: Exactly what I say.

---

*Hekate: Patron of successful wars, object of a Boiotian cult (later associated with sorcery).

Koryphaios(w): What dreadful thing has happened?
Come, tell us: we're all your friends.
Lysistrata: It isn't easy
to say it; yet, God knows, we can't hush it up.
Koryphaios(w): Well, then? Out with it!
Lysistrata: To put it bluntly,
we're dying to get laid.
10 **Koryphaios**(w):   Almighty God!
Lysistrata: Why bring God into it?—No, it's just as I say.
I can't manage them any longer: they've gone man-crazy,
they're all trying to get out.
Why, look:
one of them was sneaking out the back door
15   over there by Pan's cave; another
was sliding down the walls with rope and tackle;
another was climbing aboard a sparrow, ready to take off
for the nearest brothel—I dragged *her* back by the hair!
They're all finding some reason to leave.
Look there!
There goes another one.
20   —Just a minute, you!
Where are you off to so fast?
First Woman: I've got to get home.
I've a lot of Milesian wool, and the worms are spoiling it.
Lysistrata: Oh bother you and your worms! Get back inside!
25 **First Woman:** I'll be back right away, I swear I will.
I just want to get it stretched out on my bed.
Lysistrata: You'll do no such thing. You'll stay right here.
First Woman: And my wool?
You want it ruined?
Lysistrata: Yes, for all I care.
Second Woman: Oh dear! My lovely new flax from Amorgos—
I left it at home, all uncarded!
Lysistrata: Another one!
30   And all she wants is someone to card her flax.
Get back in there!
Second Woman: But I swear by the Moon-Goddess,
the minute I get it done, I'll be back!
Lysistrata: I say No.
If you, why not all the other women as well?
35 **Third Woman:** O Lady Eileithyia!* Radiant goddess! Thou

---

*Eileithyia: Goddess of childbirth.

intercessor for women in childbirth! Stay, I pray thee,
oh stay this parturition. Shall I pollute
a sacred spot?*

Lysistrata: And what's the matter with *you?*

Third Woman: I'm having a baby—any minute now.

Lysistrata: But you weren't pregnant yesterday.

Third Woman: Well, I am today.
Let me go home for a midwife, Lysistrata: 40
there's not much time.

Lysistrata: I never heard such nonsense.
What's that bulging under your cloak?

Third Woman: A little baby boy.

Lysistrata: It certainly isn't. But it's something hollow,
like a basin or—Why, it's the helmet of Athena!
And you said you were having a baby.

Third Woman: Well, I am! So there!   45

Lysistrata: Then why the helmet?

Third Woman: I was afraid that my pains
might begin here in the Akropolis; and I wanted
to drop my chick into it, just as the dear doves do.

Lysistrata: Lies! Evasions!—But at least one thing's clear: 50
you can't leave the place before your purification.*

Third Woman: But I can't stay here in the Akropolis! Last night I dreamed
of the Snake.

First Woman: And those horrible owls, the noise they make!
I can't get a bit of sleep; I'm just about dead.

Lysistrata: You useless girls, that's enough: Let's have no more lying.
Of course you want your men. But don't you imagine   55
that they want you just as much? I'll give you my word,
their nights must be pretty hard.
                    Just stick it out!
A little patience, that's all, and our battle's won.
I have heard an Oracle. Should you like to hear it?

First Woman: An Oracle? Yes, tell us!

Lysistrata: Here is what it says: 60
    WHEN SWALLOWS SHALL THE HOOPOE SHUN
    AND SPURN HIS HOT DESIRE,
ZEUS WILL PERFECT WHAT THEY'VE BEGUN
AND SET THE LOWER HIGHER.

First Woman: Does that mean we'll be on top?   65

Lysistrata: BUT IF THE SWALLOWS SHALL FALL OUT

---

*purification: A ritual cleansing of a woman after childbirth.
pollute a sacred spot: Giving birth on the Akropolis was forbidden because it was sacred ground.

AND TAKE THE HOOPOE'S BAIT,
A CURSE MUST MARK THEIR HOUR OF DOUBT,
   INFAMY SEAL THEIR FATE.
Third Woman: I swear, *that* Oracle's all too clear.
70 **First Woman:**   Oh the dear gods!
Lysistrata: Let's not be downhearted, girls. Back to our places!
   The god has spoken. How can we possibly fail him?

                  [*Exit* LYSISTRATA *with the dissident women.*]

Choral Episode

Strophe

Chorus(m): I know a little story that I learned way back in school
   Goes like this:
   Once upon a time there was a young man—and no fool—
   Named Melanion; and his
5   One aversi-on was marriage. He loathed the very thought.
   So he ran off to the hills, and in a special grot
   Raised a dog, and spent his days
   Hunting rabbits. And it says
   That he never never never did come home.
10   It might be called a refuge *from* the womb.
   All right,
            all right,
                 all right!
   We're as bright as young Melanion, and we hate
   the very sight
   Of you women!
A Man: How about a kiss, old lady?
15 **A Woman:** Here's an onion for your eye!
A Man: A kick in the guts, then?
A Woman: Try, old bristle-tail, just try!
A Man: Yet they say Myronides
   On hands and knees
20   Looked just as shaggy fore and aft as I!

Antistrophe

Chorus(w): Well, *I* know a little story, and it's just as good as yours.
   Goes like this:
   Once there was a man named Timon—a rough diamond, of course,
   And that whiskery face of his
25   Looked like murder in the shrubbery. By God, he was a son

Of the Furies, let me tell you! And what did he do but run
From the world and all its ways,
Cursing mankind! And it says
That his choicest execrations as of then
Were leveled almost wholly at *old* men.   30
All right,
       all right,
           all right!
But there's one thing about Timon: he could always stand the sight
of us women.
A Woman: How about a crack in the jaw, Pop?
A Man: I can take it, Ma—no fear!   35
A Woman: How about a kick in the face?
A Man: You'd reveal your old caboose?
A Woman: What I'd show,
    I'll have you know,   40
    Is an instrument you're too far gone to use.

Scene 3

[*Reenter* LYSISTRATA.]

Lysistrata: Oh, quick, girls, quick! Come here!
A Woman: What is it?
LYSISTRATA: A man.
    A man simply bulging with love.
                     O Kyprian Queen,*
    O Paphian, O Kythereian! Hear us and aid us!
A Woman: Where is this enemy?
Lysistrata: Over there, by Demeter's shrine.
A Woman: Damned if he isn't. But who *is* he?
Myrrhine: My husband.   5
    Kinesias.
Lysistrata: Oh then, get busy! Tease him! Undermine him!
    Wreck him! Give him everything—kissing, tickling, nudging,
    whatever you generally torture him with—: give him everything
    except what we swore on the wine we would not give.
Myrrhine: Trust me.
Lysistrata: I do. But I'll help you get him started.   10
    The rest of you women, stay back.

[*Enter* KINESIAS.]

---

*Kyprian Queen: Aphrodite.

Kinesias: Oh God! Oh my God!
   I'm stiff from lack of exercise. All I can do to stand up.
Lysistrata: Halt! Who are you, approaching our lines?
Kinesias: Me? I.
Lysistrata: A man?
KINESIAS: You have eyes, haven't you?
LYSISTRATA: Go away.
Kinesias: Who says so?
Lysistrata: Officer of the Day.
15 **Kinesias:**   Officer, I beg you,
   by all the gods at once, bring Myrrhine out.
Lysistrata: Myrrhine? And who, my good sir, are you?
Kinesias: Kinesias. Last name's Pennison. Her husband.
Lysistrata: Oh, of course. I beg your pardon. We're glad to see you.
20   We've heard so much about you. Dearest Myrrhine
   is always talking about Kinesias—never nibbles an egg
   or an apple without saying
   "Here's to Kinesias!"
Kinesias: Do you really mean it?
Lysistrata: I do.
   When we're discussing men, she always says
25   "Well, after all, there's nobody like Kinesias!"
Kinesias: Good God.—Well, then, please send her down here.
Lysistrata: And what do *I* get out of it?
Kinesias: A standing promise.
Lysistrata: I'll take it up with her.

                                        [*Exit* LYSISTRATA.]

Kinesias: But be quick about it!
   Lord, what's life without a wife? Can't eat. Can't sleep.
30   Every time I go home, the place is so empty, so
   insufferably sad. Love's killing me, Oh,
   hurry!

[*Enter* MANES, *a slave, with* KINESIAS'S *baby; the voice of* MYRRHINE *is heard off-stage.*]

Myrrhine: But of course I love him! Adore him—But no,
   he hates love. No. I won't go down.

[*Enter* MYRRHINE, *above.*]

Kinesias: Myrrhine!
   Darlingest Myrrhinette! Come down quick!
Myrrhine: Certainly not.
35 **Kinesias:**   Not? But why, Myrrhine?
Myrrhine: Why? You don't need me.

Kinesias: Need you? My God, *look* at me!
Myrrhine: So long!

[*Turns to go.*]

Kinesias: Myrrhine, Myrrhine, Myrrhine!
   If not for my sake, for our child!

[*Pinches Baby.*]

          —All right, you: pipe up!
Baby: Mummie! Mummie! Mummie!
Kinesias: You hear that?
   Pitiful, I call it. Six days now   40
   with never a bath; no food; enough to break your heart!
Myrrhine: My darlingest child! What a father *you* acquired!
Kinesias: At least come down for his sake.
Myrrhine: I suppose I must.
   Oh, this mother business!   [*Exit.*]
Kinesias: How pretty she is! And younger!
   The harder she treats me, the more bothered I get.

[MYRRHINE *enters, below.*]

Myrrhine: Dearest child,   45
   you're as sweet as your father's horrid. Give me a kiss.
Kinesias: Now don't you see how wrong it was to get involved
   in this scheming League of women? It's bad
   for us both.
Myrrhine: Keep your hands to yourself!
KINESIAS: But our house
   going to rack and ruin?
Myrrhine: *I* don't care.
Kinesias: And your knitting   50
   all torn to pieces by the chickens? Don't you care?
Myrrhine: Not at all.
Kinesias: And our debt to Aphrodite?
   Oh, *won't* you come back?
Myrrhine: No.—At least, not until you men
   make a treaty and stop this war.
Kinesias: Why, I suppose
   that might be arranged.   55
Myrrhine: Oh? Well, I suppose
   I might come down then. But meanwhile,
   I've sworn not to.
Kinesias: Don't worry.—Now let's have fun.
Myrrhine: No! Stop it! I said no!

                                    —Although, of course,
I *do* love you.

Kinesias: I know you do. Darling Myrrhine:
    come, shall we?

60 **Myrrhine:** Are you out of your mind? In front of the child?

Kinesias: Take him home, Manes.

[Exit MANES with BABY.]

There. He's gone.

Come on!

There's nothing to stop us now.

Myrrhine: You devil! But where?

Kinesias: In Pan's cave. What could be snugger than that?

MyrrhinE: But my purification before I go back to the Citadel?

Kinesias: Wash in the Klepsydra.*

Myrrhine: And my oath?

65 **Kinesias:**   Leave the oath to me.
    After all, I'm the man.

Myrrhine: Well . . . if you say so.

I'll go find a bed.

Kinesias: Oh, bother a bed! The ground's good enough for me.

Myrrhine: No. You're a bad man, but you deserve something better
    than dirt.

[Exit MYRRHINE.]

Kinesias: What a love she is! And how thoughtful!

[*Reenter* MYRRHINE.]

Myrrhine: Here's your bed.
    Now let me get my clothes off.

70   But, good horrors!
    We haven't a mattress.

Kinesias: Oh, forget the mattress!

Myrrhine: No.
    Just lying on blankets? Too sordid.

Kinesias: Give me a kiss.

Myrrhine: Just a second.   [*Exit* MYRRHINE.]

Kinesias: I swear, I'll explode!

[*Reenter* MYRRHINE.]

Myrrhine: Here's your mattress.
    I'll just take my dress off.

But look—

***Klepsydra:** A water clock beneath the walls of the Akropolis. Kinesias's suggestion borders on blasphemy.

where's our pillow?
Kinesias: I don't *need* a pillow!
Myrrhine: Well, *I* do.   75

> [*Exit* MYRRHINE.]

Kinesias: I don't suppose even Herakles*
would stand for this!

[*Reenter* MYRRHINE.]

Myrrhine: There we are. Ups-a-daisy!
Kinesias: So we are. Well, come to bed.
Myrrhine: But I wonder:
is everything ready now?
Kinesias: I can swear to that. Come, darling!
Myrrhine: Just getting out of my girdle.
But remember, now,   80
what you promised about the treaty.
Kinesias: Yes, yes, yes!
Myrrhine: But no coverlet!
Kinesias: Damn it, I'll be
your coverlet!
Myrrhine: Be right back.   [*Exit* MYRRHINE.]
Kinesias: This girl and her coverlets
will be the death of me.

[*Reenter* MYRRHINE.]

Myrrhine: Here we are. Up you go!
Kinesias: Up? I've been up for ages.
Myrrhine: Some perfume?   85
Kinesias: No, by Apollo!
Myrrhine: Yes, by Aphrodite!
I don't care whether you want it or not.

> [*Exit* MYRRHINE.]

Kinesias: For love's sake, hurry!

[*Reenter* MYRRHINE]

Myrrhine: Here, in your hand. Rub it right in.
Kinesias: Never cared for perfume.
And this is particularly strong. Still, here goes.   90
Myrrhine: What a nitwit I am! I brought you the Rhodian bottle.
Kinesias: Forget it.
Myrrhine: No trouble at all. You just wait here.

> [Exit MYRRHINE.]

---

*Herakles: Greek hero (Hercules) known for his Twelve Labors.

Kinesias: God damn the man who invented perfume!

[*Reenter* MYRRHINE.]

Myrrhine: At last! The right bottle!

Kinesias: I've got the rightest
95   bottle of all, and it's right here waiting for you.
      Darling, forget everything else. Do come to bed.
Myrrhine: Just let me get my shoes off.
                                  —And, by the way,
      you'll vote for the treaty?
Kinesias: I'll think about it.

[MYRRHINE *runs away.*]

      There! That's done it! The damned woman,
100   she gets me all bothered, she half kills me,
      and off she runs! What'll I do? Where
      can I get laid?
                        —And you, little prodding pal,
      who's going to take care of *you?* No, you and I
      had better get down to old Foxdog's Nursing Clinic.
105 **Chorus**[(m)]: Alas for the woes of man, alas
          Specifically for you.
      She's brought you to a pretty pass:
      What are you going to do?
      Split, heart! Sag, flesh! Proud spirit, crack!
110   Myrrhine's got you on your back.
Kinesias: The agony, the protraction!
Koryphaios[(m)]:   Friend,
          What woman's worth a damn?
      They bitch us all, world without end.
Kinesias: Yet they're so damned sweet, man!
115 **Koryphaios**[(m)]: Calamitous, that's what I say.
      you should have learned that much today.
Chorus[(m)]: O blessed Zeus, roll womankind.
          Up into one great ball;
      Blast them aloft on a high wind,
          And once there, let them fall.
120   Down, down they'll come, the pretty dears,
      And split themselves on our thick spears.

[*Exit* KINESIAS.]

Scene 4

[*Enter a Spartan Herald.*]

Herald: Gentlemen, Ah beg you will be so kind
      as to direct me to the Central Committee.
      Ah have a communication.

[*Reenter* COMMISSIONER.]

Commissioner: Are you a man,
  or a fertility symbol?
Herald: Ah refuse to answer that question!
  Ah'm a certified Herald from Spahta, and Ah've come   5
  to talk about an ahmistice.
Commissioner: Then why
  that spear under your cloak?
Herald: Ah have no speah!
Commissioner: You don't walk naturally, with your tunic
  poked out so. You have a tumor, maybe,
  or a hernia?
Herald: You lost yo' mahnd, man?
Commissioner: Well,
  something's up, I can see that. And I don't like it.   10
Herald: Colonel, Ah resent this.
Commissioner: So I see. But what *is* it?
Herald: A staff
  with a message from Spahta.
Commissioner: Oh, I know about those staffs.
  Well, then, man, speak out: How are things in Sparta?
Herald: Hahd, Colonel, hahd! We're at a standstill.   15
  Cain't seem to think of anything but women.
Commissioner: How curious! Tell me, do you Spartans think
  that maybe Pan's to blame?
Herald: Pan? No, Lampito and her little naked friends.
  They won't let a man come nigh them.   20
Commissioner: How are you handling it?
Herald: Losing our mahnds,
  if y' want to know, and walking around hunched over
  lahk men carrying candles in a gale.
  The women have swohn they'll have nothing to do with us
  until we get a treaty.
Commissioner: Yes. I know.   25
  It's a general uprising, sir, in all parts of Greece.
  But as for the answer—
                Sir: go back to Sparta
  and have them send us your Armistice Commission.
  I'll arrange things in Athens.
                And I may say
  that my standing is good enough to make them listen.   30
Herald: A man after mah own haht! Seh, Ah thank you.   [*Exit* HERALD.]

Choral Episode

Strophe

Chorus^(m): Oh these women! Where will you find
  A slavering beast that's more unkind?
    Where's a hotter fire?
  Give me a panther, any day.
5 He's not so merciless as they,
    And panthers don't conspire.

Antistrophe

Chorus^(w):We may be hard, you silly old ass,
  But who brought you to this stupid pass?
    You're the ones to blame.
  Fighting with us, your oldest friends,
10 Simply to serve your selfish ends—
    Really, you have no shame!
Koryphaios^(m): No, I'm through with women for ever.
Koryphaios^(w): If you say so.
  Still, you might put some clothes on. You look too absurd
15 standing around naked. Come, get into this cloak.
Koryphaios^(m): Thank you; you're right. I merely took it off
  because I was in such a temper.
Koryphaios^(w):   That's much better.
  Now you resemble a man again.
                    Why have you been so horrid?
  And look: there's some sort of insect in your eye.
  Shall I take it out?
20 **Koryphaios**^(m):   An insect, is it? So that's
  what's been bothering me. Lord, yes: take it out!
Koryphaios^(w): You might be more polite.
                    —But, heavens!
  What an enormous mosquito!
Koryphaios^(m):   You've saved my life.
  That mosquito was drilling an artesian well
  in my left eye.
25 **Koryphaios**^(w): Let me wipe.
  those tears away—And now: one little kiss?
Koryphaios^(m): No, no kisses.
Koryphaios^(w): You're so difficult.
Koryphaios^(m): You impossible women! How you do get around us!
  The poet was right: Can't live with you, or without you.
30 But let's be friends.

And to celebrate, you might join us in an Ode.

Strophe 1

Chorus^(m and w):Let it never be said
    That my tongue is malicious:
    Both by word and by deed
I would set an example that's noble and gracious.   35
    We've had sorrow and care
    Till we're sick of the tune.
    Is there anyone here
    Who would like a small loan?
      My purse is crammed,   40
      As you'll soon find;
And you needn't pay me back if the Peace gets signed.

Strophe 2

    I've invited to lunch
    Some Karystian rips*—
    An esurient bunch,   45
But I've ordered a menu to water their lips.
    I can still make soup
    And slaughter a pig.
    You're all coming, I hope?
    But a bath first, I beg!   50
    Walk right up
    As though you owned the place,
And you'll get the front door slammed to in your face.

Scene 5

[*Enter* SPARTAN AMBASSADOR, *with entourage.*]

Koryphaios^(m): The Commission has arrived from Sparta.
        How oddly they're walking!
           Gentlemen, welcome to Athens!
  How is life in Lakonia?
Ambassador: Need we discuss that?
  Simply use your eyes.
Chorus^(m):   The poor man's right:
        What a sight!

---

*Karystian rips: The Karystians were allies of Athens but were scorned for their primitive ways and loose morals.

5   **Ambassador:**   Words fail me.
But come, gentlemen, call in your Commissioners,
and let's get down to a Peace.
Choragos^(m):   The state we're in! Can't bear
a stitch below the waist. It's a kind of pelvic
paralysis.
Commissioner: Won't somebody call
        Lysistrata?—Gentlemen,
we're no better off than you.
10   **Ambassador:**   So I see.
A SPARTAN: Seh, do y'all feel a certain strain
early in the morning?
An Athenian: I do, sir. It's worse than a strain.
A few more days, and there's nothing for us but Kleisthenes,
that broken blossom.
Choragos^(m): But you'd better get dressed again.
15   You know these people going around Athens with chisels,
looking for statues of Hermes.*

Athenian: Sir, you are right.

Spartan: He certainly is! Ah'll put mah own clothes back on.

[*Enter* ATHENIAN COMMISSIONERS.]

Commissioner: Gentlemen from Sparta, welcome. This is a sorry business.
Spartan [*to one of his own group*]: Colonel, we got dressed just in time. Ah
20   sweah, if they'd seen us the way we were, there'd have been a new wah
between the states.
Commissioner: Shall we call the meeting to order?
                    Now, Lakonians,
what's your proposal?
Ambassador: We propose to *consider peace.*
Commissioner: Good. That's on our minds, too.
                    —Summon Lysistrata.
We'll never get anywhere without her.
25   **Ambassador:**   Lysistrata?
Summon Lysis-*any*body! Only, summon!
Koryphaios^(m):   No need to summon:
here she is, herself.

[*Enter* LYSISTRATA.]

---

*statues of Hermes:** The usual representation of Hermes was with an erect phallus. Statues of Hermes were scattered through Athens and were attacked by vandals just before the Sicilian Expedition.

Commissioner: Lysistrata! Lion of women!
　This is your hour to be
　hard and yielding, outspoken and shy, austere and 　　　　　　30
　gentle. You see here
　the best brains of Hellas (confused, I admit,
　by your devious charming) met as one man
　to turn the future over to you.
Lysistrata:　　　　　　　That's fair enough,
　unless you men take it into your heads
　to turn to each other instead of to us. But I'd know 　　　　35
　soon enough if you did.
　　　　　　—Where is *Reconciliation?*
Go, some of you: bring *her* here.　　　　　　*[Exeunt two women.]*
　　　　　　　And now, women,
　lead the Spartan delegates to me: *not roughly*
　or insultingly, as our men handle them, but gently,
　politely, as ladies should. Take them by the hand, 　　　　40
　or by anything else if they won't give you their hands.

[The SPARTANS *are escorted over.]*

There.—The Athenians next, by any convenient handle.

[The ATHENIANS *are escorted.]*

Stand there, please.—Now, all of you, listen to me.

*[During the following speech the two women reenter, carrying an enormous statue of a
　naked girl; this is Reconciliation.]*

　I'm only a woman, I know; but I've a mind,
　and, I think, not a bad one: I owe it to my father 　　　　45
　and to listening to the local politicians.
　So much for that.
　　　　　　Now, gentlemen,
　since I have you here, I intend to give you a scolding.
　We are all Greeks.
　Must I remind you of Thermopylai,* of Olympia, 　　　　50
　of Delphoi? names deep in all our hearts?
　Are they not a common heritage?
　　　　　　　Yet you men

---

*Thermopylai: A narrow pass where, in 480 B.C., an army of three hundred Spartans held out for three days
against a superior Persian force.

go raiding through the country from both sides,
55 Greek killing Greek, storming down Greek cities—
and all the time the Barbarian across the sea
is waiting for his chance!
              —That's my first point.
An Athenian: Lord! I can hardly contain myself.
Lysistrata: As for you Spartans:
Was it so long ago that Perikleides*
came here to beg our help? I can see him still,
60 his gray face, his sombre gown. And what did he want?
An army from Athens. All Messene
was hot at your heels, and the sea-god splitting your land.
Well, Kimon and his men,
four thousand strong, marched out and saved all Sparta.
65 And what thanks do we get? You come back to murder us.
An Athenian: They're aggressors, Lysistrata!
A Spartan: Ah admit it.
When Ah look at those laigs, Ah sweah Ah'll aggress mahself!
Lysistrata: And you, Athenians: do you think you're blameless?
70 Remember that bad time when we were helpless,
and an army came from Sparta, and that was the end of the Thessalian
    menace,
the end of Hippias and his allies.
                And that was Sparta,
and only Sparta; but for Sparta, we'd be
cringing slaves today, not free Athenians.

[*From this point, the male responses are less to* LYSISTRATA *than to the statue.*]

A Spartan: A well shaped speech.
75 **An Athenian:**   Certainly it has its points.
Lysistrata: Why are we fighting each other? With all this history
of favors given and taken, what stands in the way
of making peace?
Ambassador: Spahta is ready, ma'am,
so long as we get that place back.
Lysistrata: What place, man?
Ambassador: Ah refer to Pylos.
80 **Commissioner:**   Not a chance, by God!
Lysistrata: Give it to them, friend.
Commissioner: But—what shall we have to bargain with?
Lysistrata: Demand something in exchange.

---

*Perikleides:** Spartan ambassador to Athens who successfully urged Athenians to aid Sparta in quelling a
rebellion.

Commissioner: Good idea.—Well, then:
Cockeville first, and the Happy Hills, and the country
    between the Legs of Megara.
Ambassador: Mah government objects.
Lysistrata: Overruled. Why fuss about a pair of legs?   85

[*General assent. The statue is removed.*]

An Athenian: I want to get out of these clothes and start my plowing.
A Spartan: Ah'll fertilize mahn first, by the Heavenly Twins!
Lysistrata: And so you shall,
    once you've made peace. If you are serious,   90
    go, both of you, and talk with your allies.
Commissioner: Too much talk already. No, we'll stand together.
    We've only one end in view. All that we want
    is our women; and I speak for our allies.
Ambassador: Mah government concurs.
An Athenian: So does Karystos.
Lysistrata: Good—But before you come inside   95
    to join your wives at supper, you must perform
    the usual lustration. Then we'll open
    our baskets for you, and all that we have is yours.
    But you must promise upright good behavior
    from this day on. Then each man home with his woman!   100
An Athenian: Let's get it over with.
A Spartan: Lead on. Ah follow.
An Athenian: Quick as a cat can wink!
                                        [*Exeunt all but the* CHORUSES.]

Antistrophe 1

Chorus[(w)]:Embroideries and
        Twinkling ornaments and
        Pretty dresses—I hand   105
    them all over to you, and with never a qualm.
        They'll be nice for your daughters
        On festival days
        When the girls bring the Goddess
        The ritual prize.   110
        Come in, one and all:
        Take what you will.
    I've nothing here so tightly corked that you can't make it spill.

Antistrophe 2

        You may search my house,
        But you'll not find   115

The least thing of use,
Unless your two eyes are keener than mine.
   Your numberless brats
   Are half starved? And your slaves?
120   Courage, grandpa! I've lots
   Of grain left, and big loaves.
     I'll fill your guts,
     I'll go the whole hog;
But if you come too close to me, remember:
     'ware the dog!   [*Exeunt* CHORUSES.]

EXODOS*

[*A* drunken CITIZEN *enters, approaches the gate, and is halted by a sentry.*]

Citizen: Open. The. Door.
Sentry: Now, friend, just shove along!
  —So you want to sit down. If it weren't such an old joke,
  I'd tickle your tail with this torch. Just the sort of gag
  this audience appreciates.
CITIZEN: I. Stay. Right. Here.
Sentry: Get away from there, or I'll scalp you! The gentlemen from Sparta
5   are just coming back from dinner.

[*Exit* CITIZEN; *the general company reenters; the two* CHORUSES *now represent* SPARTANS *and* ATHENIANS.]

A Spartan: Ah must say,
  Ah never tasted better grub.
An Athenian: And those Lakonians!
  They're gentlemen, by the Lord! Just goes to show,
  a drink to the wise is sufficient.
10 **Commissioner:**   And why not?
  A sober man's an ass.
  Men of Athens, mark my words: the only efficient
  Ambassador's a drunk Ambassador. Is that clear?
  Look: we go to Sparta,
  and when we get there we're dead sober. The result?
15   Everyone cackling at everyone else. They make speeches;
  and even if we understand, we get it all wrong
  when we file our reports in Athens. But today—!
  Everybody's happy. Couldn't tell the difference
  between *Drink to Me Only* and

---

*Exodos: Final scene.

The Star-spangled Athens.
What's a few lies,
washed down in good strong drink?   20

[*Reenter the* DRUNKEN CITIZEN.]

Sentry: God almighty,
he's back again!
Citizen: I. Resume. My. Place.
A Spartan [*TO AN ATHENIAN*]: Ah beg yo', seh,
take yo' instrument in yo' hand and play for us.
Ah'm told   25
yo' understand the in*tri*cacies of the floot?
Ah'd lahk to execute a song and dance
in honor of Athens,
and, of cohse, of Spahta.
Citizen: Toot. On. Your. Flute.

[*The following song is a solo—an aria—accompanied by the flute. The* CHORUS OF
SPARTANS *begins a slow dance.*]

A SPARTAN: O memory,   30
Let the Muse speak once more
In my young voice. Sing glory.
Sing Artemision's shore,
Where Athens fluttered the Persians. *Alalai,**
Sing glory, that great   35
Victory! Sing also
Our Leonidas and his men,
Those wild boars, sweat and blood
Down in a red drench. Then, then
The barbarians broke, though they had stood   40
Numberless as the sands before!
O Artemis,
Virgin Goddess, whose darts
Flash in our forests: approve
This pact of peace and join our hearts,   45
From this day on, in love.
Huntress, descend!
Lysistrata: All that will come in time.
But now, Lakonians,
take home your wives. Athenians, take yours.
Each man be kind to his woman; and you, women   50

---

*Alalai:** War cry.

be equally kind. Never again, pray God,
shall we lose our way in such madness.

KORYPHAIOS^(Athenian):   And now
let's dance our joy.

[*From this point the dance becomes general.*]

CHORUS^(Athenian): Dance, you Graces

                              Artemis, dance

55   Dance, Phoibos,* Lord of dancing

                        Dance,

    In a scurry of Maenads,* Lord Dionysos

                    Dance, Zeus Thunderer

            Dance, Lady Hera*

    Queen of the sky

                Dance, dance, all you gods

    Dance witness everlasting of our pact

60   *Evohi Evohe**

    Dance for the dearest

           the Bringer of Peace

    Deathless Aphrodite!

Commissioner: Now let us have another song from Sparta.

Chorus^(SPARTAN): From Taygetos, from Taygetos,

65   Lakonian Muse, come down.

Sing to the Lord Apollo

    Who rules Amyklai Town.

*Sing Athena of the House of Brass!**

Sing Leda's Twins,* that chivalry

70   Resplendent on the shore

Of our Eurotas; sing the girls

    That dance along before:

Sparkling in dust their gleaming feet,

75   Their hair a Bacchant fire,

And Leda's daughter, thyrsos* raised,

    Leads their triumphant choir.

---

*Phoibos:** Apollo, god of the sun.

*Maenads:**Female worshipers of Bacchus (Dionysus).

*Hera:** Wife of Zeus.

*Evohi Evohe:** "Come forth! Come forth!" An orgiastic cry associated with rituals of Bacchus.

*House of Brass:** Temple to Athena on the Akropolis of Sparta.

*Leda's Twins:** Leda, raped by Zeus, bore quadruplets, two daughters (one of whom was Helen) and two
sons.

*thyrsos:** A staff twined with ivy and carried by Bacchus and his followers.

Chorus^(S and A): *Evohé!*

　　　　　Evohaí!
　　　　　　Evohé!
　　　　　　　　We pass
　　　　Dancing
　　　　　　dancing
　　　　　　　　to greet
　Athena of the House of Brass.

CRITICAL THINKING QUESTIONS

1. Before Lysistratra can confront the men who value war, she must first win over
   the women. As she attempts to convince them that they are the key to saving
   Greece (line 23), Lysistrata relies on several *appeals*. Identify and evaluate the
   effects of at least two of these appeals.

2. a. Read the argument between the Commissioner and Lysistrata in Scene I,
      beginning with line 43 and continuing through line 246. The *issue question*
      is clear: Should the Greeks continue to engage in war or work toward peace?
      List the *support* offered by the Commissioner and the *support* offered by
      Lysistrata.
   b. After examining the support used by both sides in this argument, consider
      what *value assumptions* underpin the two arguments. Underlying the Com-
      missioner's argument is the assumption *(warrant)* that the two genders
      each have a natural place in the world. What assumptions (warrants) un-
      derlie Lysistrata's argument?
   c. In her speech to the Commissioner, Lysistrata uses *argument by analogy*
      (see Glossary) in lines 194 through 215. Is this an effective argumentative
      strategy to use with her audience? Why or why not?

WRITING TOPICS

1. The use of logic and reason often leads to successful argument. However, the
   women in *Lysistrata* have found no success in attempting to reason with their
   men and, therefore, have moved to a cruder tactic. In this case, the women are
   using what is sometimes referred to as "the carrot and the stick." The carrot is
   the reward offered for accepting their argument while the stick is the punishment for not accepting the argument. For the Greek women, what forms do
   their carrots and sticks take? Describe an instance in contemporary society
   where rewards and punishments are used in an attempt to persuade.

2. *Lysistrata* has recently been revived on Broadway. What attraction does this
   two-thousand-year-old play hold for contemporary theater audiences? What

is Aristophanes's message about war? Does this message have an audience in today's world? If not, why not, and if so, who is carrying forward this message?

3. Read the poem, "Apostrophe to Man" by Edna St. Vincent Millay (page 605). Both the poem and the play present strong moral arguments against war. Is it valid to generalize that women are more likely to be antiwar than men? Why or why not? Use specific examples from history and contemporary times to support your viewpoint.

NONFICTION

ᐱᐱ

Francis Bacon (1533–1592)
Of Revenge

Revenge is a kind of wild justice, which the more man's nature runs to, the more ought law to weed it out. For as for the first wrong, it doth but offend the law, but the revenge of that wrong putteth the law out of office. Certainly in taking revenge, a man is but even with his enemy, but in passing it over, he is superior, for it is a prince's part to pardon. And Solomon, I am sure, saith, "It is the glory of a man to pass by an offense." That which is past is gone and irrevocable, and wise men have enough to do with things present and to come; therefore they do but trifle with themselves that labor in past matters. There is no man doth a wrong for the wrong's sake, but thereby to purchase himself profit, or pleasure, or honor, or the like. Therefore why should I be angry with a man for loving himself better than me? And if any man should do wrong merely out of ill nature, why, yet it is but like the thorn or briar, which prick and scratch because they can do no other. The most tolerable sort of revenge is for those wrongs which there is no law to remedy, but then let a man take heed the revenge be such as there is no law to punish; else a man's enemy is still beforehand, and it is two for one. Some, when they take revenge, are desirous the party should know whence it cometh. This the more generous. For the delight seemeth to not be so much in doing the hurt as in making the party repent. But base and crafty cowards are like the arrow that flieth in the dark. Cosmus, duke of Florence, had a desperate saying against perfidious or neglecting friends, as if those wrongs were unpardonable: "You shall read," saith he, "that we are commanded to forgive our enemies; but you never read that we are commanded to forgive our friends." But yet the spirit of Job was in better tune: "Shall we," saith he, "take good at God's hands, and not be content to take evil also?" And so of friends in a proportion. This is certain, that a man that studieth revenge keeps his own wounds green, which otherwise would heal and do well. Public revenges are for the most part fortunate, as that for the death of Caesar, for the death of Pertinax, for the death of Henry the Third of France, and many more. But in private revenges it is not so. Nay rather, vindictive persons live the life of witches, who, as they are mischievous, so end they unfortunate.

WRITING TOPIC

Bacon tells us, "Vindictive persons live the life of witches, who, as they are mischievous, so end they unfortunate." Furthermore, he claims, "This is certain, that a man that studieth revenge keeps his own wounds green, which otherwise would heal and do well." In Brady Udall's story, "He Becomes Deeply and Famously Drunk," Archie does, indeed, find peace and no longer studies revenge. However, in Ed Vega's story, "Spanish Roulette," Sixto is intent on carrying out his vengeful act. Although he knows that his own end will certainly be unfortunate, he argues that he cannot in good conscience live his life just ignoring what has taken place. He must act. Bacon counsels us, "That which is past is gone and irrevocable, and wise men have enough to do with things present and to come; therefore they do but trifle with themselves that labor in past matters." In evaluating Sixto's argument in favor of taking revenge for what has been done to his sister, what is your position? Should Sixto carry out his vengeful act, or should he ignore his offense and move on with his life? Writing in the first person, explain your decision and the reasoning behind it.

John Crawford (b. 1978)

Lies

Naturally, the common people don't want war, but after all, it is the leaders of the country who determine the policy, and it is always a simple matter to drag the people along, whether it is a democracy, or a fascist dictatorship, or a parliament, or a communist dictatorship. Voice or no voice, the people can always be brought to the bidding of the leaders. This is easy. All you have to do is tell them they are being attacked, and denounce the pacifists for lack of patriotism and exposing the country to danger. It works the same in every country.

—Hermann Goering, speaking at
the Nuremberg Trials
after World War II

You glad to be back?" The question was dripping in sarcasm, and though it was too dark to see his face, I knew a smile was on it.

I answered with a long, drawn-out "Sshhhiiitt."

"Well, man, I don't know. I figured now that you had a break and all, you be like ready to do this shit. Get it over with, you know." Sellers was jealous, and I couldn't blame him. I had just returned from two weeks of leave in America, and it was my first night back on duty. The city smelled familiar, with its plumes of smoke hidden in the darkness. Much more familiar than America had.

The two of us were sitting at OP 2, and had been for about thirty minutes before Sellers had spoken. He slumped back in a small canvas folding chair next to me. We would sit in the same kind of seats back at Florida State, tailgating for football games. His body armor and Kevlar were heaped against the lip of the building at his feet, and he bided his time by spitting puddles of Skoal onto the dusty roof.

The wire-framed chair I sat in wasn't nearly as comfortable. After the briefest   5 of moments, it began to dig into your legs and send them to sleep. My Kevlar was on the table in front of me, next to the 240 machine gun that stayed at this position. Links of rounds draped out of it and swirled once in a loop before pouring into a green metal box marked "7.62 linked."

In one hand, a cup of coffee was chilled by the night wind, while in the other was a burning cigarette. The rotations on the roof were long and dull, and it was no oddity for a soldier to smoke an entire pack or dip a can of snuff in one sitting.

"Fuck, man, I think going home made it worse," I said in between puffs of smoke.

"Whatever. I'd do anything to go home. You think now that Mitchell fucked up they'll put me on the list?"

"Shit, they hate you about as much as him. No way you're going home. Anyway, you don't want to. Believe me. Nothing's the same." The commander had picked who would go on leave by a drawing, but it was no surprise when soldiers who weren't favored by the chain of command were skipped over.

"You know I got on the plane to come back to Iraq on my first wedding an-   10 niversary?" I continued, looking out.

"No shit, man? Well, at least you were there for part of it, got to see your wife and all."

"Yeah, I guess. You know a reporter asked her how that made her feel? Me leaving on our anniversary? Can you believe that cunt? Fuck, it was harder to leave home this time. I almost didn't come back."

"Shit, man, I wouldn't if it had been me. You'd never see my ass again." Sellers spit again on the roof as if to emphasize his disgust.

We were both full of it. I never considered not coming back, and neither would he. We were still volunteers of a sort, and no matter how shitty things got, I couldn't justify deserting.

"Talk to Kim lately?" I asked, hoping to change the subject.   15

"Naw, haven't called her in a few weeks."

The silence that followed was profound, and Sellers spit again. It was a quiet night, and because the curfew wasn't being enforced anymore, the occasional car would light up the streets as it flew by. It was cold out this time of year, and all the locals were boarded up in their homes. Slivers of light escaped through cracks under doors and in walls. For a moment I was jealous. Would I trade with them if my family had been somewhere down among the shanties? In that moment, I would be just fine with living in a hovel as long as someone who loved me was there. That's better than the nicest house in northern Virginia any day.

"Well, why haven't you called her?" I finally asked, and after another silence, Sellers answered, his voice slowed by the handful of pills he had taken earlier.

"It was just fucked up. Every time we talked, I was just complaining about things here, and I think she got tired of my bitching. We haven't really had a good conversation in a while. . . . Shit, man, I don't know what's up."

20 As little as he had said, it was thick with desperation that I'm sure he didn't mean to show. When I had first met Sellers, he had been head over heels for this woman. At night he slept with the old pitted mannequin leg he had named after her. He was always a little off, but there was no doubt that he dug that chick.

The two of us had spent way too many nights like this one, and I had started to feel like I knew Kim about as well as I knew my own wife—as well as anyone really knows anyone, I guess. The despondency was more troubling because I knew exactly what he was going through. We didn't talk about it directly, no one did, but everyone was aware of each other's business. Eyes and ears picked up details, and rumors encapsulated us all—who was getting divorced, whose wife had run off with their kids. All our relationships back home had met their thresholds and broken. We had been away from home for only ten months. So much for true love.

"So what was home like, anyway? I can barely fucking remember it." Sellers glanced over at me as he asked, and I stalled for a moment by lighting another cigarette.

"America was fucking awesome, bro. All the cars were brand new, and trees all over the place, and so many girls you couldn't believe someone ever talked you into leaving in the first place. And the freedom was the best; you could up and go to the gas station or wherever anytime you wanted."

I didn't tell him that being alone, with no one to watch your back, left you feeling naked and helpless. I spent most of my time watching the rooftops and side roads, looking into my rearview mirror to make sure no one was creeping up on my car from behind. I didn't mention that every Arabic-looking person I saw gave me a funny feeling of anger inside, and that every time I saw someone sitting contentedly inside a coffee shop or restaurant, I wanted to yell at them, wake them up.

25 "You know my wife and I went to some army post near our house, right? We went to the PX there to see if they had cheaper refrigerators than in DC. They had active-duty soldiers stationed at the gates, and this really fat fuck comes up to me, leans in the window, and wants to see both our IDs, and he's not even polite about it. So I hand them to him, and he says that the decal station is closed and I have to come back the following Monday. So I tell him that I'm back from Iraq on leave and I won't be there long enough to come back. This fat fuck tells me, too bad, that I need to turn the car around and leave. And the whole time his weapon is slung across his back, no magazine in it, and his hands are in his pockets—fucking disgrace,

right? They finally let me in, but I had to argue with the NCOIC. I couldn't help thinking that if I could manage to get that fat bastard in my trunk and deliver him hog-tied and duct-taped to the airport, that he should have to take my place here. I think it's a fair deal, like you don't have to come back if you can get someone to take your spot."

Sellers laughed at my story. We all wanted to be heroes when we got back. There was this illusion that none of us would ever have to buy a drink again, that everyone would treat us differently. The only ones excited to see me get off the plane were the reporters. They swarmed in like angry bees. "Are you happy to be home? Did you miss your family?" Of course I fucking did—now get out of the goddamned way. The families themselves—some were so desperate to greet their husbands, sons, and fathers that they would hurl themselves through the crowd of reporters. Others hung back, unsure of how to react to a stranger who looked so familiar.

"When I was a kid, I went to camp, and I remember some of the other kids crying at night and bawling that they wanted to go home. I hated that pussy shit, but man, I wanna go home. I don't know how much longer I can do this. That shit broke me, going home and then leaving again. It's better just to stay here."

Sellers thought about my words for a second or two. "Man, fuck that, I don't care. I'd give anything for leave."

I knew that all over Iraq there were a hundred forty thousand other poor fuckers who were saying the same thing. I dug out another crumpled Iraqi cigarette, losing half the tobacco before I lit it. I hoped a sniper was watching.

"I just don't fucking care anymore, and I don't know what to do," I said under my   30 breath, more to myself than to my friend, but he heard and responded just the same.

"I heard that, man. All you can do is just keep on keeping on. I mean, I'm sure Kim and I will work things out, it's just that things are weird right now." Hearing the confidence in his voice, I couldn't help but feel disgust at how wrong it all was. Nothing was gonna work out—not for him, not for any of us. Our lives were crumbling so that we could pretend to help people who pretended to appreciate it.

"Everything cool with your wife and shit?"

"Yeah, she's great." I put out my cigarette and lit another one, sucking in a deep breath of poison, holding it, then letting it go. I couldn't and wouldn't tell him what was really going on. None of us talked about stuff like that. And as Baghdad slept beneath me, I tried to believe my own lies.

CRITICAL THINKING QUESTIONS

1. Who is lying to whom? List at least two claims about lies that Crawford implies in this chapter entitled, "Lies," from his book, *The Last True Story I'll Ever Tell.*

2. Reread the excerpt from Herman Goering, speaking at the Nuremberg Trials after World War II, which leads into Crawford's essay.
   a. What is Goering's opinion of leaders and people? Do you agree or disagree? Provide specific examples to support your viewpoint.
   b. Read Wilfred Owen's poem *"Dulce Et Decorum Est"* at the end of Chapter One. What perspective does the poem bring to Goering's view of war and leaders?

RESEARCH/WRITING TOPIC—Military Service: Voluntary or Mandatory?

John Crawford was a member of a National Guard unit that was deployed to Iraq in February 2003, remaining for over a year to patrol Baghdad. As he says, he and Sellers were "volunteers of a sort" (paragraph 14). When the United States pulled its military forces out of Vietnam in 1973, the draft, which enforces mandatory military service, was abolished. However, with the demand for military troops created by conflicts in Afghanistan and in Iraq—and as of the time of this writing in 2006, no end in sight for U.S. troops serving in Iraq—some U.S. Congress members have talked about resurrecting the draft. Should the draft be reinstated, and if so, who should be required to participate?

Cochise (1812?–1874)
[I am alone][1]

This for a very long time has been the home of my people; they came from the darkness, few in numbers and feeble. The country was held by a much stronger and more numerous people, and from their stone houses we were quickly driven. We were a hunting people, living on the animals that we could kill. We came to these mountains about us; no one lived here, and so we took them for our home and country. Here we grew from the first feeble band to be a great people, and covered the whole country as the clouds cover the mountains. Many people came to our country. First the Spanish, with their horses and their iron shirts, their long knives

---

[1] A Chiricahua Apache, Cochise delivered this speech in 1872, to protest a peace settlement which would relocate his people to a barren reservation in New Mexico.

and guns, great wonders to my simple people. We fought some, but they never tried to drive us from our homes in these mountains. After many years the Spanish soldiers were driven away and the Mexican ruled the land. With these little wars came, but we were now a strong people and we did not fear them. At last in my youth came the white man, your people. Under the counsels of my grandfather, who had for a very long time been the head of the Apaches, they were received with friendship. Soon their numbers increased and many passed through my country to the great waters of the setting sun. Your soldiers came and their strong houses were all through my country. I received favors from your people and did all that I could in return and we lived at peace. At last your soldiers did me a very great wrong, and I and my whole people went to war with them. At first we were successful and your soldiers were driven away and your people killed and we again possessed our land. Soon many soldiers came from the north and from the west, and my people were driven to the mountain hiding places; but these did not protect us, and soon my people were flying from one mountain to another, driven by the soldiers, even as the wind is now driving the clouds. I have fought long and as best I could against you. I have destroyed many of your people, but where I have destroyed one white man many have come in his place; but where an Indian has been killed, there has been none to come in his place, so that the great people that welcomed you with acts of kindness to this land are now but a feeble band that fly before your soldiers as the deer before the hunter, and must all perish if this war continues. I have come to you, not from any love for you or for your great father in Washington, or from any regard for his or your wishes, but as a conquered chief, to try to save alive the few people that still remain to me. I am the last of my family, a family that for very many years have been the leaders of this people, and on me depends their future, whether they shall utterly vanish from the land or that a small remnant remain for a few years to see the sun rise over these mountains, their home. I here pledge my word, a word that has never been broken, that if your great father will set aside a part of my own country, where I and my little band can live, we will remain at peace with your people forever. If from his abundance he will give food for my women and children, whose protectors his soldiers have killed, with blankets to cover their nakedness, I will receive them with gratitude. If not, I will do my best to feed and clothe them, in peace with the white man. I have spoken.

CRITICAL THINKING QUESTIONS

1. Use the rhetorical appeals—*ethos, pathos, logos*—to analyze Cochise's speech. Find specific examples and describe their effect on you.

2. Describe the *persona* (see Glossary) Cochise presents. Cite specific language that creates this image.

WRITING TOPIC

Cast yourself in the role of General Gordon Granger, commander of the district of New Mexico, with whom Cochise was negotiating. As General Granger, how would you respond to Cochise's speech?

Alex Epstein and Yaron Brook

The Evil of Animal "Rights"

Scientists are closer than ever to finding cures for AIDS, cancer and other deadly illnesses. But more research and testing are needed and much of it must be done on animals. But will it occur? Not if the animal "rights" terrorists plaguing Huntingdon Life Sciences have their way.

Huntingdon tests new medical products on animals—mostly rats and mice—to help determine if the products are safe and effective for human use. According to a recent story in *The Wall Street Journal,* "There has been a series of violent attacks on people and property linked to the company. Eleven cars belonging to Huntingdon employees have been firebombed, a senior manager had a caustic substance thrown into his eyes by a protester, and the company's managing director was seriously beaten by masked assailants."

The terrorists ally themselves with a group called Stop Huntingdon Animal Cruelty (SHAC). The group publishes information about Huntingdon and its shareholders, stockbrokers and customers, and encourages its members to stage loud protests outside these businesses and the homes of their employees. The "protests" often include violence, breaking and entering, property damage and death threats. Lacking adequate police protection and fearing for the lives of their employees, many of the targeted companies, including Merrill Lynch, Citibank, Charles Schwab and British Biotech, have cut off all association with Huntingdon, bringing it to the brink of bankruptcy.

SHAC's leaders disavow any connection to the violence—but they do not condemn the terrorists responsible for it. After all, it is the violence that scares away Huntingdon's associates and brings SHAC closer to its goal of shutting down Huntingdon. However, that is only the beginning—"When Huntingdon closes, we'll be moving on to the next one," says SHAC founder Greg Avery.

5   Ominously, the crimes against Huntingdon are not isolated incidents; animal rights terrorists commit more than 1,000 crimes annually. Some animal rights leaders are even openly in favor of criminal action. According to Alex Pacheco, director

of People for the Ethical Treatment of Animals (PETA), arson, property destruction, burglary, and theft are "acceptable crimes" when used for the animals' cause.

There is no question that animal testing is absolutely necessary for the development of life-saving drugs and medical procedures. Millions of people will die unnecessarily if it is not permitted. Animal rights activists know this, but still demand that animal testing be prohibited. Chris De Rose, director of Last Chance for Animals writes: "If the death of one rat cured all diseases, it wouldn't make any difference to me."

This is pure man-hatred.

It is common to write off terrorist activity and the vicious statements of animal rights leaders as "extremist," while maintaining that the majority of people in the animal rights movement have benevolent intentions. But man-hatred is not limited to a few leaders, it is inherent in the very notion of animal "rights." According to PETA, the basic principle of animal rights is: "animals are not ours to eat, wear, experiment on, or use for entertainment." To abide by this principle, we must leave animals free—to overrun and destroy our property, to eat our food, even to kill our children. As Michael Fox, vice president of The Humane Society explains, "The life of an ant and that of my child should be granted equal consideration."

This is a formula for human extinction since human survival and progress depend on our ability to kill animals when they endanger us, eat them when we need food, run tests on them when we fight disease. Without horses for transportation and oxen for plowing, without furs to keep us warm and meat to sustain us, mankind's ascent from the cave to civilization would have been impossible. Today, animal rights advocates want to make the progress of medical science impossible—so that rats may live. The only goal of a doctrine that demands such a sacrifice of man to animals can be the annihilation of man.

To attribute rights to animals is to ignore the purpose and justification of 10 rights—to protect the interests of man. Rights make it possible for individuals to coexist peacefully, trade and produce, provide for their own lives, and pursue their own happiness, free from the threat of violence. Animal "rights"—which demand man's destruction—are the antithesis of rights. By attempting to destroy the essential, life-preserving medical testing industry, SHAC and their allies reveal the man-hatred contained in the notion of animal "rights." Our lives depend on rejecting this evil idea.

CRITICAL THINKING QUESTIONS

1. Language is a powerful tool in argument because a writer's choice of words can strongly influence the reader. Look at the use of language in the Epstein and Brook essay. Point out specific words that push the reader toward an emotional response.

2. Review the list of **common fallacies** in Chapter Two. Putting yourself in the role of an animal rights advocate, can you identify any fallacies in Epstein's and Brook's argument?

Allan Gurganus (b. 1947)

Captive Audience

From 1966 to 1970, I disappeared from snapshots. I hid, even from my parents' camera. See, I was ashamed, of the uniform. I'd tried for "conscientious objector" in my Carolina county and was laughed out of the office. So, avoiding six years in a federal pen, I spent four in bell-bottoms, floating just off Southeast Asia. Buddies wore their caps cocked, making this assigned life feel more personal. I wore my uniform as a prisoner wears his. Why am I finally "coming out" about all this? I never ever speak of it. The new war drives me. My "service" years I freeze-dried. Till last week, I kept them stashed in the dark rear corner of a lead-lined meat locker. Now they're thawing—fact is, "My name is Allan and I am secretly . . . B-32-37-38." Name, hometown and serial number, that's what Iraqi captors ask of our latest P.O.W.s. These kids' faces are banged up, squinty. Eyes shocked and awed at gunpoint, they recall me to myself. Such dulled innocence drives me to confess.

If you live long enough, you can become your own parent. I am now that to me, even a granddad. Against the Defense Department, I so long to defend my former grandson self and all these other kids. A graying 55-year-old homeowner can see just how young 18 really is! I served in another such Children's Crusade. I'm qualified to call it a disaster. Even the generals who were in charge back then admit that now. The same guys are helping plan this new one. I was a kid enlisted, against his will, to do the heavy lifting for a nation launched on a mission botched from the start. The entrance imperative: all macho force. The exit strategy? None whatever. Only very young kids would be fool enough to go that far and do as told. Some claim they didn't even mind. I myself remember. And, for me, and for this new crop, I mind. I'm watching.

I know these trapped boys from the inside. Perfect physical specimens, they are cocksure about absolutely everything because they know next to nothing. From a commander's perspective, of course, that's very good. These kids signed up mostly to get some education. Their parents couldn't swing the loans. No college otherwise. All they know of war is from Dolby-deafening action movies. Mainly these kids rage in the fist of the hormonal, the impulsive, the puppy-playful. Girl-crazy, full of stock-car lore and vague dreams of executive glory—great soldier material.

It's spring here, and my jonquils have never been more plentiful and lush, but I walk around as if hooked by black extension cord to CNN, memories de-icing. It comes from my feelings for them. For those idiotic gung-ho kids who really believe they are making up the rules, who consider they are rugged individualists (and therefore take orders beautifully). Many probably never had a plane ride before (it sure was long!), only to sleep all night under a tarp in a sandstorm sitting up against some truck (nobody my age could walk for a week after doing that). And already they write home: "Don't worry about me, Mom. We'll straighten out this mess fast. Just keep my Camaro washed good." I also sent such letters. It is reassuring to reassure. Love becomes a kind of sedative for whatever killing chores you're forced to do tomorrow.

I want to tell you, I have never known a loneliness like it. It's Dante's 11th   5 circle, to be dressed in ugly clothes exactly like 4,000 others, to be called by a number, to be stuck among men who will brag and scrap and fight but never admit to any terror, any need. To sleep in bunks stacked five high, to defecate in booths without doors, you sitting with knees almost meeting the knees of a hunched stranger. To know that you are so much smarter than the jobs assigned, to guess that you are serving in a struggle you can neither approve nor ever understand because the old guys in charge—guys whose sons are safe, golfing at home—they don't speak the local language, either.

During the soldiers' first week, except for blowing sand, it might all seem a lark. Decisions are made by others who give you enough trigger-finger wiggle room so that you can feel a bit expressive, as baby-faced as terrifying. Such volunteers are as intentionally cut off from the effects of their killing as any placated 8-year-old glazed over the lethal thumb work of his Gameboy. These G.I.'s imagine glory, girlfriends waiting at home. The geopolitical picture is as far beyond their reach as the notion that learning a Kurdish dialect just might save their lives.

After my own tour of duty ended, I slouched home and simply sat there for six days, scared to leave my parents' house, too tired to drive a car. "So . . .what are your plans?"—my father saw my state yet chose to treat me with all the tender care of a corporate job interviewer. But Mom must have noticed that the family album featured no photos of me since the draft. So she gathered up my medals, awards for nothing more than my offering my body as another vote against the Cong. Mom assembled these little trophies I was meant to care about. A pretty red-and-yellow ribbon and its bronze coin called the Vietnam Expeditionary. Mom bought a craft-shop shadow box, a nice one too, real wood, and lined with red velvet-like plush for displaying family heirlooms. She arranged my citations under glass, protecting them. But I'd won too few to make a really pleasing pattern. So Mom dipped into my old Boy Scout badges, fleshing out my history with the brass of "God and Country." Then she added my childhood Sunday School pin for perfect attendance. "You see? Impressive." She handed it over. I thanked her and sat staring down at it. Whenever my folks visited, I would get it out and prop it up somewhere until they left. It usually stayed in the attic, where it dwells, I guess, today. In some cardboard box stacked with letters I've really been meaning to answer since '79 or so. But thanks anyway, Mom. Not your fault. Not mine. But whose then?

The latest captured Americans from a downed helicopter squat here on camera, and you see their inexperience in how they're big-eyed scared as kids at their first horror flick. Boys hang their heads with a shame almost sexual. They're blaming themselves for crashing, guilty at how sand can spoil the rotor blades of our most costly chopper. These kids mainly "volunteered," to get ahead. And now, this learning curve. They are prisoners because to start at Burger King, even for a go-getter like Larry here, would get him to only assistant manager in, say, three or four years, and you can't do too darn much on 12 grand a year, can you? These are the ambitious kids, the "good kids," the ones who wanted to make something useful and shapely of their lives.

Now they know that Mom will see them, captured, on "Alive at Five." They know she'll cover her mouth while screaming: "Al, come quick. It's Larry! They got our Larry!"

10   My parents believed in honor, duty and rendering up firstborns to Uncle Sam. For them Sam was at least as real as Santa. Avuncular, if some-what overdressed in stripes and gambler's goatee, he tended to look stern and to point right out at you. So when he knocked at our door and said he wanted me, my folks grinned: "He's hiding in the back bedroom, writing essays for the draft board all about peace and Quaker stuff. Though, fact is, he grew up Presbyterian. We'll go get him. Won't take a sec. You comfortable there?"

This week's young captives might just be released. Some will come home, back to their folks' ghetto stoops or trailers or tract houses strung with computer-generated welcomes, personalized, too. Their college years are still ahead of them. So look on the bright side. Bones that young knit fast. And, after a while, even after all the pain and not knowing why they did it, they will get to call this "their" war. And, of course, the medals will be splendid.

CRITICAL THINKING QUESTIONS

1. As you may recall from the discussion of *evidence,* citing personal experience in an argument can bring forth a highly emotional response. Of course, the degree to which personal experience is able to elicit such a response depends completely upon audience. Since "Captive Audience" appeared in the *New York Times,* we can assume a wide variety of people read the piece. Explain how two readers might react quite differently to the author's description of his experience when his mother made a box for his medals.

2. Sometimes *tone* can be difficult to interpret in a piece of writing. If someone says, "That sure was a great party," we can tell by her tone of voice that she actually thought the party was about as dull as any party could be. However, without the clues in vocal inflections, we might come away asking, "So did she really like the party or did she hate it?" Reread the last sentence in "Captive

Audience" and explain the tone you believe the author intended these words to carry. What clues has the author already given readers throughout the essay?

3. Gurganus describes the situation as he returns from the Vietnam War. Why does the returning soldier not want to leave his parents' home?

WRITING TOPIC

Gurganus does not offer the reader a specific *claim* in his writing, yet he seems to be making a statement about war and its effects on young soldiers. In a single sentence, compose a claim you believe might be appropriate for this selection, citing specific words, phrases, images, and sentences from the essay as *evidence*.

Constance L. Hays (1961–2005)

What Wal-Mart Knows about Customers' Habits

Hurricane Frances was on its way, barreling across the Caribbean, threatening a direct hit on Florida's Atlantic coast. Residents made for higher ground, but far away, in Bentonville, Ark., executives at Wal-Mart Stores decided that the situation offered a great opportunity for one of their newest data-driven weapons, something that the company calls predictive technology.

A week ahead of the storm's landfall, Linda M. Dillman, Wal-Mart's chief information officer, pressed her staff to come up with forecasts based on what had happened when Hurricane Charley struck several weeks earlier. Backed by the trillions of bytes' worth of shopper history that is stored in Wal-Mart's computer network, she felt that the company could "start predicting what's going to happen, instead of waiting for it to happen," as she put it.

The experts mined the data and found that the stores would indeed need certain products—and not just the usual flashlights. "We didn't know in the past that strawberry Pop-Tarts increase in sales, like seven times their normal sales rate, ahead of a hurricane," Ms. Dillman said in a recent interview. "And the pre-hurricane top-selling item was beer."

Thanks to those insights, trucks filled with toaster pastries and six-packs were soon speeding down Interstate 95 toward Wal-Marts in the path of Frances. Most of the products that were stocked for the storm sold quickly, the company said.

Such knowledge, Wal-Mart has learned, is not only power. It is profit, too.   5

Plenty of retailers collect data about their stores and their shoppers, and many use the information to try to improve sales. Target Stores, for example, introduced a branded Visa card in 2001 and has used it, along with an arsenal of gadgetry, to gather data ever since. But Wal-Mart amasses more data about the products it sells and its shoppers' buying habits than anyone else, so much so that some privacy advocates worry about potential for abuse.

With 3,600 stores in the United States and roughly 100 million customers walking through the doors each week, Wal-Mart has access to information about a broad slice of America—from individual Social Security and driver's license numbers to geographic proclivities for Mallomars, or lipsticks, or jugs of antifreeze. The data are gathered item by item at the checkout aisle, then recorded, mapped and updated by store, by state, by region.

By its own count, Wal-Mart has 460 terabytes of data stored on Teradata mainframes, made by NCR, at its Bentonville headquarters. To put that in perspective, the Internet has less than half as much data, according to experts.

Information about products, and often about customers, is most often obtained at checkout scanners. Wireless hand-held units, operated by clerks and managers, gather more inventory data. In most cases, such detail is stored for indefinite lengths of time. Sometimes it is divided into categories or mapped across computer models, and it is increasingly being used to answer discount retailing's rabbinical questions, like how many cashiers are needed during certain hours at a particular store.

10   All of the data are precious to Wal-Mart. The information forms the basis of the sales meetings the company holds every Saturday, and it is shot across desktops throughout its headquarters and into the places where it does business around the world. Wal-Mart shares some information with its suppliers— a company like Kraft, for example, can tap into a private extranet, called Retail Link, to see how well its products are selling. But for the most part, Wal-Mart hoards its information obsessively.

It also takes pains to keep the information secret. Some of the systems it uses are custom-built and designed by its own employees, the better to keep competitors off the trail. Companies that sell equipment and software to Wal-Mart are bound by nondisclosure agreements. Three years ago, Wal-Mart summarily announced that it would no longer share its sales data with outside companies, like Information Resources Inc. and ACNielsen, which had paid Wal-Mart for the information and then sold it to other retailers.

"When you look at their behavior, you can tell that Wal-Mart considers data to be a top priority," said Christine Overby, a senior analyst for consumer markets at Forrester Research. Over the years, she said, Wal-Mart executives have spent handsomely for their systems, paying $4 billion in 1991 to create Retail Link and signing onto innovations like bar codes and electronic data interchange, a forerunner of the Internet, well ahead of the pack. Wal-Mart is also driving manufacturers to invest in radio frequency identification. By next October, the company will require its biggest suppliers to tag shipments to some of its distribution centers with tiny transmitters that would eventually let Wal-Mart track every item that it sells.

With so much data at Wal-Mart's corporate fingertips, what are the risks to consumers? Most have no clue that their habits are monitored to such an extent.

There are no signs—like the ones for Wal-Mart's anti-shoplifting cameras—advising customers that information is being collected and stored. And there is no giveback: Wal-Mart doesn't use loyalty cards and rarely offers promotions based on past purchases.

It is aware, however, that shoppers are concerned about privacy. On its Web site, Wal-Mart posts a privacy policy that states, in part: "We take reasonable steps to protect your personal information. We maintain reasonable physical, technical and procedural measures to limit access to personal information to authorized individuals with appropriate purposes."

Not everyone agrees. "People don't know that Wal-Mart is capturing information about who they are and what they bought, but they are also capable of capturing a huge amount of outside information about them that has nothing to do with their grocery purchases," said Katherine Albrecht, the founder and director of Caspian, a consumer advocacy group concerned with privacy issues. "They can find out your mortgage amounts, your court dates, your driving record, your creditworthiness." 15

One source of information can be a credit card or a debit card, Ms. Albrecht said. Wal-Mart shoppers increasingly use the cards to pay for purchases, particularly in the better-heeled neighborhoods where the company has been building stores recently.

Some companies specialize in what is known as data enhancement, in which a customer's name and address, or a telephone number, can open the door to additional information. "If Wal-Mart had a customer database and wanted to start e-mailing their customers, we could append their e-mail addresses," said Sarah Stansberry, director of marketing for AccuData America, a company based in Fort Myers, Fla., that specializes in such services but does not use credit card records. With e-mail addresses, AccuData can track names and home addresses, she added. Other information follows: "We can access what they paid for their house, and their mortgage," though not driving records. The company has not done any work for Wal-Mart, she said.

Ms. Dillman said that she did not think Wal-Mart had ever tried to squeeze data from credit cards to learn more about customers' buying habits. Indeed, she said, it wouldn't be necessary. "We can do that without the credit card information," she said. "We can look at what's happening in the market, and look at what's happening in other markets that are similar."

Wal-Mart uses its mountain of data to push for greater efficiency at all levels of its operations, from the front of the store, where products are stocked based on expected demand, to the back, where details about a manufacturer's punctuality, for example, are recorded for future use. The purpose is to protect Wal-Mart from a retailer's twin nightmares: too much inventory, or not enough.

"They recognize that technology is a critical tool for them to have an efficient supply chain," said Kathryn Cullen, a principal at Kurt Salmon Associates, a 20 consulting firm, who said that she has not advised Wal-Mart. "They track the purchases and very quickly route that back to their suppliers so they can be replenished. They are very strict with their suppliers, but they give them the data that they need."

Armed with sales results from past weeks and months, Wal-Mart meets with each of its suppliers to establish sales goals for the coming year. Suppliers are actively encouraged, so to speak, not to miss those goals. A manufacturer that fails to meet its sales target—or has data-documented problems with orders, delivery, restocking or returns—can expect even tougher negotiations in the future from Wal-Mart, which is renowned for its steeliness in such situations.

Still, achieving sleeker operations is not the whole story. In many ways, data are used to forecast and drive Wal-Mart's business. "We use it in real estate decisions, understanding what the draw is like and what the customers will be like," Ms. Dillman said, referring to the company's planning for new stores, including the number of shoppers it expects to attract to each.

When it comes to Sam's Club, Wal-Mart's membership warehouse chain, "we know who every customer is," she added. So Wal-Mart does a kind of outreach, contacting nearby convenience store owners, for example, to let them know that "the items they buy, they could save money on by buying at Sam's."

At Wal-Mart, problems are referred to as "exceptions," and technology is essential for what Ms. Dillman calls "exception management." Within the company's empire, "we keep watching everything that just happened," she said. "We are pretty near real time. We can tell people that they need to go do something, and we are within hours, depending on the event."

25   The "event" may be a truck's failure to drop off or pick up something, or the delivery of a load of shoes missing their mates. It could be the absence of an important product in a store's backroom, or in the distribution center that serves that store. Or it could be an act of nature like the hurricanes that descended, one after another, on Florida and other parts of the Southeast this year.

Eventually, some experts say, Wal-Mart will use its technology to institute what is called scan-based trading, in which manufacturers own each product until it is sold.

"Wal-Mart will never take those products onto its books," said Bruce Hudson, a retail analyst at the Meta Group, an information technology consulting firm in Stamford, Conn. "If you think of the impact of shedding $50 billion of inventory, that is huge."

The impact will probably be felt by suppliers, he added, but none are likely to complain.

"You can see the pattern of Wal-Mart's mandates, and as Wal-Mart grows in power, it is getting more dictatorial," he said. "The suppliers shake their heads and say, 'I don't want to go this way, but they are so big.' Wal-Mart lives in a world of supply and command, instead of a world of supply and demand."

30   Consumers willingly turn over plenty of information. For example, cashing a payroll check at Wal-Mart requires a two-step process, said an assistant manager in a Wal-Mart in Saddle Brook, N.J., who asked to be identified only by her first name, Mary.

"First you enter your Social Security number into the system, twice," she said, pointing to the number pad hooked up to a register in the checkout lane. "The cashier can enter it, but some people don't like to share that information." Next a customer must enter his or her driver's license number, the assistant manager said. If payroll checks are cashed regularly at Wal-Mart, there is no need to keep punching in the Social Security number, only the driver's license number: "The system will recognize you the next time."

All of that information winds up at the company's office in Bentonville, the assistant manager added.

Ms. Dillman said it was "separated out, along with any personal identifiable information," and warehoused in a way that requires special permission to gain access. For check approval—when a customer writes a personal check to pay for something at a Wal-Mart, for example—"we don't keep it any longer than we need it for that transaction," she said. "All it's linked to is the checking account number, when we scan your check," she added. "We don't mine that data. We don't use it for anything other than the transaction."

Historically, Wal-Mart's focus has been on the products it sells, not to whom it sells them. One of the most difficult pieces of information to harvest is which customer bought what. Such information is expensive, too.

"When you are in the everyday-low-price market, you tend not to gather a lot of information about customers directly because you don't spend a lot of time with them gathering name, address, telephone numbers through a loyalty card," said Gene Alvarez, a vice president at the Meta Group. "That is the proper focus, because when you want to get customer-intimate, you have to offer a loyalty program, and there's the cost of that loyalty program."

Wal-Mart has discovered the potential of its own Web site in learning more   35
about customers. Ms. Dillman said the site was beginning to allow users to buy a product online and have it delivered to a store near them, an option that Sears Roebuck and other retailers have had for years. Naturally, some personal information would have to be submitted as part of the transaction. "You can do some association there, what products are of what interest," Mr. Alvarez said.

But Wal-Mart executives tend to care more about how products sell as part of a larger basket. "Me knowing what you specifically buy is not necessarily going to help me get the right merchandise into the store," Ms. Dillman said. "Knowing collectively what goes into one shopping cart together tells us a lot more."

Analyzing what ends up together in that cart drives Wal-Mart's pricing, other experts said. Shoppers might buy cold medicine along with chicken soup and orange juice during flu season, but not all of those products need to be priced at rock-bottom, said Ms. Overby, the Forrester analyst. "They might say, 'If we get really good at pricing the cold medicine and promoting it and letting people know that, hey, we have that product in stock and also at the best prices,' then they get people into the store," she said. "The other items in the basket might not be the lowest price in town, but the entire basket will be 10 to 20 percent less."

Still, as Wal-Mart recently discovered, there can be such a thing as too much information. Six women brought a sex-discrimination lawsuit against the company in 2001 that was broadened this year to a class of about 1.6 million current and former female employees. Lawyers for the women have said that Wal-Mart has the ability to use its human-resources database to calculate back pay for the plaintiffs as well as to determine whether women were fairly promoted and paid. The judge hearing the case, which is pending in a federal court in San Francisco, has agreed.

The database is unusually detail-rich, said Joseph Sellers, a lawyer for the plaintiffs. "They've put into their work force database the information that bears on virtually every facet of compensation," he said. "They have performance reviews, along with seniority, the time spent with the company, which store they worked in. So you can compare people working in the same store, to measure whether men and women are paid differently."

40   If that comes to pass, it will be a rare moment indeed, with Wal-Mart's carefully assembled data being channeled for a purpose Wal-Mart did not desire.

RESEARCH/WRITING TOPIC—Marketing Tactics and Personal Privacy

In this article, a retail analyst is quoted as saying, "Wal-Mart lives in a world of supply and command, instead of a world of supply and demand." He is speaking of Wal-Mart's relationship with those who produce the products sold in Wal-Mart stores, as well as with the customers who buy those products. One issue that arises from these relationships is Wal-Mart's extensive use of customer data collection. As with any subject appropriate for argument, this one has two legitimate perspectives. From the perspective of business, the collection and use of data is a profitable marketing tool; from the perspective of personal privacy advocates, the collection and use of data is a serious threat. After examining the evidence for both sides of the issue, develop an argument that supports one side of this controversy. In arguing your position, be sure to address the opposing viewpoint (see the section in Chapter Three, "Counterarguments: Concessions and Refutations").

John F. Kennedy (1917–1963)
Inaugural Address, January 20, 1961

My Fellow Citizens:

We observe today not a victory of party but a celebration of freedom—symbolizing an end as well as a beginning—signifying renewal as well as change. For I have sworn before you and Almighty God the same solemn oath our forebears prescribed nearly a century and three quarters ago.

The world is very different now. For man holds in his mortal hands the power to abolish all form of human poverty and to abolish all form of human life. And yet the same revolutionary beliefs for which our forebears fought are still at issue around the globe—the belief that the rights of man come not from the generosity of the state but from the hand of God.

We dare not forget today that we are the heirs of that first revolution. Let the word go forth from this time and place, to friend and foe alike, that the torch has been passed to a new generation of Americans—born in this century, tempered by war, disciplined by a cold and bitter peace, proud of our ancient heritage—and unwilling to witness or permit the slow undoing of those human rights to which this nation has always been committed, and to which we are committed today.

Let every nation know, whether it wish us well or ill, that we shall pay any price, bear any burden, meet any hardship, support any friend or oppose any foe in order to assure the survival and success of liberty.

This much we pledge—and more. 5

To those old allies whose cultural and spiritual origins we share, we pledge the loyalty of faithful friends. United, there is little we cannot do in a host of new cooperative ventures. Divided, there is little we can do—for we dare not meet a powerful challenge at odds and split asunder.

To those new states whom we now welcome to the ranks of the free, we pledge our word that one form of colonial control shall not have passed merely to be replaced by a far more iron tyranny. We shall not always expect to find them supporting our every view. But we shall always hope to find them strongly supporting their own freedom—and to remember that, in the past, those who foolishly sought to find power by riding on the tiger's back inevitably ended up inside.

To those people in the huts and villages of half the globe struggling to break the bonds of mass misery, we pledge our best efforts to help them help themselves, for whatever period is required—not because the communists are doing it, not because we seek their votes, but because it is right. If the free society cannot help the many who are poor, it can never save the few who are rich.

To our sister republics south of our border, we offer a special pledge—to convert our good words into good deeds—in a new alliance for progress—to assist free men and free governments in casting off the chains of poverty. But this peaceful revolution of hope cannot become the prey of hostile powers. Let all our neighbors know that we shall join with them to oppose aggression or subversion anywhere in the Americas. And let every other power know that this Hemisphere intends to remain the master of its own house.

To that world assembly of sovereign states, the United Nations, our last best hope in 10 an age where the instruments of war have far outpaced the instruments of peace, we renew our pledge of support—to prevent its becoming merely a forum for invective—to strengthen its shield of the new and the weak—and to enlarge the area to which its writ may run.

Finally, to those nations who would make themselves our adversary, we offer not a pledge but a request: that both sides begin anew the quest for peace, before the dark powers of destruction unleashed by science engulf all humanity in planned or accidental self-destruction.

We dare not tempt them with weakness. For only when our arms are sufficient beyond doubt can we be certain beyond doubt that they will never be employed.

But neither can two great and powerful groups of nations take comfort from their present course—both sides overburdened by the cost of modern weapons, both rightly alarmed by the steady spread of the deadly atom, yet both racing to alter that uncertain balance of terror that stays the hand of mankind's final war.

So let us begin anew—remembering on both sides that civility is not a sign of weakness, and sincerity is always subject to proof. Let us never negotiate out of fear. But let us never fear to negotiate.

Let both sides explore what problems unite us instead of belaboring the problems that divide us.

15   Let both sides, for the first time, formulate serious and precise proposals for the inspection and control of arms—and bring the absolute power to destroy other nations under the absolute control of all nations.

Let both sides join to invoke the wonders of science instead of its terrors. Together let us explore the stars, conquer the deserts, eradicate disease, tap the ocean depths and encourage the arts and commerce.

Let both sides unite to heed in all corners of the earth the command of Isaiah—to "undo the heavy burdens . . . (and) let the oppressed go free."

And if a beach-head of cooperation can be made in the jungles of suspicion, let both sides join in the next task: creating, not a new balance of power, but a new world of law, where the strong are just and the weak secure and the peace preserved forever.

20   All this will not be finished in the first one hundred days. Nor will it be finished in the first one thousand days, nor in the life of this Administration, nor even perhaps in our lifetime on this planet. But let us begin.

In your hands, my fellow citizens, more than in mine, will rest the final success or failure of our course. Since this country was founded, each generation has been summoned to give testimony to its national loyalty. The graves of young Americans who answered that call encircle the globe.

Now the trumpet summons us again—not as a call to bear arms, though arms we need—not as a call to battle, though embattled we are—but a call to bear the burden of a long twilight struggle, year in and year out, "rejoicing in hope, patient in tribulation"—a struggle against the common enemies of man: tyranny, poverty, disease and war itself.

Can we forge against these enemies a grand and global alliance, North and South, East and West, that can assure a more fruitful life for all mankind? Will you join in that historic effort?

In the long history of the world, only a few generations have been granted the role of defending freedom in its hour of maximum danger. I do not shrink from this responsibility—I welcome it. I do not believe that any of us would exchange places with any other people or any other generation. The energy, the faith and the devotion which we bring to this endeavor will light our country and all who serve it—and the glow from that fire can truly light the world.

And so, my fellow Americans: ask not what your country will do for you—ask 25 what you can do for your country.

My fellow citizens of the world: ask not what America will do for you, but what together we can do for the freedom of man.

Finally, whether you are citizens of America or of the world, ask of us the same high standards of strength and sacrifice that we shall ask of you. With a good conscience our only sure reward, with history the final judge of our deeds, let us go forth to lead the land we love, asking His blessing and His help, but knowing that here on earth God's work must truly be our own.

CRITICAL THINKING QUESTIONS

1. Notice how short the paragraphs are in this address. What effect does this structure have on the listener or reader?

2. What *rhetorical devices* do you see Kennedy using in this address? Make a list of pairs of words Kennedy uses, such as *united/divided* or *not because/but because*.

3. In what sense does this address argue for power, and in what sense does it argue for responsibility?

WRITING TOPIC

Read one other inaugural address by a U.S. president (www.bartleby.com/ 124, "Inaugural Addresses of the Presidents of the United States"). Summarize and compare the arguments offered by Kennedy and the president you selected.

Abraham Lincoln (1809–1865)

Second Inaugural Address, March 4, 1865

At this second appearing to take the oath of the presidential office, there is less occasion for an extended address than there was at the first. Then a statement, somewhat in detail, of a course to be pursued, seemed fitting and proper. Now, at the expiration of four years, during which public declarations have been constantly called forth on every point and phase of the great contest which still absorbs the attention, and engrosses the energies of the nation, little that is new could be presented. The progress of our arms, upon which all else chiefly depends, is as well known to the public as to myself; and it is, I trust, reasonably satisfactory and encouraging to all. With high hope for the future, no prediction in regard to it is ventured.

On the occasion corresponding to this four years ago, all thoughts were anxiously directed to an impending civil war. All dreaded it—all sought to avert it. While the inaugural address was being delivered from this place, devoted altogether to *saving* the Union without war, insurgent agents were in the city seeking to *destroy* it without war—seeking to dissol[v]e the Union, and divide effects, by negotiation. Both parties deprecated war; but one of them would *make* war rather than let the nation survive; and the other would *accept* war rather than let it perish. And the war came.

One eighth of the whole population were colored slaves, not distributed generally over the Union, but localized in the Southern part of it. These slaves constituted a peculiar and powerful interest. All knew that this interest was, somehow, the cause of the war. To strengthen, perpetuate, and extend this interest was the object for which the insurgents would rend the Union, even by war; while the government claimed no right to do more than to restrict the territorial enlargement of it. Neither party expected for the war, the magnitude, or the duration, which it has already attained. Neither anticipated that the *cause* of the conflict might cease with, or even before, the conflict itself should cease. Each looked for an easier triumph, and a result less fundamental and astounding. Both read the same Bible, and pray to the same God; and each invokes His aid against the other. It may seem strange that any men should dare to ask a just God's assistance in wringing their bread from the sweat of other men's faces; but let us judge not that we be not judged. The prayers of both could not be answered; that of neither has been answered fully. The Almighty has his own purposes. "Woe unto the world because of offences! for it must needs be that offences come; but woe to that man by whom the offence cometh!" If we shall suppose that American Slavery is one of those offences which, in the providence of God, must needs come, but which, having continued through His appointed time, He now wills to remove, and that He gives to both North and South, this terrible war, as the woe due to those by whom the offence came, shall we discern therein any departure from those divine attributes which the believers in a Living God always ascribe to Him? Fondly do we hope—fervently do we pray—that this mighty scourge of war may speedily pass away. Yet, if God wills that it continue, until all the wealth piled by the bond-man's two hundred and fifty years of unrequited toil shall be sunk, and until every drop of blood drawn with the lash, shall be paid by another drawn with the sword, as was said three thousand years ago, so still it must be said "the judgments of the Lord, are true and righteous altogether."

With malice toward none; with charity for all; with firmness in the right, as God gives us to see the right, let us strive on to finish the work we are in; to bind up the nation's wounds; care for him who shall have borne the battle, and for his widow, and his orphan—to do all which may achieve and cherish a just and lasting peace, among ourselves, and with all nations.

CRITICAL THINKING QUESTIONS

1. What do you see as Lincoln's primary purpose in this address?

2. Identify passages that illustrate each of the rhetorical appeals—*pathos, logos, ethos.*

3. a. List several *value assumptions* about leadership that Lincoln's address illustrates.
   b. Can you think of individuals who represent the leadership values you listed above? Try to think of persons, living now or from recent history.

WRITING TOPIC

Based on your responses to question 3, write a paragraph in which you define leadership; include specific examples and description to elaborate. Besides showing what leadership is, you can use comparison and contrast—that is, provide examples of what leadership is *not*—to develop your definition. (See also O'Brien's story, "The Things They Carried," page 556.)

George Orwell (1903–1950)
A Hanging

It was in Burma, a sodden morning of the rains. A sickly light, like yellow tinfoil, was slanting over the high walls into the jail yard. We were waiting outside the condemned cells, a row of sheds fronted with double bars, like small animal cages. Each cell measured about ten feet by ten and was quite bare within except for a plank bed and a pot for drinking water. In some of them brown, silent men were squatting at the inner bars, with their blankets draped round them. These were the condemned men, due to be hanged within the next week or two.

One prisoner had been brought out of his cell. He was a Hindu, a puny wisp of a man, with a shaven head and vague liquid eyes. He had a thick, sprouting mustache, absurdly too big for his body, rather like the mustache of a comic man on the films. Six tall Indian warders were guarding him and getting him ready for the gallows. Two of them stood by with rifles and fixed bayonets, while the others handcuffed him, passed a chain through his handcuffs and fixed it to their belts, and lashed his arms tight to his sides. They crowded very close about him, with their hands always on him in a careful, caressing grip, as though all the while feeling him to make sure he was there. It was like men handling a fish which is still alive and may jump back into the water. But he stood quite unresisting, yielding his arms limply to the ropes, as though he hardly noticed what was happening.

Eight o'clock struck and a bugle call, desolately thin in the wet air, floated from the distant barracks. The superintendent of the jail, who was standing apart from the rest of us, moodily prodding the gravel with his stick, raised his head at the sound. He was an army doctor, with a gray toothbrush mustache and a gruff voice. "For God's sake, hurry up, Francis," he said irritably. "The man ought to have been dead by this time. Aren't you ready yet?"

Francis, the head jailer, a fat Dravidian in a white drill suit and gold spectacles, waved his black hand. "Yes sir, yes sir," he bubbled. "All iss satisfactorily prepared. The hangman iss waiting. We shall proceed."

5   "Well, quick march, then. The prisoners can't get their breakfast till this job's over."

We set out for the gallows. Two warders marched on either side of the prisoner, with their rifles at the slope; two others marched close against him, gripping him by arm and shoulder, at though as once pushing and supporting him. The rest of us, magistrates and the like, followed behind. Suddenly, when we had gone ten yards, the procession stopped short without any order or warning. A dreadful thing had happened—a dog, come goodness knows whence, had appeared in the yard. It came bounding among us with a loud volley of barks and leapt round up wagging its whole body, wild with glee at finding so many human beings together. It was a large woolly dog, half Airedale, half pariah. For a moment it pranced around us, and then, before anyone could stop it, it had made a dash for the prisoner, and jumping up tried to lick his face. Everybody stood aghast, too taken aback even to grab the dog.

"Who let that bloody brute in here?" said the superintendent angrily. "Catch it, someone!"

A warder detached from the escort charged clumsily after the dog, but it danced and gamboled just out of his reach, taking everything as part of the game. A young Eurasian jailer picked up a handful of gravel and tried to stone the dog away, but it dodged the stones and came after us again. Its yaps echoed from the jail walls. The prisoner, in the grasp of the two warders, looked on incuriously, as though this was another formality of the hanging. It was several minutes before someone managed to catch the dog. Then we put my handkerchief through its collar and moved off once more, with the dog still straining and whimpering.

It was about forty yards to the gallows. I watched the bare brown back of the prisoner marching in front of me. He walked clumsily with his bound arms, but quite steadily, with that bobbing gait of the Indian who never straightens his knees. At each step his muscles slid neatly into place, the lock of hair on his scalp danced up and down, his feet printed themselves on the wet gravel. And once, in spite of the men who gripped him by each shoulder, he stepped lightly aside to avoid a puddle on the path.

10   It is curious; but till that moment I had never realized what it means to destroy a healthy, conscious man. When I saw the prisoner step aside to avoid the puddle, I saw the mystery, the unspeakable wrongness, of cutting a life short when it is in

full tide. This man was not dying, he was alive just as we are alive. All the organs of his body were working—bowels digesting food, skin renewing itself, nails growing, tissues forming—all toiling away in solemn foolery. His nails would still be growing when he stood on the drop, when he was falling through the air with a tenth-of-a-second to live. His eyes saw the yellow gravel and the gray walls, and his brain still remembered, foresaw, reasoned—even about puddles. He and we were a party of men walking together, seeing, hearing, feeling, understanding the same world; and in two minutes, with a sudden snap, one of us would be gone— one mind less, one world less.

The gallows stood in a small yard, separate from the main grounds of the prison, and overgrown with tall prickly weeds. It was a brick erection like three sides of a shed, with planking on top, and above that two beams and a crossbar with the rope dangling. The hangman, a gray-haired convict in the white uniform of the prison, was waiting beside his machine. He greeted us with a servile crouch as we entered. At a word from Francis the two warders, gripping the prisoner more closely than ever, half led, half pushed him to the gallows and helped him clumsily up the ladder. Then the hangman climbed up and fixed the rope round the prisoner's neck.

We stood waiting, five yards away. The warders had formed in a rough circle round the gallows. And then, when the noose was fixed, the prisoner began crying out to his god. It was a high, reiterated cry of "Ram! Ram! Ram! Ram!" not urgent and fearful like a prayer or cry for help, but steady, rhythmical, almost like the tolling of a bell. The dog answered the sound with a whine. The hangman, still standing on the gallows, produced a small cotton bag like a flour bag and drew it down over the prisoner's face. But the sound, muffled by the cloth, still persisted, over and over again: "Ram! Ram! Ram! Ram! Ram!"

The hangman climbed down and stood ready, holding the lever. Minutes seemed to pass. The steady, muffled crying from the prisoner went on and on, "Ram! Ram! Ram!" never faltering for an instant. The superintendent, his head on his chest, was slowly poking the ground with his stick; perhaps he was counting the cries, allowing the prisoner a fixed number—fifty, perhaps, or a hundred. Everyone had changed color. The Indians had gone gray like bad coffee, and one or two of the bayonets were wavering. We looked at the lashed, hooded man on the drop, and listened to his cries—each cry another second of life; the same thought was in all our minds; oh, kill him quickly, get it over, stop that abominable noise!

Suddenly the superintendent made up his mind. Throwing up his head he made a swift motion with his stick. "Chalo!" he shouted almost fiercely.

There was a clanking noise, and then dead silence. The prisoner had vanished, and 15 the rope was twisting on itself. I let go of the dog, and it galloped immediately to the back of the gallows; but when it got there it stopped short, barked, and then retreated into a corner of the yard, where it stood among the weeds, looking timorously out at us. We went round the gallows to inspect the prisoner's body. He was dangling with his toes pointed straight downwards, very slowly revolving, as dead as a stone.

The superintendent reached out with his stick and poked the bare brown body; it oscillated slightly. "*He's* all right," said the superintendent. He backed out from under the gallows, and blew out a deep breath. The moody look had gone out of his face quite suddenly. He glanced at his wristwatch. "Eight minutes past eight. Well, that's all for this morning, thank God."

The warders unfixed bayonets and marched away. The dog, sobered and conscious of having misbehaved itself, slipped after them. We walked out of the gallows yard, past the condemned cells with their waiting prisoners, into the big central yard of the prison. The convicts, under the command of warders armed with lathis, were already receiving their breakfast. They squatted in long rows, each man holding a tin pannikin, while two warders with buckets marched around ladling out rice; it seemed quite a homely, jolly scene, after the hanging. An enormous relief had come upon us now that the job was done. One felt an impulse to sing, to break into a run, to snigger. All at once everyone began chattering gaily.

The Eurasian boy walking beside me nodded towards the way we had come, with a knowing smile: "Do you know sir, our friend (he meant the dead man) when he heard his appeal had been dismissed, he pissed on the floor of his cell. From fright. Kindly take one of my cigarettes, sir. Do you not admire my new silver case, sir? From the boxwallah, two rupees eight annas. Classy European style."

Several people laughed—at what, nobody seemed certain.

20   Francis was walking by the superintendent, talking garrulously: "Well, sir, all has passed off with the utmost satisfactoriness. It was all finished—flick! Like that. It iss not always so—oah, no! I have known cases where the doctor wass obliged to go beneath the gallows and pull the prisoner's legs to ensure decease. Most disagreeable!"

"Wriggling about, eh? That's bad," said the superintendent.

"Ach, sir, it iss worse when they become refractory! One man, I recall, clung to the bars of hiss cage when we went to take him out. You will scarcely credit, sir, that it took six warders to dislodge him, three pulling at each leg. We reasoned with him, 'My dear fellow,' we said, 'think of all the pain and trouble you are causing to us!' But no, he would not listen! Ach, he wass very troublesome!"

I found that I was laughing quite loudly. Everyone was laughing. Even the superintendent grinned in a tolerant way. "You'd better all come out and have a drink," he said quite genially. "I've got a bottle of whiskey in the car. We could do with it."

We went through the big double gates of the prison into the road. "Pulling at his legs!" exclaimed a Burmese magistrate suddenly, and burst into a loud chuckling. We all began laughing again. At that moment Francis' anecdote seemed extraordinarily funny. We all had a drink together, native and European alike, quite amicably. The dead man was a hundred yards away.

CRITICAL THINKING QUESTIONS

1. The powers of peace and order have structured this execution perfectly, and all the details seem so right, so correct. What small event allows Orwell to see past all the trappings of justice being carried out?

2. Why does everyone laugh at the end? Surely an execution cannot be humorous.

WRITING TOPIC

Although some states still carry out the death penalty, it continues to be an issue that divides Americans. Orwell gives his readers a glimpse into the reality of ending the life of a "healthy, conscious man." How do the narrative details of this essay affect your view of capital punishment?

Katherine Anne Porter (1890–1980)

To Dr. William Ross

March 4, 1951

Dear Dr. Ross,

I cannot possibly sign the oath of allegiance you sent me, and I'm sorry I was not told in your first letter that this would be required of me, for a good deal of time and trouble would have been spared both of us.

This is the first time I've encountered this dangerous nonsense, but I have known from the beginning what my answer must be. My memory goes back easily thirty years to the time this law was passed in Colorado, in a time of war, fright and public hysteria being whipped up by the same kind of people who are doing this work now. Only now we're worse for thirty years of world disaster.

I believed then, and still do believe, that this requirement of an oath of allegiance was more of a device for embarrassing and humiliating honest persons than an effective trap for traitors and subversive people. We, all of us, do quite a lot of ceremonial oath-taking on many important occasions of life as an act of faith, a public testimony of honorable intention, and it is the mere truth that an oath binds only those persons who meant to keep their promises anyway, with or without an oath. The others cannot be touched or controlled in any such way. We all know this so why assist at such a cynical fraud.

I'm entirely hostile to the principle of Communism and to every form of totalitarian society, whether it calls itself Communism, Fascism, or whatever. I feel indeed that Communism and Fascism are two names for the same thing, that the present struggle is really a civil war between two factions of totalitarianism. But Fascism is older, more insidious, harder to identify, easier to disguise. No one can be a Communist without knowing what he is doing. A man may be a most poisonous Fascist without even in the least recognizing his malady.

5   It is not the oath itself that troubles me. There is nothing in it I do not naturally and instinctively observe as I have and will. My people are the old stock. They helped to found colonies, to break new trails, and to survey wildernesses. They set up little log cabin academies, all the way from Virginia and Pennsylvania to Kentucky and clear into Texas. They have fought in all the wars, they have been governors of states, and military attachés, and at least one ambassador among us. We're not suspect, nor liable to the questionings of the kind of people we would never have invited to our tables.

You can see what the root of my resentment is. My many family branches helped to make this country. My feeling about my country and its history is as tender and intimate as about my own parents, and I really suffer to have them violated by the irresponsible acts of cheap politicians who prey on public fears in times of trouble and force their betters into undignified positions.

Our duty, Dr. Ross, is to circumvent them. To see through them and stop them in their tracks in time and not to be hoodwinked or terrorized by them, not to rationalize and excuse that weakness in us which leads us to criminal collusion with them for the sake of our jobs or the hope of being left in peace. That is not the road to any kind of safety. Nothing really effective is being done here against either Communism or Fascism, at least not by the politicians because they do not want anything settled. Their occupation and careers would be gone. We're going to be made sorry very soon for our refusal to reject unconditionally the kind of evil that disguises itself as patriotism, as love of virtue, as religious faith, as the crusador against the internal enemy. These people are themselves the enemy.

I do not propose to sit down quietly and be told by them what my duty is to my country and my government. My feelings and beliefs are nothing they could understand. I do not like being told that I must take an oath of allegiance to my government and flag under the threat of losing my employment if I do not. This is blackmail, and I have never been blackmailed successfully yet and do not intend to begin now.

So please destroy the contract we have made, as it is no longer valid. I know I run some little risk of nasty publicity in this matter. I hope not. I am not in the least a martyr. I have no time for heroics and indeed distrust them deeply. I am an artist who wishes to be left in peace to do my work. I hope 1that work will speak in the long run very clearly for me and all my kind, will be in some sort my testimony and my share of the battle against the elements of corruption and dissolution that come upon us so insidiously from all sides we hardly know where to begin to oppose them.

10   You may say this is a great how-do-you-do about a small matter. I can only say it is not a small matter when added to all other small matters of the kind that finally make an army of locusts.

Dr. Ross, I thank you for your courteous letter and hope you will take my word that this letter has nothing personal in it. That towards you I intend nothing but human respect in the assurance that I believe I understand your situation which must be extremely difficult.

What has this kind of meanness and cheapness to do with education? What is wrong that undesirable applicants for the faculty are not quietly discovered and refused before they are appointed? Why must a person like me be asked to do a stupid, meaningless thing because one person with a bad political record got into your college once?

No, I can't have it, and neither can you. The amusing side of all this brou-ha-ha is I really did not expect to have any occasion to mention the flag or the laws of Colorado or the Communist Alger Hiss or even the Fascist Senator McCarthy. I meant to talk about literature, life understood and loved in terms of the human heart in the personal experience. The life of the imagination and the search for the true meaning of our fate in this world, of the soul as a pilgrim on a stony path and of faithfulness to an ideal good and tenacity in the love of truth. Whether or not we ever find it, we still must look for it to the very end.

Any real study of great literature must take in human life at every possible level and search out every dark corner. And its natural territory is the whole human experience, no less. It does not astonish me that young people love to hear about these things, love to talk about them, and think about them. It is sometimes surprising to me how gay my classes can be, as if we had found some spring of joy in the tragic state to which all of us are born. This is the service the arts do, and the totalitarian's first idea is to destroy exactly this. They can do great harm but not for long. I am not in the least afraid of them.

With my sincere good wishes, and apologies for this overlong letter,

Yours,

Katherine Anne Porter

CRITICAL THINKING QUESTIONS

1. Why does the writer make the loose distinction between Communism and Fascism? Does she imply by this definition that Dr. Ross may be a Fascist?

2. When she describes her role as a teacher, how does that affect her appeal to *ethos?*

WRITING TOPIC

The fallacy of *ad populum* substitutes content with a "just plain folks" appeal, which sometimes "disguises itself as patriotism." With that idea in mind, what does Katherine Anne Porter see as her duty?

Tom Regan (b. 1938)
Religion and Animal Rights

In its simplest terms the animal rights position I uphold maintains that such diverse practices as the use of animals in science, sport and recreational hunting, the trapping of furbearing animals for vanity products, and commercial animal agriculture are categorically wrong—wrong because these practices systematically violate the rights of the animals involved. Morally, these practices ought to be abolished. That is the goal of the *social* struggle for animal rights. The goal of our *individual* struggle is to divest ourselves of our moral and economic ties to these injustices—for example, by not wearing the skins of dead animals and by not eating their decaying corpses.

Not a few people regard the animal rights position as extreme, calling, as it does, for the abolition of certain well-entrenched social practices rather than for their "humane" reform. And many seem to imagine that once this label ("extreme") is applied, the need for further refutation evaporates. After all, how can such an "extreme" moral position be correct?

I addressed this question in a recent speech, reminding my audience of a few "extreme" moral positions we all accept:

Rape is *always* wrong.

5   Child pornography is *always* wrong.

Racial and sexual discrimination are *always* wrong.

I went on to note that when an injustice is absolute, as is true of each of the examples just cited, then one must oppose it absolutely. It is not reformed, more humane child pornography that an enlightened ethic calls for; it is its abolition that is required—it is this *extreme* position we must uphold. And analogous remarks apply in the case of the other examples.

Once this much is acknowledged, it is evident (or at least it should be) that those who oppose or resist the animal rights position will have to do better than merely attach the label "extreme" to it. Sometimes "extreme" positions about what is wrong are right.

Of course, there are two obvious differences between the animal rights position and the other examples of extreme views I have given. The latter views are very generally accepted, whereas the former position is not. And unlike these very generally accepted views, which concern wrongful acts done to human beings, the animal rights position concerns the (alleged) wrongfulness of treating animals (nonhuman animals, that is) in certain ways. Those who oppose or resist the animal rights position might seize upon these two differences in an effort to justify themselves in accepting extreme positions regarding rape and child abuse, for example, while rejecting the "extremism" of animal rights.

10   But neither of these differences will bear the weight of justification. That a view (whether moral or otherwise) is very generally accepted is not a sufficient reason for accepting it as true. There was a time when the shape of the earth was very generally believed to be flat, and when the presence of physical and mental handicaps was very generally thought to make the people who bore them morally inferior. That very many people believed these falsehoods obviously did not make them true. We won't discover or confirm what's true by taking a vote.

The reverse of the preceding also can be demonstrated. That a view (moral or otherwise) is not generally accepted is not a sufficient reason for judging it to be false. When those lonely few first conjectured that the earth is round and that women are the moral equals of men, they conjectured truly, notwithstanding how grandly they were outnumbered. The solitary person who, in Thoreau's enduring image, marches to a different drummer, may be the only person to apprehend the truth.

The second difference noted above is more problematic. That difference cites the fact that child abuse and rape, for example, involve evils done to human beings, while the animal rights position claims that certain (alleged) evils are done to non-human animals. Now, there is no question that this does constitute a difference. The question is, is this a *morally relevant difference*—a difference, that is, that would justify us in accepting the extreme opposition we judge to be appropriate in the case of child abuse and rape, for example, but, which most people resist or abjure in the case of, say, vivisection. For a variety of reasons I do not myself think that this difference is a morally relevant one. Permit me to explain why.

Viewed scientifically, this second difference succeeds only in citing a biological difference: The victims of rape and child abuse belong to one species (the species *Homo sapiens*) whereas the (alleged) victims of vivisection and trapping belong to other species (the species *Canis lupus,* for example). But biological differences *inside* the species *Homo sapiens* do not justify radically different treatment among those individual humans who differ biologically (for example, in terms of sex, or skin color, or chromosome count). Why, then, should biological differences *outside* our species count morally? If having one eye or deformed limbs does not disqualify a human being from moral consideration equal to that given to those humans who are more fortunate, how can it be rational to disqualify a rat or a wolf from equal moral consideration because, unlike us, they have paws and a tail?

Some of those who resist or oppose the animal rights position might have recourse to "intuition" at this point. They might claim that one either "sees" that the principal biological difference at issue (namely, species membership) *is* a morally relevant one, or does *not* see this. No *reason* can be given as to why belonging to the species *Homo sapiens* gives one a superior moral status, just as no *reason* can be given as to why belonging to the species *Canis lupus* gives wolves an inferior moral status (if wolves have a moral status at all). This difference in moral status can only be grasped immediately, without making an inference, by an exercise of intuitive reason. This moral difference is "self-evident"—or so it will be claimed by those who claim to "intuit" it.

However attractive this appeal to intuition may seem to some, it woefully fails to bear the weight of justification. The plain fact is, people have claimed to "intuit" differences in the comparative moral standing of individuals and groups *inside* the human species, and these alleged "intuitions," we all would agree, are painful symptoms of unquestioned and unjustifiable prejudice. Over the course of history, for example, many men have "intuited" the moral superiority of men when compared with that of women, and many white-skinned humans have "intuited" the moral superiority of white-skinned humans when compared with humans having different skin colors. If this is a matter of intuition, then no reason can be given for this superiority. No inference is (or can be) required, no evidence adduced. One either "sees" it, or one doesn't. It's just that those who do "see" it (or so they will insist) apprehend the truth, while those whose deficient intuitive faculties prevent them from "seeing" it fail to do so.

I cannot believe that any thoughtful person will be taken in by this ruse. Appeals to "intuition" in these contexts are symptomatic of unquestioned and unjustifiable moral prejudices. What prompts or encourages men to "see" their moral superiority over women are the sexual prejudices men bring with them, not what is to be found in the existence of sexual differences themselves. And the same is true, *mutatis mutandis*, of "seeing" moral superiority in racial or other biological differences between humans.

That much established, the weakness of appeals to intuition in the case at hand should be apparent. Since intuition is not to be trusted when questions of the comparative moral standing of biologically different individuals *inside* the species *Homo sapiens* are at issue, it cannot be rational to assume or insist that such appeals can or should be trusted when questions of the comparative moral standing of individuals *outside* the species are at issue. Moreover, since appeals to intuition in the former case turn out to be symptomatic of unquestioned and unjustifiable moral prejudices, rather than being revelatory of some important moral truth, it is not unreasonable to suspect that the same diagnosis applies to appeals to intuition in the latter case. If true, then those who "intuit" the moral superiority of all members of the species *Homo sapiens* over all members of every other species, also emerge as the unwitting victims or the willful perpetrators of an unquestioned and unjustifiable moral prejudice.

"Speciesism" is the name given to this (alleged) prejudice. This idea has been characterized in a variety of ways. For present purposes let us begin with the following twofold characterization of what I shall call "categorical speciesism."

Categorical speciesism is the belief that (1) the inherent value of an individual can be judged solely on the basis of the biological species to which that individual belongs, and that (2) all the members of the species *Homo sapiens* have equal inherent value, while all the members of every other species lack this kind of value, simply because all and only humans are members of the species *Homo sapiens*.

20   In speaking of inherent value, both here and throughout what follows, I mean something that coincides with Kant's famous idea of "end-in-itself." Individuals who have inherent value, in other words, have value in their own right, apart from their possible utility for others; as such, these individuals are never to be treated in ways that reduce their value to their possible usefulness for others; they are always to be treated as "ends-in-themselves," not as "means merely." Categorical speciesism, then, holds that all and only humans have this kind of value precisely because all and only humans belong to the species *Homo sapiens*.

I have already indicated why I believe that appeals to intuition cannot succeed in establishing the truth of categorical speciesism as so characterized. How, then, might the prejudicial character of speciesism be established?

Part of that answer is to be found when we pause to consider the nature of the animals we humans hunt, trap, eat and use for scientific purposes. Any person of common sense will agree that these animals bring the mystery of consciousness to the world. These animals, that is, not only are *in* the world, they are aware *of it*—and also of their "inner" world. They see, hear, touch and feel; but they also desire, believe, remember and anticipate.

If anyone questions my assessment of the common sense view about these animals, then I would invite them to speak with people who share their lives with dogs or cats or horses, or others who know the ways or wolves or coyotes, or still others who have had contact with any bird one might wish to name. Common sense clearly is on the side of viewing these animals as unified psychological beings, individuals who have a biography (a psychological life-story), not merely a biology. And common sense is not in conflict with our best science here. Indeed, our best science offers a scientific corroboration of the common sense view.

That corroboration is to be found in a set of diverse but related considerations. One is evolutionary theory, which implies that (1) the more complex has evolved from the less complex, that (2) members of the species *Homo sapiens* are the most complex life form of which we are aware, that (3) members of our species bring a psychological presence to the world, that (4) the psychological capacities we find in humans have evolved over time, and that (5) these capacities would not have evolved at all and would not have been passed on from one generation to the next if they (that is, these capacities) failed to have adaptive value—that is, if they failed to offer advantages to our species in its ongoing struggle to survive in an ever-changing environment.

Given these five points, it is entirely consistent with the main thrust of evolutionary theory, and is, indeed, required by it, to maintain that the members of some species of nonhuman animals are like us in having the capacity to see and hear and feel, for example, as well as to believe and desire, to remember and anticipate. 25

Certainly this is what Darwin thinks, as is evident when he writes of the animals we humans eat and trap, to use just two instances, that they differ psychologically (or mentally) from us in degree, not in kind.

A second, related consideration involves comparative anatomy and physiology. Everything we know about nature must incline us to believe that a complex structure has a complex reason for being. It would therefore be an extraordinary lapse of form if we humans had evolved into complicated psychological creatures, with an underlying anatomical and physiological complexity, while other species of animals had evolved to have a more or less complex anatomy and physiology, very much like our own in many respects, and yet lacked—*totally* lacked—any and every psychological capacity. If nature could respond to this bizarre suggestion, the verdict we would hear would be, "Nonsense!"

Thus it is, then, that both common sense and our best science speak with one voice regarding the psychological nature we share with the nonhuman animals I have mentioned—those, for example, many people stew, roast, fry, broil and grill for the sake of their gustatory desires and delights. When the dead and putrefying bodies of these animals are eaten, our psychological kin are consumed.

Recall the occasion for this review of relevant scientific considerations. Categorical speciesism, which I characterized earlier, is not shown to be a moral prejudice merely because those who accept it are unable to prove its truth. This much has been conceded and, indeed, insisted upon. What more, then, would have to be established before the charge of moral prejudice could be made to stick? Part of that answer is to be found in the recent discussion of what common sense and our best science contribute to our understanding of the nonhuman animals we have been discussing. Both agree that these animals are fundamentally like ordinary human beings—like you and me. For, like us, these animals have a unified psychological presence in the world, a life-story that is uniquely their own, a separate biography. In the simplest terms *they are somebody, not something.* Precisely because this similarity is so well established, grounded in the opinions, as Aristotle would express this, of both "the many and the wise," any substantive moral position at odds with it seems dubious to say the least.

30   And categorical speciesism, as I have characterized it, *is* at odds with the joint verdict of common sense and our best science. For once the appeal to intuition is denied (and denied for good reasons), the onus of justification must be borne by the speciesist to cite some unique feature of being human that would ground the attribution of inherent value exclusively to human beings, a task that we now see is all but certain to end in failure, given the biographical status humans share with those nonhuman animals to whom I have been referring. Rationally considered, we must judge similar cases similarly. This is what the principle of formal justice requires, what respect for logical consistency demands. Thus, since we share a biographical presence in the world with these animals, it seems arbitrary and prejudicial in the extreme to insist that all humans have a kind of value that every other animal lacks.

In response to this line of argument people who wish to retain the spirit of speciesism might be prompted to alter its letter. This position I shall call modified speciesism. According to this form of speciesism those nonhuman animals who, like us, have a biographical presence in the world have *some* inherent value, it's just that the degree of inherent value they have *always is less* than that possessed by human beings. And if we ask why this is thought to be so, the answer modified speciesism offers is the same as categorical speciesism: The degree of value differs because humans belong to a particular species to which no other animal belongs—the species *Homo sapiens.*

I think it should be obvious that modified speciesism is open to many of the same kinds of damaging criticisms as categorical speciesism. What, we may ask, is supposed to be the basis of the alleged superior value of human beings? Will it be said that one simply "intuits" this? Then all the same difficulties this appeal faced in the case of categorical speciesism will resurface and ultimately swamp modified speciesism. To avoid this, will it be suggested that the degree of inherent value an individual possesses depends on the relative complexity of that individual's psychological repertoire—the greater the complexity, the greater the value? Then modified speciesism simply will not be able to justify the ascription of superior inherent value to all human beings when compared with every nonhuman animal. And the reason it will not be able to do this is simple: Some nonhuman animals bring to their biography a degree of psychological complexity that far exceeds what is brought by some human beings. One need only to compare, say, the psychological repertoire of a healthy two year old chimp, or dog, or hog, or robin to that of a profoundly handicapped human of any age, to recognize the incontrovertible truth of what I have just said. Not all human beings have richer, more complex biographies than every nonhuman animal.

How are speciesists to get around this fact—for get around it they must, be- cause fact it is. There is a familiar theological answer to this question; at least it is familiar to those who know something of the Judeo-Christian religious traditions, as these traditions sometimes have been interpreted. That answer states that human beings—all of us—are inherently more valuable than any other existing individual because we are spiritually different and, indeed, unique. This uniqueness stems from our having been created in the image of God, a status we share with no other creature. If, then, it is true that all humans uniquely image God, then we are able to cite a real (spiritual) difference between every member of our species and the countless numbers of the millions of other species of creaturely life. And, if, more- over, this difference is a morally relevant one, then speciesists might seem to be in a position to defend their speciesism (and this is true whether they are categorical or moderate speciesists) in the face of the demands of formal justice. After all, that principle requires that we judge similar cases similarly, whereas any two individu- als—the one human, the other of some other species—will not be relevantly sim- ilar, given the hypothesis of the unique spiritual worth of all human beings.

Now I myself am not ill-disposed to the idea of there being something about us humans that gives us a unique spiritual worth, nor am I ill-disposed to the idea that the ground of this worth is to be found or explicated in the idea that we hu- mans uniquely "image" God. Not surprisingly, therefore, the interpretation of these ideas I favor, while it concedes this (possible) difference between humans and the rest of creation, does not yield anything like the results favored by speciesism, whether categorical or moderate. Let me explain.

The position I favor is the one that interprets our divine "imaging" in terms   35 of our moral responsibility: By this I mean that we are expressly chosen by God to be God's vice-regent in the day-to-day affairs of the world; we are chosen by God, that is, to be as loving in our day-to-day dealings with the created order, as God was in creating that order in the first place. In *this* sense, therefore, there *is* a morally relevant difference between human beings and every other creaturely expression of God. For it is only members of the human species who are given the awesome freedom and responsibility to be God's representative within creation. And it is, therefore, only we humans who can be held morally blameworthy when we fail to do this, and morally praiseworthy when we succeed.

Within the general context of this interpretation of our unique "imaging" of God, then, we find a morally relevant difference between God's creative expression in the human and God's creative expression in every other aspect of creation. But— as should be evident—this difference *by itself* offers neither aid nor comfort to speciesism, of whatever variety. For to agree that only humans image God, in the sense that only humans have the moral responsibility to be loving toward God's cre- ation, in no way entails either that all and only humans have inherent value (so- called categorical speciesism) or that all and only humans have a superior inherent value (modified speciesism, as I called it). It is perfectly consistent with our unique status as God's chosen representative within creation that *other* creatures have in- herent value and possess it to a degree equal to that possessed by human beings.

Granted, our uniqueness lies in our moral responsibility to God and to God's creation, including, of course, all members of the human family. But this fact, assuming it to be a fact, only answers the question, "Which among God's creatures are capable of acting rightly or wrongly (or, as philosophers might say, 'are moral agents')?" What this fact, assuming it to be one, does not answer are the questions, "To which creatures can we act rightly or wrongly?" and "What kind of value do other creatures have?"

Every prejudice dies hard. Speciesism is no exception. That it is a prejudice and that, by acting on it, we humans have been, and continue to be, responsible for an incalculable amount of evil, an amount of truly monumental proportions, is, I believe, as true as it is regrettable. In my philosophical writings over the past fifteen years I have endeavored to show how this tragic truth can be argued for on wholly secular grounds. On this occasion I have looked elsewhere for support—have in fact looked to the original saga of creation we find in *Genesis*—in the hope that we might there find a religious or theological account that resonates with the secular case for animal rights. Neither case—not the secular and not the religious—has, or can have, the conclusiveness of a proof in, say, geometry. I say "can have" because I am reminded of Aristotle's astute observation, that it is the mark of an educated person not to demand "proof" that is inappropriate for a given subject matter. And whatever else we might think of moral thought, I believe we at least can agree that it is importantly unlike geometry.

It remains true, nonetheless, that my attempt to explain and defend as egalitarian this view of the inherent value of humans and other animals must face a number of important challenges. For reasons of length, if for no other, I cannot on this occasion characterize or respond to all these challenges, no even all the most fundamental ones. The best I can do, before concluding, is describe and defuse two of them.

The first begins by observing that, within the traditions of Judaism and Christianity, *every form of life,* not simply humans and other animals, is to be viewed as expressive of God's love. Thus, to attempt to "elevate" the value of nonhuman animals, as I might be accused of having done, could be viewed as having the unacceptable consequence of negating or reducing the value of everything else.

40   I think this objection misses the mark. There is nothing in the animal rights philosophy (nothing, that is, in the kind of egalitarianism I have endeavored to defend) that either denies or diminishes the value of fruits, nuts, grains and other forms of vegetative life, or that refuses to accept the possibility that these and the rest of creation are so many ways in which God's loving presence is manifested. Nor is there anything in this philosophy that disparages the wise counsel to treat all of creation gently and appreciatively. It is an arrogant, unbridled anthropocentrism, often aided and abetted in our history by an arrogant, unbridled Christian theology, not the philosophy of animal rights, that has brought the earth to the brink of ecological disaster.

Still, this philosophy does find in humans and other animals, because of our shared biographical status in creation, a kind of value—inherent value—which other creatures fail to possess, either not at all or at least not to the degree in which humans and other animals possess it. Is it possible to defend this view? I believe it is, both on the grounds of a purely secular moral philosophy and by appeal to Biblical authority. The secular defense I have attempted to offer elsewhere and will not repeat here. As for the Christian defense, I shall merely reaffirm the vital importance (in my view) of *Genesis 1*, as well as (to my mind) the more than symbolic significance of the covenant, and note that in both we find Biblical sanction for viewing the value of animals to be superior to that of vegetables. After all, we do not find carrots and almonds included in the covenant, and we do find God expressly giving these and other forms of vegetative life to us, as our food, in *Genesis'* first creation saga. In a word, then, vegetative life was meant to be used by us, thus giving it utility value for us (which does not mean or entail that we may use these life forms thoughtlessly or even irreverently).

So much for the first challenge. The second one emanates from quite a different source and mounts a quite different objection. It begins by noting the large disparities that exist in the quality of life available to those who are affluent (the "haves") and those who are poor (the "have-nots"), especially those who live in the so-called "Third World." "It is all fine and good to preach the gospel of animal rights to those people who have the financial and other means to practice it, if they choose to do so," this objection states, "but please do spare us your self-righteous denunciation of the struggling (and often starving) masses of people in the rest of the world, who really have no choice but to eat animals, wear their skins, and use them in other ways. To condemn these people is to value animal life above human life. And this is misanthropy at its worst."

Now, this particular variation on the familiar theme of misanthropy (at least this is familiar to advocates of animal rights) has a point, up to a point. The point it has, is that it would be self-righteous to condemn the people in question for acting as they do, especially if we are acting worse than they are (as well we may be). But, of course, nothing in what I have argued supports such a condemnation, and this for the simple reason that I have nowhere argued that people who eat animals, or who hunt and trap them, or who cut their heads off or burst their intestines in pursuit of "scientific knowledge," either are or must be evil people. The position I have set forth concerns the moral wrongness of what people do, not the vileness of their *character*. In my view, it is entirely possible that good people sometimes do what is wrong, and evil people sometimes do what is right.

Indeed, not only is this possible, it frequently happens, and among those circumstances in which it does, some concern the actions performed by people in the Third World. At least this is the conclusion we reach if we take the philosophy of animal rights seriously. To make my meaning clearer, consider the following example. Suppose we chance upon a tribe of hunter-gatherers who annually, on a date sacred to their tradition, sacrifice the most beautiful female child to the gods, in the hope that the tribe will prosper in the coming year. In my view this act of human sacrifice is morally wrong and ought to be stopped (which does *not* mean that we should invade with tanks and flame-throwers to stop it!). From this moral assessment of what these human beings do, however, it does not follow that we should judge them to be evil, vicious people. It could well be that they act from only the best intentions and with nothing but the best motives. Nevertheless, what they do, in my judgment, is morally wrong.

45   What is true of the imaginary case of this tribe, is no less true of real-life cases where people in the Third World raise and kill animals for food, cruelly subject other animals to forced labor, and so on. Anytime anyone reduces the inherent value of a nonhuman animal to that animal's utility value for human beings, what is done, in my view, is morally wrong. But it does not follow from this that we should make a negative moral judgment about the character of the human moral agents involved, especially if, as is true in the Third World, there are mitigating circumstances. For it often happens that people who do what is morally wrong should be *excused* from moral blame and censure. A person who shoots a family member, for example, in the mistaken belief that there is a burglar in the house, does what is wrong and yet may well *not* be morally blameworthy. Similarly, those people in the Third World who act in ways that are prohibited by respect for the rights of animals, do what is wrong. But because of the harsh, uncompromising exigencies of their life, where they are daily faced with the demand to make truly heroic sacrifices, where indeed it often is a matter of their life or their death that hangs in the balance, the people of the Third World in my view should be excused from our harsh, uncompromising judgments of moral blame. The circumstances of their life, one might say, are as mitigating as any circumstances can be.

In light of the preceding remarks, I hope it is clear why it would be a bad reading of the philosophy of animal rights, to charge its proponents with a hearty appetite, if not for animal flesh then at least for self-righteousness. When we understand the difference between morally assessing a person's act and that person's character, and when we take cognizance of the appropriateness of reducing or erasing moral blame in the face of mitigating circumstances, then the proponents of animal rights should be seen to be no more censorious or "self-righteous" than the proponents of any other moral philosophy.

The challenge to lead a good, respectful, loving life just in our dealings within the human family is onerous and demanding. How much more onerous and demanding must it be, therefore, if we widen the circle of the moral community to include the whole of creation. How might we begin to meet this enlarged challenge? Doubtless there are many possible places to begin, some of which will be more accessible to some than to others. For my part, however, I cannot help believing that an appropriate place to begin is with the food on our plates. For here we are faced with a direct personal choice, over which we exercise absolute sovereign authority. Such power is not always within our grasp. How little influence we really have, you and I, on the practices of the World Bank, the agrarian land-reform movement, the call to reduce armed conflicts, the cessation of famine and the evil of abject poverty! These large-scale evils stand beyond the reach of our small wills.

But not the food on our plates. Here we are at liberty to exercise absolute control. And here, then, we ought to be asking ourselves, "Which of those choices I can make are most in accord with the idea of the integrity of creation?"

When we consider the biographical and, I dare say, the spiritual kinship we share with those billions of animals raised and slaughtered for food; when, further, we inform ourselves of the truly wretched conditions in which most of these animals are raised, not to mention the deplorable methods by which they are transported and the gruesome, blood-soaked reality of the slaughterhouse; and when, finally, we take honest stock of our privileged position in the world, a position that will not afford us the excuse from moral blame shared by the desperately poor who, as we say, "really have no choice"—when we consider all these factors, then the case for abstaining from animal flesh has the overwhelming weight of both impartial reason and a spirituallyinfused compassion on its side.

True, to make this change will involve some sacrifices—in taste perhaps, in   50
convenience certainly. And yet the whole fabric of Christian *agape* is woven from the threads of sacrificial acts. To abstain, on principle, from eating animals, therefore, although it is not the end-all, can be the begin-all of our conscientious effort to journey back to (or toward) Eden, can be one way (among others) to re-establish or create that relationship to the earth which, if *Genesis 1* is to be trusted, was part of God's original hopes for and plans in creation. It is the integrity of this creation we seek to understand and aspire to honor. In the choice of our food, I believe, we see, not in a glass darkly, but face to face, a small but not unimportant part of both the challenge and the promise of Christianity and animal rights.

CRITICAL THINKING QUESTIONS

1. The author systematically destroys all the arguments we commonly hear for eating meat. Does he convince you to become a vegetarian? If so, why? If not, why not?

2. Whether or not you are convinced by Regan's argument, what do you consider to be his most effective *evidence?*

WRITING TOPIC

Regan says, "The challenge to lead a good, respectful, loving life just in our dealings within the human family is onerous and demanding. How much more onerous and demanding must it be, therefore, if we widen the circle of the moral community to include the whole of creation." While you may not be ready to include the "whole of creation," create a moral argument advocating a change in our behavior toward some particular creature in this world.

Frank Schaeffer and John Schaeffer

My Son the Marine?

When two Marine recruiters showed up at our Salisbury, Mass., home in dress blues, they bedazzled my younger son, John. He had talked to recruiters from the Army, Navy and Air Force too, but his eyes lit up while the Marines spoke. I watched, inwardly alarmed. John seemed to relate to these stern, clean men with their insanely flawless uniforms in some basic way that I could barely comprehend. My wife, Genie, looking concerned and a bit drawn, turned to one of the men and asked, "But when he's done with the Marines, I mean—what will he have?"

The recruiter said, "Have, ma'am? I don't understand."

"I meant, what will he get out of it?"

The man's cheeks flushed. "He'll be a United States Marine, ma'am!"

5   There were no promises of college funds, "signing bonuses" or great "civilian opportunities" later on in life. Instead, the Marines promised that if John joined the Corps, he would find standards that had not been lowered. A young man wanting to measure himself against the tradition of maximum endurance would not be disappointed. "Boot camp's still tough as hell," one of the recruiters told us.

When the men left, John said to me, "I'm not sure I want to go into the military, Dad. But if I do, it'll be the Marines. Otherwise, what's the point?"

I was born in Switzerland to American missionaries, the youngest of four children. Perhaps because they were overprotective of me after I contracted polio—I wore a leg brace—my parents home-schooled me, and then sent me to private schools in England and Wales.

Genie and I married in 1970 and moved to America ten years later. In September 1980, our son John was born. From the moment he entered our lives to his last high school poetry reading, I doted on him. He made the meaning of life clear to me.

So when he finally decided to join the Marines, I had no picture of how things would go. I felt ignorant. I vaguely imagined my son leaving for boot camp, and then after he graduated, being sent off to the ends of the earth. Why the hell was John going into the Marines?

10   It had been hard enough sending my two older children off to college. The normal separations were just about unbearable. Our daughter, Jessica, went to New York University, and our other son, Francis, to Georgetown. Couldn't John have gone on to college first? No other parent in our affluent town on the North Shore of Boston had a son or daughter who was going into the military, let alone as an enlisted recruit.

When I told another parent of John's decision to join the Marines, the man was incredulous. "He's so bright and talented and could do anything!" the man said. "What a waste!"

The day John left for boot camp at Parris Island in South Carolina, I woke very early. I had to get him to the local recruiting office by 4:30. At our front door, John and his mother hugged and she cried steady, silent tears. John told his mother he loved her.

At the recruiting office, I looked at my son as he shook the staff sergeant's hand and thought, *What is he trying to prove?* More than once during the last few months, I had asked him, "Why do you want to do this?" Sometimes he'd say, "I want self-discipline." The best answer he gave was, "I just do." We parted with a hug and a handshake. "I'll miss you, boy," I said. "I'll write every day."

"Okay."

"I love you, John."   15

"I love you, Dad."

Driving home, I lost my way twice on a road I'd driven a thousand times. I'd never experienced pride and fear as one emotion before. *Oh, Lord, please protect my boy and bring him home safe!* was all I could think as I peered forlornly into the gloom while trying to remember my way home.

After a brief call letting us know he'd arrived—plus two form letters sent by the Marines—John was not allowed to contact us. I bought a book by Thomas E. Ricks called *Making the Corps,* which, with its day-by-day account of boot-camp training, quickly became my bible. I followed John's activities: drill marching; classes in subjects like Tactical Weapons of Opportunity (i.e., using things like rocks and sticks to smash the enemy with when a rifle wasn't handy); and physical training— miles of running, thousands of repetitions of exercises, pugil stick fighting, and endless humps (marches in full combat gear and pack).

Writing to John was a poignant experience. There was something so unequal about writing to him from the lap of luxury when he had essentially died and gone to hell.

For the first time in both our lives, my son was beyond my help. Did he have it in   20 him to become a Marine? I knew that John's idea of a good time was to curl up in front of the fireplace and reread his favorite bits of *The Hobbit.* When he caught fish, he let them go. How could my son become a Marine? What sort of a person would he be when the Corps was done with him? Would John be absolutely devastated if he failed? I felt sick.

But he did not fail. Three months after John had left us, Genie and I went down to Parris Island for his graduation. We stood in the stands for the ceremony and watched our son parade in, third man from the front, a tall Marine—my son.

I wiped my eyes and looked around. It occurred to me that this was the first time I'd been in an integrated crowd of this size dedicated to one purpose and of one mind. We were dark-skinned, weather-beaten, Spanish-speaking grandfathers; black kids wearing head rags; Southern-accented mothers with big hair and tight sweat suits; and some people who looked like us.

The platitudes my educated friends mouthed about "racial harmony" and "eco- nomic and gender diversity" were nothing compared to the spirit shared among the people gathered in the stands that day to honor our Marines. Our children would room together as they had in boot camp, drink together, work together, united by a high purpose: the defense of our country and loyalty to the Corps.

Nearly two years later, I was packing my bags to fly down to Florida to visit John at his new base, where he was a squad leader and had been nominated by his platoon to represent it as "Marine of the Quarter," the best performer of his unit for that time period. My biggest worry was whether I would have trouble checking the cooler full of food I was bringing to John. It was September 10, 2001.

25   The next day, all flights were canceled, and civil air traffic over the United States was shut down for the first time in history. The cooler of food was forgotten. I was so scared for John. I longed to hold on to my son for dear life.

I finally spoke to him the next day, on September 12. He sounded calm and confident.

"Hey, Dad, this is worse for you than for me," he said.

"How's that?"

"All you have to do with yourself is worry, but we have a job to do." He paused. "Dad? I love you."

30   After I hung up the phone, I stared at the television. There were fire-fighters, cops and military personnel struggling to find survivors and thousands of dead. I felt deeply frustrated at being able to do nothing. At least I knew that I could look the men and women in uniform in the eye. My son, after all, was one of them.

CRITICAL THINKING QUESTIONS

1. In analyzing an argument, we look at the choices authors make: Why do writers choose to begin their pieces in these ways? Why do they place the evidence in this order? Why do they use a particular metaphor or descriptive phrase? In "My Son the Marine?," why did the writers choose to mention the son's "last high school poetry reading"? How do the writers use similar information later in the piece? How does this information relate to the title?

2. Although we cannot point to an *explicit* claim in "My Son the Marine?", we can articulate an *implied* claim. What might the authors want their readers to believe after reading this piece?

3. Compare and contrast the authors' use of rhetorical appeals *(ethos, logos, pathos)* in this essay to Alan Gurganus's use of appeals in "Captive Audience" (page 668). Based on your critical analyses of the two arguments, which one is more persuasive?

WRITING TOPIC

Think of a personal experience that was meaningful to you. If you were to relate this experience to other people, write out a sentence in which you succinctly state what would you like them to conclude (your *claim)*. Now write out a description of your personal experience so that readers will understand your claim without seeing it stated in a specific sentence. As a simplistic example, your description of an automobile accident might imply that drinking and driving is not a good thing to do.

Suzanne Winckler (b. 1946)

A Savage Life

Every few years I butcher chickens with a friend named Chuck who lives near the farm my husband and I own in northern Minnesota. Chuck buys chicks and takes care of them for the 10 weeks it takes them to mature. I share in the feed costs, but my main contribution—for which I get an equal share of birds—is to help slaughter them.

One day last fall, Chuck, two other friends and I butchered 28 chickens. We worked without stopping from 10 a.m. *to* 6 p.m. By the time it was over we had decapitated, gutted, plucked, cleaned and swaddled each bird in plastic wrap for the freezer. We were exhausted and speckled with blood. For dinner that night we ate vegetables.

Butchering chickens is no fun, which is one reason I do it. It is the price I pay for being an omnivore and for eating other meat, like beef and pork, for which I have not yet determined a workable way to kill.

The first time I caught a chicken to chop its head off, I noticed, as I cradled it in my arms, that it had the heft and pliability of a newborn baby. This was alarming enough, but when I beheaded it, I was not prepared to be misted in blood or to watch it bounce on the ground. Headless chickens don't run around. They thrash with such force and seeming coordination that they sometimes turn back flips. When I first saw this, three things became clear to me.

I realized why cultures, ancient and contemporary, develop elaborate rituals for cop- 5
ing with the grisly experience of killing any sentient creature. I understood why so many people in my largely bloodless nation are alarmed at the thought of killing anything (except insects) even though they eat with relish meat other people process for them. I saw why a small subset of my contemporaries are so horrified by the thought of inflicting pain and causing death that they maintain people should never kill anything.

One risk I run in this self-imposed food-gathering exercise is leaving the impression, or perhaps even furtively feeling, that I am superior to the omnivores who leave the killing of their meat to someone else. I don't think I am. Slaughtering my own chickens is one of two opportunities (gardening is the other) where I can dispense with the layers of anonymous people between me and my food. I have no quarrel with them. I just don't know who they are. They are not part of my story.

Killing chickens provides narratives for gathering, cooking and sharing food in a way that buying a Styrofoam package of chicken breasts does not. I remember the weather on the days we have butchered our chickens, and the friends over the years who've come to help, who have included a surgical nurse, a cell biologist, a painter of faux interiors, a Minnesota state representative who is also a logger, a zoologist, a nurse with Head Start and a former Army medic who now runs the physical plant at a large hospital. I can measure the coming of age of my partner's two kids, who were tykes the first time we butchered chickens 10 years ago, and who this go-round were well into puberty with an array of pierced body parts.

My mother, who was born in 1907, belonged to the last generation for whom killing one's food was both a necessity and an ordinary event. Her family raised chickens for the purpose of eating them, and her father taught all his children to hunt.

My survival does not depend on killing chickens, but in doing so I have found that it fortifies my connection to her. It also allows me to cast a tenuous filament back to my feral past. In 1914, Melvin Gilmore, an ethnobotanist, wrote, "In savage and barbarous life the occupation of first importance is the quest of food." Having butchered my own chickens, I now feel acquainted with the savage life.

As exhilarating as this may be, I do not thrill at the prospect of beheading chickens. Several days before the transaction, I circle around the idea of what my friends and I will be doing. On the assigned morning, we are slow to get going. There are knives and cleavers to sharpen, vats of water to be boiled in the sauna house, tables and chairs to set up, aprons and buckets to gather, an order of assembly to establish. In their own ritual progression, these preparations are a way to gear ourselves up. I feel my shoulders hunch and my focus is narrow. It is like putting on an invisible veil of resolve to do penance for a misdeed. I am too far gone in my rational Western head to appropriate the ritual of cultures for whom the bloody business of hunting was a matter of survival. But butchering chickens has permitted me to stand in the black night just outside the edge of their campfire, and from that prospect I have inherited the most important lesson of all in the task of killing meat: I have learned to say thank you and I'm sorry.

CRITICAL THINKING QUESTIONS

1. If as the author states, "I do not thrill at the prospect of beheading chickens," then why does she do it?

2. In a closing statement, the author tell us, "But butchering chickens has permitted me to stand in the black night just outside the edge of the campfire." What does she mean by choosing this metaphor?

WRITING TOPIC

Slaughtering chickens affords the author an opportunity to "dispense with the layers of anonymous people between me and my food." Can you support this opportunity? Do you agree that it is valuable to have direct knowledge of the source of your food?

Richard Wright (1908–1960)
from *Black Boy*

One morning I arrived early at work and went into the bank lobby where the Negro porter was mopping. I stood at a counter and picked up the Memphis *Commercial Appeal* and began my free reading of the press. I came finally to the editorial page and saw an article dealing with one H. L. Mencken. I knew by hearsay that he was the editor of the *American Mercury*, but aside from that I knew nothing about him.

The article was a furious denunciation of Mencken, concluding with one, hot, short sentence: Mencken is a fool.

I wondered what on earth this Mencken had done to call down upon him the scorn of the South. The only people I had ever heard denounced in the South were Negroes, and this man was not a Negro. Then what ideas did Mencken hold that made a newspaper like the *Commercial Appeal* castigate him publicly? Undoubtedly he must be advocating ideas that the South did not like. Were there, then, people other than Negroes who criticized the South? I knew that during the Civil War the South had hated northern whites, but I had not encountered such hate during my life. Knowing no more of Mencken than I did at that moment, I felt a vague sympathy for him. Had not the South, which had assigned me the role of a non-man, cast at him its hardest words?

Now, how could I find out about this Mencken? There was a huge library near the riverfront, but I knew that Negroes were not allowed to patronize its shelves any more than they were the parks and playgrounds of the city. I had gone into the library several times to get books for the white men on the job. Which of them would now help me to get books? And how could I read them without causing concern to the white men with whom I worked? I had so far been successful in hiding my thoughts and feelings from them, but I knew that I would create hostility if I went about this business of reading in a clumsy way.

I weighed the personalities of the men on the job. There was Don, a Jew; but I distrusted him. His position was not much better than mine and I knew that he was uneasy and insecure; he had always treated me in an offhand, bantering way that barely concealed his contempt. I was afraid to ask him to help me to get books; his frantic desire to demonstrate a racial solidarity with the whites against Negroes might make him betray me.

Then how about the boss? No, he was a Baptist and I had the suspicion that   5 he would not be quite able to comprehend why a black boy would want to read Mencken. There were other white men on the job whose attitudes showed clearly that they were Kluxers or sympathizers, and they were out of the question.

There remained only one man whose attitude did not fit into an anti-Negro category, for I had heard the white men refer to him as a "Pope lover." He was an Irish Catholic and was hated by the white Southerners. I knew that he read books, because I had got him volumes from the library several times. Since he, too, was an object of hatred, I felt that he might refuse me but would hardly betray me. I hesitated, weighing and balancing the imponderable realities.

One morning I paused before the Catholic fellow's desk.

"I want to ask you a favor," I whispered to him.

"What is it?"

"I want to read. I can't get books from the library. I wonder if you'd let me   10 use your card?"

He looked at me suspiciously.

"My card is full most of the time," he said.

"I see," I said and waited, posing my question silently.

"You're not trying to get me into trouble, are you, boy?" he asked, staring at me.

15   "Oh, no, sir."
"What book do you want?"
"A book by H. L. Mencken."
"Which one?"
"I don't know. Has he written more than one?"
20   "He has written several."
"I didn't know that."
"What makes you want to read Mencken?"
"Oh, I just saw his name in the newspaper," I said.
"It's good of you to want to read," he said. "But you ought to read the right things."
25   I said nothing. Would he want to supervise my reading?
"Let me think," he said. "I'll figure out something."
I turned from him and he called me back. He stared at me quizzically.
"Richard, don't mention this to the other white men," he said.
"I understand," I said. "I won't say a word."
30   A few days later he called me to him.
"I've got a card in my wife's name," he said. "Here's mine."
"Thank you, sir."
"Do you think you can manage it?"
"I'll manage fine," I said.
35   "If they suspect you, you'll get in trouble," he said.
"I'll write the same kind of notes to the library that you wrote when you sent me for books," I told him. "I'll sign your name."
He laughed.
"Go ahead. Let me see what you get," he said.
That afternoon I addressed myself to forging a note. Now, what were the names of books written by H. L. Mencken? I did not know any of them. I finally wrote what I thought would be a foolproof note: *Dear Madam: Will you please let this nigger boy*—I used the word "nigger" to make the librarian feel that I could not possibly be the author of the note—*have some books by H. L. Mencken?* I forged the white man's name.
40   I entered the library as I had always done when on errands for whites, but I felt that I would somehow slip up and betray myself. I doffed my hat, stood a respectful distance from the desk, looked as unbookish as possible, and waited for the white patrons to be taken care of. When the desk was clear of people, I still waited. The white librarian looked at me.
"What do you want, boy?"
As though I did not possess the power of speech, I stepped forward and simply handed her the forged note, not parting my lips.
"What books by Mencken does he want?" she asked.
"I don't know, ma'am," I said, avoiding her eyes.
"Who gave you this card?"
45   "Mr. Falk," I said.
"Where is he?"

"He's at work, at the M——Optical Company," I said. "I've been in here for him before."

"I remember," the woman said. "But he never wrote notes like this."

Oh, God, she's suspicious. Perhaps she would not let me have the books? If she had turned her back at that moment, I would have ducked out the door and never gone back. Then I thought of a bold idea.

"You can call him up, ma'am," I said, my heart pounding.

"You're not using these books, are you?" she asked pointedly.

"Oh, no, ma'am. I can't read."

"I don't know what he wants by Mencken," she said under her breath.

I knew now that I had won; she was thinking of other things and the race question had gone out of her mind. She went to the shelves. Once or twice she looked over her shoulder at me, as though she was still doubtful. Finally she came forward with two books in her hand.

"I'm sending him two books," she said. "But tell Mr. Falk to come in next time, or send me the names of the books he wants. I don't know what he wants to read."

I said nothing. She stamped the card and handed me the books. Not daring to glance at them, I went out of the library, fearing that the woman would call me back for further questioning. A block away from the library I opened one of the books and read a title: *A Book of Prefaces.* I was nearing my nineteenth birthday and I did not know how to pronounce the word "preface." I thumbed the pages and saw strange words and strange names. I shook my head, disappointed. I look at the other book; it was called *Prejudices.* I knew what that word meant; I had heard it all my life. And right off I was on guard against Mencken's books. Why would a man want to call a book *Prejudices?* The word was so stained with all my memories of racial hate that I could not conceive of anybody using it for a title. Perhaps I had made a mistake about Mencken? A man who had prejudices must be wrong.

When I showed the books to Mr. Falk, he looked at me and frowned.

"That librarian might telephone you," I warned him.

"That's all right," he said. "But when you're through reading those books, I want you to tell me what you get out of them."

That night in my rented room, while letting the hot water run over my can of pork and beans in the sink, I opened *A Book of Prefaces* and began to read. I was jarred and shocked by the style, the clear, clean, sweeping sentences. Why did he write like that? And how did one write like that? I pictured the man as a raging demon, slashing with his pen, consumed with hate, denouncing everything American, extolling everything European or German, laughing at the weaknesses of people, mocking God, authority. What was this? I stood up, trying to realize what reality lay behind the meaning of the words . . . Yes, this man was fighting, fighting with words. He was using words as a weapon, using them as one would use a club. Could words be weapons? Well, yes, for here they were. Then, maybe, perhaps, I could use them as a weapon? No. It frightened me. I read on and what amazed me was not what he said, but how on earth anybody had the courage to say it.

Occasionally I glanced up to reassure myself that I was alone in the room. Who were these men about whom Mencken was talking so passionately? Who was Anatole France? Joseph Conrad? Sinclair Lewis, Sherwood Anderson, Dostoevski, George Moore, Gustave Flaubert, Maupassant, Tolstoy, Frank Harris, Mark Twain, Thomas Hardy, Arnold Bennett, Stephen Crane, Zola, Norris, Gorky, Bergson, Ibsen, Balzac, Bernard Shaw, Dumas, Poe, Thomas Mann, O. Henry, Dreiser, H. G. Wells, Gogol, T. S. Eliot, Gide, Baudelaire, Edgar Lee Masters, Stendhal, Turgenev, Huneker, Nietzsche, and scores of others? Were these men real? Did they exist or had they existed? And how did one pronounce their names

I ran across many words whose meanings I did not know, and I either looked them up in a dictionary or, before I had a chance to do that, encountered the word in a context that made its meaning clear. But what strange world was this? I concluded the book with the conviction that I had somehow overlooked something terribly important in life. I had once tried to write, had once reveled in feeling, had let my crude imagination roam, but the impulse to dream had been slowly beaten out of me by experience. Now it surged up again and I hungered for books, new ways of looking and seeing. It was not a matter of believing or disbelieving what I read, but of feeling something new, of being affected by something that made the look of the world different.

As dawn broke I ate my pork and beans, feeling dopey, sleepy. I went to work, but the mood of the book would not die; it lingered, coloring everything I saw, heard, did. I now felt that I knew what the white men were feeling. Merely because I had read a book that had spoken of how they lived and thought, I identified myself with that book. I felt vaguely guilty. Would I, filled with bookish notions, act in a manner that would make the whites dislike me?

65   I forged more notes and my trips to the library became frequent. Reading grew into a passion. My first serious novel was Sinclair Lewis's *Main Street*. It made me see my boss, Mr. Gerlad, and identify him as an American type. I would smile when I saw him lugging his golf bags into the office. I had always felt a vast distance separating me from the boss, and now I felt closer to him, though still distant. I felt now that I knew him, that I could feel the very limits of his narrow life. And this had happened because I had read a novel about a mythical man called George F. Babbitt.

The plots and stories in the novels did not interest me so much as the point of view revealed. I gave myself over to each novel without reserve, without trying to criticize it; it was enough for me to see and feel something different. And for me, everything was something different. Reading was like a drug, a dope. The novels created moods in which I lived for days. But I could not conquer my sense of guilt, my feeling that the white men around me knew that I was changing, that I had begun to regard them differently.

Whenever I brought a book to the job, I wrapped it in newspaper—a habit that was to persist for years in other cities and under other circumstances. But some of the white men pried into my packages when I was absent and they questioned me.

"Boy, what are you reading those books for?"

"Oh, I don't know, sir."

"That's deep stuff you're reading, boy."   70

"I'm just killing time, sir."

"You'll addle your brains if you don't watch out."

I read Dreiser's *Jennie Gerhardt* and *Sister Carrie* and they revived in me a vivid sense of my mother's suffering; I was overwhelmed. I grew silent, wondering about the life around me. It would have been impossible for me to have told anyone what I derived from these novels, for it was nothing less than a sense of life itself. All my life had shaped me for the realism, the naturalism of the modern novel, and I could not read enough of them.

Steeped in new moods and ideas, I bought a ream of paper and tried to write; but nothing would come, or what did come was flat beyond telling. I discovered that more than desire and feeling were necessary to write and I dropped the idea. Yet I still wondered how it was possible to know people sufficiently to write about them? Could I ever learn about life and people? To me, with my vast ignorance, my Jim Crow station in life, it seemed a task impossible of achievement. I now knew what being a Negro meant. I could endure the hunger. I had learned to live with hate. But to feel that there were feelings denied me, that the very breath of life itself was beyond my reach, that more than anything else hurt, wounded me. I had a new hunger.

WRITING TOPICS

1. Wright wants a library card in order to read and grow intellectually. Perhaps today he would have been looking for access to a computer. Read about the computer divide. Fifty years later, are we still dividing access to knowledge according to wealth if not race?

2. Have you ever wanted or needed something that someone else in power has denied you? If so, did the situation make you angry? Like James Baldwin and other African-American artists, especially jazz musicians, Richard Wright spent years living in France. Look up the meaning of the word expatriate. Can you imagine situations that would lead you to leave your country?

3. After reading the excerpt from Richard Wright's *Black Boy*, read Langston Hughes's poem, "Democracy," on page 601. Explain how the situation Wright describes illustrates Hughes's words, "compromise and fear."

CHAPTER ACTIVITIES
AND TOPICS FOR WRITING ARGUMENTS

1. Suppose you are a professional athlete who has just signed a multimillion dollar contract. Assuming money is power, you certainly will have the power to do many things, but once you have bought Mom and Dad a nice retirement home and satisfied your own desire to trek through the Himalayas, what next? To what degree do you have responsibilities to your fellow human beings? Create a specific plan for using your assets, and argue that it is the best choice

(literature suggestions: Brooks's "The Boy Died in My Alley," Milton's "When I Consider How My Light Is Spent," and Kennedy's "Inaugural Address").

2. Here is a hypothetical situation: The United States is at war in the Middle East, and China has stepped into the conflict. Our government has stated one objective in this war is to restore human rights to the besieged countries. However, everyone understands that this war is also over oil: We win and life goes on normally; we lose and gas goes up to six dollars a gallon while our economy unravels and depression looms. And in this ground war, fought by high-tech infantry, Americans are dying in large numbers. The draft has been reinstated, and your number is called. It's the front lines for you. But there is an alternative. The Scandinavian countries as well as Canada have denounced this war and openly accept conscientious objectors. What are your responsibilities? What do you do? Make a decision and support it (literature suggestions: Aristophanes's *Lysistrata,* Crawford's "Lies," Gurganus's "Captive Audience," and Schaeffer and Schaeffer's "My Son the Marine?").

3. Killing animals is an emotional issue for many people. Read "The Evil of Animal 'Rights'" by Aaron Epstein and Yaron Brooks and "A Savage Life" by Suzanne Winckler; as you read, make notes of the authors' uses of the appeal to *pathos*. In a small group, discuss the animal rights issue. Focus on the various subtopics that fall under this broad heading, such as factory farming, animals in the entertainment and fashion industries, and lab experimentation. Now share your notes on the essays, and as a group, record clear instances of the appeal of *pathos*. In particular, point out words, phrases, and examples. Discuss whether these emotional appeals are legitimate or merely covering up a lack of credible evidence. Finally, decide which of the two arguments uses emotional evidence more effectively. As you evaluate the two arguments, keep in mind that *effective* does not always equate to *legitimate*.

4. Since we seem to share the desire to vanquish our enemies, revenge is sometimes called *sweet*. But is revenge sweet? We often applaud the person who has suffered unfair treatment when he or she finally triumphs. And we, ourselves, cannot help but feel a twinge of joy when the court finally forces that unscrupulous car dealer to pay us back the money he unjustly took from us and to offer an apology. But is revenge always sweet? Situations often are not as simple and clear-cut as they appear on the surface. Read the stories, "Spanish Roulette" by Ed Vega and "He Becomes Deeply and Famously Drunk" by Brady Udall, the poem, "Bully" by Martín Espada, and the paragraph, "Of Revenge" by Francis Bacon, and then write an extended definition of the word *revenge*. In your extended definition, you might include examples from history, literature, and personal experience, but also be sure to focus on the conflicts this impulse for revenge creates in people.

5. While Abraham Lincoln and John F. Kennedy were superior national leaders, everyday persons also take on the responsibilities and risks of leadership, as illustrated by the characters, Jesus in Brady Udall's "He Becomes Deeply and Famously Drunk,"and Robert, the blind man, in Raymond Carver's "Cathedral." On the other hand, Lieutenant Jimmy Cross in Tim O'Brien's "The Things They Carried" believes he has neglected his duties as the leader of his platoon. If you were conducting a leadership workshop for your college or local community, how could you use these five individuals to illustrate key points of your presentation? What other examples, contemporary or historical, fictional or factual, might you use to illustrate leadership qualities?

6. The term, "white lie," suggests that, in some situations, lying may be justified. Depending on the context, some persons may attempt to justify lies when they feel that the negative consequences of telling the truth outweigh the virtue of honoring the truth. For some people, however, lies are always unacceptable; for them, "white lie" is an oxymoron, a contradiction in terms that creates a *slippery slope*. Moving beyond the personal to the political arena, is a government ever justified in withholding information that directly impacts its citizens? Recently, this issue question has been debated in relation to national security and war on terrorism. In an essay, take a stand on this issue; support your position with evidence from history and current events. (literature suggestion: Crawford's "Lies")

COLLABORATION ACTIVITY: CREATING A ROGERIAN ARGUMENT

For this activity, you will work in small teams to research, write, and present a Rogerian argument on a contemporary issue that has emerged from your exploration of readings in this chapter. The Writing Topics, following many of the selections, can help you identify an issue. For a discussion of the Rogerian Argument and a suggested organizational approach to the assignment, please see Chapter Three.

Following are guidelines for this collaboration activity:

* Identify an issue.
* Divide the research/writing responsibilities as follows:
  * Student one: introduction section
  * Student two: body section, affirmative position
  * Student three: body section, opposing position
  * Student four: conclusion, summation, and middle-ground position.

Following are characteristics of effective collaboration. The team member should:

* Contribute by collecting information related to the issue.
* Take responsibility by completing his or her assigned work on time.
* Engage with team members by listening to and considering other viewpoints.

Sample Issue: The Justice or Injustice of Reparations
Acknowledging the injustice of the internment of Japanese Americans during
World War II, in 1988 the U.S. Congress voted to issue a formal apology and to
pay reparations. Today some people argue that other groups also are deserving of
payments for past wrongs and unjuries. African Americans and Native Americans
are two of these groups. On the other hand, other people argue that wrongs done
to these groups were committed in the distant past, and, therefore, reparations are
not justified. Select one of these two groups and address the issue question: Should
the U.S. government pay reparations for past wrongs to——?

Literature suggestions: "The Red Convertible," "The Reservation Cab Driver,"
and "In Response to Executive Order 9066" in Chapter Four; "Ballad of Birmingham"
in Chapter Six; "America," "Fight the Power," and "[I am alone]" in Chapter Seven.

MAKING CONNECTIONS

Chapter Seven: Power and Responsibility

Individual responsibility and political forces
Forché, "The Colonel"; Merrill, "Casual Wear"; Aristophanes, *Lysistrata;* Gurganus, "Captive Audience"; Porter, "To Dr. William Ross"

Knowledge and individual power
Bambara, "The Lesson"; Hawthorne, "The Birth-Mark"; Udall, "He Becomes Deeply
and Famously Drunk"; Hughes, "Theme for English 'B'"; Wright, from *Black Boy*

The individual and ethical choices
Gordimer, "Terminal"; Hawthorne, "The Birth-Mark"; Olds, "The Promise";
Pastan, "Ethics"; Orwell, "A Hanging"

Personal dilemmas in daily life
Vega, "Spanish Roulette"; Brooks, "The Boy Died in My Alley"; Espada,
"Bully"; Frost, "Mending Wall"; Schaeffer and Schaeffer, "My Son the Ma-
rine?"; Winckler, "A Savage Life"

Cross-Chapter Connections

The individual and civic duty
Blake, "London" (Chapter One); Crane, "The Bride Comes to Yellow Sky,"
Plato, From *Crito* (Chapter Four); Ballou, "Last Letter to His Wife" (Chapter Six); Whitman, "Beat! Beat! Drums!", Crawford, "Lies," Kennedy, "Inaugural Address," Porter, "To Dr. William Ross" (Chapter Seven)

Glossary

Active voice the construction of a sentence in which the subject of the sentence is the doer of the action, as opposed to *passive voice,* in which the object of the action is in the subject place. "John hit Joe" is active voice, while "Joe was hit by John" is passive voice.

Ad hominem the fallacy of personal attack. Instead of arguing with someone's position, one attacks the person. "Mrs. X has had two affairs and does not deserve our vote."

Ad populum the fallacy of substituting content with a "just plain folks" appeal.

Allegory a work which may be seen totally or in part to represent a similar political or moral situation. *Aesop's Fables* or the *Stories of Brer Rabbit* are famous allegories.

Alliteration the repetition of an initial sound, usually of consonants, for example, *a fearsome food fight.*

Ambiguity intentionally vague meaning, sometimes leading the reader astray in argument or adding multiple levels of interpretation to literature.

Analogy in argument, creating an explanation through point-by-point comparison, for example, comparing the perceived moral deterioration of the modern world with that of ancient Rome.

Anecdote a brief story used within a larger work in order to illustrate an idea.

Annotation a critical or explanatory note.

Appeal to authority in argument, an appeal for support based on the widely accepted credibility of the witness; for example, suggesting that Dr. Spock, the noted baby doctor, held a similar position to your own on the subject of toilet training.

Archetype a recurring image that evokes very basic associations seen in universal patterns of human experience.

Assertion also called the *claim* or the *thesis,* it is the speaker's or writer's statement of his or her position in an argument.

Assumption   in argument, an idea which the writer or speaker feels no need to support, prove, or justify since the writer believes his or her audience will certainly hold it to be true. See also *Warrant.*

Audience   the readers or listeners for whom the writer composes, thus shaping or influencing the final product.

Begging the question   to use an argument that assumes exactly what the argument attempts to prove; for example, gun control goes against our freedom because it takes away our individual rights.

Caricature   a comic portrait of a person based on the exaggeration of several traits.

Character   the representation of a person in literature. A one-dimensional character is called a *flat* character, while one who is realistically complex is called a *round* character.

Claim   in argument, the main point, thesis, or assertion of the argument—what the speaker or writer wants his or her audience to think or do about an issue.

Cliché   a word or phrase overused and outworn to the point of losing its impact; for example, *the bottom line* or *put the pedal to the metal.* In literature, plot situations can be termed *cliché* or hackneyed.

Climax   the high point of interest and intensity after which the plot moves toward its conclusion. See also *Denouement.*

Conceit   in writing or speaking, the use of an elaborate or striking metaphor.

Concession   in argument, recognizing and acknowledging the validity of a portion of the opposition's point of view. In making a concession, the arguer can strengthen his or her *ethos* by demonstrating the character trait of fair-mindedness.

Conflict   the opposition that creates tension in literature. The opposing forces may be *external* when a character conflicts with other people, or they may be *internal* when a character faces conflicts within him or herself.

Connotation   the emotional or social meaning attached to a word beyond its literal, objective meaning. For example, in James Fenimore Cooper's story, "The Slaughter of the Pigeons," the word "slaughter" suggests a wanton and brutal assault. See also *Denotation.*

Crisis   the point of uncertainty and tension, leading to the plot's *climax.*

Deduction   the reasoning process that begins with a generalization, applies that generalization to a particular instance, and then draws a conclusion based on that application. See also *Induction.*

Denotation   the dictionary definition of a word—its literal and explicit meaning. See also *Connotation.*

Denouement   the climax or final coming together of all plot elements in a drama or narrative once the conflicts are resolved. See also *Climax.*

Diction   the speaker's or writer's choice of words.

Didactic   when an author wishes to teach a lesson or instruct his or her audience through his or her writing.

Documentation   a systematic way of attributing sources of words and concepts, usually following MLA or APA parenthetical style.

Dramatic irony   a situational irony in which an audience's wider understanding highlights a character's limited vision.

Either-or reasoning   sometimes called the *black and white* or *false dilemma fallacy;* in argument, such reasoning is characterized by oversimplification that presents an issue only in two ways, either X or Y.

Ellipses   the three periods used to indicate words left out of a direct quotation; for example, "I shall never . . . return to this area of the country."

Emphasis   in writing, the use of repetition, syntax, and word placement to draw the reader's attention to a word or idea.

Equivocation   in argument, the intentional use of a word which has more than one interpretation and thus misleads the reader or listener.

Ethos   the appeal first mentioned by Aristotle through which the writer or speaker evokes his or her credibility and trustworthiness; for example, a teenager wishing to stay out past curfew might ask his or her parents, "Have I ever done anything to lead you to mistrust me?"

Euphemism   a word used in place of a harsher or more emotional word, for example, "passed away" used instead of "died." Such words sometimes can mask the truth of an issue.

Evidence   in argument, there are many types of evidence, but the most common are personal experience or first-person accounts, *logos* or the use of facts and objective reports, *ethos* or the use of character and credibility, and *pathos* or the use of value-based and emotional appeals.

Exposition   that portion of a drama or narrative which introduces the facts of setting, plot, and character to the audience.

Fact   verifiable information; a statement that can be proven true or false. "Texas is located near New Jersey," is stated as a fact although, of course, it is false.

Fallacy   illogical reasoning; often an intentional flaw created to manipulate the evidence and mislead one's audience, but sometimes an unknowing flaw in reasoning due to one's carelessness or ignorance.

False analogy   a false comparison, sometimes expressed as "comparing apples and oranges." People might say that like Rome, America is destined for destruction; however, modern America is quite unlike ancient Rome.

Figurative language   language using imaginative comparison, such as *metaphor* and *simile.*

Flashback   a return, out of chronological order, to an earlier point in the plot, often used in fiction and film.

Foil character   a minor character designed to reflect the qualities of a major character through contrast.

Foreshadowing   a hint or suggestion of what is to come.

Image   a reference in text which calls to mind vivid details of sight, sound, smell, taste, and touch.

Induction   a process of reasoning that begins by one's examining details in order to arrive at a generalization. In moving from specific evidence to articulating a probable conclusion, one makes an *inductive leap*. When one moves hastily from inadequate evidence to a generalization, this leap in reasoning represents flawed reasoning, commonly called *jumping to a conclusion.*

Inference   S. I. Hayakawa defines it as "a statement about the unknown based on the known." Unlike a fact, an inference cannot be proven true or false since it is a probable explanation or an interpretation of evidence.

Interpretation   moving beyond line-by-line explication of a work to an examination of themes, implications, and broader meanings.

Irony   a humorous or sarcastic statement whose words mean the opposite of their usual use, or in literature, the contrast between a character's perception and the truth known to the reader or audience.

Issue   a topic of argument that generates tension because both sides have some reasonable aspects to their arguments.

Logos   in argument, the rhetorical appeal that Aristotle identified as the arguer's use of reasoning and logic to persuade his or her audience to accept the claim.

Metaphor   without using "like" or "as," this device describes something as if it were something quite different. "That man is an angel."

Mood   the emotional quality of a work created through the writer's choice of imagery and setting. One might say Shakespeare's *Romeo and Juliet* is a "tragic and somber" play, while Harvey Fierstein's *On Tidy Endings* is "both funny and sad, yet, uplifting."

Narration   the recounting of a series of plot events in order to tell a story. A *narrator* relates these events to the reader.

Non sequitur   in argument, a common fallacy, meaning "it does not follow"; the reasoning does not follow logically between clauses within a sentence or between consecutive sentences.

Pathos   the quality in literature that arouses pity; in argument, an emotional or value-based appeal. When an emotional appeal replaces content, it is called the fallacy of *ad misercordium* or appeal to pity and fear.

Persona   literally translated as a "mask"; the identity or image the writer presents in poetry, fiction, or nonfiction.

Plagiarism   a writer's failure to give credit for words or concepts from another source.

Plot   the chain of events in literature, what happens next.

Point of view   the speaker or narrator of a work through which the audience or readers perceive the details of plot and character. The point-of-view may be omniscient, limited, or objective, as well as first-, second-, or third-person.

Post hoc **fallacy**   Incorrectly attributing a cause and effect relationship; often called the false cause fallacy.

Premise   the main idea, hypothesis, or underlying principle in an argument.

Protagonist   the central character or actor in literature.

Red herring   the fallacy of leading the reader astray by bringing up a different issue as bait to capture the reader's interest, thus distracting him or her from the real issue.

Refutation   attempting to prove an argument wrong.

Rhetorical question   asking a question as a way to involve the reader in the issue at hand. In this way, the writer sets him or herself up to answer the question that has been planted in the reader's mind.

Stacking the evidence   the writer or speaker purposefully ignores opposing evidence to create a one-sided argument.

Stream-of-consciousness   a narrative technique in which the author may reveal the emotions, perceptions, and thoughts of a character on a conscious or unconscious level.

Subplot   a story that runs parallel to the main plot of a narrative, sometimes reinforcing the central theme.

Syllogism   in argument, Aristotle's three-part method of deductive reasoning, beginning with a major premise, followed by a minor premise, and ending with a conclusion.

Syntax   the arrangement of words, phrases, and clauses forming sentences.

Theme   a recurring, unifying idea running through a piece of literature. To discover *plot*, readers ask the question, "what happens next?", whereas, to discover *theme*, readers answer the question, "why?"

Tone   a speaker's or writer's attitude toward his or her subject and audience, often conveyed through diction.

Tragedy   traditionally the fall of a great person through his or her own errors in judgment. In modern literature, the term is often applied to the downfall of less highly placed characters.

Tragic flaw   a character's shortcoming which leads to disaster, for example, greed, lust, pride, or merely poor judgment.

Voice   the writer's personality or image constructed by the reader, often conveyed to the reader by the writer's sentence style and diction. See also *Persona* and *Tone*.

Warrant   a general principle or premise, stated or unstated, which the arguer assumes his or her audience accepts as valid or true; often a value-based principle. For example, in opposing abortion, prolife advocates assume that life has human value from the moment of conception.

ᐱᐱ Authors' Biographical Notes ᐱᐱ

Abbey, Edward (1927–1989)   Although born and raised on a farm in Pennsylvania, Abbey lived in the Southwest from 1947 until his death. A passionate defender of the wilderness, his book, *Desert Solitaire* (1968), helped to launch the environmental movement. His novel, *The Monkey Wrench Gang* (1975), about a group of environmental guerrilla's plot to blow up Glen Canyon Dam of the Colorado River, is credited with influencing radical environmental groups such as Earth First!

Alexie, Sherman (b. 1966)   A Spokane/Coeur d'Alene Indian, Alexie was born on the Spokane Indian Reservation in Wellpinit, Washington. Alexie is a prolific and versatile writer, known for his realistic portrayal of contemporary Native American reservation life and his comedic tone. His first collection of short stories, *The Lone Ranger and Tonto* (1993), received a PEN/Hemingway Award for Best First Book of Fiction. Alexie's first novel, *Reservation Blues,* was published in 1995, followed by *Indian Killer* (1996), which was named a *New York Times* Notable Book. Alexie also has several collections of poetry, including *The Business of Fancydancing* and *I Would Steal Horses,* and was a screenwriter for *Smoke Signals,* which won two awards at the Sundance Film Festival in 1998.

Aristophanes (c. 446 B.C.–c. 386 B.C.)   Aristophanes's plays, featuring lyric poetry, fantasy, and comedy, provide a political and social—and often satirical—perspective on classical Athens. His plays continue to be read and performed. Most popular in modern times has been *Lysistrata,* with its engagingly clever and comic heroine, ribald humor, and antiwar message.

Bacon, Francis (1561–1626)   Bacon was an English author, a courtier, philosopher, and an advocate of inductive reasoning in science.

Bambara, Toni Cade (b. 1939)   Bambara grew up in New York City and became a welfare investigator and a community activist. In 1970, she adopted the name "Bambara" from a signature she found in her great-grandmother's trunk. She has edited anthologies of black literature and published two collections of short stories, *Gorilla, My Love* (1972) and *The Sea Birds Are Still Alive* (1977).

Bass, Rick (b. 1959)   Bass, who lives in northwest Montana, is the author of fourteen books of fiction and nonfiction, including *The Watch* (1994), *The Sky, the Stars, the Wilderness* (1977), *Wild to the Heart,* and *Colter: The True Story of the Best Dog I Ever Had* (2000).

Bradstreet, Anne (1612?–1672) Born in England, Bradstreet grew up in a Puritan household. At age sixteen, she married Simon Bradstreet, who had recently graduated from Cambridge. Sailing with Puritan John Winthrop's fleet to the New World in 1629, Bradstreet and her husband were among the settlers of the Massachusetts Bay Colony in the New World. Despite the harsh conditions in rearing a family in the wilderness, Bradstreet continued to pursue her childhood interest in writing poetry. A collection of her poetry, *The Tenth Muse,* was printed in England in 1650.

Brooks, Gwendolyn (1917–2000) Brooks won the Pulitzer Prize in 1950 for her collection of poetry, *Annie Allen.* Since then she continued to write and was named the poet laureate of Illinois in 1969. Her poems reflect the diction and syntax of black street life. *The Bean-Eaters* was published in 1960, followed by *Beckonings* in 1975 and *To Disembark* in 1981.

Carson, Rachel (1907–1964) A scientist and writer, Carson's *The Sea Around Us* won the 1952 National Book Award. Her book, *Silent Spring* (1962), alerted the nation about the dangers of widespread and indiscriminate use of pesticides and chemical fertilizers. In 1963 the National Wildlife Federation recognized Carson as Conservationist of the Year.

Carver, Raymond (1938–1988) Raised in a working-class environment in the Pacific Northwest, Carver worked at many jobs while writing stories about the lives of everyday working people who feel trapped by their surroundings. His writing has been collected in *Fires: Essays, Poems, and Stories* (1989).

Chopin, Kate (1851–1904) In defiance of contemporary restraints, Chopin often wrote about strong, independent, female characters. She also wrote frankly about her characters' sexual feelings and, for that reason, caused a literary scandal. Her novels have recently found a sympathetic audience.

Cleary, Michael (b. 1945) Cleary grew up in upstate New York and now teaches college English in Fort Lauderdale, Florida, where he writes poetry. His first book of poems is *Hometown,* published in 1992.

Clifton, Lucille (b. 1936) A graduate of Howard University, Clifton has published seven books of poetry and fifteen children's books. She now teaches creative writing at the University of California, Santa Cruz.

Cochise (1812?–1874) A Chiricahua Apache leader, Cochise's people lived in the Southwest. Following the Civil War, as white settlers' numbers increased in the West, U.S. government soldiers and Apaches engaged in frequent and hostile conflicts. In 1871 a U.S. colonel and Cochise negotiated a peace settlement, but when Cochise discovered that the terms included relocating his people to a barren reservation, he rescinded his agreement. In 1872 Cochise again entered into negotiations with the U.S. government, during which he delivered the speech, "[I am alone]." Cochise succeeded in negotiating a compromise, and his people were relocated to a reservation along Apache Pass in southeastern Arizona.

Cooper, James Fenimore (1789–1851) Considered by critics to be the first successful American novelist, Cooper created the character Natty Bumppo in his famous

Leather-Stocking Tales, depicting life on the frontier. The collection includes the well-known novels *The Last of the Mohicans* (1826) and *The Deerslayer* (1841).

Corso, Gregory (1930–2001) Corso was a poet who gained fame as one of the Beat Poets along with Allen Ginsberg and Jack Kerouac. After a childhood in orphanages and foster homes, Corso became interested in literature while in a prison in New York. His book, *Mindfield: New and Collected Poems,* was published in 1998.

Crane, Stephen (1871–1900) Crane spent his brief life involved with writing: working with newspapers, serving as a war correspondent, and composing fiction. "A Bride Comes to Yellow Sky" was produced as a result of the year he spent traveling in the West. His best-known novel, *The Red Badge of Courage,* was published in 1895.

Crawford, John (b. 1978) Although born in Lexington, Kentucky, Crawford grew up Palatka, Florida. Crawford was on his honeymoon and only two credits away from graduating from Florida State University, when he received notice that his National Guard unit would be deployed to Iraq. His unit remained in Iraq for over a year, patrolling Baghdad. While serving, Crawford began writing his first-person account of his experiences, which became the book, *The Last True Story I'll Ever Tell.* Published in 2005, the book became a *New York Times* best seller. Crawford now lives in Tallahassee, Florida, and is completing his first novel.

Crumb, Robert (b. 1943) As a young artist, Robert Crumb was influenced by Harvey Kurtzman, the creator of *MAD* magazine. He went on to write the *Fritz the Cat* series and, while living in San Francisco, created ZAP Comix. He remains one of the central figures in the underground comix movement, and today his cartoon images have made him an icon of popular culture.

Cullen, Countee (1903–1946) This African American poet, who graduated from New York University and later earned a master's degree from Harvard University, became an important part of the movement known as The Harlem Renaissance. His collections of poems include *Color* (1925), *Copper Sun* (1927), *The Black Christ* (1929), and *On These I Stand* (1947).

Davis, Lydia (b. 1947) Born in Northampton, Massachusetts, Davis is the author of the novel, *The End of the Story* (1995), and five collections of short fiction, including *Almost No Memory* (1998), *Break It Down* (1986), *Story and Other Stories* (1983), *Sketches for a Life of Wassily* (1981), and *The Thirteenth Woman* (1976). She was selected as a finalist for the PEN/Hemingway Award for *Break It Down* and has received fellowships from the National Endowment for the Arts and Ingram Merrill Foundation. In 2003 she received a MacArthur Fellowship. Davis, who lives in upstate New York, also translates French and teaches at Bard College.

Dickey, James (1923–1997) Born in Buckhead, Georgia, Dickey flew combat missions in World War II and also served in the U.S. Air Force during the Korean War. A poet, novelist, and essayist, Dickey received a number of awards, including the 1966 National Book Award for Poetry; also, Dickey was invited to read at the inauguration of President Jimmy Carter (1977). Among his collections of poetry are *Buckdancer's*

Choice (1965), *The Strength of Fields* (1979), and *The Whole Motion: Collected Poems, 1945–1992* (1992). Dickey's novel, *Deliverance* (1970), an international best seller, was made into a popular movie.

Dickinson, Emily (1830–1886)   Born in Amherst, Massachusetts, Dickinson rarely left her family home throughout her life. From a prominent family, she received more formal education than most of her peers, male or female. Dickinson's poems are noted for their syntactical and rhythmic improvisation, their conciseness, and their profundity. However, her poems were not published until after her death, first in the collection, *Poems* (1890). Despite her lack of recognition as a poet during her lifetime, critics consider Dickinson to be one of America's most important poets.

Dillard, Annie (b. 1945)   Dillard, born in Pittsburgh, Pennsylvania, won the 1975 Pulitzer Prize for general nonfiction for *Pilgrim at Tinker Creek*. Author of essays, a memoir, poetry, and literary criticism, her many published works include *An American Childhood* (1987), *The Writing Life* (1989), *Mornings Like This: Found Poems* (1995), and *For the Time Being* (1999).

Eliot, T. S. [Thomas Stearns] (1888–1965)   Although born in St. Louis and educated at Harvard, Eliot emigrated to England and became a British citizen in 1927. *Prufrock and Other Observations* was published in 1917 during World War I. He won the Nobel Prize for Literature in 1948.

Emerson, Ralph Waldo (1803–1882)   The son of a prominent Unitarian minister in Boston, Emerson graduated from Harvard University in 1821 and briefly attended Harvard's Unitarian Divinity School. Emerson was ordained to be a preacher at a Boston Unitarian church in 1829, but increasingly skeptical about Christianity, he resigned in 1832. His first book, *Nature* (1836), reveals Emerson's passion for idealistic philosophies, ancient and modern, particularly, Transcendentalism. Besides his writings, Emerson was a frequent lecturer and a prominent figure on the social and intellectual landscape of the nineteenth century. His many published books include essays, journal writings, and the texts of his sermons, lecturers, and letters.

Erdrich, Louise (b. 1954)   Erdrich is the author of three novels, *Love Medicine, The Beet Queen,* and *Tracks.* She has also written two volumes of poetry and is the coauthor with her late husband, Michael Dorris, of *The Crown of Columbus.* Erdrich was born in Minnesota to Chippewa and German parents.

Espada, Martín (b. 1957)   An attorney who was born in the housing projects of Brooklyn, Espada's poems often highlight the social inequities of urban America. His book, *Rebellion Is the Circle of a Lover's Hands,* won the Peterson Poetry Prize in 1991.

Fierstein, Harvey (b. 1954)   Fierstein wrote a series of one-act plays, *Torch Song Trilogy,* between 1976 and 1979. An acclaimed actor on and off Broadway, he also wrote the book for the musical version of *La Cage aux Folles.*

Forché, Carolyn (b. 1950)   After attending schools in Michigan and Ohio, Forché moved to the Southwest where she lived among Pueblo Indians. Later, she documented civil rights violations in El Salvador for Amnesty International. Her published books of poetry include *Gathering the Tribes* in 1975, *The Country between Us* in 1981, and *The Angel of History* in 1994.

Franklin, John Hope (b. 1915)   A history professor and author, Franklin has served as the chair of the President's Initiative on Race. His books include *Racial Equality in America* (1976) and *The Color Line: Legacy for the Twenty-first Century* (1993). Currently, Franklin is associated with Duke University.

Frost, Robert (1874–1963)   Frost was born in San Francisco but is best known for his relationship with New England, where he lived most of his life. *A Boy's Will,* his first collection of poems, was published by 1913, and Frost continued to write and publish poetry through 1962. He won four Pulitzer Prizes for his work and will be remembered for reading his poems, "Dedication" and "The Gift Outright," at the inauguration of President John F. Kennedy in 1961.

Gilbert, Jack (b. 1925)   Gilbert won both a Guggenheim Fellowship and a grant from The National Endowment for the Arts but later chose to live quietly and away from publicity. He has published four collections of poetry: *Views of Jeopardy* (1962) *Monolithos* (1984), *The Great Fires: Poems 1982–1992* (1994), and *Refusing Heaven* (2005).

Giovanni, Nikki (b. 1943)   Born in Knoxville, Tennessee, Giovanni is a poet, writer, lecturer, and professor of creative writing. She has published many books of poetry, as well as an autobiography, *Gemini: An Extended Autobiographical Statement on My First Twenty-five Years of Being a Black Poet* (1971).

González, Genaro (b. 1949)   A psychology professor at the University of Texas at Pan American, González received the National Endowment for the Arts Creative Writing Award in 1990. His book, *Only Sons* (1991), is a collection of interconnected stories about characters who live along the Mexican-American border.

Goodall, Jane (b. 1951)   Born in Yorkshire, England, and attending both London and Oxford Universities, Goodall became famous for her groundbreaking primate research conducted in Africa. Today she lectures and raises funds for her foundation. Her most famous book, *In the Shadow of Man,* recounts her first experiences observing chimps in the wild.

Gordimer, Nadine (b. 1923)   Born an English-speaking Jew in South Africa, Gordimer resented the white supremacist attitudes embodied in the system of Apartheid. Her fiction most often centers on the relations between blacks and whites in South Africa. She received the Nobel Prize for Literature in 1994.

Grahn, Judy (b. 1940)   After growing up in New Mexico where she worked at several blue-collar jobs, Grahn moved to California and founded the Diana Press. Her work includes volumes of poetry and the nonfiction work, *Another Mother Tongue: Gay Words, Gay Worlds* (1984).

Gurganus, Allan (b. 1947)   A writer and an artist, Gurganus has taught fiction at a number of universities for the past thirty years. His most recognized work is a novel, *Oldest Living Confederate Widow Tells All,* published in 1989. His fiction is most often set in the American South. Openly gay, Gurganus explores themes of homosexuality in his novel, *Plays Well with Others,* published in 1997.

Hardy, Thomas (1840–1928)   A major British novelist, Hardy also wrote poems throughout his career. *Tess of the D'Urbervilles* and *The Mayor of Casterbridge* are two of his many novels. At age sixty, he turned entirely to poetry, publishing *Late Lyrics and Earlier* in 1922. *Winter Words in Various Moods and Metres* was published posthumously in 1928.

Hawthorne, Nathaniel (1804–1864)   A Massachusetts author whose fiction draws on romance and psychological realism, Hawthorne found much of his material in New England's Puritan history. Besides his many short stories, he is best known for his novels *The Scarlet Letter* (1850) and *The House of Seven Gables* (1851).

Hayden, Robert (1913–1980)   Hayden was a professor of English at several universities, primarily at Fisk University. During his teaching years, he published multiple volumes of poetry, including *The Night-Blooming Cereus* in 1972.

Hays, Constance L. (1961–2005)   Hays worked as a reporter for *The News and Observer* in Raleigh, North Carolina, and, since 1986, for the *New York Times*, where she covered the food and beverage industry for three years. Her book, *The Real Thing: Truth and Power at the Coca-Cola Company*, was first published in 2004 as an eBook.

Heaney, Seamus (b. 1939)   An Irish poet, Heaney won the Noble Prize for Literature in 1995. *Government of the Tongue* was published in 1988, and *The Redress of Poetry* in 1995. In 1998, he published *Opened Ground: Selected Poems 1966–1996*.

Hemingway, Ernest (1899–1961)   Hemingway, an author and journalist, wrote the novels, *The Sun Also Rises* (1926), *A Farewell to Arms* (1929), *For Whom the Bell Tolls* (1940), and *The Old Man and the Sea* (1952). He won the Nobel Prize for Literature in 1954.

Hendrie, Laura (b. 1954)   Born in Colorado Springs, Colorado, writer Hendrie has worked as a bartender, ditch-digger, and for the U.S. Forest Service. Her novel, *Remember Me,* is set in Queduro, New Mexico, and *Stygo,* a book of short stories about small-town life, is set in Colorado. Hendrie's awards include a Rosenthall Foundation Award, the Mountains and Plains Regional Booksellers' Award, and finalist for the PEN/Hemingway Award, 1995, all for *Stygo.*

Hogan, Linda (b. 1947)   Hogan, a member of the Chickasaw tribe, grew up in Oklahoma and Colorado in a military family. Her writings center on the traditional, indigenous relationship of humans to the land, animals, and plants. *Seeing Through the Sun* won the American Book Award in 1986.

Houston, Pam (b. 1962)   Born in Trenton, New Jersey, Houston received her BA from Denison University and then attended graduate school at the University of Utah. She has published several books, including fiction, nonfiction, and poetry. Houston's collection of stories, *Cowboys Are My Weakness* (1992), won the Western States Book Award, and *Waltzing the Cat* (1999), also stories, won the Willa Cather Award for Contemporary Fiction. Her novel, *Sight Hound,* was published in 2005. Houston has been a hunting and whitewater rafting guide in the American West and Alaska and now teaches creative writing at the University of California, Davis.

Hughes, Langston (1902–1967)   Born in Joplin, Missouri, Hughes became a major force in the Harlem Renaissance. He was among the first successful African American writers in the United States and published poetry, novels, and plays as well as children's books and song lyrics.

Huxley, Aldous (1894–1963)   The grandson of the famous English biologist T. H. Huxley, Huxley pursued a wide range of intellectual interests throughout his life. He was a prolific writer, best known for *Brave New World*, written in 1932.

Jewett, Sarah Orne (1849–1909)   Born in South Berwick, Maine, Jewett began publishing stories and sketches in her twenties, when she developed a correspondence with the prominent author Harriet Beecher Stowe. Among Jewett's books are *A White Heron and Other Stories* (1886) and *The Country of the Pointed Firs* (1896).

Jones, Edward P. (b. 1950)   Born and raised in Washington, D.C., Jones was a winner of the PEN/Hemingway Award and the recipient of a Lannan Foundation Grant and National Endowment for the Arts fellowship. Since earning degrees at Holy Cross College and the University of Virginia, he has spent his career as a professor of fiction writing at a range of universities, including Princeton. His first book, *Lost in the City*, was short-listed for the National Book Award. Jones won the 2004 Pulitzer Prize for Fiction for his novel, *The Known World.*

Kenan, Randall (b. 1963)   Although born in Brooklyn, New York, Kenan grew up in North Carolina and received his BA in English from the University of North Carolina in 1985. A former editor at Alfred A. Knopf, he currently teaches creative writing at the University of North Carolina. Kenan's literary awards include grant recipient for the New York Foundation of the Arts, 1989; MacDowell Colony Fellowship, 1990; and the Lambda Literary Award, Gay Men's Fiction, 1993, for *Let the Dead Bury Their Dead*, which includes "The Foundations of the Earth." In 1999, Kenan published *Walking on Water: Black American Lives at the Turn of the Twenty-First Century.*

Kennedy, John Fitzgerald (1917–1963)   Kennedy was the thirty-fifth president of the United States (1961–1963). Born in Brookline, Massachusetts, Kennedy graduated from Harvard University and served in the Navy during World War II. In 1953 he was elected to the U.S. Senate, and in 1955 his book, *Profiles of Courage*, won the Pulitzer Prize for History. Elected president of the United States in 1960, Kennedy became the country's first Roman Catholic president. Kennedy was assassinated in Dallas, Texas, on November 22, 1963.

King, Martin Luther Jr. (1929–1968)   One of the most prominent civil rights leaders of the twentieth century, King was born in Atlanta and was the grandson and son of ministers. After receiving degrees from Morehouse College and Crozier Theological Seminary, he attended Boston University, earning his PhD (1955) and DD (1959). In his decade of leadership of the civil rights movement, King was influenced by the example of Mahatma Gandhi who led a bloodless rebellion against British colonial rule in India. King instituted training for his nonviolent campaign of protest. In 1963 King delivered his famous speech, "I Have a Dream," and in 1964, "Letter from Birmingham Jail" was published. King received the Nobel Prize for Peace in 1964, but in 1968, at the height of his work for civil rights, King was assassinated in Memphis, Tennessee. Among his published works are *The Measure of a Man* (1968), *I've Been to the Mountaintop* (1994), and *A Knock at Midnight: Inspiration from the Great Sermons of Reverend Martin Luther King, Jr.* (1998).

Kinnell, Galway (b. 1927)   Kinnell grew up in Providence, Rhode Island, and attended Princeton University where he and poet W. S. Merwin were classmates.

Besides writing poetry and teaching at colleges and universities, Kinnell has been director of an adult education program in Chicago, a journalist in Iran, and a field worker for voter registration in the South in the 1960s. Among his poetry collections are *What a Kingdom It Was* (1960), *Body Rags* (1969), *The Past* (1985), and *Imperfect Thirst* (1994).

Klinkenborg, Verlyn (b. 1952) Klinkenborg, who received a PhD from Princeton University, is a member of the editorial board of the *New York Times*. His books include *Making Hay* (1986), *The Rural Life* (2002), and *Timothy, or Notes of an Abject Reptile* (2006). Living on a farm in upstate New York, he often writes first-person pieces about his experiences.

Knight, Etheridge (1933–1991) Knight, who grew up in the South, was sentenced to twenty years in Indiana State Prison for a robbery in 1960. *Poems from Prison* was published in 1968, and he won the American Book Award in 1987 for *The Essential Etheridge Knight* (1986).

Kramer, Peter D. (b. 1948) A professor of clinical psychiatry at Brown University, Kramer's book, *Listening to Prozac: A Psychiatrist Explores Mood-Altering Drugs and the Meaning of Self* (1993), was a national best seller. He is a contributor of numerous articles to journals and the author of a monthly column in *Psychiatric Times*.

Lee, Cherylene (b. 1953) Born and raised in Los Angeles, Lee, a fourth generation Chinese American, is a prize-winning writer whose fiction and poetry have appeared in many anthologies. With the production of *Arthur and Leila* (1993), Lee gained national recognition as a playwright. Her plays have been produced in a variety of venues, including the Mark Taper Forum in Los Angeles and the Pan Asian Repertory in New York. In 2004, two plays by Lee, *Antigone Falun Gong* and *Mixed Messages*, premiered.

Le Guin, Ursula K. (b. 1929) A highly versatile writer, Le Guin is perhaps best known for her science fiction and fantasy works, notably, *The Left Hand of Darkness* (1969), *The Lathe of Heaven* (1971), and *The Dispossessed* (1974). Less overtly political, her more recent book, *Buffalo Gals and Other Animal Presences* (1987), examines fundamental relationships between human and nonhuman animals. In addition to science fiction awards, Le Guin has received a National Book Award and a Newberry Honor Medal for children's literature.

Leopold, Aldo (1876–1944) A conservationist, forester, professor, and writer, Leopold was a founding member of the Wilderness Society in 1934, and an influential advocate of an ecological perspective on wildlife and land management issues. In his book which addresses this concept, *The Sand County Almanac* (1949), Leopold uses a reflective, meditative prose style, which contributes to the book's universal appeal.

Levertov, Denise (1923–1997) Levertov was a nurse in London during World War II and later moved to New York where William Carlos Williams guided her career as a poet. She has published widely, her recent books being *Evening Train* and *New and Selected Essays*, both published in 1992.

Lincoln, Abraham (1809–1865) Born in a cabin in Hardin County, Kentucky, Lincoln became the sixteenth president of the United States. Shortly after his inauguration on March 4, 1861, the Civil War began. In 1863 he issued the Emancipation Proclamation, laying the groundwork for the passage of the Thirteenth Amendment, which outlawed slavery forever in the United States. Several weeks after he delivered his Second Inaugural Address on March 4, 1865, he was assassinated by John Wilkes Booth. Lincoln died on April 15, 1865.

London, Jack (1876–1916)   Born in San Francisco, London began earning his own living at age fifteen, by working in a canning factory, a laundry, and as a sailor. Fully aligned with working-class persons, he joined the Socialist Labor Party. London produced a number of works of fiction, among them, *The Call of the Wild* (1903), *Son of the Wolf,* and *South Sea Tales* (1912).

Madonna, Paul (b. 1972)   Born in Pittsburgh, Pennsylvania, Madonna received his BFA from Carnegie Mellon University in 1994. While a senior, he interned at *MAD Magazine* with the title of "first art intern." Since 1994 Madonna has lived in San Francisco, where he continued to practice his art by making minicomics, which he distributed freely. In 2004 the *San Francisco Chronicle* and SFGate.com began publishing his strip, "All Over Coffee." Madonna's art also is featured regularly in galleries and restaurants.

Marquis, Don(ald) (Robert Perry) (1878–1937)   A newspaper columnist, humorist, poet, playwright, and author of about thirty-five books, Marquis was born in Walnut, Illinois. He is best known for his books of humorous poetry about Archy the cockroach and Mehitabel the cat.

McKay, Claude (1890–1948)   Originally from Jamaica, McKay was an important figure during the Harlem Renaissance when black writers found their voice in America. He wrote novels and plays but is best remembered for his poems. *Home to Harlem* was published in 1928.

Meinke, Peter (b. 1932)   Meinke was born in Brooklyn, New York, and attended Hamilton College. He received his doctorate in literature from the University of Minnesota. His poetry has appeared in many magazines and journals since the 1970s. *Liquid Paper: New and Selected Poems* was published in 1991. He now teaches at Eckerd College in St. Petersburg, Florida.

Meloy, Maile (b. 1972)   Meloy, who was born in Helena, Montana, now lives and writes in California. A regular contributor to literary journals and periodicals, such as *Ploughshares* and the *New Yorker,* Meloy also has published several books of fiction, including *Half in Love* (2002), a collection of stories set in the American West, and a novel, *A Family Daughter* (2006).

Merrill, James (1926–1995)   Independently wealthy, Merrill published poetry throughout his life, beginning with *First Poems* in 1951 and ending with *Selected Poems* in 1992. During that time, he won two Pulitzer Prizes and two National Book Awards.

Millay, Edna St. Vincent (1892–1950)   Millay published many volumes of poetry during her lifetime and was also recognized as a dramatist, lecturer, short story writer, and actress. Although her reputation began to decline in the 1930s, a modern interest in feminism and women writers has allowed her work to regain a position of respect in American literature. Her *Collected Poems,* edited by Norma Millay, was published in 1956.

Miller, Arthur (1915-2005)   Although *Death of a Salesman* (1945) continues to be his most successful play, Miller had a long career as a playwright, winning both the Pulitzer Prize and the New York Drama Critics Circle Award. His play, *The Crucible*

(1953), grew out of his disdain for the anticommunist fervor of the McCarthy-era House Un-American Activities Committee.

Milton, John (1608–1674)   Milton worked for Oliver Cromwell during the civil war between the king and Parliament but was arrested when the monarchy was restored. During the last fourteen years of his life, he retired from public life and wrote his epic poems, *Paradise Lost* (1667) and *Paradise Regained* (1671).

Momaday, N. Scott (b. 1934)   A Kiowa who often explores Native American history and culture in his writing, Momaday received his doctoral degree from Stanford University. His novel, *House Made of Dawn*, won a Pulitzer Prize in 1969 and helped to spark the Native American renaissance.

Murray, Pauli (1910–1985)   Murray, who grew up in Durham, North Carolina, worked to dismantle the barriers of race and gender and founded the National Organization of Women (NOW) in the early 1970s. She published *Proud Shoes: The Story of an American Family* in 1956, *Dark Testament and Other Poems* in 1970, and her autobiographical *Song in a Watery Throat: An American Pilgrimage* in 1987.

Ng, Fae Myenne (b. 1957)   Born in San Francisco and raised in Chinatown, Ng's first novel, *Bone* (1993), received widespread recognition. Her award-winning stories have been published in many periodicals, including *Harper's* magazine. She has won the Pushcart Prize for short fiction and a McDowell Fellowship.

Nye, Naomi Shihab (b. 1952)   An American singer and writer with Palestinian roots, Nye has published children's books as well as poetry. Her poetry collections include *Hugging the Jukebox* (1982), *Words under the Words: Selected Poems* (1995), and *Fuel* (1998).

Oates, Joyce Carol (b. 1938)   Oates, a prolific writer who has published over one hundred stories and forty books, is a professor at Princeton University. Her novels, *Because It Is Bitter, and Because It Is My Heart* (1990) and *What I Lived For* (1994), received widespread critical attention.

O'Brien, Tim (b. 1946)   After graduating from college, O'Brien served as an infantry man in Vietnam, where he won the Purple Heart. Upon returning home, he began to write about his war experiences. His novel, *Going after Cacciato* (1978), won the National Book Award.

Okita, Dwight (b. 1958)   An American of Japanese descent, Okita was born and raised in Chicago. His collection of poems is *Crossing with the Light* (1992).

Olds, Sharon (b. 1942)   A professor and writer, Olds is a much-published contemporary American poet. Her poetry collections include *The Father* (1992), *The Wellspring* (1995), *The Gold Cell* (1997), and *Blood, Tin, Straw* (1999). Olds lives and teaches in New York City.

Oliver, Mary (b. 1935)   Oliver was born in Cleveland and attended Ohio State and Vassar. She first published a collection of poetry in 1963, *No Voyage and Other Poems*. Her book, *New and Selected Poems*, won the National Book Award for poetry in 1992.

Orwell, George (1903–1950)   A writer and socialist, Orwell lived in poverty and associated with laborers early in his writing career. He later fought in the Spanish civil war and went on to write *Animal Farm* (1945) and *1984* (1949), both illustrating his distaste for totalitarian governments.

Owen, Wilfred (1893–1918)   Owen was an English poet who died in France during World War I at the young age of twenty-five before his career ever began. Twenty-four of his poems were published after his death.

Paley, Grace (b. 1922)   A fiction writer and teacher of creative writing, Paley was born and raised in New York City. Perhaps reflecting her native New York City, her stories often bristle with humor and toughness in their tone and theme. Paley has several published volumes of stories, including *The Little Disturbances of Man* (1959) and *Enormous Changes at the Last Minute* (1975), a collection of short fiction and poetry, *Long Walks and Intimate Talks* (1991), and a book of poetry, *New and Collected Poems* (1992). In 1993, she won the Rea Award for the Short Story.

Pastan, Linda (b. 1932)   Pastan lives in Potomac, Maryland, and was the Poet Laureate of Maryland from 1990 to 1995. Her book, *PM/AM: New and Selected Poems* was nominated for the National Book Award.

Peacock, Molly (b. 1947)   Peacock has published five volumes of poetry, as well as a memoir. For her work as a writer, she has received numerous fellowships, including a Danforth Foundation Fellowship and on five occasions a Woodrow Wilson Foundation Fellowship. She lives in Toronto and New York City.

Plato (427–347 B.C.)   A Greek philosopher born in Athens, Plato was an *idealist*. He wrote thirty dialogues in which Socrates, an Athenian philosopher twenty-five years older than Plato, is the principal speaker.

Porter, Katherine Anne (1890–1980)   A fiction writer, who also played small parts in films and worked in journalism, Porter is considered a Southern writer. Her book, *Collected Stories,* won both the National Book Award and the Pulitzer Prize in 1967.

Quiñonez, Ernesto (b. 1966)   *Bodega Dreams* is the first novel by Quiñonez. He currently teaches fourth grade in the New York public schools and is writing his second novel.

Randall, Dudley (1914–2000)   Randall founded Broadside Press in 1965, where he published African American writers. His collected poetry is found in *More to Remember: Poems of Four Decades* (1971) and *A Litany of Friends: New and Selected Poems* (1981).

Ray, Janisse (b. 1962)   Ray, born in Appling County, Georgia, received her BA from Florida State University in 1984, and her MFA from Montana University in 1997. A writer and an environmental activist, Ray's awards include the Southern Environmental Law Center Award for Outstanding Writer on the Southern Environment, 2000, and the Southern Book Critics Circle Award for nonfiction for *Ecology of a Cracker Childhood,* which includes "Forest Beloved."

Regan, Tom (b. 1938)   A leading philosopher in the animal protection movement, Regan's book, *The Case for Animal Rights* (1984), brought the subject of animal rights to new levels of serious discussion within scholarly circles. He is a professor of philosophy at North Carolina State University.

Rich, Adrienne (b. 1929)   Rich was a Phi Beta Kappa graduate of Radcliffe in 1951, the year she published her first collection of poetry, *A Change of World.* Since then, she has won many awards, including the National Book Award for poetry in 1974. *An Atlas of the Difficult World* was published in 1992.

Rilke, Rainer Maria (1875–1926)   One of the most famous German poets, Rilke served as secretary to the French sculptor Rodin. He published *New Poems* in 1907. Later, living in Switzerland, he wrote *Sonnets to Orpheus* (1923) and *The Duino Elegies* (1923).

Robinson, Edwin Arlington (1869–1935)   Robinson created psychological portraits of small-town citizens in his poems and received three Pulitzer Prizes for his work.

Rodriguez, Richard (b. 1944)   His book, *Hunger of Memory: The Education of Richard Rodriguez* (1982), focuses on the issues of education and ethnic identity. *Days of Obligation* (1992) was nominated for the Pulitzer Prize. Rodriguez appears on the "The News Hour with Jim Lehrer" on PBS.

Roethke, Theodore (1908–1963)   Roethke grew up in Michigan and attended the University of Michigan and Harvard University. He won the Pulitzer Prize for poetry in 1954 for *The Waking: Poems 1933–1953*. He also won two National Book Awards for poetry.

Rogers, Pattiann (b. 1940)   Rogers has won grants from the National Endowment for the Arts and the Guggenheim Foundation. She has published several books of poetry, including *Splitting and Binding* (1989) and *Firekeeper: New and Selected Poems* (1994). In *The Dream of the Marsh Hen: Writing as Reciprocal Creation* (1999), Rogers explores her writing process.

Rukeyser, Muriel (1913–1980)   Born in New York City, Rukeyser was a poet and social activist who published many books of poetry, including *Body of Waking* (1958) and *Collected Poems* (1978).

Sandburg, Carl (1878–1967)   Sandburg grew up in Illinois and often wrote about Chicago, for example, in *Chicago Poems* (1916) and *Smoke and Steel* (1920). In 1939, he received the Pulitzer Prize for History for his biography of Lincoln, and in 1951, won again for poetry for his *Complete Poems of 1950*.

Sanders, Scott Russell (b. 1945)   Born in Memphis, Sanders has published many essays, novels, and children's books. His latest books are *Hunting for Hope* (1998) and *The Country of Language* (1999). He is a professor of English at Indiana University.

Setterberg, Fred (b. 1951)   A native Californian and graduate of the University of California at Berkeley, Setterberg won a creative writing fellowship from the National Endowment for the Arts in 1982 and the creative nonfiction award from Associated Writing Programs for *The Roads Taken: Travels through America's Literary Landscapes* in 1993. He has been teaching writing at the University of San Francisco since 1993.

Sexton, Anne (1928–1974)   Sexton was born in Newton, Massachusetts. She attended poetry workshops in the late 1950s in the Boston area and began writing poetry at age twenty-eight. Sexton received the Pulitzer Prize for *Live or Die* (1967) and taught creative writing and continued writing poetry until her death by suicide.

Silko, Leslie Marmon (b. 1948)   Silko grew up on the Laguna Pueblo Reservation and has taught English at Navajo Community College, the University of Arizona, and the University of New Mexico. She has published poetry and fiction since 1974, including the novel, *Ceremony* (1988).

Snyder, Gary (b. 1930)   Born in San Francisco, Snyder studied Asian languages at University of California, Berkeley, worked as a logger, studied Buddhism in Japan, and shipped as a crew member on oil tankers. His poems draw on images from nature, Native American culture, and Buddhism. Of his many books of poetry, *Regarding Wave* was published in 1970.

Song, Cathy (b. 1955)   Song, who lives in Hawaii, first published *Picture Bride* in 1983, for which she won the National Book Critics Circle Award. Her collection of poems, *School Figures,* was published in 1994.

Soto, Gary (b. 1952)   Born in Fresno, California, Soto is the author of many books of poetry, two novels, a memoir, and numerous young adult and children's books. His collection, *New and Selected Poems* (1995), was a National Book Award finalist, and his memoir, *Living Up the Street* (1985), received an American Book Award. Other honors include the Andrew Carnegie Medal, the United States Award of the International Poetry Forum, and the Bess Hokin Prize and Levinson Award. Soto, who has received fellowships from the Guggenheim Foundation and the National Endowment for the Arts, lives in northern California.

Stafford, William (1914–1992)   Stafford earned his doctorate from Iowa State University. He was a conscientious objector during World War I and later taught at Lewis and Clark College in Oregon. His 1963 collection of poetry, *Traveling through the Dark,* won the National Book Award for poetry.

Stevens, Wallace (1879–1955)   Born in Reading, Pennsylvania, Stevens attended Harvard for three years and then received his law degree at New York law school in 1903. After briefly practicing law, he began to work for the Hartford Accident and Indemnity Company and moved with his wife to Hartford, Connecticut, which became his lifelong home. While prospering as a businessman in the 1930s (he became vice president of Hartford in 1934), Stevens also was fully engaged in writing and publishing his poetry. Placing the individual at the center of his poems—the self as observer and creator—Stevens is often considered to be the twentieth-century, modernist interpreter of nineteenth-century American transcendentalism. Many critics consider *The Collected Poems of Wallace Stevens* (1954) to be one of the most influential books of modern poetry.

Strand, Mark (b. 1934)   Although born in Canada, Strand was named U.S. Poet Laureate in 1990. *Selected Poems* was published in 1980 and *The Continuous Life* in 1990. In 1993, he received the Bollingen Prize. In 1999, Strand won the Pulitzer Prize for Poetry, 1999, for *Blizzard of One: Poems,* and in 2004, he received the Wallace Stevens Award for outstanding and proven mastery in the art of poetry.

Swift, Jonathan (1667–1745)   Swift was an Irish essayist, poet, and satirist.

Terkel, Studs (b. 1912)   Terkel is associated with Chicago, where he lives and works. He most often focuses his attention on working-class, everyday people. His book, *Race: How Blacks and Whites Think and Feel about the American Obsession,* was published in 1992.

Thoreau, Henry David (1817–1862)   Thoreau wrote the classic, *Walden, or Life in the Woods* (1854), based on his experience of living a simple life in a cabin by Walden Pond near Boston. An outspoken social critic, he opposed slavery and the Mexican War of 1846 to 1848. His published lecture on civil disobedience influenced Martin Luther King Jr.

Udall, Brady (b. 1957)   Udall, who grew up in the Southwest, is a graduate of Iowa Writers Workshop. He found critical recognition with his collection of short stories, *Letting Loose the Hounds,* published in 1997. In 2001, Udall published his first novel, *The Secret Life of Edgar Mint.* His fiction is set in the small towns of Arizona and Utah. Udall currently teaches at the University of Idaho.

Updike, John (b. 1932)   A writer and lecturer, Updike has published many novels and collections of short stories, including *Pigeon Feathers and Other Stories* in 1962. Contemporary urban and suburban people are the focus of Updike's stories. In a series of four novels—*Rabbit Run, Rabbit Redux, Rabbit Is Rich,* and *Rabbit at Rest*—Updike dramatizes the life of Harry "Rabbit" Angstrom who confronts the realities of his present life while longing for his idealized vision of a past life. Updike's recent novels include *Brazil* (1994) and *In the Beauty of the Lilies* (1996).

Vega, Ed (b. 1936)   Vega is a Puerto Rican fiction writer who has lived in New York since 1949. In 1985, he published *The Comeback,* a novel satirizing ethnic autobiography and the identity crisis. *Casualty Report,* his third book, was published in 1991.

Villanueva, Alma Luz (b. 1944)   Villanueva's fiction often appears in anthologies. Her novel *Desire* was published in 1998. *Weeping Woman: La Ilorna and Other Stories* came out in 1994.

Walker, Alice (b. 1944)   Born in Eatonton, Georgia, Walker attended Spelman College and received her BA from Sarah Lawrence College. A poet, writer, lecturer, and professor, Walker also coproduced the film documentary, *Warrior Marks* (1993). Walker has won numerous awards for her poems and novels, including the 1983 Pulitzer Prize for fiction and the American Book Award for *The Color Purple.* Other publications include *Revolutionary Petunias and Other Poems* (1973) and the novel, *Possessing the Secret of Joy* (1992).

Walker, Margaret (Abigail) (1915–1998)   Born in Birmingham, Alabama, the daughter of college professors, Walker published *Jubilee* in 1966, a novel that imagines the Civil War and emancipation from the slave's point of view. Her collection of poetry, *For My People,* was published in 1942.

Warren, Robert Penn (1905–1989)   Warren won the Pulitzer Prize in 1947, 1957, and 1978. Additionally, he was named the first American Poet Laureate in 1985. His most acclaimed novel is *All the King's Men,* published in 1946. His poetry collections include *Promises* (1957) and *New and Selected Poems* (1985).

Welty, Eudora (1909–2001)   Welty is the author of numerous works of fiction, including *The Optimist's Daughter,* which won the Pulitzer Prize in 1972. Born in Jackson, Mississippi, Welty roots the actual settings of her stories in the Southern region she knows firsthand. Meanwhile, the thematic implications far extend those geographic borders.

Whitman, Walt (1819–1892)   Whitman worked as a journalist in the New York area most of his life, but with the publication of *Leaves of Grass* in 1855, he assured himself of an important place in world literature. His poetry focuses on the American landscape and its people.

Wilbur, Richard (b. 1921)   Wilbur is a prolific poet who has taught at Harvard University, Wellesley College, and Wesleyan University. His many books include *The Poems of Richard Wilbur* (1963), *Waking to Sleep* (1969), and *The Mind-Reader* (1976).

Winckler, Suzanne (b. 1946)   Winckler is a freelance writer whose focus is the natural world. She has written several volumes in the *Smithsonian Guide to Natural America* series, as well as articles for *Atlantic* and *Audubon*. Her book, *Prairie: A Natural History,* was published in 2004.

Woolf, Virginia (1882–1941)   Woolf was a major English novelist who quickly became the center of the Bloomsbury Group before World War I. Her novels, *Mrs. Dalloway* and *To the Lighthouse,* published in 1925 and 1927, are always counted as major examples of the modern novel. Bouts of depression led to her suicide in 1941.

Wordsworth, William (1770–1850)   Wordsworth was the English poet who introduced Romanticism with its interest in nature. The natural world, Wordsworth believed, held the power to heal some of the abuses inflicted upon society by urbanization. He is most famous for *The Lyrical Ballads* (1798) and *The Excursion* (1814).

Wright, James (1927–1980)   Wright was born in Martins Ferry, Ohio. After serving in World War II, he attended college, receiving a Fulbright Scholarship to the University of Vienna and his PhD from Washington University. He taught at Hunter College in New York from 1966 to 1980. His many volumes of poetry include *The Branch Will Not Break* (1963), *Collected Poems* (1971), and *This Journey* (1982). Wright won the 1972 Pulitzer Prize for *Collected Poems.*

Wright, Richard (1908–1960)   Born in Roxie, Mississippi, Wright graduated as valedictorian of his high school class in 1925, although during his youth he was often close to starvation. Fifteen years later, he published his novel, *Native Son,* and in 1945, his autobiography, *Black Boy,* brought him widespread critical acclaim.

ᐱᐱ Text Credits ᐱᐱ

⋀⋀ Author/Title Index ⋀⋀

✿ Subject Index ✿